THE
BOOK
OF
SYMBOLS

REFLECTIONS ON ARCHETYPAL IMAGES

THE
BOOK
OF
SYMBOLS

REFLECTIONS ON ARCHETYPAL IMAGES

Editor-in-Chief
AMI RONNBERG

Editor
KATHLEEN MARTIN

TASCHEN

Preface

There couldn't be a better way to describe the significance and guiding principle of *The Book of Symbols: Reflections on Archetypal Images* than with these words by Meister Eckhart: "When the soul wants to experience something she throws out an image in front of her and then steps into it." It is an evocation of the image as a threshold leading to new dimensions of meaning. Symbolic images are more than data; they are vital seeds, living carriers of possibility. Eckhart's words also explain why a book of images matters in a world as chaotic and complex as our own.

C. G. Jung was once asked for advice from someone who had in mind to publish a lexicon of symbols. His response was not to do it, since each symbol would require an entire book. We found a way around this by focusing on a specific image. The image both limits and opens up: it is *this* particular image, it grounds the symbol in *this* experience, and yet, with the right image the archetypal reality is evoked. If we couldn't find the right image, we didn't include this particular symbol; when we did, it brought a sense of joyous recognition—like a door opening to some hidden delight. Paul Klee said it well: "Art doesn't reproduce the visible. It renders visible."

Poetry, like symbols, expresses that which cannot be said. When poets awake, it becomes night, said W. S. Merwin. We have tried to keep some of this nighttime perspective, by including poetry, as yet another reflection on symbols. Like the poet who carefully observes nature, in the guidelines we encouraged the writers to study the "luminous particular" of the physical object. Seeing in this way makes another world shine through. Since we were limited to a very brief text, we could only hope, at best, to catch a glimpse of the archetypal reality. At times, readers may disagree with a particular vision of a symbol. Even so, if this provokes alternative associations we feel that the entry has been successful. "A poem wants another poem," said T. S. Eliot, and we hope that our reflections will inspire readers to continue their own. During the years we were often asked why we would make another book about symbols when there are so many. Our answer was always that there isn't one that brings the perspective of the image. The ancient Egyptians had only one word for both writing and drawing. And it is a similar understanding of image and text working together that makes this a unique work on symbols. This is also why we decided not to edit the texts into a uniform style but to let the many voices of the writers be heard. It is as if each symbol needs its own expression. At the same time the editor and Jungian analyst Kathleen Martin brought her profound knowledge of the workings of the psyche to this project.

We are deeply grateful to the many writers for the commitment to this project and for taking up the challenge to write about a symbol in a few hundred words. A small group of writers, in particular, gave abundantly of their time and talent. The fact that *The Book of Symbols* is the result of a group effort is made clear by naming the Archive for Research in Archetypal Symbolism as the "author." It is to this organization that the entire project owes its existence.

However, a project such as this has many parents. The idea for *The Book of Symbols* came from Sam Bercholz at Shambhala Publications, who had previously published two volumes of the ARAS publication project: *An Encyclopedia of Archetypal Symbolism*, and the second subtitled *The Body*. The roots of the archive itself reach back to a series of conferences, beginning in the 1930s and continuing throughout most of the twentieth century. They were arranged by Olga Froebe Kapteyn, took place in Ascona, Switzerland, and were named Eranos, from the Greek, meaning a "shared feast." Each year, scholars from East and West, and from diverse academic disciplines, were invited. C. G. Jung became a lifelong contributor and often presented his initial ideas for his later writings. It was the magic of a particular theme that tied the speakers together across cultures and disciplines. To one kind of magic was added another—the images that Frau Froebe collected and exhibited on the walls in the lecture hall and which gradually formed a remarkable archive. In time a copy of this archive was given to the Bollingen Foundation in New York, which gradually grew into the present ARAS under the passionate care of Jessie Fraser and is now housed at the C. G. Jung Center in New York. The materials were given an archetypal structure by Joseph L. Henderson, and branches were added in San Francisco, Los Angeles and Chicago. Recently, the 17,000 images and accompanying texts became available online at www.aras.org through the efforts of Thomas Singer and Carol Sellers Herbert. Finally, without the stewardship of Charles H. Taylor who served for many years, in turn as president, treasurer and editorial chairman, there would be no publication project. It is in gratitude to his selfless service that *The Book of Symbols* is dedicated to him.

Present and former members of the archive board and a number of ARAS associates have made essential annual contributions to our work. These include in particular Robin Jaqua and John Jaqua, whose passion for the archetypal images was a constant encouragement and inspiration throughout the years, Lucia Woods Lindley and Daniel Lindley, Charles H. Taylor, Nancy Furlotti, Ann Paras, Carol Sellers Herbert and Sarah Griffin Banker. In addition, Rose-Emily Rothenberg, Arlene TePaske Landau, Deborah A. Wesley, Anne Pickup, Philip T. Zabriskie and Beverley Zabriskie, Mary Ottoway and James Ottoway, Judith Harris and Tony Woolfson, Carol Shahin, the estate of Elizabeth Caspari, Melinda Haas, Maude Ann Taylor, Thomas Kirsch, Thomas Singer, Virginia Beane Rutter, Penny Etnier Dinsmore, Joyce King Heyraud, Peter Mudd, Joseph L. Henderson, Barbara Blatt, Maxson McDowell, Nancy Field, Chie Lee, George R. Elder, Mary Wells Barron, Sheila Zarrow, Stephanie Fariss, Thomas Elsner, Beverly Parent and Paul Levine have been generous in their support. The C. G. Jung Institutes in Chicago, Los Angeles, New York and San Francisco made grants that have been great encouragement. Faithful members of the Friends of ARAS in New York, too numerous to mention, have together made critically useful gifts.

During the many years of preparation the editorial committee has been meeting regularly and reviewing the texts, which often inspired passionate discussions. Past and present members include Sarah Griffin Banker, Diane Fremont, Melinda Haas, Robin Jaqua, Maxson McDowell, Laurel Morris, Ann Paras, Bruce Parent, Anne Pickup, Charles H. Taylor and Philip T. Zabriskie. Their wise counsel helped give form to this volume as it now exists. The editorial committee is part of the larger board, with representatives from each of the C. G. Jung Institutes in Chicago, Los Angeles, San Francisco and the C. G. Jung Foundation in New York. Together they have helped steer this gargantuan project to a successful landing.

But were it not for the staff, this volume would have remained in the chaos where everything has its beginning. Throughout we worked as a group, defining the direction of this project and refining the organization. Each member, a working artist in her own right, brought unique skills to the process. Karen Arm, managing editor, reviewed the art history and created ingenious databases where texts and images could be tracked on the computer from beginning to completion. Anne Thulin, assistant editor, scanned and organized all the images. Her sense of structure made it possible to locate all the materials, including the 1,500 images that didn't make it into this volume. She became a part-time detective, trying to find the many owners across the globe in order to obtain permission to use the more than 700 images. Kako Ueda, assistant editor, shared this enormous task and also gathered reference materials from the vast resources in ARAS and the Kristine Mann Library, which helped to inform the texts. Allison Langerak, ARAS online editor, worked on the many finishing details. In addition, Eric Muzzy gave generously of his computer expertise, Ann Withers worked on poetry permissions, Leslie Bialler offered useful advice on poetry, Michael N. Flanagin and Deborah A. Wesley read the manuscript, Vera Manzi-Schacht checked names, Patricia Llosa, Ellen Krüger and Gina Speirs helped track down many images and without Nancy Furlotti this book would never have reached Taschen. I also want to thank Florian Kobler, the editor at Taschen, who is as wise as he is generous with his time and expertise. For a project that took more than 13 years to complete, there were numerous others who gave of their time and talents. We are deeply grateful to them all.

Ami Ronnberg

Introduction

All of the original essays in this volume are accompanied by images that represent art from around the world and from every era since human beings first depicted, on rocks and cave walls and in simple tools and objects, psyche's imaginal forms. The same forms appear uniquely in an individual's dreams and fantasies. The intention was not to describe at any length the artistic features or contextual history of these images but rather to allow them to serve as points of departure for the essays that follow.

Together, image and text open up a symbol, telling something about what its intrinsic qualities evoke. A symbol mysteriously unites disparities. Thus, the reader will find that we have avoided pat definitions and equations since these tend to constrain a symbol. A still vital symbol remains partially unknown, compels our attention and unfolds in new meanings and manifestations over time. Physics, neurobiology and genetics, for example, have recently provided many new symbolic images. Consistent with the archive's appreciation for C. G. Jung's researches into the psyche, each essay suggests how a given symbol reflects intrapsychic landscapes and field phenomena in which structures and functions, shifting, mercurial energies and processes of transformation participate. Etymological roots, the play of opposites, paradox and shadow, the differentiated ways in which diverse cultures have engaged a symbolic image have all been employed as vectors of meaning.

Of course, symbolic energies get incarnated in all the stuff of life through our unconscious projections, which can obscure as well as illuminate. Our writers have taken pains to be true to the integrity of a symbol and of the empirical realities on which its qualities get "hooked." Such precision is important in discerning how a symbol might be understood, for symbols reveal themselves in specificities. An elephant's habits of relationship, love of water, massive size, huge ears and strong and flexible trunk have specifically associated it with fertile rain clouds and thunder, the earth goddess Lakshmi, the removing of obstacles and the solidity and weight of interior ground. At the same time, the essays, like the symbolic energies they describe, flow into each other in ways that mirror psyche's unexpected convergences. You might read the entry on Breath, for example, and then be intuitively drawn to Wind and Bird. Our hope is that a wide range of readers will find *The Book of Symbols* absorbing, and that in turn it will stir their own reflections, insights and symbolic imaginings.

My thanks to Laurel Morris for suggesting my participation in this project. To the many independent writers from the fields of psychology, religion, art, literature and comparative myth, who authored the essays, my sincerest gratitude. Special thanks is due Kathie Carlson and John Mendelsohn for their help in the beginning stages of the book. An immense debt of gratitude is owed writers Michael N. Flanagin, Mary E. Martin, Priscilla Young Rodgers, Ami Ronnberg, Sherry Salmon and Deborah A. Wesley for their distinguished contribution to the book over a period of years. To the ARAS staff, Karen Arm, Anne Thulin and Kako Ueda at the archive, and Allison Langerak at ARAS online, my profound appreciation and admiration for the work you do. And to Ami Ronnberg my heartfelt gratitude for the privilege and pleasure of our collaboration.

Kathleen Martin

About the Authors

Drawing upon Carl Gustav Jung's work on the archetype and the collective unconscious, the Archive for Research in Archetypal Symbolism (ARAS) is a pictorial and written archive of mythological, ritualistic, and symbolic images from all over the world and from all epochs of human experience.

The collection of 17,000 photographic images, accompanied by commentary on their cultural and historical context, probes the universality of archetypal themes and provides a testament to the deep and abiding connections of all life.

www.aras.org

Contributors

MAIN CONTRIBUTORS
Kathie Carlson, Michael N. Flanagin, Kathleen Martin, Mary E. Martin, John Mendelsohn,
Priscilla Young Rodgers, Ami Ronnberg, Sherry Salman, Deborah A. Wesley

CONTRIBUTORS
Polly Armstrong, Frank Barth, Barbara Blatt, Martin Brauen, Susan Bumps,
Vicky Burnett, John A. Cook, Priscilla Costello, Delia Doherty,
Claire Douglas, Ruthann Duncan, Josephine Evetts-Secker, Zoë Francesca, Mara Freeman,
Diane Fremont, Joan Golden-Alexis, John A. Gosling, Melinda Haas, Molly Hall,
Valerie Harms, Charlene M. Henry, Suzanne Ironbiter, Robin Jaqua,
Timothy Gus Kiley, Adam Klein, Margaret Klenck, Ellen Krüger,
Laura Lombard, Michele McKee, Laurel Morris, Jolinda Osborne,
Hallfríður Ragnheiðardóttir, Rose-Emily Rothenberg, Meredith Sabini,
Michael S. Schneider, Dennis Patrick Slattery, Richard Smoley,
Jon Swan, Charles H. Taylor, Maude Ann Taylor, Pamela D. Winfield

MANAGING EDITOR
Karen Arm

ASSISTANT EDITORS
Anne Thulin and Kako Ueda

ARAS ONLINE EDITOR
Allison Langerak

CONSULTING EDITORS
Michael N. Flanagin, Timothy Gus Kiley,
Deborah A. Wesley, Mary Wolff

PHOTOGRAPHIC CONSULTANT
Christopher Gallo

EDITORIAL ASSISTANTS
Aurelie Athan and Gayle Homer

Bibliography

References appear within the text in parenthesis and include the author's last name and page number/s. The complete list of bibliographic references is located at the end of the text.

BIBLIOGRAPHIC ABBREVIATIONS

Certain references that are frequently used throughout the book are cited within the text in abbreviated form. The abbreviations are listed here in alphabetical order:

(ARAS 2An.001) refers to records from the Archive for Research in Archetypal Symbolism (ARAS) in New York and San Francisco, which are also available at www.aras.org.

(ARAS 1) Moon, Beverly. Ed. An Encyclopedia of Archetypal Symbolism. Vol. 1. Boston and London, 1991.

(ARAS 2) Elder, George R. An Encyclopedia of Archetypal Symbolism: The Body. Vol. 2. Boston and London, 1996.

(CW) Jung. C. G. The Collected Works. Vols. 1-20, 1957–1979. Please note, that paragraphs and not pages are used for Jung's Collected Works.

(*Compt.*) Compton's Interactive Encyclopedia. 1999.

(de Vr) de Vries, Ad. Dictionary of Symbols and Imagery. Amsterdam, 1984.

(de Vries) de Vries, Ad and Arthur de Vries. Elsevier's Dictionary of Symbols and Imagery. Amsterdam, 2004.

(DoS) Chevalier, Jean and Alain Gheerbrant. A Dictionary of Symbols. London and New York, 1996.

(ECI) Roberts, Helene, E., Ed. Encyclopedia of Comparative Iconography. Vols. 1-2. New York, 1998.

(Enc.Brit.) The New Encylopaedia Britannica. Chicago, 1988.

(EoR) Encyclopedia of Religion. Ed. Mircea Eliade. Vols. 1-16. New York, 1987.

(ERE) Hastings, James, Ed. Encyclopedia of Religion and Ethics. Vols. 1-12. New York, 1917.

(IDB) The Interpreter's Dictionary of the Bible. Vols. 1-5. Nashville, 1962.

(MM) Cavendish, Richard. Man, Myth, and Magic: An Illustrated Encyclopedia of the Supernatural. Vols. 1-24. New York, 1970.

CREATION
AND
COSMOS

Egg

An oval mass of gold appears centered amongst swirls of white on a silvery ground. The oval is stable and self-contained; the swirls are liquid, full of energy, dynamic, expanding. The Indian image of a cosmic egg goes back to the Vedas. *Brahmanda*, the egg of Brahma the Creator, contains the phenomenal world. *Hiranya-garbha* is the golden womb, germ or embryo, luminous incubator. The egg's shell bifurcates, like two bowls, into earth and sky; the yolk is the sun. It is a primal scene: an ovum in a sea of sperm; the daily birth of the sun out of eastern waters massaged by wind; breath/spirit moving with the waters of life, and light emerging, making form visible; the opening of an eye.

In many creation myths, the universe is hatched from an egg, which has everything within itself and is needful only of brooding (von Franz, 265). Often it is a bird, or birdlike deity, combining the chthonic and the spiritual, that lays and broods the egg. Orphism, for example, tells how sable-winged Night laid her wind-egg in the abyss of Tartarus, and from it shining Phanes, or "whirlwind Love," is born (Aristophanes, 51). In myths of ancient Egypt, the Great Cackler (a celestial goose), or an ibis-form of Thoth, god of the moon and of wisdom, lays a cosmic egg containing Re, the solar bird whose heat creates the world. Much earlier, in the Upper Paleolithic period, approximately 12,000 B.C.E., circular, oval and elliptical painted egg forms began to appear as symbols of regeneration and rebirth. They survive today in the Easter ritual of painting eggs and rolling them on the earth for the springtime renewal of vegetation after the torpor of winter (Gimbutas, 213). Each spring, possibility returns in thousands and thousands of eggs. Jellylike eggs of fish and frogs shimmer in shallow waters. In nests of all kinds, turtles and other reptiles lay eggs contained in leathery membranes, while birds lay and brood variously tinged and dappled eggs whose hard protective shells are both permeable to respiratory gases and relatively impermeable to water.

Just as life gestates in the egg, so in ancient healing rituals would initiates withdraw into a dark cave or hole to "incubate" until a healing dream released them reborn into the upper world, in the same way the chick crawls out of the egg. Similarly, in deeply introverted, self-reflective states, brooder and brooded become one in egglike, nuclear processes of crystallization. Here, too, the egg evokes the beginning, the simple, the source. The egg is the mysterious "center" around which unconscious energies move in spiral-like evolutions, gradually bringing the vital substance to light. Alchemy depicted the germ of the egg contained in the yolk as the "sun-point," the infinitesimally small, invisible "dot" from which all being has its origin. It is also the creative "fire-point" within ourselves, the "soul in the midpoint of the heart," the quintessence or golden germ "that is set in motion by the hen's warmth" of our devoted attention (CW 14:41).

Aristophanes. *The Birds*. Ann Arbor, MI, 1961.
Gimbutas, Marija. *The Language of the Goddess*. SF, 1989.
von Franz, Marie-Louise. *Shadow and Evil in Fairy Tales*. Boston, 1995.

1. The contrast between the dynamic and the stable reflects the natural and symbolic relationship of sperm and egg, water and sun, perceived world and perceiving eye, primordial fluidity and centered form. Cosmic egg, from a manuscript of *Bhagavata-Purana*, painting on paper, ca. 1730 C.E., Punjab Hills, India.

2. Lid of an alabaster jar, with newly hatched fledgling surrounded by four eggs. Painted wood with ivory tongue, from the tomb of Tutankhamun, 18th dynasty (ca. 1332–23 B.C.E.), Egypt.

3. A divine bird man, perhaps the creator god Make, holding the egg from which the universe was hatched. Pigment on stone, possibly late 18th century to mid-19th century C.E., Orongo, Easter Island (Rapa Nui), Polynesia.

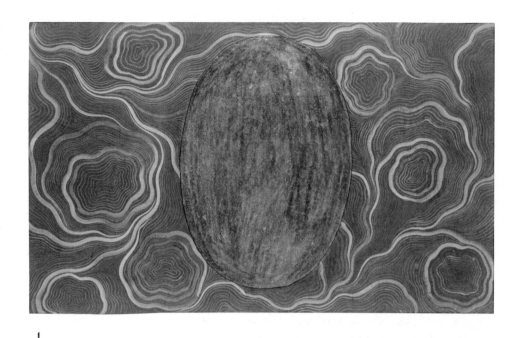

1

2

3

Breath

Nose almost touches nose in a mystical sharing of breath between god and king. With his right hand, the pharaoh, Sesostris I, wearing the pleated royal headdress, touches the head of the creator god Ptah. Responding, the deity, mummiform to signify his immortality, embraces the king and breathes into him life, stability, prosperity and health, "all joy" (ARAS, 2Ag.035).

Breath animates the clay of our being. It is the lusty cry of the newborn, and the essence of wind, spirit, muse, sound. Our feeling states manifest in changes of breath, from the panicky shortness of breath to the sighs "too deep for words" of intense sorrow. Breath carries other things like disease, harsh words and rank odors. Everything "breathes." Think of a woods on a spring day, the susurration of leaves, the rippling grasses, the trembling of dappled light. "The Tao is the breath that never dies. It is a Mother to All Creation," says the *Tao Te Ching* (37). Classical Greece perceived breath as something vaporous within, dew-like, sometimes visible, blending and interacting with the air (Onians, 48). To hear, see, smell or speak was to send out breath, sometimes as a ray or as fire; the breath mixed with the "intelligence" in the breath of others, and taken back in, added to one's knowledge. Breath was identified with consciousness, locating both thought and feelings in the lungs, which interacted with the heart, blood and pulse. "In men of understanding the eyes and tongue and ears and mind are rooted in the midst of their breasts" (ibid., 70). And the gods as inspiration, Latin *inspirare*, "to breathe," might be experienced in a sudden influx of love, courage, wrath, prophecy or brilliance.

That breath is imagined as essence and exchange is consistent with its chemical reality. Breathing is the taking-in of oxygen and the release of carbon dioxide from the body by a complicated internal pumping mechanism that changes the air pressure inside the body, and so causes oxygen-filled air to enter. Breath links animal and plant life: Animals require oxygen and release carbon dioxide, while plants need carbon dioxide and yield up oxygen. The body stores almost no oxygen, so that breathing is an urgent matter; death is literally, as in the Inuit language, "losing your breath." Because breath is what quickens the body, it is equated with soul, which is thought to take wing on the last breath of life.

Do we breathe or are we breathed? The Sanskrit *prana*, "breathing forth," refers to the source and force of life and the vibratory energy of all manifestation (EoR, 11:483–5). The sacred texts of India describe the vital breath of the living being, rhythmic and pulsating, as the microcosmic form of the alternating day and night, activity and rest, of cosmic time. In the interval between successive creations, the god Vishnu, having withdrawn the universe back into himself, sleeps, floating on the cosmic ocean in the coils of the serpent Ananta, "Endless." His breathing is deep, sonorous, rhythmical, "the magic melody of the creation and dissolution of the world" (Zimmer, 35ff). It is the song of the immortal gander, the soft *ham-sa* of divine life-breath within the body of the universe and the nucleus of the individual. "Just as spokes are held together in a wheel-hub, everything is held together in the breath" (Chandogya Upanishad, Vii.15:1, 189). The yogi, in controlled inhalation-*ham*, exhalation-*sa*, hears the same melody as the inner presence of the Atman, or supreme self, being revealed.

Laozi. *Tao Te Ching*. NY, 1993.
Roebuck, Valerie J. *The Upaninsads*.
New Delhi and NY, 2000.
Zimmer, Heinrich. *Myths and Symbols in Indian Art and Civilisation*. NY, 1946.

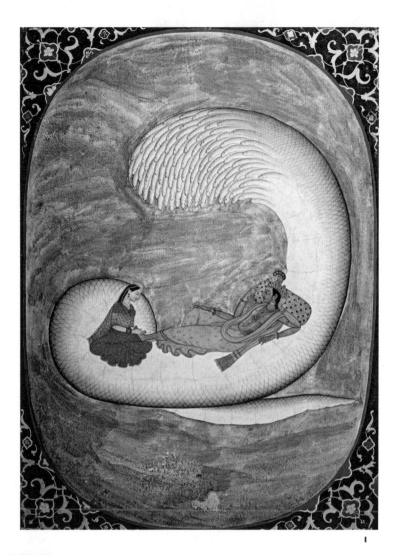

1

2

1. Within the Golden Egg, the god Vishnu reclines on the fluid coils of the primordial sea, his breath the flowing in, flowing out of endless creations. Painting on paper, ca. 1760 C.E., India.

2. The immortal Ptah breathes on the Egyptian pharaoh, investing him with renewed power and strength. Relief, detail from the Pillar of Sesostris I, 12th dynasty (ca. 1971–28 B.C.E.), Egypt.

Star

It does not prevent me from having a terrible need of, shall I say the word—of religion—then I go outside in the night to paint the stars ....
Vincent van Gogh, in a letter to his brother Theo, Arles, September 1888

Twinkling in the more than 100 billion galaxies of the universe, the sheer numbers of stars are almost unimaginable. The stars of deep space that we see through telescopes on a clear, dark night are so ancient and so far away that their light has taken millions, even billions of years to travel to us. There are no peoples in the world who have not projected into the starry heavens the preeminent forces and myths of their cosmos. The great goddess—Inanna, Ishtar, Aphrodite—was everywhere the radiant evening-and-morning star, arc of the mysteries of sleep, dream, death and regeneration. We watch and wish on stars, pray to stars and see in them the phosphors of our psychic firmament. For thousands of years stars have oriented the wanderer, sailor and pilgrim just as consciousness navigating its unknown darkness takes its bearings from the scintillations of psyche's imaginal forms. Stars tell us of the infinite, the visionary, of something in ourselves that is starlike, star stuff. In loss, we look up and find in the beckoning incandescence of a single star the longed-for soul of the departed.

Out of galactic clouds of gas and dust, a star forms over millions of years into an immense ball, self-luminous with radiation from trillions of nuclear reactions at its core, and is held intact and bound to other stars and planets within its galaxy by the gravitational pull of dark matter (Greene, 295). Though Plato described it as "the moving likeness of eternity," a star eventually implodes under its own weight when its nuclear fuel is exhausted. If it is a massive star, its death can create a supernova, a series of explosions that blow off the star's outer layers in a radioactive cloud that causes a brilliance equal to a billion suns and finally ends as a black hole where the gravity is so strong that even light cannot escape it.

Long before we knew the phenomenal nature of a star, it suggested a nuclear, enigmatic "point" or "monad" whose source of gravity was mysterious and abysmal. Egyptian Nut, the lovely goddess of the night sky, was depicted as giving birth to the stars and taking them up against her dark belly (Clark, 50), the way unconscious gives birth to consciousness and darkly encompasses the luster of its individual spark. In the Pyramid Texts, the deceased was directed to become an "imperishable star" and so live forever (Quirke, 50). Alchemy adopted the theme in its goal of bringing the conflicting "many" of the self into a luminous and unified "one." Evocative of the magnetic "center" and its capacity to order and synthesize, the pole star, in Egypt known as "that place" or "the great city," was perceived as the node of the universe, the center of its regulation and the seat of the high god who presides over the cosmic circuit of stars (Clark, 58). In unmoving solitude in the midst of the heavens as at the center of a mandala, the pole star appeared to the Chinese as the stillness of an emperor surrounded by his glittering court, and alchemy described it as the fiery heart of its spirit Mercurius.

Stars are also felt as ambivalent; we speak of our good stars and evil stars. The ancients discovered in the "wheel of the stars" a divinatory map, or zodiac, based on the orbits of the sun, moon and planets in relation to the fixed star constellations. Astrology brought the outer heavens into correspondence with the inner by calculating the position of the heavenly bodies at the moment of an individual's birth. The "writing in the heavens" could seem fated, however. *Heimarmene*, the "compulsion of the stars," referred to unconscious patterns of behavior that felt unalterable and determinative; it was a goal of religious rites and of healing process even in their oldest forms to bring these patterns under conscious agency, thereby breaking their compulsive power.

Stars continue to stir us at the deepest levels. The black hole has been compared to alchemy's "black blacker than black" of psychic fragmentation and

1. *Untitled (Stars no. 1)*, detail, by Karen Arm, acrylic on canvas, 1999, United States.

absolute despair. M. L. von Franz thought of it as an image of the soul outside the "event horizon" of space and time—existing beyond death in a state of unextended intensity, or "psychification" (p. 139). Alchemists called the imagination a celestial or supercelestial star because of its ability to shed light on, transform and transcend the fetters of existence (CW 12:394). Paracelsus used the term for the numinous "light of nature," which he believed was innate uniquely in each individual and also in animals as an inborn spirit. Only self-knowledge, he believed, can teach us of this "quintessence," and the learning is unconventional, engaging intuition, feeling, fantasy and dreams: "As the light of nature cannot speak, it buildeth shapes in sleep" (CW 8:390–391). These, too, are like stars, reflections of eternity in the dark pool of our being.

Clark, Robert and Thomas Rundle.
Myth and Symbol in Ancient Egypt. London, 1959.
Greene, Brian. *The Fabric of the Cosmos*. NY, 2004.
Quirke, Stephen. *Ancient Egyptian Religion*. NY, 1992.
von Franz, Marie-Louise. *Psyche and Matter*. Boston, 1992.

2

2. *Starry Night, Arles*, by Vincent van Gogh, oil on canvas, 1888, France.

3. Five-pointed stars as emblem of gods and immortal souls. Painting from the tomb of Iry-nufer, 1305–1200 B.C.E., Theban Necropolis, Egypt.

3

Sun

To have the whole air!—
The light, the full sun
Coming down on the flowerheads ...
Theodore Roethke, "The Shape of the Fire"

So when earth,
After that flood, still muddy, took the heat,
Felt the warm fire of sunlight, she conceived ...
Ovid, Metamorphoses, Bk 1:432–434

Loveliest of what I leave behind
is the sunlight ...
Praxílla of Sícyon

How easy it is to be captivated by the sheer splendor of the sun's shining, by its capacity to make manifest a world it seeds with its own fire. How naturally we imagine our own capacity to know and to create, as the bright sun of consciousness. How many of the thousands of sense perceptions imprinted upon the body and mind over a lifetime are authored by the sun; how instinctively flora and fauna turn their faces sunward, as if to the Center. And if in temperate zones sunlight may be taken for granted, its more rare occurrence in frigid climes can be experienced as a kind of grace: "benign ... forgiving ... run through with compassion in a land that bore so eloquently the evidence of centuries of winter" (Lopez, xx).

The nuclear fusion reactions at the core of "our hot, stable, brightly burning star" (Greene, 171) convert 4,000,000 tons of matter into energy every second, a small amount of which supports life on earth. To sun worshippers over millennia, solar rays have seemed to transfer magical properties of fertility, creativity, prophecy, healing and even (for the alchemists) a living potentiality for wholeness that dwells in every individual. No wonder then that the sun has evoked the illustrious, worldly prestige and authority of rulers and royalty who wear the sunlike crown, the world-transcending intelligence of the "enlightened one," the

pellucid vision of the haloed saint, and the *solificatio* or achievement of highest illumination by the initiate of mysteries. As the heavenly warrior, the sun's blazing light turns back the darkness of primeval chaos; as the hunter, his arrowlike rays unerringly hit the target. The majestic solar dynamism embodied in lion, tiger, horse and ram is also reflected in the soaring eagle and the hawk. Casting its maternal gaze over the world, the sun is the eye of the Mother of All; as the omniscient, all-seeing Eye of Allah, it is the exacting guardian of universal order.

But just as the Hindu god Rudra in his aspect as "fire, lightning and the sun" destructively "devours flesh, blood and marrow" with his burning, "atrocious" heat (Kramrisch, 15), so also the ferocity of the sun exhausts the body, boils the brain and drives to madness. The merciless "solar" intellect preternaturally exposes the burgeoning creative idea or intuition taking root in darkness, or, ablaze with self-love, voraciously pursues its boundless lust for knowledge. The familiar Greek myths of Icarus and Phaethon are instructive: To fly too near the sun is to lose one's ground(edness); to become identified with the inflammable, archetypal energies that far exceed mortal limitation is to court destruction and death.

For the alchemists, the alchemical Sol carried, like its physical counterpart, an amalgam of energies. On the one hand, Sol is the bright "day" life of the psyche as well as the sulphurous "active substance" that compels it toward specific goals. As King Sol it represents the authority of particular principles investing consciousness; as the "ailing" king, their waning and disintegration. But Sol was also the "gold," the "yellow balsam," the *veritas*, or truth, behind the capacity of consciousness for self-healing and rejuvenation through immersion in moist, lunarlike feelings, moods and dreams reflecting the magical and mercurial. The regenerated "Sun of the Philosophers" was both transparent and opaque, a sun and a consciousness paradoxically both light and shadow.

1. Jyoti (Light). Spirit and matter—the transparency of consciousness and the crystallization of light as form—coalesce in the golden disk of the sun. Tempera painting with gold, ca. 18th century, India.

As Ovid's recounting of the myth of the flood suggests, earth and sun have always been partners in the conception and nurturing of life. With the phenomenon of global warming, and consequent overturning of the natural order, the ages-old alliance may be irrevocably compromised. But for the moment we can still rejoice in the mutual revealing of the loveliness of the world manifested under the loveliness of sunlight, or watch a kiting falcon turn a burnished gold as it momentarily catches the full blaze of a late afternoon sun, and imagine the ancient solar deity, wings spread protectively over the earth.

Greene, Brian. *The Fabric of the Cosmos*. NY, 2004.
Kramrisch, Stella. *The Presence of Siva*.
Princeton, NJ, 1981.
Greek Lyrics. Chicago, 1960.
Lopez, Barry Holstun. *Arctic Dreams*. NY, 1986.

2

3

4

2. The power over the earth of the falcon-headed sun-god Horakhti (Horus-of-the-Horizon), is particularly evident at sunrise and sunset. His flower sun rays, directed at the worshipping Taperet, evoke the cardinal power of creation and the primordial opening of the cosmic lotus bud, when light first emerged in the world. Painted wood stele of Lady Taperet, 22nd dynasty (1070–712 B.C.E.), Egypt.

3. The concentrated energy of the "Sunburst" mandala is at once symmetrically contained and creatively dispersed through multiple rays. Surrounded by golden phoenixes, birds and plants, the mandala evokes the

celestial order and beneficence over which the sun presides, and its earthly reflection in shah and empire. Opening folio from an album *Shamsa ("sunburst")*, inscribed with the titles of Shah Jahan (1628–58), ca. 1645, India.

4. The sun's elemental power of fertility, nurturing light and warmth, and a more ambiguous capacity for fierceness, is conveyed in the figure of Sun Woman, whose hut is also a sun-wheel. *Sun Woman in Her Hut*, by Tjamalampuwa, ochre on bark, 1954, Melville Island, Australia.

Moon

I was a stranger on earth.
Stepping on the moon, I begin
the gay pilgrimage to new
Jerusalems
in foreign galaxies.
Heat. Cold. Craters of silence.
The Sea of Tranquility
rolling on the shores of entropy.
And, beyond,
the intelligence of the stars.
Stanley Kunitz, *The Flight of Apollo*

Mother, the moon is dancing
in the courtyard of the dead.
Federico Garcia Lorca,
Dance of the Moon in Santiago

Not a soul ever visits my hut
Except the friendly light of the moon,
Peeping through the woods.
Saigyō

Thank goodness for the moon's inconstancy—the loveliness, the fearsomeness, the portentousness of its measured concealments and revealments; the apportioned variability of its shadow and light. How reassuring the cadence of lunar time, its allowances for increase and necessary diminishment. How potent the "nocturnal predominance" (James Joyce) of the moon and of the particular mode of consciousness we think of as "lunar." How myriad are the moon's enchantments: the way that objects and spaces, ordinary by day, assume a cool essentiality under moonlight; the way the moon will reflect itself in a river, and in the innumerable mental, emotional and physical liquidities of living beings. The way that ocean and sea are "kneaded by the moon" (Thomas Hardy); how it soothes, as "nurse of the dew," the fiery excesses of the sun. The way the moon "hangs in the vacant, wide constellations" (Tu Fu, "Full Moon"); how its resplendent currencies can incite to creative, spiritual, magical, sexual, prophetic and lunatic disposition.

The celestial body nearest to Earth, the moon's kinship with the planet is evident in the dominions of the ancient lunar deities. Embodied in the progenerative "Bull of Heaven," or in the cow-headed Hathor, whose milk nourishes the world, in Nana-Sin the celestial physician, or black-cloaked Isis, whose "misty radiance nurses the happy seeds under the soil" (Apuleis), the moon presides over conception, pregnancy and birth, over the agricultural cycles of sowing and reaping, over every kind of coming into being. She is mistress of moisture; of the juices of life including sap, spittle, semen, menstrual blood, the nectar and poisons of plant and animal. She governs the humid vapors that promote decay, the moisture that falls as

1

1. Earth's ancient affinity with the moon is evoked by the gentle inclination of autumn flowers basking in its splendidly reticent light. *Full Moon and Autumn Flowers by the Stream*, by Ogata Gekko (1859–1920), fan-shaped wood-block print, Meiji period, ca. 1895, Japan.

rain or dew, the ebb and flow of every body of water; the favorable or unfavorable outcome of every navigation. As lord of ecstasy the moon reigns over all intoxications and inspirations. As Thoth, the baboon-headed god of measure and due proportion, it presides over learning, wisdom and writing as well as magic and spells. The moon is the mystic vessel containing the milky soma of immortality; the ship of souls that transports the dead to heaven, or the Manichean "elect" to the Pillars of Glory. In radiant fullness, the "circle without blemish" (Tu Fu, "Full Moon") is the Buddhist symbol of tranquility and perfect truth.

Because the moon spins on its own axis in the identical time it takes to orbit the Earth, its lighted "near side" is always turned earthward, just as its perpetually dark "far side" is always turned away. "Everyone is a moon," wrote Mark Twain, "and has a dark side which he never shows to anybody." For alchemists, it is the task of the adept to navigate this unchartered territory of the soul, and bring it, so far as possible, into consciousness. The dangers of the undertaking are intrinsic to the allurements and the gravitational pull of Luna herself. The adept can emerge from the far side of the psyche initiated into self-knowledge, or become irretrievably lost in the darkness. Similarly, spiritual ravishment by the moon spirit can inspire to transformative heights and depths, or to vaporous fantasies that draw the individual out of reality. The lunar chill emanating from one's own shadow can numb the soul, its desolation mirrored in the face of the moon:

White as a knuckle and terribly upset.
It drags the sea after it like a dark crime;
it is quiet
With the O-gape of complete despair. I live here.
Sylvia Plath, "The Moon and the Yew Tree"

It is disconcerting to think that one day space shuttles crowded with human tourists might regularly travel to the moon, or that moon miners might excavate her ancient innards. For now, however, we have not entirely demythologized the moon. We can still look up and see the lunar hare or frog or moonflower. Selene, the "Shining One," still looks upon us with her womanly gaze. In the invisibility of the new moon Hecate, the crone, yet guards the secrets of death and regeneration. And Artemis, the maiden hunter, still skims the heavens with star-hounds at her heels. The moon remains Earth's friend and muse, guiding us to new Jerusalems or four and a half billion years into the past. And still, in the night sky, her "same clear glory extends for ten thousand miles" (Tu Fu, "Full Moon").

2

2. The moon's phases are changing appearances in recurrent cycles of "becoming visible."

3. The formidable and invigorating power of the feminine as mediator and image of the self is embodied by the figure of Luna standing in the curve of the crescent moon. From the wedding book *Le nozze di Costantio Sforza e Camilla d'Aragona*, 1480, Italy.

LVNA.

Crescent

High up in the branches of a tree silhouetted against an evening sky glows a slender arc of light, the crescent of the new moon. A modern image, it is rooted, perhaps, in the ancient symbol of the Sumerian moon tree, "the house of the mighty mother who passes across the sky" (Harding, 48). Like the horns of a white cow, the crescent moon curves delicately around space that is black and hollow, yet fecund with the promise of light to come as the moon swells into fullness. The crescent's boatlike shape conjures Babylonian Ishtar, the "Ship of Life" who bears the seeds of all living things (Jung, 370). It is Byzantium's Io and her daughter Keroessa, "the horned" (ERE 12: 145). It evokes the maiden aspect of the Greek triple-headed moon goddess, the breathtaking beauty and potency of the kore: Athena, Persephone, Artemis, "goddess of the night, glory of the stars," who holds a crescent moon or wears one in her hair. So, too, does the Christian Madonna rest her feet on the crescent moon, a paradoxical image of chaste virgin and vessel of divine birth.

The horns of the crescent moon are also of the masculine principle, the Mesopotamian moon god, the great bull who fecundates cows, marshland and human women with his spermatic dew. The word crescent is from the Latin word *crescere*, to increase; thus the crescent as new moon was a time to make wishes, plant seeds and turn over silver coins in one's pocket to make them increase along with the moon's silver. Prayers of gratitude met the ever-returning sliver of light that superseded the dangerous "lunacy" and terrifying void of the dark moon.

However, the crescent itself has a sharp edge. As the sickle of death, the Artemian bow of slaughter, the alchemical Luna as bride who is "not only lovely and innocent, but witch-like and terrible," the crescent moon attests to the captivating beauty and potential danger of the "animated" unconscious psyche (CW, 14, 24ff). The crescent that begins the moon's waxing is identical with the crescent that completes the moon's waning. The bright maiden and anima soul is one with the aged crone. Crescent reminds us of the mortality of everything that begins life, the transience of everything that comes into consciousness. Yet the nature of the crescent is not the completion of the circle or the confinement of what lies within. Rather, it suggests the horned gateway of the moon's eternal cycling and if it promises an end to every beginning, it equally signifies the promise of beginning wherever there is end.

Harding, M. Esther. *Woman's Mysteries, Ancient and Modern.* NY, 1972.
Jung, C. G. *Dream Analysis: Notes of the Seminar Given in 1928–1930.* Princeton, NJ, 1984.
Sierksma, Fokke. *The Gods as We Shape Them.* London, 1960.

The bright crescent of a new moon shines from its leafy matrix as daylight fades, heralding the ascendancy of the night. *Le Seize Septembre*, by René Magritte, oil on canvas, 1956, France.

Eclipse

Eerily beautiful sign of conjunction, a single spot of photospheric light shining through a gap on the moon's edge, or limb, appears "as a brilliant gem set on a band of ghostly, subdued coronal light," the so-called "diamond ring effect" (Mechler, 112). It occurs in a total solar eclipse seconds before the moon overlies the entire surface of the sun, casting the earth into untimely nightfall.

For our prescientific ancestors who feared the permanent extinction of the sun's vital light, the less than eight minutes spent in the 2,000 mph path of the umbra (shadow) of a total solar eclipse must have felt like an interminable time before the sun's seemingly miraculous reappearance. The wonder of the eclipse is that the apparent size of the sun and moon are nearly identical. This is caused by the fact that the sun's diameter is 400 times greater than the moon's and at the same time 400 times more distant. The chance capacity of the moon to eclipse the sun's glowing core while revealing its fiery corona is considered by modern astronomers—who routinely view jeweled nebulae and the birth of stars—as one of the most sublime sights a human can witness. Traditional cultures everywhere, however, typically perceived the sun to be enshrouded by demonic forces as the midday breezes ceased, temperatures dropped and birds began to roost. The entire village would gather to banish the baleful effects by firing arrows at the malign spirits, frightening them off with drums or torchlight, sacrificing humpbacks or dwarfs or burying lamps underground in imitative magic.

Eclipse, from the Greek *ekleipsis*, means abandonment, failing, cessation, omission or flaw. Solar eclipses happen when a dark or new moon, often mythically portrayed as inauspicious or dangerous because hidden, passes in front of the sun. A solar eclipse was experienced as the abandonment of the earth by the "omission" of its emblem of creation, life, warmth, light and consciousness. Out of time, darkness reigns, however briefly, associating eclipse with ominous possibilities—plague, earthquake, apocalypse, the death of a ruler or a savior. In partial eclipses, the planes of the orbits of the sun and moon are not perfectly aligned, and the moon cuts into only a portion of the sun's body, deforming it. Many peoples imagined an eclipse of the sun as a wounding or devouring of the solar principle by cosmic snake, jaguar, demon or dragon, forces of the night, dark and chthonic; in China the ideogram for eclipse and eat (*ch'u*) are identical. Others portrayed eclipse as pursuit and incestuous coitus between divine siblings. Alchemy represented solar eclipse as the descent of *Sol* into the lunar "fountain," or an encompassing of the masculine by the feminine—Osiris by Isis, Christ by the Virgin Mary. Such images combined the themes of union, dissolution, deathly marriage or the "dead balance" of opposites canceling each other out. Yet it also portended the possibility of rebirth in the psychic matrix, or out of the symbolic coitus, the conception of a new spirit of double nature, solar and lunar.

Lunar eclipses occur at the time of a full moon, when the moon passes through earth's shadow. The sunlight that normally illuminates the moon's surface is blocked, and the moon dims to a coppery red or grayish color. Rarely does the moon completely disappear, since some sunlight reaches it through the earth's atmosphere, but its lunar brilliance is obscured. Visible from the side of the earth facing the moon, lunar eclipses may be partial or total. Totality can last for almost two hours and the entire eclipse for four. Lunar eclipse is depicted as a shadowing of the moon's soulful luminosity by earthly "corruption," or is a theft of the moon's life-giving dew of feeling, inspiration, emanation, reverie, dream and fruition. In a Hindu myth, the severed head of the demon Rahu pursues the moon, the "effulgent cup from which the gods drink the Amrita," the elixir of immortality. Eclipses occur when Rahu is able to grasp and swallow the heavenly cup, but passing through his disembodied head and neck, the "boon-bestowing orb" reappears (Zimmer, 175-6).

Eclipse means that the ordinary lights on which we depend are temporarily quenched. Nightly, sleep eclipses our waking awareness, which sinks exhausted into the liquid realm of dreams. More afflicting, the light of nature within ourselves can be eclipsed by affects, moods, traumas and compulsions. Eclipse conveys the idea of the ego being overshadowed by the unconscious or the ego itself blocking the essential source of illumination. But while life can be eclipsed in many ways, the symbolism and science of celestial eclipse attest to a provisional extinguishing of the light, inevitably followed by its welcome resurgence.

Mechler, Gary, et al. *The Sun and the Moon.* NY, 1995.
Zimmer, Heinrich Robert. *Myths and Symbols in Indian Art and Civilization.* Princeton, NJ, 1972.

1

2

1. A photograph shot from a planetarium in Utah records the sun's final flash of jewel-like brilliance before the moon conceals it in a total solar eclipse. A rare marvel, this phenomenon is unlikely to recur at the same site for three or four centuries.

2. The immortal head of the Balinese demon Kala Rauh (Rahu in India) swallowing the sun. Ceiling painting from a temple shrine.

Comet

A great light blazes through the night sky in a photograph from the beginning of the twentieth century. This brilliant, uncanny visitor that slowly travels across the darkness is a comet. Through the ages, comets have inspired both wonder and dread. As a bad omen, the comet signaled the disruption of the established order, but it also heralded the appearance of something new under the sun.

A comet is actually a "dirty snowball" of cosmic ice and dust, which travels from the far edges of the solar system (Krupp, 315). As it orbits near the sun, the ice vaporizes into a glowing gas that surrounds the nucleus, and forms a tail that can extend for millions of miles (Chapman, 4–5).

The word comet derives from *kometes*, a Greek word meaning "the long-haired," (Partridge, 112) referring to the comet's hairlike tail. In the *Iliad*, Achilles connects this feature with the comet's supposed malevolence, "Like the red star from his flaming hair / Shakes down disease, pestilence and war" (Krupp, 313). And when Electra saw Troy going up in flames, she was said to have torn her hair out with grief, and was then placed by the gods among the stars as a comet (Bell, 54).

The elliptical orbit of comets is tilted in relation to the flat plane of planetary orbits, and may take a few years or many centuries to complete (Chapman, 5–6). Before the discovery of their periodic return, comets seemed unpredictable, interrupting the annual transit of constellations and the reassuring regularity of the planets. For cultures around the world, comets were portents of natural disaster, particularly of flood, famine and plague (DoS, 226).

Political, social or religious upheaval was often connected with the appearance of comets. The death of the Aztec king Montezuma at the hands of the Spanish and the murder of Julius Caesar both coincided with the sighting of comets (DoS, 226). The Norman Invasion in 1066 was preceded by the return of Halley's Comet. It has been speculated that the star of Bethlehem that announced the birth of Christ was a comet's unexpected brightness (Krupp, 307, 314).

Because of their origination in the heavens and their suddenness and brightness, comets, like meteors and UFOs, are potent hooks for psychic projections. Jung speculated that they represent "strange contents" from the collective unconscious that oppose the values held consciously by the culture. On account of their strangeness and their intimation of revolutionary change, such contents cannot be integrated directly. They thus get projected on unusual natural phenomena and interpreted as "menacing omens" or marvelous signs (CW 10:608–10).

What we now know about comets is that seemingly random, they actually make cyclical returns; perhaps the changes they portend can also be said to have continuity, to be part of a larger pattern. Recent research theorizes that comets have seeded the earth, from its earliest days, with carbon-rich molecules, the forerunners of the amino acids that form DNA. Thus the "strange contents" that have been so often feared may be the very essence of creative beginning (Broad, C1).

Bell, Robert E. *Dictionary of Classical Mythology.* Oxford and Santa Barbara, CA, 1982.
Broad, William J. "The Comet's Gift: Hints of How Earth Came to Life." *The New York Times* (April 1, 1997).
Chapman, Robert DeWitt and John C. Brandt. *The Comet Book: A Guide for the Return of Halley's Comet.* Boston, 1984.
Krupp, E. C. *Beyond the Blue Horizon: Myths and Legends of the Sun, Moon, Stars, and Planets.* NY, 1991.
Partridge, Eric. *Origins.* NY, 1958.

Halley's comet photographed in France during its
passage on May 26, 1910. Retouched vintage
photograph, France.

Ocean

*It wasn't a heavy sea—it was a sea gone mad!
I suppose the end of the world will be some-
thing like that ...*
Joseph Conrad, *The Secret Sharer*

*One lovely autumn afternoon, I saw a beautiful
white gull sailing along the volute of a breaker
accompanied by his reflection in the wave.*
Henry Beston, *The Outermost House*

*There was neither non-existence nor existence
then; there was neither the realm of space nor
the sky which is beyond. What stirred? Where?
In whose protection? Was there water, bottom-
lessly deep?*
***Rig Veda,** 10.129 Creation Hymn*

Whether we are inveterate inlanders or dwell perpetually on the tide line, we have an oceanic memory.
Indeed, such are the correspondences between ocean
and our psychic depths that the two might be visible
and invisible forms of the same reality. In the one, as
in the other, subterranean and celestial fluidities coalesce. Their most abyssal regions are largely impenetrable. "Living fossils" in the sea, like the archaic energies in the psyche, have remained largely unchanged
over millions of years, lurking in the icy darkness of
the bottom waters. Whole ecosystems, untouched by
sunlight, flourish in the sea just as networks of accumulated experience flourish in the psyche, enhancing
the waters regardless of our knowledge of their existence. In each of us, salty, amniotic waters run in our
mnemonic veins. Tidal currents course through our
deeps and shallows, yielding to the rhythmic pull of
moon and sun. The undulations of our myriad intensi-

ties combine in ever-changing patterns reflected on our
surfaces, just as the patterns of wave trains—
"intermingling, overtaking, passing, or sometimes engulfing one another" (Carson, 109–10)—are endlessly
reconfigured over the face of the sea.

Ancient and primal, the ocean is our mother of
mothers, the Great Round within whose fluid containment life began and from whose fertile precincts the
first bold pioneers scuttled out upon the sand. For eons
her "wild and clear call" has summoned poet and ar-
gonaut, contemplative and castaway to the "dark glory"
of her nurturing, mysterious reaches. You can be lulled
like a cosmic child in the cradle of her shoals, just as
the ego surrenders to the universal mergence of sleep
and dream. You can be lifted on a rearing whitecap, or
borne on a wave of creative inspiration, and be carried
shoreward with transporting exhilaration. You can be
cleansed by the arctic ice of her impersonal majesty,
baptized in the coruscating radiations of her phospho-
rescent fire. Just as her innumerable progeny, flashing
their bioluminescent lamps now here, now there, will
light your way over her darkness, so on the mythic
night sea journey, the glittering, intuitive, "living lights"
in the psyche will help negotiate the depths.

We are droplets in the vast liquidity of the sea, and
just as the ocean can swallow whole our titanic ships
and jumbo jets, so our little vessels of human consciousness are liable to engulfment by the deepest waters of psyche. Its vital energies can loom like mythical sea monsters: sucking us up, spitting us out,
dismembering. The churning of its abyss can activate
archetypal epicenters of potentially shattering force.
Shipwrecked by the elemental dynamism of emotional
storm waves, we sink into a bottomless, cold, sepul-
chral gloom that no ray of sunlight can penetrate. In

1. *Untitled (Ocean no. 1)*, detail, by Karen Arm,
painting on paper, 1994, United States.

1

much the same way the surpassing power of the ocean, whose continuous saltwaters sweep 40 million square miles (nearly 71 percent) over the terrestrial surface, vitiates the sovereignty of the mainland. In the disequilibria of her trenches—which may extend seven miles beneath sea level, the deepest place(s) on the planet—earthquakes are bred. Their convulsive shocks give birth to seismic sea waves that rise up like gigantic renegade tides, overrunning the coastal habitations that form the tenuous boundary between sea and land. Lethal storm waves lashed by hurricane winds and borne up by storm tides invade the "ordered world" and batter it into chaos. Even the teeming abundance at the ocean's sunlit surfaces can detonate a pandemonium of competing appetites.

Yet like the upwelling and sinking downward of diverse currents; the displacement of upper layers by the rich, revitalizing, colder waters from below, the inexhaustibly fertile, ever-changing waters of psyche are sustaining and rejuvenating. Traversing its Great Waters brings one side(dness) face to face with its opposite shore. The bitter salt of engagement with unknown depths can be transmuted into wisdom. "Journeying birds alight here and fly away again all unseen, schools of great fish move beneath the waves, the surf flings its spray against the sun" (Beston, 2).

Beston, Henry. *The Outermost House*. NY, 1981.
Carson, Rachel. *The Sea Around Us*. NY, 1961.

3

2. The gods and the demons work together, churning the milk ocean in order to obtain the elixir of immortality. *The Churning of the Milk Ocean*, gouache on paper, late 19th century, Uttar Pradesh, India.

3. Waves as the restlessness of the sea and the psyche. *Hatō Zu ("Rough Waves")*, by Ogata Korin, double screen, 1704–9, Japan.

River

Orinoco, Achelous, Mississippi, Nile ... Ganges, Hudson, Danube ... Styx and Lethe ... Namings of moving waters flowing between two banks, waters rolling as Time itself, as if veins of the Great Mother Earth. River is vital fluidity; the rivers move through both the upper world and the lower world, over ground and underground, inside and outside: rivers of fertility and prosperity, rivers of forgetting, rivers of binding oath, rivers of commerce, rivers of blood and rivers of water, rivers of rebirth, rivers of death, rivers of sorrow, all presided over in our mythic history by beneficent deities, dreadful nixies or changeable river spirits. Rivers have been central to civilizations locating along their banks, offering fresh or freshening water, living fish, clay, fertile soil, flood cycles and waterways as famously along the Nile, Tigris and Euphrates. The rivers have been the abode of immortals who have offered these many gifts as well as the gifts of purity, cleansing, grace and a mythic passage to the "other shore." Nefarious water spirits can just as easily take life, claiming the bodies of those who drown in swift and unpredictable currents. The river speaks of life as flow, freedom, movement, dangerous currents, drowning, running ever along, running its course, flooding, also as confinement, direction, holding, channeling. The river reminds us that we can never rise above our source; all rivers flow downhill from their source, finally terminating in a sea or confluence. Creatures can be driven to swim upstream, like the salmon, and others just go with the flow; rivers carry things and are transporting in ways both literal and metaphorical. And rivers can run dry, their beds worn and empty, signs of a changing course or season, nature living in time. Language is a river of words ... a river of poetry and music transporting the head of Orpheus; rivers are weary, strong, flowing, sparkling, gushing, falling, rapid, smooth, heavy, bright. Everything that lives partakes of the quality of riverness.

Mythologies speak of how the great waters came to earth as river. The rivers diverged into four in Paradise and into seven in ancient India ... waters of life flowing from the source into the world need to multiply. The Ganges, the holiest of the three holy rivers in India, flows from Vishnu's toe through heaven, earth and the world below. Once upon a time the Holy river of Ganga wound round Mount Meru three times in the city of Brahma. Then one day Bhagiratha prayed for the river Ganga to descend from the highest abode of the gods to earth and beyond to the depths that they may reach and revive the 60,000 Sagaras, his ancestors, whose ashes lay in the underworld. His prayers were answered, but the might of the holy waters was far too much for the earth to withstand, so Shiva offered his matted hair to catch the river in her descent so that her landing might be softened for humankind. She emerged from Shiva's hair in seven streams, one of which is the Ganges. In the underworld, the waters cascaded and flowed over the ashes of the 60,000, at which point their souls rose to the heavens. Over a million Hindus journey to Varanasi, where the three holiest streams meet, each year to bathe in her waters, cleansing themselves of the karma of previous lives, and assuring an auspicious rebirth. The waters of the river can promise rebirth, as the River Jordan was a baptism of souls into a new life in spirit. "Shall we gather at the river?"

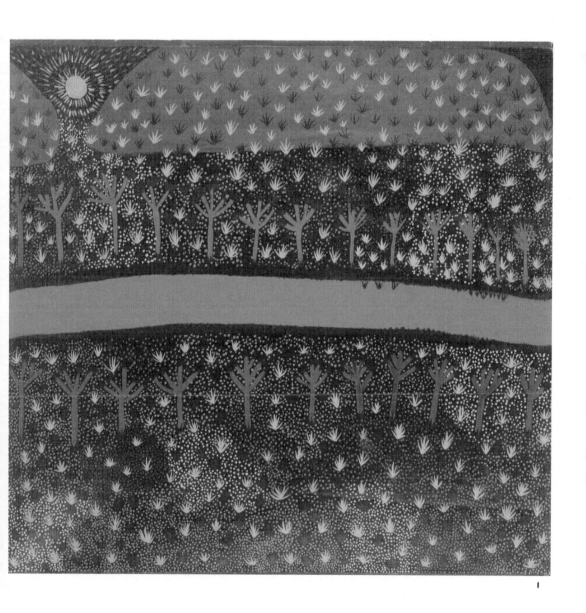

1

1. The Dreaming of the artist Lily Sandover Kngwarreye,
Sandover River, painting, 1989, Australia.

Alongside the image of rebirth is the river crossing, an age-old symbol of crossing over to the other shore, the land of the dead. To die is to "cross over." In Greek mythology Charon ferries the dead across the river Styx in the underworld. The river is a boundary between lands and between the living and the dead. Crossing is a transition and a metaphor for the possibility of traveling between the mind's two shores, the conscious and familiar shore and the unconscious farther shore.

And the river is a teacher. Human beings attempt to alter rivers to better use their power. We build dams to harness power and we straighten river courses to increase their speed and power. Up to a point, nature supports us in this. Yet, "For centuries, the Yellow River symbolized the greatness and sorrows of China's ancient civilization, as emperors equated controlling the river and taming its catastrophic floods with controlling China. Now, the river is a very different symbol of the dire state of China's limited resources at a time when the country's soaring economic growth needs more of everything" (Yardley).

Bachelard, Gaston. *Water and Dreams: An Essay on the Imagination of Matter.* Dallas, 1983.
Roebuck, Valerie J. *The Upaninsads.* New Delhi and NY, 2000.
Yardley, Jim. "A Troubled River Mirrors China's Path to Modernity." *The New York Times* (November 19, 2006).

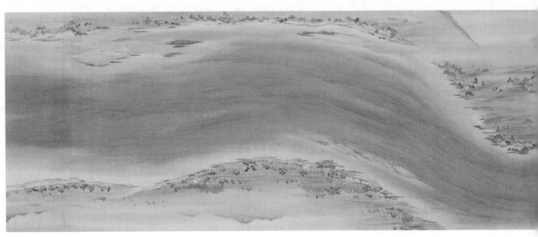

2

2. The complete scroll depicts the river from Kyoto to Osaka, one of the largest slices of topography ever presented in a continuous composition. *Both Banks of the Yodo River*, detail, by Maruyama Ōkyo, ink and color on silk, 1765, Japan.

3. The river Nile personified as a male figure, having breasts of a woman and a large stomach as an indication of fertility. From the *Book of the Dead of Pennesuttawy*, Third Intermediate period, 1070–712 B.C.E., Egypt.

Lake / Pond

The lake is a large tranquil eye. The lake takes
all of light and makes a world out of it.
Through it, the world is already contemplated,
already represented. It too might say,
'The world is my representation of it.'
Gaston Bachelard, *Water and Dreams*

To come upon a lake is to come upon a fluid expanse of mystery, apparently still and yet moving. At lake's edge the earth is suddenly missing, gives way to another medium and appears again at the shore beyond. Hence our word "lacuna" is derived from "*lac*" or lake, and signifies something omitted or missing, a hiatus. The lake, for many peoples, has been a symbol of the land of the dead, of life gone missing into the fluid substance and darkness of another world. The contained reflecting presence of a lake has evoked many mythical ideas. For example, the lake has been seen as earth's open liquid eye at the edge of knowledge where all that is solid dissolves into a two-way mirror of the soul—a sometimes visionary, at other times hungry eye that looks up from the underworld below. Standing at water's edge and gazing out over the surface, we pause and give way to dream, reflection, imagination and illusion; to other worlds below and beyond in ourselves, making lake symbolically the entry, for good or ill, into psyche's unconscious dimensions.

Upon the surface of the lake's reflective eye, the image of earth and sky are inverted at the water's edge. The lake seems to say, "as above, so below," and turns its image of the world upside down. Similarly, the world is presented through the lens of our own eyes upside down, and perception must be "righted" by the brain to present as reality. But at lakeside, rightness is suspended to bring forth a surreal and imaginal dimension, a "more real" space of psychic fluidity where the soul says, "The world is my representation of it."

Harboring underwater life-forms populating its silt, and sometimes deceptively safe to swim in, the lake is so calm and inviting and yet dark and deep.

Lakes have given rise to fantasies of nymphs, seductive nixies and various water demons that live below the surface in jeweled kingdoms and may approach wandering onlookers and swimmers to pull them seductively into the deep. One takes a dive only to be trapped by surprisingly dense marsh and reed growth, and drowns entangled in the seemingly soft green grasses. Lake nymphs and nixies play, as does the lake itself, between surface and depth, illusion and reality. With reflections and fantasies of the heart's desires, these imaginal creatures beguile their victims, drowning them in the paradisal wishes of the unconscious mind. The Lady of the Lake of Arthurian legend was benevolent toward those of knightly virtue and commitment who respected the wisdom of the feminine waters. But as Vivienne, she was the magician Merlin's undoing, not because he lacked respect for the magical dimension, but because loving it too much he was finally imprisoned in it.

Perhaps we think and dream so intimately next to the lake because it reflects us best as the most "body-like" of the bodies of water. Different from an ocean or a great river, the scale of a lake can be encompassed by the human imagination, and lakes, like us, live and die. A lake begins dying as soon as it is formed, taking in sediment from contributing rivers or streams, filling with accumulating organic debris and ever so slowly, as the stretches of geological time progress, turning to marsh, bog and finally land. At the same time the lake is continually taking in water and letting it go, flowing in an apparent stillness and constancy, demonstrating the give and take necessary to support life (*Enc. Brit.*, 13:600). Sustaining mother who provides water, food and favorable climate to those who inhabit her shores, the lake requires in turn a subtle balance of power between human nature and spirit to insure the natural life of her precious waters.

Bachelard, Gaston. *Water and Dreams: An Essay on the Imagination of Matter.* Dallas, 1983.

In Georgia O'Keeffe's painting the lake is mirror of
earth and sky. The "as above, so below" dual reality of
reflection and matter combine to suggest a reclining
female form that evokes the beauty of this world and its
impermanence. *Lake George*, 1922, United States.

Whirlpool

Hiroshige's wood-block image depicts the whirlpools at Awa, their gentle involutions centered at the foreground of an expansive landscape, suggesting transition amid seeming permanence. It is a meditative and tranquil image of whirlpools, the forceful currents brought about by an interaction of rising and falling tides. Carrying associations similar to those of the spiral, these currents are symbolically depicted in relation to the center, unaffected by the impelling forces that surround it. When coastal and ocean bottom configurations are both narrow and deep, however, a whirlpool may exhibit a fearsome downdraft, changing its aspect. The vortex produced by these currents can appear to create an aperture, falling away into immeasurable depths, sucking all things into the void and then disgorging them again. For this reason, the whirlpool is often personified as a monstrous force. In Homer's *The Odyssey*, the whirlpool Charybdis swallows the sea down in the "yawning maw" of its funnel, exposing the black sand at the bottom of the abyss, and then vomits it back up "like a cauldron seething over intense fire" (Homer, 217), suggesting what it still might be for consciousness to be caught in the maelstrom energies of psyche.

Many nautical myths combine the benign and violent aspects of the whirlpool, allowing the chaotic maelstrom (from Dutch for "whirling stream") to function as an initiation, and the center of the vortex to reveal a vision normally hidden from human perceptions. In eleventh century Teutonic myth, sailors entered a maelstrom that opened up onto an island of giants, their hidden gold temporarily unguarded (Rydberg, 320). In the same sense, whirlpools suggest portals to other worlds and times, and in many literary representations, there is a sustained moment where the observer is witness to the underworld. A Cherokee myth details the adventures of two tribesmen on a canoe at the mouth of Suck Creek. One was seized by a fish and never seen again. The other was saved after he "reached the narrowest circle of the maelstrom." Here the water opens and as if looking down through the roof beam of a house, he can see at the bottom of the river a great company, which beckons to him, but before they can seize him the swift current catches him up out of their reach (Mooney, 340). In another story, the abyss has a different aspect (and the depths of psyche can feel equally ambivalent): Edgar Allen Poe's "Descent into the Maelstrom" is based on the whirlpools located near the Lofoten Islands off the coast of Norway. Poe describes a state of calm intelligibility at the heart of the funnel, a transition from dread to hope, discovering in the gulf a "narrow and tottering bridge which ... is the only pathway between Time and Eternity."

Mooney, James. "Myths of the Cherokee." *Nineteenth annual report, 1897–98* (30, 1900).

Poe, Edgar Allan and David D. Galloway. *The Fall of the House of Usher and Other Writings: Poems, Tales, Essays, and Reviews.* London and NY, 2003.

Homer. *The Odyssey.* NY, 1963.

Rydberg, Viktor, Rasmus Björn Anderson, James W. Buel and Norroena Society. *Teutonic Mythology: Gods and Goddesses of the Northland.* NY, 1907.

Landscape With the Whirlpools at Awa, by Hiroshige,
wood-block print, 1857, Japan.

Waterfall

Hokusai's wood-block print depicts a waterfall of which the name, Amida, reflects the perceived resemblance between the waterfall's round gorge and the luminous halo of Amida, the Buddha who presides over the Western Paradise. The swirling current of the waterfall is contained within the almost perfect circle of rock before cascading in white streams down the black face of the sheer cliff to seemingly abysmal depths. The human figures in the foreground preparing a picnic are diminutive in proportion to nature's splendor (Singer, 323).

A waterfall is a cataract, a "breaking" or "downrushing" of water over a precipice. We hear the ceaseless thundering of a waterfall before we see its seething, perpendicular rapids and the enveloping mists born of torrential, continuous downpour uniting highest and lowest. In its natural setting of rainforest, woods and mountains, the force and beauty of a waterfall seem sublime and sacred. "Amid the waters, under the high cliff … even the sluggish soul can rise to the noblest concerns," wrote the fourteenth-century humanist Petrarch of his favorite haunt, a waterfall in Vaucluse, Provence, the source of the river Sorgue (Petrarch, 105, 124).

The descent of a great mass of water can also overwhelm us. The waterfall has been imagined as a stream feeding the dark realms of the underworld and circling up to issue again from craggy heights. It has suggested the descent of the immutable into an ever-dividing stream that defies capture, cannot be contained, is eternal movement, eternal change, generating life and death. One can be broken in the tonnage of the waters: "Deep calls to deep at the thunder of your cataracts; all your waves and billows have gone over me," cries the Psalmist to his god (42.7). In Chinese tradition, the waterfall represents the autumnal, yin aspect of the dragon's water power; it plunges into the water, its claws are the spouts of foam (Desai, 3).

Human beings have learned to exploit the waterfall's hydroelectric power in order to drive technology, but in so doing they destroy the waterfall and devastate the land to which it belongs and contributes ecologically. The waterfall itself is an emblem of balance. Chinese landscape paintings portray the waterfall in contrast to the upward movement of the rock face over which it descends, and the dynamic movement of its rushing waters with the stillness of the rock.

Desai, Helen. *Unpublished Essay.*
Avery Brundage Asian Art Museum. SF, 1997.
Petrarca, Francesco. *Letters from Petrarch.*
Bloomington, IN, 1966.
Singer, Robert T., et al. *Edo, Art in Japan 1615–1868.* Washington, DC, 1998.

Amida Waterfall on the Kiso Highway, by Hokusai 1760–1849), from the series *A Tour of Waterfalls in Various Provinces,* wood-block print, Japan.

Flood

Floodwaters overwhelm foundering swimmers helplessly whirled in the sea's chaos around a rocklike ark, its doors closed on the last possibility of salvation. Earlier even than the Biblical legend, there is a Sumerian version of the great deluge, the *Epic of Atrahasis,* which describes casualties of flood strewn about the rivers like dragonflies. In the Babylonian *Epic of Gilgamesh*, the hero Utnapishtim rides out a cosmic flood with his family and animals until coming to rest, as Noah does, on a solitary mountaintop.

Flood evokes not only mythic but true-to-life images of terrifying devastation—water in gigantic force as torrential rains, overflowing sea levels, massive tidal waves—breaking through all the barriers we have set against such inundation. Houses, unmoored, are carried away in the furious currents with survivors clinging to the rooftops; lives are indifferently tossed into the vortex, trees swept away and cultivation leveled, returning some portion of the world to its original elements. Nature's autonomy in the mingled flood-frenzy of the heavens and the deep has often been depicted in myth as angry, punishing deities, or merely the impersonal activity of the gods.

Floods are especially frightening because they intimate unpredictable forces of like nature within ourselves. Times of great stress and change, when consciousness can be submerged by flooding anxieties and affects. Incursions from the unconscious that can penetrate defenses and swamp a hard-pressed ego, uprooting its foothold in reality. Collective flooding where members of a group, caught up in waves of numinous emotions or ideas, lose touch with solidifying values. Myths tell us that survival of a flood may depend on foresight, guile or luck, attention to warnings that come from unusual sources like visions or dreams and shelter in vessels of insulating containment. In many stories a single human family starts life again, or a small group of animals that when the storm is over fish up a clod of earth, reminding us that rebirth begins with the nurturing of the smallest bit of matter.

Floods are not only destructive. The moon's gravity draws the waters of the seas encompassing the earth, creating tidal movement that cyclically floods coastal areas, fostering lush vegetative growth and protects fertile feeding and breeding grounds for hosts of creatures. In some myths, a deluge routinely marks the end of immense intervals of time. The waters have no form in themselves, but give birth to multiple forms, which, once separated from the source, are vulnerable to aging, change and decay and in time must be renewed; thus the flood represents cosmic ablution and a new beginning (Eliade, 212). Each yearly occurrence of the flooding of the Nile in ancient Egypt was a repetition of the moment of creation, but also recalled the primeval waters of nothingness "out of which matter emerged but in which the world hangs in delicate balance." And, in the seeding of the dark, rich silt left by the floodwaters in the fields, was the promise of new life (Quirke, 26, 50, 57). Alchemy intuited in the image of flood the dissolution of psychic structures that no longer serve the integrity of the self, and the self's ark-like preservation of those that do (Edinger, 81). We can be flooded in ways that link us with mythic inundations and transformations. We can also be flooded by simpler forms of excess, which our ancestors, too, must have known—overwhelming feelings of love, the sheer joy of existence, erotic passion and religious longing, or, like Dylan Thomas, the ebullience of the creative moment:

> My ark sings in the sun
> At God-speeded summer's end
> And the flood flowers now.
> **Prologue**

Edinger, Edward F. *Anatomy of the Psyche.* La Salle, IL,1985.

Eliade, Mircea. *Patterns in Comparative Religion.* Lincoln, NE, 1996.

Gossen, Gary H. and Miguel León-Portilla. *South and Meso-American Native Spirituality*. NY, 1993.

Quirke, Stephen. *Ancient Egyptian Religion.* NY, 1992.

1

2

1. " … all the fountains of the deep burst forth,
and the windows of heaven were opened" (Genesis
7:11). The Biblical cosmic deluge as illustrated in an
early Christian manuscript.

2. In a seal from Sumerian times, a boat holding a flood
survivor and an honored ancestor or god floats serenely
on the stilled waters. Life will have a new beginning.
Third century B.C.E.

3. A yarn painting from contemporary Mexico illustrates
the pre-Conquest Huichol myth of Watakami, the
original worker. Instructed by the earth goddess
Takutsi, he is hewing a canoe from a great tree trunk in
which to ride out the coming flood (Gossen, 312ff).

3

Bubble

In physical reality, a bubble exists as a watery transparent object filled with air or gas. Its smooth, glassy surface mirrors rainbow colors of light, intermingling in fluid movement. The weightlessness of the bubble allows it to float freely on invisible currents of a gentle breeze, but its fragility soon causes it to burst and dissolve into mist.

In contrast, the archetypal symbol of a bubble exists in the psyche beyond time and space. It constitutes an invisible reality imaged by mystics throughout the ages, a round nothingness that is paradoxically the primordial source of all. The unseen forces within the archetypal bubble symbolize the oneness, which can be likened to the Tao as described in the *Tao Te Ching* (ch. 25):

> There is something formless yet complete
> That existed before heaven and earth.
> How still! How empty!
> Dependent on nothing, unchanging.
> All pervading. Unfailing.
> One may think of it as the
> mother of all things under heaven.
> I do not know its name,
> But I call it "Meaning."
> If I had to give it a name,
> I should call it "The Great."

Throughout history, the translucent bubble has inspired contemplation of the infinite and the eternal. In ancient Egypt the Ba soul, or ghost that appeared after death, flew in and out of the tomb as a weightless bubble. Like the circle or sphere, the globular roundness of the bubble connotes oneness, wholeness, totality, completion and spiritual perfection. The translucency of the bubble introduces, in addition, the numinosity, ethereality and spirituality associated with the celestial light of heaven. The painting of Kukai, founder of the Shingon school of Buddhism, illustrates the golden luminosity of the spiritualized bubble. He is shown in a devotional posture, seated on a lotus floating in a luminous circle. This image symbolizes the beginning of spiritual awareness in the divine boy. The bubblelike enclosure of the figure excludes all reference to the world beyond and imparts a timeless, supernatural quality (ARAS, 1:254).

The bubble has a shadow side as well. For example, the bubble that bursts suggests an elusive idea or delusive scheme, denoting untrustworthiness and instability. Someone lacking cogent thought is called a "bubble head," and a burp or intestinal gas may be called a bubble. And bubbling evokes the image of a boiling witch's cauldron, the frightful brew of nightmares.

There are more positive projections than negative ones for the elusive bubble, such as flying dreams, flying golden balls, drifting vessels and colorful balloons. A happy child is filled with bubbling effervescence and bubbling laughter. Bubbles carry children to lands of make-believe, where fairies and elves represent a life of enchantment. And the song that goes "I'm forever blowing bubbles, pretty bubbles in the air" evokes a sense of lightness of spirit and a creative imaginative way of life. As the shining soap bubble soon dissolves into thin air the archetypal symbol of bubble conveys—beyond the certainty of the body's demise—the hope of the soul's eternal life.

1

2

1. In this 15th-century Japanese hanging scroll by an unknown artist, Kukai is depicted as the Divine Child in a bubblelike enclosure. Detail of *Kobo Daishi (Kukai) as a Boy (Chigo Daishi)*.

2. "Inside the Bubble of Love," detail from *The Garden of Earthly Delights*, by Hieronymous Bosch, oil-on-wood triptych, ca. 1504, the Netherlands.

Air

To ancient Egyptian eyes, this small ivory headrest from Tutankhamun's tomb pictured a vast landscape: Shu, the god of air, lifts a support for the king's head, which was imagined as the sun. On either side are lions, whose backs were thought of as mountains rising at the east and the west ends of the world. So Shu, as air, fills the space between earth and heaven, keeping the sky from falling down onto the earth. As well as keeping them separate, air was a mediator between earth and sky, bringing prayers up to heaven and light and divine commands down to humankind (Bonnefoy, 1:103).

Air is atmosphere, and breath, distinguishing in cosmogonic terms, that which is necessary for animal life. Originally, earth's atmosphere lacked free oxygen and the heat and ultraviolet radiation of the sun made life on land impossible. Simple cells absorbed nutrients from the sea, and later primitive plants evolved photosynthesis as a way of using the sun's energy to make food. Through photosynthesis, plants processed carbon dioxide, storing the carbon in their tissues and releasing free oxygen into the atmosphere where it could be used in the metabolism of animal life.

Invisible and material, air is a thin shell of gasses, composed of nitrogen, oxygen, small amounts of carbon dioxide and argon traces. Clinging tightly to our planet because of gravity, air is moving restlessly in the whirls and flows that we experience as weather. Air in motion—inhalation and exhalation, the potency of the wind—captures our imagination. On air we project the presence of spirit, soul, deity. Some of the early Greek philosophers saw air as the divine ether from which everything in the universe arose. In Plato, air is said to be the eventual home of the soul after the dissolution of the body (Peters, 4). Even into Christian times, the air between earth and the moon was imagined to be filled with spirits: gods, ghosts of the dead, witches, magicians and angels (ERE 1:256). Spirits of illness were said to inhabit the cold or nighttime air and evil demons to live in the lower atmosphere and work their influence on humankind (Buttrick, 1:73).

Indeed, air is the medium of disparate things. Sound waves are wondrously carried on the air; but air is also how viral microbes are communicated from one person to another. Air is what draws the singing fire in the hearth and spreads the flames of destruction. Air pressure builds into the tension that breaks in crackling storms, brings the refreshing rain after heat, the warming trends after frigidity, and also the cataclysms of hurricane, drought, flood and tornado. Human beings, in their turn, drastically affect the composition of air with their pollutants and emissions, compromising air's capacity to filter the harmful rays of the sun and maintain climatic balance.

Symbolically, air derives much of its content from chemical processes in which solid matter is volatilized, vaporized or distilled (Edinger, 117ff). Airiness can be descriptive of quickness of mind, imagination, ideation and abstraction, or, on the other hand, a lack of true substance or ground. Alchemically, however, air is associated positively with sublimation, the elevating of the concrete to its symbolic meaning. Air has to do with space and perspective. Egyptian Shu's original role was to separate Nut and Geb, heaven and earth, so that the discriminated forms of creation and consciousness might come into being. Air is about relationship as opposed to identification. When the psychic environment is too "close," or suffocating, or when one is compulsively immersed, we speak of taking a breather, catching our breath, getting some air. Paracelsus, the sixteenth-century physician and alchemist, wrote that humans are composed of two kinds of life forces, the natural and "the aerial, wherein is nothing of the body" (CW 13:200). Jung translated this to mean that we experience a psychic reality as well as a physiological one. Shakespeare, writing at approximately the same time, gave the name of Ariel to the mercurial agent of fantastical happenings in *The Tempest*: "I come to answer thy best pleasure; be't to fly, / to swim, to dive into the fire, to ride / on the curl'd clouds … " (1.2.222–225). Thus is air inspiration, shimmering and magical, supporting the wings of flight, stiffening the sails of the ship, moving the waters of stagnation.

Bonnefoy, Yves and Wendy Doniger. *Mythologies. Chicago, 1991.*

Buttrick, George A. Ed. *The Interpreter's Dictionary of the Bible.* Nashville; Abingdon, 1991.

Edinger, Edward F. *Anatomy of the Psyche.* La Salle, IL, 1985.

Peters, Francis E. *Greek Philosophical Terms.* NY, 1967.

Wilkinson, Richard H. *Reading Egyptian Art.* London, 1992.

Shu, the Egyptian god embodying air, shoulders an
ivory headrest for supporting the head during sleep.
The image alludes to the correspondence between the
head and the sun. Both are associated with
illumination; both are lowered in the evening, the sun
to set and the head to sleep and both rise again at
daybreak, suggesting resurrection after death
(Wilkinson, 159). From the tomb of Tutankhamun,
18th dynasty (ca. 1332–23 B.C.E.), Egypt.

Sky

There was a time when we lived at a great and respectful distance from the sky. The sky was a huge, inverted blue bowl, a vast tent, or Biblically, a great metallic plate arched over the earth (EoR, 13:346). It was the home of God or it was God, or the great goddess Nut bending over, sheltering the world. The sky was so vast, so high, so far away that only birds and mountains could reach it. We stood looking up at the starry night sky or at the endless radiant blue of daytime, and knew our own smallness. No wonder that sky came to stand for God—for God's immensity but also for divine power. Lightning and thunder crashed from it. Light from the sun, moon and stars streamed down. Life-giving rain poured onto the earth.

In human mythology there have been many sky gods (Nut is the rare goddess), and very frequently they have been the ones who at the beginning created everything that is. For a time, in many myths, this god and his realm were close to the earth, in easy contact. Then, abruptly, often with violence or anger, the sky and the divine beings moved upward and away. After this the divine sky was distant, hard to reach, seemingly indifferent to earth life (EoR, 13:348–50). Other gods presided over love, war, fertility, and it was to them that sacrifices were made and temples built on earth (James, 12). But the distant god who was the sky, or of the sky, stood for the highest authority and power, and is sometimes referred to as "the most high." He embodied the idea of order—cosmic order. To humankind, struggling in a chaotic world, the predictable movements of the stars and planets, the regular alternation of day and night, the repeated appearance and disappearance of the moon, showed that there was basic order in the universe.

Now we can venture into the sky on planes and rockets and leave our footprints on the moon. We say now that "sky" is the upper part of the envelope of gasses (primarily nitrogen and oxygen) that enclose the earth. The old image of "sky" rests uneasily next to the modern idea of "space." Now depth psychology sees the image of the star-studded sky as a visualization of the flickering sparks of consciousness within the dark vastness of the unconscious psyche. In Buddhism, "the pure clarity of the sky is metaphorically an illustration of Buddha [enlightened] Mind" (Beer, 31). Apparently, though, some of the old symbols of the sky god are still alive. One of the Apollo astronauts was stirred to write of his experience in terms of infinity. Saying of the universe, "There is no end," he expressed his conviction that some creator must have "placed our little world, our Sun and our Moon where they are in the dark void" (Cernan, 209).

Beer, Robert. *The Encyclopedia of Tibetan Symbols and Motifs.* Boston, 1999.
Cernan, Eugene and Don Davis. *The Last Man on the Moon.* NY, 1999.
James, E. O. *The Worship of the Sky-God.* London, 1963.

2

1. Image of cerulean infinity, sky intimates both unbounded freedom and unearthly void.

2. Nut, the sky goddess of the ancient Egyptians, arches protectively over the circular world. Incised relief on a sarcophagus, 380–300 B.C.E., Egypt.

Cloud

In the painting by the American artist Georgia O'Keeffe, we are high above the clouds, looking down through open patches to the earth below. This lovely panorama depicts clouds as both natural phenomena and poetic evocations of limitless freedom and tranquility.

The natural qualities of clouds embody both a connection to and a release from the terrestrial. Formed by the evaporation of the world's water, clouds float suspended between the earth and the upper reaches of the atmosphere. Clouds are part of shifting, global weather patterns, reflectors and repositories of solar energy and the source of lightning, thunder and rain. There are ten main cloud families or genera, divided into three groups according to altitude. With their distinctive external shapes and internal structures, certain cloud forms are associated with rain, snow or hail, or with fair weather (*Enc. Brit.* 3:396–7; 17:601–2).

Clouds are part of an endless, reciprocal exchange between the ethereal and the earthly, moving between formlessness and form. In many cultures, clouds were regarded as the wellsprings of cosmic fertility. The cloud was associated both with life-giving rain and the fertility principle itself, which activated the receptive earth. Because of clouds hovering between heaven and earth, it has been an image that conveyed the hiddenness as well as the manifestation of the divine. Before Islam's Allah revealed himself, he existed as a cloud in a primal, undifferentiated state (DoS, 206–207). In

Mayan cosmology, the creator took the form of a cloud, from whence he created the universe (EoR, 3:546). In the Hebrew scriptures, God is present as a pillar of cloud to Moses and the Israelites in their long exodus from Egypt. The fourteenth-century Christian mystical text "The Cloud of Unknowing," alludes to the dark cloud that closes one off from God. This "cloud" is penetrated not by reason, but by intuitive love that is met from above by the piercing light of the divine (MM 4:489).

Symbolically, the cloud also evokes the endlessly shifting imagery that hovers in psyche's in-between spirit-matter nature. In clouds we see the angels, dragons and animals, geometric forms and religious symbols that form the background of psychic process. Such images are playful, anticipatory, inspiring, ominous. Or, still "nebulous," they can intimate a darkening mood, a coming storm of affect or on the other hand, resolution of an oppressive state of tension. Ignorance and deception, confusion and pessimism can cloud the mind. We can "live in the clouds," unrelated to grounding realities. But cloudiness can also suggest the ephemeral fantasies that provide a welcome diffusion of consciousness. The Chinese sage is even likened to a cloud: he transforms himself through spiritual practice, losing the ego's fixity and undergoing a metamorphosis merges himself with the formlessness of infinity (DoS, 207).

1. This evocative painting reminds us that clouds have served as symbols of the mind's ability to project its own inner, imaginative meanings upon outer phenomena. *Above the Clouds I*, by Georgia O'Keeffe, oil on canvas, 1962–3, United States.

2. Christ is surrounded by a seven-fold nimbus. This image refers to the apocalyptic vision of Jesus' "coming with clouds," recorded by St. John in Revelation 1:7. *Silos Apocalypse*, detail, by Beatus of Liébana, illustrated by Prior Pedro, ca. 1073–1109.

3. Io's submission to Jupiter (Zeus in Greece) in the form of a cloud expresses the human longing for union with God. On a more obvious level, the undulating embrace of her warm sensuous body by the misty cloud mass—which fails to conceal the god's face and hands—is an image of profane ecstasy. *Jupiter and Io*, by Correggio, oil on canvas, ca. 1530, Italy.

1

2

3

Wind

The four wooden snakes used in the Navajo ceremonial called "Windway" express by means of their various colors, wavelike form and affinity with the undulating, fiercely rising serpent and the feathered bird that glides and swoops, all the potential motions of the wind—from the soft breezes of the dawn to the dust storms and whirlwinds that blow across the mesa. *Wind exists beautifully*, they say. *Back there in the underworlds, this was a person it seems.* For the Navajo, wind is the unifying force of nature, encompassing primordial mists, light and darkness, the greatness of the mountains and the four cardinal directions. It was the wind that brought up the Holy People, human and four-legged, from speechless existence in the underworlds to life on the earth's surface, and gave them language, thought and leadership. Wind enters the individual at conception, and the wind causes the movement of the unborn child.

Wind is actually air in motion, caused by the differences in the temperature of earth's atmosphere and the pressure exerted by the cooler, heavier air on the lighter, heated air. Though invisible, wind affects us with remarkably distinct sensations. In the wind is the fragrance of spring flowers, dry leaves and mown hay, the scents of prey and predator. Wind touches cheek or hand in benefaction and greeting. Wind howls, moans, roars and sighs.

It is this animated nature of wind and the spectrum of its character with which some autonomous, wild force within the psyche has found age-old correspondence. *Wind existed first, as a person, and when the Earth began its existence Wind took care of it.* Wholly independent of our bidding and control, wind evokes an unseen, felt spirit of generation, inspiration and religious ecstasy. The Aztec Quetzelcoatl, another feathered serpent, was an embodiment of the wind, representing the fertilization of the corn and the mysteries of death and rebirth. Wind is the Greek *pneuma*, Arabic *ruh*, Hebrew *ruach*, the divine breath that broods over the primal waters of creation. Wind "blows where it lists," dispersing the seeds of transformation and growth, and itself is phallic, spermatic, impregnating and conceptual, Holy Spirit and mercurial spirit, the "rush" of attraction, the vinculum or connecting bond that brings things together.

On wind we have projected the unpredictable factor that moves us and carries us, sometimes directing our course or forcing us to change course. The hero Odysseus received the gift of fair winds for his voyage home from Troy, but his sailors thoughtlessly released the foul winds pent up in a leather satchel and caused their captain 20 years of wandering. Wind fills our sails, the slightest breeze more favorable than none, since windless states make us vulnerable to siren longings. The skilled sailor knows in what direction the wind is blowing, its velocity and pressure, how to move with the wind, or against it, and keep the vessel afloat.

There are "ill winds" that connote misfortune or a spirit of incoherence or even madness. Symbolically reflecting our experience of the libido that manifests in boisterous, gusting passions and furious outbursts of temper, wind can be truculent, typhonic, the force of gale, hurricane and twister, toppling the sturdy trees, taking out power lines and devastating our firm structures. Words and affects can be "full of hot air," fiery, parching or blustery, frigid and cutting. Wind is all these things. Gentle, cradling, pushy, violent, it gets us, settles over us, flows within us, "breezes beautifully." *It is this, it is a person*, they say.

Matthews, Washington. Ed. *Navaho Legends*. Boston and NY, 1897.
McNeley, James Kale. *Holy Wind in Navajo Philosophy*, p. 9–10. Tucson, AZ, 1981.

Ritually employed by the Navajo, the four feathered
wooden snakes depict the black wind of the east, the
blue wind of the south, the yellow wind of the west and
the white wind of the north (Matthews, 76). Ca. 1903.

Rain

The quality of mercy is not strain'd,
It droppeth as the gentle rain from heaven
Upon the place beneath …
Shakespeare, *The Merchant of Venice* (4.1.80–82)

It was not like our soft English rain that drops
gently on the earth; it was unmerciful and
somehow terrible; you felt in it the malignancy
of the primitive powers of nature. It did not
pour, it flowed. It was like a deluge from
heaven, and it rattled on the roof of corrugated
iron with a steady persistence that was mad-
dening.
W. Somerset Maugham, *Rain*

The water upon which all of life depends descends to earth as raindrops both gentle and torrential. Rain is a miraculous visitation of heavenly power, natural and immense, necessary and feared, cleansing, releasing, dissolving, flooding, relieving and sweet. Rain precipitates growth, change, refreshment, purification and … disaster. The image of rain in the mythologies of many peoples represents the penetration of the earth below by descending celestial, fertilizing powers and points to the sacred marriage of heaven and earth. The divine sperm falling like the golden shower of Zeus upon Danae impregnates the earth to sustain and renew all life, serving as a primal image of the bestowal of grace, mercy and abundance. Yet rain can also come as the language of divine retribution, in the destructive waters of the deluge. As symbol and metaphor, the details of nature's rains reflect inner psychic dispositions. When we are flooded, we are emotionally overwhelmed.

When it rains, we withdraw inward, move to an interior place, seek shelter. The sky above, aloof, inspirited and superior, darkens, storms and finally lets go its waters, corresponding to grayness, disruption, moodiness, the tearful rains of sorrow or perhaps to much needed release and even the gentle joy of "Singin' in the Rain."

Beneficial healing by the celestial influence of such "rain" cleanses that which is dark and trapped in emotional blindness, or in the parched earth within, inert, barren of life, stuck in unconsciousness or in certainty, and in need of the dissolving and propagating rains. The alchemists saw the falling rain as the "washing" of this *nigredo* state, illuminating and reanimating what felt dead and dark. This divine intervention of grace occurring at the darkest point preceded a new *coniunctio*, a psychic union of emotion, body, imagination and mind in a new level of consciousness.

In mythic lore, humanity out of balance with the divine nature of life symbolically invites flood or drought. Peoples the world over have created rain dances and rituals to invoke beneficent treatment by the sky god, or sometimes the rain mother, who dispenses rain. Nearly all the world's mythologies include references to a divine flood wherein the sky deities wipe out worlds before recreation or repopulation in a new age. Thus does Yahweh proclaim, "I will cause it to rain upon the earth forty days and forty nights; and every living substance that I have made will I destroy from off the face of the earth" (Genesis 7:4). When the waters are flooding, the people must seek higher ground; a new perspective that holds one above the inundation is necessary.

1. The blue of water and sky dominate this image, an expression of human beings amidst nature's immense and complex circulation of water, rising from below, condensing above and descending again as rain. *A Sudden Shower Over Ohashi,* by Hiroshige, from the series *One Hundred Famous Views in Edo,* wood-block print, 1856–8, Japan.

As an inexorable force of nature, rain is an immense power dwarfing the individual will or the collective arrogance of humankind. The poisonous emissions of our technologies have been answered by the anomalous rains and flooding of global warming. Writers like W. Somerset Maugham have portrayed vengeful rain as the counterpoint to power-driven strivings that seek to subdue nature. But there is also the rain of blessing and balance. When the last of a line of true African Rain Queens died in 2001 in Petersburg, South Africa, three days of unseasonable rains were reported in the area beginning on the day of her death (*The New York Times*, June 30, 2001). Similarly, the humble quality of Hiroshige's image, depicting people sheltered under umbrellas and moving to and fro across a bridge in a wide waterscape, might be seen as a right attitude to the preeminence both of the rain, and the task of making a crossing.

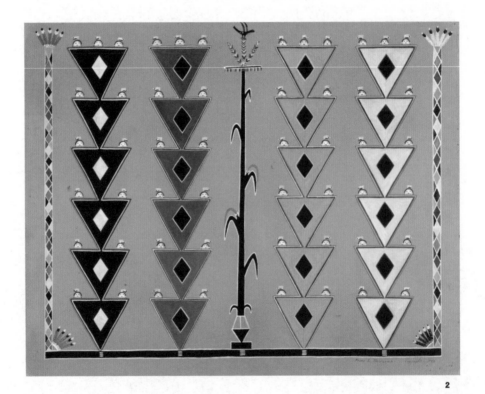

2

2. Navajo sandpainting depicting rain clouds and cloud people, rainbow rope and seeds in the water. Rain as an animating principle. *Cloud People*, by Franc J. Newcomb, before 1933.

3. Cowherds seek Krishna's protection from the rain. Krishna as a protective mountain or "higher ground" through whom the tremendous forces of nature can be met. Different levels of fear and calm can be viewed in this image of a deep psycho-spiritual event. Miniature, ca. 1700, India.

Storm

In the winter of 1842, the great British artist J. M. W. Turner was a passenger on the paddle-steamer Ariel as it left Harwich harbor in the midst of a snowstorm. Odysseus-like, Turner had, he later recounted, asked the ship's sailors to lash him to the mast so that he could observe the roiling weather. This painting, almost abstract brushstrokes evoking swirling snow and waves, was the artist's record of his four-hour ordeal at the mercy of the storm (Bockemühl, 69).

Storms are defined as violent atmospheric disturbances that bring rain, hail, or snow, often accompanied by strong winds, thunder and lightning. The storm, transcending human initiative and control, can be a spectacular meteorological phenomenon, making it a natural metaphor for spontaneous upheaval in the ordinary affairs of life that can be annihilating or transformative.

Worldwide, storms were seen as manifestations of the sacred, expressions of celestial and generative power that were communicated to the terrestrial realm. Storm gods wielding thunderbolts were personifications of an aspect of nature capable of volatility and violent acts of destruction; yet the same gods were responsible for providing life-giving rain. In many cases, storm gods had evolved from, or were sons of, creator sky-gods, and became spouses of the Great Mother—fertilizers of the earth and sources of vital energy and universal order (EoR, 9:488). Often associated with mythic animals like the bull and the ram, which embodied such dynamic energies, these sons of cosmic power became saviors, healers or gods of vegetation who would die and be resurrected with each new agricultural year (Stevens, 182).

The storms of literature often signify a character's inner turmoil, grief and eros. King Lear's maddened howls mix with those of a raging storm when his two eldest daughters betray him. In *Wuthering Heights*, wild storms reflect the tempestuous atmosphere of erotic passion between Heathcliff and Cathy. The orphaned Dorothy finds her world turned upside down when the vortex of a tornado carries her to the bewitched Land of Oz.

Symbolically, storm evokes psychic tension gradually building to the bursting point, or more sudden inbreakings of highly charged transpersonal energies. Such tempests may leave the psychic landscape in devastation or flooding, and they may refresh and cleanse it. The darkening storm clouds of potential affect can presage open conflict or outright war within the psyche and can manifest in a corresponding storm of chaos without. Analogously we speak of the distant thunder of war machines and the gusting winds of change. Lightning can strike as cataclysmic reversals of destiny, but also as revelatory insight. Creative and emotional dry spells are resolved in cathartic breakthroughs of libido that arrive like a deluge of fecundating rain. As Shakespeare's play *The Tempest* portrays, storm conjures the energies of elemental spirits, spent fury and order overthrown. Says the storm-summoning magician Prospero:

> ... *I have bedimm'd*
> *The noontide sun, call'd forth the mutinous winds,*
> *And 'twixt the green sea and the azur'd vault*
> *Set roaring war ....*
> **(5.1.48–50)**

Berrin, Kathleen and Esther Pasztory. *Teotihuacan: Art from the City of the Gods.* NY and SF, 1993.
Bockemühl, Michael. *J. M. W. Turner, 1775–1851.* Cologne, 1993.
Stevens, Anthony. *Ariadne's Clue.* Princeton, NJ, 1999.

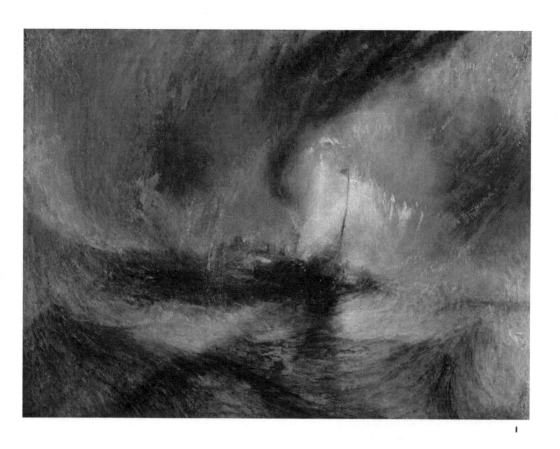

1. *Snow Storm—Steamboat Off a Harbor's Mouth*, by J. M. W. Turner, oil on canvas, 1842, England.

2. Volcanic stone is an apt medium for this storm-god relief from Teotihuacan, Mexico. The bifurcated tongue, four pointed upper teeth and curled upper lip evoke a deity associated with war and warriors as well as water, earth and fertility. Tlamilolpa-Metepec, 200–750 C.E. (Berrin, 171).

Thunder

Stormy of countenance, the Japanese god Raijin makes thunder as he pounds on a great ring of drums. The crash of thunder can still unnerve us. While science has explained thunder as the explosive expansion of heated air in lightning's path, it was in former times the signature of the highest, earthshaking gods: Thor, Zeus, Yahweh, Indra, Baal, Taranis. Always ambivalent, the gods of thunder and lightning could bring either death and destruction or fertility and new life to humankind and its surroundings.

Thunder, on its own, was the voice of the almighty, majestic and terrifying, heard variously as an expression of anger, assent or simply presence. The Hindu Upanishad (Brihad-aranyana 5, 2, in Radhakrishnan) tells us that the original cosmic father Prajapati instructed his offspring—gods, humans and demons—by means of three identical claps of thunder, which each clan heard differently according to the needs of its nature. "Restrain yourselves," the unruly gods heard; "give," avaricious men understood the thunder to say; "be compassionate" came through to the cruel demons.

Some peoples have imagined the sound of thunder as the bellowing of a divine bull, the clashing wings of the giant thunderbird, the roar of a magical jaguar or the rumbling wheels of Thor's great cart pulled across the heavens by huge goats. In the *I Ching, the Book of Changes*, thunder is the symbol of great physical or psychic shock, which may terrify and temporarily disorient or daze the beholder, but can also stimulate reflection and self-examination. In nature, thunderstorms precede spring rains and reawaken the divine life force (Wilhelm, 298). The same theme appears in the rituals of the American Great Plains' Pawnee Indians, who believed that in winter the gods withdrew from the earth. The first thunder of spring was an announcement that the gods were at last returning, and the people immediately prepared a ceremony of welcome for them. Songs, sacrificial offerings, recitations of sacred history and censing with sacred smoke marked the great moment.

Thunder evokes the portentous rumblings of psyche, a clap that brings us to attention from dormant awareness. Thunder signifies movement, release, a breaking in or breaking through, which shifts energy and gets things flowing, or, on the other hand, foreshadows violent storms, psychic chaos, a "lowering of the boom." Whatever is "thunderous" transcends the ordinary noise of timely existence, reverberating in deep layers of memory as thundering hooves, the cannons of war, sublime applause. Thunder is electric, heated, revelatory, full of lightning, shaking us to the core, leaving us thunderstruck.

Radhakrishnan, S. *The Principal Upanishads.* NY, 1953.
Wilhelm, Richard and Cary F. Baynes. *The I Ching; or, Book of Changes.* NY, 1950.

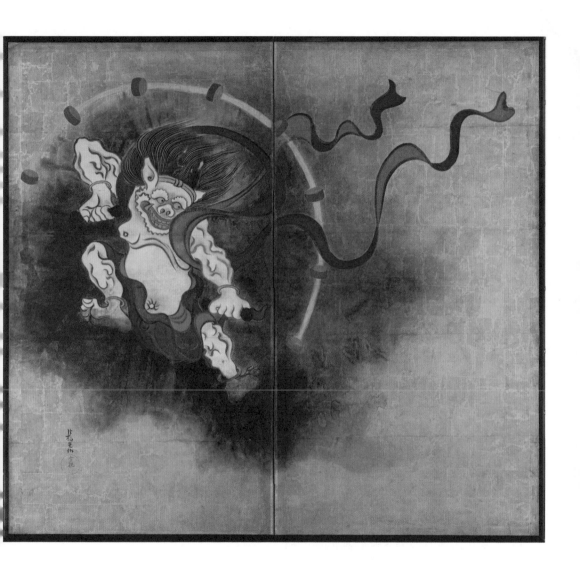

Raijin, Japanese god of thunder, detail from
Gods of Wind and Thunder, by Ogata Korin
(1658–1716), screen painting, Japan.

Lightning

Dazzling and awful, the brilliance, speed, unexpectedness and killing power of lightning have been attributed to deities like Baal, who stands on his cosmic mountain above the watery abyss brandishing his thunder mace in one hand and a lightning spear in the other. At the top, the spear seems to open into the buds of a greening tree, suggesting lightning's potency, not only as a weapon to fight off chaos and evil powers, but also as a means of fertilizing the earth and releasing saving waters (ARAS, 2cf.006). Mexican myth places the discovery of maize at the moment when a flash of lightning split open a rock and revealed the original seed (Miller, 106). Sometimes the lightning flash is imagined as the fecundating ejaculation of a virile god. The Chinese symbol for lightning, *shen*, refers to the positive, expansive forces of the universe, which, coming with the rain, support life (EoR, 12: 203f).

Physically, lightning is the sudden, visible discharge of atmospheric electricity. Air masses within thunderclouds are subject to violent heating and cooling, resulting in a separation of positive and negative electrical charges. These amass in different parts of the cloud and periodically leap toward each other, generating intense heat and light when they meet. The resulting lightning takes place mostly within or between clouds, but sometimes negatively charged particles jump toward the ground, causing positively charged particles to gather in the earth; the positive charge, jumping to complete the electrical circuit, results in a "negative to ground" lightning flash. The heat of lightning unites nitrogen and oxygen, forming nitrate and other compounds that infuse the rain and replenish the nutrients in the soil *(Compt)*. The rarity of reverse lightning occurs when *positive* charges rush from the cloud to the ground, creating a lightning channel through which electrons shoot from the ground back up to the cloud. Reverse polarity tends to carry more charge and is associated with mysterious lights whimsically called sprites, elves and trolls that hover above a storm (Blakeslee, 1).

The much more destructive aspect of lightning is imaged as the thunderbolt, a single flash of lightning representing the "terrible swift sword" or the hurled, crackling missile of a mighty deity meting out retribution. Lightning splits trees, sets forests on fire, shatters buildings and strikes us dead. Intimating its symbolic capacity to "level," lightning often strikes the highest object in its path. For Hinduism and Buddhism, the lightning bolt is embodied in the *vajra*, a weapon of spiritual transformation that "mercilessly destroys" the ego's inflated illusions (Beer, 233). Imagination has seen in lightning a revelation of the divine or an omen of disaster. Sometimes signaling the advance of high winds and violent storms and followed by deafening peals of thunder, lightning evokes unexpected, overpowering shifts in the physical or psychic landscape (CW 9.1:553ff).

But lightning is also quintessentially illumination. Shamanism knows the mystical experience of *qaumaneq* ("lightning"), which, contacting the unconscious, opens up the psychic realms of clairvoyance (EoR, 9, 487f). Lightning is warning and clarification, the in-breaking of nature, momentous and electrifying. "Struck by lightning" is how we describe not only astonishment and paralyzing shock, but also the intuition that "comes in a flash," the sudden awareness that "strikes home," and those stunning insights, inspirations and conversions that represent our own cloud-to-ground enlightenments.

Beer, Robert. *The Encyclopedia of Tibetan Symbols and Motifs*. Boston, 1999.
Blakeslee, Sandra. "Lightning's Shocking Secrets; Clues to Tornadoes and Other Mysteries." *The New York Times* (July 18, 2000).
Miller, Mary and Karl Taube. *The Gods and Symbols of Ancient Mexico and the Maya*. NY, 1993.

1. *Lightning Field*, by Walter De Maria, a permanent earth sculpture of 400 stainless steel poles arranged in a grid array measuring 1 mile by 1 kilometer; average pole height is 20 feet 7 inches, pole tips form an even plane, 1977, New Mexico. Photo by John Cliett. ©Dia Art Foundation.

2. Sudden, dangerous, vigorous, lightning is the essence of creator-gods like Baal, the god of ancient Canaan (Syria). He holds the lightning spear, or "thunderbolt," with his left hand. In his right hand, he brandishes a mace; a dagger protrudes from his belt. Limestone relief, 1600–1400 B.C.E.

Rainbow

When I bring clouds over the earth, and the bow is seen in the clouds, I will remember my covenant between me and you and every living creature of all flesh; and the waters shall never again be caused to flood to destroy all flesh.
Genesis 9:15

After the storm, the rainbow appears, emblem of promise. So it was in the Biblical story of the flood when the inundating waters of divine judgment abated; and so it has been ever since: Rainbow is the sign of renewal, the transmuting changes of the heart and the *eros* of covenant between heaven and earth.

A complex optical phenomenon as wondrous as the fanciful ways we depict it, the rainbow is formed when sunlight (or moonlight) strikes a "screen" of raindrops, drizzle or fog. The droplets act as a prism, refracting and then reflecting the white light of the sun. To an observer standing between the sun and the rain, an arc of concentric colors appears—the limpid spectrum that forms the rainbow.

Poets have called the rainbow "the dyes of heaven," "a glittering robe of joy" and "a celestial kaleidoscope" (Whelan, 23, 26, 62). The Book of Revelation describes a rainbow, "like an emerald," surrounding the throne of God. Alchemy portrays the rainbow as a form of the *cauda pavonis*, or peacock's tail of brilliant hues, alluding to the lapis that unites all qualities (CW 14:392). Tibetan Buddhists find in the rainbow's ephemeral translucence an intimation of the spirit transcending the nature of reality, the "rainbow body" achieved through intense, solitary meditation. Desire disappears, replaced by luminous awareness and bliss so complete that if one dies in such a state, the body itself dissolves into rainbow-colored light, leaving only hair and nails behind.

For many, however, the rainbow represents the imaginal bridge that links the visible world and all that is invisible, magical and supernatural. Fantasy peoples the rainbow's unseen perimeters with angels, fairies and elves that guard abounding treasure, the bright gold and luminous pearls of wisdom, creativity and mercurial play. Myth has portrayed the rainbow as the highway over which psyche's supernal emissaries bring their messages to consciousness. From the rainbow bridge the Japanese divine couple Izanagi and Izanami stir the primal sea of potential with a jeweled spoon whose droplets coalesce into living matter. The spirits of the Hopi kachinas, or ancestors, descend from the celestial realm of the dead to the land of the living by means of the rainbow, whose earthly counterpart is the ladder descending into the kiva.

Yet the rainbow is poignantly evanescent. The Norse myth of the Ragnarok depicts the rainbow bridge collapsing under the weight of the insurgent "sons of the giants" who come to destroy earth at the end of time. Does the story intimate, perhaps, that the energies of alliance embodied by the covenantal rainbow could, just in the nature of things, or just because of human nature, shift back into submerging chaos? In the meantime, the breathtaking, differentiated hues of the rainbow continue to materialize, dissolve and come into being again and again, suggesting the feeling-toned process between known and unknown that is our fragile bridge of expansive possibility.

Lee, Raymond L. and Alistair B. Fraser. *The Rainbow Bridge*. University Park, PA, 2001.
Whelan, Richard. *The Book of Rainbows*. Cobb, CA, 1997.
World Meteorological Organization. *International Cloud Atlas. Abridged Atlas*. Geneva, 1956.

1. Divine symbol of covenant above the once-flooded land, a rainbow offers its promise to Noah and his sons. Manuscript illumination from the Vienna Genesis, 6th century, Syria.

2. Japan's brother-sister creator deities Izanagi and Izanami stand on the celestial rainbow bridge to stir the cosmic sea. A sacred bird sits in the middle of the island of Japan coalescing out of the water. Hanging scroll by Nishikawa Sukenobu, 18th century, Japan.

3. Touching earth, and yet unearthly, a shimmering arch of prismatic raindrops. Photograph by Robin Jaqua.

1

2

3

Dew

Eos, the winged goddess of dawn, dispenses dew from twin amphoras as she flies above the earth. The lovely lightness of the image conveys the celestial grace of the goddess who brings from above to below the renewing moisture.

Science has explained dew as water droplets condensed from the air at night onto cool surfaces. This mystery of the darkness that leaves all the plant life glistening at first light has contributed to dew's symbolic potency. For the ancients, the refreshment and cooling balm of the dew was evidence of divine visitation and divine gift—of Eos, or the rainbow messenger Iris, or the starry, overarching Egyptian Nut in her night-sky aspect. Because of its "heavenly" source, others saw in the dew tonic and panacea, even a mystical mirror in which the world was reflected. Buddhist literature speaks of Kuan Yin emerging from the center of the lotus with her vase of the "sweet dew" of compassion (Matthews , 94). Ethereal, evanescent, vanishing with the appearance of the sun, dew was the imaginal food of spirits, or the form that souls took following the cremation of the body (ERE 4:698).

Dew's relation to both night and dawn has also made it a portent of transpersonal intervention and illumination. In the biblical Exodus, dew heralds the "manna," the bread that God sends to feed the Israelites in the wilderness: "and in the morning dew lay round about the camp. And when the dew had gone up, there was on the face of the wilderness a fine, flake-like thing, white as hoarfrost" (16:13–4). For the early Christians, dew symbolized the gift of the Holy Spirit, a boon from heaven that revitalized parched souls. Borrowing in part from these sources, alchemy found in the dew a synonym for the *aqua sapientia*, the mercurial water of wisdom (Abraham, 53). Not merely an intellectual form of understanding, but incorporating feeling values, the "dew" alluded to psyche's capacity to freshen and reanimate the personality desiccated by unconsciousness of its soul-stuff. The illumination of these contents, like glistening drops of dew, represents the "moisture that heralds the return of the soul" (CW 16:483ff).

Abraham, Lyndy. *A Dictionary of Alchemical Imagery*. Cambridge, UK, and NY, 1998.
Matthews, John. *The Grail: Quest for the Eternal*. NY, 1981.

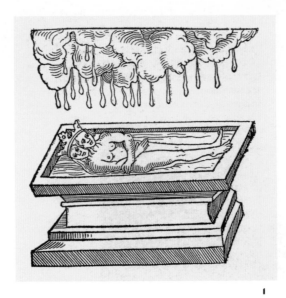

2

1. The dew falling from heaven signals "resuscitation," the potential for a new way of being embodied after the "death" of the old life. Wood engraving from the alchemical text *Rosarium Philosophorum*, 1550, Germany.

2. A Greek vase depicts Eos, the goddess of dawn, bestowing dew on the earth, a blessing known to anyone who rises early and walks barefoot in the grass.

Fog

This monumental Japanese painting—it is 260 feet long—invites us into the world of fog. Studying it from right to left, in the tradition of Japanese scroll-viewing, we move from forbidding blackness through a somber middle ground to delicate tracery and translucency to what finally appears to be hazy light. The symbolism of fog is just as variable.

The darkest images arose in Scandinavia, where Niflheim, a mythical wasteland of freezing mist and fog populated by monsters, also included the realm of the dead (Orchard, 118). "[F]og in my throat" was Robert Browning's metaphor for approaching death (in *Prospice*). Fog may arise from the work of demonic beings in fairy tales or surround Shakespeare's witches, who comment on the "fog and filthy air" (*Macbeth* 1.1.16). In Asian legend, it may represent strange moods in which spirits appear (Biedermann, 139). Widely, though, fog is taken to represent confusion, uncertainty, indefiniteness, a state between the real and the unreal. Here it is opposed to the brilliant light of certainty.

While fog seems vaporous, we feel it, because it is formed by the condensation of very small water droplets around microscopic dust particles in the air. Fog limits horizontal vision. Less dense, it is called haze or mist. Unlike clouds, its base is on or near the ground and its symbolism is associated not with the sky, but with the earth realm. Sometimes fog is seen as enfolding, blanketing. T. S. Eliot imagined fog as a yellow cat that "rubs its back upon the window pane" and finally "curled once about the house and fell asleep" (Eliot,

4). Contemporary poet Nan Hunt refers to fog as, "The mummy wrap of soft white / that hints of resurrection."

Fog is not favorable to direct action. Ships, planes and fast-moving humans are delayed or stopped. A slower, more cautious awareness arises. Symbolically, the world of clear rational thought gives way to dreaminess, ambiguity, a kind of knowing that is more nuanced, less absolute. This knowing is perhaps more valued in the East than in the West. Zen sage Keizan Zenji puts it:

Though clear waters range to the vast
blue autumn sky, How can they compare with
the hazy moon on a spring night!
Most people want to have pure clarity,
But sweep as you will, you cannot empty
the mind.
Maezumi, iii

Biedermann, Hans. *Dictionary of Symbolism.* NY, 1994.
Eliot, T. S. *The Love Song of J. Alfred Prufrock, The Complete Poems and Plays: 1909–1950.* NY, 1952.
Hunt, Nan. "What Will You Do?" Unpublished original poem. Copyright Nan Hunt.
Maezumi, Hakuyu Taizan. *The Hazy Moon of Enlightenment: On Zen Practice III.* LA, 1977.
Orchard, Andy. *Dictionary of Norse Myth and Legend.* London, 1997.

Fog is the medium in which the elements of a classic Japanese nature study are obscured, and materialize. *Forest*, by Senju Hiroshi, *fusuma* (sliding door) painting, 2001.

Snow

In Hiroshige's graceful print, the midair suspension of snowflakes suggests an almost magical suspension of time. Snow is the harbinger of winter, the season that slows down the world. Snow's ineluctable motion stills as it piles, drifts and blocks the way where it will: "As a little snow, tumbled about, anon becomes a mountain" (Shakespeare, *King John*, 3.4.176).

Snow is crystals of ice that form from atmospheric vapor and fall as flakes. The crystalline structure of snowflakes prevents them from packing together tightly, resulting in air gaps that make snow an excellent heat insulator. Covered by a layer of powdery snow, the warmed ground only partially freezes, remaining permeable to moisture and protecting the plants and animals it shelters from the effects of frigid climates. Literally "blanketing" the earth, silent snow is often experienced as insulating the senses from the distractions of the outer world. The snow-covered landscape appears to be sleeping, even dreaming. In the cycle of seasons, snowy winter slumber precedes awakening in spring.

Yet snow can also be amazingly active—glittering, twirling, blowing, transforming environments in ways as various as its own physical forms, so that cultures like the Inuit have a myriad different ways of describing "snow" (Hall, 103). Snow is ambiguously magical and dangerous, gentle and overpowering. It may bury everything beneath it, yet it retains an affinity with the heights, clinging to rooftops and tree branches, lingering atop mountains in every season, an image of detached purity and majestic wisdom.

For such reasons snow's brilliance is felt to be cold. More like moonlight than sunlight, snow's cool-white, reflected light often symbolizes purity and "chaste" retreat from warm human touch. Paradoxically, snow can also reflect so much light that it ceases to illuminate, but instead blinds, creating blizzard "whiteouts" or burning eyes unprotected by snow goggles. Containing like all symbols powerful opposites, snow seems to bind fire and ice. In many world cultures, snow becomes the "snow maiden," a regal but remote form of the archetypal feminine who inspires passion only to drain from her lover the lifeblood of emotional warmth. Her beauty, like that of snow, is fascinating but inhuman and potentially deadly. On the other hand, snow can image psychic "frozen ground" as protectively repressed or dissociated feelings. Only in due time, perhaps, can such feelings thaw, when there is a consciousness able to withstand the melting.

Slight, yet also grand, the aesthetics of snow inspire awe. A formal perfecting power resides within snowflakes, mostly hexagonal crystals, all of which are individually unique—a staggering statistical idea. In *Black Door with Snow*, Georgia O'Keeffe reveals each individual flake as a potential emissary of beauty. Snowflakes may delicately outline tree branches or telephone lines, or amass to reduce an entire landscape into its basic topography. Even the snowball aspires to become that platonically perfect form, a sphere. Snow creates simple beauty and activates fantasies of transformation. Thus we can understand why medieval alchemists so greatly rejoiced upon seeing white sublimate suddenly "falling like snow" in their retorts—a key event in making the elusive philosopher's stone (Abraham, 184).

Abraham, Lyndy. *A Dictionary of Alchemical Imagery*. Cambridge, UK and NY, 1998.
Hall, Edward T. *The Silent Language*. Greenwich, CT, 1963.

1. Tiny crystals of snow almost imperceptibly amass to transform an entire landscape. *Snow Falling on a Town, Mariko, Station No. 21*, from the *Fifty-three Stations of the Tōkaidō Road*, by Hiroshige, woodblock print, 1851-2, Japan.

2. Magical in its crystalline beauty, a snowflake.

1

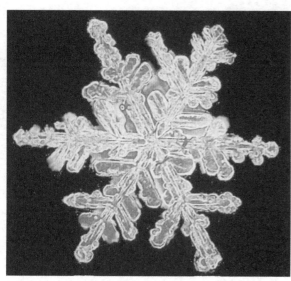

2

3. The artist David Hammons with snowballs he signed and sold in New York City. *Blizzard Ball Sale*, 1983, United States.

4. The almost-motionless motion of snow reveals each flake as an ephemeral but unique creation. Science tells us that no flake is ever identical with another. *Black Door with Snow*, by Georgia O'Keeffe, oil on canvas, 1955, United States.

Fire

Fire enkindles nature in solar heat, stellar brilliance and flashes of lightning, seethes and smolders in subterranean regions, erupts spontaneously in rippling ground fires or soaring infernos. All living things are in some way fertilized, tempered, ripened or destroyed by forms of fire. Probably a million years before hominids knew how to make fire, they stoked the embers of naturally occurring fires and learned "that fire could be manipulated like a dangerous ally" to provide warmth, light, deterrence to predators and insects and also the "hypnotic attraction of living 'activity' in the emptiness of a moonless night" (Kingdon, 56). Visible fire gradually intimated an invisible fire animating our substance and manifesting in the multiple flickers and excitations of psychic life. Friction ignites the hidden fire of wood and stone, as in ourselves it transposes

possibility into conception. A single flame-point illuminates darkness, focuses or mesmerizes the eye, ascends in the vapors of inspiration and offering. The fire of passions sweeps through the body, consuming and germinating, just as conflagration can blacken the forest and engender new growth.

The first sparks of human self-discovery coincided with fire-making and fire-tending. Everywhere, fire was imagined as a deity, part animal, part spirit, living, breathing, eating, propagating; a trickster and shape-shifter whom we engage and propitiate. The Egyptian goddess Sekhmet displays the lioness-like, burning ferocity of the desert, breathes life into the pharaoh, breathes fire against his enemies, in blood-lust transforms into the "powerful" as the avenging, incinerating Eye of the sun-god Re (Hart,187–8). Hinduism's

1

2

1. Death and cremation, as well as the meditative tapas, or heat, of the Tantric practitioner, are conveyed by this image from a manuscript of *Bhagavata-Purana*, painting on paper, ca. 17th century, Rajasthan.

2. *Untitled*, by Karen Arm, acrylic and oil on canvas, 1997, United States.

Agni, primordial Fire, vitalizing warmth of the waters and plants, self-immolating as the contained flame of hearth and altar, reincarnated daily from the fingers of holy maidens twirling the kindling fire drill, intensifies as ruddy, howling Rudra, the "fierce essence of fire," blazing, devouring fire, the fever of madness, the raging arrows of death, the "inseminating fury of sex" and the ardor of the ascetic (EoR, 5:341; Kramrisch,15ff, 78). Encircled by a ring of flames Shiva, Lord of Yoga, or red-tongued Kali, the goddess Time, unveils our illusions of existence by dancing them into ash at the cremation grounds strewn with corpses. Fire's disturbing ambiguity applied to the "masters of fire"—the potter, smith, metallurgist, alchemist, shaman and witch, and to the inner as much as to the outer fire. "Sulphur" was the name alchemy gave to its "secret fire," a tincturing agent that was the key to the opus because it brought out the vital essence of matter. Sulphur could be creative, hellish, healing and stinking. Its fire is sometimes golden and luminous, sometimes it burns in the depths but gives off no light or it glows but does not consume—all ways of expressing the unknown "inflammable element" and "motive factor" behind the mystery of unconscious compulsion and conscious will (CW 14:151).

In myth as in reality, fire sometimes merely destroys, but often destroys so that from the purified residue or ashy essence a new world may come into being.

The Greek Heraclitus imagined a kind of fiery ether as the primary constituent of the cosmos and the soul as composed of similar fire. Many religions have depicted a divine spirit indwelling us as a fire that can be fanned or quenched. Because fire-making is the discovery that defines us as humans, in many creation myths fire is portrayed as a priceless gift from the gods, a fortuitous discovery or titanic theft. As the materials and structures of civilizations have been built and renovated by fire-craft, so is the stuff of the self worked by the libidinal fires of urges, instincts, affects and desires. Their intensity brings things to the surface, releases and propagates golden seeds, calcinates, sublimates, refines and tortures, hardens and shapes what is overly pliable and melts or evaporates what is rigidly hard. "It is through fire that Nature is changed," wrote Eliade (p. 170), making it the "basis of the most ancient magics," and in its symbolism carrying, even now, our terrors and hopes of transmutation.

Eliade, Mircea. *The Forge and the Crucible.* Chicago, 1978.
Hart, George. *A Dictionary of Egyptian Gods and Goddesses.* London and Boston, 1986.
Kingdon, Jonathan. *Self-Made Man: And His Undoing.* London and NY, 1993.
Kramrisch, Stella. *The Presence of Siva.* Princeton, NJ, 1981.

3

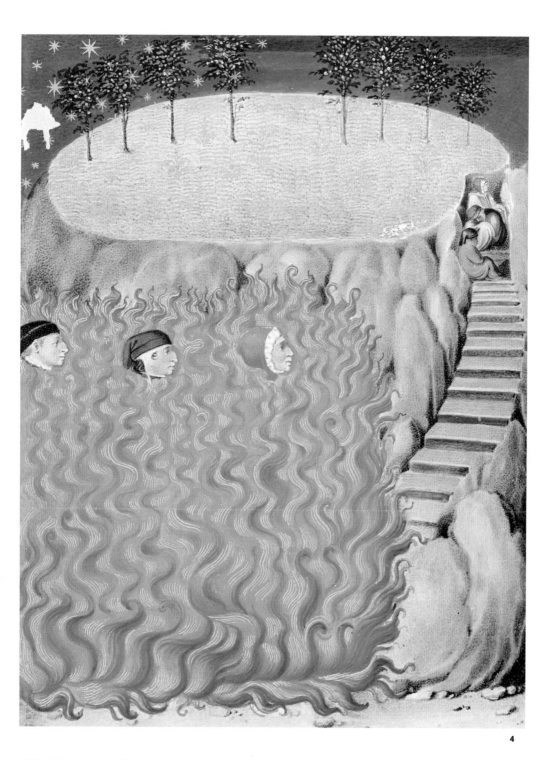

4

3. Wrathful, sulphurous fire rains from heaven to destroy Sodom and Gomorrah, in a depiction of the Biblical story. *Landscape with Lot and His Daughters*, detail, by Herri met de Bles (ca. 1510–72), oil on wood, Flanders.

4. *Passing Through the Fire of Purgatory*, manuscript illustration from Dante's *Divine Comedy*, 15th century C.E.

Spark

… Poor Man, a Spark
From Non-existence struck by Wrath divine, …
Night VII, page 48 (lines 964–5), (1742–45),
William Blake (Butlin, 54–5)

In Hildegard's vision, the brilliantly fiery, eyelike orb of the Creator God shoots a tongue of flame into the dark chaotic sphere, sparking the creation of heaven and earth and kindling the hearts of humankind within the lowly lump of clay, "each soul a spark awakened from the great living fire" (ARAS, 5Dk.199). The origins of the word spark attest to its fertile, spermatic quality as well as its animating, vital essence. The Greek *spargan* means to swell, teem, abound and then break or burst forth, also relating to a sprout or germinating plant life. In Latin, *spargere* is to strew or scatter, as seeds of activating light might be sown in the darkness of fixity or stagnation (Partridge, 645).

A spark is an incandescent particle thrown or remaining from a fire, the tiniest of which, left unextinguished in hearth or campfire, can burst to life again ferociously enough to consume a whole house or rage into a forest conflagration. Thus the spark embodies the incendiary potential of ideas, which can plant the seed for a new invention, scientific discovery or artistic creation, as well as spark a revolution powerful enough to reconfigure the entire world order. Sparks fly when opposite electrical charges join or conflict, and when passions ignite between two people, whether in love, anger or enmity.

One can imagine the awe inspired in ancient humans the first time that two stones struck together released sparks, as though from hiding deep within. Many Native American tribes venerated flint, a hard quartz that sparks when struck with steel, regarding it as a god of fire, and using it as a lucky charm to protect against bad magic and aid in the search for buried gold (MM 20: 2707). The early stone tool and hand-axe were "charged with mysterious power," analogous to the thunderbolt, as both could emit sparks and inflict injury. The meteorite, a ball of fire falling to earth like a spark from the anvil, was seen as the product of the nuptial impact between the god of thunder and the goddess of earth (Eliade, 29ff). The early smiths who fashioned sacred tools from this sidereal ore were themselves venerated as godlike.

In Blake's image, a lightning-like streak carves a zigzag path through the pressing, earthen darkness, culminating in a glowing spark with a radiant infant nestling at its center. Thus the spark simultaneously bursts forth, breaks in and creates a space of potential growth for the tiny germ of new life. Sixth century Greek philosophers talked of the soul being made out of star-stuff. The Gnostics saw the soul of a human as a spark or seed of light from the greater fire of God, left behind or fallen in his Creation, imprisoned in the darkness of matter, awaiting restoration to the realm of light. This soul spark formed the secret backbone of humankind, without which there would be no redemption (Rudolph, 109).

In the alchemical fantasy of the scintilla, infinitesimal sparks are found in multiple forms in the earth, or finely mingled in the depths of the dark water. When contemplated, these sparks shine in the darkness like fishes' eyes and, when gathered together, form the alchemical gold. Jung found that these processes corresponded with his clinical observations of the multiple centers of the psyche. They depict how a human being can become conscious of, or "gather together," the luminous substance of the personality, extracted from complexes and unconscious projections into a more integrated whole (CW 14: 42ff).

Butlin, Martin. *The Paintings and Drawings of William Blake: Text.* New Haven, CT, 1981.
Eliade, Mircea. *The Forge and the Crucible.* NY, 1962.
Partridge, Eric. *Origins.* NY, 1958.
Rudolph, Kurt and R. McL. Wilson. *Gnosis: The Nature and History of Gnosticism.* SF, 1983.
Siegfried, T. *Life's Story Starts with Chemistry of the Stars.* ://whyfiles.org/siegfried/story26/, 2007.

1. Hildegard of Bingen's (1098–1179) illuminated vision of the spark of creation. From *Liber Scivias (Know the ways of the Lord)*, Book II, from a facsimile, 12th century, Germany.

2. Watercolor illustration, detail, by William Blake, from Edward Young's *The Complaint: or Night-Thoughts on Life, Death, & Immortality*, Night VII, ca. 1795–7, England.

Dawn

... look, love, what envious streaks
Do lace the severing clouds in yonder east:
Night's candles are burnt out, and jocund day
Stands tiptoe on the misty mountain tops
Shakespeare, *Romeo and Juliet*, Act III.v, 9–12

Though first appearing as the merest attenuation of darkness, dawn, the beginning of daybreak, nevertheless signals an inevitable resurgence of light. Whether alluding to the incipient universe, or to the momentary flicker of an idea or feeling in its earliest apprehension; whether naming the interlude of communion engendered by the pristine clarity and shared focus of the whole of creation poised at the brink of sunrise, dawn evokes annunciation, beginning, approach, coming into being.

Weaving variegated semblances of light into the fabric of the universe, dawn may, on the one hand, restore the form and texture of an ordered world. For some, every dawn is a new creation, crafted by the deity from the transformed chaos of "night." On the other hand, in early popular Hindu tradition dawn represents the intoxicating allure of the "primal power of existence," introducing the surprising, the "spontaneously charming," the "incorrigibly unintentional" into the ongoing process of creation (Zimmer, 258). And in the Arctic darkness, during the ten days when the sun disappears following the winter solstice, Inuit whale hunters and their wives gather on the roofs of their igloos to await the "breaching" of the dawn, a shred of light that shines and fades immediately on the southern horizon, anticipating the gradual return of daylight and a prosperous hunting season in the spring (Lowenstein, 128).

Alchemy associates dawn with the operation of *separatio* and the splitting of the cosmic egg that separates heaven and earth. In the opening, the interstice of chaos, consciousness is born. Dawn is also a symbol for the purificatory stage of the *albedo* or "whitening." Similarly, the initiatory ordeals of baptism are brought to a conclusion at dawn when the "newly born," washed in the fount and dressed in pristine white robes, assume their new identity.

Typically, dawn is depicted as a beautiful young woman, like Eos, the goddess of Greek mythology whose saffron- and rose-tinted light announces the momentous and conspicuous advent of her brother Helios. In ancient Egyptian mythology, the red streaks of dawn represent the blood of the cow goddess Hathor as she labors to deliver her calf—the sun—who is born anew each morning (Clark, 87–9). Likewise, the chariot of the Vedic goddess Usas, laden with riches for humankind, is drawn through the sky by tawny cows or by red-gold horses. Just as cows break out in the morning from their night enclosure, Usas breaks open the darkness; as the swollen udder of the cow yields life-giving milk, so Usas "uncovers her breast" to bestow beneficent light (Doniger, 179–181).

Dawn, however, is not without paradox. Romeo's aubade, or lyrical lament at the arrival of dawn and, hence, of the impending separation of the two lovers, suggests her other side. The lovely Usas, for instance, though bedecked with the bright ornaments of a dancing girl and "smiling like a lover," also steals away the youthfulness of mortals like a gambler who pilfers another's stakes. And while Dawn rouses the sleeper, urging him into life and the fulfillment of the responsibilities of work, family and religious obligations, she also separates the weary from night's brief, healing reprieve.

Nevertheless, most mortals willingly surrender to Dawn's more graceful blandishments. As Walt Whitman observes, "We found our own O my soul in the calm and cool of the daybreak."

Clark, Robert Thomas Rundle. *Myth and Symbol in Ancient Egypt*. London, 1959.
Doniger, Wendy. *The Rig Veda: An Anthology: One Hundred and Eight Hymns, Selected, Translated and Annotated*. Harmondsworth, Middlesex, UK, and NY, 1981.
Lowenstein, Tom. *Ancient Land, Sacred Whale: The Inuit Hunt and Its Rituals*. London, 1993.
Zimmer, Heinrich Robert. *The King and the Corpse: Tales of the Soul's Conquest of Evil*. NY, 1948.

Interposed between night and day, dawn's prelusive light parts the melting black edges of earth and sky.

Sunrise

All poets and heroes...are the children
of Aurora, and emit their music at sunrise.
Henry David Thoreau, Walden

Anyone who has waited in anticipatory silence for the sun to glide like a molten hallelujah out of the sea, or ventured forth as the vast engine of the city comes alive in the morning sunlight reflecting off river and skyscraper; anyone whose creative thought or intuition crosses the threshold from inception to epiphany resonates with the ages-old veneration of the daily or seasonal rising of earth's own life-sustaining star:

> *... Of all forms, yellow, all-knowing,*
> *The supreme goal, the one light, giving heat.*
> *Thousand-rayed, existing in a hundred forms,*
> *The sun rises as the breath of creatures.*
> **Prasna Upanishad, Question 1:8**

The Latin word for the rising, or morning, sun is *oriens*; the name given also to the direction from which it rises: the East, or the Orient. We are "oriented" when we face or point toward the East; an "orient" gem is one that is lustrous or glowing. The noun *oriens* is formed on the verb *orior*: rise or become visible. By extension, the verb means "growing" or "springing forth," "origination," "coming into being" and birth.

Decisively marking the division of time between night and the day it brings into being, sunrise is symbolic not only of the creation of the world, but of the birth of consciousness—the "day" of psychic life—and the ego that is its presiding and orienting luminary. And just as the sunrise is emblematic of the savior god who sinks into the land of the dead, only to ascend again, so the daily resurgence of consciousness from the "little death" of sleep and dream is a rehearsal of resurrection. So, too, the hero who successfully negotiates the nighttime perils of the soul will reappear at sunrise, refulgent with the flame of newly won knowledge. Alchemy, as well as numerous myths, distinguishes sunrise from dawn. As daybreak, the latter is suggestive of the "first light" of spiritual, symbolic or psychic illumination, while sunrise evokes its infusion with the fire, blood and energic heat of lived experience.

To be sure, sunrise is not always a welcome event. The Egyptian goddess who raises the sun is "she who annihilates ... [who] comes out of the darkness." Though the goddess certainly dispels the last vestiges of night, and may represent a spirit who destroys the enemies of the sun god Re, the epithet likely refers to the annihilating quality of the sun (ARAS, 2An.084). Similarly, the bloody human hearts torn from sacrificial victims and ritually offered by the ancient Aztecs to strengthen the sun deity in his daily ascent, is suggestive of the raw, digestive force that thunders "out of the darkness" to devour life as well as sustain it. T. E. Lawrence described the scorching desert sun that "came up like a drawn sword and struck us speechless"(Brooks, 144). Commenting on the chakra Manipura, "lustrous like a gem," located at the region of the solar plexus, a Sanskrit text observes that through meditation "on the region of Fire, triangular in form and shining like the rising sun...the power to destroy and create (the world) is acquired" (Avalon, 366, 369). Preeminently, however, sunrise evokes birth, new beginning, manifestation. And on a spring morning, who would question why the poet "wakes up early" to greet the rising sun:

> *Hello, sun in my face.*
> *Hello, you who make the morning*
> *and spread it over the fields*
> *and into the faces of the tulips*
> *and the nodding morning glories,*
> *and into the windows of, even, the*
> *miserable and the crotchety—*
>
> *best preacher that ever was,*
> *dear star, that just happens*
> *to be where you are in the universe*
> *to keep us from ever-darkness,*
> *to ease us with warm touching,*
> *to hold us in the great hands of light—*
> *good morning, good morning, good morning.*
>
> *Watch, now, how I start the day*
> *in happiness, in kindness.*
> **Mary Oliver, Why I Wake Early**

Avalon, Arthur. *The Serpent Power: The Secrets of Tantric and Shaktic Yoga.* NY, 1974.
Brooks, Geraldine. *Nine Parts of Desire: The Hidden World of Islamic Women.* NY, 1995.
Roebuck, Valerie J. *The Upanishads.* London; NY, 2003.
Thoreau, Henry David. *The Variorum Walden.* NY, 1962.

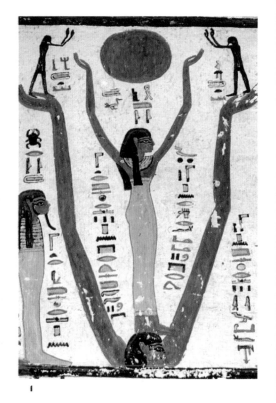

1

2

1. In a cosmic feat of levitation, the goddess "She who annihilates" raises the orange-black globe of the sun above the worshipping horizons of the east and west. Detail from a wall painting in the tomb of Ramses VI, ca. 1145–37 B.C.E., Valley of the Kings, Egypt.

2. A serenely majestic, saffron sun emerges from gold-tinted clouds. Central scroll from *Triptych of Flowers and the Rising Sun*, by Sakai Hoitsu, ink and color on silk, after 1824, Japan.

Solstice

Solstice is a turning point. The sun "stops" at its zenith in the summer solstice of late June in the northern hemisphere, and at its nadir in the winter solstice of late December; it is "that curve which forms the golden swing in the sky" (Calasso, 41).

In these countervailing extremes of light and darkness is the evocation of a limit reached in the arc of a life, a mood, a capacity, or in the hegemony of consciousness or unconscious. The Midsummer Night of the summer solstice is a night of fairy magic and dream, earth's extravagant, sun-imbibed bloom and the lust and tenderness of lovers. Since ancient times, traditional celebrations—roundels, or circular dances; feasting; the lighting of bonfires—on the summer solstice mark this longest day and yearly pinnacle of the sun's intensity: "On a summer midnight, you can hear the music / Of the weak pipe and the little drum / And see them dancing around the bonfire" (T. S. Eliot, "East Coker"). At the same time, the summer solstice signifies the reaping of the first harvest and the beginning of the sun's gradual descent into darkness. The winter solstice is the shortest day of the year, the time of Saturn's dominion, of mown harvest, darkness, chill, death and the age-old presentiment of light's extinction. But the winter solstice is also the point where the descent ends and the reascent begins; at the Saturnalia on this day, the roles of master and slave were reversed, signifying the notion of direction inverted (Vitale, 11ff).

The winter solstice has been mythologized as the birth of the divine light in a time of great darkness, and the overcoming of death in the sun's eternal rejuvenation. In Ireland's New Grange, the winter solstice sun penetrates a long passageway to an inner room of intricate spirals and sun disks carved into cave walls to "capture" the new light, as one might grasp a flicker of hope or a spark of meaning, which changes everything. The *I Ching* describes the winter solstice as a time of resting, for the life force is still underground and the natural, spontaneous movement that the light engenders is only just beginning (Wilhelm, 97, 170). Yet it does begin, and it is this imperceptible movement that makes the solstice never merely the triumph or defeat of light in relation to darkness. Rather, solstice reflects a numinous simultaneity of the sun's standing at an extreme and turning into the opposite, a divine rotation of ascent and descent that makes of light and darkness one.

Calasso, Roberto. *The Marriage of Cadmus and Harmony.* NY, 1993.
Vitale, Augusto. "Saturn: The Transformation of the Father." *Fathers and Mothers.* Ed. Patricia Berry. Dallas, TX, 1990.
Wilhelm, Richard. Tr. *The I Ching; or Book of Changes.* Princeton, NJ, 1967.

1

2

1. Play on a swing evokes the limit and return played out
in every solstice. Detail from miniature painting, ca.
1760, India.

2. Sunrise illuminates the great circle of monoliths at
Stonehenge on the summer solstice. Wiltshire, England.

Dusk

Arched by a bridge, the waters of the Sumida River reflect the first twinkling stars of dusk, while along the riverbank a geisha follows behind the lantern carried by her unseen escort. In the background, the Sanya canal leads to the gate of the red-light district of Yoshiwara, where restaurants and pleasure houses are just coming to life.

Dusk is the interval between day and night, a darkening that still holds within itself the final, residual luster of the sun, now mythically embarked on its night-sea journey. It is this soft, gradual dissolution of the diurnal light simultaneous with the rising of the moon and the evening stars that evokes such a mixture of elements: the erotic, seductive, melancholy, quiescent, night's magical or sinister possibilities, solitude, cessation and return. Among the Inuit, twilight was the time when the shadow of a shaman could separate from his body and transparently enter invisible realms (Seidelman, 47). In the same sense, consciousness at dusk may yield to the psychic tow of the unconscious, senses and perceptions attune themselves differently and the psychic landscape undergo a blurring and blending of things. Dusk brings enchantment and uncanny manifestations. Animals of the night awaken and become active, unveiling themselves in pairs of glowing eyes, the flittering wings of bats, an owl's hooting or the amorous incandescence of fireflies. Our own repressed, crepuscular energies surface, mythically portrayed as a quickening of the spirit world and the supernatural, haunting apparitions, and shape-shifting from human into were-animal, vampire and alter-ego.

Dusk signifies the evening of day and the evening of life, or the evening of time as the "twilight of the gods" when earth's light is swallowed. There is pensive intimacy and release in the lengthened shadows and lowering darkness when what has burned brightly has already relinquished itself to the coming night, and day is done.

Seidelman, Harold and James Turner,
***The Inuit Imagination.* NY, 1994.**

Evening View of Matsuchiyama and Sanya Canal, from the series *One Hundred Views of Edo*, by Hiroshige, wood-block print, ca. 1857. Japan.

Sunset

Two heavily cloaked figures silhouetted on a high hill watch a winter sunset, emphasizing by contrast the aureate reds, yellows and purples of the sun's descending striations. Every evening the sun sinks toward the horizon, meeting earth with heaven, and slipping under the boundary of our perspective, carries with it something of ourselves into the netherworld of the imagination. To one culture the sunset is reminiscent of a great, striped, crepuscular tiger; to another it is the falling golden eagle of the gods. "Enormous wings out of the west, the sad red splendid light," wrote the American poet Robinson Jeffers. We often watch the sunset as we might the last embers of a dying fire, peacefully or pensively reflecting on the inevitable repetition of death and rebirth, the declination of an individual life or the completion of a cycle. Some Australian aboriginal tribes depicted the sunset as the more intimate drama of consciousness nightly descending into the timeless realm of sleep and dream in order to find renewal from psyche's latent spark of creative fire. The sun woman burns up her stock of fuel by the end of each day, and at night goes down into the underworld for fresh supplies of firewood. Or she has a lover among the dead and every night descends into the underworld to be with him, at sunrise reappearing dressed in her lover's gift, a red kangaroo skin (MM 20:2719).

If, however, sunset pertains symbolically to a fertilizing conjunction in the underworld, it is also emblem of all that is sunlike within us encompassed by darkness. Because it is the direction of the sunset, the west is the mythic land of the spirits where the night-sea journey of the hero begins. Long ago, our ancestors must have watched the sunset with awe and trepidation, hoping they might participate in the sun's eternal circuit and rejuvenation. Later this became elaborated as a journey of spiritual transformation and rebirth, or psychologically, as an incubation in the unconscious by which its energies become integrated with consciousness. In the rich mythology of ancient Egypt the headless goddess of the Western Mountain draws the evening sun into her embrace, or the sun in its barque enters the mouth of the goddess Nut, delicately arched as the night sky. The portal of the netherworld opens, dissolving all familiar orientation of the day. Evoking our experience of besieging unconscious forces, the sun makes its way through the pitch black of the night sea, battling chaos and extinction, threatened by the vast, eclipsing coils of the primal serpent Apophis and its attendant monsters. Only in the last of the 12 hours of night, does the exhausted sun reach the containing womb of the goddess and is reborn through the gates of her vulva at dawn.

Sunset is variously depicted as the surrender, union or tension between the relatively fixed solar element and the watery, changeable element, signified by the ascendance at twilight of the waxing and waning moon. Sunset has even been portrayed mythically as the end of time when all creation returns to the primal ocean of preexistence. Within time, sunset closes the day and opens us, in the lengthening shadows, to the possibilities of a different order. There is release in that, allowing us, in the words of Roethke, "To stare into the after-light, the glitter left on the lake's surface, / When the sun has fallen behind a wooded island."

Jeffers, Robinson and Albert Gelpi. *The Wild God of the World: An Anthology of Robinson Jeffers.* Stanford, CA, 2003.
Roethke, Theodore. *The Collected Poems of Theodore Roethke.* Garden City, NY, 1975.

Sunset, detail, by Caspar David Friedrich, oil on canvas, ca. 1830–5, Germany.

Night

Night I embrace, a dear proximity ...
Theodore Roethke, *In Evening Air*

Uncanny, impending potency, resonant of animal, human and god, emanates from the Navajo depiction of night. Suspended in ebony space, a pensive moon, under a scattering of mist, dominates the sky. Behind her, in perfect equilibrium, a veiled sun reinforces her sovereignty in the wake of a vanished day. "Only the dark, dark night shows to my eyes the stars," wrote Walt Whitman; here, spidery intersecting lines trace the path of the Milky Way amid celestial Rabbit Tracks, the trail of the Great Serpent and other heavenly configurations.

Like a finely woven shawl, Night enfolds the world in the interval between dusk and dawn. Bringing silence, healing and a cool hiatus from the sun's burning heat and light, night evokes the restorative darkness and repose, the veiling of sunlike consciousness, that follows upon the tumultuous splendor and striving of day. But to "night eyes" and ears the coming of darkness is also an awakening: a numinous world manifested in the lambent play of fireflies, the secret rustling of night foragers, the flickering of bat wings at moonrise. During the night, Walter Otto observes, "Knowledge flares up, or descends like a shooting star— rare, precious, even magical knowledge" (p. 119).

An Orphic myth depicts Night as she who was "in the beginning," a black-winged bird with awe-inspiring oracular powers. The goddess conceived of wind, and she laid a silver egg in the immense lap of Darkness. From this egg, Eros, the golden-winged god of love, was born (Kerényi, 16–7). Just so does Night birth in the soul an oceanic feeling of kinship, not only with the lover with whom one sleeps "while the dark earth spins with the living and the dead" (Pablo Neruda, "Night on the Island," 24–5), but with ancient ancestors and future descendants, universes seen and unseen, gods and creatures of time and eternity.

For many however, the "proximity" of Night's own "dark side" is experienced as a sinister enshrouding by all that is menacing, terrifying and unpredictable. Rather than rendering the world an "immense similitude," the onset of darkness may intensify a feeling of otherness: night as friend to predator, betrayer, thief and nightmare, the restless "undead" who drain the blood of the living. Or, as a mirror of the watery abyss, the night sky may evoke the loneliness of the void on the edges of which earth and its inhabitants seem small and insignificant.

Night has often symbolized encroaching old age and bodily death, the final "lights out" of an individual life. As such, it may be anticipated with loathing or as a welcome release. On a cosmic scale, Hinduism's Night of Brahma signifies an "interval of non-manifestation" following the cataclysmic end of a cycle. While Vishnu sleeps on the cosmic ocean during this all-encompassing "night of nights," the primordial integrity and loveliness of the universe are reincubated (Zimmer, 20, 37–9).

Psychologically, night may evoke the unconscious in both its positive and more threatening aspects. Like Nut devouring the sun, the unconscious swallows ego consciousness during intervals of sleep. Depressive moods, a state of "unknowing," lassitude and absence of meaning characterize the "dark night of the soul." On the other hand, the sense of a divine epiphany occasioned by the sight of a jewel-encrusted night sky may reflect "constellations" of burgeoning insight in the unconscious of the viewer, the myriad "little lights" that gradually reveal themselves to consciousness.

Writing about the Greek god Hermes, the "seductive and lethal" companion of the night, whose golden wand put souls to sleep and awakened them again, the mythographer Karl Kerényi observed: "The night of generation and the night of dying, do we not carry these in us?" Does not Nut's night aspect make possible the regenerative motion toward dawn? The descent of night upon consciousness need not signal a permanent death of the ego, but only a temporary darkening out of which a fuller vision and apprehension of the "deity within" might emerge.

Kerényi, Karl. *The Gods of the Greeks.* London, 2002.
Neruda, Pablo. *The Captain's Verses.* NY, 1972.
Otto, Walter Friedrich. *The Homeric Gods: The Spiritual Significance of Greek Religion.* London, 1979.
Quirke, Stephen. *Ancient Egyptian Religion.* NY, 1992.
Whitman, Walt. *Leaves of Grass, and Selected Prose.* NY, 1949.
Zimmer, Heinrich Robert and Joseph Campbell. *Myths and Symbols in Indian Art and Civilization.* Princeton, NJ, 1972.

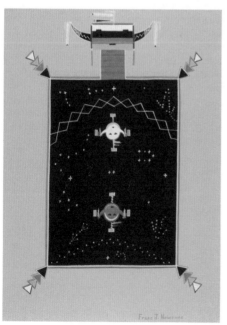

1. Myriad stars, evoking the glittering souls of the dead, shelter within the graceful, overarching body of the Egyptian sky goddess Nut, here manifested as night. Underneath her the lady Taperet prays to Aton. Painted wood stele, 22nd dynasty (1070–712 B.C.E.), Egypt.

2. Colorful rainbow spots guard the horned sun and moon in this Navajo sandpainting of Father Sky's night aspect. Jagged lines of male rain extend from the turquoise-covered face of the sun. In front of him, a luminous moon, her face coated with white quartz, emits straight lines of female rain. *Night Sky*, by Franc J. Newcomb, 1936.

2

Darkness

Out from the darkness
back into the darkness—
affairs of the cat
Issa

Throughout our lives—in the daily circadian rhythms of sleep and waking, the creative process of play and invention, the thought waiting for emergence out of the depths of the unconscious; during periods of introversion when the allure of the outer world is stilled and the transpersonal encountered at the horizon of consciousness—we, like the cat, repeatedly come out of the darkness and go back into darkness. Darkness is our first reality, the looming riddle of our becoming. Like the macrocosmic galaxy hypothetically plunged in a globe of "dark matter" and permeated with mysterious "dark energy," so our own microcosmic being, quickening in the womb, is enveloped by the dark matter and dark energy of our ancestral inheritance.

Darkness is defined most simply as the absence of light, and our experience of the one may initially take shape as the obverse of our experience of the other. We think of light, for instance, as clarifying and delineating. The world comes into being at daybreak. Darkness, on the other hand, as Rilke reminds us, absorbs and merges the many into one:

But the darkness pulls in everything:
shapes and fires, animals and myself,
how easily it gathers them!—

While light is quick, propulsive, transparent, darkness is still and waiting and opaque. Light beams, transmits, radiates; darkness extinguishes, eclipses, swallows. Darkness is tunnel, abyss, maw, the city in blackout, the locked closet, the roach scurrying over the countertop before the kitchen light goes on. It is the veiled face and cloaked body. It is the massive iceberg concealed beneath the pitchy surface of the sea, the miasmic land of the dead, the "nighttime nothingness" of the shadowed edge of the moon.

As absence, darkness attracts human projections of moral or mental deficiency, often translated in terms of sin or evil: the Koran's chapter Light, for example, describes the deeds of the disbeliever as "darkness on a vast abysmal sea…layer upon layer of darkness." A "heart of darkness" in Joseph Conrad's imagination is one governed by abhorrent passions and base instincts that tempt the "unlawful soul" beyond the defining boundaries of humanity. For Sylvia Plath, darkness is intimate and impending:

I am terrified by this dark thing
That sleeps in me;
All day I feel its soft, feathery turnings,
its malignity.

Darkness often evokes the teeming formlessness of the beginning: "Darkness there was" the Rig Veda declares, "at first concealed in darkness this All was undiscriminated chaos." Or it may suggest an impoverishment of spirit or substance. Hinduism's Kali Yuga or "dark age," for instance, lacking the ordering force of dharma, the holy law, is rife with hubris, greed and war. Alchemy associates the imagery of darkness with *nigredo*—the stage in which the ego is confronted not only with the weight of its earthliness and unlived possibilities, but also with its capacity for evil.

1

1. Inscrutably, darkness presides over the brooding
latency and ghostly luminescence of sea and sky. *North
Pacific Ocean, Stinson Beach*, by Hiroshi Sugimoto,
gelatin silver print, 1994.

Yet what appears to be only absence, emptiness and obscurity may actually point to a luminosity, presence and fullness of being peculiar to darkness' domain. Is it not, after all, alive and stirring?

I'm getting the spirit in the dark
I'm getting the spirit in the dark
People movin, aw, ain't we groovin?
Just getting the spirit in the dark.
Aretha Franklin, *Spirit in the Dark*

According to the fourth century Christian writer Gregory of Nyssa, it is only after one has quenched the brilliant light of the reasoning mind that one may enter most immediately into the presence and knowledge of god: "Moses' vision of God began with light, afterwards God spoke to him in a cloud. But when Moses rose higher and became more perfect, he saw god in the darkness."

Preeminently, darkness is the precinct of initiation. In the enchanted forest, the shamanic cave, the black pool or the well, the darkened theater, the alcheringa time, the Asclepian temple one comes face to face with the agony and the muted rapture of death and (re) birth. The experience of initiatory darkness, as evoked by T. S. Eliot, is, to be sure, one of paradox and ambiguity:

O dark dark dark ...
I said to my soul, be still,
and let the dark come upon you ...
I said to my soul, be still and wait without hope
For hope would be hope for the wrong thing;
wait without love,
For love would be love of the wrong thing; ...
Wait without thought,
for you are not ready for thought:
So the darkness shall be the light,
and the stillness the dancing.

But if one consciously enters into the darkness and endures its enshroudment; if catlike, one learns to see and to hear acutely in its recesses, the darkness will gradually reveal the treasures concealed there. In the process, darkness will become the mysterious and familiar source of transformation and inspiration, growth and healing to which, repeatedly, we gratefully return:

You darkness, that I come from,
I love you more than all the fires
that fence in the world ...
Rainer Maria Rilke, *You, Darkness*

of Nyssa, St. Gregory, Jean Daniélou and Herbert Musurillo. *From Glory to Glory: Texts from Gregory of Nyssa's Mystical Writings.* Crestwood, NY, 1979.

2. The "Black Sun" of the alchemical stage of the
nigredo signifies an eclipse of the ego's standpoint due
to an incursion of the unconscious. Though depicted
as an encounter with death, the presence of the angels
testifies to the necessity of this provisional darkening
in order to achieve the opus. *Viridarium chymicum*,
1624, Germany.

Stone

The sharp and ragged stone from Stenness, Scotland, points toward the sky, half of its length buried underground. We will never know the exact meaning invested in this monument, but it still moves us after four thousand years. In raising the stone to an upright position its sculptural form is revealed, creating a powerful presence and new meaning. In fact, it was this act of giving meaning to their world—of turning stone into symbol—that made our earliest ancestors fully human. Our relationship with stone is so ancient and intimate that we have named the beginning of human history the Stone Age.

Stones were among our earliest tools and weapons, often shaped into beautiful perfection; these were symbols of power, increasing the might and effectiveness of early men and women coping with their environment. Throughout the ages stone has been part of human life. Stones heated by fire could be used for cooking, and stone structures housed the living or the dead. In Germany the spirit of the dead remained in the tombstones, just as in Africa stones carried within them the spirit of an ancestor. A stone could signify a god or become a place of worship, such as the Ka'aba, the meteoritic black stone in Mecca, the central object of Islamic pilgrimage. Another famous meteorite is the black stone of Pessinus, an epiphany of the Phrygian goddess Cybele (ARAS, 1:52, 326).

Yet, the mineral world is viewed as the lowest form of creation. It takes outside force to move or change a stone; we throw one and it remains inert. There are many expressions in our language that reflect this lowly aspect of the stone. We say that someone is stupid, blind or deaf as a stone. Stone lacks sensation or feeling, and we accuse someone of having a heart of stone. When Medusa, in Greek myth, turns someone into stone, its psychological meaning is that he or she regresses to a less conscious state. Our worst fear freezes us into stone, robbing us of our ability to act.

We are fascinated by the dense nature of stone that refuses us access. In her poem "Conversation with a Stone," Wislawa Szymborska writes:

I knock at the stone's front door.
"It's only me, let me come in."
"I don't have a door," says the stone.

The closed world of the stone invites our imagination to play; sometimes we assign gender to stone. Standing stones, from ancient *menhirs* to modern sculpture, seem to have a phallic quality. "Rocks" and "stones" are slang for testicles. The meteor's association with fire and sky also adds to the masculine quality of stone. In Hinduism lingam, or the active creative principle, appears as a pillarlike stone while the feminine receptive element, the yoni, is carved into a circular stone hollow. Thus, stone represents feminine matter as well and in personified form becomes the earth mother. The god Mithra was born from a rock, and in many traditions we are told how rocks give birth to precious stones. Like embryos they ripen within the living rock before being mined or "born" (Eliade, 43–52). Then again, the stone as the hermaphrodite of the ancient alchemists combined all opposites: of male and female, child and old man, beginning and end or ignorance and wisdom.

The notion that something is "written in stone" makes it unalterable and fixed—contrary to the mercurial nature of the stone that defies all categories. The word "mercurial" comes from the Roman god Mercurius, who alone was able to cross over borders between heaven, earth and the underworld, a transgression forbidden to all others. Mercurius was also the guardian of borders in the form of an erect phallic stone called herm (from his Greek name Hermes). For the alchemists Mercurius became the unifying spirit, often used interchangeably with the stone (CW 14:715).

1. This raised monument from Stenness, Scotland, made of local flagstone, stands more than 12 feet high but is only 12 inches thick. Originally, it was part of a circle of 12 standing stones, out of which only four survive (Clarke, 40). The Stones of Stenness, ca. 2400 B.C.E.

Compared to our brief human life span, stone becomes a symbol of endurance; indeed it suggests the concept of eternity. Yet, the common stone surrounds us everywhere, and we give it little value. For the alchemists, the "mean, uncomely stone, cheap in price" became the indestructible material of transformation into the "Philosopher's Stone." Their idea that it is "a stone and not a stone" suggests that perhaps the much sought-after stone is to be understood in a psychological way. The Arabian alchemist Morienus expressed it even more directly: "This thing [the philosopher's stone] is extracted from *you*: *you* are its mineral, and one can find it in you" (Jung, 210). This tells us that we must patiently work throughout our life, like the ancient alchemists, "with love and approbation" to transform what we least value—the dead, ignorant or false aspects of ourselves—into the true stone, wise and eternal.

Clarke, D.V., et al. *Symbols of Power at the Time of Stonehenge*. Edinburgh, 1985.
Eliade, Mircea. *The Forge and the Crucible*. Chicago, 1978.
Jung, C. G. and Marie-Louise von Franz. *Man and His Symbols*. Garden City, NY, 1964.

2

3

4

2. Stone suggests essential hardness. Stone axes dating from the time of Stonehenge, ca. 3000 B.C.E., England.

3. One of the names of this carved stone is Akwanshi, which means "dead person in the ground." Monolith in phallic form as a memorial to ancestors of the Ekoi peoples (ca. 1500–1900), Nigeria.

4. Burmese monks at prayer before the Golden Rock at Shwe Pyi Daw (the "Golden Country"), the Buddhist holy place.

Mountain

Fuji—the majestic paraphrase of Japan itself—floats above the visitors streaming to its popular temple-shrines. Their figures, tiny in relation to the mountain, can be seen wherever Kano Motonobu's stylized clouds part to demarcate the stages of their pilgrimage. Three seated Buddhas represent the state of enlightenment sought by the zigzag parade of pilgrims nearing the top.

Visible from a dozen provinces, Fujisan is the "center of the world" in a country that is 85 percent mountainous—an active volcano that is paradoxically the guardian of the nation. Originally a place for the disposal of the dead, medieval Japan's pine-covered slopes sprouted *yama-miya* (mountain shrines) inhabited by *yamabushi* (mountain-sleepers), whose *Shugendō* practices included ceremonial mountain-climbing to absorb magical powers (EoR, 13:302–5). Blending indigenous Shinto with Chinese Buddhist and Taoist beliefs, these hermits meditated on the transcendent realms the mountain peaks themselves intimated. The mountain sleepers developed rituals for worshiping *yamo no kami* (mountain spirits) and guarding against the sudden bewitchment of *tengu* (mountain demons) (ARAS, 1:39–41; Bonnefoy 2:1059). For even the most sacred of Japan's mountains, Fuji, was imagined as not only the entrance to Amida Buddha's Paradise, but also the fearful "man-hole" (*hito-ana*), the volcanic vent that was the entrance to fiery hell (Clark, 10).

The mountain is one of our very oldest images of deity, distant sky gods of thunder and rain, gods of erupting intensity, divine metallurgists fanning the volcanic bellows of creativity. Even older, perhaps, is the mountain as the mother goddess of Asia Minor and India. The mountain is the throne from which she rules and protects, seated, immobile, eternal. Her snowmelt and rainfall stream down the mountainside fertilizing everything. Wild animals and raptors shelter in her slopes and clefts. Rock materializes her bulk and gravity, the greatness of her thighs and breasts, her towering, gigantic, generative strength. Gestating within the mountain's hollow, uterine interior are precious metals, an image alchemy adopted to describe the mysterious *prima materia*, the undifferentiated stuff we start with when we mine our depths, which gradually reveals its potential forms and values (Abraham, 131). Here, too, was evoked the dwelling of invisible, supernatural forces of potential, for the great mountain mother encompassed not only the living, but the spirits of the metals and the spirits of the dead. Epic kings like Frederick Barbarossa or the legendary Islamic martyrs, the Seven Sleepers of Ephesus, were said to be slumbering, sealed inside mountains, awaiting rebirth.

Mountainous domes of hardened magma or upward-swelling sedimentary rock, the earth's massive ranges and intercontinental rings slowly compressed by moving plates into fractured folds or cataclysmically transformed by avalanche or volcano: These suggest the thrust and shift of deep tectonic forces (Greek, *tekton*, "builder") that orient us out of the void, the flowing lava that reshapes our landscapes. Mountains are associated with revelation and transition; the mountaintop is where Moses meets God, where Jesus is transfigured. Mountains suggest arduous, painstaking ascent and sublimation, the widened perspective, the peak experience, the thin air of headiness and sublimity. The Babylonian ziggurat at whose summit a sacred marriage was celebrated and the funereal pyramids of Egypt are modeled on the mountain and its intangible heights where earth and heaven meet; they reflect the mythic goal of sacred quests and the pinnacle of self-knowledge. Luther, however, viewed mountains as grotesque irregularities amidst ordered creation (EoR, 10:130), and Buddhists imagine no mountains filling the perfect emptiness of Nirvana. Yet India's Mount Meru, 84,000 miles high, is the Himalayan prototype of Indian temple-domes and center of a quadrated universe. In the American Southwest, the Navajo homeland nestled within the Four Sacred Mountains of the Four Directions. Jung in his travels encountered the Pueblo sage, Mountain Lake, who asked him, "Do you not think all life comes from the mountain?" (Jung, 251).

Abraham, Lyndy. *A Dictionary of Alchemical Imagery.* Cambridge, UK, and NY, 1998.
Bonnefoy, Yves. *Mythologies.* Chicago, 1991.
Clark, Timothy. *100 Views of Mount Fuji.* Trumbull, CT, 2001.
Jung, C. G. and Aniela Jaffé. *Memories, Dreams, Reflections.* NY, 1989.

1

2

1. The path to self-realization is portrayed as an ascent to the summit of Mount Fuji, which rises 12,000 feet above sea level—soaring here above even the sun and the moon. *Mandala of Pilgrimage to Mt. Fuji,* by Kano Motonobu (1476–1559), hanging scroll, Japan.

2. Botticelli's intricately chambered mountain would fit inside the hollow cavity of Dante's Inferno, which it depicts. By purging oneself of the traits that cast one into these hellish depths, one could ascend Mount Purgatory and regain Paradise. Manuscript illustration, ca. 1500, Italy.

Valley

A valley is the opposite of a peak; it is the lowest point in a lofty landscape. Opening up like a cupped hand, the valley creates a gulf between mountains and hills. It is often an area of plenitude, amassing rainfall and providing rich earth for vegetation, a longed-for destination after rugged treks. Because water chooses the lowest place to gather, a river or glacier may incise a valley, its contours the result of channel erosion, transport and deposition of debris. Valleys are the living fossil record of powerful geologic and fluvial forces, of weathering and the gradual shifting of mantle rock. Hiroshige's almost abstract depiction of the Kasatori Pass contrasts the soft greenness of a valley with the sharp angles of blue and gray mountains, evoking the sinuous movement of life between high and low. The flow of travelers following the curves of the landscape seems as eternal as the ancient pines that line their path. The valley is associated with the earthy, the humble and also with the womb as source, linking us with the Way and oneness: "Those on the Way of Tao, like water / Need to accept where they find themselves; / And that may often be where water goes / To the lowest places, and that is right" (Laozi, 41). A valley can also be empty and deserted. We depict states of emotional heaviness as the vales of life, shadowed oppressively by mountainous burdens or looming fears—the vale of tears, the lonesome valley. At the same time, the "valley of the shadow of death" is where the psalmist feels the immanent presence of the deity and is comforted; Ezekiel's visionary valley of dry bones, perceived with prophetic meaning, shifts into a locus of hope and reanimation. Dwarfed by the majestic heights of the towering, pneumatic mountains and the "peak experience" of transcendence they intimate, the valley conveys a sense of experience that is *not* transcended, but imparts a deep and sustaining effect. "Soul is at home in the deep, shaded valleys," said a Dalai Lama of Tibet (Hillman, 119ff). Similarly, the pharaonic burial site, the Valley of the Kings, in Egypt, denotes a place of immortality and quiet observation, permanently defined by its surrounding cliffs and wadis and is emblematic of stillness and rest.

Hillman, James. "Peaks and Vales." *On the Way to Self Knowledge: Sacred Tradition and Psychotherapy.* Ed. Jacob Needleman. NY, 1976. Laozi. *Tao Te Ching: A New Translation.* NY, 1994.

Ashida, Station 27: A Green Valley with Trees, from
the series *The Sixty-Nine Stations of the Kisokaido*, by
Hiroshige, wood-block print, 1834–42, Japan.

Cave

The discovery of Pech-Merle by two teenagers in 1922 restored to humanity one of our first refuges and earliest galleries of permanent sacred art—the underground cavern. Dating from the Upper Paleolithic era (10–30,000 years B.C.E.), Pech-Merle imagery included an anthropomorphic element, like this hint of a primordial breast, with its suggestion of the cave as a mother, and imprints of children's feet. Although some caves are formed by abrupt geological forces—pockets of volcanic gas, tubes of lava, earthquakes—it is the glacially slow seepage of groundwater that creates the iciclelike stalactites and the eternal calm of the legendary limestone caverns of Paleolithic France and Spain. Deep in their labyrinthine corridors, a water drop or falling stone echoes through a world of absolute darkness and constant temperature. Our ancestors felt their way along these cool walls, balancing flickering cups of burning oil in their hands, listening for the breath of massive cave bears, before reaching astonishingly realistic animal paintings—proof of humanity's long fascination with artistic technique and symbolic images.

By providing a passage between this world and the underworld, or between life and the land of the dead, caves evoke the primordial functions of the earth mother as both womb and tomb. The Aztecs traced their origin to Seven Caves (*Chicomoztoc*), a primordial event mirrored in the creation myths of the Pueblo, Hopi and Zuni, recalling their emergence from a cavernous earth-womb. Ancient and medieval poets depicted the entrance to Hades or Hell as a plummeting cave, drawing on these maternal associations to portray a place of death, return, initiation and rebirth. According to Eliade, traditional miners compared their art of drawing precious metal out of the earth's body, where it gestated in caverns, to the art of obstetrics

(Eliade, 41). Similarly, Ovid tells his ancient Roman readers that in the primitive age of Saturn, humans made their first homes in caves (Ovid, 6), just as Jupiter was sheltered from Saturn in the Cretan cave of Mount Ida, protectively fed by bees and goats.

In the cave's complete darkness, the dramatic symbol of light was forcefully manifested. When the insulted Japanese sun-goddess Amaterasu withdrew into a cavern, she plunged the world into darkness. She was cajoled out only when the gods aroused her curiosity by holding a mirror at the cave's entrance to reflect her own brilliance. Plato taught that the world itself is a cave to the ignorant, who watch shadows on its walls cast by a celestial light that the enlightened perceive directly. Psychologically, entering a cave can have the quality of introversion, incubation, regression to the source, psychic withdrawal or hibernation. The cave can represent a refuge, but also a confined and archaic perspective. A wanderer may become lost or disoriented in the cave, or experience a "cave-in," reflecting how solid containment may give way to crushing self-doubt. Alchemy depicted the cave as a form of the alchemical *vas,* and religious lore has seen the cave as a space of conversion and the climax of a spiritual quest. Mohammed heard the voice of Allah reverberating in a cavern, just as in Orthodox Christian icons Jesus is born not in a stable, but in a cave. The Star of Bethlehem overhead directs its beam into the opening of the cave, illuminating the new god sheltered in the secret interior of mother earth.

Eliade, Mircea. *The Forge and the Crucible.* NY, 1962.

Ovid. *Metamorphoses.* Bloomington, IN, 1955.

1. The enormous long-lost caverns of Spain and France provided paleolithic people with refuges, primitive temples and galleries of sacred art. In the sanctuary of Le Combel, at Pech-Merle in the French Dordogne, rows of ochre-red dots accentuate a natural stalactite formation, drawing the eye to the semblance of a stone breast. The dots are thought to have been placed by blowing ochre through a hollow bone or imprinting using palms or fingers.

2. An Olmec "earth monster" from the slopes of Chalcatzingo, Mexico, gazes at climbers about to enter its yawning mouth. Hollowed-out over 2,500 years ago and carved with images for conjuring rain, the face encloses a shallow cave-opening. Here, rites were staged that were most likely visible to the villagers below.

3. The warm pink interior of a conch shell combined with the concavities of a woman's body evoke the seductive entrance of a cavern. *Pink Cave,* by Louisa Chase, oil on canvas, 1983, United States.

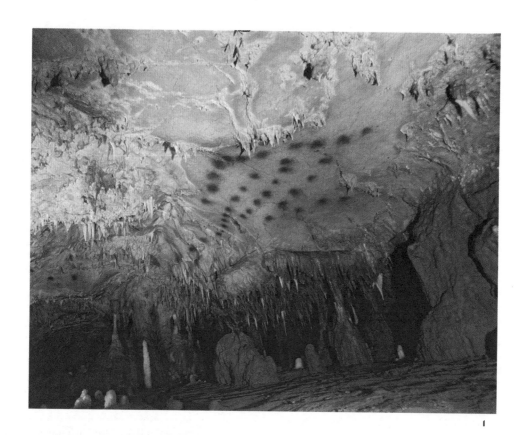

1

2

3

Salt

A magnified photograph of salt crystals reveals their cubic (quaternary) structure, suggesting unity, differentiation and balance. In dry and concentrated form salt is so strong that pillars of salt support the ceilings of enormous mines thousands of feet underground. Yet in the presence of water salt quickly dissolves and becomes a clear and colorless liquid, the primary solute in all the oceans of the world.

The salt sea was our beginning. Only when the primal ocean contained essential salty electrolytes and oxygen could primitive life on earth develop billions of years ago. In the ocean of the later Paleozoic era, when vertebrate life evolved, the concentration of salts was perhaps one-third as great as it is today, and it is this lighter concentration of salt that we carry in our mammalian blood, in amniotic fluid, sweat, tears and semen. For humans, the exact degree of saltiness is crucial, and if we drink the saltier seawater of today's ocean it draws the water out of our cells and we die of dehydration. Accordingly, our taste buds have evolved so that too much salt tastes bitter, as poisons do, while small to moderate amounts, without which we die, are pleasing.

Salt is so valuable, especially where it is rare or difficult to obtain, that ancient Roman soldiers were provided with a salt allowance, the *salarium* from which our word "salary" derives. So too we say a person is "worth his salt." The savor salt adds to food as a condiment has long tied it to rites of hospitality in the Mediterranean and Near East. Through the shared bonds developed at mealtimes, salt came to be a token of agreement among the Hebrews: Salt is to accompany all offerings, including those to Yahweh, and is a sign of covenant. Salt's function in seasoning made it a metaphor for the wit, wisdom, earthiness or spice we bring to our assimilation and expression of experience.

However, alchemy's *sal,* or salt, was not "the common salt," but a personification—based, nonetheless, on the real qualities of salt—of the "arcane substance" and mystic principle of transformation. Salt was associated with baptismal waters; the wetness and coldness of the moon as feeling; with "marination" in corrosive disappointment, sadness and bitterness; with the *albedo,* or cleansing, in the "solution" of salt tears until bitterness was dissolved and transmuted into the salt of wisdom. Because salt preserves and sterilizes, drawing out water and making it impossible for bacteria to survive, it suggested an agent that fosters something incorruptible within. Salt burns, is sharp and bitter to the taste, and swallowed brine can be toxic, assigning salt symbolically to the elements and effects of both fire and water. The mining or evaporation of salt evoked processes of extraction and "firing," purification through the suffering of affects, which left a fine residue of understanding. Salt was a main ingredient of glass, emblem of the "raw batch" of matter out of which, through the opus, derived the solid, transparent and indestructible self.

The alchemists were aware of the paradoxical properties of salt: It is necessary to life and poisonous; it enhances food and can make it bitter; it stings and it heals; it kills microbes and can destroy tissue. Its sterilizing effect gave rise to the notion of sowing the ground with salt to make it barren. Lot's wife, in the biblical story of Sodom and Gomorrah, is turned into a pillar of salt because she looks back at the destroyed city of Sodom; she cannot relinquish what has already exhausted its possibility (Genesis 19:26). Jung observed that "wisdom is the comforter in all psychic suffering ... where there is bitterness, wisdom is lacking, and where there is wisdom there can be no bitterness" (CW 14:330). The salt of the wise discriminates with life-enhancing precision what is too little of one or too much of the other.

Salt and the Alchemical Soul: Three Essays by Ernest Jones, C. G. Jung and James Hillman. Ed. Stanton Marlan. Woodstock, CT, and NY, 1995.

1. A photographic enlargement showing the cubic structure of salt crystals.

2. Lot's wife turned into a pillar of salt. Illustration from the *Sarajevo Haggadah*, 14th century, Spain.

1

2

Desert

Georgia O'Keeffe's desert paintings stand in stark contrast to her earlier portraits of soaring, neon-lit Manhattan skyscrapers that she produced before her solitary journey to New Mexico, where she fell under the spell of a wilderness that changed her forever. Fascinated by the pure light beating down on desiccated trees and sun-bleached skulls, she turned away from the New York art world and retired to an adobe hermitage near Abiquiu to absorb the desert's enchantments. By trusting her instincts in this way, O'Keeffe reenacted an exodus that visionaries had made for centuries in order to confront questions of life, death and spirit easily drowned out by the frenetic fashions of the city. One can enter the desert as much to lose as to find oneself. Even in the fourth century, Christian monastic withdrawal and retreat "instinctively sought the desert" in a quest for solitude and rejection of worldliness (Walker, 154).

The desert, of course, is a mixture of things. Its conditions are often inimical: vast, waterless expanses without demarcation; scorching heat and paralyzing cold, storms that create whirlwinds and walls and columns of sand that bury in minutes what does not keep moving. The desert may be experienced as a mere dust bowl, or a featureless wasteland where death stalks as the elements. Sheer deprivation exaggerates basic needs into hallucinatory longings, conjuring both literal mirages (a natural refraction of light caused by the desert's prismatic atmosphere) and haunting fantasies of tantalizing voluptuaries and airy banquets. Yet the desert also reveals dreamlike cactus and panting reptiles, exotic birds that seem to survive on dew and camels that find nourishment in thorns—metaphors to artists like O'Keeffe of the endurance demanded of the desert-dweller to gain admission to its theater of wonders. With similar adaptability nomadic peoples have survived in the deserts of Arabia, Africa, China, America, Russia and Antarctica.

As a psychic landscape the desert often exemplifies protracted periods of alienation, spiritual thirst and creative tedium, disorientation and depletion, and also mortification, purification, redemption and initiation. Biblical writers knew unrelieved desertlike stretches of emptiness and despair, the howling domain of the satanic Lord of the Flies. Or the desert was a transitional space of wandering, exile, temptation and waiting for promise. Many ancient peoples imagined the desert as heated seas of sand, badlands into which the outcast and scapegoat were banished. The Egyptians conceived the desert bordering the lush Nile and its fertile black silt as a desolate place ruled over by the god Set, from whose *deshret*, or "red land," disordering forces of passion and violence swept into the civilized borders of conscious life. The desert was where the warm cat-goddess Bastet became the lioness Sekhmet, as fierce and fiery as the desert sun.

Whether it is the physical or the imaginal desert, some who venture there are not fortunate. One can die in the desert from the shriveling intensity of heat, cold or lack. But if it is a place of trial, it is also one of encounter—with angels, as well as devils and djinns. O'Keeffe herself discovered not just parching aridity in the desert, but flash-floods of inspiration mirrored in sporadic, torrential rains and erosive winds that swept through a fantasy world of pinnacles and arches of colored stone, so that after first setting up her easel against this primordial background in 1929, she lived there until she was almost a hundred years old. Much earlier, when St. Anthony hungered in the desert, he was said to have been fed by a raven, emblem of the unforeseen sustenance in the psyche activated by extremity. One looks and listens, begins to detect the unique, unnoticed signs of life. Just as in the desert water sleeps in the heart of a plant (Ondaatje), so are there hidden sources of vitality in the desert spaces of the soul. And these are sometimes prefigured in dreams, which, like stars invisible in the overbright city, disclose themselves in the black crispness of the desert night.

Ondaatje, Michael. *The English Patient*. NY, 1992.
Walker, Williston et al. *A History of the Christian Church*. NY, 1985.

1. Georgia O'Keeffe saw the desert as a place of wondrous forms and dazzling colors that transformed her from an urban artist into a visionary painter of such works as *Bear Lake (Desert Abstraction)*, oil on canvas, 1931, United States.

2. An aerial photograph of the Sahara reveals an extreme landscape scoured by dry winds, seen here engulfing a palm oasis beneath never-resting waves of sand.

1

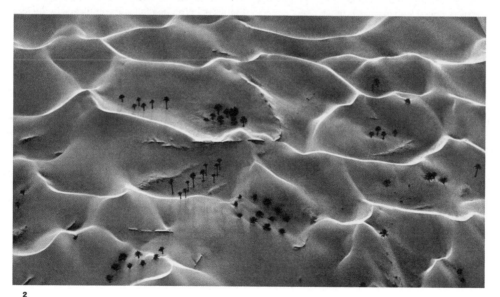

2

Forest/Jungle

A small boy reaches for the hand of his young sister and summoning courage, the two children take in the perspective of a huge, ancient forest. Any human being is rendered small and young by a great forest, seemingly endless and eternal. The nineteenth-century Swedish painter Edvard Bergh was being faithful to Germanic fairy tales of children who are forced by circumstance to wander off into a wilderness where every cracking branch signals a goblin's approach and every dark stump transforms into a prowling animal. When one is lost in its depths, a forest becomes fiendishly alive as the evening gloom swallows the last sunray and cuckoos yield to mournful owls.

Once, the great oaks of Germany and the evergreens of Scandinavia formed an unbroken canopy, part of the immense forest that stretched from Ireland to Japan. Before walking upright, our humanoid ancestors lived in the trees of the arid forests of Africa. A sultry, teeming rainforest such as the vast Amazon is home to most species of trees as well as 90 percent of organisms of every kind (Tudge, 17). In a jungle, army ants, anacondas, brilliant, parti-colored birds, plate-sized spiders, cats, apes, elephants and strangler fig-vines coexist, interact, compete and prey upon each other, a paradigm of the mythic great mother's endless unfolding and impartiality.

The forest, with its exotic forces, is "outside" the inhabited precincts of consciousness, as village, city, household or castle. But the boundaries are often depicted as tenuous; many tales begin with the protagonist living "at the edge of a forest," just as, inevitably, the worlds of typical and archetypal impinge upon each other. An unusual presence comes out of the forest or a magical animal is sighted there. One chances into the forest as into a daydream, and loses one's bearings. The forest is a place of loneliness, entanglement, healing, regression, loftiness and obstruction, spontaneous growth and continuous decay. Kindly or perverse elves materialize out of grasping roots or pricking brambles. The munificent and devouring witch, libidinous satyr, the devil, magician, sorceress, angel and fairy abide in the forest. Like the animal spirits they share their wisdom, show the way or rend one in pieces. A youth coming of age or a shamanic initiate would go to the forest seeking a vision. Many spiritual and psychological journeys begin, as Dante's did in the *Divine Comedy*, by entering the "dark wood" of psychic wilderness. And because the forest has a "mysterious impenetrability ... things suddenly appear and disappear, and there are no paths, anything is possible" (Jung, 178).

We think of the forest as timeless, one tree replacing another, and all together enduring through ages as other life dissolves. But the forest is also the source of the building materials of civilization. For centuries, peoples all over the world set about felling their old-growth deciduous hardwoods and cone-bearing softwoods in the spirit of the American folk-hero Paul Bunyan, the fanciful lumberjack giant who chopped away forests with an oversized ax. We have decimated our forests and their wildlife, deranging ecological balance, and the city has become an urban jungle of unchecked sprawl.

One can disappear into the forest, escaping life. But the Hindu notion of a life span includes becoming a *vanaprastha*, or "forest-dweller," once the responsibilities of house-holding are over. It was in the legendary Deodar Forest of ascetical refuge where the cast-off phallus of Lord Shiva became a fiery pillar connecting heaven and earth, and the form of the original lingam. To the sacred groves of antiquity devotees of the deity came for healing and communion. A Japanese torii gate opens simply on the natural shrine of a pine forest. Somewhere in the midst of the forest we may also happen upon a sanctuary set apart in virgin country. Perhaps it is drenched with rain, muffled with snow, or hanging moss makes the trees look ghostly. Perhaps 300-foot redwoods, drinking the Pacific mists, compose nature's sublime temple. What is primeval in ourselves is animated by the primeval forest. Can we dare to lose it? Innermost nature, just as it is, and wholly enchanted.

Jung, C. G. *Nietzsche's Zarathustra*. Princeton, NJ, 1988.

Tudge, Colin. *The Tree*. NY, 2006.

1

2

3

1. Two small children on the threshold of an evergreen world animated by whispering shadows, bearlike boulders and, in the distance, a reassuring patch of light. *In the Forest*, detail, by Edvard Bergh, oil on canvas, 1868, Sweden.

2. "Midway upon the journey of our life, I found myself within a forest dark." So Dante begins his *Divine Comedy*. *The Dark Wood*, by Gustave Doré, engraving ("Inferno 1"), 1868, France.

3. A fairy-tale world of flamboyant birds, flesh-hungry alligators, acrobatic monkeys and, no less at home in this zoological paradise, a primeval man and woman. *Jungle*, by Tonie Roos, oil on linen, 1977, Sweden.

Marsh

The tomb painting of a hunting party in a marsh of the Nile Delta is apparently not of an actual event in the life of the deceased nobleman Ti; the boat, for example, is much too flimsy, and a hippo would hardly be holding in its jaws its most feared predator, the alligator. Rather, the image is an evocation of the afterworld, the so-called Field of Rushes, recalling the marsh in its primeval, eternal form, untouched by human history or labor (ARAS, 2Ad.098). In turn, the actuality of a marsh is suggestive of a particular ancient Egyptian conception of existence after death.

Marshes, whether they are nontidal (occurring along the boundaries of lakes, ponds or rivers) or tidal (occurring along coastlines and influenced by the tidal cycles of the sea), are freshwater, saline or brackish wetlands. They are sometimes inundated, mostly by surface- or groundwater. Rich in nutrients and minerals, they are also pH neutral, so that they sustain abundant, diverse animal life and vegetation adapted to the saturated soil. Sediment and pollutants settle to the floor of the marsh, preserving the cleanliness of the waters at the surface, and microorganisms use nutrients that in excess would compromise oxygen levels. Marshes store floodwaters and act as buffers to stormy oceans (US, EPA).

The fecund ooze of the marsh, and the in-between reality of murky water and dry, insular ground, is emblematic of what, to the ancient Egyptian, death represented: a state of hidden "becoming," a source of new life, purification and constant renewal, a "passing from one kind of time to another, from life yesterday to life tomorrow" (Clark, 165). Every summer, with the swelling of the Nile River from the highland rains, the marshes and low-lying fields in the Nile Valley were returned to the form of primordial waters. And every autumn, the fields would reappear, covered with a layer of fertile silt (Quirke, 50–1). Thus the soaking of the marsh intimated the watery energies of dissolution that

underlie the substance of being. A cow might be seen peering through the rushes and transform into a momentary vision of the motherly "cow of the waters" out of which land emerges like a calf. In a marsh might be found fishes teeming in the water, waterfowl making their habitat among the reeds and bulrushes, and also snakes, alligators or crocodiles hidden at the edges of the marsh, sunning themselves on the sand or swimming in the same water where muskrats make their elaborate huts and multipetalled lotuses rise from the mud among cattails, grasses and riddling insects. Clutches of eggs, and hatchlings, signs of beginnings, appear side by side with predatory forces of annihilation. "Alive with creaking and buzzing, flapping and cawing" a writer describes the marshes of the Florida Everglades in December (Bilger, 84).

The marsh continues to be an apt metaphor for those developmental transitions or temporary passages within a larger process where consciousness experiences itself in the muck between the permanently dissolved and the yet to be, a space of extreme potential and extreme vulnerability, vital, slippery, unpredictable and emergent. And just as this happens more than once in a lifetime or an individuation, so for the ancient Egyptians the Field of Rushes signified not a single stage to be passed through and never entered again, but an entire cosmic circuit over and under the earth, where, as in the psyche, continuities of form incarnate in the specificities of being.

Bilger, Burkhard. "Swamp Things." *The New Yorker* (April 20, 2009).
Clark, Robert Thomas Rundle. *Myth and Symbol in Ancient Egypt.* London, 1959.
Quirke, Stephen. *Ancient Egyptian Religion.* NY, 1992.
U.S. EPA. *Marsh.* www.epa.gov/owow/wetlands/types/marsh.html.

Bas-relief from the tomb of Egyptian dignitary Ti, portraying the deceased in the Field of Rushes, ca. 5th dynasty (2600–2390 B.C.E.).

Beach

Border and boundary of a sea or lake, the beach is a narrow margin of sand or shingle continuously created, shifted and destroyed in the rhythm of the tides. It represents the convergence of three vast worlds: sky, sea and land. One stands on the beach as if at the edge of the known world, gazing across the water into the unknown. The innumerable grains of sand on the shore, the distant horizon, the boundless waters under an infinite sky, may inspire feelings of awe, or simply of dwarfed insignificance. Though Whistler's *Trouville* is serene, his beach, like all beaches, is unrelentingly affected by the sea's potent forces. Twice daily tides drag the shore. Waves roil the land's debris and make their own deposits. Temperature differentials between land and water summon nearly incessant winds across the strand.

Psychologically the beach evokes for us the daily experience of the slim shore between conscious and unconscious lapped and buffeted, shifted and changed, temporarily submerged and once again delineated in the tidal rhythms of waking and sleeping. There are "deposits" from dream and fantasy, the play of the imagination, the clarity of awareness. Sometimes what the psyche tosses onto the shore can, like the jellyfish, only be experienced but not assimilated. As the perspective and rhythms of the beach and the movement between water and land can liberate one's feelings and expand one's sense of space, time and being, so does the exchange between the depths of the psyche and consciousness.

Yet, the beach is also vulnerable to the elemental forces of the sea. The dry land can be inundated. Tidal wave and earthquake belong to Poseidon, whose great horses, their wild manes flying in the sea foam, thunder in a pounding surf. Analogously, there can be seismic shifts in one's conscious state; we can get inundated by tempestuous affects, overwhelmed by psychic shocks. D. H. Lawrence captures the autonomous nature of such energies: "It is the moon that turns the tides. The beaches can do nothing about it" (p. 509). The inundating sea in time recedes, though it may alter the terrain of the shore, and ultimately may wear it away in gradual evolution or more radical change.

Lawrence, D. H. *The Complete Poems.*
NY, 1964.

Harmony in Blue and Silver: Trouville, by James
Abbott McNeill Whistler, oil on canvas, 1865, France.

Island

On curling waves of sleep, one might drift to an island like this one depicted by a Swedish artist: dark as the unknown, green with life, isolated and eerie. Islands have ever harbored our conscious fantasies and unconscious projections. They evoke escape, solitude, refuge or captivation. Figuring in the myths and stories of cultures all over the world, there are bleak, veiled islands of the dead, or islands of the blessed, eternally fertile, their trees dripping honey. There are islands of loneliness and exile, magical islands inhabited by fabulous beings, islands where the shipwrecked find solid ground and unexpected adventure. Homer's Odysseus is sensually captive to the nymph Calypso on her island for seven years; Shakespeare's Prospero conjures a redemptive tempest from his island of rough magic. King Arthur lies dead, or merely sleeping, in the mists of the fairy island Avalon. Islands are formed from the rifting of a continent or accumulations of sand on a continental shelf. Undersea they are often connected to the mainland. Volcanic islands can emerge in mid-ocean from the drifting of tectonic plates over volcanic "hot spots," or like Iceland, from the surfacing of an oceanic rift. Intensely fascinating to the imagination, islands evoke split-off portions of consciousness, animated by psyche's watery depths. They represent isolating secrets, the accumulated sediment of remote memories, taboo desires, dissociated trauma. They can be "magnetic and evasive" and may have subtle, insidious effect (von Franz, 89). Such reefs are connected to the total personality in hidden ways or can seem utterly unrelated. In creation myths, islands portray the beginnings of consciousness, small, vulnerable bits of earth fetched up from the bottom of the cosmic sea that are easily resubmerged. Island may express insularity as alienation, self-absorption or inaccessibility, but also a state of introversion, a blessed retreat from inundating stimuli, or the capacity to stand alone. Island can represent the locus of a psychic factor that maroons one from what is most vital in the self. Or, it may express the unforeseen, inviolable space where the treasure of self is found.

von Franz, Marie-Louise. *An Introduction to the Interpretation of Fairy Tales.* Dallas, 1982.

Island, by Suzanne Nessim, painting, 1990, Sweden.

PLANT WORLD

TREES

MAGICAL PLANTS AND FLOWERS

Tree

How we long to achieve the growth the tree fosters in itself, the reach and rootage, the sturdiness and balance between high and low, the way it meets each season, holding its ground, spare or blooming. Every sort of creature nestles in the tree's sheltering, motherly branches, hides in her hollows and is fed by her substance. Our hominid ancestors were arboreal, only descending when ice ages shrank the primal forests, and the dexterity of our hands and strength of our limbs developed in our climbing and swinging from trees. We and the tree seem alike, upright in the trunk, long-armed, slender-fingered, toeing the earth. In myths humans are sometimes transformed into trees, and the sighing of the tree and its resinous tears are both tree-like and human and speak of endurance, entanglement,

and also fixation. As we have a soul, so it seems there is an animating spirit in the tree that we have imagined as a snake, a bird, or a genie in a bottle buried at the roots. The tree shows us how, from a tiny, bare seed of potential, the self can come into existence, centered and contained, around which occur incessant processes of metabolism, multiplying, perishing and self-renewal. Water and minerals are drawn up to the leaves of a tree from the earth through deep roots and millions upon millions of orderly, conducting, threadlike vessels in the trunk and branches. The tree holds its flat, perforated leaves as high as possible to absorb carbon dioxide from the air and fire from the sun. The chlorophyll that makes the leaves green traps photons of sunlight and splits molecules of water, so that oxy-

1

1. Georgia O'Keeffe's dizzying view of the pine tree outside her New Mexico home allows us to climb into an age-old world of wonders sought by shamans and seers, who traditionally used trees as bridges to the realms of the spirits. *The Lawrence Tree*, oil on canvas, 1929, United States.

2. An Egyptian tomb painting portrays the goddess Isis in the form of a leafy sycamore tree suckling a pharaoh in the afterworld, reinforcing the tree's association with eternity and the mysteries of rebirth in the womb of the primal Mother (ARAS, 2Ak.057). Painting from the tomb of Pharaoh Thuthmose III (ca. 1479–26 B.C.E.), Valley of the Kings, Egypt.

gen floats away into the atmosphere, giving us breath (Tudge, 252ff). The tree knows how to find nourishment even in the dead stuff, assimilates its own deciduous rot and the earth's animal and vegetable decay.

We have left the bodies of our dead in trees, cradled in its boughs awaiting rebirth or curled up like an embryo in the hollowed-out trunk because the tree signifies regeneration and impinges on the heavens and the underworld, realms of eternity. And so the tree is also a cosmos encompassing psychic spheres of refreshment, creativity and initiation transcending space and time. In Scandinavian myth one of the three great roots of the cosmic ash or yew tree, Yggdrasil, reaches down into the realm where the frost giants dwell. Here lies Mimir's Well filled with the waters of wisdom and memory. Another root descends into the realm of the dead, while beneath the third is Asgard, the abode of the gods (Orchard, 186). Close by live the Norns, three sisters who spin the web of destiny and water the tree from the sacred spring of Urd. Meanwhile, goats and harts nibble on Yggdrasil's leaves and bark, and the great serpent Nidhogg gnaws at its roots. A magnificent eagle perches on the topmost bough and the squirrel Ratatosk runs up and down the trunk carrying insults between the bird above and the snake below in an everlasting tension and balancing of opposites (Davidson, 26–27).

Alchemy made the tree a central symbol of its opus, because the tree depicted the nature of intense inner life and development that follows its own laws and can reveal the "evergreen" within the individual. The alchemists did not forget that the tree may represent not only a place of awakening to new life, but also of suffering—mythic suspensions of sacrifice, ordeal, suicide, execution and reversal. A treasure guarded by snakes or dragons at the tree's gnarled roots alluded to the difficulty of achieving the goal, the extraction of the self from the tangle of unconscious factors (CW 13:304ff). Nevertheless intuitive fantasies portrayed the tree bearing the sun, moon and stars as luminous gold and silver fruits, the "metals" of the planets hanging from branches, or the tree filled with flowers or singing birds, all expressive of spiritual enlightenment, the integration of many different forces of life and the fructifying imagination essential to symbolic process. At the top is the beautiful symmetry of the tree's corona signifying the union of opposites. But while the alchemists saw this as the consummation of the work, the reality of the tree—and of psyche—is that such moments of obtainment are usually followed by new cycles of desiccation and growth.

Davidson, Hilda Roderick Ellis. *Gods and Myths of Northern Europe*. London and NY, 1990.
Orchard, Andy. *Dictionary of Norse Myth and Legend*. London and NY, 1998.
Tudge, Colin. *The Tree: A Natural History of What Trees Are, How They Live, and Why They Matter*. NY, 2006.

3

4

3. Alchemy's Philosophical Tree materializing in a glass retort, engraving, ca. 1470 C.E.

4. Psychic life and its sacred symbols as a tree rooted in invisible realms extending beyond the boundaries of consciousness. Inverted "Tree of Bliss" from a Turkish prayer book, 18th century.

Oak Tree

Ansel Adams' photograph of a white oak silhouetted against the Sierra foothills reveals the twisting branches and massive trunk characteristic of a fully grown oak. They are shapes that have become imprinted in the human imagination, along with the oak's broad leaf and stippled fruit, the tiny acorn.

Ancient Europe was once covered so densely with oaks that Julius Caesar encountered Germanic tribes who had never reached the end of these hardwood forests. Intimating the grandeur and vastness of the mythic World Tree and axis mundi, the oak's commanding presence made it the most widely worshipped of trees. A member of the beech family, the oak could live a thousand years and grow over ten stories tall. Like the disseminated divine matter of creation stories, the oak's substance became the raw material for every kind of human fabrication. Carpenters fashioned its wood into bridges, pews, keels, barrels, coffins and thrones admired for their strength and beauty. The soft bark of one variety still furnishes winemakers with cork stoppers; a more durable English variety provided shipbuilders with lumber for the imperial British fleet, consuming entire forests that had earlier sheltered Merlin and Robin Hood.

The acorn, too, proved invaluable. Ancient legends tell of an era before agriculture when humans relied upon acorns as a staple food. Even after the cultivation of grain, acorns served as fodder for wild beasts and livestock. An oak starts producing acorns when it is at least 20 years old and then just once a year in the fall. While, remarkably, the whole of the mighty oak is contained in potential in the acorn, only about one acorn in ten thousand actually becomes a tree.

Evoking what is royal, solid and eternal, oaks are traditionally associated with cycles of birth and death, especially in the seasonal rituals around the mythic year kings. Ancient druids (from the Celtic word for oak, *daur*) dragged oak logs at yuletide, the winter solstice, and heaped them onto midsummer bonfires to mark the cyclical demise of springtime's Oak King, who was succeeded by autumn's Holly King (Williamson, 58ff). Virgil claimed an oak gave birth to the first humans, just as Norse gods whittled Embla, the first woman, from an oak tree (and Ask, the first man, from an ash tree). On the other hand, in Northern Europe where the oak tree "belonged to the dead," its occasionally hollow trunk provided a much sought-after coffin. Similarly, the alchemist's "philosophical tree" was often a hollow oak, a maternal vessel in whose cleavage the alchemical king installed his bath of symbolic rebirth, suggesting an inner feminine dimension of the seemingly virile tree that corresponded to the soul stuff of the adept (CW 14:70ff).

Gathering force throughout its span of life from acorn to spreading giant, the oak represents invincible, august strength. Virgil wrote that violent thunderstorms could not uproot the oak, with its roots anchored in Tartarus and its branches reaching into the heavens. Drawing down lightning as natural conductors, these ancient, legendary oaks were sacred to the thunder-gods Zeus and Jupiter in Mediterranean Europe and Thor and Donar in Northern Europe. Lightning was believed to cling to the oak's branches in the form of mistletoe, which James Frazer called the oak's "seat of life" since it remained green in winter and turned golden when the oak was felled. But the oldest known oak-cult was in northeastern Greece at Dodona, where the oaks' rustling leaves were heard as the communications of an oracle. Athena gave Jason a talking oak-beam from Dodona for the hull of his ship, the Argo. It guided the Argonauts to Colchis, where Jason found the Golden Fleece nailed to another oak.

Symbolically, as well as physically, oak continues to extend its branches and bear new fruit. In the alchemical fairy tale "The Spirit in the Bottle," the dark, mercurial spirit of transformation is hidden in the roots of an oak tree. Jung found this image of the treasure-containing oak to be a beautiful evocation of the self, the unconscious core of the personality, a "royal figure" among all the other contents of the unconscious (CW 13:241ff). Like the oak whose roots extend into the mineral realm, the self is rooted in the chemical elements of the body and extends, in a psychological sense, into infinite heights and depths. As a mature oak unfolds from an acorn, so does psychic individuality unfold from some small intimation of self that, brought into consciousness, grows and gives leaf over time to a multiplicity of images. Mirroring the oak's solidity, the self is the perduring center that can withstand fiery outbursts of affect and psychic flooding. "Oak" transports, and humbles—so perfectly is imperial nature embodied in its form.

Williamson, John. *The Oak King, the Holly King, and the Unicorn.* NY, 1986.

1

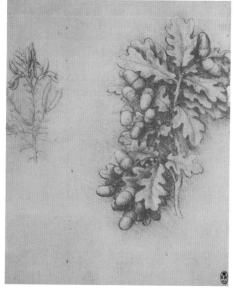

2

1. The majestic white oak can grow to be very old, has a deep root system and usually stands alone. It has a great deal of strength and can endure floods, storms and even fire but attracts lightning. In contrast, the red oak is smaller and the leaves stay on until next spring. *Oak Tree, Sunset City, Sierra Foothills, California*, by Ansel Adams, photograph, 1962, United States.

2. Drawn from natural observation in the red-chalk technique he may have originated, da Vinci's skillfully modeled acorns suggest why folk traditions considered the fruit of the oak to be sexually symbolic. Each phallic kernel is enclosed within a feminine casing, just as a mature oak combines masculine strength with feminine soulfulness. *Sprays of Oak Leaves and Dyer's Greenweed*, by Leonardo da Vinci, ca. 1503–4, Italy.

Olive Tree

Able to root, grow, bear fruit and sustain itself in the dry, rocky soil of the Mediterranean landscape to which it is native, the olive tree evokes the resilience, regeneration and fertility that establish, and succeed, whole civilizations. Van Gogh's painting expresses the spirit of the olive tree, the gnarled trunks that exist for centuries, even a thousand years or more, and their branches that over time are buffeted and twisted by the wind until they resemble waves on hillsides above bustling societies and ancient ruins.

Olive trees perpetually renew themselves from their roots (Psilakis, 209). They resurrect after fire by sprouting new shoots and are able to grow back even if their tops and trunks decay. Cultivated olive strains cannot grow by themselves from seed but must be grafted onto wild olive trees. Saint Paul employed the image in reverse as a metaphor, reminding the Gentile Christians that they were shoots of the wild olive tree, which, contrary to nature, had been grafted on the cultivated olive tree of Jewish Christian believers, whose roots and branches were Israel (Romans 11:13–24). The olive was the Tree of Life for the ancient peoples of Greece and Rome, the Biblical Hebrews and the Muslims. Its fruit, processed with lye or salt, its rich, delectable oil and its wood provided food, light, medicine, fuel and building materials. Evergreen olive branches, their shapely leaves green on one side and silvery gray on the other so that they shimmered in the sun, crowned brides, war heroes and athletic victors who embodied the immortals. Olive oil anointed kings, holy objects for ritual and sacred spaces, and lighted the lamps of home and temple for centuries. Those who approached the Asclepian sanctuary of healing at Epidaurus came "crowned with the wreath of the pure olive," signifying transcendence of destructive forces and rebirth. Before going to Crete to slay the Minotaur, the legendary Theseus dedicated to Apollo an offering with branches from the holy olive tree on the Acropolis (Psilakis, 164ff). Olive garlands and branches were common in the worship of the god Zeus and at the Panathenaea, the games honoring Zeus' daughter Athena, warrior-goddess of the city-state.

So essential to the religious, practical and economic life of Greece was the olive that in the sixth century B.C.E., the ruler Solon introduced strict laws for its protection (ibid.). Mythically, however, it was Athena who gave the olive as a gift to the Greeks, who were cultivating it in Crete as long ago as 3500 B.C.E. or earlier (*Enc. Brit.* 8:917). Athena and Poseidon, the divine lord of the seas, held a contest to determine who would rule Attica. Poseidon struck the rock of the Acropolis with his trident, causing a saltwater spring to burst forth. Athena planted an olive tree beside the rock and her gift was deemed of the greater value; she won Attica and Athens was named in her honor.

Athena's militant aspect primarily served the defense of Athens and its perpetuation as the thriving center of Greek culture. The olive tree's association with life made it the emblem not only of Athena but also of the Roman goddess Pax, or Peace. Messengers seeking truce or asylum would carry an olive branch wrapped in wool (Biedermann, 245). In the biblical story of Genesis, it was an olive branch that the dove brought back to Noah, signifying the recession of the floodwaters and the restoration of harmony between human and divine. That is the olive—symbol of the quintessence that survives the dissolution of the old forms and renews itself from the roots up.

Biedermann, Hans. *Dictionary of Symbolism.* NY, 1994.
Psilakis, Nikos. *The Olive Wreath: The Wreaths of the Olympic Winners, Symbolic and Moral Background.* Heraklion [Crete], 2003.

Gnarled, swirling, silvery, Van Gogh's olive trees
seemingly draw together earth and sky in timeless
witness to successions of human endeavor. *Landscape
with Olive Trees*, oil on canvas, 1889, France.

Pine Tree

With a few brushstrokes, a Japanese painter conveys the strong standing presence of pines amid the gray mists of winter. Associated with Confucius and the Taoist immortals, the pine is a favorite subject of Chinese and Japanese painters and poets. Because of its hardiness and the fact that it retains its green leaves even through the winter, the pine has become a symbol of long life, immortality, constancy, courage, strength in adversity and steadfastness unaffected by the blows of nature. Weathered pines are seen as images of the spirit and wisdom of old age. The ninth-century Chinese poet Bo Ju-yi wrote of the old pines growing in his courtyard: " ... they are 'useful friends' to me, and they fulfill my wish for conversations with 'wise men'" (Eberhard, 237–8).

Of all the trees, pines are the most ancient. More than one hundred species grow in the world's cool and mountainous regions. Bristlecone pines of the western United States are known to be the oldest living plants on earth. One in Nevada (since cut down by a chain saw) possessed over 4,800 growth rings; it was "the oldest single living organism ever known" (Balog, 37). All of the pines, evergreen and marked by their needle-like leaves and seed-bearing cones, evolved much earlier than the broad-leaved trees, which drop their leaves in winter. Human veneration of these trees is equally ancient. Species of pine were sacred to Egyptian and near-eastern deities, and to Greek and Roman gods and goddesses, including Zeus, Artemis, Dionysus and Poseidon.

In the Western world as in the East, the pine tree is an image for immortality, and also fertility, creativity, regeneration and good luck. Yet the pine tree also evokes the suffering, dying and resurrection of vegetation deities and youthful son-lovers of eternal return.

The pinecone with its myriad seeds formed the top of the thyrsus, or staff, of Dionysus, the ancient god of the vine associated with indestructible life, the wine culture, intoxication and subterranean rebirth in outer and inner worlds. Attis, the beautiful youth loved by the Phrygian goddess Cybele, castrated himself and died beneath a pine tree when, in a jealous rage, she robbed him of his sanity. Cybele turned him into a pine tree, and violets grew from the drops of his blood. At the festival of Attis, a sacred pine tree was cut down and carried in a procession, its branches hung with violets, signifying nature's endless cycles of death and renewal.

As it does the Christmas tree, the pinecone often crowned the mythic Tree of Life, abode of the Great Mother, fecund source and vessel of nurturance, healing and transformation. Concretely, in fact, medicinal remedies made from the pine tree are legendary: Smoke from burning pine needles cures coughs; pine resin was eaten as a tonic against aging and used on wounds to prevent infection; pine needle tea is recommended for colds and scurvy. Modern analysis has shown that a cup of strong pine-needle tea yields more vitamin C than the average lemon (Vitale, 232). Myth and reality conflate in the wondrous pine tree of whose most ancient forms the gnarled and twisted trunks are near 5,000 years old, and still growing.

Balog, James. "92 Ways of Looking at a Tree." *Sierra* (90/6, 2005).
Eberhard, Wolfram. *A Dictionary of Chinese Symbols*. London and NY, 1986.
Vitale, Alice Thoms. *Leaves: In Myth, Magic & Medicine*. NY, 1997.

Pine Trees, detail, by Hasegawa Tōhaku, screen, 16th century, Japan.

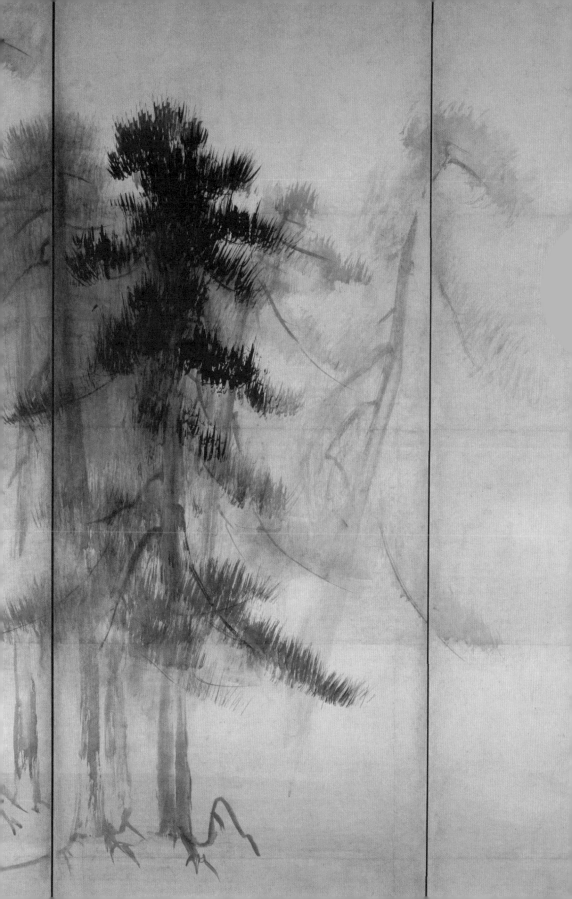

Palm Tree

The Egyptian date-palm (*Phoenix dactylifera*) is named after the palm of the hand that its fronds resemble. Considered a grass rather than a tree despite its tall sturdy trunks, a palm ripens its kernels enclosed in fleshy rinds (dates) or in hard protective shells (coconuts). The Egyptian variety pollinates at dawn, creating a mist that gave rise to the phoenix legend, the mythical bird reborn in a cloud of fire, smoke and ashes in the palm's fronds. Raising one's palm in a salute served as a traditional gesture of adoration in Egyptian depictions of triumph or rebirth (Wilkinson, 29). In this spirit, palms greeted the deceased into the Fields of Reeds, the swamplands of the afterlife that required minimal labor, symbolizing a victorious rebirth. The date-palm was sacred to the sky-goddesses Nut and Hathor, who distributed food and drink to the deceased from its fronds. Nut poured out the water of immortality, while the hanging pair of date-clusters (illustrated here) were meant to recall the breasts of Hathor—"queen of the date-palm"—to whom the *ba*-soul hastened after death to drink her sacred milk (Goodenough, 7:94–6). The vertical waves of the pool signifying the "distant water of the beyond" from which all life rises and returns (Wilkinson, 137). The swaying palms along the banks of the Nile came to be associated with the sacred river's power to restore the dead to life. Indeed, it was customary to leave food in tombs made from palm products.

Perhaps the Mesopotamian date-palm was the prototype of the biblical Tree of Life in Eden, as earlier Sumerian cylinder-seals suggest (Langdon, 5:179). Later, the palm entered the Christian story. Jubilant crowds spread palm leaves before Jesus when he made his entry into Jerusalem, an event ritualized on Palm Sunday. Ashes from the fronds saved from the previous Palm Sunday are imposed on penitents' foreheads on Ash Wednesday, marking the beginning of the season of Lent. Apocryphal legend has it that when the Holy Family fled into Egypt across the Sinai they rested under a palm tree. When Mary could not reach the tree's fruits, Christ commanded it to bend down, whereupon the palm revealed a hidden spring and offered them drink. In gratitude, Jesus promised that its shoots would be planted in paradise (Schiller, 118–19). Similarly in the Koran, when Mary experienced the throes of childbirth by a palm tree, an angel comforted her: "Your Lord has provided a brook that runs at your feet, and if you shake the trunk of this palm tree it will drop fresh ripe dates in your lap. Therefore rejoice" (Dawood, 32ff). Jewel-like images of the palm tree appear in Hindu art, often associated with lovers. The vertical trunk suggests the lingam, the palm leaves, spreading at the crown (and sometimes containing a beautiful woman), the yoni. The tree of the desert oasis, the palm offers a vision of refreshment—sexual pleasure and the fruits of erotic union, redemption in the wilderness, compassion for the suffering and bliss to those, like the Egyptian Pashedu, who gratefully kneel to drink "distant water of the beyond" in the palm tree's cool shade.

Dawood, N. J. *The Koran*. Harmondsworth, Middlesex, 1968.
Goodenough, Erwin R. *Jewish Symbols in the Greco-Roman Period*. Princeton, NJ, 1954.
Langdon, Stephen. *Mythology of All Races: Semitic Mythology*. Boston, 1918.
Lurker, Manfred. *The Gods and Symbols of Ancient Egypt*. NY, 1980.
Schiller, Gertrud. *Iconography of Christian Art*. Greenwich, CT, 1971.
Wilkinson, Richard H. *Reading Egyptian Art*. London, 1992.

1. Eternal waters in the afterworld refresh a palm tree, heavily laden with dates and bursting with lush fronds. Pashedu, the necropolis foreman to whom this ancient Egyptian tomb mural is dedicated, kneels in reverence to drink from the same pool. Wall painting, 1295–1185 B.C.E., Deir-el Medina, Thebes, Egypt.

2. The longing of a young woman for her departed lover is dreamily transferred to the green trunk of a palm-tree associated with vital fluids and bountiful produce. Painting, early 19th century, Punjab, India.

Roots

... whatever you have to say, leave
the roots on, let them
dangle

And the dirt
just to make clear
where they came from.
Charles Olson, These Days

In Eugène Atget's spare photograph, gnarled and tenacious roots secure a tree to the earth and support its trunk, which invisibly reaches skyward. The primary root is, botanically, the first part of a plant to appear when a seed germinates. Anchoring the seedling, the root pushes down into the soil, searching the darkness for nutriments and a foothold in viable ground. From the primary root, other roots grow and spread, extending themselves to absorb water and dissolved minerals from the inorganic realm to feed and aerate the living stem.

Root matter is foundation, origin and source. When we speak of a "root cause" or the "root of the problem," we mean its basis. The root of a word carries its primary meaning. A musical root is the note from which a chord is built. Cultural lore acknowledges a root principle in certain edible plants. The ancient Greeks believed that wild carrots excited the passions (de Vries, 83). The radish, from the Latin *radix*, or root, became a favorite theme in Japanese art, signifying that the humblest form of life can attain Buddhahood (Baird, 95).

Cultural, ethnic and geographical roots link one with ancestral origins and the deep strata of evolutionary process and its psychic matrix in "sacred time." Family trees of material and mythic substance develop from such roots, like the biblical "root of Jesse," and continue to grow with each generation. Likewise the roots of an individual extend into layers of personal and archetypal ground. The quality of such rooting, fostered by experience, mirroring and imagination, affects the capacity to thrive, generate new growth and creatively blossom. Roots that find only meager subsistence in rocky soil can struggle with circumstances so inimical they would seem not to support life at all. The power of roots is that they find a way.

Rootlessness, on the other hand, connotes desultory movement from place to place, or from one identity to another. The feelings of shallowness, instability, and depersonalization that characterize pathological narcissism, borderline states, affective and dissociative disorders suggest a disconnection with one's authentic, nourishing ground. To "put down roots" means to settle into something, materialize potential or recognize a locus of belonging. War, terrorism, famine and disease increasingly separate peoples from the cultural, religious and symbolic structures that have supported their identity, a cruel uprooting. Roots, however, can both anchor and entrench. Vital roots can take the form of a seemingly chaotic mass, and roots that once were vital can get impacted.

Our psychological roots descend to the deepest psychosomatic level. In the alchemical fairy tale recorded by Grimm, "The Spirit in the Bottle," the mercurial life spirit is discovered in a sealed bottle hidden among the roots of a great oak tree, which extend into the inorganic realm. A related image in alchemy is that of the Philosopher's Tree rooted, not in the ground, but in the heavens or in the sea. Symbolically, it conveys the idea that a treelike process of growth in which consciousness is transformed originates in the unconscious dimension of psyche, whose dynamic energies are imaged in the archetypal forms.

Baird, Merrily C. Symbols of Japan. NY, 2001.

1. Roots ground a tree like the toes of an ancient foot. Untitled photograph by Eugène Atget, ca. 1924–5, France.

2. Vibrantly colored, these roots grow in a seemingly chaotic mass. *Tree Roots*, by Vincent van Gogh, oil on canvas, 1890, France.

3. Mangrove trees root in tidal shores, trapping debris, silt and mud. In the lagoons at Trincomalee and Negombo, such roots are the home of the Sri Lankan crab. Mangrove tree, hand-colored photograph from *The Lagoon Cycle* (1972–82), a 350-foot-long mural created by Helen Mayer Harrison and Newton Harrison, Sri Lanka.

1

2

3

Kabbalistic Tree

For the Kabbalist, the Tree of Life serves, among other things, as a kind of filing system for all archetypes. There are many versions of the Tree. The one shown here, taken from a 1652 work by the occultist Athanasius Kircher, is the best-known type. The *sefirot*, portrayed as ten circles, are connected with divine names and principles. The paths connecting the *sefirot* symbolize the connections between the different levels of the cosmos. At the top is the Infinite, the "Horizon of Eternity." Next is the *mundus archetypus*, the "archetypal world," associated with the angelic hierarchies. Lower levels indicate the realms of the planets and the elements, with Malkuth, "Kingdom" or earthly reality, at the bottom.

How did the world arise out of nothing? How does it sustain its existence on the unfathomable depth of the void? How can we on earth make our way back to the divine? The Kabbalah provides powerful and sublime answers to these questions. Meaning "tradition" in Hebrew, it is the esoteric teaching of Judaism. Like all such teachings, it is ultimately about the many levels, visible and invisible, that connect the primordial unity with the reality we experience every day.

The Kabbalistic Tree of Life presents the essence of this teaching. This "ladder of lights," as it is sometimes called, can be traced back to the mystical Judaism of thirteenth-century Spain and gives a succinct yet profound picture of the universe as envisaged by the Kabbalists. The Tree has informed and inspired countless mystics, Jewish, Christian and others. For all its apparent obscurity, it is not a particularly difficult or intricate system; one could memorize it in an evening. One could also spend a lifetime contemplating it and still find new things to learn.

The most familiar version of the Tree of Life depicts ten circles (symbolizing the *sefirot* or "principles"; the singular is *sefirah*) arranged in three columns or "pillars." This system gives a flexible but dynamic view of the workings of existence that can be applied to everything from the creation of a cosmos to the baking of a cake. At the top is Kether, or "Crown," the dimensionless point at which something begins to appear out of nothing. At the bottom is Malkuth, or "Kingdom," our familiar, solid reality. Between these, the other

eight *sefirot*, with names like Tiphereth ("Beauty") and Yesod ("Foundation"), symbolize the forces of expansion, contraction and equilibration that beget and maintain all things.

The Kabbalistic Tree is far more than an intellectual system. It is a profound tool for expanding the horizons of consciousness. Some Kabbalists ascend to higher states of awareness by visualizing themselves rising through the *sefirot*. Others may meditate on one of the several Hebrew names of God (each of which is associated with a particular *sefirah*). A Kabbalist who wishes to evoke rigor or severity will focus on the left side of the tree, called the "Pillar of Strength"; another who wishes to foster loving kindness works with the right, the "Pillar of Mercy."

None of the pillars or *sefirot* is better or worse than the others. What is most important is to experience these principles directly and bring them into balance. This is the work of the central column, called the "Pillar of Mildness," sometimes called the "Pillar of Consciousness." It is consciousness at all levels that enables us to choose between mercy and rigor, between expansion and contraction, at each moment of our lives.

Perhaps the central teaching of this profound symbol is that there is a single structure that underpins all things. This is the immanent aspect of God: the side of the absolute that we can know and experience. It is as much a part of ourselves as it is of the external world. The Kabbalah teaches that this divine system has an order and a beauty of its own, and that by coming to know and align ourselves with it, we may promote greater harmony both within ourselves and in what is around us.

Halevi, Z'ev ben Shimon. *Kabbalah: Tradition of Hidden Knowledge*. London, 1979.
Scholem, Gershom Gerhard. *Major Trends in Jewish Mysticism*. NY, 1961.
Scholem, Gershom Gerhard. *Kabbalah*. Jerusalem, 1974.
Smoley, Richard and Jay Kinney. *Hidden Wisdom: A Guide to the Western Inner Traditions*. NY, 1999.

Kabbalistic Tree of Life as ten circles, by Athanasius Kircher, drawing, 1652, Germany.

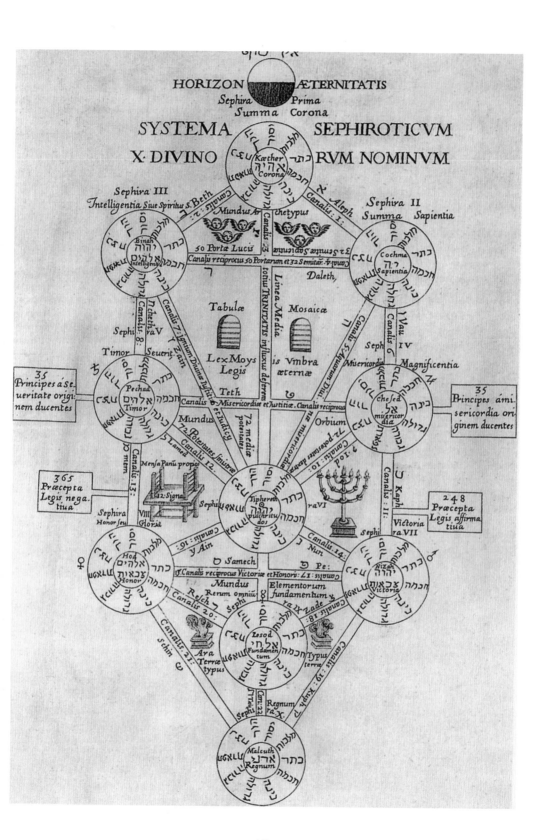

Yakshi

In a niche of the elaborately carved stone gateway to the great Buddhist stupa at Sanchi, a graceful, seminude female figure can be seen intimately entwined with a mango tree. The sensuous nymph is a *Yakshi*, an expression of the divine life-force that surges through all living things, especially as it is manifested in the growth and flowering of vegetative life. The female *Yakshi*, in particular, is identified with the life of the tree. In the Indian view, the tree draws its sustenance directly from subterranean waters absorbed through its roots and transformed into vital sap. The sap rises, channeled and propelled up the central trunk of the tree toward the light. As it reaches its apex, like a fountain it spills out and over into the many branches of the tree, bringing the tree to maturity in a canopy of foliage, blooming flowers and abundant fruit.

An anthropomorphic embodiment of this process, the *Yakshi* here specifically expresses the mango's burgeoning life. As her raised left arm grasps an upper limb, it forms a graceful curve that continues the arched crown of the tree, while her right arm, amorously wrapped around a lower limb, curves downward like another branch. Her right foot, planted solidly at the base of the tree, parallels the sturdy trunk, while her raised left foot set behind her touches or perhaps even kicks the trunk of the tree to induce it to flower. The abundant ripe mangos, dangling in tight clusters, have as their counterpart the *Yakshi*'s full rounded breasts, while her soft, fleshy body, sportively bent in the classic *tribhanga* pose, is emblematic of the ideal of feminine beauty. Her jeweled belt, pendant earrings, necklace and numerous bangles serve to emphasize her nudity and charged sexuality while reminding us that *Yakshis* are boon-granters and guardians of wealth.

The benign and benevolent *Yakshi* here at Sanchi represents only one side of the *Yakshi* nature. In early Hindu, Buddhist and Jain literature, she is portrayed more as an ogress than a nymph. She haunts the forests and marginal areas outside the village from where her frightening screams can be heard at night. Furtively she accosts travelers and passersby, deluding them with her maya, entrapping them in their own desires and delusions, the all-consuming "wheel of samsara."

This very life energy, however, the same force that brings the trees to flower, also drives the awakening of consciousness. Hinduism and Buddhism neither deny nor suppress this life force, but use, control and direct it toward the goal of self-transcendence and liberation. Beneath the *Yakshi* in the photograph, we can dimly perceive the massive dome of the stupa—the ultimate symbol of transcendence. *Yakshi* and stupa appear together, entranceway and goal, aspects of the same sacred complex.

Auspicious and fetching, a Yakshi adorns the east gateway of the Great Stupa at Sanchi, ca. 50 B.C.E., India.

Garden

Eighteenth-century patron Rana Jagat Singh II of Kotah, India, cultivated the arts as one might cultivate a fine garden. The Kotah master to whom this painting is attributed has honored his patron by depicting him enthroned in the center of a flourishing garden, divided into four sections of pink and orange blossoms, lush vegetation and fountains flowing with water. Women attendants serve Jagat Singh and a lunar light surrounds him, as if to suggest that like the dews associated with the moon, his largesse is a source of refreshment and fruitfulness (Welch, 18–19).

A garden begins in the intimacy of a hand touching the earth, sifting and turning the soil, scattering seed or burying tubers, absently plucking one form of vegetation to give breathing space to another. We plant, tend and nourish gardens, gather and prune them, all the while negotiating the claims of nature's forces. We must be observant, mindful of the garden's needs, said the poet Stanley Kunitz, who compared the tiers of his garden to the stanzas of a poem. The garden expresses fusion, secrets, changeability, possibility and an "exchange between the self and the atmosphere" (p. 62ff). Gardens, in turn, provide us with food, herbs and medicinals. They nurture us with the fragrance of flowers, soil, mulch and compost, the vividness of colors and shapes, the interplay of the elements, the presence of songbirds, small animals, humming insects and stirrings in the dark.

Most often gardens are set apart from the pressures of ordinary life for pleasure and contemplation. In many languages the word for garden signifies enclosure, bringing to mind walled gardens, secret gardens or mythical gardens—hidden, supernatural worlds transcending time and disorder. The garden paradise is the imagined locus of our beginning and end, the original matrix and mandala of life, fed by underground sources of living waters. The Garden of Eden, the Elysian Fields, the Pure Land or Western Paradise of Buddhism, the Garden of the Hesperides where Zeus and Hera were wedded are all enclosed paradisial garden worlds whose inhabitants are divinely protected. The paradisial garden variously reflects our fantasies of an idealized inner space of potential wholeness and hidden design, or a preconscious state of innocence and harmony. Medieval Christianity projected on the Virgin Mother the soul of the paradisial cosmic garden: inviolate, self-generating and contained.

The gates of entry to secret gardens are typically invisible, narrow, difficult to find. Just as in processes of individuation one repeatedly circles the more accessible aspects of the personality, only gradually moving closer to the center, so in dream or myth one might have to circumambulate the outer garden wall many times before the portal to the interior garden is revealed. Physical or imaginal, gardens are often arranged to reflect designs of wholeness, a quaternary form, for example, with a fountain, tree or image of a deity in the center.

In almost all cultures and religions, the garden represents a sacred space, a uniting of the conscious self with its unconscious source. Muslims speak of gardens as states of bliss and call Allah "the gardener." The spare gardens of Japan are commonly not viewable all at once; they gradually reveal themselves in spaces opening along pathways and waterways where one may stroll and contemplate. The Zen dry gardens, stripped to the very essence, convey the eternal through an abstract and mystical design, making gardening a path to enlightenment.

1. Garden as proliferation and creative blooming: Patron of the arts Rana Jagat Singh II of Kotah enthroned like a ruler in a lush garden. Kotah master, opaque watercolor and gold on paper, ca. 1750–1800, India.

We can never wholly domesticate a garden any-more than we can wholly domesticate the soul. Even our most compulsive efforts to control or manipulate the garden are subject to the autonomy, randomness and surprises of nature. Priapus, Saint Augustine reminds us, embodies the endlessly proliferating spirit of the garden. And how easily the untended garden returns to wilderness, its matted overgrowth and tangled vines encroaching on all our emblems of civilization.

Kunitz, Stanley and Genine Lentine. *The Wild Braid: A Poet Reflects on a Century in the Garden.* NY, 2005.
Welch, Stuart Cary. *Gods, Kings, and Tigers: The Art of Kotah.* Munich and NY, 1997.

2

3

2. A monk sits in contemplation in a dry garden at
Daisen Monastery in Kyoto. The Zen dry garden
expresses nature's forms and rhythms as an abstracted
essence. Ripples of sand convey the idea of water,
mounds of sand earth rising up, a balance of yin-and-
yang representation.

3. A detail from a Roman fresco in Livia's garden room.
The image simultaneously conveys a natural garden
progressing through the seasons and stretching into the
misty distance, an occult garden where all the seasons
timelessly coexist. From an underground room in a villa
near Prima Porta, on the Via Flaminia, late 1st century,
B.C.E., Italy.

Flower

The ancient Greek counterpart to Flora, the Roman goddess of flowers, was named Chloris, meaning "green." Zephyr, the gentle west wind, enamored of Chloris, pursued her, and as he overtook the maiden, flowers spilled from her lips, and they were subsequently married.

Flowers are the hallmark of spring. There is no surer sign of renewal in the world, of awakening and rebirth. The young, budding shoots of violets, snowdrops and crocuses push up even through the impacted earth and late snows of winter's end. Delicate, fragrant cherry and apple blossoms signal anticipated fruits; other flowers are themselves vegetation's radiant, culminating bloom. Their ephemeral blossoms have associated flowers with all the brilliant forms that quickly fade. The transitory soul, for example. Or Kore, the divine maiden who, picking flowers, was herself plucked by Hades and carried to the underworld to become its queen. Or the lovely, short-lived mythic youths of antiquity: Narcissus, who wasted away, spellbound by his own reflection; Hyacinthus, felled by Apollo's misguided arrow; Adonis, for whom the briefly petalled anemone memorializes the blood of his mortal wound from a boar. Yet flowers are, in truth, remarkably resilient. Their aggressive roots invade rough, inauspicious soil. They assert their bright growth on the rocky banks of highways and out of asphalt cracks. Wildflowers gloriously latch onto walls and railings, and fill jungles, deserts and woods. Rare species of orchid thrive in swamps.

All of nature is enticed into the flower's proliferation. The stamen forms golden pollen grains that produce male gametes. These sperm are transferred to the stigma or tip of the pistil, and burrow down through the pistil to ovules at its swollen base. In the fusion of sperm cell and ovule a seed is formed. Most flowering plants are hermaphroditic, but some have either a stamen or a pistil. Cross-pollination of flowers is provided by bees, wasps, butterflies and moths, birds, bats and other mammals, water and the fructifying wind: "There's April in the west wind, and daffodils," said the poet John Masefield. Color, fragrance and sweet, golden nectar in the cup of the flower invite and guide the many pollen carriers.

Is anything more sensual than the flower? Its green sepals forming the calyx, its shy buds unfurling to reveal a corolla of velvety petals, its heady perfumes, the edible and cosmetic essences of rose, jasmine, lily, freesia? In Pampore, India, the lavender-blue *crocus sativus* that flowers for just two weeks in October is plucked at dawn and the stigmas carefully removed to make saffron, that costliest spice with which the Hindu deities Krishna and Radha were traditionally anointed (Bharadwaj, 36–7). Flowers are incorporated into ritual and sacrament the world over, as emblems of eros, beauty, perfection, purity, fertility, joy and resurrection. The simplest form of the flower with a radial shape is a natural mandala linking the flower symbolically with the wheel and eternal, cosmic movement around a mystic and orienting center. The flower's hermaph-

1. Flora, the Roman goddess of flowers. *Primavera*, detail, by Sandro Botticelli, tempera on panel, ca. 1482, Italy.

roditic qualities suggest the joining of opposites in self-becoming. Visible above yet rooted in the invisible below, the flower symbolically bridges the manifest and unseen worlds, realms of latency and potentiality and those of active generation. The poppy, for example, associated with the grain goddess Demeter, combines bright, many-hued blooms with narcotic properties inducing painlessness, slumber or death. The four-petalled "blue flower" of alchemy signifies both the darkness of the *prima materia,* as the shadowy, unknown self, and the quadratic, unifying totality of the *lapis.*

We flourish in concert with the flower. It is emblem of the hidden "seeding-place" within ourselves, supported by multiple, participating energies. The Holy Spirit makes itself known in the secret redolence of flowers. The lush rose intimates the presence of Aph-rodite and the Virgin Mary. In Buddhism, the lotus signifies enlightenment and the "golden flower" of Chinese alchemy the achievement of the "diamond body" through the interior circulation of light. A European alchemical text describes the synthesis of the four elements, the hoped for unity in multiplicity of nature and psyche as the goal of the opus: It is "as if it were a meadow decked with colours and sweet-smelling flowers of divers kinds, which were conceived in the earth by the dew of heaven" (CW 14:389).

Bharadwaj, Monisha. *The Indian Spice Kitchen.* NY and London, 1997.

Clark, Kenneth. *Leonardo da Vinci: An Account of His Development as an Artist.* NY and Cambridge, UK, 1939.

2

3

2. Mayan whistle depicting most probably Xochiquetzal or "Flower Feather," goddess of love, erotic pleasure and spiritual transformation. Ceramic, ca. 550–850, Jaina Island, Campeche, Mexico.

3. Possibly a figure of one of the Graces, Thalia (bloom) evokes spring; virginal, feminine beauty and all that is lovely and fleeting. *Primavera*, painting from a bedroom of Villa Arianna, 89 B.C.E.–79 C.E., Stabiae (near Pompeii), Italy.

Iris

A low bridge zigzags through a stand of blue irises with fresh green stalks. On a golden Japanese screen, the irises are perpetually alive, a vivid reminder of both springtime's renewal and absent love. In the painting, the artist alludes to an episode in the tenth-century literary classic, the *Tales of Ise*. After a failed love affair, the story's hero, accompanied by a group of friends, leaves the capital for the east in order to start life anew. At a bridge that passes through blooming irises, they compose a poem about nostalgia, love and loss (ARAS, 1:367).

The iris is a genus of about 300 species of flowering plants that for millennia have been prized for their dazzling colors. The number of the iris' stunning natural varieties has been augmented by the extensive use of selective breeding. The flower ranges in color from near black to blue and violet through vermilion, orange, yellow and white, and is often variegated with strongly contrasting hues (Westrich, 17). It is this multicolor display of the iris that is responsible for its appellation. Iris, meaning "rainbow" in classical Greek, was the messenger of the Olympian gods. Her emblem was the rainbow of many colors, the bridge by which she traveled between heaven and earth with her divine messages. Analogously, the "iris" is what gives the eye its color.

Striking not only for its colors, however, but also for its sensual nature, the iris has phallic, sword-shaped leaves surrounding distinctive blossoms consisting of three erect petals and three larger outer petallike sepals. The latter suggest, as in Georgia O'Keeffe's *Black Iris*, the form and enticement of the feminine genitalia, even if the artist denied that she had such imagery in mind (Wright, 65). While the flower of the iris is not noted for its scent, "essence of violet" perfume is made from orrisroot, derived from the varieties of iris that grow, not from a bulb, but a rhizome, a creeping underground stem (*Enc. Brit.* 6:384).

Medicinal properties accompany the sensual pleasures of iris. On an Egyptian hieroglyph of an iris carved in stone 3,500 years ago was a list of medicinal plants. The ancient Greeks documented the flower's internal and external uses (Westrich, 9, 12). Traditionally, Japan celebrates an Iris Festival in May, when the flower is publicly displayed and men and women wear irises in their hair; young men drink tea made from iris bulbs and take baths in which irises have been floating, in order to insure good health and virility (ARAS, 1:367). The iris is also believed to protect against disease and evil spirits (Baird, 85).

The diverse, exquisite hues of "iris," reflected in flower, rainbow and eye, correspond, in the alchemical fantasy, to the "peacock's tail," the brilliant *omnes colores* that represent the integration of all qualities in the Stone. Just as Iris heralded the approach of the gods, so, psychologically, the show of "many colors" heralds the transcendent self in which the many facets of the personality, once opposing each other, are brought into a unity (CW 14:388ff).

Baird, Merrily C. *Symbols of Japan*. NY, 2001.
Lehner, Ernst and Johanna Lehner. *Folklore and Symbolism of Flowers, Plants and Trees*. NY, 1960.
Westrich, Josh and Ben R. Hager. *The Iris: The Rainbow Flower*. NY, 1989.
Wright, Susan. *Georgia O'Keeffe: An Eternal Spirit*. NY, 2009.

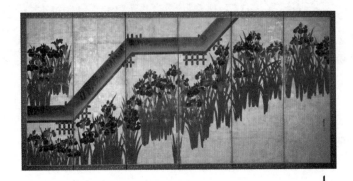

2

1. *Irises and Zigzag Bridge*, by Ogata Korin, painted screen, ca. 18th century, Japan.

2. Lusty, mysterious, this iris reflects the deep reproductive patterns underlying romance and life. *Black Iris*, by Georgia O'Keeffe, oil on canvas, 1926, United States.

3. The goddess Iris was a messenger of the gods, and traveled on a rainbow between Olympus and the earth. Iris was honored by the planting of her flower on the graves of women, since it was she who led their souls to the Elysian Fields (Lehner, 64). The Niobides Painter, 5th century B.C.E., Greece.

3

Lily

After sending up a tall stem from its bulb underground, the lily plant amazes us by unfolding large, gleaming white flowers, which release a penetrating fragrance. Held high on its leafy stem, this pristine flower has been connected with queenly divinities from the time of Bronze Age Crete, where it represented the island's reigning goddess. In ancient Greece it was sacred to Hera, Queen of Heaven, and was said to have arisen from drops of her breast milk as they fell to earth during the creation of the Milky Way.

"Lily" encompasses almost 4,000 species in more than 280 genera, and is found in every part of the world. Not only white, the lily includes the gorgeous pinks, blues, yellows and reds of tulip, daffodil and hyacinth. Balancing the delicate, scented beauty of the blossoms, earthy, tuberous roots have medicinal, toxic and intoxicating properties. The Mexican pulque, for example, is derived from the lily. Onion, leek, garlic and asparagus are edible and odorous forms of the lily.

Mythically, the short-lived lily has also represented the *puer*, the beautiful youth who dies before reaching maturity. Narcissus, who was captivated by his own image reflected in a pool, wastes away and is transmuted into a "narcissus," or daffodil. Hyacinthus, the young prince beloved of Apollo, was also fancied by the West Wind, who in a jealous rage mortally struck the youth's skull. The blood of the dead boy became the hyacinth. It is the white lily, however, that flowered in Christian symbolism, the lily of mercy balancing the flaming sword of judgment. Beginning in the twelfth century, the lily was identified with the purity, innocence and chastity of the Virgin Mary. The lily depicted in many images of the Annunciation evokes an attitude of receptiveness to "other" uncontaminated by merely personal desires or aspirations (Edinger, 26ff).

Yet the whiteness of lily is not unalloyed. While "lily-white" can mean an irreproachably spotless character, it can also denote the thing that is deceptively shadowless, or, like lily-white political bodies, is intentionally dedicated to the exclusion of color. In the East the images of purity and sanctity were largely expressed by the lotus, a form of water lily. It is also associated with feminine beauty in China, where an emperor of the Qi dynasty, carried away by the beauty of a concubine, exclaimed, "Wherever she steps, a lily springs up." This gave rise to the "golden lily," the tiny foot of the Chinese woman who underwent foot-binding.

The calyx or cup of the lily is particularly distinct; thus the lotus has embodied manifestation, center, heart or spiritual vessel from which is born the divine within. Equally reflective of the vital source, the deep calyx of the lily shaped into trumpet, bell and chalice shoots up in every hue from the dark earth at springtime, heralding resurrection and renewal. Highly regenerative, the lily surfaces even after fire or drought. Alchemy honored the lily as evoking the very essence of Mercurius, the spirit of psyche's unconscious depths and transforming opus. As the quintessence, the longed for goal of the adept, lily represents psychic integrity that is no longer pulled apart by affect. The alchemical lily is "incorruptible" and "eternal," "the noblest thing that human meditation can reach" (CW 14:689). United in love as one after long opposition, the red lily represents psyche's solar, masculine energies; the white lily the lunar and feminine that counters the combustible nature of the sun.

Edinger, Edward F. *The Christian Archetype.* Toronto, 1987.

1. White lilies emblematic of the primordial goddess are depicted in a fresco painted on the wall of a Cretan house, ca. 1650 B.C.E., Greece.

2. A Greek goddess emerges from the calyx of a lilylike flower, mythic container and birthplace of the divine. Stone, Greco-Roman, 1st century B.C.E–4th century C.E.

3. Announcing the conception of the divine child, the Archangel Gabriel presents Mary with a white lily, signifying her virgin nature. *Annunciation*, detail, by Gaudenzio Ferrari, oil on panel, ca. 1512–3, Italy.

2

1

3

Lotus

Out of dark water, a golden-centered, many-petalled pink lotus emerges on a slender stem. Surrounded by closed or partly opened lotus buds and leaves, it faces the viewer. A pale-skinned lotus-clothed woman and a blue-skinned lotus-clothed man face one another. Sitting on a dark-green shore, they exchange love-gazes. Each presents a cut lotus to the other. Only their faces and hands appear out of the layered petal wrappings.

The Indian sacred lotus, *nelumbo nucifera*, is a pink perennial water flower. Like other lotuses, its roots sink into the murky soil of a pond or river bottom. From there, stems rise above the water surface to present bright flowers to the sun. The cuplike seed pod is surrounded by a many-layered wreath of lotus petals, which at dawn open to full bloom in time to greet the sun as it rises. Throughout the day the flowers turn to face the sun as it moves across the southern sky and after sunset the lotus petals close into a tight bud around the seed pod in the center. The flowers have the unusual ability of controlling their temperature; they create a warm place for bees and other pollinators. Lotuses and water lilies of other families may be white, yellow or blue. In Egyptian myth, a lotus emerges out of the dark waters of the primeval sea as emblem of the spirit of life, luminous and fragrant, disclosing, sometimes as a divine child, the sun god Re; in the form of the beautiful blue lotus of the Nile valley, it is sacred to the goddess, the womb from which golden life arises. The yearly flooding of the Nile was a repetition of this "first time" "when the waters receded to reveal the first shallows out of which a lotus-flower could bloom to support the sun-god" (Quirke, 26).

"Mud-born" (*pankaja*) is a Sanskrit poetic term for the Indian lotus. As a poetic image and visual icon, the lotus symbol evokes the realization that all life, rooted in mire, nourished by decomposed matter, growing upward through a fluid and changing medium, opens radiantly into space and light. The mire and fluidity symbolize the grosser, heavier qualities of nature, including the mind's nature. The flower, beautifully multipetalled, symbolizes the array of subtler, more lucid qualities, with the golden hue, the radiance of spirit, at its center.

The lotus twosome in the Basohli painting is Radha and Krishna. Their erotic relationship manifests an Indian philosophical principle that Spirit (*Purusha*, symbolized by Krishna) and Nature (*Prakriti*, symbolized by Radha) are eternal principles. They exist for one another: she for his vision of her creation, he for her bliss in spiritual union with him. The central open lotus suggests the center of a meditative or ritual focus—the heart, hands, eyes, feet, an internal or external image. Meditative practice, according to the principles of yoga, links or yokes such a psychophysical focus to its spiritual center, as the petals of a lotus all link to the flower's center.

As is typical for Hindu and Buddhist sacred images, Akshobya, Buddha Imperturbable, sits on a lotus throne and manifests spiritual luminosity. He touches the ground as his witness that the samsaric world, all that arises and passes away, does not disturb him. And yet he is not separate from it. Just as a lotus lives in a murky mud-bottomed pond, so nirvana, of which he is an image, is not apart from samsara, nor samsara from nirvana. The Sanskrit mantra "Om mani padme hum (literally "Om the jewel in the lotus hum")" expresses this seating of Buddha-mind, the enlightening jewel, in the psychophysical world.

The esoteric yogas of India and Tibet picture a sequence of chakras, vital energy centers in the subtle body, as lotuses of particular hues and petal numbers. At the top of the head is a thousand-petalled lotus. Their colors and petal numbers reflect their place in the spectrum from red to violet and white light, and their energies correspond with the energies of the universe. The colors, shapes and energies manifest through meditation, chanting and visualizations stimulated by such images as Radha, Krishna, Buddha, their lotus eyes or hands, or a lotus flower.

Clark, T. Rundle. *Myth and Symbol in Ancient Egypt*. NY and London, 1959.
Quirke, Stephen. *Ancient Egyptian Religion*. NY, 1992.

1. Radha and Krishna as nature and spirit. *The Lotus World*, gouache on paper, 18th century, Punjab Hills, India.

159

2

3

2. A woman smelling a lotus. Tomb of Djehuty, 18th dynasty (ca. 1550–1295 B.C.E.), Luxor, Egypt.

3. *Tathagata Akshobhya (Buddha Imperturbable)*, gilt bronze with silver and copper inlays, 15th–16th century, Guge, Western Tibet.

4. Mayan figure emerging from water lily, the lotus of the Americas, perhaps referring to the resurrections of Hun Hunaphy, father of the Hero Twins. Ceramic, 600–900, possibly from Jaina, Campeche, Mexico.

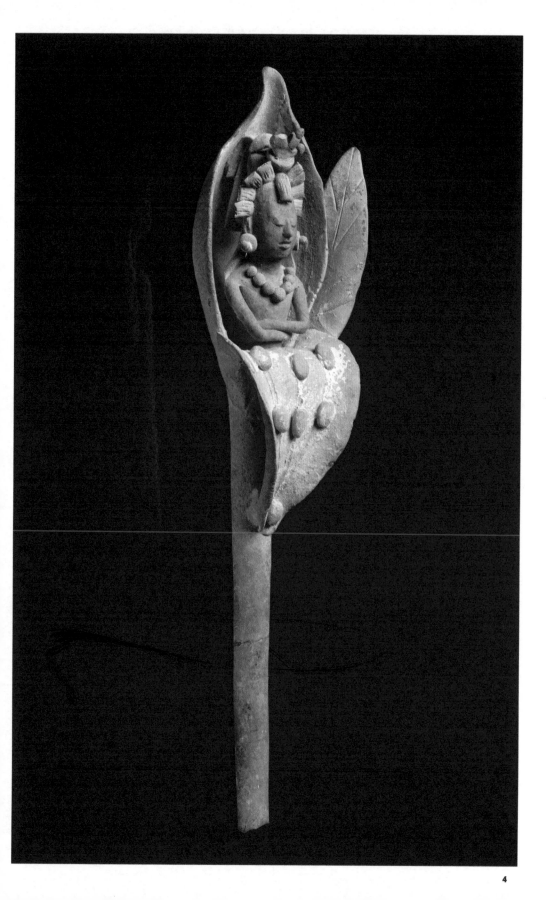

Rose

Under the summer roses
When the flagrant crimson
Lurks in the dusk
Of the wild red leaves,
Love, with little hands,
Comes and touches you
With a thousand memories,
And asks you
Beautiful, unanswerable questions.
Carl Sandburg, Under the Harvest Moon

Let our banquet have roses ...
Horace, Odes, 1.36.15

What would the feast of life be like without the "flagrant crimson" or the chaste simplicity, the playful exuberance, or the serene composure of the rose? For at least six millennia, its five-petaled wild ancestors and their thousands of cultivated descendants have delighted the eye, soothed the soul and borne testimony to a myriad human rites and passages. Appealing to the haughty as well as the humble, roses evoke the evanescence of innocence and youth, enwreathe the victor, memorialize the martyr, are woven into flags of nationhood and the banners of royal bloodlines. Above all, roses signify love, in all its earthly and heavenly hues: what or who we love in the present; the one we loved and have lost, and the longing for something nameless—embodied in the form and color of roses, and in the perfume that "suddenly ... lies on the air like fame" (Rilke, 149)—that both beckons and mysteriously eludes us.

Roses are equally at home being tended by angels in the Garden of Paradise or decorating a florid Victorian valentine. Rosewater or rose oil has enhanced complexions, been used against plague, washed and purified the Mosque of Omar, and been incorporated in the preparation and burial of the dead. The scent of roses has remained the most popular, for the longest time, of any flower's fragrance, evoking both the seductive love magic of Cleopatra, and the "odour of sanctity" of the Virgin Mary. Though roses are associated with several male deities, they are preeminently the flower of the Great Goddess, resonant of her sensuality, fertility and regal compassion. Sacred to Venus (Aphrodite), they float on the wind in Botticelli's famous painting of her birth from Ocean; the devotees of the Phrygian Cybele "shadow the Mother and her retinue with a snow of roses" (Lucretius Carus, 2.627). And in Apuleius' second-century novel *The Golden Ass*, though roses are the antidote for the magic-gone-amuck that has transformed the hero Lucius into a donkey, they are always just out of reach until strategically placed in a festive procession for the Egyptian goddess Isis, who subsequently calls Lucius to priestly service.

For alchemists, the entire process of psychic transformation takes place sub rosa (under the rose). Denoting silence, the phrase purportedly originated in the story of Eros' gift of a rose to Harpocrates, the god of silence, in grateful recognition of his discretion regarding the illicit amours of Eros' mother Aphrodite. In alchemy, however, the crossed branches of the white and red rose not only allude to the "love affair" and "marriage" of opposite natures, and to the *albedo* and

1. The angelic blossom of blessing and the quintessential emblem of earthly love coalesce in the voluptuous petalage of this crimson rose. *Cramoisi Supérieur*, botanical illustration from *Journel des Roses* (August 1883).

2. As a single two-colored flower, the alchemical red-and-white rose is the western version of the "golden flower" of Chinese alchemy: the many-petaled "light of the inmost regions" (*The Secret of the Golden Flower*) where the *filius philosophorum* is born. Illustration from the *Ripley Scrowle*, by Sir George Ripley, 1588, Germany.

1

2

rubedo as understanding and realization of psychic processes, but also to the silence necessary to the interior nature of the work and to the womb or "rose" within whose petalled folds the Self is secretly conceived.

But while the endearing qualities of roses are indisputable, so is their notorious thorniness. Literally, the prickles or thorns of roses are protective, dissuading predators from making a banquet of their delectable blooms; they may also serve as armored reservoirs to forestall dehydration in the stems, especially of those, like the desert rose, that live in hot climates. Although this suggests at a psychic level that a certain amount of thorniness is a positive attribute, thorns may also represent a prickly defensiveness that precludes intimacy. In the fairy tale "Sleeping Beauty," the spindle that pricks Briar Rose and drugs her into a hundred years' sleep is replicated in the imprisoning hedge of briers that entangles and lethally wounds her would-be suitors. In the fairy tale "Snow-White and Rose-Red," on the other hand, the phallic thorniness of their own aggression and the "prick" of reality is exactly what the two sisters need in order to outgrow the cloyingly "rosy" sweetness and goodness—devoid of any shadow—that suffuses their idyllic, exclusively feminine world with mother. As an emblem of Dionysus, the thorns of the rose as well as its alluring scent suggest the potential dangers of the subterranean aspect of psyche. In Keats' "Ode to a Nightingale," for instance, the "soft incense ... in the embalmed darkness" of the musk rose and white hawthorn intimates the poet's melancholic love affair with death.

Bringing together both earthly and otherworldly grace, as well as piercing sorrow, the Virgin Mary, perhaps more than any other religious figure, bears the sobriquet "Rose." In the poem "Ash Wednesday," in which the two—the Rose and the *Mater Dolorosa*—are identified, T. S. Eliot captures the mute eloquence of both the Queen of Heaven and the Queen of Flowers:

Lady of silences
Calm and distressed
Torn and most whole
Rose of memory
Rose of forgetfulness
Exhausted and life-giving
Worried reposeful
The single Rose
Is now the Garden
Where all loves end

Dante Alighiere. *The Divine Comedy of Dante Alighieri.* Toronto and NY, 1986.
Horace. *The Odes and Epodes of Horace.* Chicago and London, 1960.
Keats, John. *Selected Poetry and Letters.* NY, 1965.
Lucretius Carus, Titus. *On the Nature of the Universe.* NY, 1951.
Rilke, Rainer Maria. "The Sonnets to Orpheus: Second Series, 6." *Duino Elegies and the Sonnets to Orpheus.* Boston, 1977.

3. The Queen of Heaven presides over tiers of souls, each forming a petal, as angel "bees" pollinate the Celestial Rose with the "peace and ardor" of divine love's eternal dwelling (Dante: *Paradiso.* Canto XXXI, 7, 17). *Paradiso,* from the *Divine Comedy,* by Dante Alighieri, illuminated manuscript, 15th century, Italy.

Thistle

Thistle is inherently discriminating. The spiny edges of its profuse leaves sting and tear like small thorns, discouraging touch. Yet the showy flower that crowns the stalk is sweetly fragrant, attracting butterflies, insects, bees and birds. Evoking one who is barbed but has a soft heart, the thistle's prickliness is associated with self-protection, impenetrability, austerity and resilience. Mythically, the thistle did not grow in the Garden of Eden; rather, the thistles and thorns appeared as a curse after the Fall, as opposed to the blessing of figs and grapes of Paradise. Indeed, farmers regard the thistle as a plague—a prolific, intractable weed—in popular belief it is seen as a gift of the Devil. Nevertheless, the thistle also conveys love that endures suffering and labor that endures hardship. Thistle is associated with the worldly love of Aphrodite as well as the loving compassion of the Virgin Mary; to thistle have been attributed properties of healing, cleansing and longevity. Scotland, whose national emblem is the thistle, celebrated its character in a tenth-century legend. Invading Vikings, hoping to stealthily attack Staines Castle, removed their boots. But the Scots had filled the castle's dry moat with thistles and the anguished cries of the enemy betrayed their presence (Heilmeyer, 26). Organically bringing sweet bloom out of rough stalk, thistle's roots are said to dispel melancholy.

Heilmeyer, Marina. *The Language of Flowers: Symbols and Myths*. Munich and London, 2001.

Thistle with Insects, by Barbara Regina Dietzsch (1706–83), gouache on vellum, Germany.

Apple

The Belgian surrealist, René Magritte (1898–1967) stirs our remembrance of a world of greater reality—or *surreality*—by the simple juxtaposition of everyday objects: Here nothing more than a green apple inside a music room makes the fruit's magical qualities spring to mind. "Snapshots of the impossible," the art critic Robert Hughes calls Magritte's work, or he might equally have said "windows into a forgotten paradise" that the taste of this seemingly ordinary apple throws open. Concealed at the aromatic core of the gleaming apple—itself so suggestive of life's initial paradise and romance's glowing honeymoon—are seeds of darkness in what is called its "ovary," an explicit reminder of the feminine pattern revealed when an apple is split lengthwise in two. Accordingly, it served as a common love-gift in ancient Greece, where the apple was imagined as an attribute of Aphrodite, the goddess of love. The fateful legend of Paris, a handsome prince who signaled his choice of the fairest among three goddesses by presenting her with an apple provided by Eris, the goddess of discord, concluded in the tragedy of the Trojan War, for Aphrodite rewarded Paris for choosing her by presenting him with the most beautiful woman alive—Helen, the immediate cause of the war. This pattern of a seemingly innocent apple inaugurating a tortuous narrative is repeated in the familiar tale of Adam and Eve in the Garden of Eden. Although Genesis (2:15–3:24) makes no explicit mention of an apple, a Latin double entendre ("apple," *malus,* also means "bad") reinforced the long-standing identification of the forbidden fruit with the apple (just as Saint Augustine equated eating it with sexual intercourse) (Bendiner, 14).

A botanical relative of the rose, the apple (*Malus pumila*) goes back to the earliest phases of human settlement; its present size and sweetness results from long domestication of its small, sour prototype. Today, the flavorful apples once dispersed by Johnny Appleseed as a means of bringing civilization into the American wilderness are often bypassed in favor of bland apples shipped in refrigerated compartments for year-round availability, while the fragrant taste of a traditional apple arouses fantasies of the lost delights of nature that play into its complex symbolism. Through Eve, both the apple and woman herself were stigmatized by medieval Christians as temptingly beautiful but with concealed wiles, which Christianity balanced by its belief that paradise was restored through Mary and her legendary gift of the tree upon which Christ was hanged as a figurative apple. The Jungian analyst Erich Neumann even renamed Giovanni da Modena's "Mystery of the Fall and Redemption of Man" (a Renaissance depiction of Christ crucified on an apple tree) as "The Restitution of the Mystic Apple to the Tree of Knowledge." He meant the name to convey the symbolic reversal of human destiny: the poignant loss of life's original sweetness and its potential transformation through the paradoxical coexistence of goodness and darkness within the feminine (Neumann, Plate 116). The apples that belonged to the Norse goddess Idun, for example, were associated with deathless youth, the very aspect that would tempt any of us to acts of thievery that Idun ironically punished by inflicting rapid aging and death. Conversely, the apple's reddish peel recalls the western sunset at the end of life, yet it was in the westernmost Garden of the Hesperides that Hercules gained immortality by stealing apples from the nymphs of the evening who guarded its orchard. Welsh legends describe Arthur and Merlin

1. By positioning his apple inside a room, René Magritte
gives it a surreal largeness, inviting us to confront its
sensuousness up close: its taut skin, its sweet flesh
around a hidden core and, as our tempted lips draw
near, the fragrance we long to recapture. *The Listening
Room*, oil on canvas, 1958, Belgium.

traveling to a similar blessed island in the western seas to be reborn after death. This insular paradise of apple orchards (where the Grail was placed for safekeeping) was known as Avalon, thought to derive from the Welsh word for apple, *afal*. Sought out by mariners as late as the eleventh century, Avalon was finally accepted as a figurative paradise, a sign that the apple's symbolism rather than its literal historicism was dawning upon the modern mind—perhaps a fall from the innocence of faith, but the first step toward conscious digestion of the apple's enigmatic sweet poison.

Bendiner, Kenneth. *Food in Painting*. London, 2004.
Magritte, René. *The Portable Magritte*. NY, 2002.
Neumann, Erich. *The Great Mother: An Analysis of the Archetype*. Princeton, NJ, 1972.

2

2. Dark temptations rear their head even in animated fantasies made for innocent children. Walt Disney's classic depiction of wickedness enticing purity with a poisoned apple is forever stamped into our collective memory. *Snow White and the Seven Dwarfs*, 1937.

3. The fall of Adam and Eve from Paradise, the grand finale to which their first taste of forbidden fruit is the opening act. Detail from *Paradise*, the left wing of the triptych *The Last Judgement*, by Hieronymus Bosch (1450–1516), oil on panel, the Netherlands.

Peach

A tray laden with succulent pinkish peaches, carried by a jade maiden, has been prepared for the goddess. She is Xiwangmu, the Queen Mother of the West, and at last her extraordinary fruits are ready. It has taken 3,000 years for them to ripen, for these are the peaches of immortality (Little, 276). Now that they have finally been picked, Xiwangmu will invite her fellow Taoist gods for a festival to eat this miraculous harvest (Eberhard, 227–8).

The tree that yields Xiwangmu's peaches grows in her palace garden in the Chinese paradise of Mount Kunlun (Little, 276). Three thousand leagues across, this world tree's tangled branches reach to the sky, serving as a ladder for gods to move between heaven and earth. Just as the tree is protected by divine guardians, peach wood contains *ling*, spiritual force, and thus is efficacious against evil spirits (Birrell, 308; Leach, 2:849).

In China and Japan the symbolism of the peach is extensive, uniting the sensual with the esoteric, the human with the divine. In appearance and taste, the peach suggests a juicy abundance that is both natural and sacred. Blossoming in the early spring, the peach tree is a sure sign of nature's regeneration. The peach, with its cleft, rounded forms has long been associated, in east and west, with the female genitalia, and with the feminine principal of fecundity and renewal (Stevens 388). Even feminine complexions resembling the coloring and texture of the peach are described as "peaches and cream," and girls blossoming into womanhood are sometimes referred to as "peaches."

The peach's evocation of life's rebirth poetically coalesces in two Chinese myths. In one, the Peach Blossom Spring, issuing from deep within a cave, gives access to a happy world beyond this mortal life (Eberhard, 228). In the other, the Little Peach Boy is discovered by a childless couple when they find a great peach floating in a stream. When the fruit is split, it gives birth to the tiny child, Momotaro, which means peach child. He goes on to heroically regain treasures from a band of demons (Piggott, 86).

Peaches are not just magical fruits and the food of immortals, but touch ordinary lives as well. Shou-Lo, a bearded old man pictured emerging from a peach, is the Chinese god of long life for humankind. And the promise of the peach is made manifest in a celebratory soup eaten in China on New Year's Day (Leach, 2:849).

It is reputed that when a soul eats of the sacred peach tree, it will enjoy three millennia of good health. But anytime we bite into the juicy flesh of a peach, we need no divine garden or glimpse of eternity. As we break the downy surface and are flooded with the peach's rich flavor, we are delivered into the present with our own sweet taste of paradise.

Birrell, Anne. *Chinese Mythology: An Introduction.* Baltimore, 1993.

Eberhard, Wolfram. *A Dictionary of Chinese Symbols.* London and NY, 1986.

Leach, Maria. Ed. *Funk & Wagnalls Standard Dictionary of Folklore, Mythology and Legend.* NY, 1949.

Little, Stephen and Shawn Eichman. *Taoism and the Arts of China.* Chicago; [Berkeley], 2000.

Piggott, Juliet. *Japanese Mythology.* London and NY, 1969.

Stevens, Anthony. *Ariadne's Clue: A Guide to the Symbols of Humankind.* Princeton, NJ, 1998.

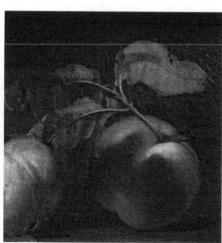

1. Xiwangmu, the Queen Mother of the West, receives from a jade maiden the peaches of immortality. *Blessings for a Long Life*, detail, scroll painting, Yuan dynasty (1260–1368 C.E.), China.

2. What could be more sensual or inviting than the blush of peaches, the soft fuzziness of their skins, the promise of their ripe, golden fruit? *Still Life With Peaches*, detail, by Jan van Huysum, oil on canvas, ca. 17th–18th century, the Netherlands.

Grape

The story of wine begins with the grape, the bright sweet fruit that seems all juice, that hangs down from green vines in heavy clusters, gleaming in late-summer light as it awaits the harvest. This beautiful fruit appears in the first image, surprisingly, as the shining cloak of a human figure, the personified god Bacchus (Dionysus, to the Greeks). Or perhaps the god *is* the bunch of grapes, an intimation that grapes, more than a simple food crop, are involved with spirit. Once the clusters are cut from the vines and crushed, mysteries begin. The crushed fruit transforms itself into a powerful new substance, wine. And the new substance transforms us as we drink it, bringing intoxication. This double transformation is the foundation of wine's symbolism.

Grapes have been cultivated and wine produced for over 6,000 years, and some of the best wines are apparently produced by grapes grown in difficult soil, attesting to the grape's tenacious life force. Genesis tells us that after the flood, Noah planted vineyards. The grapevine was often equated with the tree of life. In Sumerian cuneiform script, the sign for "life" was a vine leaf (Stevens, 390). Later, but still in ancient times, the Greek god of wine, Dionysus, alternately "exalted and terrified" the souls of his worshippers with the juice of the grapes (DoS, 1115), which in Cretan myth the god and his satyrs trod "with dancing steps" (Kerényi, 59).

Wine (along with women and song) has long stood for the exuberant pleasures of life and release from care and duty into joy and abandon. Dionysus and his cults brought this spirit into Greek life, and along with it, the darkness of the vine. For the crushing of the grapes and their running, bloody-looking juices also signified the dismemberment of the god, mirrored in the rending and eating of living animals, and sometimes human beings by frenzied, intoxicated devotees. Like the grape's grasping, proliferating vines, the powers of the dark god can possess us in unpredictable disinhibitions, dissolution, ecstasy and aggression. The ancient gilded cup in the third image shows a divine figure seated among bearing grapevines, but the figure is not Dionysus. It's Jesus, who said of himself, "I am the true vine and my Father is the husbandman," and told his followers, "I am the vine, you are the branches ... " (John 15:1–5). Here, like the pagan deity of earlier times, the crucified and resurrected Christ is identified with the grape, crushed to make the life-giving wine. In the sacrament of the Eucharist, the consecrated wine signifying the blood of the savior is offered to the faithful, uniting them in everlasting life. Yet in the Book of Revelation, the grape's more violent mysteries are apparent: At the end of time earthly life will be thrown into "the great winepress of the wrath of God" from which will flow an immense river of blood (Rev. 14:20). In Islam, the faithful are forbidden to drink the wine of this world, but in imagination divine wine flows strongly, especially in Islamic mysticism. The mystic poets equate wine with divine love, and intoxication with the ecstasy of losing oneself in God. The Persian poet Rumi wrote, in the thirteenth century, "Before a garden, a vine or a grape existed in this world, our souls were intoxicated with immortal wine" (DoS, 1115).

Jalal al-Din Rumi. *The Soul of Rumi.* NY, 2002.
Kerényi, Karl. *Dionysos: Archetypal Image of the Indestructible Life.* Princeton, NJ, 1976.
Stevens, Anthony. *Ariadne's Clue.* Princeton, NJ, 1998.

1. In this ancient Pompeian fresco, buried for 800 years by the eruption of Mt. Vesuvius, we see grape-wreathed Bacchus and the volcano, its slopes covered by trellised vineyards. The foreground serpent was probably a positive spirit quite at home in the household chapel where this fresco decorated one wall. First century.

2. Grape-bearing vines, symbolic of the resurrection of the dead, cover the ceiling of a tomb chamber from ancient Egypt. Detail from a wall painting in the tomb of Nakht, 18th dynasty (1550–1295 C.E.).

3. This detail from an early Christian chalice was discovered in the ruins of ancient Antioch, in Turkey, only in the 20th century. It shows Christ seated among grapevines, much as the Greek god Dionysus had been portrayed centuries earlier. Silver, 500–550 B.C.E.

Pomegranate

A maiden kneeling on half a pomegranate holds her cloak in a gesture that signifies epiphany. The presence of winged Eros at her shoulder denotes that the one who discloses herself is divine—here, the goddess Persephone (Kerényi, 144). The smooth, hard, rosy shell of the *pome granate,* or "seedy apple," crowned by a golden aureole, opens up to reveal blood-red fruit and numerous seeds, the basis for the pomegranate's mythic dynamism throughout the ancient Mediterranean. According to a Phrygian myth, a fertilized stone phallus engendered a hermaphroditic being, Agditis, who, castrated by the gods, became the goddess Cybele (Daniélou 90); from the blood of the castration sprang the first pomegranate tree. The priests of Attis, a castrated son-lover of the earth goddess carried pomegranates in their hands or wore them on their heads in wreaths (Kerényi, 136). Along with the fig and apple, the pomegranate is associated with the underworld and the mysteries of the death, conception and rebirth of vegetation, personified by divine young men or maidens. The pomegranate's seeds and blood-colored flesh were emblematic of this eternal renewal of the life of the world in which the human initiate might also participate. The pomegranate was sacred to Hades, who seized Persephone, the daughter of the grain goddess Demeter, into the land of the dead. When Demeter in grief withheld the grain from the earth, Zeus agreed to have Persephone returned to her mother. But Hades gave the maiden "a single sweet pomegranate seed," which meant that she must spend a third of the year with him as his spouse and the Queen of the Dead (ibid., 133). The pomegranate played a part in the Eleusinian Mysteries, honoring the two goddesses as the feminine source and continuity of life, and also in the phallic, Dionysian Holoa festival and the Thesmophoria. In some rites, the initiate was allowed to eat nothing except the seeds of the pomegranate; in others, the eating of this fruit was forbidden. As a votive offering to the subterranean aspect of the Great Goddess in particular, the pomegranate suggests, in a psychological sense, the bitter depths and majestic forces of the unconscious encountered in the taking in of the fertile, dreadful seeds of the self.

Daniélou, Alain. *The Phallus: Sacred Symbol of the Male Creative Power.* Rochester, VT, 1995.
Kerényi, Karl. *Eleusis.* NY, 1967.

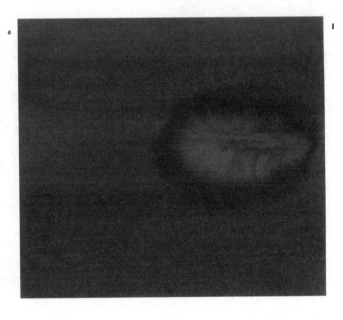

1. *Pomegranate Seed*, by Elizabeth J. Milleker,
gouache and sumi-ink painting, 2003, United States.

2. A girl with Eros kneeling on a half-pomegranate,
terra-cotta, ca. 400–323 B.C.E., Greece.

Mushroom

There is something uncanny about mushrooms. Above ground, mushrooms appear suddenly, overnight, where no plant was visible before. They are oddly weightless. They seem to be plants, but they are not green. Eaten, they are sometimes gourmet treats, sometimes poison. Sometimes mushrooms cause visions. Small wonder that these little plants, the largest of the fungi, have been (and still are in some places) seen as magical—demonic or divine. The ancient stone carving from El Salvador, with its flowerlike halo, seems to be divine—or at least, benign.

Mushrooms vegetate underground in masses of dense, white, tangled threads called *mycelium*, which if conditions are suitable, can live for hundreds of years. Umbrella-type mushrooms have gills under their caps from which spores develop and scatter in the wind, sprouting filaments that become new mycelium (*Compt.*). Mushrooms have been eaten and cultivated in many parts of the world for thousands of years. In China and Japan, a diet of agaric mushrooms was associated with legendarily long life. Current medical research indicates that compounds from this same mushroom bolster the immune system and allow greater tolerance for the drugs used in chemotherapy, perhaps also reducing levels of cancer incidence. Eighteenth-century travelers in Siberia reported that a special mushroom, fly agaric, was used by a number of tribes as an intoxicant and was regarded as sacred (Kiple, 1:330). Probably this use goes back much farther, perhaps to the Stone Age (EoR, 15:284). Siberian and Alaskan shamans used the mushroom to increase physical strength and to induce trances. In some of these groups, evil spirit-beings were believed to inhabit the mushrooms, and could only be controlled by shamanic magic (Andrews, 154).

The western European imagination associates mushrooms with mold, decay, rotting leaves, slimy toads. "Toadstool" is the popular term for a toxic mushroom. Fantasy holds that mushrooms are to be found in witches' brews and are the property of fairies. Or that "fairy rings" of wild mushrooms sprouting when their underground root system gradually expands, leaving an empty center, are fairy dancing-grounds that can hold a human captive. Generations of English-speaking children remember Alice's classic meeting in Wonderland (Carroll, 49–57) with the philosophical caterpillar seated on a mushroom. Alice grew taller when she nibbled a fragment from one side of it, and shorter after tasting the other side—experiences that may resonate today with what we know about mushroom-induced hallucinations of body size.

In pre-Hispanic cults of the sacred mushroom still alive in Mexico and Central America, special mushrooms (*Psilocybe* species) are ritually eaten for the purpose of healings, divination and producing visionary states (Wasson, 142ff). Mushroom stones, like the one from El Salvador, were probably used in the ancient predecessors of these cults even as long ago as 1500 B.C.E (EoR, 12:49).

Symbolically, the mushroom evokes unexpected manifestations of what is already proliferating in invisible, vegetative dimensions. What "mushrooms" into conscious life can function to enchant, expand, alter, nourish, but also to poison. The "mushroom cloud," for example, signifies explosive devastation and nuclear change. Mushrooms have ever been associated with bivalent spirits and the sacred rituals that conjure their potency. When a contemporary Mazatec Indian in Oaxaca, Mexico, was asked why the sacred mushroom was called *nti si tho,* "that which springs forth," the Mazatec answered, "The little mushroom comes of itself, no one knows whence, like the wind that comes we know not whence nor why" (Wasson, 147).

Andrews, Tamra. *Nectar & Ambrosia.* Santa Barbara, CA, 2000.
Carroll, Lewis. *Alice's Adventures in Wonderland and through the Looking-Glass.* NY, 1946.
Kiple, Kenneth F. and Kriemhild Coneè Ornelas. *The Cambridge World History of Food.* Cambridge, UK, and NY, 2000.
Wasson, R. Gordon and Mycological Society of America. *The Hallucinogenic Fungi of Mexico.* Cambridge, MA, 1961.

A foot-high ritual mushroom, stone, 400 B.C.E.–250
C.E., El Salvador.

Mandrake

A dense growth of fantasy, superstition and legend surrounds—almost buries—this modest looking plant, which has been known for more than 3,000 years. Common in Mediterranean lands, its large rosette of dark green leaves grows close to the ground above a long, fleshy forked root, which often resembles the legs and crotch of a human being. Mauve or blue flowers give way to pungent orange fruits that look like eggs in a nest.

Not so strangely, the mandrake (also called mandragora) was associated with fertility from earliest times: in Egyptian art; in the Biblical Song of Songs; in Genesis, where barren Rachel bargains for the root and finally conceives a son. Greek legend speaks of it as the plant of the seductress Circe's magic brew, which turned men into swine. As an aphrodisiac, it was widely known from China to Arabia and Persia, to Shakespeare's England.

Shakespeare also knew of its medical uses. Cleopatra begs, "Give me to drink mandragora / That I might sleep out this great gap of time / My Antony is away" (*Antony and Cleopatra*, 1.5.6–8). Root and leaves of the plant are poisonous, but in the right dosage it relieved convulsions, depression and insomnia. First used by the ancient Greeks and Romans, mandrake was the earliest known anesthetic, bringing a temporary deathlike stupor against even the pain of major surgery or amputation (Thompson, 3). Modern chemical analysis supported the ancient medical claims and found that mandrake contains a number of poisonous hallucinogens, including atropine and scopolamine (Biedermann, 216). In Roman times, a "wine" of mandragora and myrrh was sometimes given to crucified prisoners to relieve their anguish before death, and at times they were taken down from the cross while only apparently dead, so escaping with their lives. In medieval Germany, the root was carved into small precious manikins with arcane powers. They were clothed, bathed, asked for advice. If properly treated, they brought good luck (Thompson, 132–133).

Despite all these magical benefits, the mandrake's was a dark power. While still embedded in the earth it was linked to diabolical forces, to death and madness, to the underworld. Elaborate ritual precautions were necessary when pulling it up. To the medieval mind, the worst danger came when the plant, dragged from the ground, gave a terrible shriek that would kill any listener or drive him insane. By the light of the moon, a black dog had to be tied to the stem of the plant, and the man, blocking his ears, fled, bribing the dog with food to move away from the plant and so pull it out of the earth; the dog itself would be killed by the shriek. Then the man could return for the mandrake, being careful not to let the plant touch the ground again, lest its powers leak back into the soil. One might take this formula as saying that ferocious dark energies are necessary to extract the magical content from the unconscious depths, and they can only do their work in the darkness and not in an everyday state of mind. However, these energies have to be sacrificed once the work is done, lest they take over the conscious life (Edinger, 117ff).

Symbolically, the mandrake is ambiguous. It gives life and brings death; it heals and it poisons. "In general, the mandrake symbolized forces humans must approach only with great caution" (Biedermann, 216). Different ages have pictured these forces in different ways: as the uncanny Hecate of the Greeks, as demons in the Muslim world, as the devil of the flesh by medieval Christians, as the unpredictable unconscious of modern depth psychologists (Edinger, Whitmont), as the mysterious dark and light world of sexuality. To know these powers we must be wise, clear-sighted and not too afraid of the dark.

Biedermann, Hans. *Dictionary of Symbolism.* NY, 1994.

Edinger, Edward F. *The Mysterium Lectures.* Toronto, 1995.

Rahner, Hugo. *Greek Myths and Christian Mystery.* NY, 1971.

Thompson, C. J. S. *The Mystic Mandrake.* New Hyde Park, NY, 1968.

Whitmont, Edward C. "The Magical Dimension in Transference and Counter-Transference." *Current Trends in Analytical Psychology.* Ed. Gerhard Adler. London, 1961.

The sleeping power of the mandrake plant, about to
be wrenched out of the earth and into the human
world. Medical manuscript illustration from the
Theatrum Sanitatis, by Ububchasym of Baldach, late
14th century, Italy; text 11th century, Baghdad.

ANIMAL
WORLD

PRIMORDIAL CREATURES

SNAIL, WORM, TOAD, FROG, TURTLE / TORTOISE, SNAKE, COBRA, CROCODILE

WATER CREATURES

FISH, WHALE, DOLPHIN, OCTOPUS, CRAB, SHELL, CLAM / OYSTER

ARACHNIDS AND INSECTS

SCORPION, SPIDER, COCKROACH, ANT, HONEYBEE , FLY / MOSQUITO, BUTTERFLY / MOTH, SCARAB

BIRDS

BIRD, FEATHER, DOVE, CROW / RAVEN, FALCON, OWL, EAGLE, PEACOCK

WILD ANIMALS

APE / MONKEY, ELEPHANT, GREAT CATS, BEAR, WOLF, COYOTE, FOX, KANGAROO, DEER, RABBIT / HARE, RAT / MOUSE, BAT

DOMESTIC ANIMALS

DOG, CAT, COW, BULL, HORSE, DONKEY, GOAT, SHEEP, PIG, HEN / ROOSTER

Snail

While I ponder
a snail
passes me by
Anonymous

It may be that the snail in this seventeenth-century Dutch flower painting has eaten of the wilting rose and fretted leaf, for snails nourish themselves on green plants and decaying vegetable matter. If the flowers are meant as reminders of mortality, the snail decrees that life moves forward, even in the smallest urges and imperceptible movements of time. The spiral-shaped whorls of the snail's silvery shell associate it with the moon's recurring cycles of rebirth and evolution; in ancient Mexico, the moon god Tecciztecatl was depicted enclosed in a snail's shell (DoS, 890). The progression of the snail is unhurried, measured, like the moon or like the unfolding of eternity. The snail's "foot," its soft, mollusk body, produces a mucus slime in order to reduce friction with the ground, and the snail travels by slow undulation on its wet highway. Some have compared the excretion and the moist substance of the snail's body to the female vulva; in other cultures such as Benin, the snail is considered a reservoir of semen (ibid.). The snail's tentacles are reminiscent of horns, that age-old emblem of male generation. Though most snails have genders and reproduce by copulation and internal fertilization, others, types of land and freshwater snails, are hermaphroditic, reproducing like their gendered cousins, but equipped to act as male or female in the mating. Snails are models of self-containment and self-sufficiency. They can withdraw completely into their helical shells, and are compactly arranged. An internal, visceral sac contains organs of digestion, excretion and respiration, and in the head are cerebral ganglia that may be called a brain. In snails with four tentacles, the two longest each contains an eye lens. Snails have adapted to every continent on earth except Antarctica. Because snails need to stay moist, they avoid the heat and sunlight, sheltering themselves in leaves, crevices or underground during the day and emerging at night, early morning or when there is dew or rain. This elicits our projections of the retiring nature that shuns the light, but also of something vital and hidden. Indeed, the lowly snail unifies opposites like masculine and feminine, time and eternity, small and great.

Addiss, Stephen and Fumiko Y. Yamamoto. *A Haiku Menagerie: Living Creatures in Poems and Prints.* NY, 1992.

Flowerpiece, detail, by Jan van Huysum, oil on canvas,
ca. 17th century, the Netherlands.

Worm

Who really respects the earthworm,
the farmworker far under the grass in the soil.
He keeps the earth always changing.
He works entirely full of soil,
speechless with soil, and blind.

He is the underneath farmer,
  the underground one,
where the fields are getting on
  their harvest clothes.
Who really respects him,
this deep and calm earth-worker,
the deathless, gray, tiny farmer
  in this planet's soil.
Harry Martinson, *The Earthworm*

The diminutive figure in her burial shroud represents Matron Clay, or Mother Earth, who, one with the worm she nourishes, is "earthworm," the humblest form of matter. Following the alchemical principle of "as above, so below," however, Blake's imagination sees in the earthworm as much a dwelling place for the divine as the loftiest aspect of the heavens (Raine, 1968, 1:122).

Blake's worm embodies the symbolic complex that has arisen around this small, simple animal. Worms are legless, naked, tubelike, segmented creatures belonging to many different phyla. Their primitive physiology, undulating movements and often slimy exteriors all contribute to their capacity to disturb us. Free-feeding or parasitic, worms have commonly been confused with insect larvae like maggots.

The worm's quiet work of breaking down matter has made it a metaphor for insidious destructiveness. The worm has symbolically been associated with death and decay, the gnawing of corpses and the fear of burial. This sense of horror is captured in the description of hell from the ancient Scandinavian *Edda*, "Dripping poison / Dropped from the roof / The Chamber walls /

Are bodies of worms" (CW 14:482). Yet the particular characteristics of the earthworm that repel many are also the things that make it so valuable to nature. The earthworm's underground tunneling and excretions aerate and condition the soil to optimally support the growth of seed and shoot.

Alchemy associated the worm with the stage of *putrefactio*, evoking the breaking down of dysfunctional attitudes that were "overripe" in order to prepare the individual's psychic ground for organic renewal. In a number of creation myths, new life arises from the worms that feed on the corpse of a primordial being (DoS, 1129). Similarly, in the myth of the phoenix, what first emerges from the ashes is a tiny worm, suggesting the "despised thing" that is paradoxically the source of the personality's luminous potential (CW 14:472).

Because of its humbleness, literally its "closeness to the earth" and its physical vulnerability, humans project on the earthworm lowliness and even groveling, "spineless" behavior. The Hebrew psalmist, feeling forsaken by God, cries out, "But I am a worm and no man; a reproach of men and despised of the people" (Psalm, 22:6). Yet, for Christianity, the same verse is a reference to "the chosen one," the Messiah. Like the fly and the grain of sand, the earthworm is an image of the *punctum*, the tiniest point where eternity resides (Raine, 1968, 2:165). Insignificant and godlike, "earthworm" is the mutability of earth and all that is of earth. Beauty, life itself, psyche, are subject to change, decay and disintegration. But just as the earth's worm can regenerate its lost segments into new, so does the worm's earth become the ground of rebirth.

Raine, Kathleen. *Blake and Antiquity.* Princeton, NJ, 1977.
Raine, Kathleen. *Blake and Tradition.* Princeton, NJ, 1968.

This etching with line engraving is from Blake's book *For Children: Gates of Paradise.* Blake instructs the viewer to recognize God in this lowest of creatures" ... for he is become a worm that he may nourish the weak" (Raine, 1977, 72). *The Worm in Her Winding Sheet,* by William Blake, 1793, England.

16 I have said to the Worm, Thou
art my mother & my sister
Publishd by WBlake 17 May 1793

Toad

Matching the quixotic expression of his human companion, a toad, luminous like the moon or like sea phosphorescence, rests on the shoulder of Liu Haichan, whose name means Master Sea Toad. Once the grand councilor for an emperor of China, Liu became an adept at inner alchemy (the circulation of light within) and a hermit, sometimes included among the Eight Immortals (Little, 330). One of his emblems is the toad whose three-leggedness signifies the three phases of the moon. The toad's lunar countenance is carried also in the petals of the flowering and fruiting peach blossom Liu holds in his left hand, and both toad and flower convey longevity, fertility and purity.

Chinese myth portrays the toad as a moon goddess of transformation and immortality. The seated toad resembles the roundness and gravity of the full moon and its large eyes and mottled skin the moon's dark patches. Its nocturnal hunting habits and mild venom have associated it with occult deities and spirits of the night and their aphrodisiac and medicinal decoctions, including ones that relieved labor pains. Bigmouthed, with a tongue attached to the front rather than the back for extension toward insect prey, the toad has been depicted as a devourer, eclipsing the sun as does the dark moon. The Aztec toad goddess Tlaltecuhtli, for example, swallowed the sun in her "maw of the netherworld," the womb of cyclical destruction and rebirth (DeGraaff, 82). Large species of toads eat almost anything, adding rodents and birds to the typical diet of beetles, spiders and ants. The toad has a wide field of vision and a keen sense of direction. Bold in its defenses, it inflates itself and rears up on tiptoe in order to enhance its size, reminiscent of the waxing moon, and toads have butted heads with snakes to drive them away (Caspari, 272). In some other cultures the toad evokes the heaviness, solidity and darkness of earth, earth mother and uterine ground that holds, generates and nurtures life. More comfortable on dry land than its cousin the frog, a toad, when the temperature drops, will burrow into leaves and earth from which its graybrown coloring makes it almost indistinguishable. The toad is more earthbound anyway, since it is able only to hop, not leap like the frog. For western alchemy, the toad is one image of the firm reality to which the volatile things of the spirit (the eagle) must be linked lest they wing away without ever getting incarnated. And in its hiddenness and swallowing aspect, the toad embodies the other side of reality, which is mortality. There are those who perceive the toad as a quintessentially homely, even ugly animal, but to some its bumpy rivulets of skin and soulful eyes are jewel-like, as is its character of wisdom and magic.

Caspari, Elizabeth. *Animal Life in Nature, Myth and Dreams.* Wilmette, IL, 2003.
DeGraaff, Robert M. *The Book of the Toad: A Natural and Magical History of Toad-Human Relations.* Rochester, VT, 1991.
Little, Stephen and Shawn Eichman. *Taoism and the Arts of China.* Chicago and Berkeley, 2000.

The Immortal Liu Haichan touching the foot of a three-legged toad, associated in China with the moon and the yin principle as longevity, wealth and money-making (Cooper, 228). *Haichan*, detail, by Yan-Hui, left hanging scroll of a pair, color on silk, Yuan dynasty (13th–14th century), China.

Frog

So naturalistic is the small blue faience frog from ancient Egypt leaning forward in a balanced squat, its skin moist-looking, its head tilted upward, the protruding eyes focused, that it seems its tongue will suddenly dart out of its wide mouth and pull an insect in, or the long hind legs, in a nimble leap, carry it to another part of the pond. The glass figurine may have been a new year's gift from one friend to another given with wishes for long life and good fortune, or it may have been an amulet. Frogs were sacred to Heqet, goddess of embryonic waters. She was the wife of Khnum, who molded material human life on his potter's wheel. Heqet helped to fashion their forms inside the womb as midwife and protector of the pregnant and newborn. The squatting birth position of a woman, where her legs are widely parted bears a striking resemblance to that of a frog. Figures with a frog's body and a woman's face and genitalia have been found dating to as long ago as 6000 B.C.E., suggesting that the notion of a frog goddess is extremely ancient.

The richness of the frog's symbolism is in this linking to womb, waters, fertility and developing life. Highly dependent on water, frogs absorb it from the environment through their permeable skins. "Singing in the rain," they croak and copulate throughout the mating season; "a brilliant, night-shattering mad opera of the universe" (Kennedy, 174). After the inundation of the Nile, millions of exuberantly singing frogs would appear as if spontaneously generating in the silty mire emblematic of the unformed matter before creation and the interval between death and rebirth. One species of frog that lives in a temperate climate freezes itself "dead" in winter and thaws back to life in the spring (Goodeve, 41). "I am the resurrection" proclaims an inscription on early Christian Coptic oil lamps bearing the image of a frog with a cross on its back (Andrews, 63). Later Christians and others not so beguiled considered the frog's insistent croaking and nocturnal habits evidence of an unclean, unchaste and devilish spirit associated with the witch and aphrodisiac sorcery.

Frogs have to lay their thousands of eggs in water, and the eggs lack shells to prevent water loss. They hatch into tadpoles, which live in the water, undergoing metamorphosis: Larval gills are replaced by air-breathing lungs, the tail is reabsorbed, limbs develop (Uhlenbroek, 46–47). Because of the much longer back legs than the front, the adult frog is often perceived as bearing an endearing resemblance to a miniature human being, or something between the human and the uncanny. In dreams and fairy tales the frog arrives, quite suddenly, out of water somewhere, just as an aspect (often princely) of self-substance emerges from the waters of the unconscious, but is not yet in fully conscious, recognizable form. In many such fairy tales, this fertile little being from the watery regions must be accepted and attended to in its frog form, however unattractive or odd it may seem, and inevitably it transforms into the soulful prince or princess.

In many different cultures, frogs have been seen as bringing the cleansing rains. Native American Haida shamans of the Pacific Northwest were said to acquire their healing powers from frogs (Kennedy, 183). On account of their extremely sensitive skins, permeable to the toxins in an environment, frogs are also the first to let us know when nature is drastically out of balance (one of the reasons why, perhaps, in fairy tales they bring in what's missing). Currently one of the most threatened group of animals on earth, they are an accurate indicator of a traumatized biosphere and of a future that might be woefully absent of their mosquito- and fly-catching, their brilliant colors, their fervent forms of every size and knobby embellishment, and their raucous song of espousal.

Andrews, Carol. *Amulets of Ancient Egypt*. Austin, TX, 1994.
Goodeve, Thyrza Nichols. "Mythic Creatures: Dragons, Unicorns, and Mermaids. Frogs: A Chorus of Colors." *Artseen* (July/August 2007).
Kennedy, Des. *Nature's Outcasts: A New Look at Living Things We Love to Hate*. Pownal, VT, 1993.
McDade, Melissa C. and Neil Schlager. *Grzimek's Animal Life Encyclopedia: Amphibians*, VI. Detroit, MI, 2003.
Uhlenbroek, Charlotte and American Museum of Natural History. *Animal Life*. NY, 2008.
Wyman, Leland Clifton and Berard Haile. *Beautyway: A Navaho Ceremonial*. NY, 1957.

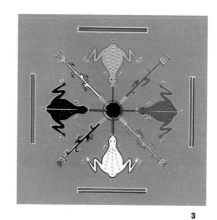

1. Embodiment of proliferating life, the frog was sacred to the Egyptian water goddess Heqet. The image of the larval form of the frog, the tadpole, was the hieroglyph meaning "one hundred thousand," similarly conveying abundance. Faience, reign of Amenhotep III (ca. 1390–53 B.C.E.), Egypt.

2. As if in deep meditation, the frog remains motionless for hours while still aware of the world around it. *Meditating Frog*, by Zen master Sengai, ink on paper, 18th century, Japan.

3. In Navajo myth frogs were originally people who planted corn (shown in the quadrants) to feed themselves (Wyman, 193). *Frogs at the Waterhole*, a copy of a Navajo ceremonial sandpainting in which frogs mark the directions of the compass, by Wilito Wilson, 1942, United States.

Turtle / Tortoise

Hundreds of millions of years are carried in the archaic form of a Galapagos turtle, the dinosaur thickness of its bowed legs and wizened skin, the rugged, intricately patterned shell, able to bear 200 times its body weight and as heavy and beautiful as stone. Dignified of bearing, paced and deliberate in its rituals, a tortoise may live to an exceptionally old age. Myths and legends depict it as earth's immense antiquity, solidity, continuity and wisdom, or in its domelike upper, and flattened lower shell, comprising the totality of the cosmos. Even the rhythms that underlie the musical nature of the universe mythically originate with the tortoise, since the Greek god Hermes fashioned the first of all lyres from a tortoise shell, and gave it as a gift to golden Apollo.

Like other turtles, tortoises have been around at least 225 million years. A marine turtle that eons ago learned to live on land, the tortoise traded fins for short legs, and the plates or scales on its back gradually increased in size as a defense and grew together to form a hard, domed shell into which it can effectively retract its head, legs and tail from predators (Young, 8). The tortoise uses its bladder as a reservoir for storing water, and by digging a trench inside the earth escapes the blazing desert sun or hibernates for months below the frost zone, oblivious to the ravages of cold and storm (Young, 14). Folk etymology attributes the names "turtle" and "tortoise" to the Latin *Tarturus*, or underworld, conveying the sense of psyche's subterranean ground supporting all the ascending levels of life and consciousness. An Iroquois myth tells how primordial water birds bring up bits of earth and place it on the back of a tortoise floating on the surface of the sea, and the earth grows and expands with the tortoise as the supporting force of its center (von Franz, 37). In Hinduism, the world rests on the back of a tortoise as the chthonic form of the creator and preserver Vishnu. Kashyapa, Old Tortoise Man, elder of elders, is lord and progenitor of all creatures (Zimmer, 5). China imagines the tortoise as mother of all the animals (Jung, 78) while in alchemy it signifies the primal matter to which the things of the spirit must be linked if they are to become incarnate. The image of the tortoise in its shell underground has a more sinister aspect: the hard, dark carapace of nature under which, in seasons of darkness and drought, life, growth, potential, creativity and hope seem imprisoned. Yet the tortoise also evokes those meditative or introverted states in which, as process or protection, libido is withdrawn from the world in order to devote its heat or moisture to the interior.

Aquatic or semiaquatic species of turtles remained at home in the sea, or in rivers, lakes, ponds or marshes. The marine turtle has a leathery, flat shell and wide, smooth flippers, which it moves like wings, allowing this agile, powerful swimmer to dive to great depths where it can remain for up to half an hour without surfacing for air. The turtle's capacity to descend into the dark, cold depths of ocean inspired ambivalent fantasies of being carried and mediated by this spirit of the sea to nethermost regions of mystery and regeneration, and also the terrifying prospect of being snapped up and pulled down into a devouring abyss of death or madness. Yet, on the huge shell of a sea turtle are carried, in Goethe's *Faust*, the little Cabiri, creative spirits and protectors of those who journey over the deep (II:2, 231, fn 2.). Male sea turtles never leave the sea, but females must in order to breed. They swim vast distances and unerringly find their way to the beaches where they can deposit their eggs in synchronization with the moon and tides, and a clutch can number as many as 200. Some turtles have found a solution to the predatory birds that wait for the hatchlings; countless females lay their eggs on the same beach at the same time, so that all the hatchlings emerge together and run for the sea in such multitudes as to confuse the birds and insure that most of the new turtles survive. Mythic lore has associated the turtle especially with the fertility and sageness of the great goddess, the moist, shadowy, lunar qualities of yin, and the primeval waters in which all things have their (supported) beginning.

Goethe, Johann Wolfgang von. *Faust: A Tragedy: Interpretive Notes, Contexts, Modern Criticism.* NY, 2001.

Jung, C. G. and Karl Kerényi. *Essays on a Science of Mythology.* NY, 1949.

Laughton, Timothy. *The Maya: Life, Myth, and Art.* NY, 1998.

Young, Peter. *Tortoise.* London, 2003.

Zimmer, Heinrich Robert. *Myths and Symbols in Indian Art and Civilisation.* Princeton, NJ, 1972.

1. The giant Galapagos tortoise provides us with an intimate feeling for the antiquity of the earth, and might itself surpass the age of 175. Photograph by Guido Rossi.

2. Vishnu, in his form as Kurma, a tortoise, holds up Mt. Mandara, the "paddle" for churning the Milky Ocean in order to extract the divine elixir of life. Gouache on paper, 18th century, India.

3. The Maya maize god escapes a funereal underworld when released from the carapace of a turtle with the help of his sons, the Hero Twins (Laughton, 97). The deity's rebirth symbolizes fresh corn sprouting from the dark earth. Ceramic, Late Classic Maya, 680–750 B.C.E.

Snake

There is no such thing as a singing snake. The sound of a hiss or rattle, notice to the unwary wanderer of the snake's presence and sometimes an ominous warning, strikes terror in many. Emily Dickinson expresses this fear eloquently:

> *But never met this Fellow*
> *Attended, or alone*
> *Without a tighter breathing*
> *And Zero at the Bone—*
> **A Narrow Fellow in the Grass**

Arms raised in awe and holding a stick or wand in his left hand, an ithyphallic male faces an enormous, sinuous snake, a serpentine line of eternally undulating cosmic energy. The erect phallus of the human mirrors the raised head of the snake—a numinous encounter with (or magical invocation of) the serpent as emblematic, primordial life force. We can almost sense the quickening of the man's breath, the "zero at the bone," as he meets this elemental spirit. Emerging with S-shaped movements from primal waters, spiraling or coiling up on itself (like the DNA in every living cell) (Narby, 60ff), striking out at lightning speed or deftly slithering away on its limbless belly and vanishing in a flash, the snake enters our mythologies as cosmic creator, progenitor, destroyer and sacred being.

How eerie a snake can seem. It smells with its flickering forked tongue. It hears through its skin and is particularly sensitive to low-frequency vibrations and tremblings of the earth, linking it with secret, subterranean, oracular mysteries of knowledge. The snake sees through lidless eyes covered by a transparent scale, never blinking, evoking a supernatural vigilance, like the cobra protectively encircling the brow of the Egyptian pharaoh, or the eye of the unconscious psyche that sees where consciousness cannot, or the mesmerizing eye of the legendary hero, or the unflinching eye of death. When the snake withdraws to shed its skin, signifying renewal, rebirth and immortality, the eye scale becomes milky, sometimes taking on an ethereal, misty blue cast as though the serpent is entering a meditative state and has access to wisdom beyond our ken. Heat-sensitive infrared radar allows some species of snake to track their prey unerringly in the dark. The jaw of the python unhinges, allowing it to ingest whole prey many times its size. These uncanny feats associate the snake with the relentless, death-dealing aspect of nature or with the instinctual psyche and "its sudden and unexpected manifestations, its painful and dangerous interventions in our affairs and its frightening effects" (CW 5:580). The snake's gender is determined by the temperature of its surroundings during gestation. Males have split hemipenes, a forked penis, and females have a split clitoris, relating these parts to the tongue and the imagery of paradisal seduction and the creative word as well as sexuality. Its unmistakable phallic shape combined with its habit of copulating for days or even weeks, either with one snake or with fifty, has identified the snake with active, penetrating phal-

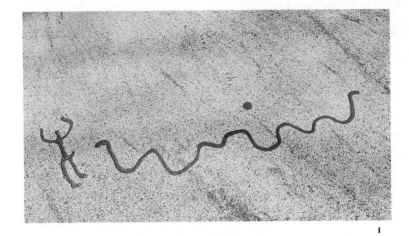

1. Man and Serpent. Rock carving, Bronze Age,
1300–500 B.C.E., Sweden.

2. Two men and a woman in an attitude of reverence
before an immense serpent, probably Zeus Meilichios,
the Attic deity who was the chthonic counterpart to the
Olympian god. Marble relief, ca. 400–375 B.C.E.,
Greece.

lic energy, fertility and potency (Stutesman, 11ff); "the wild braid of creation" poet Stanley Kunitz called an entwined pair of snakes hanging from a tree in his garden ("The Snakes of September," 221).

Valiant, epiphanic and terrifying, snakes flare up out of the earth or from under leaf litter or rocks or the dark waters of rivers or the darkness of the psyche. The underworld realm of the dead that snakes mythically inhabit is also the fecund ground from which new life emerges, a place of healing, initiation and revelation, dominion of the ancient Great Goddess. The snake is the theriomorphic form of countless deities including Zeus, Apollo, Persephone, Hades, Isis, Kali and Shiva. In the Tantric traditions of India, the feminine cosmic energy of the kundalini lies asleep like a coiled serpent at the base of the spine. Awakened in processes of yogic meditation, this serpent, Shakti, rises through the subtle body, the two nerve currents flowing on either side of the spinal cord, passes through and opens the energy centers, or chakras, to unite in the crown with Shiva in ecstasy and transcendence (ARAS, 1:351–2).

Sacred also to Asclepius, the divine healer of ancient Greece, the snake embodied the demon or "genius" of the physician and was often depicted entwined around his staff. A patient came to the sanctuary seeking "incubation" in the innermost chamber, where, in sleep, one's innermost depths could "accomplish their curative potentialities" in the form of a dream. The analogue of this was the actual visitation of the sanctuary snake, emblem of "a hidden force, dark and cold, but at the same time warm and radiant that stirs beneath the surface of the waking world and accomplishes the miracle of cure" (Kerényi, 34). Particular species of snake are now known to physically possess extraordinary medicinal properties even in their venom, which can also sicken or kill. The snake has thus always conveyed power over life and death, making it, everywhere, a form of the ancestral spirit, guide to the Land of the Dead and mediator of hidden processes of transformation and return.

Gimbutas, Marija. *The Language of the Goddess.* SF. 1989.
Kerényi, Karl. *Asklepios.* NY, 1959.
Kunitz, Stanley and Genine Lentine. *The Wild Braid: A Poet Reflects on a Century in the Garden.* NY, 2005.
Narby, Jeremy. *The Cosmic Serpent.* NY, 1999.
Stutesman, Drake. *Snake.* London, 2005.

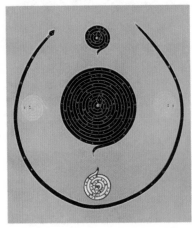

3

4

5

3. Within the boundaries set by the guardian snake of the mandala, coiled, three-dimensional-looking serpents are restfully contained. *Coiled Mountain*, a copy of a sandpainting of the Navajo Shooting Chant, one of the most important healing ceremonies, by Franc J. Newcomb, United States.

4. In the foreground, a young man being treated by a physician, perhaps in a dream; in the background, an image of the innermost sanctuary where the physician's

chthonic counterpart, the sanctuary snake, visits and licks the sleeping patient. Stone relief, ca. 380–370 B.C.E., Greece.

5. A pair of intertwined serpents, in the form of a yantra, or sacred diagram, probably from the Tantric tradition of India. The snakes represent the sun and moon, components of the subtle body, spiraling around the world axis. Gouache on paper, 18th century C.E., Punjab, India.

Cobra

The sovereign "eye" of the high god of ancient Egypt, the heat or "anger" of the blazing sun, was depicted as a cobra of intense, fixating vision and burning venom. Called "the rising goddess," or "the fiery goddess," a gilded, rearing cobra encircled the brow of pharaohs, a sign of their sanctified kingship and the god's power to strike in all his manifestations, including that of the crowned king. Found among the dazzling treasures of the pharaoh Tutankhamun's tomb was a pendant known as "the great enchantress," a goddess with a woman's head and a cobra's body nursing the young king, and a golden cobra Netjer-Ankh, "the living god," which served Tutankhamun as a protective device.

Who would think of going up against a cobra? With a deep, hair-raising hiss, it warns by rearing a third of its body and by means of specialized muscles in the neck and ribs flares its patterned hood. Egyptian cobras deliver their extremely toxic venom in a deadly bite. When they need to flee, spitting cobras are able to also spray their poison (usually nonfatal) through a tiny opening in the front fangs. They aim at the eyes and will hit the mark from four to eight feet away, blinding the aggressor (Mayell, 2005). The king cobra, the largest venomous snake in the world, can grow to a length of more than 18 feet, so that the third it rears may be taller than a man, though it actually prefers to avoid confrontation (San Diego Zoo). The Indian cobra has a pair of circular marks on the back of its hood that resemble eye spectacles, visible when it rears, "balancing to and fro exactly as a dandelion tuft balances in the wind" (Kipling, 305). A hatchling cobra is able to spread its hood, strike and spit from the day it is born (San Diego Zoo).

Easily mythologized as the image of annihilation—terrifying, mesmerizing, self-sufficient, lightning quick—the cobra is nevertheless as much an emblem of deathlessness as it is of death, for time winds into eternity, which once again gives birth to time. India depicts the cobra as a form of the *naga*, the serpent residue of the destroyed cosmos at the end of an age and also the stuff of a new beginning. This cobra is mythically the most ancient of serpents, Vritra, who coils around the mountain that guards eternity before creation. Likewise, the cobra encircles the waist, wreathes or is the sacred thread, amulet or ornament of divine Rudra-Shiva, Kali and Ganesha, creator-destroyers who hold the universe within their substance. The cobra spreads its protective hood above the sacred lingam, or over the infinity of the meditating Shiva, Brahma and Buddha. It signifies the inscrutable ferocity and fascination of the "wild god of the world" and his appalling sensuality and asceticism. Cobralike, Rudra flashes consuming fire from his third eye, and death from his striking arrows, but is also healer and protector from the poisonous fangs of existence; "The serpents, in the polyvalence of their meaning, cling to Rudra, the healer, who knows how to control them; they shed their skins as symbols of renewal" (Kramrisch, 429).

For the Egyptians, too, the cobra represented not only the inevitability of death, but its antidote in the mysteries of rebirth and the establishment of order, to which the cobra aligned itself as a killer of rodents. The cobra as Apophis serpent was the enveloping chaos that each night threatened to swallow the sun, and at the same time its opposite, "the power of life to defend itself inviolate against dissolution and the spirits of non-being" and a warding off of the enemies of king, kingdom and cosmos (Clark, 94). In our psychological age, the Apophis materializes in the coils of suffocating anxiety, the ego's intimation of its tenuous mastery. Fear of the unconscious, observed Jung, will result in its instinctive forces, if persistently disregarded, rising up in opposition, changing into a venomous serpent; and the more negative the attitude the more dangerous the unconscious becomes (CW 5:450). And if it is the cobra, will give fair warning.

Clark, Robert Thomas Rundle. *Myth and Symbol in Ancient Egypt.* London, 1959.
Kipling, Rudyard. "Rikki-Tikki-Tavi." *Kipling: A Selection of His Stories and Poems.* Ed. John Beecroft. Garden City, NY, 1956.
Kramrisch, Stella. *The Presence of Siva.* Princeton, NJ, 1981.
Mayell, Hillary. "Cobras Spit Venom at Eyes with Nearly Perfect Aim." *National Geographic News* (February 10, 2005) http://news.nationalgeographic.com/news/2005/02/0210_050210_cobra.html.
San Diego Zoo. *Animalbytes.* www.sandiegozoo.org/animalbytes/t-cobra.html.

Unearthed in 1923 in the newly opened tomb of
Tutankhamun, Netjer-Ankh, a fiery cobra of gilded
wood with eyes of translucent quartz, protects the
deceased pharaoh in the underworld. The height of the
reared front of the snake is 22¼ inches, true to life.
Ca. 1332–23 B.C.E., Egypt.

Crocodile

*Beware of pointing the way to him who may be
looking for me until we reach Crocodile Town,
that lies at the edge of the Marshes ...*
Delta Cycle (Clark, 194)

Facing each other in an identical posture of respect are a divine crocodile and an Egyptian noblewoman whose safe passage to the afterlife is conveyed by the peaceful ambience in which they meet. Here, the chthonic deity Geb, familiarly depicted as a human figure incarnating the earth's green, sprouting vegetation, takes the form of the crocodile at the riverbank of the underworld, linking the notion of renewal with the energies of dissolution. In another of its symbolized aspects, a crocodile, still as a log, with only its eyes and nostrils breaking the surface, can suddenly explode from the water, propelled by its powerful musculature and tail, and snatch, drown and dismember its prey, a terrifying image of the submerged potential for sudden devouring and disintegration, particularly at the brink of things. In ancient Egypt, the divine crocodile Sobek was revered and propitiated especially at the dangerous riverbanks, the places where the marshes concealed animals, or where difficult currents heightened the risk of shipwreck (Quirke, 73–75). He was mothered by the more aggressive waters of the goddess Neith, the primeval watery round. Sobek evokes chaotic pulling under, taking back, rending apart, but in his aspect as "the Rager" personifies the pharaoh's capacity to obliterate enemies of the kingdom (Hart, 201). At the ceremony the Weighing of the Heart of the dead, the monster Ammit, a combination of crocodile, lion and hippopotamus, swallows the heart that has failed to achieve the psychic balance pleasing to Maat, the underlying order of the universe that brings together chaos and cosmos in right proportion.

In a literal sense, crocodiles, including the alligators, caimans and gharials, are living dinosaurs, the last representatives of the group of archosaurian reptiles that once dominated the earth (*Enc. Brit.* 16:388). Crocodiles have been around for 230 million years, and may even have been the image of the leviathan in the Biblical story of Job: "Who can penetrate its double coat of mail? Who can open the doors of its face? There is terror all around its teeth" (Job 41:13–15). An opportunistic carnivorous feeder that thrives on small live prey as well as carrion, the crocodile wears a heavy armor of bony plates with protrusions containing nerve fibers so sensitive that even the slightest movement of a fish or a heron in the water is detected. By mouth and habitat a threshold creature often associated with the swamping, imprisoning primal muck of the Great Mother, the crocodile also shares in her paradox as the vital mire of beginning and becoming. Related to the flying pterosaurians as well as lizards, crocodiles build nests and lay eggs, which the female broods, and the hatchlings make birdlike cheeping sounds. In the same maw that can sever and crush, the mother gently rolls unhatched eggs between her tongue and palate to allow her young to break out, then gently carries them in her mouth down to the water from her onshore nest and will fiercely protect them from predators for a year or more (Angier, F4).

The regulation of the crocodile's body temperature is determined by that of the ambient environment. Thus, lord of the fertile waters from which it hunts and mates, the crocodile emerges from the water to nest and bask, and like the sun shaking off the dark wetness of night, embodies the rebirth of the light and the ascendance and ferocity of the solar. Or, in the reverse, an Australian myth imagines Crocodile as an ancestor who survived the flames of a hut fire by plunging into the waters of the deep, and now carries its burnt-bark hut on its mighty tail (Morphy, 176).

Still invoked as a protective presence and initiatory spirit of psyche's archaic, fertile and perilous processes, the crocodile itself is in danger from being overhunted for its skin, losing its native habitat to human encroachment and getting displaced to untenable environments in the exotic pet trade. That full-grown crocodilians, like other large reptiles, are turning up in the backyards and front porches of coastal housing developments gives pause. At the heart of our relation to nature, is there an ominous imbalance to which nature is responding with its ancient corrective?

Angier, Natalie. "Not Just Another Pretty Face."
The New York Times (October 26, 2004).
Clark, Robert Thomas Rundle. *Myth and Symbol
in Ancient Egypt*. London, 1959.
Hart, George. *A Dictionary of Egyptian Gods
and Goddesses*. London and Boston, 1986.
Morphy, Howard. *Ancestral Connections: Art and
an Aboriginal System of Knowledge*. Chicago, 1991.
Quirke, Stephen. *Ancient Egyptian Religion*.
NY, 1992.

1. At the entrance to the underworld, the noblewoman Here-Ubekhet prostrates herself before the deity Geb, in the form of a crocodile, and drinks from the waters that will unite her with the gods and assure safe passage to the afterlife. Painting on papyrus, ca. 1000 B.C.E., Egypt (ARAS, 2AP.004).

2. The "crocodile smile." A crocodile opens its jaws to help cool and heat its body, and because it requires less muscle power to open than to close them. The huge saltwater crocodile of Australia has a bite-force stronger than any other living animal, yet its counterpart at the Nile allows the African plover to step inside its open mouth and safely feast on the parasites that attach themselves to the crocodile's gums and palate.

Fish

The Swiss artist Paul Klee, who guarded his own inner life, felt a protective kinship with his luminous *Goldfish*. Seemingly startled by our intrusion into its hidden seabed, Klee's fish stares at us warily, as if we coveted its gold-embroidered scales, while its timid companions dart away to hide among the aquatic weeds. Actually a fisherman himself at one time, Klee abandoned his fishing rod after interior misgivings guided him to give up his predations and, instead, to wait patiently at the shore of consciousness for fishlike revelations. Capable of drifting into artistic reverie as if gently slipping underwater, Klee noted in his diary that his paintings were like dreams flowing beneath the waking surface of life, dreams that could be plucked out like his gilded fish, glistening with the incandescence of a primeval world. "A kind of stillness glows toward the bottom," Klee writes in a poem, "From the uncertain a something shines not from here, not from me, but from God" (Klee, 312).

Moderns rarely locate God at the bottom of the sea, but the ancients instinctively did. Streaming nets of writhing eels, inexplicable seahorses, birdlike stingrays, glowing lantern fish and electric fish charged with 300 volts fostered a sense of religious wonder. To ancient poets the sea intimated the great mother as matrix of being, whose son-lovers were fish. To understand water, they hinted, one must study the fishes; to understand a fish, one must study water. From a fish's streamlined contours, slime-coated scales and cold-blooded sinuosity one can in fact intuit the nature of its all-surrounding element, water. From our modern psychological viewpoint, a fish is the living content of its fluid medium, the unconscious psyche, the invisible nature of which is made tangible through its symbolic images, which with patience can be drawn up to instruct us in its secrets.

As the world's earliest vertebrate, fish appeared in the ocean half a billion years ago; when landlocked within evaporating seas, they survived by evolving into four-legged amphibians and reptiles, the ancestors of our own warm-blooded species. Fish easily symbolize our lost participation in their archaic, unconscious world, one that fairy tales often portray as a lost golden ring that a fish returns as a gift in its mouth or inside

its stomach. The fish's primal innocence suggested to Christians that it had been spared during the Great Flood. They portrayed those awaiting baptism as fish swimming around Christ's ankles, and Christ himself either as a fish (*ichthys*) or as a "fisher of men" (an epithet shared not only with Saint Peter, but with the Buddha and Orpheus). After early Christians were baptized in a font known as a piscina (fishpond), they occasionally donned fish costumes to signify their reclaimed nature (Eisler, 72–3).

The Christian *pisciculi* ("little fish") can be seen as semiconscious souls in need of a *cura animarum* ("cure of souls") due to a one-sided development of consciousness portrayed in such ways as the wounded and barren fisher-king in the Grail legend, and as the zodiacal symbol, Pisces. An astrological depiction of two fish swimming in opposite directions in its constellation of stars, Pisces is traditionally ascribed to the past 2,000-year age in which one fish swims vertically toward the spirit and the other horizontally toward matter. These two fish ably characterize our present split between the unconscious and conscious psyche, a split equally serious whether one sees it as spirit lacking embodiment or matter lacking spirituality. Alchemy reflected a promising development within our age to reunite these divergent fish, and like Klee, pointed to the image of the fish eye, a symbol of a still unrealized archetype of the Self that comprehends spirituality and matter in a single mercurial nature (CW 9ii:103ff). While most fish "sleep" in the sense of spending some time in an energy-saving state, they do not close their eyes, which are lidless, suggesting the all-seeing eye of God (CW 14:45). Alchemists imagined the fish eyes as shining sparks within primal matter that intimate ever-aware multiple luminosities within the dark waters of psyche, a marvel we may behold ourselves by gazing into the unsleeping eye of Klee's *Goldfish*.

Eisler, Robert. *Orpheus the Fisher*. London, 1921.

Martin, Stephen A. *The "Young" Paul Klee*. Unpublished thesis. Zurich, 1980.

Klee, Paul. *The Diaries of Paul Klee: 1898–1918*. Berkeley, 1964.

Verdi, Richard. *Klee and Nature*. NY, 1985.

1

2

3

1. Paul Klee painted *The Goldfish* after a visit to the
Naples Aquarium, where he beheld an otherworldly fish
gliding toward him, bathed in ghostly light, purer in its
ultramarine world than any creature he could imagine
in Paradise. Oil and watercolor on cardboard, 1925,
Germany.

2. Ganga, the goddess of the sacred Ganges, sits upon
her fish mount as she prepares to descend from the

river's Himalayan source to the vast plains of India.
Opaque watercolor and gold on paper, ca. 1815 C.E.,
Himachal Pradesh, India.

3. The mythic dimension of fishing; the sea from which
the fishers draw their catch abounds with marine
creatures of supernatural size. Fishing is depicted here
as a heroic contest with nature. Roman mosaic, 3rd
century C.E., Tunisia.

Whale

Whale is the spirit of the Deep, the creature that mirrors its incomparable size and swallow—as ocean, unconscious, memory, night, womb and underworld. Sometimes, glimpsing in the distance white pearls of briny exhalation, the breaching head and dark flukes, we have thought of the cosmos (be)coming out of the primeval waters. In a constellation of silvery stars in the dark abyss of space we have discerned the swimming shape of Cetus, the Whale, whose astral eye feels like the eye of an intelligence within ourselves that is more than the ego.

Our ancestors called the whale "dragon," "sea-monster" and giant "fish," projections that carried innate fears of how easily existence and reason are swallowed. In the myth of the Night Sea Journey, the solar hero trapped in the "belly of the whale" harrows hell and overcomes death by finding a way out. With the help of a god of culture he is disgorged, or cuts away the heart of the whale or sets a fire, images of human consciousness severing connection with the matrix of nature. Tikigaq Inuit whalers portrayed the soul of primal woman and primal whale as one; her igloo was a "whale," its passage of reassembled whalebones an "area of birth, death, danger and initiation"; in some stories "woman and whale are one and the same victim" (Lowenstein, 39). When the men hunted the bowhead whale, their wives remained inert and passive in a form of shamanic male-female magic with which to lure the whale into passively surrendering itself so that its death might reanimate igloo, community and landscape (Lowenstein, 37ff). The Hebrew "Leviathan" at first meant an attribute of the Creator and may have literally referred to the great crocodile, but the word symbolically came to represent an adversary of immense proportions and devilish ferocity, an image adopted and amplified by whalers: " ... all the subtle demonisms of life and thought; all evil, to crazy Ahab, were visibly personified ... in Moby Dick. He piled upon the whale's white hump the sum of all the general rage and hate felt by his whole race from Adam down ... ," wrote Melville in his famous novel.

What did we slay when we massacred the whale in the frenzied conflict between our terror of and attraction to the dark void of our unknown being? The blue whale can grow to 100 feet long and weigh 200 tons, the largest creature ever to have existed; the sperm whale has the biggest brain on earth. The toothed whales—sperm, orca and dolphin—as well as the huge, more solitary toothless whales that filter tiny crustaceans through sievelike flexible plates of baleen, possess brain structures similar to our own and evolved spindle cells, neurons that link to functions like self-awareness, compassion and linguistic expression perhaps 15 million years earlier than humans (Siebert, 7–8). The rhythms and refrains of the humpback whale, with a million information-carrying changes of frequency, represent the single most elaborate vocal display in the natural world (Saunders, 132). Oriented to the magnetic fields of earth by particles of iron oxide in their brains, whales travel vast distances to breeding grounds, court, copulate, give birth and suckle their infants undersea; recognize themselves and their companions, invent tools, play, learn, teach and help one another, grieve and dream.

In the protected birthing grounds of Baha's Laguna San Ignacio, gray whales, some with old harpoon scars, have recently been coming (sometimes with their young) alongside the boats of whale-watchers. "The baby gray glided up to the boat's edge and then the whole of his long, hornbill-shaped head was rising up and out of the water directly beside me, a huge ovoid eye slowly opening to take me in. I'd never felt so beheld in my life," says a writer (Siebert, 4). Does the whale sense that the human ego, so long detached, yearns to reclaim its ancient mother? Then we might sound our depths in the spirit of the consummate Sounder, and let imagination assume buoyant bulk and insulating blubber, store oxygen in muscles, slow the heart rate to meet the pressure of the bottom and descend from our illuminated surfaces to the ocean floor of primordial activity, lighting the darkness with explosions of sonar, navigating the passages of ocean canyons, the debris of submerged volcanoes, and all the pulsing, appetitive forms stirring and swelling the sea within.

Lowenstein, Tom. *Ancient Land: Sacred Whale; The Inuit Hunt and its Rituals*. NY, 1999.
Saunders, N. J. *Animal Spirits*. Boston, 1995.
Siebert, Charles. "Watching Whales Watching Us." *The New York Times Magazine* (July 12, 2009).

1. Humpback whale (*Megaptera novaeangliae*) breaching near whale-watching boat, Southeast Alaska, United States.

2. Over his head and back, a Kwakwaka'wakw (Kwakiutl) shaman wore this articulated whale mask, with moving flukes and pectoral fins, during winter ceremonial dances to encourage the whale spirit to bestow long life and prosperity (Saunders, 132). Baleen whale mask, 19th century, British Columbia.

Dolphin

Quintessential saviors of the shipwrecked and drowning, dolphins are the nimble "sea-people" (Bacchylides of Ceos) who can be relied upon to buoy us up and carry us back to shore, protect us from marine marauders, keep us company in our lone passages through treacherous channels and, if we're lucky, escort our ships out of trouble before they founder in the first place. The reasons for wild dolphins' long history of beneficence toward us is a mystery, but their role as our rescuers from imminent submergence is attested in outer reality as well as in our dreams. There is something suggestive in the similarity of the Greek words for dolphin (*delphis*) and for womb or uterus (*delphys*). Just as the goddess Aphrodite is born from the surf and is often shown on the back of a dolphin, the streamlined creatures who are so conspicuously attuned with their marine world are emissaries of the womb of ocean, where all life arose and to which the whales, rare among mammals, returned to live after having spent some evolutionary time as earth dwellers.

Dolphins are smaller, toothed whales, like porpoises, pilot whales and the killer whales or Orcas. Famous for their acrobatic leaps and spins, and their elegant arcing motion over the surface of the sea, dolphins have a mysterious capacity to lift people, not only physically but emotionally. It is not just that (some) dolphins have a perpetual "smile" formed by the curve of their beaklike snout, or that, with or without our projections, they clearly delight in their watery medium, their social life, their hunting skills and freedom. Or that their coloration—spotted, or criss-crossed or uniform or countershaded—blends with light near the surface of the water, or with the darkness where the light fades out deeper down, camouflaging them or breaking up their lineaments, so that they seem to become water, light, or shadow. There is something else, more subtle, a way that dolphins seem to tune into our energy fields, to scan us from the inside out, discerning what is right or amiss with us, and even alter our "frequency" to restore the balance.

Though we have idealized dolphins in near angelic terms, they are also aggressive and tough, can turn themselves into effective missiles, smashing the gills of sharks or teaching a human trainer in a captive dolphin show what's what. Orcas are known as the "wolves of the sea" because of their cooperative hunting techniques, their preying on other mammals, including whales, their close-knit pods and their marine version of group "howling." Dolphins are sometimes tricksterish, and they don't mind playing a practical joke or two on humans swimming around them, though it is all in fun. The most famous myth of the dolphin is that of the rescue of the Greek poet Arion. The crew of his ship, bent on stealing his treasure, insisted he kill himself or jump in the sea. The master lyrist asked if he might sing a final song. His singing was so beautiful that when he jumped into the sea, the listening dolphins caught him up and brought him to shore. Dolphins have been known to burst into a fanfare of whistles on the occasion of reciprocal human help in rescuing dolphins. It's nice to think that "music" binds the two species.

A naked young man, his hair blowing in the wind, rides
on the back of a dolphin. Silver coin, 5th century
B.C.E., Greece.

Octopus

Appearing in the depths like an amorphous phantasm, all head and feet (cephalopod), the eight-tentacled sea mollusk octopus has received humanity's deepest imaginings about the mysteries of dissolution and regeneration. An elusive mandala-in-motion, the image of octopus brings together extremely negative and positive attributes, a paradox that expresses the hidden connections between chaos, emptiness and the ordering capacity of the psyche.

Symbolically, octopus often belongs to the fateful round of the Great Mother. Like other archetypal "monsters of the deep," ancient mariners seem to have considered it one of the most grotesque and frightening terrors of the sea, capable of pulling whole ships down to a watery grave. A recurring motif in decorative Minoan and Greek art, was the octopus also a model for the many-headed Hydra, or for the paralyzing Medusa—to whose big, round head, staring eyes and tentacles of hair the octopus bears an uncanny resemblance? The Greeks dubbed both the octopus and their great sea-hero Odysseus "polumetis" (loosely translated as "wisdom" and "magical cunning"). Perhaps the sea monsters who menaced Odysseus and his crew personified the terrifying undifferentiated aspects of the classical Greek psyche, understood as dangerous, capable of sucking in and emptying out, until mastered by the creative and clever Odysseus? Related to the astrological sign of Cancer, the moon, the summer solstice and the depths, the octopus resembles its cousins—the whirlpool, the spider's web, the wheel and the spiral—in representing both the mystic center, and the unfolding of creation through dissolution.

Highly intelligent, challenging even the higher vertebrates, octopuses lost the invertebrate's need for a shell as a result of their extreme agility and mobility. They range in size from a tiny 2 inches to an arm span of 33 feet; if a tentacle is wounded or breaks off, another will grow in its place. Their sense of touch is exquisite, and the eyes of an octopus very closely resemble the highly developed human eye. Octopuses can "read" letterlike shapes. An extreme shape shifter, elastic and liquid, octopus changes colors freely with its emotional state or to blend in with the environment for protection—from grey to red, pink, white, blue and greens. When approached peacefully, underwater divers experience strong empathic connections with the octopus. When threatened, it withdraws backward, obscuring itself and disappearing in a dark inky cloud.

Having often succumbed to a case of maligned and mistaken identity, the image of the octopus symbolically depicts an encounter with the depths of the psyche, in all its ambivalence, suffering and seeming chaos. Both remote from, and yet similar to humanity, having a special affinity with the fluidity and dynamics of psychological process, the "soft alien intelligence" (De Luca Comandini, 91) of the octopus symbolizes totality-in-motion, activating the imagination, which in turn promises new possibilities of awareness. The healing potential of this deep awareness, which instinctively seeks possible connections and opens questions, is expressed in charming folk wisdom: In rural areas of Japan, where the octopus was credited with human emotions and desires, talismanic images of a seven-tentacled octopus were employed in the fight against whooping cough. When a cure came about, the eighth leg was drawn in, and the image of the octopus set afloat on the currents of a strong river.

Baird, Merrily C. *Symbols of Japan*. NY, 2001.

Caspari, Elizabeth. *Animal Life in Nature, Myth and Dreams*. Wilmette, IL, 2003.

De Luca Comandini, Federico. "The Octopus: Metamorphosis of an Imaginal Animal." *Spring* (1988).

Saunders, Nicholas. *Animal Spirits*. NY, 1995.

1. Painted vessel decorated with octopus. Terra-cotta, Late Minoan, ca. 1500 B.C.E., Palaikastro, Crete.

2. A ceremonial octopus mask with movable tentacles and hinged jaws manipulated by cords. By a Kwakwaka'wakw (Kwakiutl) artist, wood, ca. 19th century, British Columbia.

Crab

Short summer night—
flowing among the rushes,
bubbles from crabs.
Buson

Fancifully depicted against a dark, wavy background suggesting the sea, a crab holds a full moon in its claws as if the moon were a mirror in which the crab sees its reflection. Or is the crab about to eat the moon, initiating the phase of its waning? Even the spiral tail the artist has given the crab replicates the lunar imagery, evoking the cosmic rhythms of the moon to which the crab is synchronized.

Crab and moon are counterparts in this fifteenth-century Armenian manuscript illustration, and in symbolism all over the world. The moon rises in the night sky; the crab in its white shell rises from watery depths. The moon waxes and wanes, cycling from dark to new to full and back. The crab also advances and retreats, oriented by lunar tides, and, depending on the species, in its movement typically scuttles sideways, or backward and forward. Moon and crab are associated with mother, night, water, feeling, and also with the changeable, moody and inconstant.

True crabs, as distinct from species of hermit and terrestrial crabs, are mostly marine crustaceans (though some live in freshwater), and they inhabit every sea in the world. The crab has a hard shell that protects its internal organs, and, unlike the crab of the drawing, five, not six, pairs of jointed legs. Only the front pair, or chelipeds, are provided with large claws, enabling the crab to grasp food quickly and bring it to its mouth, and to defend itself against attackers. Crabs have been endowed with highly effective physical sensors. Bristles and hairs on the body and especially on the walking legs are touch receptors alerting the animal to hard surfaces as well as water currents. Compound eyes with thousands of optical units protrude from the front of the shell on short stalks, see very well and can be lowered into sockets for protection. Crabs hear and make species-unique sounds. Their antennae have smell detectors that help in mating, finding food and escaping predators.

Imagination has amplified the observed qualities of the crab. We picture the big claws and wide mouth devouring even the moon as Time. Myths of giant crabs dragging ships down to their doom reflect the catastrophic reversals and profound regressions that seem to reach, crablike, out of the void to pull us under. Yet regression is not essentially negative. The dark of the moon brings renewal, and the dark of the unconscious, psychic rebirth in the womb of the sea-mother. The tough carapace of the crab has been a metaphor of defensiveness that belies inherent insecurity, but it can also represent the firm circumscribing of boundaries to safeguard what's violable.

In western astrology the crab is the emblem of the fourth sign of the zodiac, Cancer, in which the moon is exalted. The time of the Crab is the summer solstice when the sun reaches its highest northern point and then retreats backward toward the ecliptic as the days get shorter. On the one hand, this is the defeat of the solar hero, and likewise the crabbing pull on the life that has reached its zenith. On the other hand, it is the Crab's balancing of progression and regression, and the dissolution of solar avidity in crescent darkness.

In the zodiacal chart the crab rules the fourth house, that of the home environment. Here, the crab denotes attunement to the natural rhythms and cycles in which we "home" ourselves, and evokes the instinct for refuge and recuperation, how we go back each day to where we dwell. The sign of the crab hovers over needful aloneness as well as convivial sharing, and the memory of resources. But it also evokes fierce self-protection from perceived intrusion, and an unconscious "watchfulness" and deep sensitivity that anticipate the shifting currents and hard surfaces of experience.

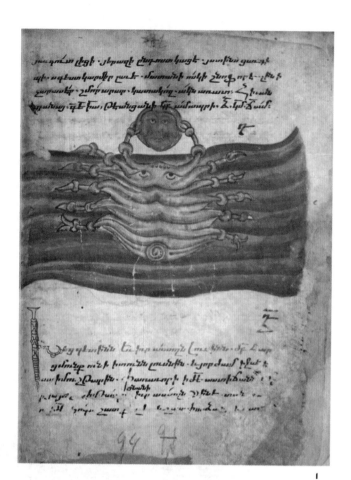

1

2

1. Biologically and mythically linked in rhythm and nature, crab and moon seem to watch each other. Manuscript, 15th century, Armenia.

2. Backward or sideways, crabs scuttle, a motion that likens them to the changeable quality of moon and sea. In China a feast of crabs celebrated the fullness of the harvest moon in autumn. *Five Crabs*, by Qi Baishi, ink drawing on a hanging scroll, 1950, China.

Shell

From time immemorial, we have held conch shells to our ears to hear the surflike sound—the eternal tides of life that engrave their markings upon us. The human ear resembles a shell, gathering vibrations of air in its outer cavity called the "conch," and directing them through the winding passages of its shell-like inner ear as sound, symbolically evoking an interior listening. "He who has ears to hear let him hear," said Jesus of the hidden meaning of his parables. Images of the Buddha with elongated ears suggest that listening with the inner ear includes keeping silent, meditating on what has been said and opening ourselves to the resonance of the source.

We have also raised the conch shell to our lips, trumpeting as gods of the sea might have, for the sound of the conch was said to lull the tumultuous waves of the sea. That the conch comes from the deep associates it with the underworld. The Mayan deity Quetzalcoatl mythically descends to Mictlan, the abode of the skeletons, as a dead conch that has fallen silent, so that worms may bore into him in order that he come to life again inside (Moctezuma, 138–9).

Shells are mysterious sea treasure, in beautiful shapes, sometimes symmetrical, often ridged and whorled, reflecting stages of growth. The recesses of a shell are reminiscent of the sacred spiral, labyrinth and

1. As if incised by the waters of eternity—a stone conch shell. Aztec, ca. 1486–1502, Templo Mayor, Mexico.

2. *The Birth of Venus,* by Odilon Redon, oil on canvas, ca. 1912, France.

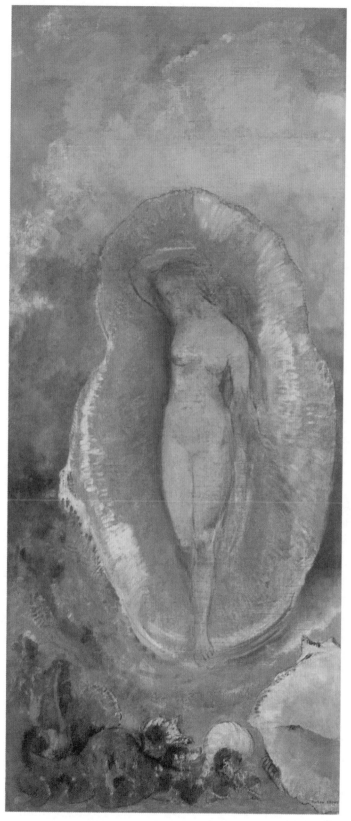

center. The intimation of marine life is also allusion to the hidden life of our interior world, sometimes surfacing, leaving its evidence in consciousness, sometimes not. A shell is an exoskeleton serving to protect the vulnerable creature that dwells within. But shells are also delicate, easily broken, not the tough carapace of defensiveness. We speak of coming out of, or going into, one's "shell," suggesting gradual, tenuous exposure to the world, or of retreat from it, in privacy, refuge or withdrawal.

The shape and depth of some shells, the lush pink of their coloring, brings to mind the female vulva, associating the shell with the allure and mystery of the feminine, and with incarnation and fertility. Aphrodite, the Greek goddess of love (to the Romans Venus), ma-

terializing out of the ocean's foam, is borne ashore on a seashell. In his celebrated painting, Odilon Redon depicts the open, vulva-shaped shell, its soft opalescence infusing the sky and the goddess lying, yet standing, asleep and yet waking, as in a vision. We adorn ourselves with shells, remembering the goddess and her beauty, her seductions. The shell and its evocation of the uterine salt-sea, the moon, tidal ebb and flow, imparts a sense of birth and rebirth; early Christian art made the empty shell an image of the soul's departure to immortality.

Moctezuma, Eduardo Matos and Michel Zabé. *Treasures of the Great Temple.* La Jolla, CA, 1990.

3

3. Figure, perhaps a deity, emerging from a shell, showing whorls of growth. Effigy vase, painted terra-cotta, Mayan, 600–800 C.E.

4. Shell-shaped and oversized, the ear of the Grand Buddha suggests wise listening. Detail from a carved cliff face, 713 C.E., Leshan, China.

4

Clam/Oyster

When we look into Georgia O'Keeffe's slightly open clamshell we see the chaste beauty of the primordial shell of existence, a reminder of the sea's salty, elemental first fruits of life. Or again, the slightly open shell imparts subtle, feeling-toned qualities: the receptive, intimate, sensual and shy. It speaks of the creative and the gestative, the introverted containment that fosters the essence of a life. At the particular angle that O'Keeffe has depicted the shell, the vulvalike shape of its opening is apparent and erotic, intimating the watery power of yin, and the virginal that yields to insemination. Bivalve, or double-shelled mollusks like the clam and its cousin the oyster, close their shells for self-protection by means of special muscles that clamp the shell tight shut, hiding every bit of flesh and confounding their natural predators. When the shell closes, a protein rubber called *abductin* stretches or compresses, depending on the species, and by doing so stores mechanical energy, enabling the shell to open when the creature needs to breathe or eat. Tiny cilia, or hairlike structures, propel water into the animal and help filter out the minute particles of food it feeds on (Denny, 72). How long ago did we begin to harvest the clam and oyster—moist, slippery, edible and aphrodisiac—and claim for ourselves the oyster's immaculate pearl? Their rough or round shells invite our projections of prying open the world with our consciousness—"the world is my oyster"—extracting its treasures, assimilating its good. The shell opening of itself evokes the wonders of revelation and incarnation. And the closing of the shell: hidden process, reticence and isolation; "clamming up," a drawing of boundaries, a gathering in; being "secret, and self-contained, and solitary as an oyster" (Dickens, "A Christmas Carol," 260).

Denny, Mark. "Features—the Rewards of Chance." *Natural History* (May 2001).
Dickens, Charles. *A Christmas Carol, and Other Haunting Tales.* NY, 1998.

Slightly Open Clam Shell, by Georgia O'Keeffe, pastel on cardboard, 1926, United States.

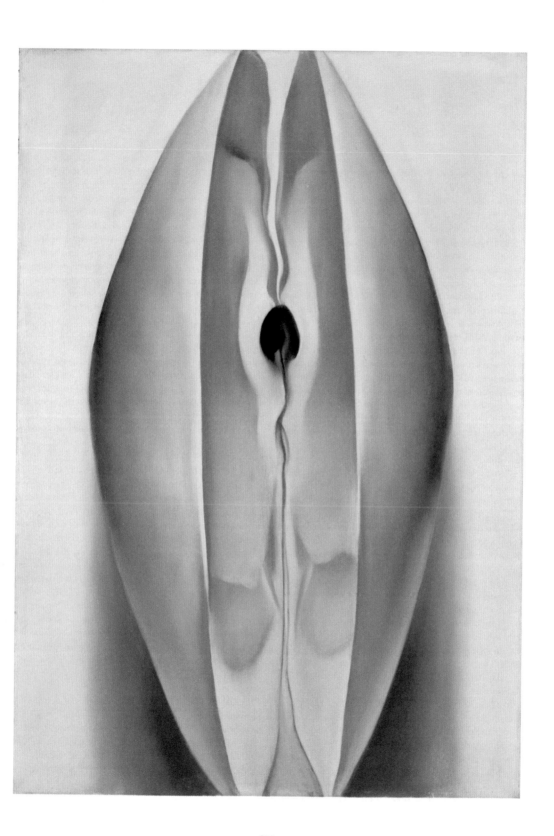

Scorpion

Since the earliest times the scorpion has embodied the bridging of fluid depths and firmer ground. Older than the dinosaur or the spider, and physically almost unchanged to the present day, the scorpion was resident in the warm Silurian environment of 400 million years ago. The oldest fossil arachnid is a scorpion. A descendant of what was likely a marine animal, it was able, because of its horny exoskeleton, to make the evolutionary shift from sea-dweller to land creature without fatal water loss.

The scorpion's uniqueness lends itself to majestic and dire projections. Incarnate in the scorpion mother that takes her newborns onto her back and carries them until their first molting, the Egyptian scorpion goddess Selket represents the capacity to survive transitions of a fundamental nature. Selket is known as the one who gives us breath; hers is the gift of immortality. The bronze from the New Kingdom era portrays her as a sphinx, in Egypt a figure of benevolence and protection. Her tail, ending in a venomous stinger, is raised, warding off enemies. Her human arms are outstretched to receive the setting sun, mediating its descent into the underworld from which it will emerge, renewed, at daybreak. With her companion goddesses Isis, Nephthys and Neith, Selket guards the coffins of the dead and the canopic jars containing their vital organs.

Yet, Selket is also associated with the scorching sun and the desolation of the wilderness. The Mayans depicted their god of war and the Christians their devil as having the fiery scorpion tail, evoking in the one case physical death, and in the other, spiritual demise, treachery and subversions of consciousness into occult domains of fascination and compulsion. Shakespeare's Macbeth, poisoned by murderous ambitions, laments, "Oh, full of scorpions is my mind, dear wife" (3.2.43). The legendary scorpion of Mali asserts "I am a creature which brings death to whatever touches me" (DoS, 835).

By nature, scorpions are solitaries shunning light. Adapted to rain forests, deserts and urban settings, they burrow in the sand and wait at the opening for prey and secrete themselves in crevices of buildings or under rocks, debris or bark. They are nocturnal hunters and fierce opponents, their mouthparts flanked by a pair of pedipalps ending in pincers, with which the scorpion seizes and tears apart or crushes its prey, and then sucks the body juices. Weapon of last resort, at the tip of the scorpion's segmented tail are two venom glands opening into a sting and surrounded by muscles; contracting, they force poison into the victim.

But if the scorpion represents death's sting, it also attests to the endless renewal embedded in endless death, making it one of the most ancient emblems of the Great Mother and her round. Like psyche transforming its primal matter—poison, antidote and panacea, self-destroying and self-healing—the scorpion mythically "slays itself with its own dart" and brings itself back to life again. Alchemy's opus engages scorpion energies in its "rending" and "recollection." Seals and cylinders, some of extraordinary antiquity, portray scorpions protecting the birthing Great Mother of Ur, or surrounding the rosette of Sumerian Inanna. The Indian scorpion goddess Chamunda is one of the seven companions of demon-slaying Durga. Seven helpful scorpions accompany Isis in her search for the scattered parts of Osiris. Greek Artemis was imagined to have set a scorpion in eternal pursuit of the arrogant and seductive Orion.

The mating dance of scorpions beautifully evokes the proximity of fruitfulness and annihilation associated with the Great Mother's creature. The male holds the female with pedipalps or pincers, their tails erect and sometimes intertwined. Leading or forcing her backward and sideways, he positions her so that she takes his sperm packet into her genital orifice; the mating act completed, she often devours him. Equally dichotomous, Scorpio, the eighth sign of the zodiac, is dominant as autumn moves into winter. Assigned to the element water, fixed, ruled by Mars and identified with the genitals, Scorpio is associated with the wine harvest and the final distillation of the grapes, with forces of fertility, intoxication, power, sexuality, degradation and transmutation. Seeking the darkness, the scorpion signifies the penetration of psyche's Plutonian depths, full of riches and dangers. Alchemy projected on the scorpion the baleful sting of latent, unearthed desires resulting in hellish dramas of self-loss as well as processes of integration.

All this is essential to the mysteries of death and rebirth, letting go and becoming, for which the scorpion is anciently famous. Thus, the alchemists are said to have celebrated "scorpion time," when base metals turned into gold. And if, in reality, the scorpion concerns itself little with such an endeavor, symbolically there is no other so well-equipped to mother it.

1

2

1. Threshold guardian, the scorpion goddess Selket is endowed with the venomous sting of death and also its antidote. Consistent with this ancient portrayal, the scorpion's toxin, affecting the nervous system, is now recognized as also having healing properties. Bronze, 1539–1295 B.C.E., Egypt.

2. Scorpio, the eighth sign of the zodiac, inhabits the fathomless night sky as the scorpion once did the sea, a creature able to negotiate the energies of disparate dimensions in the service of quintessential transformation. Manuscript illustration, 18th century, United States.

Spider

If anything perfectly embodies nature's arsenical magic, it is a spider sitting at the center of its newly spun orb, waiting for prey. Under the coppery "spider moon" of late summer, or wet with dew at first light, ubiquitous, sometimes tattered webs shimmer on trees, shrubs, caves, rafters, crypts and blades of grass. All the momentary, intricate matrices of visible and invisible life are conjured in the spider and its captivating web.

Believed to be 300 million years old, spider embodies the ancient soul of existence reverberating with creativity and predation. Nature has made the spider a most uncanny being, a trapeze artist dangling from its silken thread and reeling itself up again, a spinner of virtuosity and a cunning hunter with a wide net. The artist Louise Bourgeois compared the spider to her mother, "a tapestry woman," and called it "subtle, indispensable, neat and useful" (Sischy).

Biologically an arthropod, like the scorpion, the spider has only an abdomen and a cephalothorax to which are attached eight legs and usually eight eyes, and mouth parts including jaws and a pair of fangs with pinchers for grabbing, stunning and holding the spider's victims. Nineteenth-century Japanese artists caricatured these traits, rendering the spider a version of the monstrous *tsuchigumo*, the gigantic earth spiders of early myth evoking nature's fateful consuming of fragile life and primal consciousness.

Spiders produce silk and their dazzling string-game magic is another solution to the problem of catching insect prey. Some species make ensnaring bolas or guyed trapdoors; males, females and newborns of other species spin webs in the form of orbs, funnels, sheets and ladders. Separate glands in the spider's abdomen produce different kinds of silk for different purposes including sacs for the spider's eggs or the trussing of large or poisonous prey. Young spiders hang on single strands of silk as the wind "balloons" them for miles. The spider reels silk from spinnerets in its rear end, in the process coating some threads with a sticky substance. An orb-making spider works its lines into a scaffold of spokes, around them safely weaves its deadlier, sticky spirals and reabsorbs torn or superfluous threads (Dawkins, 38ff).

Like a latticed window whose center looks on eternity, the spider's web intimates the instinctual patterns of behavior out of which psyche's dark and luminous agency is felt, mythically identifying the spider with divine creator, culture-hero, trickster and benefactor. In a Hopi creation story, Grandmother Spider lives in an underground kiva that mimics the trap-door spider's dwelling and recalls the Hopi's emergence from the "underworld." A Navajo tale describes Spider-Woman lodging behind the hero's ear, whispering secret advice and mediating his transit between physical and subtle dimensions, all within life's encompassing web. The spider Anasi of West African tradition is an unscrupulous buffoon but also a trickster that outwits larger creatures such as the elephant or lion (Courlander, 135). The spider's ever-renewed, wheel-like web has been compared to the radiating sun. In Hindu Myth the veiled *Maya* is spinning the world of illusion out of her substance and drawing it back in.

Concealing and revealing, medieval spiders protectively veil the Holy Family and the prophet Muhammad from their enemies, while E. B. White's miraculous Charlotte writes on her web in order to save a pig. The action hero Spider Man exploits the versatile spinnerets embedded in his human hands. Ovid associated the spider with the grace and ruthlessness of Athena, primordial moon goddess and, later, Olympian embodiment of the virtues of world-creating consciousness and its crafts. Arachne, from whom spiders get the name arachnid, was a maiden so fabulously gifted at spinning that she boastfully challenged Athena to a contest and their brilliant tapestries were judged equal. The goddess so persecuted Arachne that she hanged herself; out of pity, Athena transformed her into a spider.

Indeed, the spider embodies the Terrible Mother's gruesome mysteries of death and dissolution, the superb tension and recoil of her web proof against the struggles of the prey. Images of her terrors are reinforced by the spider's killing or paralyzing its victims with venom from hollow fangs, and the female's habitual devouring of the typically smaller male after mating. Evoking our own propitiatory hedges against fate, the male may offer a diversionary, silken parcel of food, pluck a thread in courtship twangs that may delay her need to feed or tie her up in silk long enough to mate and flee (Dawkins, 38ff).

Spider suggests fetter, noose and the "devil's snare." We speak of webs of conspiracy and lies. The cyberspace "Web" tantalizes us into endless sites of data, relationship, illusion and perversion. Our hapless entanglements in misunderstood circumstances are

1

2

1. The artist welcomed spiders into her home as small heroines who rid her of mosquitoes, and also admired the "connection-making" conveyed by their webs. *Spider*, by Louise Bourgeois, watercolor and ink on paper, 1994. Private collection, Photo: Beth Philipps.

2. The Japanese artist Hokusai (1760–1849) portrays the spider as a devouring monster whose immense size is suggested by the small human skulls hoarded under its belly. Spider venom, however, is rarely effective on human beings. Book illustration.

the stuff of the "spider." So are fatal attractions of sex or ambition, and dismembering enmeshments of identity. The defenses of the self can draw the traumatized soul into webs of encapsulating, schizoid fantasy and addiction. There is the lonely weaving of solitary, autistic worlds and the sinister bindings of madness.

Unapologetic, spider is nature, forever spinning its strings of vitality and devastation. The very matter of psyche can become a mercurial web of stuckness. Equally, the signal threads of dream and vision vibrate with meanings that can be grasped, feeding the soul and its transformations. Says the noble and predatory Charlotte, "A spider has to pick up a living somehow or other, and I happen to be a trapper."

Courlander, Harold. *A Treasury of African Folklore.* NY, 1996.

Dawkins, Richard. *Climbing Mount Improbable.* NY, 1996.

Sischy, Ingrid. "Interview with Artist Louise Bourgeois, October, 1997." Procuniar Workshop. http://www.procuniarworkshop.com/home/index/article/26.html

White, E. B. *Charlotte's Web.* NY, 1952.

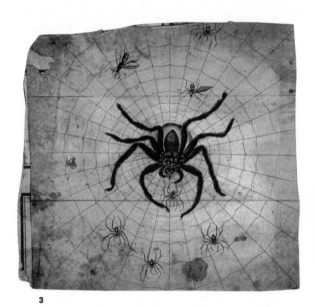

3

4

3. A tattoo design of a spider being at the center of her web. Painting by George Burchett, ink and watercolor, early 20th century, England.

4. This engraved gorget amulet depicts a spider ringed by a mandalalike web—spider as creator, protector and ancestral guide. Shell, North American Woodland period (1300–1500 C.E.).

5

5. Here, the French Symbolist painter Odilon Redon suggests the tricksterish aspect of spider. Redon's compatriot, Joris-Karl Huysmans, described this drawing as a "terrifying spider, its human face lodged in the middle of its body" in his novel *A Rebours. The Smiling Spider*, charcoal on paper, 1881.

Cockroach

Three hundred million years ago, in the dense, humid forests of the Carboniferous era, 800 species of cockroach thrived. The earliest ancestor of the cockroach may be as much as 450 million years old. The cockroach existed when the landmass of the earth divided into continents, and eventually its populations spread to all of them, even the Arctic. It survived the ice ages and thaws that extinguished whole groups of other life. It witnessed the evolutionary emergence and advance of Homo sapiens, which it exploited for its survival.

We can be unnerved by the sight of a single cockroach, all the more so an infestation producing a heaving sea of scuttling movement, trembling antennae and the strong odor of animal pheromones, as if the force of the tide might pull us back into chaos. The cockroach represents an elemental power *profoundly* archaic, entrenched and adaptable, which slipping through the walls of our defenses, proliferates in the chthonic and the primal, eludes our calculated attempts at repression and, disappearing from one room of our existence, inevitably reappears in another. Its segmented body (head, thorax and abdomen) is ovoid and flattened, giving it the ability to move through narrow cracks. Many cockroach species have two pairs of wings for flight that can also fold against the body, allowing it to get into or out of tight places. Functioning as an early warning system that supports amazingly speedy escapes, its six flexible, jointed legs have tiny, hairlike bristles sensitive to minute changes in the environment, as well as ears on each knee joint so attuned to the earth's internal vibrations they can pick up an earthquake registering .07 on the Richter scale (Copeland, 28–9). Its grasshopper-like mouthparts make it possible for the cockroach to eat almost anything, including fingernail clippings, human hair, glue, paint, soap and paper (Embery, 51–2).

Our fantasies and projections have demonized the cockroach, associating it with nuisance, disorder, poverty and plagues. Western patriarchal tradition consigns it mythically to the bowels of the earth, to nature's "criminal element" or the Great Mother's feared "underside" of witchcraft and destruction. Yet, there are many who recognize in the cockroach a venerable elder linked to primordial beginnings, a household protective spirit insuring good fortune, a mentor of heroic adaptation to everything from merely onerous circumstances to nuclear upheaval, an emblem of continuity and an embodiment of the tough, survivalist spirit of the immigrant and outsider that societies have treated like vermin. Entomologists and others have noted the intelligence of the cockroach, its responsive companionship and its magical beauty and variety: the hissing Madagascar cockroach, for instance, the golden cockroach, the pale green Cuban cockroach, the Central and South American "Cockroach of the Divine Face," with its 12-inch wingspan. Folk tales of Africa and the Caribbean have portrayed the cockroach as the cunning hero of the downtrodden that outsmarts the great; recent novels make it a spokesperson for the ethics of ecofeminism.

Worldwide, the cockroach has long been a source of human food and medicines for a host of human ailments, suggesting a secret affinity with us. Though it may carry the contaminants of an environment, like inner-city tenements where it was once thought to be the source of high levels of asthma, the cockroach itself has not been found to cause disease. But the cockroach is not a creature of the light, which perhaps fosters our aversion to it. It prefers to be hidden, prefers darkness and the earth, like the leaf-litter of forests, where it is ecologically essential to the production of compost. The cockroach is also a frequent and familiar visitor to the netherworld of our dreams, often signaling by its antique presence the activation of an old complex or an impending regression. And who better than this ancient one to pick up the energies brewing at psyche's archetypal core?

Copeland, Marion. *Cockroach*. London, 2003.
Embery, Joan. *Joan Embery's Collection of Amazing Animal Facts*. NY, 1983.

1

2

1. Ancient cockroach trapped in amber, approximately 90 million years old, New Mexico, United States.

2. *Hanging, Execution Series,* by Catherine Chalmers, gelatin silver print, 2000, United States.

Ant

Unnoticed by a family engrossed in chores, half a dozen ants circle about in small, tireless activity, mirrored by their human counterparts. Since antiquity, writers and artists such as this unknown Spanish painter have chosen the ant to convey the virtue of industry at physical, psychological and spiritual levels. In the Greek myth of Psyche and Eros, for example, tiny ants embody the methodical, discriminating work that helps Psyche, or soul, to sort the seeds of her relationship to the divine principle of Love (von Franz, 116ff). In the illuminated manuscript here, the Christian Holy Family is shown humbly employed, despite the splendid garments that signify their spiritual majesty. The Virgin Mary embroiders while her husband Joseph planes wood. Rendered much smaller to emphasize his youth, Jesus plays with a tethered bird. The unusual addition of ants at his feet suggests that just as the almost invisible activity of the ants has purpose, so does the child's apparently idle play anticipate his future task of freeing souls from their tethers.

Found throughout nature, ants belong to rigorously organized communities dominated by an egg-laying queen; a solitary ant would soon perish. An ant will pass its existence feeding another with nectar, or serve in ant nurseries or as a fearless soldier, weaver or carpenter, or even as a "dairy-ant" herding honey-dew aphids (Chinery, 16). Such diligence inspired Solomon in the Hebrew scriptures to urge, "Go to the ant, thou sluggard, and consider her ways and get wisdom." In the Christian story, Christ's upbringing in a carpenter's shop served to sanctify labor. Industriousness became prognostic of the soul's redemption, a doctrine that would shape the Protestant work ethic and revolutionize Reformation Europe. LaFontaine retold Aesop's fable of the hard-working ant laying up food for winter.

At the same time, ants can infest households and their stings containing tissue-dissolving enzymes are fiery. African driver ants are swarm raiders, their intensely sharp mandibles capable of stripping even large vertebrates to the bone (Morris, n.p.). Depending on the species, ant nests can extend above the earth in microclimatically regulated dirt mounds or hills of multiple chambers and galleries (Hölldobler, 373), or several feet underground. Tall anthills, often inhabited by snakes, are adorned by religious devotees with flowers and incense. The anthill leading into the earth mythically associates the ant with the ambivalent magic of psyche's instinctual, subterranean forces that wreak chaos as well as support order. The American Navajos counted the ant among its "intangible evils," and their healing ritual, "the Red Antway," counteracted infestations of all "unappeasable animals" (Reichard, 326) that, like the ant, were denizens of the Navajo underworld (Wyman, 20). Nevertheless, it was the mythic Ant People who first built houses and the anthill was taken as the prototype of the Navajo's dome-shaped hogan with its rooftop opening (ibid., 90). In the Navajo hero-quest, it is the ant that helpfully gathers up the fragments of the hero's shattered body (ibid., 23), suggesting psyche's capacity to bit by bit bring dissociated substance into cohesion.

Hinduism has found in the ant an emblem of the smallness of a unit of time—the endless succession of universes, ambitions, countless rebirths, Indras and Brahmas, saviors and gods (Zimmer, 3ff). The swarming anthill recalls the milling crowds of a modern metropolis, especially if viewed from mountaintop or skyscraper, putting all vanities in perspective. Yet the ant is also sacred, evoking subtle realities easily dismissed, but charged with potency: "Nothing could be more dangerous and delicate than an anthill. It is the earth's ear. It is the place where the leftovers of sacrifices are left. It is the home of the snake. It is the threshold of the world below the earth" (Calasso, 207).

Calasso, Roberto. *Ka*. NY, 1998.
Chinery, Michael. Ed. *The Kingfisher Encyclopedia of Animals*. NY, 1992.
Hölldobler, Bert and Edward O. Wilson. *The Ants*. Cambridge, MA, 1990.
Morris, Dale. "Army Ants." *BBC Wildlife Magazine* (December 2002).
Reichard, Gladys. A. *Navaho Religion: A Study of Symbolism*. NY, 1963.
von Franz, Marie-Louise. *The Golden Ass of Apuleius*. Boston, 1992.
Wyman, Leland. *The Red Antway of the Navaho*. Santa Fe, NM, 1965.
Zimmer, Heinrich. *Myths and Symbols in Indian Art and Civilisation*. NY, 1946.

1. Tiny ants crawl at the feet of the Holy Family. Illuminated manuscript, 1461–1500 C.E., Spain.

2. Devotees adorn the sacred anthills of India, in which snakes may take up residence. Ant nests can extend above and below the earth.

Honeybee

Honey-making is a world-creating art, essentially an alchemical "warmth process" initiating somewhere deep within the interaction of sun and flower, where nectar and pollen form, and carried forward by the sun-loving bee, who collects and consumes it, digesting and metabolizing it through her body, thickening it with the fanning of her wings into its highest consummation. To the ancient Egyptians, among the first to raise bees, the honeybee was the creature that transformed the warmth of the sun's rays into golden sweetness. In Hinduism, deities Indra, Krishna and Vishnu are called "the nectar-born" and the sound of the rising Kundalini serpent, awakened from its coiled state, is compared to the humming of bees.

Yet the honeybee is most often associated with the great mother goddess, since the queen bee, created by feeding an ordinary larva only on "royal jelly," a glandular substance, dominates honeybee society. Her chemical, aromatic pheromones, spread by contact with the worker bees give a hive its distinctive identity (Hubbell, 20). Numbers of drones mate with a queen in flight, dooming them; the rush of air opens the male's abdomen to release his organ, which, once it has entered the queen's vulva and ejected his sperm, is left "dangling from the queen like a trophy" (Longgood, 117). The one and only mating flight of a virgin queen provides her with all the sperm she can store, and then she lives her life in the darkness of the hive, laying up to 2,000 eggs a day, her sole function (ibid, 77). Worker bees, who cannot produce fertilized eggs because their ovaries are atrophied, feed and care for the nursery and the queen, build the comb, feed the drones, defend the hive and forage for nectar and pollen. A mere pound of honey requires about 25,000 trips between flower and hive, and contains the essence of over two million flowers. Ancient honey gatherers disregarded the perils of cliffside and stinging bees to reach into a black, womb-like crevice and remove the ovoid honey-dripping hive. The new honey was tested by holding a handful; a tingling on the palm meant it was toxic and if ingested, could lead to madness or death. Our ancestors linked bees and caves to the nurturance of ambivalent infant gods like Zeus and Dionysus, or to the earth's creation, or imagined a universal hive at the center of the earth or envisioned a great beehive issuing forth gods, goddesses and humans (Andrews, 116).

Comb-building bees fill themselves with honey, hook together in long loops and, through a sort of meditative process, turn the honey into wax, which they secrete from their abdomens and sculpt into clusters of intricate hexagonal cells so ingeniously formed that a mere one and a half ounces of wax can hold four pounds of honey, the container and contained being different manifestations of one and the same substance (Burroughs, 4). Thus Christ was referred to as "honey in the rock," for soul is to body as honey is to comb – divine essence housed in an earthly vessel (Psalm 81:16).

It is no wonder that the intricacy of the honeycomb and the honey-making process was identified

1. Hieroglyph of "Nesu-bit" ("He of the sedge and the bee"), King of Egypt. The bee was the symbol of the Lower Kingdom of Egypt and the sedge of Upper Egypt. Here both are united in a heraldic image (Wilkinson, 115). Stone, 12th dynasty.

2. Honey-gatherer, cave painting from the La Araña Caves, 6,000 to 8,000 years old, Spain.

with divine wisdom, or that the sweet touch of its golden product on the tongue could inspire poetry, truth-saying and prophecy, and even propitiate gods and monsters. In mystery religions, purifying honey was poured over the hands and tongues of initiates and, associated with immortality by its sunlike color, given at later stages of initiation as a sign of new life and transformation, while the ultimate goal of Sufi mystics was to melt like honey into the godhead. Equated with the bliss of nirvana in India and heavenly pleasures in China, honey also connotes earthly sexual pleasure. Early poets describe eros as "bitter honey" because Cupid, the honey thief, stings with arrows that intoxicate with both the sweetness and the agony of sexual desire, the ultimate outcome of which is new life. Alchemically, sticky honey, like desire, binds and coag-

ulates, and is said to initiate the incarnation of spirit, while Paracelsus identifies the "prime matter" of the honeybee's gold as "the sweetness of the earth which resides in naturally growing things" (Edinger, 87, 90).

Andrews, Tamra. *Nectar & Ambrosia: An Encyclopedia of Food in World Mythology.* Santa Barbara, CA, 2000.
Burroughs, John. *Locusts and Wild Honey.* Boston and NY, 1907.
Conversations with Håkan Rönnberg, beekeeper.
Edinger, Edward F. *Anatomy of the Psyche.* La Salle, IL, 1985.
Hubbell, Susan. *A Book of Bees.* NY, 1988.
Longgood, William. *The Queen Must Die.* NY, 1985.

3. *The Beekeepers*, detail, by Pieter Bruegel the Elder (ca. 1525–69), pen and brown ink on paper, the Netherlands.

4. Swarming bees attack honey thieves in a Dictaen cave sacred to the Great Mother. Black figures on a Greek amphora, ca. 550 B.C.E., Vulci, Italy.

Fly/Mosquito

Where there are people
There are flies, and also
There are Buddhas
Issa

Mosquito at my ear—
Does it think
I'm deaf?
Issa

Most of us perceive the fly merely as a nuisance and pest, maddening beast and human with its relentless buzzing or whining, its biting and deft avoidance of the flyswatter. The ancient Egyptians, however, found in the fly's tormenting persistence a model of the skilled soldier on the attack and even created a military badge of honor as a golden, lifelike rendering of the fly (Andrews, 62).

True flies, of the order *Diptera*, are insects having only two wings. Among the more than 85,000 species are the houseflies, horse flies, black flies, sand flies, mosquitoes and tsetse flies familiar and oppressive to us. We forget that flies are beneficial scavengers, predators and parasites of insect pests, pollinate plants and destroy noxious weeds. The Inuit carried amulets of flies, perceiving the fly to be invulnerable because it was so hard to catch. Like Sila, the spirit who controlled the capricious weather, flies were "masters of the air" with equally unpredictable moods (Seidelman, 25, 36). Among the Tlingit, the mosquito's characteristic sucking of blood corresponded to the shaman's capacity to "suck out" sickness or evil from his patients emphasized by the wearing of a fierce-looking, red-lipped ritual mosquito mask, the pointed proboscis carved to resemble a long beak (Wardwell, 101).

In general, flies are less identified with spirits of the air and gifts of healing than with earthliness at its most graphic as disease, death, offal and putrefaction. Females of many species, like the mosquito and horse fly, use their piercing mandibles to suck blood necessary for egg production and houseflies and robber flies have a proboscis with small teeth for tearing the skin around sores and wounds to increase the flow. Houseflies travel from feces to human food, transferring infective organisms. (*Enc. Brit.* 21:667–8). Maggots, the larvae of flies, eat decaying organic matter; how fat they are and the state of pupal cases left behind when they turn into flies help forensic scientists to determine how long a body has been decomposing (Osborne, 105ff). In the Northwest Coast regions familiar to the Tlingit, as well as in very temperate lands, mosquitoes occur in stupendous, devouring hordes, associating them with cannibals and ogres from whose ashes they are imagined to have originated.

The habits of survival which converge with their role in the lethal transmission of disease have mythically made the fly a creature of the diabolical and its possession: "The evil spirit lies like a fly at the door of the human heart," says the Talmud (ERE, 2:299). The Baal-Zebub, Lord of the Flies, a Philistine deity, became in the Christian scriptures a synonym for Satan. Medieval demonologies depicted Satan as a fly with death's heads on its wings. In Persian myth, the enemy of deified Light assumes the form of a fly (Biedermann, 138). While the angelically beautiful butterfly signifies the soul transcending the body at death, the fly recalls our reduction to carcasses: "A fly buzzed when I died," begins a poem by Emily Dickinson. Alchemically, the fly would be an aspect of the *nigredo*, linked with the stuff of pestilence, disorder and filth, with the "buzzing" in one's head around putrid, long-repressed matter. Yet, consistent with the discipline of the adept and perhaps the Egyptian warrior, the fly teaches us not to evade this mortifying mess, but to engage it frontally and make it fruitful.

Andrews, Carol. *Amulets of Ancient Egypt.* Austin, TX, 1994.
Biedermann, Hans. *Dictionary of Symbolism.* NY, 1994.
Osborne, Lawrence. "Dead Men Talking." *The New York Times Magazine* (December 3, 2000).
Seidelman, Harold. *The Inuit Imagination.* NY, 1994.
Wardwell, Allen. *Tangible Visions.* NY, 1996.

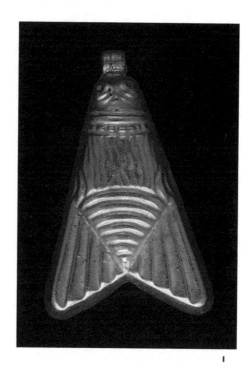

1. Fly as military zeal: Golden ornaments such as this one from the 18th dynasty were awarded to skilled soldiers in ancient Egypt. Ca. 1540–1295 B.C.E.

2. Fly as devil: Wings emblazoned with death's heads, Satan is depicted as a lethal fly (Gettings, 52). Wood engraving from Collin de Plancy's *Dictionaire Infernal*, 1863, France.

3. Mosquito mask of a Tlingit shaman. It was found in his grave house. Wood, ca. 1830–50, Alaska.

Butterfly / Moth

Kneeling before one another a young man and woman kiss, as a magically large butterfly hovers above the blossoming flowers, a reminder of erotic release and the imbibing of the sweet nectar of first love. From ancient times the butterfly, *psyche*, has signified not only the mystery of physical metamorphoses, but also the loveliest transmutations of the soul.

There are more than a hundred thousand known species of butterflies and moths, insects that have two sets of scaly, often vividly colored wings, slender bodies and sensitive antennae. Auditory organs between the thorax and abdomen detect the ultrasonic echo-locating signals of a primary predator of these delicate beings, the bat. Moths are millions of years older than butterflies, more subdued in coloring and mostly nocturnal, navigating by moon or stars. Butterflies are diurnal creatures, navigating by the sun.

All over the world the gossamer beauty of the butterfly, its winged nature and breathtaking release from a pupal cocoon have symbolized the soul reborn out of chrysalislike containment. The butterfly begins as a caterpillar emerging from an egg. The caterpillar must eat enough plant life to last the entire lifespan of the butterfly, since butterflies drink only sugary nectar, which provides no protein or fat. Feeding voraciously, the caterpillar outgrows several skins until it exudes a thin, silken thread by which it hangs from tree or leaf as its final skin slowly hardens into a chrysalis. Like an alchemical *vas*, the chrysalis is both the "golden" (*chryseos*) vessel of transformation and the object transformed; swaying gently in the wind, it gives no outward sign of the concealed unfolding within as the old forms dissolve and the embryonic tissue is restructured.

The butterfly is one of our most poetic images of psyche's self-renewal beyond even traumatic endings. Australian aborigines imagined butterflies as returning souls that entered the afterlife in the form of earthbound caterpillars (Saunders, 128). To the Aztecs butterflies represented the heroic souls of sacrificed enemy warriors or of women who died in childbirth. Emblematic of their doomed suffering was the goddess Itzpapalotl, a star deity depicted as a butterfly surrounded by stone knives and associated with the eclipse of the sun. In the East, the quiescent but transforming pupa has seemed a model of "spiritual evolution through serene contemplation" (Caspari, 46).

The shadow of butterflies and moths is in their fluttering movement, which has suggested not only the flickering of fire or the twinkling of stars, but erraticism, anxiety or inconstancy of desire. The Latin American word *mariposa* means both butterfly and prostitute (Saunders, 128). The mass, twilight fluttering of moths is darkly associated with the energies of compulsive devouring.

Yet the fragility and transience of the moth and butterfly, which may live a few hours or a few months; the butterfly's bright flowerlike colors, its drinking of fragrant nectars and the way buttery grains of pollen adhere to its body; the moth's self-consuming attraction to the light, have made both creatures exquisitely potent images of ardent longing. The Greek myth of Eros and Psyche tells the story of passion, doubt and separation between the soul and her beloved and the torturous process that precedes their reunion. This drama is enacted in ourselves in countless ways, as libido pursues the objects of psyche's desire, ways that can be poignantly self-destructive as well as redolent of promise.

Caspari, Elizabeth. *Animal Life in Nature, Myth and Dreams*. Wilmette, IL, 2003.
Saunders, Nicholas. *Animal Spirits*. NY, 1995.

1

3

2

1. A human "pupa" awaits transformation.
Frontispiece to *For Children: The Gates of Paradise*,
by William Blake, 1793, England.

2. Butterfly as the transforming spirit of young love.
By Bahram-e Sofrekesh, opaque watercolor and gold on
paper, Persian, ca. 1640.

3. An ornament from the ancient city of Mycenae
depicts a golden butterfly, emblematic of immortality,
ca. 1600 B.C.E.

Scarab

Though "scarab" applies to a whole family of stout-bodied beetles, it is the *scarabeus sacer*, the dung beetle of the Western Desert that has so captured the mythopoetic imagination. This "sacred scarab" embodies the Egyptian god Khepri who propels the sun out of the darkness of the underworld and across the sky in its diurnal journey (Quirke, 35–6). Here, in an illustration from the Egyptian *Book of the Dead*, Khepri encompasses the sun rising out of the night sea. Shu, the god of air, supports the solar barque, while Nut, the goddess of the sky, receives the brilliant orb to which she gives birth each day.

The dung beetle has the remarkable instinct of rolling balls of animal dung along the ground to its underground cache where the dung will be stored for food. Unlike the images of the scarab, however, it is not its front legs but its feathery-looking hind legs with which the beetle rolls the balls of dung. The ball is sometimes so large that the beetle is forced into an almost vertical position; yet, persistent and resolute, the scarab manages to negotiate obstacles in the way.

African cultures featured the dung beetle in myths of the beginning, as the creature able to bring up a piece of primordial earth from the watery abyss. But the scarab's pushing of its dung ball resonated especially in the imagination of the ancient Egyptians. Khepri, associated in particular with the sun of the morning, was depicted in lifelike form as the black dung beetle, sometimes with its wings spread, or as the figure of a man with a scarab beetle head. *Kheper*, from which Khepri gets his name means "to take shape" or "to come into being," evoking the sun and solar consciousness taking visible shape with day. But Khepri's blackness also suggests that it is an invisible force that upholds solar energies, an unconscious that propels consciousness into its awakenings and discriminated forms, creativity and perpetual motion.

The scarab's relation to the rising of the sun made it an emblem of rebirth. This symbolism was reinforced by the fact that besides the dung ball it rolls for food, the scarab fashions from sheep dung a pear-shaped ball in which to lay its eggs and feed its larvae. Pupae resembling tiny mummies, their wings and legs encased, rise out of the earth in which the dung ball containing the beetle's eggs was embedded, giving all the appearance of spontaneous self-creation.

So much did the scarab evoke the qualities of immortality, sublimation and transcendence that its dwelling, a subterranean, vertical shaft leading to a horizontal passage, may have been imitated in the architecture of Egyptian tombs (Andrews, 51). Hundreds of thousands of scarab amulets were crafted in Egypt out of precious and semiprecious stone, metal and glass. Their flat undersides were inscribed with images of animals, gods, kings and other designs, and they drew power to the living in the form of seals or jewelry (Andrews, 50), or were placed with the dead in the tomb as symbols of new life (Lurker, 105). Funerary texts illuminate the notion that at death the heart, seen as the center of life, feeling, action and memory, would be weighed against the feather of Maat, the goddess of order and proportion. If the heart failed to balance, it would be devoured by a monster, prohibiting entry into the afterworld. Heart scarabs were a magical means of preventing such an outcome, even, presumably, if the life lacked virtue (Andrews, 56). Attached or sewn to the mummy bindings over the chest, their purpose was "to bind the heart to silence during the weighing" (ibid.). Many were inscribed with pleas to the heart not to betray its owner: "Do not contradict me with the judges...do not make my name stink to the gods" (Wilkinson, 77). Here, the image of the scarab may be said to signify, on the one hand, a well-concealed defense against authenticity; and on the other, the balance and essence required for a "coming into being" as a linking of finite and infinite dimensions of self.

Andrews, Carol. *Amulets of Ancient Egypt*. Austin, TX, 1994.
Lurker, Manfred. *The Gods and Symbols of Ancient Egypt*. NY, 1980.
Quirke, Stephen. *Ancient Egyptian Religion*. NY, 1992.
Wilkinson, Richard H. *Reading Egyptian Art*. London, 1992.

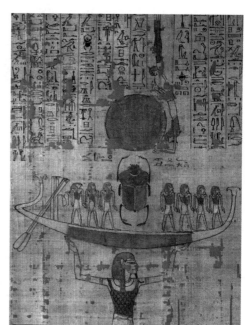

1. Transcending the boundaries of darkness and underworld, the scarab god Khepri emerges with the rising sun. Illustration from *The Book of the Dead of Anhai*, 20th dynasty (ca. 1100 B.C.E.), Egypt.

2. Changing "heads" as the day progresses, the solar deity is Khepri in the morning, while the noonday sun at the zenith manifests as the falcon-headed Ra and the sun of the evening as the ram-headed Khnum. Wall painting from the tomb of Nefertari, 19th dynasty (ca. 1270 B.C.E.), Valley of the Queens, Egypt.

Bird

Know that the psyche has its own
Fame, whether known or not, that
Soul can flame like feathers of a bird.
Grow into your own plumage, brightly,
So that any tree is a marvelous city.
James Applewhite, *Prayer for My Son*

Recently, a small carving of a bird was found in a cave in Hohle Fels, Germany. It turned out to be one of the oldest works of art ever found. It is only two inches long but very powerful in its simplicity. It is an image of a water bird, its wings folded as if it is about to dive. It makes us realize that 30,000 years ago someone was able to move between the worlds—like the bird who can move between the elements—from the outer world of the senses to an inner vision. Something moved this carver to begin to shape a piece of ivory into a new form, an image of a bird. And with this, something was changed, the world was no longer the same. It was this shift into a creative act that made us human.

The flight of birds must have stirred our imagination from the moment we saw them ascending toward the sky. Birds don't seem to be bound by the same laws of nature that we are. With the very lightness of thought they defy gravity, equally at home in the air as on earth. Some can even swim under water. Forming a link between heaven and earth, conscious and unconscious, the bird is almost universally seen as a symbol for the soul or anima, as the breath of the world, or the world soul hidden in matter.

It is their feathers, sometimes in glorious colors, which make birds unique in the animal world. The only other species having feathers were perhaps some dinosaurs, from which the birds descended. In contrast to snakes, their eternal mythical adversaries, birds are warm-blooded, allowing them to thrive throughout the seasons. Their incredible lightness is created by air pockets lacing their bones (Embery, 25). Birds are among the most intelligent animals; they use their beaks and claws to create complex tools, some talk, have a sense of humor and make up new words, others are capable of what looks like deception (Blakeslee, 1, 4). They return year after year, sometimes from the opposite side of the globe, to the same nest, evoking a sense of home. The Plains Indians compared the sacred circle of the nests to their own tepee, where, according to Black Elk, "the Great Spirit meant for us to hatch our children" (Neihardt, 165). Throughout the brooding and hatching of the eggs, the helpless offspring continue to be tended by their protective parents, sometimes even after they learn to fly. Although other animals can fly, none presents the unrivaled, elegant and varied flight of birds. Their specialized feathers allow them to hover and soar, turn in midair, stoop or dive at an incredible speed or like humming birds even fly backward.

1

2

1. Birds seemed to have such remarkable power that they were associated with the creation of the world. In a Native American creation myth, a water bird dives into the ocean and brings up a ball of mud, which forms the beginning of dry land. Mammoth-ivory sculpture, 30,000 years old, Hohle Fels, Ach River Valley, Germany.

2. Detail of a painting by Habib Allah, from *The Language of the Birds (Mantiq al-Tayr)*, a Persian book of poems by Farid al-Din Attar about birds on a pilgrimage in search of enlightenment, ca. 1600, Iran.

In our desire for boundless freedom, we identify ourselves with the flight of birds. In our imagination we transcend the ordinary world by leaving the earth and the weight of the body. Wings lift us. "Hope is a thing with feathers," says Emily Dickinson. Plato declared, "The function of the wing is to take what is heavy and raise it up into the region above where the gods dwell." According to Black Elk, "The most important of all the creatures are the wingeds, for they are nearest to the heavens." With wings we can look at things from both the perspective of earth and heaven at the same time. Intuition and inspiration seem to arrive unexpectedly on wings out of thin air as the first sign of any creative act. All kinds of winged beings connect us with the world beyond: the white dove of the Holy Spirit and Aphrodite, the black crow and raven, the angel, equally half-bird half-human, daimon and duende, as the voices of destiny, Mercury, the winged spirit of alchemy, the ancient shamans who flew to other worlds on their magical wings and imagination itself is winged. They return, each with their unique message.

It is also their song that makes birds so remarkable. Their voices are not only the voice of the spirit, as we usually think, they are also the voices of the instincts deep down in our body; the sound of blood and bone, tissue and nerves—the instincts of the animals.

The birds' singing wakes us up in the morning, they call us to our lives. The birds know their way, they read the signs of the seasons. They know when it is time to break up and leave for the next long journey. Having built in what seems like both sextant and compass, they take directions from above and below. They follow the sun, moon and stars, and when covered by clouds, the earth's magnetic field, as they fly across continents and oceans (Chinery, 202). Deep inside us our own instincts guide us where to go. We know what is true. And we respond in turn with our own singing. "Song is existence," said Rilke. We embody the spirit through song. In this dialogue of ascending and descending, listening and expressing we may find our own soul bird, guiding us on our journey.

Blakeslee, Sandra. "Minds of Their Own: Birds Gain Respect." *The New York Times* (February 1, 2005).
Brown, Joseph Epes. *Animals of the Soul: Sacred Animals of the Oglala Sioux.* Rockport, MA, 1997.
Chinery, Michael. Ed. *The Kingfisher Encyclopedia of Animals.* NY, 1992.
Embery, Joan. *Joan Embery's Collection of Amazing Animal Facts.* NY, 1983.
Gallo, Christopher. Personal communication. 2009.
Neihardt, John G. *Black Elk Speaks: Being the Life Story of a Holy Man of the Oglala Sioux.* NY, 1972.

3

4

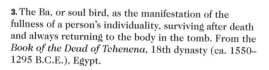

3. The Ba, or soul bird, as the manifestation of the fullness of a person's individuality, surviving after death and always returning to the body in the tomb. From the *Book of the Dead of Tchenena*, 18th dynasty (ca. 1550–1295 B.C.E.), Egypt.

4. A flock of crows or ravens cleaning the corpses to the bare bones. This is the *nigredo*, the darkest place, the deepest depression, which according to the alchemists signals both an end and a beginning. Often, large flocks of birds have negative connotations, such as the man-eating Stymphalian birds in Greek mythology or the murderous seagulls in Hitchcock's classic film *The Birds*. *Viridarium chymicum*, 1624, Germany.

5. A line drawing showing both the external and internal structure of a bird, as if suggesting transcendence. *A Bird*, by Bert Kupferman, pen and ink drawing on watercolor paper, 2008, United States.

Feather

So many of the qualities we associate with birds are distilled in the image of a single feather: lightness, mobility, air, wingedness, balance, flight and joy. Part of the magic of feathers is that, unique to birds, the most heavenly of creatures, they are thought to have evolved from the scales of primordial reptiles, attesting to the unity of heaven and earth. We now know that there were feathered dinosaurs that likely originated flight, just as mythically the Mayan feathered serpent god Quetzalcoatl combines the numinous elements of bird and snake.

Epidermal outgrowths consisting of shafts and veins interlaced with tiny barbs, feathers serve various functions. Some aid in flight, others insulate the body, still others offer bright display important in mating rituals. American Indians used feathered bird-skins cut into strips and woven into blankets as insulation. Inhabitants of the Arctic stitched water-bird skins into their parkas in order to waterproof them (Hausman, 44–6). But everywhere in the world, feathers were also believed to be endowed with magical powers, which accrued to the individual who wore ritual dress or used implements adorned with feathers. Feathers have decorated medicine bundles, ceremonial rattles, drums and staffs, war bonnets, helmets and crowns. Representing the altered states of consciousness described as ecstatic flight between earth and the spirit world, feathers covered the shamanic cap or robe. Sticks decorated with feathers were ritually employed by Indians to carry prayers aloft and by the Maori to transport the soul of a deceased chief to the realm of the gods (Eliade, 492). Hindu *Apsaras*, or flying genies, and Christian angels have wings of brilliant feathers, allowing

them to be swift, celestial messengers. In ancient Egypt, the ostrich feather was the hieroglyph for Maat, goddess of right order. In later dynastic times, it was thought that the heart of the deceased was weighed against the feather of Maat. Depending on the result, the dead entered the land of the blessed, or was swallowed into the void, suggesting that the heart of one who had lived life in balance should be at the end "light as a feather."

Feathers are sensitive to the slightest wind, and thus are emblems of psyche's capacity to pick up "invisible and imperceptible currents" (von Franz, 49). If we take note of these and follow up on them, as happens in some fairy tales, we can be shown new possibilities, or discover where psychic energy is tending. Thoughts, intuitions, imagination are often depicted as feathers that are caught up and carried on the breath of inspiration. Feathers form the wings with which one can transcend the concrete, escape confinement and soar to creative heights or spiritual vision. Alchemy conveyed by the changing colors of the feathers of the bird of spirit the stages of the opus: In the *nigredo* they were black, since much was still in the dark; in the *albedo*, white, since understanding had brought things into the light; and in the *rubedo*, red, for the actualization of the insights that had dawned.

Eliade, Mircea. *Shamanism*. NY, 1964.
Hausman, Gerald. *Turtle Island Alphabet: A Lexicon of Native American Symbols and Culture*. NY, 1992.
von Franz, Marie-Louise. *The Interpretation of Fairy Tales*. Boston, 1996.

1. A single-flight feather embedded in limestone, found near a 150-million-year-old fossil linking dinosaurs to birds. Bavaria, Germany.

2. Each feather of this war bonnet belonging to Chief Yellow Calf of the Arapaho Plains Indians symbolizes an honor of battle. The tips of the feathers were decorated with hair, suggesting scalp locks.

3. Maat, the goddess of Right, the realization of the eternal order of the universe, is signified by the ostrich feather, which she wears as crown. Detail from an Egyptian wall relief, 19th dynasty (1320–1200 B.C.E.), Egypt.

1

2

3

Dove

O my dove, in the clefts of the rock,
in the covert of the cliff,
let me see your face,
let me hear your voice,
for your voice is sweet,
and your face is comely.
Song of Solomon 2:4

Innocence, beauty and simplicity are the legend-ary virtues of the docile, inquisitive bird with the softly feathered, round body, elegant head and bright eye. Sweetly, it watches from the rafters at divine births, hovers in amorous pairs at depictions of lovemaking and marriage, takes wing as the spirit of hope, herald of good tidings and emblem of peace. Its cooing, bill-ing, pattering are homely and companionable. Proba-bly since cave-dwelling times we have been fascinated with this celestial, yet obliging creature that was capa-ble of relationship with us and embodied sacred forces with which we have integral bonds. Great mother god-desses of love and fecundity like Babylonian Ishtar, Phoenician Atargatis, and Greek Aphrodite took the form of the dove. Rome's love-goddess was one with the bringer of quiescent death as Venus Columba, Venus the Dove, whose catacombs and burial sites were "*columbaria*," or dove cotes (Walker, 253).

By nature monogamous, doves are the quintessen-tial lovebirds, whose courtship ritual, the "bow-coo," species-specific bowing postures accompanied by coo-ing, precedes copulation (Grzimek, 249). A female pi-geon may let the courting male "feed" her like a nest-ling by putting her beak in his, resembling a kiss. Male and female doves share the building of the nest, the in-cubation of the eggs and the feeding of the young with crop milk that sloughs off the epithelial lining of the crop, or throat. Always, the prolific dove has been as-sociated with the mystic, erotic attraction and devo-tion that bring things into fertile union. Alchemy's dove, as the soul rising out of the chaotic waters of the *nigredo* or descending from heaven to meet them, me-diates a marriage between our lofty aspirations and the churning affective life that bubbles up from below. In the myths of Babylonia and Judaism, a dove circles the subsiding waters of the primal flood and returns with the olive branch, sign of renewal after inundation. As the fertilizing wind of the Holy Spirit, the dove impreg-nates the Virgin Mary, and at the baptism of Jesus con-secrates her human-divine son.

Doves, especially the highly intelligent rock dove from which our domestic and feral city pigeons derive, have superb flying and navigational skills, fostering our projections of angelic intermediaries. Supported by hollowed bones with reserves of oxygen, a tapered fu-selage and immense breast muscles, the dove can ex-ceed speeds of 60 mph and sustain them over long dis-tances, or fly up and down the rock face of massive cliffs. Over 2,500 years ago, doves carried the names of Olympic winners from Athens to other city-states, were the aerial messengers of Egypt and China and have carried messages in war since the beginning of re-corded history. Carrier pigeons saved thousands of lives in World Wars I and II, often arriving grievously wounded at their destinations (Blechman, 30ff).

Not everyone loves the dove. There are those who despise the city pigeon as a nuisance, and poison, elec-trocute or net it for slaughter in recreational "pigeon-

1. A snow-white dove. Detail from a painting by Ferdinand von Wright (1822–1906), Finland.

2. *Purgatio.* A pristine dove descends into dark waters, activating processes that will bring high and low together. From the alchemical manual *De sapientia veterum philosophorum,* 18th century.

1

PVRGATIO

2

shoots." By 1914, we had gunned into extinction the beautiful, red-breasted passenger pigeon that used to darken the skies with its numbers (Weisman, 244–45). Yet, for thousands of years, the rushing sound of a dove's rapid wing beats has meant the advent of a supernal emissary, the saving inspiration that out of the blue alights at the critical time, or, as the luminous soul departing, presses its wings into eternity. A medieval alchemist compares the wings of the dove to "spotless and simple thoughts and contemplations" (CW 14:205n). In southwest Africa, the dove is host for the ancestor spirit of gentleness, laughter and song. Even the droppings of the dove were once considered an incomparable fertilizer. The dove, no depredator, depends on flight and fertility for its survival. And survives, moreover, in the soulful imagery that transcends the violence of our polarities.

Blechman, Andrew D. *Pigeons*. NY, 2006.
Grzimek, Bernhard. *Grzimek's Animal Life Encyclopedia: Birds, II*. Detroit, 2003.
Walker, Barbara G. *The Woman's Encyclopedia of Myths and Secrets*. SF, 1983.
Weisman, Alan. *The World without Us*. NY, 2007.

3

3. A haloed dove as the Holy Spirit, one of the three parts of the Godhead. Detail from a 14th-century painting of the Christian Trinity, Italy.

4. A child bids farewell to her doves on a Greek relief intended as a grave marker for a young girl of the 5th century B.C.E. The doves represent the soul stuff from which the mortal body is separating.

Crow / Raven

Here among the docks and the skunk-cabbages, [Silverspot] unearthed a pile of shells and other white, shiny things. He spread them out in the sun, turned them over, lifted them one by one in his beak, dropped them, nesting on them as though they were eggs, toyed with them and gloated over them like a miser. This was his hobby, his weakness...
Ernest Thompson Seton, Wild Animals I Have Known

*Striding along
as though he were tilling the fields—
the crow*
Issa

*Dear Friend,
... Quickened toward all celestial things by crows I heard this morning—accept a loving caw from a nameless friend.*
Emily Dickinson, in a letter to Mrs. Edward Tuckerman, Amherst, Massachusetts, April 1885

Though ubiquitously familiar, crows and ravens inevitably retain an aura of the uncanny. Like dark angels come to set the balance of the natural order to rights, they strut and flutter through the landscapes of desert and arctic, tropics and urban sprawl, over tilled farmland and the shifting soil of the human imagination. They are not inconspicuous; they show themselves without apology. They are destructive as well as helpful. Their communications—announced by the sharp caws of crows or the gruff croak of ravens—can both "quicken us toward all celestial things," or seem obtrusive, disquieting, disruptive of the status quo. Like the mythic Raven who was known by Northwest Pacific Coast Indians as "Real Chief," the "Great Inventor," the "One Whose Voice Is to Be Obeyed" (Marzluff, 112), ravens and crows are ministers of veiled mysteries. They arouse in us a sable-plumaged, elemental spirit—a daemon—who answers to their summons with a loud, joyously raucous caw of recognition.

For more than 12 million years, crows and ravens have applied their splendid intelligence to the art of living by their wits. They are master opportunists. They seek and find. They take, or thieve. They don't necessarily wait for doors or anything else to be opened unto them; they do it themselves, with their stout, knifelike beaks. Their tool-making and complex language capabilities excite our admiration. Their mischievously brilliant exploitation of human culture excites our pique. They have acquired notoriety as carrion eaters and scavenging "gallows birds" who peck out corpses' eyes. They ravage the eggs and nestlings of other songbirds; relentlessly harrow the raptor depredators of their own. They enjoy sliding on their backs or bellies down a snowy hill, thieving laundry from a clothesline, singing duets with their mates, sunbathing, smearing their skin with crushed ant oil, mounting razzle-dazzle flying exhibitions, finding shiny treasures to cache and lovingly mull over.

We never grasp the full measure of the birds. They subvert our attempts to do so, just as the tricksters, shamans, magicians and culture heroes they embody in folklore and myth subvert our fondest notions of human superiority, put in question what constitutes the reality of sacred or profane, rearrange our moral landscape. Consider the progenitor and shaman Raven, who brings humans into being by coaxing them out of their (clam)shell, steals daylight for them through trickery or by opposing the falcon of night, brings them fire and water, teaches them how to sow seed and to hunt—and then "plays" with his creatures and occasionally kills and eats them. Just so does the crow or raven daemon perched in our psyches open doors, steal treasures for us from hidden places, coax us out of our narrow, conventional shells—and also mercilessly confuses us, trips us up, puts us down and sometimes devours us. The Norse god Odin's famous ravens Hugin and Munin ("Thought" and "Memory") wander shamanlike through the "nine worlds," prying and probing beneath the surface of things in order to bring the hidden truth to the ears of the god. The Thought and Memory that peck away at our own illusions and pre-

1. Rounded wings "rowing" against a white sky, a solitary crow navigates a sea of clouds. *Untitled*, by Joseph Cornell, collage, 1970, United States. © The Joseph and Robert Cornell Memorial Foundation/ Licensed by VAGA, New York, NY

tensions can at times affect us as "grim, ungainly, ghastly, gaunt, and ominous bird(s) of yore" (Poe, "The Raven"). The alchemical stage of the *nigredo*, after all, was known to the artifex as the "raven" or "raven's/crow's head" (*capus corvi*). Depicted by images of a raven perched on the shoulder of a skeleton who stands atop a black sun, or of the birds scavenging a field of human corpses, they evoke the mortification, in the deepest sense, of being reduced to the bare bones of psychological verity.

Though the crow is also the divinatory bird of Apollo, it is not so much the blazing sun god of unremitting heights, but the Apollonian consciousness that falls in love with Crow Maiden, the dark and light of the moon. What the birds draw us toward is a way of being in the world established on a different kind of consciousness. Like the three-legged crow or raven who sits in the center of the sun in Chinese and Japanese iconography, such consciousness will bear a certain resemblance—at once knowing, roguish, compassionate and playful—to the enigmatic birds.

Dickinson, Emily. *Selected Poems and Letters of Emily Dickinson*. NY, 1959.

Marzluff, John M. and Tony Angell. *In the Company of Crows and Ravens*. New Haven, CT, 2005.

Poe, Edgar Allan and Richard Wilbur. *Poe; Complete Poems*. NY, 1959.

Seton, Ernest Thompson. *Wild Animals I Have Known, 1898*. Quoted in *Crows: Encounters with the Wise Guys*. Ed. Candace Savage. Vancouver and Berkeley, CA, 2005.

2

2. Like cuneiform imprinted on the sun, a gregarious conventicle of crows is depicted in eloquent and precise detail. *Crows*, screen section, ink and gold on paper, Edo period (1615–1868), Japan.

Falcon

One of the earliest images of kingship in Egypt, and in human culture, was the far-flying, far-seeing falcon. Its outstretched wings evoked the vast spread of the sky. Its fierce, round eyes suggested the sun and moon. Its speckled breast resembled the feathery clouds spotting the empyrean, and its breath was imagined as the winds. Thus the falcon was the emblem of the high god or "distant one," and the king was the god's earthly representative or incarnation (Frankfort, 37). The Falcon Horus ultimately became the title of kingship, and the "personification of divine and regal power"(Quirke, 61).

This elegant hawk easily calls up such symbolism. Circling and then dropping from the skies like a feathered bullet, a falcon reaches speeds in excess of 200 miles per hour to snap the neck of its prey "at one fell swoop," linking it with the imagery of supernatural vision, expert surveillance and lightning strike, which has also, for some, expressed the idea of war as one power swooping down on another. Both far and near, falcons made their dwelling in the upper reaches of ancient Egyptian palaces and temples, as they do today in urban high-rises. Sculptors portrayed the falcon perched on the nape of the pharaoh's neck, protectively encompassing his head with its long, pointed wings, suggesting guardian agency from a supernal region. Sometimes the falcon form was shown surmounting the palace, pictured as the rectangular "serekh," in which the pharaoh was housed, or as subjugating the king's rivals beneath its impressive talons. With extraordinary powers of sight, the falcon can recognize small objects a mile away; its immense orblike eyes are 30 times more color-sensitive than our own and are equipped with a double fovea for true stereoscopic perception. What to human eyes is the blurred flight of a dragonfly registers in the falcon's brain four times more slowly, helping it to stun its victim in midflight (Macdonald, 21f). While another favorite creature of Egyptian iconography, the cobra, is the chthonic representative of the sun's fiery, penetrating, burning eye, which can "rise up" in the violence of defense, the falcon is the celestial form, and sometimes the two are pictured together as the high god and the king. But the "eye" of the primeval sun that originally protects against the waters of disintegration is a falcon eye.

The peregrine falcon is named from the Latin peregrinus, meaning someone from foreign parts, and thus a "wanderer," making the falcon the spirit of peregrination, "sailing" on its tapered wings just as the sun sails over the sky and the sun-boat sails into night and underworld, or consciousness crosses the great water into the unconscious. The peregrine would represent the flight of intuition that shows the way to distant places of experience, much the way the falcon has made its own expansions into global dispersion and migratory routes up to 18,000 miles long (Slater, 54) between Siberia and South Africa or Alaska and Argentina. Because of its capacity to fly high, to travel far and wide and to see even ultraviolet light, the falcon is mythically a messenger and sojourner between worlds earthly and unearthly. Carvings of the falcon on enduring stone steles at mortuary sites in Egypt helped assure the pharaoh of rebirth, for just as the Falcon Horus rose triumphantly out of darkness and death at sunrise, so did the deceased pharaoh's ba—his falcon-headed soul—ascend into eternity (Lurker, 49). Their sharp, powerfully gripping claws class the falcon among the raptors (from Latin raptere, "to seize," the root also of "rapture"); mystics have likened the falcon's spiraling upward flight to contemplative ascent and seen its spectacular dive for prey as spirit seizing the human heart. In Hinduism, the falcon is the one that steals from the heavenly abode of its guardians the divine soma, elixir of immortality and inspiration, and wings it from psyche's eternal realm into the consciousness of human beings.

Frankfort, Henri. *Kingship and the Gods.* Chicago, 1978.
Lurker, Manfred. *The Gods and Symbols of Ancient Egypt.* NY, 1980.
Macdonald, Helen. *Falcon.* London, 2006.
Quirke, Stephen. *Ancient Egyptian Religion.* NY, 1992.
Slater, P. J. B. *Encyclopedia of Animal Behavior.* NY, 1987.

Discovered inside one of Egypt's earliest mortuary
vaults, the inscribed image shows the pharaoh as a
sharp-eyed serpent guarded by the vision, swiftness and
power of the divine falcon. *Stele of the Serpent King*,
Reign of the Serpent King, 1st dynasty (ca. 3000
B.C.E.), Egypt.

Owl

The earliest known rendering of an owl is about 30,000 years old and appears on the limestone wall of the Chauvet Cave in southern France. With its ear tufts, round face and vertically barred body, the image strongly suggests the large eagle owl that was common at the time on the Eurasian continent. These owls are the greatest raptors of the night, as eagles are of the day. With large eyes evolved for acute perception in near darkness, ears that can locate the rustle of a rodent in total darkness, and wings softly feathered at the tips to be silent in flight, they quietly await their prey, descend without warning and seize it with uncanny suddenness and finality (Terres, 664). Their "far reaching sonorous *oohoo* or *oohu* with emphasis on the first syllable, from which the species' imaginative German name *Uhu* is derived" has a melancholy, haunting sound, and their "giggling, laughing, growling and rattling" (Voous, 91) in sexual communication evoke a magical half-human quality. Hunters of the night, owls are rarely seen by day, but when they are they seem to stare at us with human intensity and concentrated attention.

Owls have extremely keen vision provided by eyes set in bony sockets that cannot move. Their heads compensate by being able to turn more than 240 degrees in either direction, reversing so swiftly some observers have had the illusion of being followed in a complete circle. Well disguised by their plumage in their natural habitats, they do not generally pursue their prey from afar, often locating themselves on a nearby branch or perch while waiting to swoop down when they see or hear small animals below. Thus it is not surprising that owls have become symbols of both acute awareness—the invisible see-er in the dark, the bird of crafty skill that accompanies Athena (Greek goddess of civilization and protector of Athens)—and of the stunning power of death: mortal terror of the stealthy visitor in the night.

In Germany and Eastern Europe, an owl alighting on a dwelling or a barn is deemed to foreshadow an imminent death, and this association extends across most of the world, including for example, the alliance in Native American mythology of the owl with Skeleton Man, god of death. But as often, the powers of death are also the powers of transformation, and the owl is symbolically bound to the renewal of life that is mythically implicit in death. One of the strongest of these associations is in renderings of the Great Goddess with owl features or companions. As Marija Gimbutas points out, there are many such images, in pottery, sculpture and other artifacts made over a period of several millennia, both prehistoric and later (p.190). As the Great Goddess gives life, so also she takes it away in the perpetual cycle of death and regeneration. She conveys the wisdom of evolution that each living creature must surrender its claim on time so that the next generation may live.

These early connections of the owl to feminine fertility and regeneration as well as to death suggest that Athena's positive qualities as patron of both the martial and the civilized arts are grounded in the older wisdom of the Goddess for whom death is as much the soil of life as darkness is the bed of day. Often today we think of the wise old owl as shrewd and clever, seeing and hearing into the darkness with eyes as sharp as Athena's, but the depth of the owl's wisdom includes not only the ability to bring what is dark into the light, but also the ability to live in the dark itself.

The ambivalence of a creature who sees and hears with superhuman talent and takes prey in the night by stealth naturally gives rise to images of mysterious power. The owl is a regular familiar of witches and the world of magic, and is illustrated often in their company. It is also a common companion to shamans, who are sometimes assisted by owls in evoking the spirits. "Siberian and Inuit (Eskimo) shamans regard them as helping spirits, a source of powerful aid and guidance, and wear their feathers on caps and collars" (EoR 11:144). In folklore, tribal tradition and mythology the owl's natural history invites us to imagine what lies beyond the veil of dusk.

Chauvet, J. M., E. B. Deschamps and C. Hilaire. *Dawn of Art: The Chauvet Cave, the Oldest Known Paintings in the World.* NY, 1996.
Gimbutas, Marija. *The Language of the Goddess: Unearthing the Hidden Symbols of Western Civilization.* SF, 1989.
Terres, John K. *The Audubon Society Encyclopedia of North American Birds.* NY, 1980.
Voous, Karel H. *Owls of the Northern Hemisphere.* Cambridge, MA, 1989.

1. The earliest known rendering of an owl from a cave in southern France, where it was discovered by Jean-Marie Chauvet and his colleagues in 1994. Ca. 30,000–32,000 years old, Chauvet Cave, France.

2. The goddess Athena and her owl. Two sides of a silver coin, 5th century B.C.E., Greece.

3. Esoteric goddess riding an owl, perhaps a depiction of a yogini. *She Who Makes a Loud Noise*, 10th–11th century, Uttar Pradesh, India.

Eagle

... while the mother-eagle
Hunts her same hills, crying the same
beautiful and lonely cry and is never
tired; dreams the same dreams,
And hears at night the rock-slides rattle
and thunder in the throats of these
living mountains.
Robinson Jeffers, The Beaks of Eagles

... and when I returned
Down the black slopes after the fire
had gone by, an eagle
Was perched on the jag of a burnt pine,
Insolent and gorged, cloaked in the folded
storms of his shoulders.
Robinson Jeffers, Fire on the Hills

It might be a primeval dawning: An eagle perches on a stake emerging out of dark, undulating waters; the red ball of the sun rises over distant hills in a soft diffusion of heat and light. The magnificent bird and majestic orb are counterparts, each evocative of sovereign ascent, ferocity of nature and lonely, heroic struggle against the powers of dissolution.

From the time of cradle civilizations, the greatness of the eagle has inspired comparison to the sun, and to supernal deities of lightning and storm, earthly rulers and imperial nations. It is hard not to be awed by the sight of an eagle perched at the summit. The sound of their wings, spanning six to eight feet, is like the rushing of mighty winds or the clapping of thunder. The Oglala Sioux felt the presence of the Great Spirit in the eagle because it soars higher than any other bird and in the sacred form of the circle (Brown, 33). The wings of angels, those messengers of unflinching gaze and transcendent vision, are eagle wings. We are carried, metaphorically, on the wings of eagles through the clouds of tempest, above the storm's disintegrating effects in order to survive and benefit from the fertile aftermath of inundation and brush fire. The eagle's huge nest of dried branches, twigs and grass in treetop or rock cliff is emblem of the "aerie" of spirit, sublimated perspective and commanding view.

Largest of the hawks, the eagle with its strong feet and great, curved talons is an aggressive predator, a quality that we have made an ambivalent part of its symbolism. The imperial eagle of the Aztecs had its own warrior society and the hearts of enemy warriors were sacrificed to the Eagle of the Sun (DoS, 324–5). Yet the eagle's hooked beak that tears prey held in its feet also delicately places bits of food in the mouths of hungry chicks, whose incubation and feeding are shared by the monogamous parents, returning to the same nest year after year. Mating couples or groups of eagles play toss and catch with prey in midair, or somersault, dive, even link talons in remarkable aerobatic displays of strength and vitality. Serpent eagles carrying away their prey have been mythologized as the victory of solar forces over those of the abysmal and chthonic. Hinduism's divine eagle Garuda "ablaze with the heat of the glowing sun," ruthlessly, eternally attacks the snake as "the vivifying liquid of the all-nourishing earth" (Zimmer, 75).

1. *The Great Solar Eagle*, by Chong Hong-Nae, watercolor and gold on silk, 1720, Korea.

2. A white tailed sea eagle in flight, Norway.

1

2

Still, just as the eagle and snake are both aspects of supreme Vishnu, the mythic domain of the eagle includes the celestial waters that refresh and mingle with the waters of the earth, which in turn evaporate to bring moisture to the heavens. An Iroquois myth relates how Oshadage, the Big Eagle of the Dew, carries a lake of dew on his back that brings water and life to the earth after parching fire. The divine lion-headed eagle Imdugud of Assyro-Babylonian myth spreads his wings after a drought, shrouding the skies in rain-bearing clouds (EoR, 4:533).

In alchemy, the eagle is portrayed as the ascension of the spirit from the *prima materia*, a way of describing how, when understanding separates from the chaos of emotion, it takes wing and can easily disappear into the ether. The alchemists believed that ascent must be answered by its opposite, which means that our loftiest illuminations must descend into integrated embodiment and be applied. Thus, inspired by the sea eagle that dives from the sunstruck sky into ocean or river and re-emerges, the mythical eagle of spirit was imagined to fly into the sun's fire, almost burning itself up, only to plunge into the deep waters of swelling life, and reemerge in phoenixlike self-renewal.

Brown, Joseph Epes. *Animals of the Soul: Sacred Animals of the Oglala Sioux*. Rockport, MA, 1997.
Zimmer, Heinrich Robert. *Myths and Symbols in Indian Art and Civilization*. Princeton, NJ, 1972.

3. *Aztec Eagle Warrior*, symbol of the sun, from the Templo Mayor, 1480, Mexico.

Peacock

Nature's extravagance has made the peacock almost more mythical than actual. Like the phoenix, he is a solar bird. His shimmering tail is emblem of the sun's expansive, fiery descent, and its radiance fanning out of darkness at dawn. Bird of immortality, the peacock enthrones the immortals, his multiple "eyes" suggesting their surpassing vision, and the all-seeing eternal.

There is an old Hindu saying that the peacock has "the feathers of an angel, the walk of a thief and the voice of a devil." The stunning tail is a courtship display that is also heavy and conspicuous, making the peacock vulnerable to predators, and also to moralizers who perceive an example of pride and fall. The peacock's gingerly strut is surely a means of maintaining balance while carrying his magnificent burden. His characteristic loud wailing associates him with the raucous crow, mythically identified with ambiguous forces—but all the more magical because of it.

And the tail is dazzling. In antiquity the peacock signified rebirth and early Christian art adopted the image as a symbol of resurrection. Pairs of peacocks accompanied the lamb on Christian sarcophagi. Renaissance versions of the adoration of the Magi, or the Annunciation, perched a peacock in the rafters, signifying auspicious events yet to unfold. The peacock molts in the fall, and unadorned for many months acquires brilliant plumage in the spring, a fact that found correspondence in the penitential season of Lent that precedes the Easter renewal. There was an old legend that the flesh of the peacock would not corrupt; thus it became identified with the divine body of Christ. Alchemy laid claim to the same flesh, imagining it as a kind of arcane "food," psychic matter that could be assimilated so as to incarnate and nourish the imperishable self.

From its origins in India, the peacock was greeted as a marvel throughout the ancient world. Byzantine and Roman imperial courts assigned the peacock to the empress, just as the eagle was the emperor's bird. For the ancient Greeks, who protected the bird to assure its propagation, the peacock belonged to Hera, the Queen of Olympus, the Roman Juno. Ovid relates how Mercury slew the hundred-eyed Argus, whom Juno had enlisted to spy upon the maiden Io, one of Zeus's conquests: "So Argus lay low, and all the light in all those eyes went out forever, a hundred eyes, one darkness. And Juno took the eyes and fastened them on the feathers of a bird of hers, the peacock, so that the peacock's tail is spread with jewels ... " (Ovid, 25). Iris, the messenger of the gods, the rainbow, shares the same iridescent colors as the peacock's tail, the *cauda pavonis*, sign of the dawning synthesis of heaven and earth, the goal of the opus.

Evoking insight that can shift what is felt as poisonous into healing medicine, the peacock was said to transmute the snake's venom into his blue throat-feathers and the snake's cunning into the "eyes of wisdom" on his tail (Beer, 85). Divine Shiva's throat had turned peacock blue when he swallowed and purified the poison of the primordial ocean. India's epic, the *Ramayana*, relates how the storm-god Indra transformed himself into a peacock in order to elude the demon Ravana, afterward rewarding the bird with hundreds of eyes in its feathers and the power to kill snakes. Indeed, it is the solar bird that has the heat to overcome fiery venom and searing drought. The peacock's cawing heralds the Indian monsoon, time of mating and lush growth; lyrical images of the season depict him fanning his sumptuous feathers and dancing in the longed-for rain.

Beer, Robert. *The Encyclopedia of Tibetan Symbols and Motifs.* Boston, 1999.

Ovid. *Metamorphoses.* Bloomington, IL, 1955.

1. Myo'o (Vidyaraja) descending from heaven on a peacock. *The Peacock King,* hanging scroll painting, Northern Song dynasty, 11th century, China.

2. A Mughal painting depicts a peacock dispatching a snake, while a peahen looks on. National bird of India, the peacock is a legendary serpent killer. *Peafowl,* attributable to Ustad Mansur, Nadir al-Asr, 1610, India

3. A peacock appears in the glass alembic, signifying the golden dawn, climax of the opus. *The Peacock,* an illustration from the alchemical manuscript *Splendor Solis,* or "*Splendor of the Sun,*" by Salomon Trismosin, school of Nuremberg, ca. 1531–2, Germany.

2

1

3

Ape/Monkey

You call this a party? The beer is warm, the women are cold and I'm hot under the collar.
Groucho Marx, *Monkey Business*, 1931

It is easy to see why, throughout our history, monkeys and apes have been the objects of our projections and thus of our worship, admiration and sometimes our derision. Their social habits, physical appearance, brain development, behaviors and talents have made the comparison to ourselves tempting and apt. Almost every major pattern of social organization exists in the world of the old and new world monkeys and the lesser (gibbons) and great apes (orangutans, gorillas, chimpanzees and bonobos). Until quite recently, we assumed that primates were alone in being able to invent and manipulate tools, or display emotions like empathy. We identify with a small monkey under a full moon in the Amazon forest hooting mournfully in the treetops, searching for a lifelong mate. And yet, swinging from the shadows of humanity's ancestral tree, "monkey" speaks to the ambivalent fantasies and images of our animal origins—to both their romanticized pristine perfection, and to the ridiculous untutored hilarity of the instincts and antics of our "monkey mind." Mischief-makers who nevertheless "seek" a code of conduct—like the three legendary mystic monkeys who "Hear No Evil, Speak No Evil and See No Evil"—monkey embodies humanity's plight, caught between the amorality and literality of instinctual expression and the drive toward social and emotional evolution.

Immortalized in Mayan myth for having been the only creature to survive the gods' destruction of Creation, venerated in ancient Egypt as Thoth, friend to the dead and the spirit of wisdom behind the Pharaoh, elevated in India as the "strong-jawed" god Hanuman, the unarmed and perfect warrior, son of the wind who moves mountains—in many older cultures clever and impudent monkey reigned supreme. But, as monkey began to range over the theological savannahs of Judeo-Christianity and Islam, the image took the projections of humanity's lust, greed and perniciousness, becoming the "perversion" of God's work. A twelfth-century bestiary opined that while monkey's whole being is "disgraceful, yet their bottoms really are excessively disgraceful and horrible." In the Middle Ages Satan was described as the *simia dei*—the ape of God—and Christian art frequently depicted this devil with a disgraceful bottom (apparently most attractive to witches) as a monkey. In the most degraded image, an ape with an apple in its mouth signified the fall of man.

In the modern era, as the "primal hordes" roamed the landscapes of scientific discovery and psychoanalysis, the image of monkey remained split, but softened somewhat, coming to represent the sobering and enlightening truth of evolutionary theory, and acting as a psychopomp into the discontented "primitive" side of human civilization and psyche, still with ambivalent overtones of repression verses free expression, and with new intimations of a patriarchal culture gone wild. And "humans are not the 'end-product' of great ape evolution. Each species within Hominidae has evolved on its own distinct pathway, although all share a common ancestry" (Grzimek, 225), which the striking mask of the African Makonde people reinforces.

In distinction to the Western trajectory, the sixteenth-century Buddhist story *Journey to the West* or *Monkey* tells the adventurous tale of a monkey who finally became a god. Always a nuisance to man and the gods, hampered by drunkenness, foolishness and pretensions—but nevertheless in search of wisdom—Monkey uses his powers of trickery, perseverance and his lust for life to attain both immortality and an ever-lasting place in the Chinese pantheon, as the "God of Victorious Strife." As with his cousin—the trickster Hermes, god of magicians and the transformations of alchemy—Monkey both shows us up as fools, but as a personification of instinctual activity also offers tremendous blessings.

A monkey's transformed body weds
the human mind. Mind is a monkey—
this, the truth profound.
**Wu Cheng'en, *Xiyouji Journey to the West*
(or *Monkey*)**

Allan, Tony, Charles Phillips and John D. Chinnery. *Land of the Dragon: Chinese Myth.* Amsterdam, 1999.
Freud, Sigmund and James Strachey. *Civilisation and Its Discontents.* NY, 2005.
Grzimek, Bernhard, et al. *Grzimek's Animal Life Encyclopedia: Mammals, I, III, V.* Detroit, 2004.
Mercatante, Anthony S. *Zoo of the Gods: Animals in Myth, Legend, & Fable.* NY, 1974.

1. A mask used as part of initiation dance ceremonies to conceal the identity of the dancer. Sculpture, wood and human hair, Makonde people, early 20th century, Mozambique/Tanzania, Africa.

2. The Hindu god Hanuman, leader of the great monkey clan, standing on a double-lotus pedestal. Bronze, 11th century C.E., Tamil Nadu, India.

3. Statue of a praying baboon, protecting a royal figure. Stone, New Kingdom, 1550–1295 B.C.E., Egypt.

Elephant

The lone bather worshipped the Ganga in her own way, not as a human suppliant but as a creature born to water. One moment she frolicked in the sacred river, splashing and spraying herself with innocent delight, then all at once she collapsed and let the stream wash over her, supine as a boulder, scoured and sculpted by the current.
Stephen Alter

Our newly emerging compact with elephants ... requires nothing less than a fundamental shift in the way we look at animals and, by extension, ourselves. It requires ... a new "transspecies psyche," a commitment to move beyond an anthropocentric frame of reference and, in effect, be elephants.
Charles Siebert

In architecture, height and mass have a wonderful effect because they suggest immediately a relation to the sphere on which the structure stands, and so to the gravitating system.
Ralph Waldo Emerson

Just about everything to do with African and Asian elephants (the last surviving species of their kind) is on a grand scale: their imposing architecture; the largesse of their souls; the eloquence with which they inhabit their splendid, and increasingly vulnerable, gigantism. Borne on cushioned feet exquisitely attuned to earth's vibrations, absorbing a thousand olfactory and tactile clues with their uncanny trunks, they travel silently and fluently over the changeable surfaces of rain forests and foothills, of African savannah and desert periphery, of the rural woodland of a Tennessee sanctuary, and the dream vistas of the human psyche. Along the way they reconfigure topography; opening dark spaces to light, removing obstacles, digging wells to underground streams. They take pleasure in each other's company, rumbling infrasonic secrets and touching faces and flanks. They celebrate and grieve. They shout uproarious greetings to old friends at favorite watering holes. Glazed with brown-gold mud, or transformed into chalky apparitions under a fine layer of dust; crowned endearingly with tufts of grass or sandy confetti, they might be architectonic tutelaries come to show the less enlightened how to truly "be elephants" in a rapidly shrinking world.

Not only are elephants intimately and devotedly related to the "sphere on which they stand," their mythical first parents were 16 elephants who emerged from the golden halves of the cosmic eggshell and ever after supported the earth on their broad backs. Their cloudlike, winged offspring had the ability to change size and shape at will, fleetly traversing the length and breadth of the world, at home in water, earth or air. Even today, poets still see elephants in the sky: the huge, dark thunderclouds, laden with rain, flashing their tusks of lightning and answering with deep, resounding trumpets the magically efficacious summons of their cousins below. It is generally believed that the presence of elephants is propitious, ensuring the fecundity, vitality and resurgence of the physical and spiritual life of the universe. Gaja Lakshmi (Lakshmi of the Elephants), the lovely Mother Earth whose maternal benevolence causes life-sustaining juices to flow through every plant and animal, is traditionally portrayed with two tuskers, one on either side, pouring potent libations of water over her lush figure. Ganesha, the beloved elephant-headed Remover of Obstacles and guardian of thresholds, bestows material and creative riches upon his devotees. And Airavata, a moon-white, six-tusked marvel who rose out of the primordial milky ocean, is the theriomorphic form and "divine vehicle" of Indra, the Lord of the Heavens and wielder of the rainbow, who unleashes the fertile potency of rain.

To be sure, elephants can also epitomize gargantuan destructiveness. The heightened aggression of a bull in musth or the near frenzy of an elephant provoked by pain, fear or rage is a proverbial emblem of the rampancy of body or mind. Elephants can leave a wasteland where they overbrowse because of continuous human encroachment on their habitat. Increasingly, elephants are becoming "disordered"—socially, emotionally and behaviorally—from the trauma of ivory poaching, hunting and government-sanctioned culling of entire herds.

1. This striking African elephant-head mask, carved from the wood of a sacred grove, conveys both refinement and forcefulness. Western Grassfields, Cameroon.

2. Elephant herds are always led by a matriarch in whose long experience and prodigious memory are distilled the intricacies of elephant culture and socialization, the care, protection and education of the young; the seasonal locations of water and browse, and a steadfastness in all exigencies that makes survival possible.

It rests with the power of humans to properly accommodate the "size" of elephants—in every sense of the word. If we allow them to simply "be elephants" and thereby show us how to "be elephants" as well, we will also make room for something of size, something that otherwise languishes, in ourselves. Just as the long evolution of elephants consists, in the main, of the adaptation of their gigantism to the intimate and myriad motions of "existence on the ground" (Darton, 119) so might we relinquish our abstraction from earthly life and inhabit our deeper animality. Accommodate the wild as well as the tame. Gain the capacity to remove obstacles and open the way. Be impregnated with our dormant "greatness": with size that has nothing in common with the grandiosity of an inflated ego, but rather with gravitas: the fullness, the weightiness, the strength within, of one's own substance.

Alter, Stephen. *Elephas Maximus: A Portrait of the Indian Elephant.* Orlando, FL, 2004.
Darton, Eric. *Divided We Stand: A Biography of New York's World Trade Center.* NY, 1999.
Emerson, Ralph Waldo. *Selections from Ralph Waldo Emerson; an Organic Anthology.* Ed. Stephen E. Whicher. Boston, 1960.
Siebert, Charles. "An Elephant Crackup?" *The New York Times Magazine* (October 8, 2006).

3

3. In this familiar depiction of the Buddha's conception, his mother Maya dreams of an auspicious white elephant that descends like a cloud to enter her womb. The overshadowing by an elephantine spirit is reflected in the Buddha's perfect wisdom, gentleness and royal authority, as well as his superb teaching skills. Stone relief, 180–72 B.C.E., India.

4. Holding a lotus flower in his trunk, and wearing kirttimukhas (faces of glory) on his foreknees, this Asian elephant evokes protective and life-sustaining energies. He carries Lord Aiyanar, a village god and son of Shiva. Cast bronze, 16th century, India.

Great Cats

The roar of regal and predatory magnificence is what makes the lion, tiger, leopard and jaguar the "Great Cats." Stalkers and ambush artists, they dispatch their prey with a single spring and bite to the neck, or if it is large bring it down under the mighty force of their rippling muscles. Their prestige is not of swiftness but strength, and lithe elegance, lusty sensuality, sumptuous pelage. Conveying protective grace and noble authority, they have inspired everything from warrior societies and shamanic magic to some of our oldest, most commanding images of majestic divinity.

The play of light and dark in their beautiful coats and natural aggression is mirrored in symbolic ambivalence. Big cats are sometimes paired with a mythic creature, the lion with the unicorn, the tiger with the dragon, evoking nature's dynamic tensions and the mixture of its energies, soulful, spiritual and bodily. Alike in their deep-chested compactness, moving and hunting in nature with silence and agility that can seem supernatural, the different types of big cat are also

uniquely associated with particular forces and mythic relationships. Lions, regal dignitaries inhabiting savannahs and traveling in prides, are the most social of the great cats. Their tawny coats and the luxuriant mane of the male, circling his head like the radiant nimbus of the sun, his fierce, pacing guardianship of territory and pride, and the female's prowess as hunter and mother, associate the lions with gold, solar splendor, heroic survival and the sunlike magnanimity and compassion of savior and sovereign. Drawn by cave artists as early as 32,000 years ago in the Chauvet cave in southern France, groups of cave lions watch and prey over the ancient plains in striking likeness to their present-day counterparts. Living on the desert margins of Egypt, lions came to represent the sentries of the eastern (sunrise) and western (sunset) horizons and the creative energies of dissolution and becoming (Shaw, 162). The warrior goddess Sekhmet, lioness, or lioness-headed, is the watchful, sometimes raging "eye" of the sun-god Ra; her breath the hot desert winds, her

2

1. The mountain lion, or puma, is technically not a "big cat" because it does not roar like the other great cats, but it is the only cat of its size in the U.S. It is solitary, nocturnal and adaptive to many environments, and after diminishing for some time is now repopulating even the eastern U.S. *Silhouetted Mountain Lion Stalking Prey*, photograph by Chase Swift, United States.

2. The soulful, carved head of one of two lions supporting a funerary bed of King Tutankhamun. Because of the tawny lion's association with the sun, it was an emblem of resurrection. Gilded wood, ca. 1332–23 B.C.E., Egypt.

body emanating a fiery glow (Lurker, 106). The Green Lion of alchemy, devouring the sun, evokes how stealthy mercurial energies of the instinctual psyche can overwhelm even the scorching heat of the intellect, subjecting the mind to violent terrors of darkness and descent.

Mysterious and wraithlike, the tiger is rendered invisible in jungle, forest or high grasses by its "magical fur cloak" of irregular body stripes, horizontal leg patterns and intricate face markings (Green, 36). The tiger signifies the stature and ferocity of the professional or momentary warrior, the pure capacity to spring into action at the critical time. On its black forehead markings every tiger carries a pattern identical with the Chinese character for "king." The tiger also crosses into fluid dimensions, loving the waters of hidden jungle pools, ocean and mango swamps (ibid.). In Chinese and later Japanese traditions the tiger is a creature of mountainous ascent and descent, and evocative of the qualities of yin as west, sunset, autumn and earth. Here and not here, the tiger is like spirit or wind, "the mysterious rustling of the wind in a bamboo thicket, a sound that has an unearthly and eerie charm" (Desai, 3).

The leopard is shy and solitary, the most nocturnal of the big cats, and so elusive that the sighting of the beautiful snow leopard living at altitudes exceeding 10,000 feet, and rarely glimpsed in its natural habitat, represents the mystic goal of spiritual journeys. The leopard is capable of stalking for great distances and extremely agile. Its elongated body and short, massive legs make it a nimble tree-climber: It can scale up a tree 30 or 40 feet with a carcass heavier than itself in order to get out of reach of competing felines. An arborial hunter, the leopard is associated with the magic and shape-shifting of shamans for whom the treetops were initiatory, numinous openings to the land of the spirits. The leopard and its cousin the jaguar have intrigued imagination because of the rosette spotting (even in black leopards) of their velvety coats. The jaguar is associated with the eclipsing of light, of consciousness undergoing encompassment by darkness and uncanny powers. Believed to den in caves, the jaguar is also linked with the underworld and its mysteries and transformations. The echo of cavernous landscapes has been associated with the voice of the jaguar and so has the bringing of fertilizing rains. In South America its hunting skills have made it "Lord of the Animals," the master of spirits.

Great cats are wild cats. They can devour. And whether we are speaking of the gorgeous animals or the vital powers within ourselves that they embody, big cats need space, habitat and respect for the value and force of their living presence in nature. We are not their prey, but we can become prey, a terrifying prospect. In dream images such as a great cat prowling in the house or the backyard, psyche warns us that physically or affectively we are identified with big cat libido and need to get some distance. To respond to such urges by killing, caging or degrading the great cat is to brutally repress one of nature's most extraordinary incarnations of creative aggressiveness and sovereign instinct. The resolution seems to be in balance and boundaries.

Brakefield, Tom and Alan Shoemaker. *Big Cats: Kingdom of Might.* Stillwater, MN, 1993.
Desai, Helen. Unpublished essay. Avery Brundage Asian Art Museum. SF, 1997.
Green, Susie. *Tiger.* London, 2006.
Lurker, Manfred. *The Gods and Symbols of Ancient Egypt.* NY, 1980.
Shaw, Ian and Paul T. Nicholson. *The Dictionary of Ancient Egypt.* NY, 1995.

3. Throughout Asia the tiger is the king of animals. Here, it is depicted with a rushing torrent of water as a parallel amplification of its power. In Japan the tiger came to be the symbol of the aristocratic warriors, the samurai. *Tiger,* by Kishi Ganku, hanging scroll, ca. 1795, Japan.

4. The sculptures of the Benin kingdom of Nigeria are prized. Almost all Benin art, from the 15th century onward, was created to honor the Oba, or king. Leopards, like this one, would be kept on royal altars signifying royal power. Ivory and copper, 19th century, Benin, Nigeria.

3

4

Bear

Evidence suggests that since Paleolithic times, human beings have made the bear an object of magico-religious veneration. Clever, curious, dexterous, the bear is so like a human in appearance and character. Yet it is also wild and massive, with its broad head, extended jaws, huge teeth, shaggy coat and heavy, powerful paws with five razor-sharp claws capable of tearing its prey limb from limb. For many peoples, this largest carnivorous land mammal, able to rise up to ten feet tall on its hind legs, has represented a sacred creature that could move between worlds, often functioning as a "tutelary figure" or spirit helper to mythic heroes. There are stories that tell of marriages and crossings-over between bears and humans. Many Native American tribes saw the bear as a master healer who in using plants to support its own health taught humans about their medicinal properties (Shepard, 100). Shamans or medicine men often dressed as bears and imitated the bear's gait in their dances to take on its healing powers, or shape-shifted into bears for their spirit journeys (Saunders, 76). To don the bearskin was to become one with a superhuman, initiating ancestor, often referred to respectfully as "brother" or "grandmother" (Eliade, 459). In Norse legend, Odin's special warriors were called "berserkers" because of the bearskins they wore to enter a trance of uncontrollable fury, superhuman strength and resistance in battle.

Immensely powerful, the bear knows about death through its ability to deal it as well as to survive it. Associated with highly potent and thus dangerous spiritual domains, the bear is also emblematic of the drastic repercussions for the uninitiated who violate them. The bear is the animal of the virgin huntress-goddess Artemis, "one unto herself" like the single bear mother, ferocious patroness of childbirth, young animals and children, and capable of dismembering anyone who intrudes upon her sphere (ARAS, 1:97). In alchemy the bear corresponds to the potentially devouring affective energies of psyche's unconscious realm that can seize us destructively, especially if we are naïve or disrespectful enough to underestimate their significance. Yet the bear is equally evocative of the mothering aspect of nature, manifested in the image of the she-bear holding and suckling her cubs upright, carrying them on her back and fiercely and tenderly teaching them to forage and hunt. Nine-year-old Athenian girls were fostered by the she-bear Artemis as members of her cult. Wearing bearskins and dancing in the forest, they contacted their own fierce natures while learning about the particularly feminine mysteries surrounding fertility and birth. In the heavens the Big Bear and Little Bear, linked to the pole star, orient geographical as well as mystical journeys, the whole vault of heaven seeming to revolve in time with the Bear's circuit.

Because the bear disappears and returns in its cycle of hibernation, it is also an emblem of rebirth. Actually not true hibernators, brown and black bears merely sleep lightly through the winter, their body temperature dropping by only a few degrees, so that they can give birth and suckle their offspring while still buried in the ground, and rouse themselves quickly if disturbed (Saunders, 76). Emerging in the spring from their "little death" they are accompanied by new life, their cubs born so tiny, naked and blind that in classical antiquity they were believed to be shapeless lumps of flesh until their mothers "licked them into shape," so creating order out of chaos. Similarly, in shamanistic societies, initiates had visions of the bear as a spirit animal that dismembered and cleansed, strengthened and reconstituted their skeleton, symbolically replacing the old structure of being with a new one capable of enduring the most imposing forces not only of the mundane world, but also of the eternal.

Clottes, Jean. *Return to Chauvet Cave: Excavating the Birthplace of Art: The First Full Report*. London, 2003.
Davidson, Hilda Roderick Ellis. *Gods and Myths of Northern Europe*. Baltimore, MD, 1964.
Saunders, Nicholas. *Animal Spirits*. NY, 1995.
Shepard, Paul and Barry Sanders. *The Sacred Paw: The Bear in Nature, Myth, and Literature*. NY, 1985.

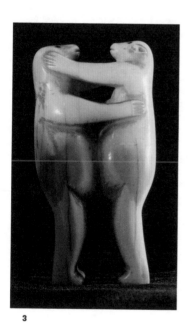

1. These bear images may have served to bring the vital substance of the animal under the influence of humans through sacred ritual (Clottes, 204). Wall painting, ca. 30,000–32,000 years old, Chauvet Cave, France.

2. The great bulk that makes a bear a bear is manifest in this grizzly.

3. Global warming threatens the existence of this huge, mighty, fierce and playful bear, almost invisible in the snow. Its survival may depend in part on mating with the brown bear. In Inuit lore, bears shape-shift into humans and humans into bears. *Two Polar Bears Embracing*, Western Inuit, walrus ivory, 19th century, Northwest Coast, United States.

Wolf

*[It is] a Heiltsuk belief that wolves do
not show themselves unless they are trying
to tell us something.*
**Ian McAllister, *The Last Wild Wolves:
Ghosts of the Rain Forest***

Possibly no other creature has stirred us to a more mystical communion with nature or a more abject fear of her dark realities than the wolf. Listening to the rough magic of a wolf howl conjures dreamscapes in which wolves are massed at the bottom of an abyss or stroll through the wilderness of urban streets, or loom, startlingly, at our front door. Skilled predators, at the top of the food chain, they evoke the vital and entirely unsentimental instinctual energies of the animal psyche. Our projections on them reveal our longing for a (re)connection with our own animal soul, and our terror that the encounter will result in the dismemberment of the ego.

Wolves are hair-raisers. Traversing the Great Distances on their slender legs and prodigious feet they appear to float, silent and spectral, like emissary spirits. The gradations of color in their variegated pelages move from white and cream and ochre to orange and brown, gray and black. They might be transmutations into form and corporeity of the diffuse light of dawn and dusk, the intervals of transition and enchantment known in folklore as "the hour of the wolf." The epithet alludes to favorite hunting times of these legendary travelers and consorters with ravens. Figuratively, it connotes the precincts of the liminal where divergent energies of light and darkness, life and death, rending and reintegration meet and merge.

In mythology, wolves are depicted as embodiments of the gaping jaws of death and unappeasable appetite. Particularly in Christian iconography they are the rapacious spoilers of sheep-like innocence. But if the dangers of the chthonic are real, it is also the chthonic in which vital immediacy is embedded. It is the wolf, at one with nature, who mediates the "voluntary death," our suffering the necessary dismemberment of self-idealization naively innocent of the dark stuff that carries our substance. Wolves theriomorphically represent the sun god Apollo as bearers of his darker, more subtle luminosity the alchemists called the light of nature. Wolves accompany the war god Mars, connoting the ability to act forcefully and effectively out of instinctual clues and discriminated cunning. Geri and Freki are the robust wolf companions of Odin, the pensive, self-sacrificing Norse god of wisdom, poetry, magic and death. Like them, the vigilant forces of nature look to the appointed times of advent and departure.

That the primordial she-wolf nurtured a civilization into being tells us something about the importance of chthonic wolfish energies as the ground of creative process, culture building and our capacity to engage psyche's energies of dissolution as well as rebirth in our repeated cycles of transformation. Without those energies, in contrast to the wolf, we will never be at home in the universe.

1. Conveying the vitality of Nature with her mother's milk, a mythic she-wolf suckles abandoned twins Romulus (the future founder of Rome) and Remus. The depiction is suggestive of the psychic roots of countless stories of abandoned human children raised by wolves. She-wolf, Etruscan, the end of the 6th–early 5th century B.C.E.; twins, by Antonio Pollaiolo, Renaissance.

2. Courage, endurance, co-operative skill in the hunt and the fierce protectiveness of their young are attributes Native Americans admired in the wolf. Wolf-head effigy, wood, ca. 800–1400, Key Marco, Florida.

3. Betrayed by the gods and bound, Fenrir, one of the giant death wolves of Nordic myth, will ultimately be loosed to bring about the destruction of the old to make way for the new. Bronze, 6th century C.E., Sweden.

1

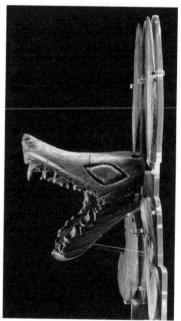

2

3

Coyote

Bow-wow-wow, ki-yi-i-i-yee-ip-ip-eow-ow-ow!
Bow-wow-ki-yi-i-i-ee-eouw-ow-ow-eow-ow-ow!
Yee-ee-ee-yeow-wow-ow-ow-ki-yip-ee-i-ow-ow!
Translation of coyote song by E. A. Brinninstool
(Dobie, 1938)

Teeth bared, necktie loosened as if at the end of a long, hot day, coyote lifts his head in a wavering howl and high-pitched yips—the song of the West. He may be getting in touch with the pack, or announcing his presence and territorial stake. Some have thought a coyote must be a cross between a fox and a wolf, but its closest relatives are actually wolves, dogs and jackals. You can see them in a coyote, but it is also its own person. Lanky, loping, the bushy tail contained but not tucked, ears high, walking on its toes, coat displaying the yellowish browns and reds of the desert; all in all a fine-looking "now you see me, now you don't" vanishing presence. In his 1938 classic *Coyote Wisdom*, the Texan J. Frank Dobie claimed the coyote survived through trickery, playing dead to attract its victims and then killing them when they unsuspectingly come nearby, tricking dogs into giving chase while its accomplices stole the chickens the dogs were guarding, and faking injuries to lure predators away from its young. The coyote is considered to be a ventriloquist, said Dobie, because when you hear a coyote's howl you can't tell which direction it's coming from, and the song of one coyote can sound like many (Dobie, 50, 57). Humans who have felt hoodwinked by the coyote have projected on it traits like greed and cunning. For others, like the Native American Crow, Old Man Coyote represented the first among the mythic gods and ancestors; he was creator of the earth, its creatures and human customs. That the world isn't perfect made coyote a refreshingly less-than-perfect spirit himself, capable of error and getting duped. Among many Native American peoples, Coyote is both creator and destroyer, a shapeshifting character whose seemingly random actions and pranks have unforeseen consequences. Navajos refer to the coyote as God's Dog (Ryden xii, xiii), and the name of the trickster Aztec God, Huehuecoyotl, means the Old, Old Coyote (Miller, 92).

Having immense stamina and agility, opportunistic in every way and quick to colonize an open ecological niche, the coyote is one of the most adaptable creatures on earth, forever defying our attempts to define or exterminate it. Thus the coyote is particularly suited to personify psyche's old, old unpredictability and changeableness, the way it adapts and extends its territory with time and evolution, its ability to be visible and invisible simultaneously, to shift shape and trip us up just when we think we have disposed of its more troublesome effects and got a grasp on it.

Dobie, J. Frank. *The Voice of the Coyote.* Boston, 1949.
Miller, Mary Ellen and Karl A. Taube. *The Gods and Symbols of Ancient Mexico and the Maya.* NY, 1993.
Ryden, Hope. *God's Dog: A Celebration of the North American Coyote.* NY, 1979.
http://news.nationalgeographic.com/news/2002/08/0806_020806_coyote.html.

Howling Coyote, ceramic with details in resinous black paint, 5th–6th century C.E., Veracruz, Mexico.

Fox

A wise fox will never rob his neighbor's roost.
English proverb

The fox's fiery red coat, flamelike ears and tail and vertical pupils in glowing amber eyes give it a volatile appearance, embodying the elusive, flickering, transformative qualities of fire itself (Wallen, 36, 82). The fox seemingly possesses its own inner light, like the shifting, mysterious "foxfire" that luminesces eerily in marsh and forest, representing a more chthonic form of consciousness than man's. In Japanese folklore, this shape-shifting fire is said to be generated by Kitsune, the fox-trickster, when he wants to become human, by using his belly as a drum (Addiss, 132ff) or, in allusion to his sexual potency and fertility, by pulling his tail between his legs and rubbing it with his forepaws until it ignites (Wallen, 69). Thus he produces an elusive glimmer that beckons from another realm—a fleeting presence that Japanese poets likened to sunlight flashing amidst rain, suddenly appearing, dazzling us, and then vanishing, like the fox itself.

Distinguishable among the canids by its long cat-like whiskers, delicate legs and strong smell, the diminutive, omnivorous fox pounces on its prey with playful, acrobatic leaps, then caches away what its small stomach cannot immediately digest (Wallen, 36-7). Though it does not hibernate, in spring the vixen's large brood sleeps tucked away in an underground den called an "earth," with bushy, white-tipped tails wrapped around noses, while the male, or "dog," regularly delivers food (MacDonald, 70). As for its legendary cunning, the red fox has been seen breaking its own scent-traces by leaping onto the backs of sheep or sweeping the snow with its tail as it runs, thereby "erasing" its tracks (Caspari, 111), as well as warily using its *vibrissae* (whiskers) to determine the size of an opening so

as not to get enclosed in a trap (Macdonald, 68-73). Apart from its regular barks, yaps and eerie banshee screams, a fox tricks its prey, according to legend, by bleating like a lost lamb, squeaking like an injured rabbit or squealing to charm rats from farm buildings.

Though often portrayed as a low-down, thieving outlaw who must be tracked down and punished, the nimble fox's notorious ability to transgress boundaries has made it one of the most successful survivors on the planet (Caspari, 110). In Homer's painting, a lithe russet fox runs through deep snow, apparently pursued by hunters and baying hounds to the sea's edge, even as the black crows above portend its approaching death (Lucie-Smith, 231). Though the tentatively lifted paw and tensed underbelly convey its trapped feeling, the cocked ears hint that the clever, fleet fox may yet find a way to elude its pursuers.

In Medieval legend, the labyrinthine passages of the wily Reynard's underground "castle" allowed him to be everywhere at once and nowhere at all, while the shimmering fluidity of his vulpine intelligence, anticipating and deluding all opponents, subverted the "proper" order of things. Called "son of the earth" by the Incas, the fox's ability to hear through the earth about far-off events made him a diviner-curer, just as the fox-guide's subterranean knowledge led North American and Siberian shamans through paths not ordinarily open or visible to humans. Thus if we approach the ubiquitous, mercurial fox—like the unconscious—on its own terms, it may guide us through the transformational spaces between oppositional states of being—between wild forest and cultivated farmland, between unconventional, intuitive intelligence and collective social norms, and between animal, human and spirit worlds, both beneficent and demonic—in the service of wholeness (Wallen, 43ff).

I

I. Red fox (*Vulpes vulpes*).

In Japan and China, no other entity has been endowed with greater "spectral potency" than the fox (Veith, 84), regarded not only as the "most subtle of all beasts," but as a *kami*— an uncanny spiritual force likened to thunder, echoes and dragons (Munsterberg, 144). Respected as a messenger of Inari, the beneficent Shinto rice goddess, but also feared as a wicked animal that can haunt and possess (EoR 5:406-7), the fox, though endowed with its own vital, earthy force, is said to long for wisdom and increasing spiritual power as well. To obtain this, it will disguise itself as a "foxy" woman and seduce scholarly young men to absorb life-essence through their semen (EoR 5:406), allowing it to become first human, then immortal, and finally a thousand-year-old, nine-tailed deity, able to pass into higher spheres (Leach, 413; Wallen, 69). These beguilements often leave its victims depleted, depressed or hysterical (Piggott, 107), and fox-possession is still a serious diagnosis in Japan. At times, a fox-spirit may sincerely love her human partner, marrying him and bearing him children, though she seldom returns the stolen life-essence and, as we see in Yoshitoshi's print, never loses the ability to revert to her former shape (EoR 5:406). So does the elusive inner feminine outfox us, slipping back into the unconscious after casting her spells.

Addiss, Stephen, et al. *Japanese Ghosts and Demons.* NY, 1985.

Caspari, Elizabeth. *Animal Life in Nature, Myth and Dreams.* Wilmette, IL, 2003.

Leach, Maria. Ed. *Funk & Wagnalls Standard Dictionary of Folklore, Mythology and Legend.* NY, 1949.

Lucie-Smith, Edward. *Zoo.* NY, 1998.

Macdonald, David W. *The Encyclopedia of Mammals.* NY, 1984.

Munsterberg, Hugo. *Dictionary of Chinese and Japanese Art.* NY, 1981.

Piggott, Juliet. *Japanese Mythology.* Feltham, NY, 1969.

Veith, Ilza. *Hysteria: The History of a Disease.* Chicago, 1965.

Wallen, Martin. *Fox.* London, 2006.

2. *Fox Hunt*, by Winslow Homer, oil on canvas, 1893, United States.

3 *Kuzunoha, the Fox-Wife, Parting from Her Child*, from the Shinkei Sanjurokkaisen series, by Tsukioka Yoshitoshi, wood-block print, 1890, Japan.

Kangaroo

A kangaroo baby peers out from the pouch of her mother in an expressive Aboriginal bark painting. In nature, the baby is born little more than an inch in length with only forelegs, nostrils and tongue well-developed; it must use its forelegs to crawl up the mother's fur and into her pouch immediately after birth. There it attaches itself fiercely to one of her four teats, which swells in response and nearly fuses with the baby's mouth until the infant is more fully developed. The full gestation period has lasted only 30 to 40 days. Unlike placental animals, which nourish their undeveloped young within the womb and expel them into abrupt separation from the mother at birth, marsupials (animals who give birth prematurely and nourish their undeveloped young within a pouch covering teats—the *marsupium*) keep their young extremely close. In the dark warmth of the maternal pouch, the baby nurses at will, cleaned and kept safe by the mother for many months until it is able to venture out on its own. The youngster, out of the pouch, returns to nurse and continues to stay close to its mother until it reaches sexual maturity, as late as two to three years of age (*Enc. Brit* 23: 399ff; Embery, 103).

The generous mothering of Aboriginal women mimics the kangaroo's maternal practices. Their infants enjoy nearly constant contact with their mother's bodies and are breast-fed on demand for three to five years. The women claim they learned it from the kangaroo Dreaming—the transpersonal realm that infuses their collective lives and links them to their ancestors (Lawlor, 165). Kangaroo offers a paradigm for nourishing whatever we give birth to, whether mani-fested as an embryonic awareness or creative project. She teaches us to hold it close and nurture it in darkness until it is developed enough to be released and expressed in the world.

Kangaroos travel in large groups called "mobs," headed by a dominant male that repels his younger rivals by biting, kicking and boxing. Well known is the kangaroo's remarkable jumping capacity, which can cover up to 25 feet in a single leap and reach heights of ten feet (*Enc. Brit.* 6:717). Mythology tells of a red kangaroo that made the "creative and supernatural Dream Journey" across the land, the first of its species to do so (Cooper, 142). Tribal totem and ancestor, it was also he who gave man the first spear-thrower and who, as culture hero, journeyed to the center of the continent, marking the land with caves, rocks and creeks as he did so. These landmarks became sacred places, permeated with Kangaroo's creative power (Willis, 286). According to legend, it was also the skin of the red kangaroo that clothed the Sun, explaining why she arrives each morning dressed in red (Guirand, 464).

Cooper, J. C. *Symbolic and Mythological Animals.* London, 1992.

Embery, Joan. *Joan Embery's Collection of Amazing Animal Facts.* NY, 1983.

Guirand, Félix. *Larousse Encyclopedia of Mythology.* NY, 1959.

Lawlor, Robert. *Voices of the First Day: Awakening in the Aboriginal Dreamtime.* Rochester, VT, 1991.

Willis, Roy G. *World Mythology.* NY, 1993.

1. Kangaroo and her baby. Bark painting, Aboriginal, 1921–8, West Arnhem Land, Australia.

2. Boxing and kicking in humanlike upright posture, two kangaroos spar. Western New South Wales, Australia.

1

2

Deer

You run like a herd of luminous deer
and I am dark, I am forest.
You are a wheel at which I stand,
whose dark spokes sometimes catch me up,
revolve me nearer to the center.
Rilke, *The Book of Hours*

Hovering in the full moon's luminous path, between above and below, stepping lightly forward between here and not-here while gazing back over its shoulder, this shimmering white deer bridges the earthly and the spiritual realms, embodying and leading us into the symbolic, intermediate realm of the soul. With its velvet coat, soft moist muzzle, brown eyes glistening beneath long lashes and slender, delicate limbs, it seems the deer's very nature to symbolize purity and sublimity. A pair of deer is often depicted flanking the throne of the Buddha, who is said to have incarnated in a previous life as a honey-voiced, golden stag whose mission it was to calm the passions of humans lost in despair and lead them to the eightfold path. The deer's graceful caution, elegant leaps, sudden appearances and swift disappearances link the animal to the alchemical Mercurius, the transformative intermediary soul substance, as well as to pilgrimage or initiation paths that are circuitous, indirect, constantly shifting direction or, like the deer, disappearing altogether (Abraham, 52). The occasional, mysterious hoof-sounds we hear in the brush along the meandering way belong to a hidden creature that teaches us to tread our path with calm reverence for the unseen and unknown.

The stag is revered worldwide for its tall, annually renewed, treelike antlers, symbols of fertility, rejuvenation, rebirth, the ebb and flow of spiritual growth and the passage of time. Stags shed their antlers every winter, and each spring they grow back with an extra branch, clearly exhibiting their age and waxing strength. By autumn, they have lost their antlers' soft "velvet" and are ready for the rutting season. The loud, barking grunts, bellowing roars and clashing antlers of competing males can be heard for miles, fostering their reputation for virility, as the triumphant stag might mate with as many as a dozen does. After a long winter gestation and spring delivery, the hungry doe will slip away to graze, leaving her curled up newborn, safely odorless and motionless, hidden by its dappled camouflage in the tall grass. Later the fawn will follow her out, learning to browse, explore and hide in plain sight. Unlike other ungulates, like sheep and goats with their hierarchical and therefore dominable nature, the more solitary, elusive and territorial deer, unwilling to breed in confined spaces, is not easily domesticated, commanding our awe and respect since ancient times (Kennedy, 33–4; Slater, 62–64).

From the Paleolithic era to the industrial age, deer provided humans with a principal source of food, as well as clothing and tools. The prolonged pursuit of this gentle animal awakened the hunter's intuition not only of the ways of the deer but of the surrounding forest. Hunting societies, from ancient Europe to medieval Japan and Native North America, acquired such a profound experience of the deer's movements that the belief was born that the creature could travel from one world to the next in a graceful bound. The Celtic lord of forest beasts, Cernunnos, adorned with leafy antlers, collects the souls of the dying and escorts them to the underworld, accompanied by the hunting goddess Flidass who, like her Greek counterpart, Artemis, rides in a deer-driven chariot. Legend tells how pregnant does swam to the island of Artemis, known as Mother Deer, to give birth, while she transformed the hunter Actaeon, when he dared spy on her bathing, into a stag to be torn apart by his own hounds, linking the deer to the mysterious passages of birth, death and transfiguration. Indeed, there is an unconscious equivalence between hunter and hunted. In a Christian legend, a stag

1. Kasuga deer mandala, ink and pigment on silk scroll, 13th century, Japan.

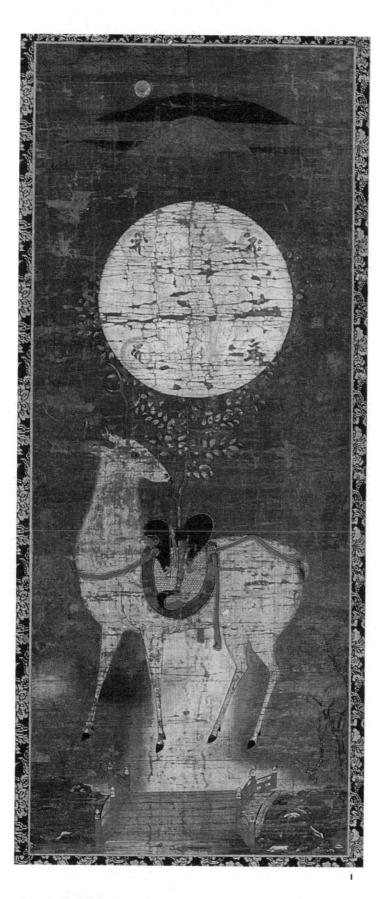

1

enters a thick forest in order to draw the soldier hunting it away from his comrades so that the stag can "hunt the hunter while he hunts," finally confronting him with a crucifix miraculously sprouting between its antlers (Giorgi, 122–3). Thus, "the hunter and the hunted are secretly identical," the seeker and the spiritual goal, as well as the pathway to it, are one and the same (von Franz, 118–21).

> *The wild deer, wand'ring here & there,*
> *Keeps the Human Soul from Care.*
> **William Blake,** *Auguries of Innocence*

Abraham, Lyndy. *A Dictionary of Alchemical Imagery.* Cambridge, UK, and NY, 1998.
Chinery, Michael. Ed. *The Kingfisher Illustrated Encyclopedia of Animals.* NY, 1992.
Giorgi, Rosa. *Saints in Art.* LA, 2002.
Kennedy, Des. *Nature's Outcasts.* Pownal, VT, 1993.
MacDonald, David W. *The Encyclopedia of Mammals.* NY, 1984.
Slater, Peter. *The Encyclopedia of Animal Behavior.* NY, 1989.
von Franz, Marie Louise. *The Interpretation of Fairy Tales.* Dallas, 1970.

2

3

2. *The Vision of Saint Eustace*, by Pisanello,
egg tempera on wood panel, ca. 1438–42, Italy.

3. Wooden drum-stand in the shape of a deer, Eastern
Zhou dynasty (771–256 B.C.E.), Hubei, China.

Rabbit/Hare

In an eighteenth-century Chinese embroidery a white rabbit stands on the moon next to a tree of life and, bathed in full moonlight, pounds the elixir of immortality with a golden pestle. The rabbit as agent of ever-lasting renewal is reflected in the Japanese tradition of preparing pounded rice cakes called *mochi* (full moon) for the celebration of the New Year. It is said that a rabbit living on the moon is constantly making *mochi*.

All over the world moon and rabbit are linked. A Mayan ceramic piece displays a plump blue rabbit upon the disk of the moon. Both the moon's and the rabbit's existence reflect in high relief the cyclical nature of life, the ever-recurring conjunction of darkness and light, death and rebirth. As each month the moon falls prey to darkness only to shine full again, so rabbits manage to live under the shadow of death. In North America, for example, they are prey to coyotes, wolves, wild cats, owls, eagles, hawks, snakes and humans, and yet they thrive.

Survival defenses of the rabbit include eyes at the side of its head, which see both forward and back, sensitive ears and nose, and the ability to run at high speed with erratic shifts in direction and sudden "freezing," which allows it to vanish from sight. Furthermore, wild rabbits, if cornered, will use their sharp claws and teeth to fight. But it is the rabbit's remarkable birthing capacity that keeps it inhabiting almost every continent of the world. Females bear up to five litters a year of three to six young and the gestation period is four weeks. Two weeks after giving birth, a doe is ready to mate again. Baby rabbits have no scent, making it difficult to detect them, and the doe, who does have a scent, can be away from the litter except for infrequent feedings because her milk has an extraordinarily high fat content.

Treading softly on the earth to nibble fresh green shoots and grasses, rabbits emerge from cover in the soft light of dawn and dusk, thresholds of transition. The diffuse light in which the rabbit reveals itself, its ability to easily vanish from sight and its lively antics have made it an embodiment of alchemy's Mercurius, the elusive, informing spirit of psyche that can bring together the mortal and immortal aspects of self. The rabbit is thus depicted as the initiate's guide in processes that lead to the obtaining of the elixir of immortality, which is also in the rabbit's possession. Perhaps because of the rabbit's association with endless regeneration and the realm of the eternal, it has been portrayed mythically as capable of heroic acts of self-sacrifice. In a Jataka story from India, the Buddha, in one of his early incarnations, appears as a rabbit, who makes a willing sacrifice of himself by leaping into a blazing fire so that he may become food for a Brahmin. In consequence, the Brahmin can fulfill his priestly duties, and the generosity of the rabbit is honored by the imprinting of his image on the moon. Often humorously, the figure of the rabbit carries the compensatory, tricksterish energies that subvert the usual order of things. The young heroine of *Alice in Wonderland* falls into a rabbit hole and seeing a white rabbit running rapidly ahead of her follows him into an uncanny, underground world. In the play *Harvey*, Elwood P. Dowd and his six-foot-tall white rabbit companion are the foil for a proper, moneyed family lacking soulful imagination (Chase, 571–607). Small often overcomes large in the escapades of the English Peter Rabbit and American Br'er Rabbit.

Rabbits are remarkably appealing as small and sometimes timid animals. Their soft fur invites touch, and their long ears and pink eyes are endearing. Rabbits are also known to dance and leap in meadows in the moonlight and to cavort in sexual play. It is only natural, then, that rabbits should join the throng around the love-goddess Aphrodite, or that the gift of a rabbit in sixth century B.C.E. Greece should be considered a token of love. Or even that *Playboy* magazine's "bunnies" should be dressed in bunny outfits. The great mother goddess in her maternal aspect is sometimes depicted with giant rabbits standing beside her, emblems of fertility and rebirth, later interwoven even into Christian mysteries as the Easter Bunny with his basket of brightly colored, magical eggs.

Chase, Mary. *Harvey*. In *Best American Plays: Supplementary Volume, 1918–1958*. Ed. John Gassner. NY, 1961.

1. Rabbit on the moon stirring the elixir of immortality.
Embroidery, 18th century, China.

2. Blue rabbit and a human figure on the moon.
Ceramic, Mayan, 550–800, Mexico.

Rat/Mouse

Running across the altar
and stealing a chrysanthemum—
the temple rat
Takamasa

Mice are so weird.
They're like humans in rodent costumes.
Noah Baumbach, *Mouse au Vin*

Typhoons ended,
the rat swims across
the flowing waters
Buson

I'm a rat, which means life is hard.
Remy, the rat chef, *Ratatouille,* **2007**

There is nothing small or mean to the soul.
Ralph Waldo Emerson,
(journal entry, Summer, 1841)

Rats and mice are hard to pin down. Elusive by nature, surreptitious, they appear and disappear like diminutive magicians. Living in tandem with human beings, they are always coming from behind. They shadow us wherever we go, perpetual stowaways on our voyage through history and our passages to brave new worlds. They slip through the cracks of our physical and psychic terrain, privy to our closeted and cupboarded secrets. Like time, hunger and guilt they gnaw incessantly. They personify the labyrinthine restlessness beneath the surface of things. Their edgy commensalism is not widely appreciated. Vilified as vermin, feared as vectors of disease and death, despised as voracious plunderers of our amber waves of grain,

mice and rats mostly exist at the margins. Denizens of basement and attic, sewer and alleyway, they furtively rummage the mountainous dumps of our collective rejectimenta. And yet, observing at dusk a happy group of rats recycling discarded Halloween treats or watching through the window of a passing bus the unmistakable silhouette foraging single-mindedly in the snowy darkness, you have to admire their tenacity, their eerie ability to beat the odds.

Like all rodents, rats and mice have prodigious incisal power. They can gnaw their way through just about anything, including brick, wood and lead. Unspecialized, omnivorous, they can adapt to almost any climate and resourcefully avail themselves of whatever they find at hand. The most prolific of any mammal, they persist, by sheer numbers, against the onslaught of their raptorial, mammalian and reptilian predators and the relentless persecutions of humankind. Curious, sociable, agile; endowed with an excellent sense of smell, fine-tuned hearing and taste buds as sensitive as ours, mice and rats are portrayed in folklore and popular culture as heroes, helpers and even five-star restaurant chefs. Gnawing through a net to free a trapped lion, dropping down a drain to retrieve a wedding ring, sewing intricate buttonholes a tailor's old hands can no longer manage, mice are suggestive of the small, invisible, intricate workings of the unconscious to overcome obstacles, even without our conscious participation. So, also, the rat companion and "vehicle" of the Hindu deity Ganesha chisels the knots that tie us up and gains entry to the bolted treasures in the psyche. As emblems of fertility, both mice and rats—especially white ones—can signify wealth, good luck and abundance, as in the Chinese Year of the Rat.

1. An Indian woman pours an offering of milk for some of the 20,000 holy rats that live in the Karni Mata Hindu temple in Deshnoke, Rajasthan. It is averred that no temple rat has ever transmitted any illness to the bevy of tourists and worshippers who flock there for blessing and good luck. Photograph taken June 20, 2002.

On the other hand, as secretive creatures active after dark, rats and mice are inevitably associated with subversive occult forces and devouring influx. Notorious as hosts of the fleas that spread Bubonic Plague to millions of people in the Middle Ages (and also killed millions of rats), they are mythic harbingers of scourge. Rats leaving a sinking ship, or mice scurrying from a house are familiar omens of imminent misfortune. Paradoxically, troops of mice and rats are often depicted in folktales as vehicles of a just vengeance, the executioners of those who escaped rightful punishment, especially for crimes against the poor and hungry.

There is a rat or mouse element within many of us: a small, feral, chthonic aspect of ourselves reprehensible in the eyes of the collective. It is tempting to relegate this "rat" to the furtive edges of consciousness, where it will remain all but invisible. But if we are willing to engage it, to give it a respectful space within which to reveal itself, its energy can become an invaluable ally. Oracular, with its ears close to the (under) ground, it can warn us of the dark patches, and mediate our way through them. It will teach us a kind of psychic street smarts, instill a scrappy determination to survive and, ultimately, reveal itself as the deity in disguise.

Baumbach, Noah. Shouts & Murmurs – "Mouse au Vin." *The New Yorker* (January 26, 2009).
Emerson, Ralph Waldo. *Selections from Ralph Waldo Emerson: An Organic Anthology.* Ed. Stephen E. Whicher. Boston, 1960.

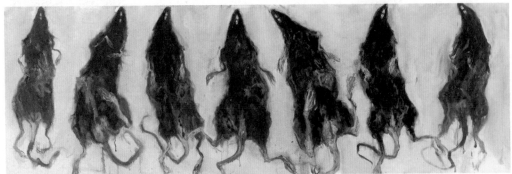

2

3

2. In this lurid depiction of rats, arranged with cold dispassion in the splayed contortions of an agonized death, the "traitors" are the human individuals whose voracious search for knowledge renders Nature barren and lifeless. *The Traitors*, by Heng Peng, painting, 1997, United States.

3. Pictured on a brass temple door from Bikaner in Rajasthan, the rat goddess Karni Mata is a 14th-century mystic believed to be an avatar of the Hindu goddess Durga. The rats carry the souls of her devotees; rare white rats are embodiments of the goddess and her kin. Brass, temple door, Bikaner, Rajasthan, India.

Bat

Embroidery on a Chinese imperial robe depicts bats in swift, darting flight above ocean waves that spiral and surge in a corresponding skyward momentum of joy. A woman would have worn this "happy occasion" robe for celebrations such as birthdays or anniversaries; the bats are emblematic of longevity and blessing.

Bats are unique mammals in many ways. They have the ability not just for gliding, but for sustained, powered flight. They hang by their hooked toes upside down in sleep and torpor and even when giving birth and nursing their young. Echo-locating bats fly with their mouths open and teeth bared, making ultrasound clicks focused and modified by sonar equipment in the shape of leaves, spikes and spears bizarrely carried on their noses or mouths. "Hand-winged" (*Chiroptera*), their thin, spidery fingers are elongated to support the rubbery membrane and living tissue that cloak these flesh-and-blood gargoyles. Bats have a clawed, opposable "thumb" and possess brain pathways consistent with those of primates, but have retained the body of a rodent. They fly like birds, by flapping their wings, but lack the feathers of either bird or angel.

Bats carry our projections of a "reverse" order that forces our perspective into the nocturnal, the underworld, and the equivalent cavernous depths of psyche. The twilight emergence of bats in the thousands or millions to forage embodies for us the concealed, primordial forces of the netherworld breaking out in expansive liberation. Fantasy has associated bats with the new moon, full moon and spirit realm, and thus with sorcery, enchantment and witchcraft. The little blood-imbibing bats native to Central and South America in early times became associated with the mysteries of death related to eternal cycles of renewal, and also with the terrors of the were-animal and vampire. Their razor-sharp teeth were reminiscent of the flint knife that cuts into the life of the sacrificial victim. The blinding bat-demon Zotz was imagined as swallowing the light of day and the "House of the Bat" was one of the corridors traversed on the way to the underworld (DoS, 71). Yet the seemingly erratic flittering of bats in the dusk which we liken to "lunatic" thoughts is not erratic at all, but sonar-guided, in the same way that there is an instinctual coherence to the seeming incoherence of the dark stirrings of psyche. In the rainforests, flying foxes are prolific pollinators of night-blooming vegetation, linking them to the sweet nectars, magical efficacy and fertility of night. A creation myth depicts the bat as the only one that can see in the creviced darkness before the world comes into being, when sky and earth are pinned together like rock.

In reality the bat is shy and gentle, fastidiously groomed and a tidy housekeeper (Ackerman, 4ff). Particularly in Asia, the bat represents the maternal aspect of the great goddess. The attunement of a mother bat and her baby is such that they can instantly recognize each other's high-pitched squeak in a nursery cave of millions and be reunited. Vampire bats are known to share regurgitated blood with starving bats and to adopt orphans (Schutt, 23–4).

Alchemy sometimes depicted the mercurial spirit of the unconscious with bat wings. It is a way of conveying not only psyche's darkness, mystery and ambivalence, but also its provision and unforeseen agency, the way it can lead consciousness into spheres requiring a different kind of orientation and in which can be found the fructifying unconventionality of nature.

Ackerman, Diane. "In Praise of Bats." *The Moon by Whale Light: And Other Adventures among Bats, Penguins, Crocodilians, and Whales.* NY, 1991.
Schutt, Bill. "The Curious, Bloody Lives of Vampire Bats." *Natural History* (November 2008).

1. Participating in the same dynamic energy, bats and waves adorn a woman's opulent "happy occasion" robe. On other parts of the robe are medallions in which emblems of longevity are encircled by five bats, signifying the five blessings of this life: longevity, wealth, tranquility, virtue and the achievement of one's destiny. *The Bat Medallion Robe*, detail, Qing dynasty, ca. 18th century, China.

2. Threshold guardian, a bat spreads its wings like a cloak above the doorway, its eyes and ears vigilant even for the subtle spirits of darkness. Florence, Italy.

3. Similar to images of the leaf-nosed vampire bat-demon Zotz, a bat man from the Maya. The blood-drinking bat of Central and South America became incorporated into the vampire lore of Europe, thus the "vampire" bat's name. Ca. 550–950, Guatemala.

Dog

There is a water over there, where the soul of one who has died must pass. And there is a dog there, a little black dog with a white spot on its throat. And one must ask permission from that dog to pass, so that one may travel on, to reach that other level, where those who have died are waiting, where those ancient relatives are living in their rancho.
Ramon Medina Silva, Huichol

With the rising of the dog-star, the living are distinguished by the Dog from the dead, for in truth everything withers that has not taken root.
Ancient alchemical text

One might imagine that humankind's first act upon standing and knowing was to tame and befriend the dog, for we have been intimately tied to our ultimate animal friend and ally for thousands of years. The uncanny superiority of his senses—his capacity to track a smell over immense distances, his sureness of direction, his keen feeling for truth of heart—have been our extension into realms where we could not venture unaided by his guidance. He can find what we have lost in the proverbial woods of the unknown, and gain nurturance from the hunt; in some cultures he was felt to commune with the spirit world. He has been willing to come into our world from his wolfish ancestry with a blossoming of unconditional love and devotion often far surpassing our own. In so doing the dog has assumed a central place in countless mythologies as a guide between the worlds of life and death, known and unknown, human and animal, and symbolically between the conscious mind and the wilderness of the unconscious psyche and soul.

In nearly every world mythology, our constant companion the dog has come to be associated with our other constant companion, death. Wild carrion devourers sniffing and consuming the dead, tame, ever hungry, digging into the depths of the earth with their paws, burying or finding bones, dogs attend death and assimilate death. Mythically fearsome death demons or abiding soul guides, they snatch human souls into the abyss of the underworld, or fetch them from it as they might snatch a morsel of meat or retrieve a ball. There are dogs that guard the gates of hell with a characteristically canine ferocity like Cerberus and Garm, the hellhound, and dogs who attend the mystery gods and goddesses of life and death: Hecate, Artemis, Osiris, Isis, Shiva, Asclepius, Hermes and others. The leash we hold on the dog links us to the energies of life and death. How we manipulate the leash says everything about how we are going to experience the ambivalent nature of the dog's death realm. The dog is keenly sensitive to its master's love or abuse.

In his role as psychopomp, threading us between the opposites of internal darkness and light, life and death, the dog appears now as wounder and at other times as healer. He hunts us down, driving us madly through our own unleashed passions toward a deeper authenticity. True to character, the dog is particularly responsive to human care, which brings out the best in him. We learn from the dog to paradoxically experience the rewards of capturing a soulful relationship to the unknown on its own terms. Bitten by the alchemical "Corascene dog," we might fall into the mouth of depression, swallowed by the devouring dog of a personal hell, becoming gruesomely bitchy, biting, trapped and hungry. Churchill referred to his own recurrent depressions as his "black dog." Sensing our despair our soul-dog may arrive and we may, if wise, finally ask the un-

1. Dogs never desert their masters, apt cause for them to be regarded in diverse mythologies and religions as accompanying their masters even unto death and as guides in the afterlife. Here, the pharaoh's two quite different dogs are depicted, one following the other. Relief sculpture, from the tomb of Sarenput II, 12th dynasty (ca. 1938–1756 B.C.E.), Egypt.

2. The dog was most likely the first animal to be domesticated. In this mosaic from ancient Pompeii, the dog is shown leashed to the four-cornered world of humankind's creation, there to serve him as his most loyal animal friend. *Cave Canem (Beware of Dog)*, from the House of the Faun, mid-1st century B.C.E., Pompeii, Italy.

1

2

derworld dog guide, maybe the Mexican Xolotl, to bring us from our darkened state, "across the ninefold river" to a new life, a rebirth. Or we might entreat the Egyptian dog-god Anubis to weigh our heart to assess its ability to love, as if asking that we be made more open to our companion animal soul that it may sniff out our path in the depths where we have lost our way.

Goethe's hero, Faust, despairing of an empty life of bookish but meaningless devotion, prays to die and asks for a guide to "distant lands." Mephistopheles appears to him first as a stray black poodle, a symbol of his own disowned and homeless soul. Mephistopheles then reveals himself as an evil whose ultimate purpose was salvation. The dog initiates us into the infernal darkness, where, if he weren't also so endearing and true, we might never find our way.

3. A woman is holding a dog with such a warm and loving attitude it inspires comparison with the unconditional bond of love between a mother and a child. Sculpture, pre-Columbian (1400–950 B.C.E.), Tlatilco, central Mexico.

4. In the mythology of the peoples from central Mexico, the dog was significant in the creation of humankind, as well as being the animal associated with an individual's passage through the underworld after death. Red-ware effigy vessel, 300 B.C.E.–600 C.E., Colima, Mexico.

5. The dark, infernal qualities of the dog are evident in this bleak and powerful image. The dog stands frozen in a hungry, possibly mad state, held tightly by a red grid that indicates a window of possibility that is no longer part of the picture. *Dog*, by Francis Bacon, oil on canvas, 1952, England.

5

Cat

The fog comes
on little cat feet.

It sits looking
over harbor and city
on silent haunches
and then moves on.
Carl Sandburg, Fog

A path runs barefoot through the forest. In the forest there are a lot of trees, a cuckoo, Hansel and Gretel, and other small animals ... When it gets dark the owl locks the forest with a big key, because if a cat got in there, then there would be some damage done.
Zbigniew Herbert, "Forest"

In the evening, all the cats who had participated in the rat-catching had a grand session at [the Swordsman's] house, and respectfully asked the great Cat to take the seat of honor. They made profound bows before her and said: "We all wish you to divulge your secrets for our benefit." The grand old cat answered: "Teaching is not difficult, listening is not difficult either, but what is truly difficult is to become conscious of what you have in yourself and be able to use it as your own."
The Swordsman and the Cat, from a seventeenth-century master's book on swordplay

Cats have a way of getting to us, of finding us where we live. From the moment they first emerged from the wild and forged their wary affiliation with human beings, they have largely defined the terms of their self-domestication. Much to the delight of their admirers, the tame and the tiger dwell within them in sinuous, if paradoxical accord. Padding proprietarily through the spaces of our mutual habitation, cats travel light, but bring whole other worlds in tow. Within their endlessly inventive ambit, primordial jungles sprout invisibly in living rooms, forest brooks overflow a water bowl, rocky outcroppings rise up from window-sills. Inveterately curious, they leave no stone un-turned. Even our flinty human hearts get kneaded into malleability under the impress of their questing little cat feet. Keep in cat company and you observe how decisively they grasp the moment with their grappling hook claws, and bring its possibilities earthward into realization. How intimately they traverse the liminal and the nighttime, gazing out from their darknesses with full-moon eyes and secret smiles. How inscruta-bly they preside over the rites and ceremonies of their feline rhythm of life. How they come and go as stealth-ily as fog; and are, and are not, the beloved creatures we think we know.

Cats have inspired potent human projections, both positive and negative. The ancient Egyptian sun god Ra may appear in the guise of a ferocious Tomcat delivering a killing blow to the Apophis serpent of pri-meval chaos. The fact that cats, like snakes, can strike with lightning quickness and precision only enhances the image. Buddhist monasteries have welcomed cats not only as protectors of the sacred texts against the destructive gnawing of mice, but as unobtrusive com-panions who share their capacity for quiet, orderly self-containment. In fairy tales, a cat may assume the role of a psychopomp whose nervy instinctual vitality com-pensates the over-refinement and "sublimated" in-stincts of the human hero or heroine. The ubiquitous *maneki-neko* (calling cat) of Japanese popular culture that beckons customers into shops and good fortune and prosperity into households is suggestive of fertile, life-enhancing feline energies.

1. Bastet shaking a sistrum and holding an aegis, with kittens at her feet. The name of the cat goddess means "she of the ointment jar," reflecting her soothing and peaceful nature, though as devoted mother she is also fierce. Late Period or Ptolemaic Period, ca. 664–630 B.C.E., Egypt.

301

In the eyes of their detractors, on the other hand, cats have often been viewed as cruel, self-serving or aloofly unloving. In Buddhist folklore, a rat dispatched to bring back medicine for the dying Buddha never completes its mission, because a cat kills and eats it along the way. Christian culture has often associated the cat with the subversive power of the devil and particularly of women who seemed noncompliant with prevailing notions of feminine (and feline!) obedience, modesty and moral rectitude. Depicted as roaming nocturnal alleyways with randy abandon, capable of stealing the souls of the dead or the breath of babies, cats were easily targeted as witches' familiars and subjected to frenzied persecution.

But individuals who have the good fortune to be beckoned by the interior cat roaming through their psyche, may find that it can lead them to the central hearth of their Original Home. Cats can mediate reunion with the instinctual native soil from which many of us have been uprooted. With their exact sense of spatial self-orientation, they can show us how to locate ourselves in the here and now. Acting as muse they can mediate the spontaneous, unpredictable play of creative energies. And who better than the cat to demonstrate, merely by example, how to claim "what we have in ourselves and to use it as our own"? Looking through the "bright carpet" (*tapetum lucidum*) that lines the retinas of feline eyes and concentrates all the separate gleams of available light, we can learn to hunt in psyche's darker landscapes for the hidden parts of ourselves and carry them out, unapologetically, into waking day.

Suzuki, Daisetz T. "The Swordsman and the Cat" quoted in *Zen and Japanese Culture*. NY, 1973. pp. 429, 431, 435.

2

4

2. The deadly resoluteness of Nature's most highly specialized stalk and pounce hunter is powerfully evoked. *Cat Catching a Bird*, by Pablo Picasso, oil on canvas, 1939, France.

3. Superb musculature, flexibility, reflexes and balance are all brought to bear in the cat's singular ability to land on all four feet when falling from a height.

4. Feline reserve and self-possession, as well as the compressed energy of the cat in repose, are etched in the supple lines of this "Kneeling Feline Figure." Calusa culture, Late Mississippian period, 1400–1500 C.E., United States.

3

Cow

And this prayer of the singer
continually expanding,
Became a cow that was there before
the beginning of the world.
Rig Veda, 10.31

Worn smooth by the elements and perhaps by the touch of her devotees, a cow nuzzles with timeless tenderness her newly born calf into position to drink her warm milk that the Indians could imagine flowing even in a sandstone replica. An altar has been placed in front of the cow, perhaps containing ceremonial balls of ghee or clarified butter made from the cow's own rich milk and reverently offered back to her in an eternal cycle. The cow's entire being radiates the gentleness of a mother's care.

The cow is the ultimate provider of riches. Her bull calves are the workers of the fields, her manure becomes fertilizer, fuel and building materials for houses; her sinews and bones turn into tools, her hide is used for clothing, her milk the ultimate nourishment, making her a wet nurse for millions of people. In ancient imaginations, the cow embodied the double transformation mysteries where the mother's blood created or built the young and then changed into milk at birth. No wonder that the cow was worshipped as the mother goddess who cares for, feeds and creates all life. She was there "before the beginning of the world." "I am thy mother who formed thy limbs and created thy beauties," says the Egyptian cow goddess Hathor (ARAS 1:87). In Scandinavia, the primeval cow Audhumla licked the salty ice-blocks of the abyss into Buri, the ancestor of the gods, while her milk, flowing as four rivers, fed the giant Ymir, from whose body the world was formed (Davidson, 27). In images of nature, the cow's milk was seen as the Milky Way, the white moonlight or the life-giving rain.

As the celestial cow, Hathor arches protectively over the earth, her stomach studded by stars. She was the mother of the sun, which was also her golden calf "of her pure mouth." The cow's great crown of horns resembles the crescent moon and is worn by the three great Egyptian cow goddesses, Nut, Hathor and Isis, who care for the soul, like they care for the sun calf, on its journey through death and rebirth. Thus the cow goddess is both of the sky and of the underworld while her sturdy body connects her to the earth. The four legs of Nut in her cow-form represent the four quarters of the earth. During India's four cosmic ages (yugas) when the moral order of life deteriorated from perfection to darkness, the cow Dharma shifts from four stable legs to a rueful three, to a shakily balanced two, and finally ends up standing on a single leg, which is our present chaotic age (Zimmer, 1963, 13–5).

The reverence for cows continues still today in India, where they roam freely through the villages, nibbling unmolested out of market food-stalls or mingle with the traffic on bustling city streets; their protection against any harm may date back even to the Rig Veda, one of their earliest scriptures. In reality, the cow's nature seems as magical as that of her mythical counterpart. The cow sleeps only an hour a day, divided into brief "cow naps." She feeds on grass, so poor in energy that it requires her to digest leisurely, masticating her cud to draw out all nutrients—her "ruminating" (which includes regurgitating the food to be chewed again) evolving into a synonym for unhurried consideration. As the plant mash enters the rumen (the first of four stomachs) it ferments at 104°F, fueling an internal furnace that keeps her warm in freezing temperature (MacDonald, 545).

It must have been the cow's patient nature, her loving devotion to her calf, her unending supply of milk, her almost trancelike stillness while chewing on the

1. Affectionately carved in high relief by a Punjabi, a cow nudges her calf gently toward her udder, protected by a double image of Krishna, the cowherd. Sandstone relief, 10th century, India

green grass of the earth that inspired so much of the Hindu tradition where a cowshed could serve as a temple for the poor, her milk and butter still an essential part of temple rituals. The cow's warm, moist mouth became a village metaphor for the loftiest of Hindu abstraction—divine liberation through loving kindness toward all things. And of course the beloved god Krishna was a young cowherd, demonstrating this principle among herds and *gopis* (cowgirls). Gandhi once wrote that the display of love toward a cow "takes the human being beyond her species…man through the cow is enjoined to realize his identity with all that lives" (Gandhi, 170). Ultimately, the milking of the cow is compared with the world's existence: " … the portion manifested as the world is but the yield of a single milking of the sublime source, the great spotted cow" (Zimmer, 1951, 346). From this cosmic vision, we may recall the simple, earthbound scene where we began of the sculpted cow with her calf and now recognize Maya prodding her offspring (ultimately our own selves) along the "cow's lane"—an ancient name for the Milky Way—to drink her milk of loving identity with all life.

Davidson, Hilda Roderick Ellis. *Gods and Myths of Northern Europe*. Baltimore, MD, 1964.
Gandhi and Homer Alexander Jack. *The Gandhi Reader*. NY, 1989.
Macdonald, David W. *The Encyclopedia of Mammals*. NY, 1984.
Zimmer, Heinrich Robert. *Philosophies of India*. Ed. Joseph Campbell. NY, 1951.
Zimmer, Heinrich Robert. *Myths and Symbols in Indian Art and Civilisation*. Ed. Joseph Campbell. NY, 1963.

2

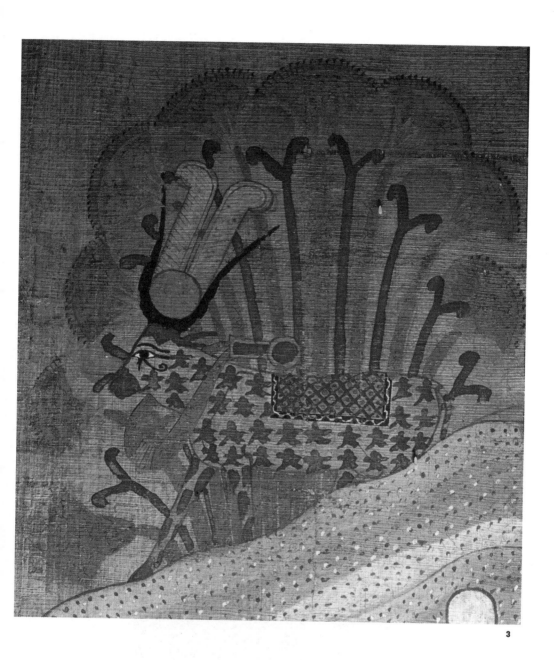

3

2. No cat or calf gets to drink from the udder of a cow in today's factorylike surroundings where cattle are bred for mass-produced food. *Cat Drinking Milk*, by Peter Zokosky, oil on canvas, 1991, United States.

3. Hathor suckled the souls of the deceased in the guise of a celestial cow, recalling her earlier personification of the Milky Way. Here she is seen as a feral cow, her body covered by stars, emerging from the papyrus stalks of the western hills, the place of burial grounds and the setting sun. Papyrus, 19th dynasty (ca. 1295–1186 B.C.E.), Egypt.

Bull

A zebu bull looks back at us from the dawn of civilization, his strength and power miraculously revealed on a seal, measuring less than two inches. His head and body are carved in profile, while his eyes and horns face the viewer. It seems that the vision of the engraver, rather than being anatomically correct, was to show the bull's inherent force, his animality and creative fecundating potency; the genital area is carefully delineated. He is standing motionless, yet he seems in the words of Stella Kramrisch "nearly spellbound with pent-up energy."

Excavated from an ancient city, this bull describes how the power of nature was harnessed to create the first civilizations. The domestication of cattle supplied sufficient food to form stable communities. The oxen (castrated bulls), the most forceful and untiring of all draw animals, were used for plowing and harvesting, corresponding to humanity's increased mastery of nature through the cultivation of land. This probably explains the extraordinary presence of bulls and cows in our cultural and religious heritage. Cattle became identical with wealth, the words "cattle" and "capitalism" sharing the same root. Wars are still fought over cattle, which was the origin of the recent genocide of the Tutsi people by extremists of the Hutu majority in Rwanda (Velten, 120–2).

In ancient belief, the overarching sky was a cow, and Hindu myth tells us that the universe was supported by the legs of a bull, signifying the four directions. The symbolic range of the bull is so encompassing that it is associated with all the four elements, indicating the tremendous power of nature, beyond human control. No wonder that the bull was worshipped as a divine being in most early civilizations. In Sumeria, the kings shared with the god the title of "The Wild Bull" (ibid., 32). The blind fury of stampeding bulls, their heads and horns lowered toward the ground, seemed much like the frenzied gods of storm-winds, destroying anything in their way. Their deep bellow and glimmering horns evoked deities of thunder and lightning. The bull's massive body seemed as solid as the earth. His life-creating virility resembled the sun and his crescent-shaped horns were associated with the moon. Like a cornucopia, the river Ganges was flowing from the horns of the Hindu bull-god Shiva in one version of the myth. Perhaps it was as the element of water that the bull was most venerated. In Egypt, the creator god Ptah in the form of the Apis bull caused the flooding of the Nile, the river's fine silt making the fields ready to sprout into new life each year. The annual flooding of the river Tigris in Mesopotamia was the result of the union between the bull-god Ninlil and the

1

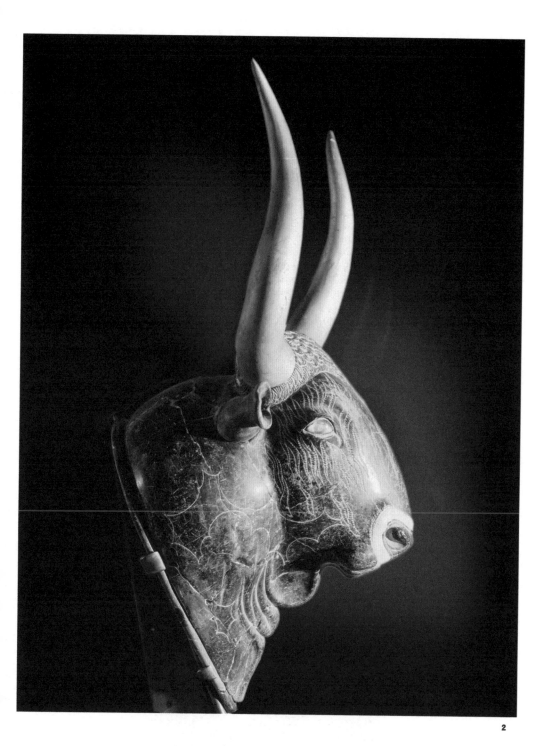

1. An ancient seal showing a majestic zebu or Brahmani bull. In later Hinduism the zebu bull is associated with Shiva. Like all bulls, the zebu or humped bull is a descendent of the extinct aurochs or wild ox that stood almost seven feet high at the shoulders. Seal, 2600–1900 B.C.E., Mohenjo-Daro, Indus Valley, Pakistan.

2. Minoan rhyton (ritual vessel) in the form of a bull's head. Wine was poured from the little round opening as from the mouth of the bull. Both the bull and the wine were aspects of Dionysus, and this rhyton shows that similar ideas existed in Crete (Kerényi, 53–4). Black soapstone with gold, 1600–1500 B.C.E., Knossos.

cow or mother goddess, making the land fertile. And the life-giving rain after a thunderstorm originated from the bull. In Sanskrit, the words for "bull" and "rain" both come from the same root, meaning both "to water" and "to impregnate" (ibid., 31–8).

In front of most Shiva temples in India, Nandi, his adoring bull, is facing the inner sanctum, which contains the lingam, the phallic symbol of Shiva's reproductive power. Nandi as Shiva's "mount," or animal form, embodies both the fierce destructive and generative aspects of the god. Nandi means "joy," one of the utterances of the god's vitality (ARAS, 2An.078). Nandi is also known as "the great inseminator." Women touch the testicles of the sculptured image in the hope of getting pregnant as they pass on their way to offer flowers to the lingam.

In Greece another bull god was worshipped for his generative power, his phallus carried in processions during his festivals and also associated with the bull. Dionysus, the god of the vine and exuberant sexuality, was called "the horned child," "the horned deity," the "bull-browed" and "the bull-born." It was in the form of the bull Zagreus that Dionysus was dismembered by the Titans but was reborn after his heart was saved. Kerényi describes the bull of Dionysus as an aspect of *zoë*, the sheer life force (p. 52) (*prana* in India). Thus,

the bull's blood as a manifestation of this energy was sprinkled over the fields in order to transmit his fertile power. In time, the bull's mere presence was enough to wake up the life force of earth and plants. Perhaps it was this "growing force" that the ancient astrologers of Mesopotamia were calling forth by naming the constellation of the fertile spring *Gut-anna*, "The Bull of Heaven" or "The Bull's Jaw," today known as Taurus the Bull (Velten, 33). Our fascination with the bull throughout history, ritualized as bull cults and bull sacrifices, still survives in present-day bull runs or bullfights. Psychologically, it is the story of our relationship to instinctual nature, where humans are confronted with the bull's thrusting animal energy as utterly "other." Astrology may still be a guide for both men and women by pointing to the essence of the astrological sign Taurus as the process of "tending" to the life force, whether in animal, garden or self. When properly mitigated, the raging bull can become surprisingly tender.

Kerényi, Karl. *Dionysos: Archetypal Image of Indestructible Life*. Princeton, NJ, 1996.
Rice, Michael. *The Power of the Bull*. London and NY, 1998.
Velten, Hannah. *Cow*. London, 2007.

3

4

3. Nandi. Guardian of all four-legged creatures, he also protects the four corners of the world. If you look into his horns you see eternity. Nandi is believed to be a fusion of the bull-god of the Indus civilization, in his creative aspect, and probably Rudra, the bull god of Aryan civilization, destroyer of cattle and men. Shiva temple, late 8th century, Kalugumalai, India.

4. Europa being seduced by Zeus disguised as a bull, who will carry her to Crete. Their union created three sons, including king Minos whose life was fated by bulls. Red-figure vessel, by the Berlin Painter, ca. 500–460 B.C.E., Greece.

Horse

A horse! a horse! my kingdom for a horse!
Shakespeare, *Richard III* (5.4.10)

They'll run forever.
They'll gallop till they die, they will …
if we don't say "stop."
They live for us … just for us …
their whole lives.
Peter Shaffer, *Equus*

Horse sense is the thing a horse has which
keeps it from betting on people.
W. C. Fields

Emerging from a long evolution stretching back nearly 50 million years comes the horse, a wild beauty, grazing peacefully on the plains, and then suddenly breaking free with snorting and fiery breath, swift as the wind. It flies across the landscape with thundering hooves as if to run out of its own skin for the love of freedom. The horse is a fabulous striving power to which we aspire for good and ill. We tamed them. They came to know us. We whispered to them and they understood us. We broke them and they gave us their service. We tied them to our plows and carts, we settled the Wild West upon their backs, and they have carried us into and through countless wars and expansive conquests. They have served as symbols of aristocracy and enticed our betting minds. Our struggle for freedom has been won through the freedom they have sacrificed for us in exchange for a powerful mutual bond and benefit. Yet our freedom can dangerously turn into a miscarriage of that sacrifice—we can become possessed by our galloping unconscious power drives and filled with inflated pride or runaway dreams of conquest. No wonder that the sacred horse sacrifice, such as the Hindu Ashvamedha, was central to many ancient peoples who held freedom, power and the mysteries of fer-

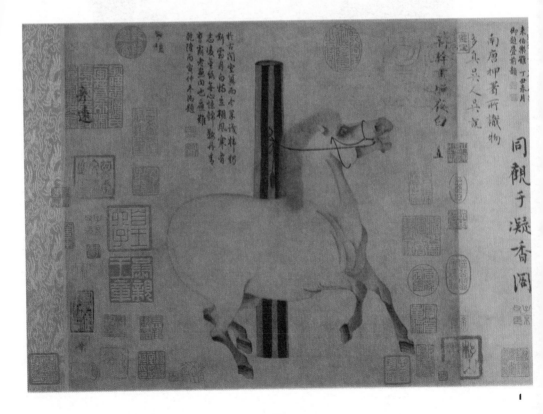

1. This is a portrait of the emperor's stallion of the same name, and successfully captures the essence of the horse's powerful and barely harnessed life spirit. It is the beginning of a long tradition of later Chinese horse painting. *Night-Shining White*, by Han Kan (742–56), Tang dynasty, China.

2. These wild horses were clearly central to the beliefs and ritual of the Paleolithic age. They were "animals of the mind more than of the Ice Age steppe." Detail from the Panel of Horses, charcoal, ca. 30,000–32,000 years old, Chauvet Cave, France.

tile life, death and renewal in balance through this ancient cult ritual. The horse, intimately tied to our psyche and civilization, has symbolically and literally brought both death and salvation.

The horse is transcendence for man. Poseidon, god of sea and quaking earth, gave the horse to mankind, but Athena of wise counsel gave us the bridle. With these gifts we have transcended the literal limits of space, time and strength by harnessing horsepower to our efforts, while in the imagination, the horse has become an even greater chthonic power animal of the cosmic beyond, magically capable of beating a hoof to bring forth springs of living water, soaring winged into the sky, driving the sun across the heavens or inspiring fear and dread as the Four Horsemen of the Apocalypse. The Norse god, Odin, "Swift One" and "Shaker," rides his eight-legged white steed Sleipnir, gathering the dead, a ride which induced such fear in the countryside folk that they would lay fodder aside for Sleipnir as he passed (Mercatante, 64), while at the end of this dark age the tenth incarnation of Vishnu as the white steed Kalki will bring forth a new world.

Mounted on horseback, heroes and dreamers ride upon very close but unknown raw powers of their animal self and intelligence, challenged with quickened libido and pulsing drive. They must tune to these and hold them well if life is to be lived as a fully embodied spiritual adventure of heart and mind. The questing medieval knight on horseback is an archetypal image of the utmost of such attunement along a dangerous path toward inner and spiritual truth, while countless fairy-tale heroes enter the woods and emerge victorious from threatening and enemied darkness only through surrender to the will and counsel of a magical horse who knows the way. In Grimm's tale "The Goose Girl," the head of the slain horse Falada takes on a guardian and oracular quality, speaking to the suffering heroine of her mother and reminding her of her origins and truth, for as the symbol of the deepest original animal nature closest to us the horse is mother, like the horse-headed Demeter, or the Celtic goddess with horse, Epona. The horse is also a warrior and sacred

to Mars, but the warrior hero's treasure lies in how he transmutes the literal powers of the horse into a new awareness. The Trojan Horse comes to mind. The cunning hero Odysseus finally puts his soldiers inside the imaginary horse, feigning defeat, and wins through the powers of imagination rather than solely by physical combat.

Hold your horses. Phaeton could not hold his and met a disastrous death. He tricked his father Apollo/Helios into allowing him to take control of the great chariot of the sun for a day, but the horses sensed a weaker hand and tore off out of control, endangering the order of the universe. There are nightmare horses of frenetic and crazy power, horses out of control, horses running away with us, getting loose, stampeding, destroying. An urge to be set free from this life can take hold. The nightmare, coming from the Indo-German "mer" meaning to "pulverize" or "crush" and links linguistically to words implying putrefaction and rotting, a process paradoxically valued by the alchemists, as decay is nature's ground for the new. They incubated the matter of their work in horse's dung, a containment referred to as the "horse's belly," imagining that the gold, or highest value, would come forth from the waste as its very ground. Thus, psychologically seeing through the horseshit without defense tames the nightmare mind and whispers to the mad horse that smells our fear. The nightmare hag-on-horseback, or the black demon-horse mount of Hel (Herzog, 66ff), breathes a dreadful and otherworldly air upon the dreamer and tugs him into a land of destructive mania and sexual violence masked by illusion. Such was the vulnerability of the adolescent protagonist of Peter Schaffer's *Equus* taken down by the demonic seduction of his nightmarish love for a horse.

Herzog, Edgar. *Psyche and Death; Archaic Myths and Modern Dreams in Analytical Psychology.* London, 1966.
Mercatante, Anthony S. *Zoo of the Gods: Animals in Myth, Legend, & Fable.* NY, 1974.

3

3. The Camargue is one of the oldest living horse breeds. From the Rhone River area of France it is believed closely related to prehistoric horse remains found in southern France. They are dark at birth but turn white after about four years, and are known to be hardy and good-natured as riding horses. *Camargue Horses*, photograph by M. Watson.

4

4. It is generally believed that the Spanish introduced horses to the Americas in the 15th century. The Nez-Perce, among other tribes, was considered wealthy through the ownership of a great many horses. *Nez-Perce warrior*, photograph by Edward S. Curtis, ca. 1910.

Donkey

Contrasting the human figures in Carpaccio's depiction of the flight into Egypt—the majesty of the sumptuously robed Mary, lovingly holding her child, and the apprehensive urgency of Joseph—is the small gray donkey on which all of them depend, carrying the mother and child to safety. The steadfastness of the donkey is legendary. Almost anyone, rich or poor, living in the world of biblical times or in many parts of the world since would have been familiar with its saving grace. A comfortable, reliable mount, the donkey has also trampled seed, turned the millstone to grind grain, pulled the plow and in donkey caravans carried staggering loads of freight to their destinations (Nelson, 62–63).

Sometimes, called an ass, and in Spanish-speaking countries a burro, the donkey is a member of the horse family; mules are hybrids of donkeys and horses. The donkey has always been considered the poor relation of the elegant, long-legged horse, so much so that it is an emblem of the humble. Yet there is something admirable and handsome in its sturdy, compact body and fine long ears. It has greater intelligence than the horse. It is more sure-footed and has the capacity to withstand the most arid landscapes and unerringly negotiate rocky, precarious terrain. There is a whole other aspect to the donkey, of course. Wild asses are not as social as horses, and adult males tend to live alone within large territories that they mark with big piles of dung, obtaining exclusive mating rights to receptive females who wander through them (Macdonald, 482–4). The long ears, and the big teeth revealed in the lusty, raucous braying of the males when fighting over females or calling to each other over long distances, have been caricatured as the randy, comical "smart-ass." Long ago the donkey was associated with Dionysian revelry and orgy, the medieval follies of the Saturnalia in which the conventional order of things was reversed, and the devilish, obscene antics and irreverent Mass at the New Year's Festival of the Ass.

It was swift wild asses, probably those whose descendents still roam African deserts from Somalia to Ethiopia, who were the first of the horse family to be domesticated; the Egyptians caught and tamed them more than 4,500 years ago (*Compt.*). Yet, because it was the beast of burden that bore the harvested corn in which the dismembered god Osiris was believed to be present, the donkey became associated with his outlawed slayer. Set is depicted with the ears of an ass and like his counterpart, inhabits the desert. His energies are the heat and chaos that both disrupt and balance Osirian order. Meanwhile, the donkey itself was demonized; Isis was imagined to hate it above all creatures. The donkey has suffered our own misguided projections of "stubbornness and stupidity," and our often brutal treatment of it; if treated kindly it is by nature an animal of perseverance and affection (*Enc. Brit.* 19:143).

Alchemy portrayed the wild ass, sometimes in the form of a unicorn, as a chthonic and redemptive spirit. In the fairy tale "The Donkey," a prince-musician is born in the body of an ass, and in "Donkey Skin," a princess fleeing her incestuous father cloaks herself in the skin of a magical donkey and works as a kitchen maid. Each is redeemed by enduring with grace and diligence being "under the donkey skin;" because they embrace the unseemly shadow of their natures, their royal splendor is ultimately restored. The donkey is an age-old vehicle for such transcendence: In the famous biblical legend in the book of Numbers, Balaam whips his ass for stopping abruptly, but the ass has stopped because its anchored instinct and inherent humility allow it to perceive an angel blocking its path, a divine presence invisible to its arrogant human rider.

Apuleius. *The Golden Ass.* Ed. Robert Graves. NY, 1951.
Lurker, Manfred. *The Gods and Symbols of Ancient Egypt.* NY, 1980.
Macdonald, David W. *The Encyclopedia of Mammals.* NY, 1984.
Youngblood, Ronald F. Ed. *Nelson's New Illustrated Bible Dictionary.* Nashville, 1995.

1. *The Flight into Egypt*, by Carpaccio, oil on panel, ca. 1515, Italy.

2. *Brown Ass*, by Bill Traylor (1854–1947), gouache on paper, United States.

Goat

And the goat shall bear upon him all their iniquities unto a land not inhabited: and he shall let go the goat in the wilderness.
Leviticus 16:22

Yes, I've fallen in love! ... Hopelessly! ... I fought against it ... fought hard ... She's a goat; Sylvia is a goat ... There she was, just looking at me, with those eyes of hers ...
Edward Albee, *The Goat, or Who is Sylvia?*
(Notes Toward a Definition of Tragedy)

Unlike its cousin, the cooperative sheep, the goat is a cunning and intelligent creature hard to contain, feisty and temperamental, oftimes funny, independent and, in a word, capricious (from the Latin *capra*, "goat"). The wild goat scrambles nimbly up the craggiest and most treacherous mountainscapes to graze upon the heights and when domesticated thrives with a built-to-suit barnyard knoll on which to perch. They can and will scale nearly any fence, turn up on the roof or even climb upon the backs of other animals. "Never turn your back on a billy goat," the saying goes, or you might get a surprise butt in the behind.

When a goat gives you that uncanny look of theirs, they seem to plot and muse with humanlike design from an alien source. Those strange light eyes, furnished with a long rectangular pupil, lend them a spooky look, but provide them with wide-angle perception and acute night vision. Many of their rowdy and otherworldly qualities, including their ability to leap as if to fly, have associated the goat with darkness and untamed passions, yet this wild ruminant has become one of the most nurturing of domesticated animals, providing milk, meat, fleece and skins to human beings. Zeus himself was suckled by the goat Amalthea. His legendary protective aegis was fashioned from Amalthea's skin, and her horn was the cornucopia of ever flowing abundance. The goat, nanny or billy, has been associated universally with fertility or potent virility, respectively. In Norse mythology this extends to the mystical ability to regenerate; Thor's chariot is drawn by two magic goats who can be cooked and eaten for dinner and return anew by morning if skin and bones are kept intact. The Norse tradition also associates the goat with protectiveness as in the famous tale "Three Billy Goats Gruff," in which a wily goat outwits a terrible troll living under a bridge.

Yet, the Judeo-Christian West has projected on the rutting billy goat's compulsive sexual drive and strong odor, together with its independence and strange look, the very devil as a black goat-man with human body, a bearded and horned goat's head and hooves, typifying carnal lust and black magic. Upon the scapegoat in Judaic lore and elsewhere, sins, shame or illness were magically transferred and it was then loosed in the wilderness. Psychological scapegoating defeats creative psychological growth, for the difficult conscious apprehension of shadows within fertilizes individuation and the ability to love, a wisdom reflected in the mythical image of the goat as the favored mount of the goddess Aphrodite. Her image later morphed into the fantasy of an evil witch traveling through the moonlit woods on a flying goat to a secret place of worship.

2

1. The he-goat, portrayed as the devil, presides over a band of wild-eyed peasants at a Sabbath, which in Goya's enlightened era would be considered an image of the mind succumbing to evil. *The Great He-Goat: Witches Sabbath*, by Francisco de Goya, oil on canvas, 1820–23, Spain.

2. The Arcadian goat-god of lust and life speaks to the animal in all of us, blurring the neat boundary between civilization and the wild. *Pan and a Goat*, from the Villa dei Papiri in Herculaneum, Roman, 1st century C.E.

The wild, lusty and independent billy goat was the inspiration for the Greek figure of Pan, the lecherous "old goat" god of the pastures of Arcadia who compels untamed earthly passions and stirs insatiable desires and panic in the wilderness of the mind. Worshipped in nature, he is a god of renewal and if the civilized human being can consciously reflect on what Pan stirs up, the god can inspire living passionate sexuality. Otherwise he can manifest in unconsciously compelled rape, sexual compulsions of all kinds and lust for power. The process of civilization was portrayed in the story of the goat-man Marsyas who was flayed by the more civilizing figure of Apollo for daring to challenge the order-bearing god to a musical contest and losing. Yet we can only take so much order and reasonable goodness before we become vulnerable to Pan's seduction. Pan shares his randy goat-ness with similar figures such as the Satyrs, the Sileni (who often accompany Dionysus) and Priapus. Dionysus, to whom goats were sacrificed, was the god of tragedy, or "goat song," from the Greek *tragos*, "goat," since the poetic forms of tragedy originated with the dithyrambic satyr play in honor of the god. Perhaps the goat association is also apt in the sense that by way of unconsciously stimulating lustful and aggressive drives into action, the Dionysian can unfold in the fatal and mad undoing of an otherwise civilized hero. The fear of such unbound passions has led some to equate them with evil. The good sheep stay with the flock, pasture peacefully in the valley and follow along, while the potent, feisty, wild and striving goat of our imagination stirs trouble and follows his own often shameless lead, at the same time often attaining the highest heights.

3

4

3. This ancient image of a billy goat seems remarkable for its gentleness and grace in contrast to other more modern images, which accentuate the coarse and lustful. *Billy Goat*, detail, relief, ca. 2551–2528 B.C.E., Old Kingdom, Reign of Khufu, Egypt.

4. The form for the casting of this famous nanny goat was fashioned from discarded found objects. *The Goat*, by Pablo Picasso, 1950.

Sheep

Soft amber light suffuses a sheep's crib, illuminating the snowy fleeces of a mother ewe and her suckling lamb. Morning, springtime, nature's magical tenderness and renewal have for thousands of years been conveyed in the birthing season of the lambs. There is no more enduring emblem of innocence than the lamb, the little creature that suckles on its knees, shyly hides behind its mother and follows the ewe in the music of gentle bleating and tinkling bells. We call our own infants "lambs" and the lamb reminds us, idyllically, of childhood simplicity, frolic and oneness with nature. One of the most exalted of all religious symbols is the lamb, because Christians called Jesus the Lamb of God for his innocence and in the belief that he was led, like a lamb, to the slaughter for our sins. Because the mildness and purity of the lamb make it especially vulnerable to the predatory and destructive, nature does not let us stay in lamblike innocence for long. In the same way that since ancient times the immaculate lamb has been offered up, so our naiveté is sacrificed in the service of adaptation and independence.

If the lamb recalls the newness of the spring sun, the full-grown wild ram, zodiacal sign of the spring equinox, signifies the light and warmth of the sun boldly resurgent after the winter darkness. Since Paleolithic times, the magnificent curling or spiraling horns of the ram have been associated with the sovereignty of the sun and the vital rutting, competing and generation of males. In the rutting season, rams run at each other in direct head-to-head clashes over hierarchy, lock horns and twist or rise up on their hind feet and crash down together. The rumble and crack of battering rams, which can be heard for miles in the mountains, thundered the fertilizing power of gods like Zeus, Indra and Thor. Amun-Re, the solar god of ancient Egypt, was portrayed as a ram, and the ram-headed creator god Khnum is depicted with a potter's wheel from which he fashions material being. Agni, the Vedic god of fire, carries his fire-sticks on the back of a ram, the emblem of the third chakra at the solar plexus, the fiery center of life force, fierce affects and audacious passions.

The mythic ram is clothed in a golden fleece shining like the sun, evoking the treasure of sunlike consciousness "hard to obtain" and prized in heroic, initiatory quests. One of the most famous is the Greek story of the hero Jason who wins the fleece after being swallowed and disgorged by the primeval dragon guarding it in a precinct of Hades. In the rebirth mysteries of the Great Mother, the god Hermes, guide of souls, is the "ram" that sires the divine child who resembles the newborn sun and signifies the leading upward of the soul from the nocturnal darkness of the underworld (Kerényi, 141–42).

The craggy heights of the great ram yield, domestically, to the vales, meadows and rocky hills of quieter landscapes. The sheep, a social animal, enjoys the comfort and companionship of the flock, whose meat, milk and wool have determined our survival. Because the sheep is easily herded, it has acquired the reputation of meekness and passivity; a "sheep" lacks initiative and discrimination, and the shadow aspect of a collective "flock" is the inability of its members to think independently. Yet one of our oldest, most enduring symbols is that of the divine Good Shepherd. Its continued potency could suggest a deep, collective longing to just be a child again. But it might alternatively suggest that to be shepherded by psyche's prescient guidance is sometimes essential to survival and growth. In the same sense, the negative aspect of "wool-gathering" is aimless daydreaming, where we can be led anywhere fantasy takes us. But myth tells us that wool-gathering can also represent the gathering of something between the natural and the supernatural, luminous and golden. In the Roman myth of Cupid and Psyche, a flock of golden sheep in a sacred grove is so fierce in the daylight that they cannot be approached, but in the evening cool under the gentler emanations of the moon, pieces of the fleece can be gathered safely from briars, just as we retrieve from the thickets of psyche the golden pieces of self (indirectly) under the moonlike luster of imagination.

Kerényi, Karl. Hermes, *Guide of Souls.* Putnam, CT, 2003..

1

2

3

1. Luminously idyllic and pastoral, the innocence of a lamb suckling its mother on folded knees. *Sheep and Lamb*, by Jacopo Bassano (1515–92), oil on canvas, Italy.

2. Profile of a ram-headed divinity of Egypt. Sacred to matriarchal, patriarchal, solar and chthonic deities, the ram with its curling horns, sometimes, as here, resembling the snake of fertility and regeneration, was emblem of nature's virile potency and life force. Limestone relief, Late Period-Ptolemaic, 400–30 B.C.E.

3. The lamb as the exalted innocence and self-sacrifice of Jesus. *Adoration of the Lamb*, detail from the Ghent Altarpiece, by Jan Van Eyck, oil on panel, 1432, Belgium.

Pig

Nestled against the sturdy, maternal bulk of a sow, a group of toddlers in China find comforting repose. Since primordial times the "uterine" animal has been linked, ambivalently, to Great Mother goddesses throughout the world. Pigs are curious and forthright creatures, voracious, social and remarkably generative. Their humanlike skin is exposed beneath scant fur; their snouts root for food, tearing up the earth; they wallow in mud. Two pounds at birth, the piglets secure the heavy teats of their mother to grow into adults of 300 to 600 pounds or sometimes significantly more. For all these reasons, pigs have been symbols of divine fruitfulness and immortality and also of slovenliness, gluttony and lust.

There is a ruthless practicality to the pig that has often been mistaken as stupidity or ignorance, which the pig personifies, for example, in the Chinese zodiac and in some Buddhist iconography. Yet the pig is actually highly intelligent and instinctually cunning in the service of survival. Omnivorous, pigs do not hoard their food for later days; they simply eat it as they find it, not discriminating fresh food from trash. In lean times, if necessary, a sow will eat her farrow. Their keen sense of smell enables pigs to discover food that is buried in the ground, and their snouts make excellent rooting tools. They loll in mud as an adaptive compensation for a lack of fur and inefficient sweat glands; given plenty of water and shade, pigs prefer cleanliness (*Compt.*).

Because it lives on waste and is capable of both nurturing and devouring its own, the pig has often been seen, in a symbolic sense, as an outsider. Ancient Egypt, for example, located "at the heart of creation the omnivorous appetite that otherwise excluded the pig from religious contexts" (Quirke, 31). The expedi-tious habits of the pig resemble the moral neutrality attributed to nature, for whom creativity and destruction, order and disorder are simply aspects of her eternal round. The Egyptian sky goddess Nut was often depicted as a pig who swallowed her piglets, the stars, every morning and bore them again each evening (Jackson, 17). When Hainuwele, the New Guinean goddess, was ritually murdered, a pig was born from her dismembered body, making pigs divine. Sharing the fate of the grain, piglets were immolated in deep pits in the earth as sacrificial offerings to Greek Demeter, the goddess of the grain, and their offal later spread over the earth to insure fertility. Initiates of the Eleusinian Mysteries honoring Demeter and her daughter Persephone, the queen of the underworld, brought piglets as expiatory sacrifice to the two goddesses. Demeter is sometimes portrayed cradling a pig in her arms.

With the rise of patriarchy and monotheism, the fecund pig's association with the divine feminine engendered prohibitions against eating pork, the shunning of swineherds, and the fantasy of pigs as receptacles for demons and all that was unclean. The Medieval Jewish, Christian and Moslem worlds denigrated "swine." Pigs became emblematic of deadly sins of concupiscence. Self-denial, separation of the body from the spirit and the glorification of chastity opposed the pig's apparent sensuality, which by then had lost all its positive, creative aspect. Even in the 20th century, "pig" was still a metaphor for the lascivious male, greedy capitalist and brute cop, and pigs are the selfish despots of George Orwell's *Animal Farm*. Yet other stories, especially children's tales like *Charlotte's Web*, *Winnie-the-Pooh* and *Babe*, reflect different attributes of the pig—innocence, sensitivity, intelligence and loyalty.

1

1. Three little children sleeping like piglets on the belly
of the mother sow. Undated photograph from China.

A symbol evolves from the interplay of nature and projection, history and imagination. Consider then, three images: the Egyptian Goddess Isis riding on a pig, her legs wide, evoking infinite proliferation, menstrual blood and cycles of death and rebirth (Shuttle, 257); Chastity, tramping her virgin foot down on a pig, a triumph of feminine restraint over feminine desire (Hall, 39); a leering, cigar-smoking pig dressed as a man, conveying a self-interested "porker" corrupting the cooperative order of things. To these add the image of the pig in itself, a keenly smart animal of prodigious size, strength and resourcefulness, and of sensibilities that contravene our entrenched perceptions.

Hall, James. *Illustrated Dictionary of Symbols in Eastern and Western Art.* NY, 1994.
Jackson, Eve. *Food and Transformation: Imagery and Symbolism of Eating.* Toronto, 1996.
Quirke, Stephen. *Ancient Egyptian Religion.* NY, 1992.
Shuttle, Penelope and Peter Redgrove. *The Wise Wound.* NY, 1988.

2

3

2. Standing on a double lotus, Marichi, the Buddhist goddess of dawn, is portrayed as a sow and her seven piglets. Bronze and silver inlay, 11th–12th century, India.

3. The serene face of a regal Egyptian pig deity is rendered simply by porcine mouth, nose and eyes, while the human female body is conveyed by two breasts. This conical terra-cotta figure is from pre-dynastic times, when the pig still had an honored role in religious life. Early Dynastic, ca. 3000 B.C.E., Egypt.

Hen / Rooster

Hens and roosters have lived in domestic partnership with us for 4,000 years or more. Until recently, the domesticated birds lived much as their wild ancestors had—in small flocks with a distinct power hierarchy, or "pecking order," and with a dominant rooster, "the cock of the walk," prevailing over the hens and the immature males.

Hens, with the ever-ready sexual participation of the roosters, are marvels of fertility. Vigilant, protective caregivers of their chicks, they are also models of devoted motherhood. The hen's energetic scratching of the ground to unearth food for her chicks, calling them to come to the meal, made for her presence in creation myths where her scratching brings the world into being. Hens brooding their eggs inspired alchemy's image of the "chick-point" of the egg as the mystic germ or center brooded into life by the henlike heat of the unconscious and the meditation of the adept. In cold or rain, chicks find protection under the hen's feathers, as she squats with her wings lowered and her feathers puffed up, an image that Jesus adopted to describe his concern for the faithful. Newly hatched chicks are active and will recognize their mother within a few hours. For her part, the hen knows her chicks, and though "mother hen" can denote overprotectiveness, the image of downy chicks nestled under the hen or following their mother about is an endearing image of springtime renewal and nature's maternal covenant. Broadly associated with fertility and rebirth, hens figure, in some parts of Africa, in women's initiation rituals as spiritual guides, and because of a widespread belief that hens, especially black ones, have an affinity with the spirit world, they are sacrificial animals used to establish contact with the departed.

Roosters—aggressive, lusty, strutting, gorgeously feathered—have engaged imagination in many ways, especially with their plangent, early-morning cries. It was an ancient belief that because evil spirits are most active in the darkness of night, the cock's crow before sunrise dispelled demons and signaled the welcome arrival of dawn: "The bird of dawning singeth all night long; / And then, they say, no spirit dare stir abroad" (Shakespeare, *Hamlet*, 1.1.181–2). The heraldic crowing of the rooster that sounds things into existence or awareness, the fiery cockscomb reminiscent of brilliant rays and the cock's fecundating power made it an emblem of the life-giving sun and illumination. The rooster was sacred to solar Apollo, and Mercury took the form of a rooster as guide to the underworld. A rooster mythically crows the Japanese sun goddess Amaterasu out of her hiding in a dark cave, when life on earth is threatened by her absence. Roosters are identified with the sun in the mythologies of India and the Native American Pueblo clans. In Zoroastrian beliefs the rooster is a symbol of light and of safeguarding good against evil, and in Christianity signifies resurrection. On a miraculous journey from paradise to hell, Islam's prophet Muhammad encounters an enormous white rooster who is also an angel. Its comb grazes the foot of Allah's celestial throne, its feet reach the earth and its wings, wide enough to envelop both heaven and earth, are adorned with emeralds and pearls. When the hour for prayer arrives, he beats his wings and crows, "There is no god but Allah!" a cry echoed by all the roosters on earth (Séguy, pl.9). Norse mythology's cosmic rooster, Goldscomb, watches the universe from the topmost branches of the world-tree Yggdrasil and reports his findings to the gods.

Exalted in some ways, chickens have also been degraded in the symbolism of cockfighting, embedded in fantasies of bloodlust and machismo, and in the images of hens as ignorant, foolish, cowardly, timid, nagging, overprotective and prone to mass panic. Such misconceptions are often leveled at women in general. Perhaps it is that chickens live so close to us that they are easy and available objects both for our spiritual imaginings and our domestic projections.

Barnhart, Robert K. Ed. *The Barnhart Concise Dictionary of Etymology.* NY, 1995.
Séguy, Marie Rose and Richard Pevear. *The Miraculous Journey of Mahomet: Miraj Nameh.* NY, 1977.

1

2

3

1. A prototypical mother hen scratches up feed for her chicks and shelters another under her feathers. Scroll, detail, 12th century, China.

2. The bold, spurred brass rooster from 18th-century Benin was probably part of a commemorative altar honoring a royal queen mother. Her position, unique among Benin women, carried authority equal to that of high-ranking men, hence the use of a male symbol to honor her.

3. A sitting hen, suggesting the psychic "brooding" essential to the processes of transformation. Nearby are a mating rooster and hen, signifying the desired conjunction of opposite forces. Manuscript illustration, 16th century, Germany.

HUMAN WORLD

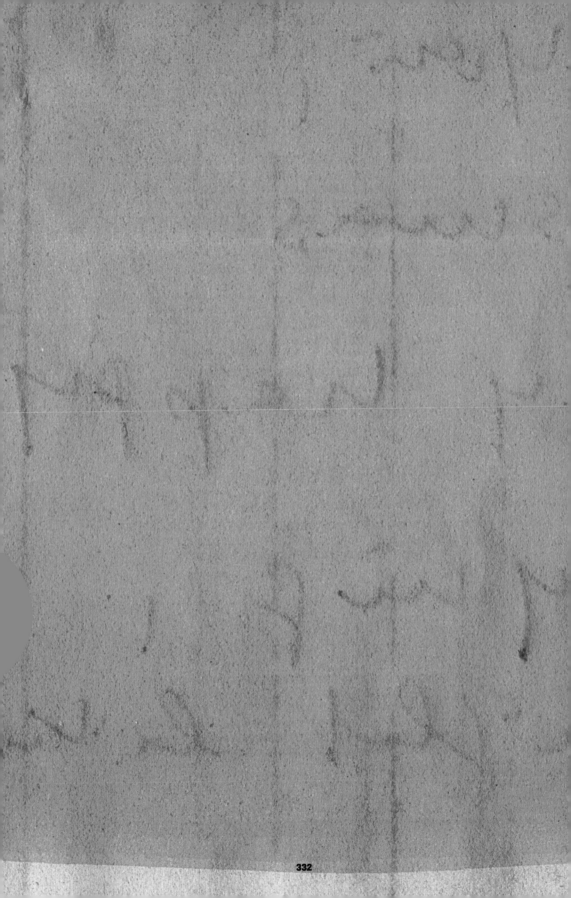

HOUSE AND HOME

HOUSE / HOME, GATE / DOOR, LOCK, KEY, WINDOW, STAIRWAY, LADDER, ATTIC, BASEMENT / CELLAR, KITCHEN, HEARTH, LAMP / CANDLE, OVEN, TABLE, CHAIR / THRONE, GLASS, MIRROR, CARPET, BROOM, BED / BEDROOM, CRADLE, TOILET, BATH / BATHING, POOL, FOUNTAIN, WELL

556

BUILDINGS
AND MONUMENTS

CASTLE, CITY, TEMPLE, NICHE, CLOISTER, TOWER, PILLAR / COLUMN, BRIDGE, TUNNEL, STREET, SCHOOL, PRISON

612

COLOR

COLOR, RED, ORANGE, YELLOW, GREEN, BLUE, PURPLE, BROWN, BLACK, WHITE, GRAY

636

SOUND

FLUTE, TRUMPET / HORN, HARP / LYRE, BELL, DRUM, SILENCE

664

Bone

Seemingly laughing, a skeleton poses jauntily before us. It suggests that something "hard" within psychic life happily endures even when the body dies. Since human and animal flesh decays rather quickly after death, leaving the bones behind, bone is a tangible reminder of the loss of life and at the same time alludes to something substantive that transcends the death of the bodily flesh.

While Judaism and Hinduism tend to avoid bone symbolism on the grounds that anything associated with death pollutes, Christianity and Buddhism engage the image of bone as the immortal part of a person. For both, this is concretized in belief in the healing, life-giving potency of particular bones. Thus Saint Peter's Basilica and Saint Paul's Church in Rome were built over the hallowed bones of their namesakes. In India, the cremated ashes and bone fragments of the Buddha were contained and venerated in reliquary structures, or stupas, which pilgrims visited in order to participate in the essence of the Awakened One dwelling in the bones. Similarly, in African Gabon culture, funeral rites for a valued ancestor include exposure of the corpse until only the hard white bones remain, fragments of which are gathered in a bundle guarded by a carved sacred figurine and placed in a special hut. Here, the ancestral spirits residing in the bones are accessible for consultation.

Evoking psyche's archetypal structure of ancestral experience that supports the personality and transcends space and time, bones are also where the mythic reanimation of a dead person must begin. As part of arctic shamanic initiations, for example, the apprentice "dies" in a dream, vision or trance and is dismembered, the bones cleaned and the flesh scraped. The skeleton is then reconstituted to support a new, shamanic embodiment that has the durability to mediate between personal and transpersonal realms. Polar hunting peoples also avoid breaking the bones of slain game animals; rather, the bones are buried in anatomical order, insuring the animal's forgiveness, reconstitution in the spirit world and willingness to be killed in future incarnations (EoR, 1:397). The symbol of the "skull and crossbones," consisting of the cranium and two crossed femurs (the longest and strongest bones in the body), came to warn of death on bottles of poison or on flags of pirate ships, yet the image probably originated as a symbol of eternal life.

Classical cultures identified the marrow of thigh bones, the fluids of brain, spine and knee, the sticky stuff of the viscera next to bones, with the dew of life, strength and generation, analogous to the sap of plants in the pulp, around the seed case (Onians, 255, 288). The Latin os, bone, refers not only to the substance of the skeleton, but metaphorically to one's inmost part, one's soul, or the hard or innermost part of trees or fruits; their seed or stone or "heart" (Lewis, 1282). Thus, the symbolic bone resonates in the saying that one feels something "in my bones," meaning one feels it with deep psychosomatic authenticity, at the very core. Perhaps this is why Ezekiel's famous vision of the valley of dried bones that are restored to life seems to associate bones with the dewlike marrow of hope that can reanimate what seems defeated.

Lewis, Charlton Thomas and Charles Short. *A Latin Dictionary.* Oxford, 1993.
Onians, Richard Broxton. *The Origins of European Thought.* Cambridge, UK, and NY, 1988.

1. Bone as the locus of immortality. This figure is probably the Zapotec equivalent of later Mictlantecuhtli, the Aztec "lord of death." Terra-cotta, 1400 C.E., Mexico.

2. The prophet proclaims words of life to a valley of dry bones. *Ezekiel Raising the Dead*, from *The Cream of Histories*, by Lütfi Abdullah et al., illuminated manuscript, tempera on paper, 1583 C.E., Turkey.

Spine

The image of an ancient Zapotec funerary urn is made in the form of a stylized backbone. At closer look, we find that there are no differentiated vertebrae along the column, and there are more projections than a backbone actually has at any one point. We begin to see a hint of tree symbolism, evoking the universal associations between humans and trees. The image lends itself to several possibilities: a stylized tree with limbs bent by ripe fruit, a cylinder displaying the beaks of many sacred birds, a phallic pole whose creative erection overcomes death and—at the same time—a backbone.

When human beings began to walk with their backs in an upright position, perhaps five million years ago, this constituted a dramatic shift toward the freeing of arms and hands. Anatomically, the backbone protects the spinal cord and consists of individual vertebrae, or bones, held together by muscles and ligaments. Most vertebrae have disks between them in order to absorb shock, which also makes it possible for us to bend or stretch. The spine enables us not only to move but to stand upright, a remarkable development that took place so long ago. The erect posture of humans requires stability, which suggests health and well-being; we slump over in sickness and depression, in sleep and in death we lie down. The spine is something we share with all animals classified as vertebrates.

The word "spine" comes from the botanical word meaning "thorn" or "prickle." Each individual vertebra has a dorsal projection called a spine and at the same time the heartwood (duramen) of a tree, like a backbone as a whole, is also known as its spine. One of the most important symbols to the ancient Egyptians was the *djed* pillar, which suggests both tree and spine. The hieroglyphic sign for the *djed* pillar means "enduring," "stable." Originally, it may have been a sacred tree stripped of its branches associated with Osiris, god of the underworld, and his perpetually erect phallus (a wooden one, according to myth, replacing the one dismembered and lost). The *djed* pillar was raised as the final act of the royal rite of succession and

seems to symbolize the resurrection in eternity of the dead pharaoh now identified with Osiris as well as the realm's stability. In Chapter 155 of *The Book of the Dead* we find words to be spoken over a *djed* pillar, which was placed at the throat of the deceased on the day of the burial: "Raise yourself up, Osiris! You have your backbone once more, O Weary-hearted One; you have your vertebrae!" (Andrews, 83)

The cerebrospinal fluid, flowing within the protection of the spinal column toward the organs of generation, was identified by the ancient Greeks and Romans with the "stuff of life." Perhaps that is why the lowest large vertebra, discounting the vestigial tailbone, was called *os sacrum*, "sacred bone," and why Jews and Muslims claimed that the resurrection of the body would commence specifically from the sacrum (Onians, 288). Furthermore, Hindu Tantrics meditate upon the backbone as the location of the three "nerves" (Skt. *nadi*) along which vital winds pass; and it may not be surprising in this context to read Jung's statement that the collective unconscious itself "is localized anatomically in the subcortical centers, the cerebellum and the spinal cord" (CW 9.I: 282).

According to Eric Neumann, the many meanings of the *djed* column symbolize essential features of the principle of integration that leads to "duration," "transformation" and the "ascent" from mere biology to consciousness (Neumann, 229ff). Sacred poles (and in the human body, the backbone) unite symbolically what is below with what is above, earth with heaven—or the ego with the realm of archetypes. This "vital link" is in fact what gives to the psyche its stability, gives to the personality what we call "backbone," a fortitude able to support the weight of an authentic life.

Andrews, Carol. *Amulets of Ancient Egypt.* London, 1994.

Neumann, Erich. *The Origins and History of Consciousness.* Princeton, NJ, 1954.

Onians, Richard Broxton. *The Origins of European Thought.* Cambridge, UK, 1991.

1

2

1. A stylized backbone stands upright to support a Zapotec funerary urn. It may symbolize the vital link between what is "above" in the psyche and what is "below," a connection that gives life support even in the midst of death. Terra-cotta, 200 B.C.E.–200 C.E., Mexico.

2. Painted djed pillar, representing Osiris' backbone, from the tomb of Nefertari, 19th dynasty, ca. 1270 B.C.E., Egypt.

Skin

Skin is associated with everything from the wonders of touch to racial profiling. Sensual, erotic, it has inspired standards of beauty captured in portraiture as well as a vast cosmetics industry and the poaching of rare animals—for compared to their hairy and often gorgeous pelts, the skin of Homo sapiens is considered naked. Skin is a responsive, tactile boundary between self and other, and the inside and outside of the individual. Vital to survival, skin is the geography where two can meet. We often refer to the quality of skin's symbolic containment or permeability: One is thin-skinned or thick-skinned; the irritating stuff of life gets "under one's skin"; one does the essential or compromising thing "to save one's skin."

The word *skinn*, of Norse derivation, refers to an outer covering or integument; a human being, a fish and an aircraft all have a skin and "to skin" describes its removal: A child falls and skins her knee, a hunter skins game before cooking. Ancient peoples flayed and wore the skins of human victims as a means of shedding, like the snake, the old skin of the year for renewal and transformation. Inside our own skins, we are not always aware of their remarkable nature. The adult human skin, if laid out flat, would cover about 21 square feet (Swerdlow, 39). In three layers, epidermis, dermis and subcutaneous fat, skin comprises 15 percent of our body weight. The biggest organ of the body, it functions to protect and cushion, is waterproof, elastic, breathable and washable.

Developing from the same fetal tissue as the brain, skin works in active concert with hormonal, vascular, immune and nervous systems. Site of the sense of touch, skin allows us to perceive via pressure, temperature and pain (ibid., 42). One of the first senses to activate in neonates and one of the last to subside in the elderly, touch is a remarkably powerful source of sensory stimulation. Infants of many species appear to thrive on tactile contact, including human children; such touch can foster greater contentedness and self-containment. Because skin is so nuanced in its reactions to natural elements, environmental circumstances and psychic fields, it serves as a barometer for physical and psychological well-being. While health and relative balance often register in the bloom of the skin, illness, undesirable contact or psychic conflict may get expressed in blushing, rashes, inflammations and allergies. Trained physicians can detect countless somatic conditions, from liver disease to infections, by the condition of the skin.

Skin is a canvas on which to portray symbolic elaborations of social standing and personal identity. In some cultures the scarified abdomen of a young woman signifies marital availability, the tattooed torso of a man, his initiatory standing. Makeup on the skin represents both play and decorative art that creates a persona for the drama of life. In fairy tales and folklore, cursed or spellbound individuals often have the skin of animals: a bird, frog, pig or fox, for example, suggesting, on the one hand, a need to redeem a psychic complex that makes one not yet human, or, on the other hand, a need to live into the animal substance or creative nature spirit one has neglected. In the Inuit imagination, one could encounter an animal that pulled back its skin to reveal a human, or a human that pulled back its skin to reveal an animal—such was the shifting, fluid nature of the psychic landscape and its interconnections.

Our relation to skin casts a huge shadow. The skins of many animals are exquisitely patterned or furred in the service of survival. But human beings also covet them as emblems of status or as high fashion so that skins have brought close to extinction the very creatures they were meant to protect. The skins of holocaust victims made into lampshades signified their ultimate dehumanization. Skin color, determined merely by the amount of melanin, or brown pigment that an individual produces, has been a main source of ethnic distinction and racism. Psychic projections around the lightness and darkness of skin have incalculably affected our perception of others and ourselves. What is "only" skin-deep is really not superficial at all, but profound and multilayered.

Swerdlow, Joel L. "Unmasking Skin."
National Geographic Magazine (November 2002).

1

2

1. Skin as our living coat of flesh. *De Cette Femme*, by Yves Tremorin, silver print, 1985–6, France.

2. A lacework of scar tissue, or keloids, adorns the back of a young Sudanese woman who receives her final scars after she has weaned her first child (Ebin, 50). The rhythmic, geometric pattern, once described as "erotic Braille," is achieved by lifting the skin with a hooked thorn, then slitting it with a blade. Photograph, 20th century, Republic of the Sudan.

Head

Throughout human history the head has been hunted, preserved, venerated, offered as sacrifice and even eaten. The uppermost part of the body, it contains the brain, eyes, ears, nose and mouth, all essential elements of human awareness, inspiration and expression. Most ancient peoples located soul, vitality, power and a daimon or genius (divine spirit) in the head. Heads are universally believed to contain the essential spirit of a person or deity. The Egyptian goddess Hathor was often portrayed as a beautiful golden head, connoting the divinity and soul of the maternal principle. In the language of images and the unconscious the head still symbolizes vital force, essence and the immortal soul.

Many practices derive from this symbolism, such as veiling or covering the head to protect it. Sneezing was believed to release some of the head's divine essence, so we say, "God bless you." Hands are placed on the head in benediction; Christ is considered the Head of the Church, with the community of followers, the Body. Phrenology, attempting to analyze personality from the shape and bumps of the head, was considered a scientific discipline in the nineteenth century. And the ubiquitous use of the guillotine during the French Revolution may have been partly a ritual attempt to redistribute energy and vitality from the dominant aristocracy to the rest of society. Without the head we are doomed, like the legendary "headless horseman" of Sleepy Hollow, to roam unmoored and in anguish.

The powerful magic contained in the head is evidenced by the worldwide practices of headhunting and beheading. Believed to contain the spirit and power of an individual, the head's removal and ritual use captured this power, which accrued to the captor, his community, the land and the power of the gods. A variation on this motif is contained in the Greek myth of Perseus and the gorgon Medusa, the terrible power of whose decapitated head passed to Perseus, and then in smaller, emblematic form to Athena, and whose blood gave birth to the Muses. Likewise, modern psychotherapists who work with "soul stuff" are referred to as headshrinkers. Endemic among Celtic peoples, headhunting and ritual beheading were part of a larger "cult of the head" including the use of skulls as sacred drinking vessels, the Grail being one such transmogrified ritual cup.

Round in shape, the head is a vessel of transformation and wholeness, akin to the alchemical "alembic," a microcosm of the spherical universe, both alpha and omega. Individuals who ingest hallucinogenic substances for the purpose of altering consciousness are called "heads." The head also symbolizes both the

I

2

1. This golden amulet was found upon the mummy of a prince. It evokes the tender maternal spirit, part bovine, part human, of the mother goddess Hathor, with whom the deceased would have been expected to identify in the otherworld. Head of Hathor, ca. 825–774 B.C.E., Egypt.

2. Colossal head, standing 5½ feet tall, stone, Olmec culture (1500–300 B.C.E.), Mexico.

seeds of new, and of immortal, life. Thus Athena's birth from the head of Zeus symbolizes the emerging soul of Greek culture. Because the head also symbolizes the immortal spirit, it is often associated with resurrection and oracular power, continuing after death, as did the heads of Osiris, Orpheus, John the Baptist and many Islamic and Christian (*cephalophoric*) saints. In Shakespeare's *Hamlet* the distressed prince attempts to consult "poor Yorick," the skull of the king's jester, but there is no magic left in the modern, angst-ridden consciousness.

Dada and Surrealist genres evoke the bizarre aspect of the linear and mechanical consciousness of the twentieth century. Only recently in the scientific age has the head come to represent reason and mind; ancient peoples considered these to reside in the heart and chest, while the head contained psyche, fertile essence and incorruptible life. Symbolically the ancient view still holds true in the unconscious of modern individuals (CW 11,13,14). Round and simple at the beginning of life, transformed into a differentiated mandala at the end and beyond, the head symbolizes the vessel and substance of life's eternal re-creations.

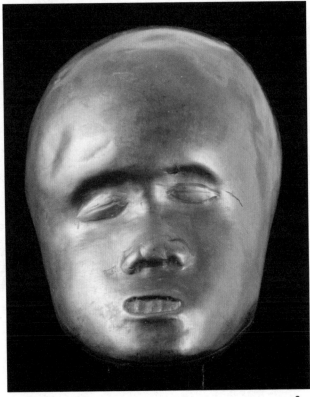

3

4

3. Head, representing a ruler or a deity such as the god of iron, 19th century, Republic of Benin, Africa.

4. Tricephalic stone head, 1st–5th century, Corleck (County Cavan), Ireland.

Brain

We know for sure only a portion of what there is to know about the brain, or the cosmos, but endlessly fascinated, we produce intriguing and playful notions about both. A contemporary Aboriginal artist depicts the Four Brains, four fields comprising the entirety of human experience within the Aboriginal cosmos from top to bottom: myths and thinking of "story brain"; relationships and emotions of "family brain"; geography/environment of "country brain"; and physical and molecular domains of "body brain." A Swedish artist portrays the "hard and gentle mothers" that protectively cover the brain. The dura mater, surrounding the brain and spinal cord, is leatherlike, tough and inelastic; the pia mater, adhering closely to the surface of the brain, is a thin membrane along which run many blood vessels that reach into the brain's substance. Just under the "hard mother" is the descriptively named arachnoid, or "spider" membrane, which has the consistency and delicate appearance of a spider web. Between the arachnoid and the "gentle mother" is a space filled with salty cerebrospinal fluid, so that the brain "floats" inside the head.

The brain itself is a soft, jellylike mass of billions of cells and their connections. Weighing two-and-a-quarter to three-and-a-quarter pounds, the human brain, by means of electrochemical energy, regulates conscious and unconscious sensation, perception and behavior, as well as the sympathetic and autonomic activities of the internal organs. In the brain stem and limbic system we experience our commonality with animal ancestors and relatives. As the "base" of the crown chakra, the brain houses our fantasies of a "higher" universal mind. The brain provides an internal representation of reality, and in so doing it also carries our symbolic projections of wholeness, the mystery of totality and the alchemical "alembic"—the distilling vessel in which the transformation of human and world takes place.

It is only recently that the brain was recognized as the locus of consciousness. For the ancients, the abode of thought and feeling was imagined to be, variously, in the heart, chest or liver. Nevertheless, the brain was imagined to be extremely potent. The Irish mixed the brain of a fallen warrior with earth, fashioning a ball to be used as a projectile weapon. Many of our ancestors ate the brains of their enemies in order to assimilate powerful mana and assume dominance. For others the brain was simply holy—in Crete, horns were thought to grow from the brain as a sign of procreative life force. In the Jewish Kabbalah, each hair on the head is a "breaking of the divine fountains" issuing from the hidden brain.

Originally a dark *rotundum,* the brain, along with the cosmos, quickly became the quintessential "black box" that we feel compelled to open in pursuit of the ancient imperative "Know thyself." A proliferation of disciplines such as neuroscience, neuroepistemology and psychoneuroimmunology now seek to unlock the "X" factor and provide access to the mystery of being. Our consequent fascination with the brain speaks to its symbolic function as an imaginal container of a timeless and unbounded process, which resolves opposites and divisions.

Observing psyche's imaginings of the brain reveals images of "geography" and brain maps, "centers" of emotion and memory, "types" of intelligence, localizations, specializations, right brain/left brain splits and the like—and recent postmodern images of "networks" and "fields," neural ecosystems, plasticity and "mirroring." In our fantasies about the brain, these complements of specialization and holistic functioning marry the perennial opposites inherent in psychological experience: fragmentation and wholeness. Subject to both brainwashing and brainstorming, our imagination about the brain is informed as much by our fantasies about our essential natures, as by scientific and technological innovation. As the terrae incognitae of the universe and the brain open to exploration, it is worth noting that as we see into images of both deep space and the brain, we also see psyche imagining itself.

The Brain—is wider than the Sky—
For—put them side by side—
The one the other will contain
With ease—and you—beside—

The Brain is deeper than the sea—
For—hold them—Blue to Blue—
The one the other will absorb—
As Sponges—Buckets—do—

The Brain is just the weight of God—
For—Heft them—Pound for Pound—
And they will differ—if they do—
As Syllable from Sound—
Emily Dickinson, ca. 1862

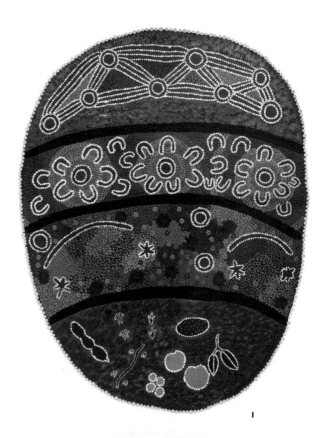

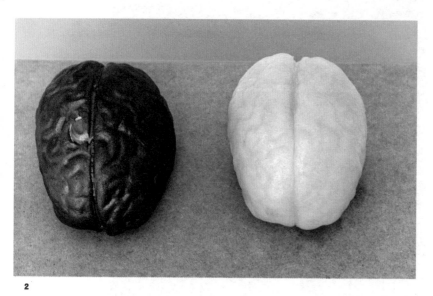

1. Desert Aboriginal iconography displays four aspects of brain function (from top): Story Brain, Family Brain, Country Brain, Body Brain. *The Brain Story*, by Rachel Napaljarri Jurrah, painting, 1994, Central Australia.

2. *Dura Mater, Pia Mater. Hard and Soft Mothers*, by Anne Thulin, sculptures in iron and rubber, 1999, Sweden.

Hair

Unadorned and disregarded by its owner, Mary Magdalene's flowing hair veils the chaste body of the penitent sinner, and at the same time conveys the faded heat of the former prostitute. Red hair, belonging to only two to four percent of the world's population, has signified erotic ardor and sexual looseness, fiery, typhonic temperament, Mars-like anger and the uncanniness of witch and devil. The red-haired Virgin Queen, Elizabeth I, made it for a time fashionable; the Inquisition viewed red hair as alien and suspect.

Hair is incredibly potent. Its root follicles, fed by tiny blood vessels, lie invisibly under the skin, associating hair with interior, involuntary fantasies, thoughts and longings. Hair tells us something about the state one's "head" is in. Dirty, lice-ridden, unkempt locks have signified derangement, but also ascetical retreat and disregard of the worldly and bodily. The quiet curls of Buddha suggest enlightened tranquility. Apollo is depicted with classically ordered sunlike locks of gold,

Dionysus with hair dark, chaotic, tangled like wild grapevines. Harry Potter's black, unruly hair signifies unconventional ideas and magical powers. Hair carries DNA and thus codes race, ethnicity and gender, but the cut or characteristics of a head of hair can also reveal individuality or conformity, freedom or inhibition, even religion, profession, political persuasion and the idols or trendsetters with whom a person identifies. The vitality of hair is stunning. Because the cells in each strand are no longer alive once the hair surfaces, cutting hair doesn't hurt, and strands that eventually fall out are constantly replaced by others, giving us on average about 100,000 in all. Hair seems to have a life of its own; like fingernails, it continues to grow after death, and ancient, fossilized human bodies with heads of hair have a spooky aliveness.

One of the first ways we register transformation is by something we do to our hair, and hair has ever played a part in initiatory process and major transi-

I

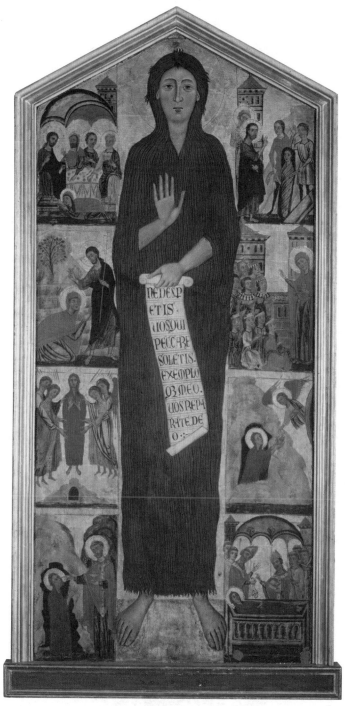

1. Samson's hair, which "no razor has ever touched," is cut by the Philistines while he sleeps on the knees of the treacherous Delilah. With the cutting goes his superhuman strength. *Samson and Delilah*, by Carlo Cignani (1628–1719), oil on canvas, Italy.

2. The Christian saint Mary Magdalene, cloaked in her red tresses, surrounded by the eight stories of her life. Wood altarpiece, by the Magdalene Master, ca. 1280 C.E., Italy.

tions. Coming-of-age rites have required the containment of the flowing hair of youthfulness, its covering with turban or scarf, or its ordering into complex constructions and adornment that signifies entrance into full membership and adult responsibility within the tribe or culture. Gray hairs evoke, variously, maturity, authority, wisdom or waning. The short "bob" adopted by women at the turn of the nineteenth century and coinciding with radical feminist movements, the invention of the bicycle and sacrifice of the corset expressed greater freedom and self-determination. The long, braided hair of some Native American men is loosed at times of mourning, among Hindu men the hair is shaved, and the tearing, cutting or veiling of hair are ways we show grief or mark separation.

Hair, once covering our animal selves, is exquisitely sensual and magnetic. There is pleasure in stroking hair, feeling its weight and texture, combing it, decorating it. A man's hair has denoted strength, virility, youth, sexiness and potency, of which he can feel robbed by baldness. A woman brushing her hair, knotting it, letting it cascade in a sign of receptiveness, running her fingers through her hair, tossing it like a horse's mane, or very short hair that regally enhances

the shapeliness of the head that crowns the body: All these have become eternal images of beauty, fertility, seduction, creativity, spiritedness and grace. There is also a shadow side. Heavenly angels were said to have been so attracted to the glorious hair of human women that they lusted after them, so that women were required to cover their heads in church or temple, connoting the relegation of their luminous thoughts and words to silence. In the Grimm's fairy tale "Rapunzel," the young girl imprisoned in a tower by a sorceress has unnaturally long tresses that look like spun gold. She embodies the plight of a possessed or encapsulated soul, where, until it is freed, the golden potentiality for true (symbolic) imagination is replaced by idealized, illusory fantasizing and the personality, dreamy and isolated, loses the ability to root in reality or live creatively in the world (Kalsched, 148–65).

Kalsched, Donald. *The Inner World of Trauma: Archetypal Defenses of the Personal Spirit.* London and NY, 1996.
Sieber, Roy, et al. *Hair in African Art and Culture.* NY and Munich, 2000.

3

4

3. This dramatic coiffure was probably inspired by the elaborate hairstyle worn by women of the Cross River region after entering adulthood. Crest mask, wood and animal skin, early 20ᵗʰ century, Nigeria (Sieber, 49).

4. Like waves of the sea from which she originates, the locks of Aphrodite combed by their divine mistress, an image repeated for centuries by mythic mermaids and human women. Marble, ca. 100 B.C.E., Greece.

Baldness

Saint Francis, who, in Giotto's painting, is preaching to the birds, was born in Assisi into a world of comfort and privilege. After a tumultuous youth, he relinquished his wealth for a life of poverty and compassionate service to the poor and the sick. When Saint Francis and his followers became clergy in the medieval Church, they were tonsured (Latin *tondere*, "to shear"), leaving only a ring of hair on their heads. In the painting, the nimbus of golden light surrounding the head of the saint echoes the tonsure, which itself imitates both Christ's crown of thorns and his crown of divine royalty (ARAS, 2:130–1).

Hair can be such a significant aspect of identity that to shave it voluntarily is often experienced as an event of great moment. Since ancient times, hair has been associated with beauty, and in men, with sexual vigor and seed, given the association of hair with the head and its life-giving fluids. To go bald was perceived as a kind of drought, like dry trees that don't leaf (Onians, 231–2). At the same time, in particular cultures and in contemporary fashion, baldness is sometimes seen as revealing and enhancing the beauty of the head. The "egghead" can denote a bookish person, or a superior intellect. Nevertheless, the story of Samson's fall after Delilah sheared his locks attests to the age-old notion of hair's magical efficacy. Men appeal to wigs, weaves and medications to reverse unwanted baldness. And for men and women alike, it can be profoundly traumatic to suffer the involuntary loss of hair because of aging, disease or chemical therapy, as the loss may disturb or permanently alter one's self-image.

The notion of inner change is crucial to the symbolic meaning of baldness. To have one's head ritually shaved conveys the idea of consecration, initiation and spiritual transformation. The hero of the mythic night-sea journey loses all of his hair because of the terrific heat in the belly of the beast (CW 11:348). Upon joining a religious order (or the military), one gives up a piece of one's individuality for the whole, a sacrifice marked by the shaving of one's hair. Like both the death's head and that of the nearly hairless newborn, the initiatory neophyte with shaven head embodies a psychic dying and rebirth.

Baldness can also signify punishment, degradation or a kind of dehumanization as in the traditional shaving of the heads of criminals, or the shaving of the heads of women who fraternize with the enemy in war. On the other hand, through shaving their hair, monks and nuns in Hindu, Buddhist and Christian religious orders make their vows visible, sever their connection to the imperative of sexual attraction and expose themselves to the direct influence of the sacred (DoS, 1015).

The symbolic strength of baldness is, perhaps, precisely because it exposes the surface of the head—the brainpan and vessel of understanding and potential change, the container of one's intimate thoughts and imaginings. While baldness is associated symbolically with receptivity to the spiritual and with new life, it also evokes psychic as well as physical nakedness and acute vulnerability. The inevitability of change may require one to submit to a state of baldness or one may make a statement with baldness, where images of beginning and end, masculine and feminine, nature and spirit lose their sharp distinctions.

Onians, Richard Broxton. *The Origins of European Thought*. Cambridge, UK, and NY, 1988.

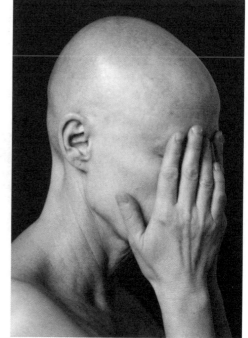

1. The tonsure of St. Francis tells of his movement from a life of privilege to one of religious service. *Sermon to the Birds*, by Giotto, fresco from the Basilica of St. Francis of Assisi, ca. 1300, Italy.

2. *Unadorned*, photograph by Katrin Brännstöm, 2001, Sweden.

Eye

Who would believe that so small a space could contain the images of all the universe? What tongue will it be that can unfold so great a wonder?
Leonardo da Vinci

Man's world is his eye.
Saying from the Bambara people of West Africa

Legend has it that humanity is descended from the tears of God. The eye retains this magic aura, shining, sparkling, withering, radiating. The eye receives and emits light, looks out and looks in, is a window on the soul and on the world, revealing and perceiving, seeing through and true. It can also see too much, or nothing at all. The eye illuminates, understands, expresses, protects, scorches and stares. We can feel truly known by the way another's eyes take us in, and despair and sorrow at being "unseen."

Loss of the eye or loss of sight can lead to something healing or creative, to the opening of clairvoyance, to the "third eye" of "inner sight," transpersonal awareness. Belonging to the psychological dynamic of dissolution, sacrifice and reconstitution, lost or missing eyes are symbolic of the potential transformation of one form of consciousness—one form of "seeing"—into another. Going both ways, this can mean "there's none so blind as those who will not see," or can refer to a "sight" and consciousness that is more dependent and responsive to an inner vision than to sense perceptions. In matters of wisdom, "second sight" has always been considered more accurate, or "visionary," than the bodily eyes. An "eyewitness" can be deceived, but the "blind eyes" of Justice see the truth. So although the eye is traditionally associated with light, insight, intelligence, reason, and spiritual awareness, the inner eyes see with a nighttime vision and darker awareness, into the wisdom of dreams and all the unconscious and emotional elements that also comprise full human understanding.

This duality of vision and consciousness conveyed by the image of the eyes is reflected again in the motif of "one eye" versus two. One-eyed vision, like that of the Cyclops, or the blasting, scorching, searching eye of the Egyptian goddess Sekhmet, or even the "eyes of god," can represent a limited, destructive, envious, and paranoid consciousness. In turn, the threatening and disastrous "evil eye" needs to be defended against and "looked back at" with apotropaic talismans. But the intense gaze of "one eye" can also represent a unity of vision in which the dualism of "inner and outer" sight feels resolved, as it is within the brain where light becomes another form of electrochemical energy. This "light of the mind" has been imaged as the "third eye," the "eye of Dharma" in Buddhism, the "eye of Wisdom" in Islam, the "eye of Shiva" in Hinduism and the "eye of God" in Christianity.

2

1. Five eye idols, alabaster and steatite, from the Eye Temple of Ishtar at Tell Brak, 4th millennium B.C.E., Syria-Israel.

2. The Eye of Horus, representing the *oudjat*, or restored "healthy and whole" eye, an amulet against death. From the tomb of Tutankhamun, 1332–23 B.C.E., Egypt.

In Hermetic symbolism, one-dimensional vision opens out into the play of opposites: the two eyes of inner/outer, blind/sighted, solar/lunar, illuminating/deadening, open/closed, all of which in turn resolve into another, more developed form of unified vision. Consciousness, which begins as a one-eyed "looking" makes a journey through psychic processes imaged as death and dismemberment to arrive transformed into a one-eyed "seeing," an enlightenment. Such is one of humanity's projections and dreams of the totality of consciousness.

Seen more obliquely, the eye corresponds metaphorically to initiation, to fleeting visions of beauty, the spirits of things, the emotional center of a storm, the essentials of experience and the secrets of the soul. Ever-watchful, Puritan minister Cotton Mather opined that squinting revealed "an Aim at low and base Ends, an unchaste eye." Nevertheless, there is much to be said for peripheral and occult vision, for keeping the eyes open but downcast and veiled, for keeping one eye in time, the other in the eternal and for exchanging the bright hawkeyed discernment—or bedazzlement—of consciousness, for the dim and blurry reality of human awareness, expression and vulnerability ... for the "Eye of the Heart."

Marshall, Bruce. Ed. *The Human Body: The Eye, Window to the World.* NY, 1984.

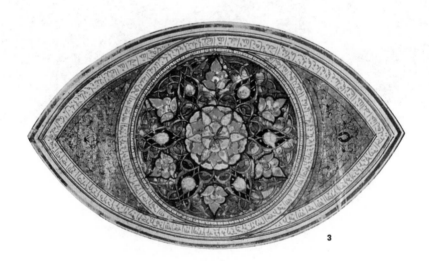

3

3. An almond-shaped mandala representing gateways to both the soul and the spiritual center. The Eye of Wisdom, detail, Islamic manuscript, 15th century.

4. *Unsighted Twin,* painted stone, Tsimshian Indian mask, one of a pair of twins, 19th century, Northwest Coast, British Columbia.

Tears

The violence and misery a woman has suffered are conveyed by the jagged lines and abstract facets of her face. In her clenched teeth is the handkerchief with which she also wipes her eyes, her tears are crystallized and caustic. As if her sorrow were inconsolable, Picasso painted this and other versions of the weeping woman in his mural *Guernica* to protest the slaughter of civilians on April 26, 1937, when German aircraft supporting Franco's Fascists bombed the Basque town.

Tears move us in a remarkable way, so much so that human ethologists consider them to be favored by natural selection for our survival. Among their physiological functions, tears serve to lubricate the surface of the eye and wash out irritants and toxins. But perhaps more important, they often elicit from others an immediate response of help, empathy or comfort. Newborns cry but don't shed tears for some weeks or months. Nevertheless, adult tears may remind us of the newborn's wet face or of the infant's pitiable crying and vulnerability.

So valuable are tears as a psychic factor that they have been depicted in myth and in dreams as precious jewels, golden amber, rain and the life-giving rays of the sun. Spontaneously, they overflow the swollen reservoirs of feeling, and the feelings may be as diverse as grief, joy, pain, excitement, compassion, relief or fear. We are not the only ones who cry. Primates, elephants and beavers are among the animals known to cry when they are upset. Human beings, however, "cry over onions, over spilled milk, over the frustration of threading a needle. We weep from unbearable sadness and simple boredom, from the thought of the future and the memory of the past" (Elkins, 25).

Tears can reveal to us unknown depths of sadness. We find ourselves suddenly tearful over some small thing that links us to a long-repressed loss or discontent. Not only physical toxins seem to be cleansed by tears but psychological ones as well. Victor Frankl, the Holocaust survivor and psychiatrist, once asked a comrade in the concentration camp how he had gotten over his edema. "I have wept it out of my system," he answered (Frankl, 87). In fairy tales, tears are often redemptive; they wash away the effects of a curse or they heal the individual or the part of the body on which the tears fall. Tears may also signify experience that is exhausting and corrosive. The Greeks of Homer's time believed that something liquid and vital in the flesh could be lost in the form of tears or sweat (Onians, 202). The Indian epic, the *Mahabharata*, tells how in order to stop the endless procession of life when Brahma first brings creatures into being, he produces the maiden Death so that all living things will repeatedly be born and repeatedly die. Death's tears of compassion for the creatures she is to kill become the terrible diseases that cause our demise, but also usher in our rebirth (Kramrisch, 123).

Indeed, tears of mourning are imagined by the Dagara people of Burkino Faso to carry the dead to the realm of the ancestors (Somé, 57). "Tears" as tree saps made into incense, myrrh, olive oil or other resins and unguents for the dead were thought by the ancients to compensate the life sap that the dead had lost (Onians, 278). Tears ritually spilled for the gods of eternal return, like Attis or Osiris, were believed to help bring about the regeneration of nature (EoR, 13: 149). The saltiness of tears intimately connects us to the primordial seawater, the containing matrix of being. In alchemy, tears belong to the operation of *solutio*; they represent a softening or melting of those aspects of the personality that have hardened and become inflexible. And as a form of the arcanum sal, or salt, tears are emblems of both bitterness and of the bitterness that in being shed can be transmuted into wisdom.

Mother, I shall weave a chain of pearls
for thy neck with my tears of sorrow.
The stars have wrought their anklets of light
to deck thy feet,
but mine will hang upon thy breast.
Wealth and fame come from thee and it is for
thee to give or to withhold them.
But this my sorrow is absolutely mine own,
and when I bring it to thee as my offering thou
rewardest me with thy grace.
Rabindranath Tagore, *Gitanjali: Song Offerings*

Elkins, James. *Pictures & Tears*. NY, 2001.
Frankl, Viktor E. *Man's Search for Meaning*. NY, 1984.
Kramrisch, Stella. *The Presence of Śiva*. Princeton, NJ, 1981.
Onians, Richard Broxton. *The Origins of European Thought*. Cambridge, UK, 1991.
Somé, Malidoma Patrice. *Of Water and the Spirit*. NY, 1994.

1. *Weeping Woman*, by Pablo Picasso, oil on canvas, 1937, France.

2. His streaming tears magically create rain. *Boinayel (Zemis) the Rain Giver*, detail, wood and shell, Taino culture, ca. 15th century, Jamaica.

3. *The Alchemy of Tears*, by Basia Irland, 1995, United States.

Ear

An ordinary man of ancient Egypt named Bai, shown in an attitude of prayer, dedicated an ear stele to the god Amun-Re, the "beautiful ram" of the sun, whose three pairs of ears in different colors signify "one who harkens to supplications." Inscribed with a single pair or many pairs of ears, Egyptian votive ear stelae made their appearance with the rise of personal devotion during the New Kingdom (1570–1070 B.C.E.). "The god who listens comes to him who calls, splendid of mien, and rich in ears," says a hymn of the time.

Antiquity suggests how important it is for us, not only the gods, *to listen*, especially to the soft-spoken "sounds" that religions hint at through their metaphor of the ear, and which are also a psychic reality. The spiritual intimation of unseen realms, subliminal or supernormal, led to an ancient culture of intuitive hearkening, as gods and humans entered into direct conversation with one another. Hebrews and Christians sought God's word, propitiating him to incline his ears to their individual cries (Psalms 88), while Jeremiah (6:10) blasted the "uncircumcised" ears of those who failed to comprehend the deity's subtleties. Long before, to put one's "ear to the ground" of nature was one of the surest means, as it is for many animals, of discriminating the landscape, receiving warning, finding direction, water, prey, knowing what was ahead or behind. Particularly in her solitary precincts, nature's sounds have ever been experienced as responses to questions and longings, and such auditory guidance seems also to express itself (silently) out of the wildernesses of psyche in fantasies, dreams, visions and, both helpfully and dangerously, in hallucinations.

Sound, the movement of waves of air molecules in the atmosphere, travels inwardly through the complex labyrinth of the human ear, in direct reversal of Plato's theory of sight as an outward projection of fire. As intricate as a winding seashell, the ear gathers these waves into its cartilaginous auricle (the outer ear, or pinna), conducts them along spiraling coils formed by the shape of vibrating sound and stimulates the eardrum (or *tympanus*) to send waves through three of the body's hardest and tiniest bones—the hammer, anvil and stirrup. These bones amplify air pressure within the eustachian tube, which applies pressure to the fluid inside the innermost chamber, the snail-shaped cochlea. The sensation of sound then travels to the auditory cortex via acoustical nerves inside tiny hairs (*the Organ of Corti*) suspended in the fluid, each hair corresponding to a different frequency. Whether responding to a sneeze or to a sonata, this remarkable act of hearing "bridges the ancient barrier between air and water, taking the sound waves, translating them into fluid waves, and then into electrical impulses" (Ackerman, 178). Since the inner chamber did not fill with fluid until animals evolved from sea to land creatures (Schwenk, 86), we can better understand the ear's other vital function of maintaining our sense of balance once we lost the support of seawater.

Hindu cosmology refers to a primordial humming sound—the mantra om—that existed before the creation of light and remains audible to sages through profoundly introverted concentration. Medieval Christians claimed that Christ (as the Word of God) was conceived in his mother's womb after a dove entered her ear, while Rabelais wildly boasted that Gargantua was somehow born from his mother's ear. The more sober Egyptian stele-artisans insisted that only the right ear received the "air of birth"; the "air of death" was received by the left ear, consistent with the widespread notion that the left side is that of the "sinister"—which, for alchemy, nevertheless seemed rich with possibility. The psychoanalyst Theodor Reik, who once claimed that "the intangible that is invisible as well as untouchable can still be audible" (p. 12), suggested in his classic text, *Listening with the Third Ear*, that we truly hear through greater use of our intuition. Alchemy understood "meditation" as a creative inner dialogue with "someone unseen," what is enacted in psychic process as "a living relationship to the answering voice of the 'other' in ourselves," by means of which, ear to ear, things unconscious and potential pass into consciousness and manifestation (CW 12:390).

Ackerman, Diane. *A Natural History of the Senses.* NY, 1990.
Reik, Theodor. *The Haunting Melody; Psychoanalytic Experiences in Life and Music.* NY, 1953.
Schwenk, Theodor, Olive Whicher and Johanna Wrigley. *Sensitive Chaos: The Creation of Flowing Forms in Water and Air.* London, 1976.

2

3

1. An ear stele absorbing the prayers of a kneeling Egyptian. Limestone, from the temple of the goddess Hathor, Deir el-Medina, ca. 1295–1070 B.C.E., Egypt.

2. With his classical gesture of a hand-cupped ear, Milarepa, the one-time murderer and later exalted Tibetan yogi (ca. 1052–1135), embodies the Buddhist role of sravaka or "hearer" of enlightening doctrines and songs. Brass, late 14th–early 15th century, Tibet.

3. This cryptic Carthaginian stele from an Algerian excavation is thought to represent the ears of an ancient goddess; etched beneath them may be the image of her divine vulva that would bring into realization the answer to the petitioner's prayers. Incised limestone, 4th–2nd century B.C.E.

4

4. Closing his eyes to external matters and blissfully absorbed in the echoing mantras that called his world into being, the Cambodian King Jayavarman VII turns his elongated ear toward us to invite interiority. The earlobes of Eastern nobles were often adorned by earrings to protect them from harmful words passing into their hearing. Stone, 12th century C.E., Cambodia.

Nose

Although the Pharaoh Sneferu was the founder of the greatest pyramid-building dynasty of ancient Egypt, his longing for immortality is better captured in his intimate nose-to-nose exchange of breath with Sekhmet, the Lion Goddess, than in the monumental tombs erected to his everlasting memory. The Egyptians considered the nose to be the most important orifice in one's body and handled it with great care during mummification, just as they maliciously sliced off the nose of an enemy's face to prevent his survival in the Land of the Dead (Meskell, 149). Their ancient linkage of the nose with life finds an echo in the discovery, in modern times, that the brain evolved from a pair of primitive olfactory sensors at the upper end of the spinal cord, establishing the antecedence of scent over the now predominant sight and hearing. Detecting scents to discriminate between edible and noxious food or to locate a sexually available mate preceded the physical emergence of the nose itself, which expanded greatly from the internal nostrils of fishes into its nature's finest culmination—the elephant's trunk, a nose capable of picking a blade of grass or uprooting a tree, to say nothing of smelling water miles away.

Among humans, the nose can detect 10,000 more flavors than the incorrectly credited tongue. Subordinated by many to the organs of sight and hearing, the nose is nevertheless associated with highly nuanced instinctual and intuitive functions—like following musky, perfumed vapors to find romance via the "right chemistry" or tracking down the scent of a crime (although the human nose has only one-fortieth the capacity of a bloodhound's). The nose's hyperdevelopment among detectives like Sherlock Holmes, who could identify the writer of a letter by waving it across his nostrils, suggests the almost psychic quality of scent. Equally impressive is the more sensate connoisseur with a "nose" for wine capable of determining its precise vintage by a pensive sniff. It follows perhaps that snobbism—literally "turning one's nose up"—reflects the primate basis of our nasal functions, and no insult is more down-to-earth than to be informed one "stinks" in any context. Rotten smells, like sulfurous brimstone, are traditionally associated with the vaults of hell, the moral sewers of life, while paradise is scented with rose and lotus, and the mere memory of a past love, like Flaubert, preserving his lover's perfumed slippers in his desk drawer, is fondly brought back to life by a single whiff.

The exterior of the nose—its shape and size—is as significant to us as its intricately winding interior. "Cleopatra's nose," Pascal famously observed, "had it been shorter, the whole face of the world would have been changed" (Pascal, 202). Ironically, the possessor of the most head-turning nose of all, Cyrano de Bergerac, wins our sympathy but loses at love in an age before plastic surgery, and a "nosy" person wins as much sympathy as an intrusive rodent. The nose's long biological development means that it connects our consciousness to the most ancient and intensely emotional parts of our brains, allowing an entire world to be recovered by the trailing scent of a Christmas spice—or in Proust's case, by a madeleine dipped in lime-blossom tea—retrieving the soul of one's past as can no other sense. The Egyptians understood that the breath passing through a goddess' nostrils to give eternal life to a deceased king would impart a fundamental reality, for the nose is like a forgotten portal to the archeology of the psyche.

Meskell, Lynn and Rosemary A. Joyce. *Embodied Live: Figuring Ancient Maya and Egyptian Experience.* London and NY, 2003.
Pascal, Blaise. *The Provincial Letters. Pensées.* Chicago, 1952.

1. Cherokee artisans fashioned this ritual "Booger Dance" mask to parody the malevolent elements in their lives, including the European settlers whose intrusive noses they mockingly imitated. Gourd, ca. 1920, Eastern Cherokee Reservation, North Carolina.

2. The Pharaoh Sneferu inhales the breath of life from the lion-headed goddess Sekhmet, as he enters into the Land of the Dead, absorbing immortality through the same sense organ that connects us all to the origins of life. Painted limestone relief, ca. 2600 B.C.E.

3. The difference the shape of a woman's nose can make in defining her attractiveness (and seemingly even her personality) before and after rhinoplasty (cosmetic nose-surgery). *Before and After*, by Andy Warhol, polymer paint on canvas, 1961, United States.

1

2

3

Mouth

By portraying the French actress Brigitte Bardot's parted mouth, the German painter Gerhard Richter echoed Andy Warhol's sensational depiction of Marilyn Monroe the previous year. But Richter chose to focus solely on Bardot's pouting lips, torch-lit with lipstick. While preserving her sex-kitten mystique with rippling paint that also suggests sound waves, he used swift strokes to give her mouth the gashlike primitiveness of a lamprey eel's.

"Every slug, insect and higher animal has a mouth," an author has noted (Ackerman, 143). And no matter how sexy, the human mouth is primarily the instrument of eating; even its role in lovemaking has the quality of a sensual devouring of the lover. The mouth is the beginning of the alimentary canal that extends to the anus, the mouth's counterpart at the lower end, and every part of the mouth contributes to the elemental function of digestion. The teeth masticate food, salivary glands add their digestive secretions, the tongue contains the taste buds, licks and assists in swallowing, the lips grasp, suck, slurp and smack contentedly. But the mouth participates in both poles of the spectrum, for all these parts also have a role in one of the most sophisticated aspects of human life, the precision of language. Moreover, the mouth carries breath, as life, spirit, soul, word, creation.

Our mouths are equipped with an extraordinary number of nerve endings, and a large portion of our sensory cortex is dedicated to the mouth's multiple activities: blowing bubbles, swallowing pills, kissing, laughing, unleashing screams, singing arias, gargling, yawning—what can the mouth not do? It appears right away in human embryos. For the very young child, it is like a small chamber of primary consciousness-bearing sensory structures, bounded on the sides by soft cheeks, portaled by the elastic lips, roofed by the hard and soft palates and with the major part of the floor formed by the tongue (Gray, 869). A small child constantly puts something in its mouth in order to find out what it is. Melanie Klein related the oral stage and its images to the development of a child's sense of outside and inside (Jackson, 100).

The smaller, outer part of the mouth, the "vestibule," at the rear becomes the cavity, down which food is swallowed through the throat. Opening wide on the hinge of the jaw, the mouth is a cavernous space that human imagination has filled with fantasies. An Indian myth tells how Krishna as a mischievous toddler ate clay for fun; his mother, Yashoda, prying open his mouth, could see the entire universe. Another Indian myth relates that the Hindu gods emerged from the mouth of the Lord of Generation, Prajapati. The demons came out of his anus, the "lower mouth," just as the anus is kissed by devotees in depictions of medieval devil worship. Spoken prayers come from the mouths of the faithful in the form of golden threads, connecting them to heaven (Biedermann, 231), or, in a thirteenth-century Japanese Buddhist sculpture, flow out as a stream of Buddhas. In the rite of the "opening of the mouth" in ancient Egypt, the lips of statues or mummies of the dead were touched with special tools allowing the image to be home to the *ka*-spirit of the deceased, and giving it the ability to consume offerings brought for its sustenance (Quirke, 94).

It is the engulfing jaws of death, however, that give us the most terrifying images of the mouth. The gigantic Cyclops of Homer's *The Odyssey* gulps down Odysseus' men, ripping their bodies apart as he eats them. The witch of Hansel and Gretel lives in the orally seductive gingerbread house, and eats little children enchanted by it. The god Saturn swallows his own children in order to prevent their supplanting him. Goya's portrayal could be a child's nightmare of the devouring father, or at another level, suggests our experience of consciousness getting gobbled up by unconscious, as affect, compulsion, regression or psychosis. One of the first signs of mythic transformation into bestial were-animal is that the mouth changes, the jaw becoming heavier and larger, the teeth sharp and fanged.

1. With swirling brushstrokes the artist depicts his
subject with such raw energy that we can easily
visualize a steamy kiss, a window-cracking scream or a
hungrily devoured meal. *Mouth (Mund)*, by Gerhard
Richter, oil on canvas, 1963, Germany.

On the other hand, the mouth is emblem of eros and its lovely kisses. The feminine mouth in particular has been an object of beauty from the fashion for the tiny, rouged, rosebud mouth to the vogue for large, sensual mouths and swollen "bee-stung" lips. Without a word being said, mouths limn a person's character or mood. The petulant mouth, smug mouth, tight mouth, sneering mouth, the upturned or downturned mouth signifying comedy or tragedy, or the way in which, in any given moment, we seem to be ingesting the world.

Ackerman, Diane. *A Natural History of the Senses.* NY, 1990.

Biedermann, Hans. *Dictionary of Symbolism.* NY, 1994.

Gray, Henry, Thomas Pickering Pick and Robert Howden. *Anatomy, Descriptive and Surgical.* NY, 1977.

Jackson, Eve. *Food and Transformation: Imagery and Symbolism of Eating.* Toronto, 1996.

Quirke, Stephen. *Ancient Egyptian Religion.* NY, 1992.

2

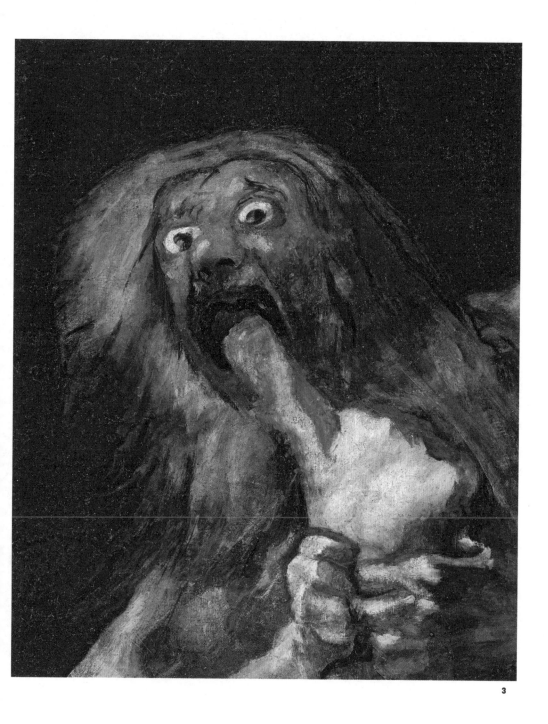

3

2. The Japanese priest Kuya opens his mouth to recite a mantra, his words appearing as an endless stream of visible Buddhas. Carved wood, by Kosho, 13th century, Japan.

3. *Saturn Devouring One of His Sons*, detail, by Francisco de Goya, oil on canvas, 1819–23, Spain.

Beard

To "beard" someone means to confront him boldly. So, it seems, does the divine Thor let us know who beards best. Imposing and content, he sits on his throne, his hands grasping—and displaying—both beard and emblematic hammer, the two rendered, in this bronze miniature, as one. The conflation between hammer and beard suggests that the beard has symbolic qualities equivalent to the thunderbolt's hurled destruction and fecundating rain.

Because hair appears on a young man's face at puberty, the beard has, of course, long been a visible reflection of the rite of passage from boy to man. The young man's beard implies phallic power, aggression and the capacity to sire progeny and assume social responsibility, including the bearing of arms. The full beard that came with greater age marked the "graybeard," an elder of wisdom and dignity. From Indra, the thundering Vedic deity, to Michelangelo's divine Creator, mythic progenitors of masculine authority—gods, heroes and those considered their offspring or earthly counterparts—have been portrayed with a virile abundance of beard. Thus, in antiquity, the rulers of Persia, Assyria, Babylon and Egypt were depicted as bearded. Egyptian rulers, who were clean-shaven, nevertheless wore a false beard as a sign of sovereignty, as was true of a ruling queen.

Just as Thor's hammer sounds the god's voice as thunder, so has the beard, encompassing the mouth and jaw, traditionally been associated with the potency of word or logos. This is further reinforced by the habit of stroking or tugging at the beard when pondering a problem. Thus, the Greek word *pogonotrophos*, "man with a beard," was once a synonym for a philosopher.

To this day, Muslims swear oaths "by the beard of the Prophet," and, indeed, Muhammad never trimmed his beard. Male professors and psychoanalysts, both of whom work with the mind by means of words, are stereotypically portrayed with beards.

Beards can also reflect shadow aspects of the masculine, both disquieting and vital. The wild man of folklore is portrayed with a rough or shaggy beard connoting his animality. Bluebeard represents a sadistic and dismembering attitude toward the feminine that can disguise itself seductively in a woman's psyche. Satan was sometimes pictured with a dark, pointed beard, resembling that of the "unholy" goat. Giants, personifying primitive affects, are often depicted with thick beards. Red beards, like Thor's, can embody passion, rage or destructiveness. Beards can make a statement counter to the prevailing political climate or collective standard. The beard was ubiquitous on youthful chins of sixties rebels and hippies. Fidel Castro's beard became emblematic of Cuban communism's defiant opposition to the West. Hostages and prisoners of war, deliberately dehumanized, have been photographed disheveled and unshaven; on the other hand, a man at leisure may relax the constraints of professional persona by temporarily growing a beard.

If beards catch the projection of intellect and eloquence, they also represent the time when it goes awry. Misbehaving or distempered dwarves of Germanic fairy tales, like "Old Rinkrank" and "Rumpelstiltskin," get their long beards caught as the means of their undoing. So can human men (and women) get tripped up in a lengthy flow of senseless thoughts or foolish words.

1. In a figure less than three inches high, the beard and hammer of a Norse god, probably Thor, are symbolically merged. Bronze, 10th century, Iceland.

2. In Michelangelo's famous image on the ceiling of the Sistine Chapel, the white-bearded, cloud-borne Creator reaches out to touch his "Adam." Detail of the Sistine Chapel ceiling, fresco, 1508–12, Italy.

3. This warrior's meticulously rendered bristles suggest an aggressive and defiant virility. *Battle of the Giants*, detail, sandstone relief, Greek, from Temple F, Selinunte, ca. 480 B.C.E., Sicily, Italy.

1

2

3

Teeth

Humbaba, demon adversary of the Mesopotamian hero Gilgamesh, was called the "Guardian of the Fortress of Intestines," suggesting, along with a face coiled like entrails, teeth capable of displaying visceral ferocity.

Bared, sharp, snapping or gnashing teeth have ever been an image of potential devouring, whether the teeth belong to an animal or a human being. Think of fanged vampires, or the sharp-toothed or snaggle-toothed witch or the "red in tooth" giants who even cannibalize children. Serving to seize prey, chew it or repel attacks, teeth evolved from the bony plates that lined the armored mouths of primitive fish, still haunting us in the image of the moist, castrating, toothed vagina, our fantasy of the unconscious powers that can chew consciousness into pieces. Unlike snakes whose backward-bending fangs prevent prey from escaping, or sharks whose thousands of replaceable teeth can shred whatever their jaws engulf, human teeth generally fulfill less formidable, if more diverse functions. Our chisel-like front incisors cut into food, our bicuspids hold a morsel of flesh in place so it can be torn loose, while our back molars grind food into digestible "bits." All this gives rise to the symbolism of aggression, of biting off portions of life for one's survival, adaptation and growth, of chewing over the stuff of life so that it can be assimilated. Symbolically, teeth represent a kind of individual psychic mill where what's too rough to take in directly can be ground up by conscious consideration, digested and metabolized. Teeth also evoke other aspects of aggression. An urbane humorist's jabbed wit is "biting," mordant. Shakespeare's King Lear bemoans, "How sharper than a serpent's tooth it is to have a thankless child" (1.4.204–5). Dragon teeth were sowed, like seed, by the mythic Cadmus to reap a crop of warriors (Onians, 233).

Our permanent set of teeth number 32, although as our dietary habits evolve, it is possible that we will produce less. Teeth are made of enamel, which, like bone, is hard and white, signifies life force and survives the decomposition of the flesh, giving the skeleton its macabre grin. Archaic hunters wore necklaces of animal teeth to acquire the vitality they embodied. Sometimes, in initiatory rites, teeth were knocked out, suggesting that something of the old way of being had to be sacrificed in order to engage a new reality. Losing teeth is a common image in dreams, often bringing to awareness conflict around assertively grasping and integrating an aspect of life one needs to claim, or a compromised capacity for aggression in general. Or it may depict a state of anxiety, a fear of affective disintegration, that one "can't hold it all together." It may also allude to the old initiatory rituals and symbolically mark a significant transition.

The exposure of teeth in gleaming smiles is regarded as a feature of beauty in the contemporary world; at other times the hiding of teeth, an aspect of the intimate (and sexual) mouth, behind hand or fan, was looked upon as a beguiling display of modesty. Young women in some cultures once darkened their teeth by chewing betel nuts to portray the charm and innocence of a toothless baby (Landau, 228ff). Other toothless mouths can represent the death's head, decay and danger of the mythic hag or trickster. In Biblical times in Israel, missing even a single tooth disqualified one for the priesthood, because an intact set of undecayed teeth was thought to reflect moral goodness. Egyptian practices of dentistry go back to about 3700 B.C.E. The Mayan offered anesthetic coca leaves when filing, adorning and replacing teeth for ritual purposes. They cut into or through the enamel of healthy teeth and inlayed them with semiprecious stones, turquoise, quartz or shell (Ring, 4–11). At the magical level, the idea of the tooth as treasure is still carried in the fantasy of the tooth fairy, who repays, in coin, each baby tooth as it falls out and is offered as a marking of passage.

Landau, Terry. *About Faces*. NY, 1989.
Onians, Richard Broxton. *The Origins of European Thought*. Cambridge, UK, and NY, 1988.
Ring, Malvin E. *Dentistry: An Illustrated History*. NY, 1993.

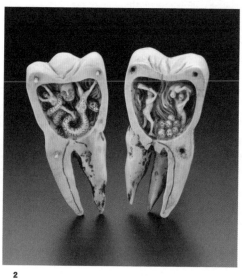

1. What makes a demon "demonic?" One thing mythologists can point to is a forbidding set of teeth; those bared by the demon Humbaba from the Sumerian epic *Gilgamesh* flash a universally recognized warning: "Keep back—my bite is fatal." Terra-cotta, from Diqdiqqah, near Ur, 2000–1000 B.C.E., Iraq.

2. An 18th-century French tooth made of ivory (a substance as hard as dental enamel) opens up to illustrate a pair of enduring myths: A noxious tooth-worm lies at the core of a toothache, and its hellish torment punishes the sufferer for moral decay.

Tongue

Few images from the pages of Greek mythology are graven deeper in our modern memory than the Gorgon Medusa, whose head of writhing snakes threatened to turn whoever beheld her to stone. We are eager to let Perseus behead her, and ourselves turn the page. Depth psychology forces us to contemplate her repellant image because the animal attributes of such "devouring mothers" clarify their natural origins: hidden in her leonine tongue is her archetypal power to destroy us or nurture us. Just as the divine physician Asclepius used Medusa's blood to revive the dead, so did her broad tongue remind the ancient Greeks of lionesses they observed licking their newborn cubs or cows lapping their calves with warm strokes to stir them into life. The lolling tongue of the Indian goddess Kali no less signifies the qualities of sustaining, nurturing and activating the forces of life, and at the same time, that she is the Absorber of all forms (Mookerjee, 62).

From the moment of birth when it enables us to suckle, the tongue serves as a mobile, muscular organ rooted to the floor of the mouth, ready for its lifelong role in eating, tasting and speaking. Unlike the spectacularly long, lightning-fast tongues of chameleons, hummingbirds or anteaters, our own tongue—with its thousands of taste buds (a parrot has only 400)—serves merely to distinguish salty, sour, bitter and sweet tastes (complex flavors depend upon scent, not taste). But just as we often refer to discriminating taste as one's "palette," "tact" (sensitivity) and "gusto" (zeal) reflect how metaphors of "good taste" originate in tactile and especially gustatory sensations. In fact, lips, tongues and genitals all possess the same ultrasensitive neural receptors (Ackerman, 132).

Ultimately, however, it is through speech that the tongue reveals its fateful power to destroy or create. The Latin word for tongue (lingua; cf. lingere, "licking") reflects the organ's "linguistic" link to language, generating countless metaphors. "To hold one's tongue" may show commendable self-control, which our complexes wrest away from us through "slips of the tongue" that blurt out uncomfortable truths. The "cloventongues of fire" that incited early Christians "to speak in tongues" were gifts of the Spirit (Acts 2:3–4), although glossolalia (from the Greek word for tongue, glossa) is not unique to Christianity, but occurs worldwide among cultures believing in spirit possession. The tongue voicing verbal abuse, sadistic menace or rumor is a conflagration: "How great a forest is set ablaze by a small fire. And the tongue is a fire, a world of iniquity … setting on fire the wheel of birth, and set on fire by hell" (James 3:5–6). Finding ourselves "tongue-tied," our embarrassment renders us speechless, a condition made permanent by the still extant practice of cutting out a criminal's tongue. Medieval Englishmen used "tongue" to signify a sound scolding, a sense that survives in our phrase, "a good tongue-lashing." Japan's Emma, the mythical ruler of hell, extricated the tongue of liars, while the Devil enjoys sticking out his own tongue, a childish insult that blends hostility with sexual suggestiveness. The milder "tongue-in-cheek" quips of the wry humorist can disguise the same intentions while "speaking with a forked tongue"—like Loki the Norse trickster—draws on images of a snake's bifid tongue (actually an organ of scent), with the implication of duplicity. Since no other internal organ protrudes out of the body, it is natural that the tongue came to express what is within us, whether cruel or benevolent, a theme first established perhaps by the primordial Egyptian Creator, Ptah, who manifested the world he had gestated in his heart only when he spoke it out loud with his tongue.

Ackerman, Diane. *A Natural History of the Senses.* NY, 1990.

Mookerjee, Ajit. *Kali: The Feminine Force.* NY, 1988.

1. As the Gorgon Medusa fixed her eyes upon her terrified victim, her scarlet tongue spilled out between her fangs, revealing her as a Devouring Mother and unexpectedly making the passage between life and death intimately moist. Red-figure Attic hydria, detail, ca. 490 B.C.E., Tarquinia, Italy.

2. When the long process of Egyptian mummification was complete, the cow goddess Hathor stepped forward and, with a gesture borrowed from nature, roused the deceased to new life with the warm surface of her tongue. Papyrus, 18th dynasty, New Kingdom (ca. 1550–1295 B.C.E.), Egypt.

1

2

Kiss

Over the doorjamb of the womb-chamber of the Konārak temple in Southern India, and among the images in niches on its facade, are small, erotic sculptures of ardent couples, or *mithuni*. Their flowing bodies melt together in passionate embrace, evoking the sexual play of both gods and mortals, and, paradoxically, the release from it in the union of the self and Supreme Self within a single being. Rapturously, the figures kiss. And here, under the arched brows and interlocked noses of two who are one, the lips merge in a state of bliss that knows nothing of a within or without, and in which there is no longer separation, desire or grief (*Brhadaranyaka Upanishad* IV:3:21; ARAS, 7Ao.044).

Behind sealed lips, we protect one of the most personal spaces of the body; we part our lips to draw in the breath of inspiration or to speak intimate feelings into the beloved's ear, finally surrendering the private self in the loving convergence of one's own lips with the lips of the other. Even when not romantic, the kiss implies affection, blessing, recognition and reconciliation. Thus the psalmist intones, "Mercy and truth are met together; righteousness and peace have kissed each other" (Psalm 85:10). The comparable climax of the Muslim hajj to the Grand Mosque of Mecca is the pilgrim's kiss upon the Black Stone of the Kaaba, an act of reverence first performed by Muhammad. In these religious traditions, kissing is a ceremonial act, a sign of bond between kin, or respect to holy relics, prayer shawls or altars or homage to one's ruler (kissing his feet) or to one's conqueror (licking the dust beneath his feet). With the bridal kiss Western culture bridged the sacred and the romantic, although such European fairy tales as "Sleeping Beauty" or "Snow White" mark the approach of true love by a kiss that awakens the soul, rather than kindles sexual libido.

However, the sensuous, unseemly kiss between Bronzino's Cupid and Venus, his mother—slipping the tip of her tongue into her son's lips—portrays a sly, incestuous carnality. To some cultures, the public display of kissing is considered scandalous, for it signals the opening act of coitus, and casual, devouring tongue-kissing has even suggested cannibalism. Jung, in fact, disagreeing with Freud that all libido was sexual, noted the pleasure infants take in sucking and observed that "kissing derives much more from nutrition than from sexuality" (CW 5:652). The empty "air-kisses" of celebrities or the shallow "spit-swapping" of teenagers can seem to cancel out any encounter between two halves of a single soul that we can still feel in the secular sculpture of Rodin's *The Kiss*. The songbirds whose crossed wings surrounded Aengus, the Celtic god of love, deteriorated into the banal "x's" that close sentimental love letters. Modern Valentines—whose puckering smooches even use kisses to veil hostility—anticipate the chilling intentions of such phrases as "kiss off" (to dismiss a stale lover), "kiss up" (to display shameless obsequiousness) and "kiss-and-tell" (to betray matters shared in confidence). More stunning is the submissive "kiss of shame" upon the devil's anus (or that of his masked proxy). Here, the disciple kisses the "nether-lips" at the opposite end of the body than the mouth, a practice of medieval Satanists at their black Sabbaths, which often inverted conventional ritual. Similarly, the "kiss of death," such as Judas kissing Jesus, reverses, in the perfidious intimacy of betrayal, all that is signified by the kiss of love. The kiss can also convey a different kind of reversal. Francis of Assisi placed squarely on the lips of a fearsome leper the "kiss of peace," communicating a spiritual love that drew the most reviled being of the age into the saint's most personal interior.

1. A kiss of passionate longing may be shunned on the chaste movie screens of contemporary India, but it is openly depicted in the sacred temple sculpture of the 13th century. Sandstone, Surya Temple, Konārak, Orissa, India.

2. Though the identity and meaning of many of the characters in Bronzino's mannerist allegory are still debated, this detail is unequivocally of Venus and her adolescent son Cupid, engaged in an amorous, incestuous kiss. *Venus, Cupid, Folly, and Time*, detail, oil on panel, 1544–5, Italy.

1

2

Neck/Throat

If we weren't so accustomed to having necks, wouldn't we think them odd? Without them, fish are more streamlined, gorillas more compact. This column that connects head and body houses vital channels carrying blood, nerve impulses, air and food. The carotid arteries ascend from the heart and branch in the neck like trees, supplying blood to the head, face, neck and the parts of the body in the cranial cavity. The jugular vein is located there too, and the neck is one of the places we can feel the pulse. The neck and throat are thus highly vulnerable, sites of choking, strangling, hanging, beheading and slitting. Predators, including the human, will "go for the jugular" of prey as a fast and efficient means of killing it. Sacrificial victims were often slain by cutting their throats and the spurting, vital blood caught in a ritual vessel, to be drunk for its magical potency or offered to the gods. The mythic vampire sinks its fangs into the neck, mixing the predatory and the erotic in its craving for blood. In the animal kingdom, wolves, antelopes and alligators telegraph their submissiveness to a stronger animal by exposing to it the most vulnerable part of their bodies, the throat.

More elaborated in the East is the symbolism of the neck as the bridge between body and mind. In Kundalini yoga, the throat is the fifth of seven chakras, or subtle body centers. The throat center is called *Visuddha*, meaning "pure," and it signifies ether, space and vacuity, wherein all the elements mingle (Mookerjee, 43, 49). The white elephant *Airavata*, vehicle of Indra, the god of storm and rain that flows from the elephantine, etheric clouds, is the animal emblem of *Visuddha*. It is the counterpart to the dark elephant of the first chakra, the *Muladhara* at the base of the spine, signifying earth and solidity. At the level of the throat chakra, however, the "insurmountable, sacred strength" of the elephant "supports the volatile substance of mind" (Jung in Mookerjee, 54); we experience reality less from the concrete than the psychical. Not only in the Indian cultures, but in many others, the symbolic emptiness of the throat identifies it with sound, sonic vibration and the sounding of the cosmos into being as Word. In the famous Hindu creation myth of the churning of the Milky Ocean, Shiva, in the form of a sacred chant, swallows the poison of death that paradoxically emerges in the attempt by the gods and demons to bring up (and possess) the elixir of immortality: "It marked his throat with sinister peacock beauty, dark blue, as if a serpent had kissed it" (Kramrisch, 152).

The human neck, especially that of a woman, is also an object of beauty and eroticism. We ornament the neck with jewels and decorate and protect it with collars, scarves and ruffs. The "bull neck" of a man suggests strength, power and seminal force. The long, slender "swan neck" of a lovely woman, gracefully curved when the head is lowered, suggests appealing delicacy and refinement. Japanese tradition emphasizes the nape of the neck of a woman as an erotic attraction that can be bared seductively. In some cultures of Burma and Africa, a very long neck is considered especially beautiful, and young girls' necks are artificially lengthened by being encased in rigid metal collars, which are gradually increased in number as the girl grows (Ebin, 12f). But as with many parts of the female body, erotic significance drives deformation: The stretching may weaken the neck, push down the collarbone and compress the rib cage.

Probably because of its function in linking, psychic conflict gets into the neck. To be "stiff-necked" connotes obduracy and inflexibility, suggesting that one can no longer take in the perspective from different angles. Perhaps it also implies a disconnect between body and head, as if they want to go in different directions, or, alternatively, a tendency to habitually look in too many directions and a need to focus on one. Is it the heart's blood gushing into the neck's big arteries that makes the throat so sensitive to feeling? It can close up when there is something too difficult to swallow. We speak of a thing so upsetting that it "sticks in the craw," comparing ourselves to a bird with a telltale lump in its throat. An allergic response makes the throat swell up, cutting off breath. Responding to exhaustion, it becomes inflamed, shutting down the creative capacity to sound. Grief, rage, panic or fear tightens the throat, creating a "bottleneck," a merging of psychic traffic, a crowding and blocking.

Ebin, Victoria. *The Body Decorated*. London and NY, 1979.
Kramrisch, Stella. *The Presence of Śiva*. Princeton, NJ, 1981.
Mookerjee, Ajit. *Kundalini: The Arousal of the Inner Energy*. Rochester, VT, 1986.

1

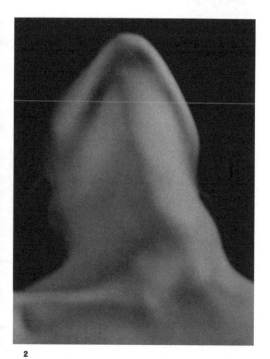

2

1. Vishnu Visvarupa, preserver of the universe, bears
what seems to be Krishna within a golden city at his
throat, marking the fifth of seven subtle energy centers
of the body. Detail, watercolor on paper, early 19th
century, Jaipur, India.

2. Surrealist artist Man Ray experiments with visual
perception, transgendering a woman's throat into the
suggestion of a phallus. *Anatomies*, photograph, 1929.

Arm

Whether one feeds the mouth with the hand, or lives "hand to mouth" or combines word with gesture, the arm is the middleman. Any symbolic image held up by the arm, such as the torch that proclaims freedom, is magnified. So versatile is the arm that it was the pictogram of activity in Egyptian hieroglyphics (DoS, 43). What's more, the basic units of measure, upon which all other proportions were based in accord with the Egyptian concept of divine "right order" or *Maat*, were the arm and the hand (ARAS, 2Am.004). Just as the arms enable the hands to touch nearly all points on our own bodies, so also do arms encompass, in their busy interactions, the world at large. Arms are innately expressive. The most centrifugal of our limbs, they naturally "move outward," often at the level of the heart, which can seem to be the locus of their agency. Strong feelings activate the arms. Perhaps the most instinctive act of a mother's love is to cradle the newborn in her arms close to the heart and breast. In dance and ritual, arms often voice a rich and spontaneous body language that defies literal translation. Arms, of course, also serve the body at the fundamental level of survival. Humans are among the creatures who forage, hunt and eat with the forelimbs. But an active hand and arm may also feed the mind by functioning as explorer and the executor of consciousness. As primate hind limbs evolved and stood erect, the manipulative power of arms and hands was released, interacting with the brain to spur the development of intelligence. Arms made humankind *homo faber*, the "maker." Strong arms build civilizations, and human labor is celebrated in universal images of powerful arms wielding tools. The same arms are capable of infinite destruction, in the aggressive force of the arm itself and in the making and deployment of "arms." The gun, arrow, grenade and other weapons vastly extend the arm's reach and capacity for annihilation. Arms can embody equally ambivalent energies of a transpersonal nature. Ritually upraised arms everywhere signify the invocation of the numinous whether for creation or destruction. The mighty arms of storm gods aim the potentially shattering lightning bolt, which also breaks up stasis and brings the fertilizing rains. Jesus enfolds the lost lamb in the crook of his arm, but also raises the sword of judgment. Shiva dances and "his flailing arms toss the mountains into the air" as the world is burnt into extinction so that it can find renewal (Kramrisch, 439). And, like the many branches of a life-giving tree within oneself, each arm of a multiarmed deity, like the ninth century Buddhist Avolokiteshvara, represents a specific spiritual attribute with far-reaching potential.

Giedion, S. *Eternal Present: The Beginnings of Architecture*. NY, 1964.
Kramrisch, Stella. *The Presence of Śiva*. Princeton, NJ, 1981.

1. From *Hand to Mouth*, by Bruce Nauman, wax over cloth, 1967, United States.

2. The many arms of a Buddhist goddess convey the scope of her boons. Copper alloy, 9th century, Sumatra, Indonesia.

3. From the outstretched hand and arm was derived the decisive linear measurement, the cubit. Drawing, from a wall relief, 19th dynasty (ca. 1292–1190, B.C.E.), Egypt (Giedion, 484).

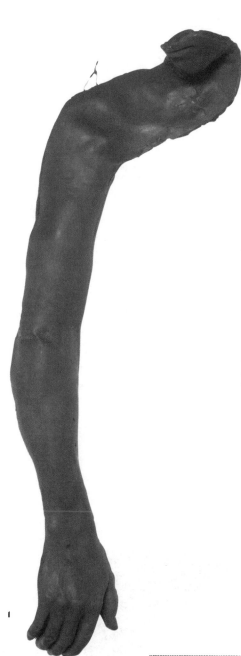

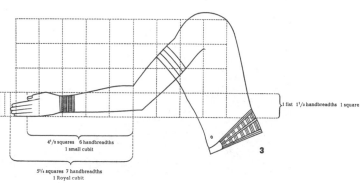

1 fist 1¹/₂ handbreadths 1 square

4¹/₂ squares   6 handbreadths
1 small cubit

5¹/₄ squares 7 handbreadths
1 Royal cubit

2

3

379

Hand

Against the containing walls of the cave of Pech-Merle, prehistoric artists apparently held their hands and blew red ochre and black cinder over them, leaving tracery visible 20,000 years later. The hands appear to ride the energy of the horses across the wall, evoking a kind of shamanic permeability of human, animal and spirit worlds. At the same time, the distinctive five fingers upraised suggest the expressive potential of emerging human consciousness brought into realization by hands like those that produced these incomparable images.

An object of fascination at the dawn of human consciousness as it is in the infancy of the human individual, the hand differs only minimally from the pentadactyl appendage of our primate cousins the chimps. In both species, the hand and its opposable thumb claim a vastly disproportionate representation in the brain. Along with the mouth and lips the hands have more neural innervation than all the rest of the body, as if reflecting the preeminence of sounding and making. In religions throughout the world, the Hand of God denotes supreme, inexorable agency. As primary instruments of the creative, the hands of the *homo faber* imitate the mythic shaping of matter into discrimi-nated being by deities who chisel, mold, sculpt, weave and forge creation. Hands signify the sovereign, world-creating reach of consciousness; they embody effectiveness, industry, adaptation, invention, self-expression and the possession of a will for creative and destructive ends. Hands are lightning rods for psychic energy. The same fingers that confer a blessing, stroke a child or tend a wound can smash a skull, drive viruses into computer systems or strike the match that sets a forest on fire. Idioms describe the manner in which, symbolically, the hand exploits its power: single-handed, even-handed, underhanded, high-handed, sleight-of-hand. Tiny hands, tied hands or a lack of hands suggests severe constraints on one's autonomy, an incapacity to grasp and claim the world, make one's desires real, form one's matter. The "Handless Maiden" of the Grimm's fairy tale, for example, can be seen as representing a feminine being-in-the-world that is psychically so bedeviled by the patriarchal attitude that the emblematic hands of self-expression are rendered passive. Or, alternatively, the story points to a need for inner reflection, rather than active handling in the world.

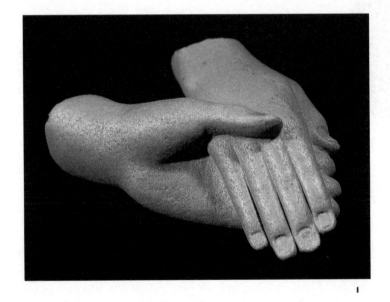

1

2

1. The lovingly held hands of a couple probably belonged to statues of Egyptian pharaoh Akhenaten and his queen Nefertiti. Sandstone, 1539–1295 B.C.E., Egypt.

2. The small, mysterious hands of Pech-Merle belonged most likely to young boys or adult women. Wall painting, ca. 25,000 years old, Pech-Merle Caves, Cabrerets, France.

Hands speak with eloquent silence: the clasped hands of lovers, the comforting hand on the shoulder of the grieving, the raised hands of prisoners of war. Hands are specifically employed in language as supplement or substitute for lips and mouth. The "signing" of the deaf, or the gestured pictographs of tribal peoples, or the hand signals of athletes, police and soldiers. Hands convey meaning that penetrates barriers of specie, nation or age: the wave of a hand in acknowledgement, the open hand as a sign of benign intent, a finger across the lips to enjoin silence. The famous Koko and other captive chimps took so readily to sign language that they began to teach their own offspring without human prompting. The string games of the Inuit and the elaborate hand dancers of Indonesia transmit tradition through stories told in ritualized movements of fingers and palms. In Hindu and Buddhist traditions, hand positions known as mudras comprise a complete symbolism in rites of devotion. Perhaps the hands of Pech-Merle similarly express the gestures of worship or tell a story, or, we may imagine, convey the greeting of primordial elders to their awed descendents.

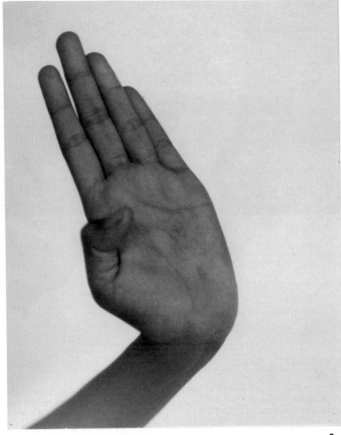

3

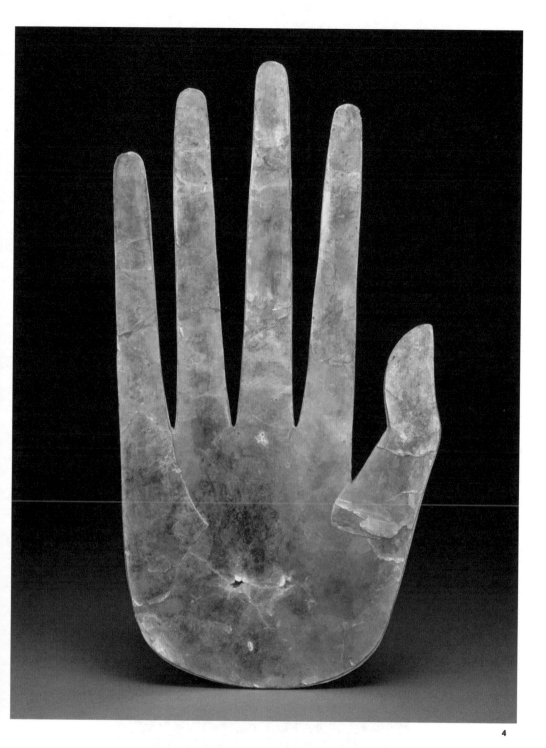

4

3. Articulated and articulate, the supple hand is that of an Indonesian dancer. Photograph by Dorothea Lange, 1958, Java.

4. What is probably a depiction of the Hand of God, a hand-shaped cutout of the American Woodland Indians conveys the authority of one who creates, ordains, blesses—and destroys. Middle Woodland period, 200 B.C.E.–400 C.E.

Finger

At the tip of an ornamental Torah pointer is a carved miniature hand with a pointing index finger that assists the reader in following the words of the Hebrew Scriptures. Neither the reader's own finger nor the pointer ever touch the scroll, a way of maintaining the Torah's sanctity (Altshuler, 122).

Fingers of flesh and blood also perform the most delicate operations. They touch with remarkable sensitivity and express word and image in eloquent gestures. With extreme precision they manipulate (from the Latin word manus, hand) the concrete matter of reality, enact the executive orders of the brain and creatively shape into existence multifarious psychic forms. Fingers pars pro toto represent the potency of the hand, so related to human consciousness. In a version of the Polynesian myth where the culture-hero Maui receives divine fire from his grandmother, it is her fingers and toes that contain the flames, like rays from the sun. In his famous painting in the Sistine Chapel, Michelangelo conceived the Creator as vital energy, a spark of which the deity transmits to his human creation Adam through the extended forefinger of his divine hand. Images of flames emanating from the fingertips of saints and the heat sometimes felt from the touch of a healer suggest that the fingers are pathways between interior and exterior realms.

Opposing the thumb to hold and grasp, each of the four fingers of the hand has individual qualities, degrees of flexibility, and the capacity to work alone or with the other fingers. No two fingerprints are alike, making the fingers a source of positive identification and forensic tracking. There are over 3,000 gestures of the hand and fingers besides the sign language used by the deaf (Stevens, 407).

So versatile and effective are the fingers that Greek mythology immortalizes them as the Daktyloi, or "little fingers," the ten sons of the Great Mother Rhea. They emerged when, in Rhea's birth pangs delivering Zeus, she dug her fingers into the earth. The Daktyloi are dwarf craftsmen, gifted and generative, evoking the wisdom and creativity of unconscious impulses that consciousness tends to overlook. These deft "fingers" can be enormously helpful.

Fingers are agents of the pleasures of touching and being touched. As the essential extremities of the hand, fingers are also world-creating, like those of divine potters molding the stuff of the cosmos. When we talk about what we have "at our fingertips," we are not just referring to convenience. We are owning the wondrous powers of invention in our distinctive digits.

Altshuler, David A. *The Precious Legacy: Judaic Treasures from the Czechoslovak State Collections.* NY and Washington DC, 1983.
Stevens, Anthony. *Ariadne's Clue.* Princeton, NJ, 1998.

1. These "fingers" point to the words of Judaism's scripture as the reader follows them. Torah pointers, 19th century, Maisel Synagogue, Prague, Czech Republic.

2. *Finger Pointing*, as accusation, emphasis or the commanding "We Want You!" of recruitment. By Roy Lichtenstein, silkscreen on paper, 1973. © Estate of Roy Lichtenstein.

Claw / Nail

In concentric curves of mineral and space, an artist has elegantly captured the structure of a raptor's talon. The beautifully designed bird-claw was cut from sheet mica about two millennia ago. This ornament from the Native American Hopewell culture embodies the fierce efficiency of the claw for clutching and tearing flesh, for ripping, piercing and manipulating. The claw's versatile potency has made it a talisman in many early cultures.

Claws are animals' natural tools for digging and climbing, defense and the killing of prey. The shape of the claws in a particular species represents an evolutionary adaptation to its hunting and food gathering habits. Bears, like eagles, have long, curved claws for catching fish; chickens have short, sturdy claws for scratching the ground. Cats have retractable claws that are implicated in balance, jumping, climbing, playing and hunting. The claws that developed into the hoof of quadrupeds, designed for fast running, and into the nails of primates and humans that protect the fingers and toes, allow for greater purchase when grasping and serve as weapons and tools.

Claws and nails seem to have a life of their own. They grow so speedily that they require regular cutting or filing, which causes no pain. Human nails continue to grow even after death. Perhaps because of their uncanny growth as well as their sharpness and defensive power, claws and nails have been seen to contain the essence or soul of the being to whom they belong. Scandinavia's mythic Norns or Fates were said to write the destiny of newborn children upon their fingernails. In fact, the genetic code of DNA is carried even in the cells of a baby's tiny nails. Nails are an indicator of health because they are sensitive to illness, toxins and physical and psychic trauma (*Enc. Brit.* 21:703).

As soul substance, fingernails had to be handled with special care after a person died (Frazer, 279). In ancient Scandinavia, for example, the uncut fingernails of corpses were the chaotic matter from which was built Naglfar, the mythic doomsday ship helmed by the giant Hrymr. The nails of the deceased were cut short for the funeral in order to delay the inevitable arrival of the grim "ship of the dead" bringing cosmic destruction (Simek, 226).

Nails have long had a part in the cosmetic display of the erotic. Since ancient Egypt, when henna was used to redden their nails, women have made fingernails a fashion statement in which danger and sexuality could be expressed in a kind of alluring masquerade. Connoting regression to or mythic contamination with unconscious energies, long nails have been associated with the indolent aristocrat, the seductive femme fatale, the "dead" vampire, witches and sorcerers.

In claw and nail a resonant continuity with our animal ancestors is evoked—ourselves as raptors or, like the cat, finding in "claw" the experience of refined play, sensuous pleasure and lightning destruction. Clawing is behind the image of "fighting tooth and nail" and concretely expresses the paradoxical energies of grasping and resisting in lovemaking. Linking us to the primal and instinctual as well as to conscious, directed manipulation, claw suggests symbolically the "sharp, curved process" of survival, interrelationship and evolutionary selection.

Frazer, James George. *Taboo and the Perils of the Soul.* London and NY, 1935.
Simek, Rudolf. *Dictionary of Northern Mythology.* Cambridge, UK, and Rochester, NY, 1993.

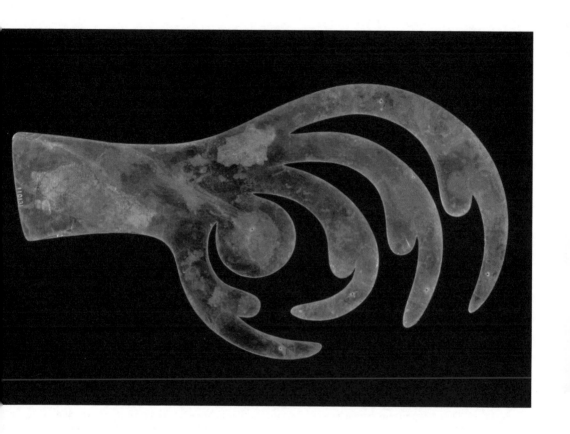

Cut from sheet mica, the elegant representation of a
bird's talon suggests the primal power of the predatory,
the savage and the soul. Bird-claw ornament, Native
American Hopewell culture, 100 B.C.E.–200 C.E., Ohio,
United States.

Breast

This breathtaking image of a clay breast fragment dotted with paint was found in the shallow waters of Lake Constance. It was found in the first decorated Neolithic building structure discovered in Northern Europe (Arnold, 23). It is a breast and more than a breast. It is natural and unnatural, a creation by nature and by human (as art), through psyche's symbol-forming capacity and expresses, through its complexity, the many underlying facets of breast imagery.

Breast is source. It is provision. It carries the potential for life within it. It is linked biologically, etymologically, psychically and symbolically with the life-giving source. The Indo-European root *bhreus,* which means to swell or to sprout, leads us back to this core meaning. Symbolically mother, breasts and the sea are linked. The sea, too, is an archetypal image of the source. Jung speculates that words for sea (such as the Latin *mare,* the German *Meer* and the French *mer*) may point back to the "great primordial image of mother" (CW 5:373).

The maternal significance of the breast is clearly one of its dominant aspects. The first human encounter is with the breast, and the Latin word for breast is *mamma.* To the newborn child the breast is mother and it is life: survival, nourishment and warmth. This functional meaning of the breast, as creator and sustainer of life, is reflected in early fertility images.

Although primarily associated with nurturance, the breast has a generative meaning as well. Note the classic psychoanalytic equivalence of penis and breast. (See, for example, Freud's studies of Dora, Little Hans and Leonardo da Vinci and, in a very different vein the writing of D. W. Winnicott.) The generative aspect of the breast is, in itself, twofold. First, the breast "makes" milk and, by extension, warmth and tenderness. Second, its making of the milk in response to the infant's need—often rather dramatically manifesting as an autonomous flow at the sound of the infant's hunger cry— is also the foundation of the infant's experience of his/her hunger creating its own needed response, that is,

it provides the basis of the capacity for generative creative response to need later in life.

The anatomical structure and function of the breast is made up of nipple, aureola and fatty tissue. The associations with receptivity, silver and the moon are all feminine. (The Egyptian hieroglyph means both breast and moon.) The word "aureola," referring to the darker circle surrounding the nipple, comes from the Latin *aurum,* meaning gold. The aureola, itself, is associated with the sun, maleness, power and creativity; thus the breast encompasses both masculine and feminine connotations. Like the penis, the aureola and nipple are made of erectile tissue that stiffens on sexual arousal.

From the basic level of anatomy to complex Christian and alchemical images, the breast expresses opposites, containing both the creative and the destructive. It represents the fiery center, the divine spark, from which comes the elixir—milk or poison. Note Isis's transforming milk, which renders one immortal, Sophia's milk of wisdom and the double nurturance from the breasts of the nurse in Frida Kahlo's 1937 painting, *My Nurse and I.*

Biologically and psychologically, the breast is inherently expressive of twoness. To psychoanalyst Melanie Klein, there is the good breast and the bad breast, the breast that supplies and the breast that withholds. The right breast is also linked with consciousness and the sun, the left with unconsciousness and the moon. Symbolically, the twoness of the two breasts suggests a constellation of opposites, while the sameness of the breasts invites a linking of those opposites—a way to get from the known to the unknown.

Associated with the erotic and the sexual, the breast connotes desire, beauty of form, fullness and artifice. It is about revealing and concealing, seducing and opening to consummation. It is about stimulating, arousing and potentially transcending time and space, however briefly. Thus it is symbolically tied to the magico-religious condition of the divine.

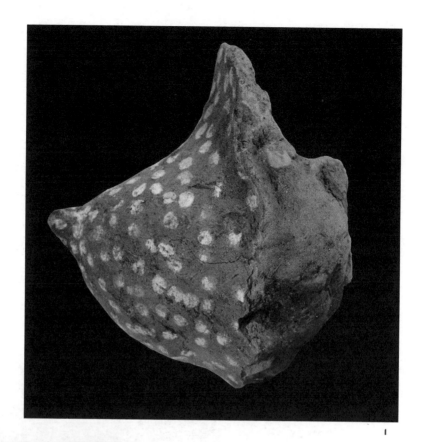

1. Breast fragment with painted dots, clay, Neolithic period, ca. 3900–3800 B.C.E (Arnold, 23).

2. In infancy the baby is one with the mother/breast. The calm, sacral feeling of this African (Mali) sculpture of a nursing child manifests the profound oneness of the mother-infant pair. The primacy of this symbol is revealed in studies that suggest that students perform better on tests when exposed to the subliminal words "Mommy and I are one" (Silverman, 1296–1308).

The breast carries power in its function and its form. In addition, many images show fear of the breast and a reaction, often violent, against its power. This ranges from difficulty separating from infant identity with the nourishing mother (images of large breasts as suffocating) to pathological and criminal forms of attack. Women's breasts have also been a battleground for control. They have been flattened, pointed, lifted, enlarged, according to the order of the day, to conform to our erotic tastes and desires.

The image of the bared breast may express supplication and a sense of vulnerability, as found in scenes of women pleading for mercy amid pillages and rape. By contrast, it can signify power and assertion of liberty, as in the French Revolution or, in a different context, the hippie movement of the 1960s.

Arnold, Bettina. "Lake Constance Yields Breast Relief." *Archaeology* (March/April, 1993).
Silverman, L. H. and J. Weinberger. "Mommy and I Are One. Implications for Psychotherapy." *The American Psychologist* (40/12, 1985).

4

3

3. The right breast drips the familiar milk, and the left flowery and fiery breast exudes otherworldly, translucent liquid nourishment. *My Nurse and I*, by Frida Kahlo, oil on metal, 12 in. x 13¾ in., collection Museo Dolores Olmedo, 1937, Xochimilco, Mexico.

4. The breast is erotic and divine, qualities that are amply present in this dancing devata (deity). This aspect appears in degraded forms as well: Magazine centerfolds portray the buxom girl next door; Times Square used to provide a coin machine that for $2.50 would open a window allowing the purchaser to feel two actual breasts for 30 seconds. Sandstone, 12th century, India.

Heart

Stop the flow of your words,
open the window of your heart and
let the spirit speak.
Rumi

The wounded yet radiant heart of Christ, encircled by a wreath of thorns, sprouting grapevines, wheat and a cross from its severed aorta and bleeding into a chalicelike font conveys the transformation of Christ's love and sacrifice into the elements of the Eucharist. So can the deepest pain, when fully held and suffered in the heart's vessel, be gradually distilled into the redemptive.

The heart is a living symbol. When we say "I love you with all my heart," we do and do not mean the heart as organ whose beats cause the circulation of blood throughout the body, whose failure could drain the body of life. We also mean the heart as feeling, as the soulful, as the heart of the cosmos, echoed and amplified in the primal pulsation of the drum. Heartbeats correspond to the contracting and expanding movements of the universe, while the heart in the body is as essential to life as the sun is to our solar system. Among the first sounds experienced in the womb are the internally resounding rhythms of the mother's heart, enveloping and echoing the quicker beats of the embryo as it grows. The heart's undeniable physical centrality to our existence has its correspondence in the undeniable reality of our emotions, variable heartbeats measuring out our feelings of affection, desire and delight, as well as pounding out our rages, fears and vulnerabilities; the heart can be pierced and melted by the darts of Eros as well as broken by love's refusal (ARAS, 2:287–89).

For many early Mesoamerican peoples, the heart's power was so valued that it was ritually sacrificed and fed, still throbbing, to the sun god weakened by his nocturnal journey through the underworld, in order to reinforce the energy and vitality of the people (Biedermann, 166). The heart, like the sun, is the central source of life, the seat of power, courage and strength. The tiny Olmec figure, embracing a heart larger than his torso, could just as well be fiercely seizing power as singing a joyous ode of praise to the light of god, the inner, invisible sun shining "as though in darkness" that this enormous heart represents. As the alchemists claim, this light is to be sought "not in ourselves," but in the god within who "deigns to make us his dwelling place," whom we encounter through passionate discourse with the feelings in our heart (CW 8:389).

In Ancient Egypt the hieroglyphic heart shaped as a vase, was the storehouse of memory and truth, the center of the personality, of understanding, will and thought as well as creative imagination. The god Ptah

1. Amulet meant to help in the underworld ordeal of the weighing of the heart. Carnelian, 7th–4th century B.C.E., Egypt.

2. *The Bleeding Heart (Lamb of God)*, anonymous, oil on tin, 19th century, Mexico.

conceived the universe in his heart and expressed those thoughts with his tongue to bring all into reality. Egyptian physicians were the first to recognize the importance of the pulse, which they called the "voice of the heart" (Milton, 62). Before the deceased were allowed to enter the underworld, they were judged in front of Osiris: The heart was weighed against the feather of Maat, goddess of truth and justice. If it was heavier or lighter, it was not in harmony with Maat, and was thrown to a hippopotamus-crocodile creature and devoured. If it weighed the same as the feather, the deceased was declared "true of voice," and granted eternal life. The heart, the only internal organ left inside the embalmed corpse, was often accompanied by small heart-shaped amulets made of red semiprecious stone, or by the heart scarab, carved from green, black or gray stone and engraved with magic spells that would prevent the heart from bearing witness against the dead person at Osiris' judgment seat. A version of this divine justice occurs in our hearts at every moment, acting as our guiding conscience, our "true voice" in the daily business of living.

The heart shares with the lotus flower and the rose the qualities of the hidden, enfolded center beneath the outer surface of things, the secret abode of consciousness, locked away, virgin and so inviolate that when we want to "let someone in," we must give them "the key." The "heart of the matter" expresses the essential core of any issue, and the heart is so identified as the center and unique essence of a human being that the idea of surgically transplanting a heart from one individual to another still meets with powerful resistance. As the seat of all emotions, positive and negative, the heart is the point of contact for linkings of hatred or love, envy or compassion, fear or courage, deepest sorrow or brightest joy.

Biedermann, Hans. *Dictionary of Symbolism.* NY, 1994.
Milton, Joyce. *Sunrise of Power: Ancient Egypt, Alexander and the World of Hellenism.* NY, 1980.

3

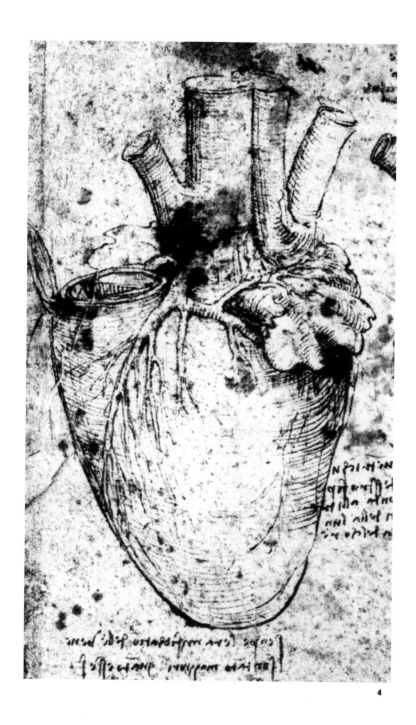

4

3. This 4½-inch-high Olmec ceramic figure from about 1000 B.C.E., thought to be one of the oldest anatomically accurate hearts, depicts the aorta, the pulmonary artery and both ventricles.

4. Drawing of heart and blood vessels, by Leonardo da Vinci, pen and brown ink, ca. 1513, Italy.

Blood

The contemporary Japanese paper artist Kako Ueda cut out her *Tree of Life* with such deft precision that we can feel the movement of her blade along our veins. At its roots, a small coffin and tiny human limbs are wrapped in capillaries beneath a skirt that maternally shelters both warm- and cold-blooded creatures in its scarlet pleats. Above them, a skull houses a spider in its tracery web—a tastefully gruesome paraphrase of the hemorrhage that nearly ended the life of the artist's mother. Intuitively, artists recognize the emotional impact of their tubes of blood-red paint: "I was walking down the road with two friends when the sun set; suddenly, the sky turned as red as blood," writes the Norwegian expressionist Edvard Munch, describing the genesis of *The Scream,* which triggered the memory of bloody carnage at his mother's deathbed when he was five (Faerna, 17). Jung also noted the intriguing parallels between the maternal Tree of Life and the human blood-system, observing how sap, imitating blood, cycles through the seasons, flowing down to its earthbound roots in winter and returning as fruit in summer, containing within its branching intricacies the entire mystery of life and death (CW 13:376). Pulsing with paradox, blood evokes life's precious value as long as it is contained within our bodies, but when it escapes in red-hot spurts, it congeals into a dark, haunting symbol of death. Spilled onto the ground, its innocent voice calls out to God to avenge Cain's fratricide of Abel (Gen 4:10), while the Greek Furies track down Orestes by his blood's incriminating scent, intent on sucking it out of him to avenge his matricide of Clytemnestra (Kuriyama, 199). To the ancient Greeks—who organized humans into categories based on four bodily fluids (or humors)—blood engendered the popular sanguine temperament associated with the sun, warmth, cordiality and magnanimity (DoS, 100). Upon this foundation, Galen relieved fiery inflammation by draining away "excess blood" (Kuriyama, 212), inspiring medieval barber-surgeons (as the red stripes of barber poles remind us) to remedy flirtatiousness and relieve sickness, banish a monk's worldly fantasies and relieve ladies at court from blushing at ribald stories by filling basins with their blood, persisting even when the bloodletting killed them off (Bettmann, 74).

Matching the salinity of Cambrian seas of half a billion years vintage, blood plasma transports red blood cells to seal wounds and carry oxygen and nutrients throughout the body, along with a smaller number of white cells to fight infection and carry away wastes. Our ambivalence toward this primordial fluid is remarkable: We belittle battle as a bloodbath, but reward the "red badge of courage" with a medal; we long for contact with a lover's warm, ruddy skin, but recoil in horror from Dracula's streaming skin-pricks in the depths of night. The Hindu artist who conceived cosmic energy flowing from the goddess Chinnamasta as a fountain of numinous blood understood that it showered down upon erotic revelry and repulsive butchery alike; equal prospects of life and death stir beneath the agonized awe of a pubescent girl at her first menstrual flow and a soldier at his first gushing wound. Blood symbolizes our *feeling* for the sacredness of life before we distance ourselves in bloodless, abstract thought—it is the soul of embodied life, forming our essential character. Sensing this, the Masai drank the blood of lions and Norwegians the blood of bears; warriors drank the blood of their slain enemies (MM 2:291) while Mayans drenched their altars with their enemies' blood to repay a debt to gods who had shed their own blood to create them (Miller, 46–47). Like Faust signing his pact with Satan in blood to lock in its drastic terms, blood commingles through the open cuts of blood brothers to seal bonds of consanguinity whether among the Knights Templar or between Huck Finn and Tom Sawyer. From archaic notions of the liver as a mass of congealed blood and from roots in countless taboos, dietary codes and sacrileges, blood resurges in the image of Christ's lifeblood spurting into a wine-chalice as he dies on a symbolic tree of life. Communion wine is then imagined as blood circulating through a grapevine to its branches—the veins and arteries that in a thousand metaphors worldwide restore us to the transpersonal heart of all things.

Bettmann, Otto L. *A Pictorial History of Medicine.* Springfield, IL, 1956.
Faerna, José Maria. *Munch.* NY, 1996.
Kuriyama. *The Expressiveness of the Body and the Divergence of Greek and Chinese Medicine.* NY, 1999.
Miller, Mary Ellen and Karl A. Taube. *The Gods and Symbols of Ancient Mexico and the Maya.* NY, 1993.

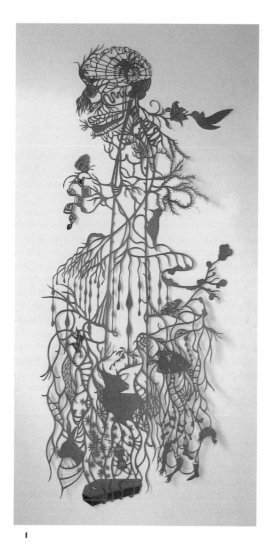

1. Circulating through an arterial silhouette, blood flows and drips along the branches of Kako Ueda's hand-cut figure, delineating the cyclical nature of life and death in freshly severed red paint. *Tree of Life*, paper, 2005, United States.

2. Although her erotic gaze makes his blue phallus become engorged with blood, the tantric coitus of Krishna and Radha seems anemic next to the headless goddess Chinnamasta, who spouts warm arcs of blood. Along with her garland of skulls and the cobra and sword in her many hands, the sight of her severed head and cup of sacrificial blood pushes us to the edge of fainting. Gouache on paper, 18th century, India.

3. Dante imagined the hell that awaited perpetrators of violence as a cataract of hot blood. In his *Divine Comedy* (Canto XII), anyone who struggled to lift himself out of this boiling river was shot back down by one of the centaurs guarding its banks. Manuscript illustration, ca. 1390–1400, Italy.

Liver

Prometheus writhes in agony in Rubens' graphic depiction of the torture to which the fire-bringer is condemned by Zeus for stealing fire from the gods and giving it as a gift to human beings. An eagle, Zeus' bird, tears the liver of the hero, and each night the liver grows back so that it can be consumed again for eons to come.

That the liver should be the focus of the Promethean punishment tells us something about the organ's symbolism and the fantasies of the ancients regarding it. We now know that the liver purifies the blood, which then passes up to the heart and lungs by way of the largest vein, vena cava (Onians, 85). The liver processes and stores nutrients, and produces proteins and cholesterol. It secretes gall or bile, essential for digestion. It regenerates so swiftly that it can be transplanted from a living donor. In ancient times, however, the liver was the object of many intriguing projections. Medical antiquity, perceiving that the liver was the largest organ in the body, and full of blood, believed that it made blood and identified the liver with life. The liver was accorded a major role in the making of specific human temperaments through the production of the "four humors," or fluids: the choleric temperament from yellow bile, the melancholic from black bile, the sanguine from blood and the phlegmatic from cold, moist phlegm. We still have the residue of this idea in adjectives like "bilious," "lily-livered" and "galling."

Another notion was, following Plato, that a principal function of the liver, situated in the lower part of the body between the diaphragm and navel, was to reflect images from the rational soul, whose seat was the head. This mirroring made the liver a natural instrument of divination, the omens of which manifested in dreams and oracular inspiration. Beginning with the ancient Babylonians, the livers of sacrificed animals were used in divining. At the moment of sacrifice, the god was identified with the animal, allowing the divine insight of the future to be read. Ancient models from Mesopotamia and from the Etruscan culture show a mapping of the cosmic structure on the microcosm of sheep livers (Nuland, 112, 114).

Because the liver was "deep-seated" in the body, and secreted bile, "it came to be regarded as the inmost spring of the deeper emotions, stirred only by powerful stimuli." The substance of these emotions, as secretions, was thought to enter the organs higher up, such as the heart and lungs (Onians, 85). The liver was variously associated with emotions like wrath, desire, grief and defiance. At the same time, the ancient Greeks believed that pain, like disease, often came at one in the form of divine arrows or predatory birds (ibid., 86). Thus, in the myth of Prometheus, who stole fire, the punishment perhaps fits the crime in two ways. First, the eagle inflicts searing pain on the "emotional" liver, which is meant to induce galling bitterness in the hero at having committed the theft. Second, the assailing of the liver consumed the imagined source of the "fire in the blood" of love and defiance that may have inspired the titanic sin.

Nuland, Sherwin B. *The Mysteries Within: A Surgeon Explores Myth, Medicine and the Human Body.* NY and London, 2000.
Onians, Richard Broxton. *The Origins of European Thought.* Cambridge, UK, 1991.

1. Forsaken in punishment, the Titan who stole fire from the gods is chained to a rock in the Caucasus Mountains, his liver the daily food of Zeus' eagle. *Prometheus Bound*, by Peter Paul Rubens, oil on canvas, 1611–18, Southern Netherlands.

2. These Egyptian stone jars were designed to conserve the internal organs of the deceased. Each organ was protected by a son of the god Horus, the human-headed for the liver, falcon for the stomach, baboon for the lungs and jackal for the intestines. Canopic jars, Late Period (5th–4th century B.C.E).

3. This Etruscan model of a sheep liver, found in Piacenza, Italy, was believed to have been used for instruction in a divining school or as an amulet. The reading of a sacrificed animal's liver for omens followed the model's division into sixteen "houses," corresponding to the gods of the divinatory sky. Bronze, end of 2nd century B.C.E.

1

2

3

Womb

The reddish, earthen Lepenski Vir pot bulges with the taut roundness of a pregnant womb, gently supported by what appear to be hands, whose sensitive touch seems to listen for the vitality and subtle movement within. In both material and form, the clay pot, whose "inside" is unseen and therefore unknown, like the cave buried deep in the earth, is a central symbol of the transformative mysteries of the womb (Neumann, 39). Pot-making, itself a sacral, creative activity, was in many ancient societies the exclusive domain of women. In traditional Native American rites and creation myths, Earth is the primary womb. Sky is her inseminator through rain as semen. Springs reveal her inner waters. Living beings—plants, animals, humans—emerge from their gestation deep within her womb, and return to it in death, to be born again. Thus the highest and most essential mysteries of the feminine are symbolized by the earth and its transformations (ibid., 47), and those reborn in rites of initiation describe themselves emerging as "fresh-baked pots" (ibid., 137). Indian temples have as their central sanctuary a *garbhagriha* or womb-house wherein one receives *darshan*, a luminous seeing of the divine. In Vedic symbolism, fire is hidden in wood as in a womb, then brought forth in fire ritual, just as divine spirit is hidden within, and brought forth through meditation and chanting om. "Where the fire is churned ... there the mind is formed" (Svetasvatara Upanishad, I.13–14, II.6). Vedic hymns sing of Hiranyagarbha, the Golden Womb or Golden Embryo, the radiant Divine that manifests through all creation (e.g. Rig Veda X.121).

The human uterus is a ruddy inverted triangular container, branching toward fallopian tubes on top and on the bottom narrowing toward the cervix, which opens into the vagina or birth canal. Inside, a moist mucous membrane, the endometrium, becomes thick during ovulation and is shed periodically as menstrual blood, unless a fertilized egg implants itself in this welcoming ground. From the combined genetic material of egg and sperm, the blood-rich placenta begins developing even before the embryo, quickly growing into the thick spongy nest we see pictured, a nourishing protective "twin" mediating between baby and mother. The embryo floats in a sac surrounded by amniotic fluid, like a tiny fish cradled in the vast ocean from which all life originates.

Alchemically, *solutio* meant the return of differentiated matter to its original undifferentiated state, and the ovoid alembic became known as the womb, or the spagyric uterus, a transformative place of the union of opposites, death and rebirth (Abraham, 219). As both birthplace and tomb, the womb is life's source as well as the gaping abyss, untiringly swallowing up mortal humankind. Psychologically, the fixed, static aspects of the personality must be reduced back to their original state through a descent into the creative unconscious, the maternal womb from which the ego is born (Edinger, 47–48). If undertaken by an immature ego, this can result in self-surrender or regression, resulting in a psychological failure to be fully born and manifest in the world. Even when undertaken by the developed ego, it is a long and perilous night-sea journey like that of Jonah in the belly of the whale, requiring heroic measures to retrieve the "treasure" therein and reemerge transformed (CW 5:509–10). This tension is suggested by the aboriginal Pregnant Mary, standing impassive in maternal reverie, carrying the man-child securely encircled under her heart, even while his fierce expression and vigorously outstretched limbs seem to press for emergence or rebirth from his confinement in the womb (Crumlin, 134).

Abraham, Lyndy. *A Dictionary of Alchemical Imagery.* Cambridge, UK, and NY, 1998.
Crumlin, Rosemary. *Aboriginal Art and Spirituality.* North Blackburn, Australia, 1992.
Edinger, Edward F. *Anatomy of the Psyche.* La Salle, IL, 1985.
Neumann, Erich. *The Great Mother: An Analysis of the Archetype.* Princeton, NJ, 1972.

1

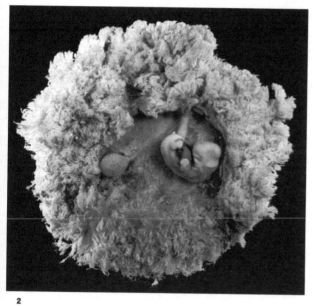

2

3

1. Clay pot with relief of hands on its belly, ca. 4850 B.C.E., Lepenski Vir, Yugoslavia.

2. Placenta with embryo.

3. This *Pregnant Mary*, carved from a single tree-branch and vividly painted with natural ochres by aboriginal artist George Mung (1921–91), bridges the two cultures of the Catholic Warmun community of Turkey Creek, Western Australia (Crumlin, 134).

401

Menstruation

The undulating foliage, issuing like a luxuriant head of hair from the flower above her head, is an evocative image that points to the spiritual dimension of menstruation and the bleeding vulva as source of growth and abundance. The composition moves us to comprehend that a woman's flowering is rooted in the soil of her blood. It exposes what she has been taught to hide, the blood gushing from her vulva, the vital energy that our culture has exiled to the menacing realms of the unconscious.

The extraordinary potency of the menstrual blood inspired ambivalent feelings in the human heart. On the one side it was believed to have curative and fertilizing properties and be an effective love potion; on the other, it was considered unclean and polluting. And so was the menstruating woman. Anything she came in contact with was considered to be contaminated. Becoming negatively taboo from the standpoint of others, she could herself become alienated from her creative source.

In primitive view the embryo of a new life is "built up" from the blood, which ceases to flow during pregnancy (Neumann, 31). By the same token, menstruation spells death and dissolution of structure. It thus becomes the germinating soil of a new cycle of possibilities. It carries an evolutionary force that mythology gives us reason to believe thrust humanity out of a state of unconsciousness.

Menstruation speaks in the poetic language of dreams. Its energy is frequently depicted as a mount, particularly the horse that moves with the liquid rapidity of the sea waves, its mane the briny foam. According to Norse mythology Sun's husband bore a horse's name. Her avatar, Freyja, goddess of love and fertility, bleeds her red-gold into the sea as she plunges the depths in search of her lost husband, Óðr, whose name denotes the intense stirrings that are the raw material of poetry and the poem itself as well.

The chord struck at a girl's first flow reverberates through her subsequent cycles. It can become her key to the music of being or throw her into discord with her own self. Many tribal societies celebrate crossing into womanhood with a ritual. Kinaaldá, a rite marking the initiation of the Navajo girl, is a reenactment of the celebration of the first flow of Changing Woman, goddess of the seasons and cycles of life. During the four-day ceremony, the initiate becomes her embodiment and is held to be endowed with powers to heal and fructify (Weideger, 34). A ritual may serve to "mold" the girl into the conventional role of wife and mother, or it may put her own individual and spiritual needs to the fore, subjecting her to a solitary quest for a dream or vision that will point to her path in life, and perhaps grant her a guardian spirit or a power animal as well. She could be called to become a medicine woman or shaman, although in other traditions and for other individuals such a calling does not come until the end of the fertile years (Høst, 4). The poetic vision, that transiting into menopause woman retains her wise blood within, is steeped in an old belief. Persecution of women, old and young, during the witch hunt of the Middle Ages is attributed to the fear of this blood (Grahn, 262).

Seclusion of the menstruating woman has been widely practiced since time immemorial, be it in a special hut or a dark corner of the house. Darkness was emphasized, for it was understood that during this phase, locked in a mysterious embrace with the black-faced moon, she is returned to the original chaos with its infinite treasures. A woman in receptive contact with her feminine "tides" often finds they lead her into her own depths and the first soundings of new life at organic, intellectual and imaginal levels. This is a gift that begs to be received. Cultural attitudes, shaped by legacies of the past, make it hard for contemporary woman to surrender to the erotic pull of the creative dimension and her own potential. Suppressing her gift, treating it with disdain, she "rides the rag" and gift becomes curse.

Grahn, Judy. *Blood, Bread, and Roses: How Menstruation Created the World*. Boston, 1993.
Høst, Annette. *Blessed by the Moon: Initiation into Womanhood*. www.shamanism.dk/Artikel - Blessed by the moon.htm.
Neumann, Erich. *The Great Mother: An Analysis of the Archetype*. Princeton, NJ, 1972.
Shuttle, Penelope and Peter Redgrove. *The Wise Wound: Myths, Realities, and Meanings of Menstruation*. NY, 1988.
Weideger, Paula. *Menstruation and Menopause: The Physiology and Psychology, the Myth and the Reality*. NY, 1976.

1

2

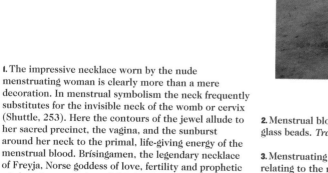

3

1. The impressive necklace worn by the nude menstruating woman is clearly more than a mere decoration. In menstrual symbolism the neck frequently substitutes for the invisible neck of the womb or cervix (Shuttle, 253). Here the contours of the jewel allude to her sacred precinct, the vagina, and the sunburst around her neck to the primal, life-giving energy of the menstrual blood. Brísingamen, the legendary necklace of Freyja, Norse goddess of love, fertility and prophetic wisdom, is a metaphor of this kind. Wood, 18th century, India.

2. Menstrual blood is playfully portrayed as a train of glass beads. *Train*, by Kiki Smith, 1993, United States.

3. Menstruating Gabonese girls in seclusion. Taboos relating to the menstrual period include a ban on sexual relations and food preparation, and exclusion from religious ceremonies. Photograph by Bruno Barbey.

Vulva

This European Stone Age sculpture on a dark-red boulder, originally covered with red ochre, was placed at the head of a stone altar in house 52 at Lepenski Vir. As if on the threshold of giving birth, the dark vaginal orifice is exposed in a droplike shape surrounded by labia swollen open. The engravings appear to manifest preengraved intimations of the stone, as if the miracle of birth is latent in it.

Vulvas—external female genitals—are distinguished by a dark opening loosely covered by labia. Through this deep orifice emerge menses, birth waters, birth blood and newborns. Similarly, water emerges through clefts in stone, plants sprout from seeds opening through earth and souls and spirits enter this world from the other side; souls reenter the hidden world in spirit journeys and at death.

Etymology observes that what is inside the vulva, what is held and covered in the womb, about to be born, is not visible from the outside. Every new birth is replete with the mystery of the other side. "This is full, that is full. The full comes from the full. The full takes from the full, and the full remains full" (Invocation, Brihadaranyaka Upanishad). Technically, the vulva includes the mons pubis and labia maiora, of adipose and fibrous tissue, and the smaller, darker labia minora, cloaking the sensitive, erectile clitoris, its prepuce and frenulum. The vestibule in the cleft between the labia minora has, opening and closing, orifices of the urethra and vagina, and the ducts of four glands.

Perhaps among the most ancient carved symbols, going back 30,000 years and still reverenced in India's goddess religion, the vulva/yoni honors the sacred power of birthing. It reminds us of our embeddedness in nature, in the mystery cycle of life and death. Temples and cave shrines replicate the female body with its deep sanctuary for *darshan*, sacred seeing. The yoni adoration scene from Bheraghat is carved below one of the 64 yogini sculptures positioned on the ground in a circular yoni shape. One enters the circle through the yoni's vestibule. Goddess worship includes smearing the yoginis with red vermilion or wrapping them in red cloth. (Yoginis are energies of the Mother Goddess.)

Prayer, meditation, ritual arts and dreams awaken remembrance of the hidden side from which all things come, which they carry within them, to which they return. The Navajo sing of how the first human beings emerged from the womb of Earth at the Rim of Emergence. The songs transform the womb-shaped Navajo dwelling, its single opening toward the east where the sun rises, into the primordial womb of Emergence. A young woman's first-menses initiation transforms her into ancestral Changing Woman impregnated by the rising sun, bringing fertility to the First People (EoR, 15:534).

The yoni genital form mirrors an occult view of the head with the fontanel opening. In subtle physiology, left and right channels, like the lower labia, wrap the central channel as the soul departs from the body through the opening at death. Shamanic healers retrieve a lost soul and blow it back into the body through the fontanel. The Hopi see the fontanel as the door through which the Creator gave life and communicated with the First People (Waters, 9–10).

As a mystical symbol, the yoni circle holds the introspective body one enters through meditation. At the center is the *garbhagriha*, the womb-space, the heart cave, where the inner spirit dwells. "What is here, that is there; what is there, that is here. The Person the size of a thumb dwells in the body. He is the lord of the past and the future. Then it is no longer hidden that this is that" (Katha Upanishad 4.10–12).

Waters, Frank and Oswald White Bear Fredericks. *Book of the Hopi.* NY, 1963.

1. Vulva sculpture, stone, ca. 6000 B.C.E.,
Lepenski Vir, Yugoslavia.

2. Pendant showing the Egyptian goddess Hathor,
gold, middle of 2nd millennium B.C.E., Israel.

3. Yoni adoration, from 64 Yogini Temple,
12th century C.E., Bheraghat, India.

Phallus

At the sight of the erect ritual phallus, contagious excitement ran like a groundswell through Dionysian rites. With foreskin and testicles intact and sometimes a painted eye evoking the all-penetrating sun, the wooden phallus was a revelation of the seminal force of life, a vision heightened by intoxicants, drumming and ecstatic dance. The Haloa festival in ancient Greece, for example, honored Dionysus as the embodiment of the phallus. Naked *phallophors* carried phalli into orgies of wine-drinking, the eating of cakes shaped like genitals and performances of lewd skits that Aristotle believed gave birth to theatrical comedy (ARAS, 2:334).

When the usually flaccid penis becomes engorged with blood at the instant of erotic excitement, filling the *corpus cavernosa* (erectile tissue) that runs along its dorsal length and the *corpus spongiosum* that forms a ventral shaft and urethral passage, it takes on the ithyphallic form that is worshipped as a *numinosum*. Seed-bearer, penetrator, begetter, the phallus was also wonderful for its association with not one, but two sacred fluids—golden urine and the semen of life. Representations of the phallus are extremely ancient. Human beings were making stone phalli almost 28,000 years ago (Amos). Ithyphallic figures were etched on cave walls such as that at Lascaux, France, as early as 17,000 to 15,000 B.C.E. The phallus and the ithyphallic god or divine shaman were often identified with the sun and its far-reaching rays, and with the crescent moon as the Bull, the Horned God or the cup into which the divine semen was poured. The serpent rearing up,

the bird in ascent, the vigorous bull, lion, horse, cock and goat, the proliferating, elongated fish are vehicles and animal forms of the phallic god. The primordial mound, *omphalos,* or upright stone, the pillar, herm and obelisk, and the plow that enters and fertilizes the earth are images of the phallus. The ancient Lord of Animals or Lord of Plants personify it. So do spermatic deities of logos, creativity, virility, fire, lightning, anger and lust.

And, to be sure, the phallus is also the violence of the creative impulse and "the sudden, obsessive invasion that plucks away the flower of thought" (Calasso, 52). In Ovid's *Metamorphoses*, the theme of Arachne's famous woven tapestry is "the gods, and their deceitful business"—Zeus, whose abductions include "Europa, cheated by the bull's disguise, Leda, lying under the wings of the swan," or Danae, to whom Zeus came "in a shower of gold" (Ovid, 132). The mortal Semele is burnt up by Zeus' heat. Dionysus copulates and abandons. Apollo impregnates Coronis, then has her slain. The brutal, violating aspect of the phallus is manifest in the rape of the individual, in the rape of the earth. Phallic power can shatter, uproot and lay waste. There are interior forms of coercive penetration, like self-destructive compulsions and invasive thoughts; or intellectual or religious transfixion, where the phallic presence overwhelms its vessel.

At the same time, we have venerated the phallus as emblem of rapturous pleasure, inseminating heat and spiritual transcendence. Nowhere is this more evocatively portrayed than in the upright stone lingam,

I

2

1. An erect fraternity of wooden and papier-mâché phalluses stand waiting in a Shinto shrine until nightfall for villagers to carry them in a sake-soaked procession. The Japanese ritual expresses "that phallic energy requires a *shintai*, a material 'god-body,' in order to manifest" (ARAS, 2:331).

2. Shaped from a branch of the erotic fig tree and as massive as the Greek maenad carrying it through the night, this extraordinary phallus provided the pièce de résistance at Dionysian festivals. Attic red-figure crater, ca. 470 B.C.E., Greece.

or phallus, in the innermost sanctuary or "womb-house" of every Shivite temple in India. The word lingam means "sign," denoting both the existence of a thing and its imperceptible essence (Kramrisch, 167). Shiva's theophany before the gods Brahma and Vishnu begins with the revelation of a pillar of fire (Shiva's severed phallus) extending down into the subterranean depths and up into the heavens. Brahma as a wild gander and Vishnu as a wild boar seek high and low to find the ends of the pillar, but it proves infinite. Now the flaming pillar splits open, and confronting the two gods is the majestic figure of Shiva, to whom they bow. In the lingam, which conveys the fiery pillar connecting heaven and earth, Shiva is manifest to the world, invisibly present as the "possession of seed," as "the wild potency of sex" (ibid., 163), as all the flamelike potentialities for creation and procreation, as liberation and annihilation. Naked, covered with ash, his hair writhing with snakes, Shiva mythically drives the wives of

the unenlightened ascetics in the Deodar Forest mad with desire. For the heat of sex is one with the "fiery ardor of the ascetic," and Shiva is Lord of Yoga (ibid., 163, 173). The lingam represents the self-containment of the yogi, who draws his seed upward in the heat of meditation. "The yogi does not deny sex, rather he transforms sexual urge and directs it away from procreation and pleasure toward intuited wisdom, toward freedom and bliss" (ibid., 164).

Amos, Jonathan. "Ancient Phallus Unearthed in Cave" *BBC News* (July 25, 2005) http://news.bbc.co.uk/2/hi/science/nature/4713323.stm.
Calasso, Roberto. *The Marriage of Cadmus and Harmony.* NY, 1993.
Kramrisch, Stella. *The Presence of Śiva.* Princeton, NJ, 1981.
Ovid. *Metamorphoses.* Bloomington, IL 1955.

3. The wild gander, a form of Brahma, ascends, while below Vishnu in his boar form dives into the ocean, each attempting to find where the lingam ends, but it is endless. *Shiva Manifesting Within the Lingam of Flames (Lingodbhavamurti),* gray stone, 12th century, Tamil Nadu, India.

4. A 28,000-year-old phallus made of siltstone. Hohle Fels, Ach River Valley, Germany.

3

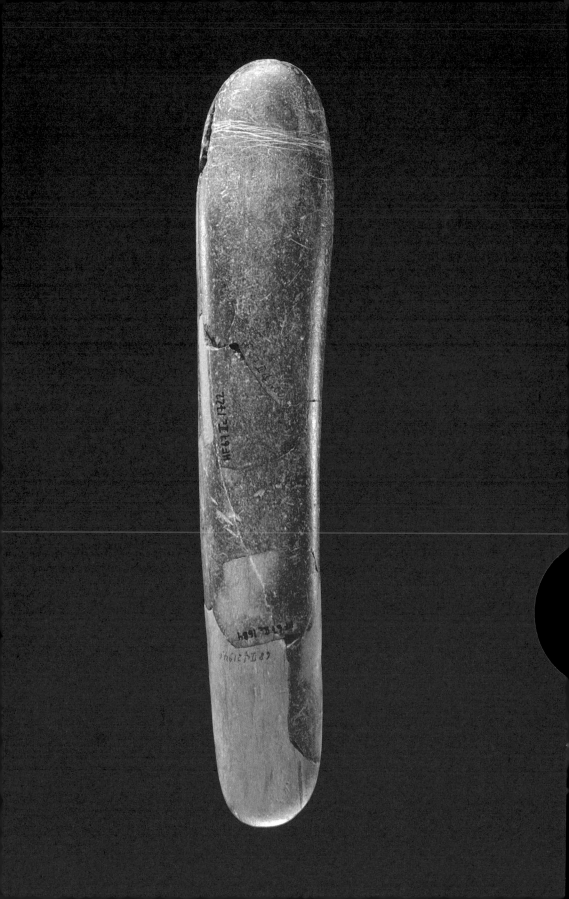

Sperm

Swimming through a chaos of competitors, these opalescent spermatozoa provide an astounding reminder that the number of sperm cells within a single seminal emission often exceeds the entire population of America (*Enc. Brit* 11:89). Yet only one among these millions will penetrate the solitary egg-cell that a woman produces during ovulation and conceive an embryo. Despite nature's lavish surplus, sperm cells are not identical clones; each brings an individual chromosomal potential from the father's genes to merge with those of the ovum, first and foremost perhaps, the X or Y chromosome that will determine the gender of the zygote. Requiring over ten weeks to mature in the testes, a sperm cell conceals the genetic history of its ancient ancestors in its miniscule almond-shaped head—3μ wide (10,000 to an inch)—40 to 60 times smaller than an ovum. Attached to a collar of mitochondria that supplies energy and a hair-thin, flagellated tail that provides motility, the head is able to "smell" the ovum and penetrate its barrier to chemically close the door upon late competitors, rendering all of us the prize of a prenatal sweepstake. Recreating this marvel in glass, artist Kiki Smith adopts sperm as a biological metaphor within the heated controversies that surround abortion, AIDS and the sociology of gender. Indeed, the miracle of sexual reproduction often casts a sordid shadow, a paradox that the Norwegian expressionist Edvard Munch captured in his painting *Madonna* (1895), depicting a pale woman weakened by the tubercular sperm cells that frame her—a specter of sexually transmitted disease or unwanted pregnancy, rather than new life.

Although semen—the viscous, milky-white fluid in which sperm cells are suspended—has always been plainly manifest, van Leeuwenhoek's microscopic discovery of spermatozoa did not occur until 1677. The "spermatic" theories of Plato and Galen that preceded his discovery claimed that semen was created in a man's head, not his testes, and traveled down his spine to its extension, the erect penis, to enter a woman upon ejaculation (Onians, 2:1–2). The Greek word *sperma* (seed) derives from *speirein* (to sow), reflecting archaic notions of the active male role in generating life in the passive feminine earth (Barnhart, 745). In a similar vein, the Koran informs its male adherents, "Your wives are to you as fields," while the Hindu *Śatapatha Brahmana* compares a farmer's furrow to the vulva and a sower's seeds to semen (EoR, 4:538). To prevent loss of this magical force and direct it toward spiritual ends, Taoist teachings instruct male practitioners to block ejaculation and force their seminal fluid back up to the brain. Traditionally, semen was imagined to derive from the purest and most potent blood—explaining why a man feels depleted after coitus—and, according to Aristotle, was able to congeal the unformed uterine blood into a human embryo (*De generatione animalium*, IV; Sissa, 136–7). In tribal New Guinea, a boy was also considered unformed until an infusion of mature masculinity was fed to him by initiatory male elders through ritual fellatio, a reflection of the widespread unconscious equation of semen and milk (La Barre, 38ff). Certain Tibetan Buddhists believe that the white male-element in semen joins with the red female-element in uterine blood to form an embryo's bones and blood, respectively. Regarding semen's mysteries, Sissa writes, "[this] extremely refined substance ... was derived from whatever was most precious and vital in the body, either the blood or cerebral matter. Within this weightless foam, the quintessence of the male was concentrated" (Sissa, 141). But in our own era that often narrowly identifies the masculine with the patriarchal suppression of the feminine, Kiki Smith's pristine glass sperm seem to seek out the feminine in the creative alchemy of life's conception, restoring a natural mutuality to male and female cells that would die apart from one another.

Barnhart, Robert K. Ed. *The Barnhart Concise Dictionary of Etymology.* NY, 1995.
La Barre, Weston. *Muelos: A Stone Age Superstition About Sexuality.* NY, 1984.
Onians, Richard Broxton. *The Origins of European Thought.* Cambridge, UK, and NY, 1988.
Piankioff, A. *Ramesses VI: Texts.* NY, 1954.
Sissa, Giulia. "Subtle Bodies." *Fragments for a History of the Human Body.* NY and Cambridge, MA, 1989.

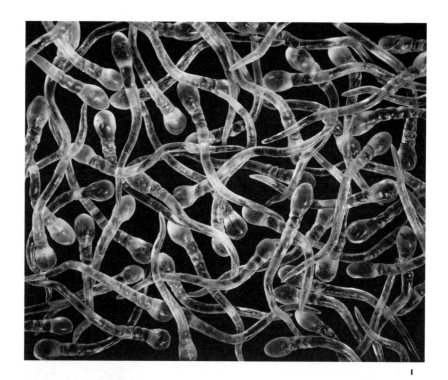

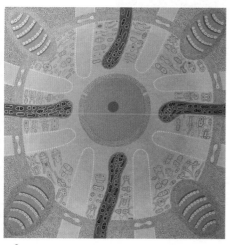

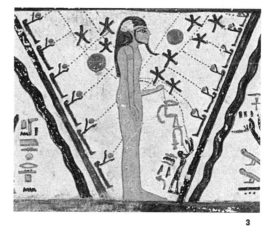

1. Glass sperm cells express the fruitfulness of nature and the extraordinary odds at play in the grandest lottery of all, generation. *Untitled*, detail, by Kiki Smith, glass and rubber, 3 in. x 108 in., 1989–90, United States.

2. Serpentine forms penetrate into the center of Creation, like sperm cells entering an egg to ignite an individual life. *Cell of the Universe*, by Dana Roman, oil on canvas, 1985, France.

3. Repeated images suggesting regeneration; sperm flowing from the ithyphallic figure named "One who hides the Hours" (Piankoff, 339) onto a child below, within a large serpent "the Enveloper" (only center visible) against a background of red disks and stars. Several goddess-raising (sun?) disks. Detail from wall texts in the tomb of Ramses VI, ca. 1145–37 B.C.E., Valley of the Kings, Thebes, Egypt.

Masturbation

Without shame and without a partner, the archaic god Min inaugurated the Egyptian pantheon in a single act of masturbation. His primordial deed was later assimilated to the more prominent sun-god Atum, who gave birth to the Egyptian ennead, or nine-member pantheon, by masturbating forth Shu and Tefnet. These two parented Geb, the earth, and Nut, the sky, who then spawned Osiris, Isis, Seth and Nephthys. Atum's solitary practice was honored in the Middle Kingdom Coffin texts where Shu declares to his progenitor, " ... you gave birth from your hand in the pleasure of emission" (Clark, 44). Over time, Egyptian priests invented a feminine partner, Iwsa'as, for their bachelor god, in the guise of his hand, and the priestesses who were ritually married to Atum bore the title "god's hand" (Shaw, 45).

Its association with cosmogonic self-creators provides masturbation, generally defined as manipulation of the sex organs to the point of orgasm, with a spiritual precedent. Scientists who have observed it among animals in the wild and infants in the womb, also provide it with a precedent in nature. Symbolically, masturbation is associated with primary rhythmical movements, the rubbing together of stones or sticks, the friction that produces a spark, hole-boring, fire-making. These images link it to procreation, creativity, speech, mind and the canalizing of psychic libido into new forms of activity (CW 5:142ff).

Kinsey's well-known discovery of masturbation's near ubiquity in males, closely followed by females, lifted its stigma in modern times. Nevertheless, ancient resistances to commandeering the soul's very fluids and forces of creation simply for pleasure run deep in the psyche. James Hillman even considers the need to prohibit the loss of the psyche's energies outside of its self-contained whole, by masturbation, to be an innate archetype (Hillman, p.55). The squandering of seed is part of the stigma attached to masturbation; another perhaps arises from the shame of having failed to win a flesh-and-blood partner. An otherwise tolerant Sigmund Freud wrote, "Masturbation contributes to the substitution of fantasy objects for reality." Biblical prohibitions against masturbation begin with the story of Onan wrongfully spilling his seed upon the ground (Genesis 38:9–10). Secular moralists and physicians conjured dire images of the consequences of "onanism": Masturbators were warned that feeblemindedness, insanity, tell-tale deformities and early death would follow.

In *Solitary Sex*, Thomas Laqueur perceives the history of masturbation as the "history of imagination, solitude and secrecy, private and public, excess, addiction, and control in different stages of our developing an individual sexual ethics once it could no longer be found in religion or an organic social order." Colin Wilson claims that the novel owes its literary existence to the faculty of imagination that masturbation fostered, beginning with the "panting, obsessive voyeurism" of Samuel Richardson's *Clarissa* in 1748 (Wilson, 90). Pornography also arose as masturbation's dark stepchild, giving rise to books that—in Rousseau's famous phrase—"can only be read with one hand" (Rousseau, *Confessions*, 34).

Whatever culture makes of masturbation in its concretized form, the recurrent theme of the self-copulating deity in myth is one of remarkable generation. Like the tail-eating *uroboros*, the hermaphroditic deities, or the divine potter who rhythmically stirs creation into being, the image of the masturbating god intimates psyche's fundamental capacity for self-becoming.

Clark, Robert Thomas Rundle. *Myth and Symbol in Ancient Egypt*. London, 1959.

Freud, Sigmund, et al. *On the Universal Tendency to Debasement in Love*. In *The Standard Edition of the Complete Psychological Works of Sigmund Freud*. London, 1964.

Hillman, James. "Towards the Archetypal Model for the Masturbation Inhibition." *The Journal of Analytical Psychology* (Vol. II, 1966).

Laqueur, Thomas Walter. *Solitary Sex: A Cultural History of Masturbation*. NY, 2003.

Rousseau, Jean-Jacques. *Confessions of Jean-Jacques Rousseau*. London and NY, 1931.

Shaw, Ian and Paul T. Nicholson. *The Dictionary of Ancient Egypt*. NY, 1995.

Wilson, Colin. *The Misfits: A Study of Sexual Outsiders*. London, 1988.

1. Masturbation has attracted ever-shifting and often self-contradictory condemnation. The madly bulging eyes and crazed expression of this Balinese figurine— busily manipulating her genitalia—display the shadowy fate imagined to result from this nearly universal practice. Wood sculpture.

2. As if the gods themselves had placed the genitals within easy reach, an Egyptian deity grips his erect phallus and brings forth Shu, the god of air, and Tefnet, the goddess of moisture, in a self-induced ejaculation. Stone statue, pre-dynastic (3150 B.C.E.).

Sexual Union

A master of Japanese wood-block prints, Hokusai (1760–1849) portrayed sexual acts with the same naturalistic feeling as his landscapes and with equal narrative detail. His exaggerated emphasis on the coupling of genitals, the physical definition of sexual intercourse, overshadows the subtler clues of the lovers' approaching orgasm. With an elegantly sparse line, he captures the woman's climax in her flung-back head, her curling fingers and toes and her eyes abandoned in the warm bliss of suckled nipples and the hot in-thrust of her partner's swollen penis, itself enlarged by desire and artistic overstatement. The litter of tissues at his feet hints that this was a night of sustained passion, perhaps even love.

With sexual intercourse, triggered by hormones and an inborn response to the erotic heat communicated by bodily excitement, musky scents, bright plumage or skimpy clothing, nature extended the possibilities of reproduction beyond the splitting of a single cell. To fission was added fusion, a sperm cell penetrating an ovum to create an individual life. The instinctual passion and pleasure that drives sexual intercourse can eclipse its biological purpose, to the point of casting aside public decorum, legal limitations and even the name of one's partner. Regardless, it is the mystery of the conjunction between opposites and the possibility of their producing a "third," a new physical, psychical or spiritual entity to which both contribute, that gives sexual intercourse its symbolic significance.

As the most compelling of opposites, feminine and masculine represent all pairs of opposites "confronting one another in enmity or attracting one another in love" (CW 14:1). Sexual intercourse intimates the twoness in oneness, and also the inherent oneness of what is apparently two. The dynamic polarity and attraction between such pairs is embedded in metaphors of friction, tension, heating, plowing, planting, flying, riding and swimming. In many creation myths, there is a preexistent, undifferentiated plenum to begin with, which divides itself into two, or creates two, who lying together bring about the multiplicity of the cosmos. From the other side, coitus (from L. *coiere*, "to come together") suggests the reunion of what has become divided, incomplete and full of longing. By no means, of course, does coitus represent a necessarily harmoni-

ous resolution to the tension of opposites. Sexual intercourse is also associated with aggression, appetite, predation and rituals of dominance and submission. At its most destructive it is merely the enactment of hostility, rape, violation, wounding or possession. This is as true of the ego's experience of being conjoined in unconscious identification with a defiling psychological factor as it is of the physical counterpart. And, because entanglement, surrender to an other, merging and orgasm are a part of the most rapturous coitus, "an archetypal drama of death and rebirth lies hidden in the conjunction" (CW 14:35).

Alchemy's entire opus had to do with the separation and synthesis of opposites, culminating in the "chymical marriage" of Sol and Luna. The alchemical fantasy prefigured the psychological process pioneered by Jung that ultimately brings about a union of conscious and unconscious. The goal of the opus was the birth of the lapis. Its psychological equivalent is the production of an internal sense of unity, a spirit of truth paradoxical and bivalent in nature. Alchemy boldly incorporated the ancient motif of the royal brother-sister incestuous *hieros gamos*, or sacred marriage, as a means of conveying the magnetism between two things, like conscious and unconscious, that are different and yet essentially of the same substance. This royal, shadowy pair engendered a "stone that is no stone"—ego and nonego, material and transcendental.

Some of the most moving evocations of sexual intercourse are the Indian and Chinese figures of loving couples—the Yub-Yum of Buddhism and the Shiva-Shakti of Hinduism. The male-female pairs are joined sexually and look into each others' eyes with utter devotion and bliss. They are sacred figures prominently displayed inside and outside temples, for they express in a profound way the many levels of what it means to be a couple. The dalliance of the gods with each other that brings about the glorious manifestation of the world, the dalliance of humans in imitation of the gods; physical and emotional love, desire and procreation, religious eros between deity and devotee, the creative "coitus" of inspiration. And the fire of sex, which, transmuted through *tapas*, the heat of yogic meditation, brings about the incandescence of union between self and Supreme Self, beyond all opposites.

1

1. For centuries, the Japanese have cultivated a taste for the graphic illustrations (*shunga*) found in traditional erotic albums (*empon*), typified by Hokusai's nakedly explicit, sensual depiction of sexual intercourse. From the album *Forms of Embracing (tsui no hinagata)*, wood-block print, ca. 1816.

2. Tibetan sacred art often depicts sexual postures that would be unthinkable on western altars. Here the Buddha Vajradhara sits locked in physical union with his consort Supreme Wisdom Visvatara; their spiritual union is evident in the penetrating gaze they direct into each other's eyes. Bronze sculpture, 18th century, Tibet.

2

Incest

And he shall be found at once brother and fa-
ther of the children with whom he consorts; son
and husband of the woman who bore him ...
Sophocles, Oedipus the King

If I've killed one man, I've killed two—
The vampire who said he was you
And drank my blood for a year,
Seven years, if you want to know.
Daddy, you can lie back now.
Sylvia Plath, Daddy

Amnon was looking
at the moon, low and round,
and saw in the moon
the hard breasts of his sister.
Federico Garcia Lorca, Thamar and Amnon

Incest is a loaded word, encompassing such different levels of meaning that our ability to entertain the
lofty idea of one is all but nullified by our recoil at another. Spiritual "incest" informs our highest religious
and artistic endeavors. Biological incest is in many
countries a (felony) crime, and in some cultures a
breach of taboo punishable by death or exile. Within
the compass of its charged energic field, a welter of fear
and desire, secrecy and seduction, innocence and betrayal moves its participants, willingly or not, between
the poles of abject sinfulness and a specialness shared
only by the gods.

The word "incest" derives from the Latin *castus*
connoting moral purity, continence, guiltlessness, freedom from pollution. The related Greek *katharos* (from
whence "catharsis") includes the idea of purity in the
sense of being clear or free of admixture; for example,
winnowed grain, unalloyed metals, "tranquil" feelings,
clean water, open spaces. As the negation of the above,
in-cest suggests the muddying of emotional waters, the
defiling or dishonoring of another, the closing off of
naïve spontaneity and trust through the breaching of
sacrosanct psychological or physical boundaries.

Mythologically, incest is often portrayed as a prerogative of the gods, hinting at its archetypal nature
and suggestive of the psychic "self-fertilization" indispensable to any creative act. In Hindu myth, for instance, the intercourse of Father Heaven, the Lord of
Generation, with his daughter Usus, the Dawn—who
is "hypostasized out of himself"—is considered "the

very core" of an essential sacrificial rite, committed for
the "good of the world" (Kramrisch, 16–17, 22). Without this primordial "rupture" of the original wholeness
of the Uncreate, neither humanity nor the ordered universe would exist. In Greek mythology the intercourse
of the mother-and-son pair Ouranos and Gaia (Heaven
and Earth) brings the race of gods into being. Similarly,
in the Biblical story of the destruction of Sodom and
Gomorrah, the daughters of Lot, finding no other men
left alive, make their father drunk and sleep with him
in order that they may "preserve offspring" who will
sire future tribes. In some historical cultures ritual incest has played a part in the sacralization of kings,
charging them with the ambivalent power attaching to
the "taboo," and insuring the purity of the bloodline.

The allegorical imagery of alchemy depicts the
psychic union of opposites at many levels as the conjunction of the brother-sister pair Sol and Luna. This
intuition of the longing of the soul for union with its
own unknown substance is a "symbolic" copulation
that potentially produces the individuated self. If the
incest motif is admittedly repugnant, it was for the alchemists the most effective way to convey the attraction between conscious and unconscious. On the other
hand, it also expresses the inherent illegitimacy of the
ego's mergings with the matrix from which it was born
and the overwhelming force, the "unholy fascination"
(CW 16:419) of unconscious contents.

Incest may come to one as a fate, committed unwittingly, as it did for Oedipus who married his mother.
It may be experienced as an urge toward an infantile
regression as enshrined in Freud's notion of the "Oedipus complex"; it may represent a symbolic attraction
at the highest spiritual level toward psychic wholeness.
However, as Jung emphatically cautions, the "absence
of [such] symbolism overloads the sphere of instinct"
(CW 16:460). Incest, when carried out literally and
concretely, is a criminal—in every sense of the word—
act of betrayal; a violation of the relational boundaries
that define the very essence of kinship. The personal
and cosmic "pollution" issuing from such "forbidden
contact" (Douglas, 162) constellates terrible and lifelong consequences.

Douglas, Mary. *Purity and Danger: An Analysis of*
Concepts of Pollution and Taboo. London, 2002.
Kramrisch, Stella. *The Presence of Śiva*. Princeton,
NJ, 1981.

1. Sol copulates with his sister Luna in this erotically forthright representation of a psychic fertilization between opposites. Woodcut, from the alchemical manuscript *Rosarium philosophorum*, 1550, Germany.

2. Oedipus is rendered childlike next to the Sphinx, who is emblematic of the "fateful" force of unconscious contents. Side of a sarcophagus, Greece, 330–23 B.C.E.

Leg

Sturdy pillars of support, legs combine the strength of the thighs, and the versatility of the knees and feet, to produce a fully erect stance as well as astonishing varieties of movement. Our dependency on the leg is felt in the long ago image of a man embracing a votive facsimile of his, offered in thanks to the god who cured its affliction. Images of the human form often embody their symbolism in the legs. The huge thighs and open legs of the Great Mother, for example, signifying her endless birthing of creation; the open legs of the prostitute evoking sexual pleasures and risks; the revealed genitals of the goddess of Tantric arts flowing with the sacred menstrual flux of the cosmos. Legs are associated with the individual journey of life. "What creature walks on four legs in the morning, on two legs at noon and three legs in the evening?" was the famous riddle posed by the Sphinx. Oedipus answered correctly that a human being walks on four legs as a crawling baby, two as an upright adult and three as an aged person leaning on a cane. Legs take us to destinations and goals and the hindering of another's legs is a sign of conquest. Ancient military monuments depict arrays of legs on the move—the warring soldiers of the conqueror; shackled legs are emblematic of those defeated and enslaved. Victorious armies often march through the broad, high legs of triumphal arches. As with other creatures, our knowing legs instinctively enact the flight or fight response. Running competitions, among the earliest of sports, unleash adrenaline-fired energies of the legs still essential for survival. The legs of synchronized marching and processions are associated both with social cohesion and the ominous potential of the mass mind. The innate rhythm of the stride is a primary foundation of music and dance expressing religious feeling and attunement with the rhythms and vibrations of nature. Shiva as Nataraja, the lord of dancers, dances the "dance of bliss in the hall of consciousness within the human heart" (Kramrisch, 440). Kali dances on the prone Shiva, bringing the potential of the supreme spirit into existence at the beginning of a new cosmic cycle (Mookerjee, 76–77). Shapely and articulated, legs are often objects of beauty, captivating artists like Degas. Legs are also sexy, entwining, acrobatic and embracing of the genitals. The hiding, exposure and elongation of female legs have driven the design of feminine costume for centuries. Innately borrowing from our finned, feathered and four-legged ancestors, our legs propel us in three mediums: earth, water and, for brief moments, air. In themselves, however, legs are mostly down to earth—common foot soldiers serving indefatigably just to get us around.

Kramrisch, Stella. *The Presence of Śiva.* Princeton, NJ, 1981.
Mookerjee, Ajit. *Kali: The Feminine Force.* NY, 1988.

1. *Legs*, by Louise Bourgeois, rubber hanging piece, each 122 in. x 2 in. x 2 in.; photograph by Rafael Lobato, 1986, collection Hirshhorn Museum & Sculpture Garden, Washington, D.C.

2. Leg as votive offering to a healing god. Marble relief, ca. 4th century B.C.E., Athens, Greece.

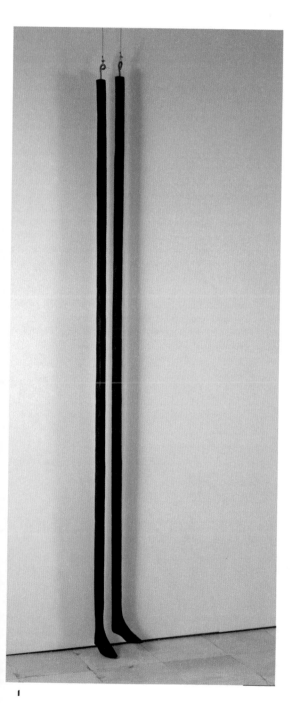

1

2

Thigh

The human contours of the 3,000-year-old ceramic hollow vessel from northern Iran equally suggest male and female. Short, sturdy legs and large feet allow the vessel to stand without support. The rounded, pear-shaped thighs accentuate the genital region with which the thighs were, for ancient peoples, synonymous. For the thigh's great muscles bind and move the femur, the longest, strongest bone in the body and the one with the most marrow, or "sap." The word femur derives from a Greek root meaning "that which engenders" and the thigh signified life, seed and procreation (Onians, 182). Thighbones, in particular, were sacrificed to the gods of ancient Greece, and in many cultures the thigh was associated with divination and the swearing of oaths. As a half-formed infant the god Dionysus was removed from his dead mother's womb by his father Zeus, who sewed the baby into his thigh until he was ready to be delivered (Ovid, 64ff). The Hebrew Scriptures portray the thigh as an organ of generation, if not a euphemism of the genitals. In the famous story of Jacob's wrestling with the angel of God, the angel touches Jacob's inner thigh, simultaneously disjointing and consecrating him; Jacob's sons are said to come from his thigh. We think of two of our strongest instincts—sex and aggression—as driving us through the thigh. Generative sensual feeling, urge and power quicken the thigh, imagined mythically in the muscled horse, lion and goat flanks of lusty centaurs and fauns. Thigh-born Dionysus inspired orgiastic ecstasy and rituals of dismemberment among his devotees. The Chinese *I Ching* warns that the thighs' tendency to act on the spur of the heart's caprice can result in humiliation (Wilhelm, 133). Weapons like guns and sabers are carried on the thigh, thus Shakespeare's "His foot Mercurial; his Martial Thigh … " (*Cymbeline*, 4.2.382). Its linking with the vital and potent makes an injury to the thigh a grievous affliction. Just as the morbidity of what were once generative, ruling values for an individual or a collective body persist until there is psychic renewal, so the incurable thigh wound of the Fisher King of the Grail is reflected in the sterility of the entire kingdom. At the opposite pole, the ubiquitous prehistoric figures of the great feminine with immense thighs suggest the potential for infinite fruitfulness.

Onians, Richard Broxton. *The Origins of European Thought.* Cambridge, UK, and NY, 1988.
Wilhelm, Richard. *The I Ching; or Book of Changes.* Princeton, NJ, 1967.

2

1. Hermes acts as midwife in the birth of Dionysus, delivering the infant god from Zeus' thigh. Neo-Attic frieze, detail, marble, Roman copy after a 4th century B.C.E. original.

2. Vessel with two feet and round thighs, ceramic, 1st millennium B.C.E., northern Iran.

Knee

Knee is the strongest joint in the body, the flexible hinge that allows us to sit on our heels as if on a pedestal or to squat into the form of a self-made chair from which to parley, or paint or toss chappatis. Sturdy knees bear the brunt of our infant crawling; scuffed knees are the medallions of childhood's exuberance. At any age we revert to the stable crawling posture of hands and knees because of injury, stealth or confining spaces. Even before we have exercised our own knees, we know the knees that comprise the hinge of a supporting lap. The unusual image of King Akhenaten and a young woman, perhaps his queen or daughter, illustrates how intimately one lap fits into another, a nesting enabled by the articulation of the knees. But the ancients also classed the fluid in the knee with cerebrospinal fluid, and considered it the sap of life, synonymous with offspring. Thus knees were seen as the seat of paternity and generation, vitality and strength (Onians, 174ff). The Latin genus, "birth," is cognate with the English "knee" (ibid.). More than any other part of the body, we depend on the knees to raise or lower ourselves. Knees are the joints most at odds with gravity, and the focal point of leverage and balance, helping to support the body and its burdens. The knee's connection with the life force is probably implicated in the symbolism of kneeling: We submit our own life force to something greater, or, as a suppliant, appeal to the life-soul of another whose knees we grasp (ibid., 180–1). One genuflects or "bends the knee" before the numinous or sacred or in obeisance to the powerful. Pilgrims crawl on their knees toward a holy shrine. The vanquished is reduced to his knees by the victor. We kneel to make declarations of love. Knees are also vulnerable. The kneecap or patella is a marvelous shield, but a sensitive one, and subject to a great deal of wear and tear. Knee injuries are extremely painful. Gangsters are known to break knees as a warning, perhaps "this time the life force, next time the life." At the opposite pole, knees secure the triangular lotus position of Buddhism and Hinduism, emblematic of axial balance, stability and sustaining the closed circuit of the energy field through which the subtle body centers of the chakras are vitalized (Mookerjee, 19).

Mookerjee, Ajit. *Kundalini.* London and NY, 1982.
Onians, R. B, *The Origins of European Thought.* Cambridge, UK, 1991.

2

1. Pharaoh Akhenaten, limestone sculpture,
ca. 1340 B.C.E., el-Amarna, Egypt.

2. The curving hinge of *Knee*, solid, strong and
highly exposed. By Anne Thulin, soil and wax sculpture,
1996, Sweden.

Foot

Our feet connect us to the earth, and in repetitive impacts, to the ground of reality. Bruce Nauman's photograph *Feet of Clay* reminds us that we are only human; the earth with which the feet have such intimate contact is also the dust to which we return in death. Yet Mother Earth is divine soil, and in the ancient rituals that honored her, devotees bared their feet in order to more directly receive her nurture (Walker, 309).

Comprised of a surprising number of small, extremely resilient foot bones that work in complex interaction with cartilage, muscles and nerves, feet help support the body and balance its weight and shifting motions. With its flexible, grasping toes, the foot negotiates the ground's unpredictable and multifarious elements. Leonardo da Vinci called the foot "a masterpiece of engineering and a work of art" (Arnot, 1). Nevertheless, the foot, located at the opposite end of the body from the self-enobling head, often signifies humility: The disciple washes the feet of the master as an act of humble respect; the master may wash the feet of the disciples as an act of surrendering love.

At the base of the erect skeleton, feet root us. Similarly, the foot evokes a character of sturdiness. A reliable, practical person "has her feet planted firmly on the ground." One perceives and acts according to one's standpoint; a capable person is sure-footed, one who thinks methodically proceeds step-by-step. Similarly, "setting foot upon" has symbolized the acquisition of lands on behalf of distant sovereigns. The foot measures pace, time and progress, and is our most natural measure of distance.

Highly sensitive, the foot can readily respond to subtle changes in the terrain and move along accordingly. Early childhood memories often spring from the pleasure or repulsion of feet encountering velvety grass, a squishy slug or the cool refreshment of streaming water. Highly erotic, the foot has been the sexualized object of adornment or fetishistic desire, including the elaborate crippling of Chinese foot binding. Feet are the resilient instruments of sport and give expression to aesthetic and religious sensibilities, from improvisation to the precise delineations of religious dance ceremonies and classical ballet. While hands evolved from two of the feet of four-footedness, feet are versatile enough to manipulate the paintbrush of fine artists who have lost the use of their hands.

Instinctively feet know when to stay put or carry us away from danger even before the head has got the message. Bound feet have often signified the conquered or enslaved. The heel of the foot is emblematic of particular vulnerability, its wounding often affecting the entire leg, and mythically it is the most human part of the foot.

Emblematic of one's material being, feet can also suggest the sequenced movement along a spiritual path, sacralized in the pilgrimages of all the great religions. Such is the rendering of Muhammad's legendary ascent to heaven. The colossal feet are actually his sandals, reputed to have reached the very platform of the Divine Throne (ARAS, 2:371). They embody the inspired footfalls of an ordinary, once illiterate man, who became the prophet of Allah.

Arnot, Michelle. *Foot Notes.* Garden City, NY, 1980.
Simon, Joan. Ed. *Bruce Nauman.* Minneapolis, MN, 1994.
Walker, Barbara G. *The Woman's Dictionary of Symbols and Sacred Objects.* SF, 1988.

1. These *Feet of Clay* remind us that we are made of earth and return to earth. Indeed, every step is a brief return. From *Eleven Color Photographs*, by Bruce Nauman, 1966–70, United States.

2. A 16th-century illuminated manuscript from Iran depicts two colossal feet, perhaps the sandals of the Prophet, standing on either side of an open Koran. Feet can symbolize pilgrimage and following the path to revealed wisdom.

3. *Anatomical Studies of the Movement of the Heel and the Ankle, and Investigations into the Calf Muscles,* detail, by Leonardo da Vinci, pen and ink, ca. 1509–10, Italy.

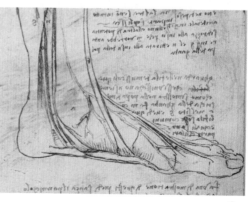

1

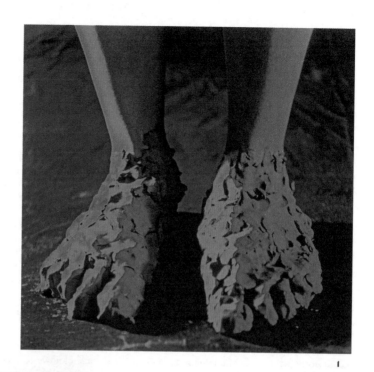

2

3

Urine

How are we to imagine urine as Bruegel must have, as something of the essence of an individual, their self-expression (even if aiming for the moon—a beautiful but unattainable goal), when, nowadays, we learn so well to contain urine, flush it, not mention it? Yet powerful and magical it was. Science tells us of the body's sophisticated filtering system, which recycles useful by-products of metabolism and concentrates the rest in this golden solution containing water, urea, salts, ammonia and some other chemical leftovers. Some of these leftovers made urine very useful in earlier times—especially in the absence of soap—for washing skin, hair and clothes, and preserving and whitening teeth. Urine dissolves oils and fats and makes dies colorfast. Early medicine prescribed it for treatment of ringworm, ulcers in the ears, snakebite (Collin de Plancy, 118), stroke and eye diseases (Horan, 75). Urine is still used in remedies for chapped skin and neutralizes the pain of some stings. In ancient Persia and India, cow's urine was considered sacred; it was used to purify priests and ritual sites. Kings were anointed with urine at their coronations, and in general it was believed that urine could wipe away physical or spiritual uncleanness (Bourke, 113).

As late as seventeenth-century Europe, urine was also tied to magic, employed in witches' spells, in the detection of witchcraft and the destruction of demons. The idea was that urine provided a magical link to the one who had produced it, and so could be used to influence or "discover" that person. It was an ingredient in love potions, and thought to reverse impotence and act as an aphrodisiac.

Alchemy elaborated the symbolic character of urine. It was golden in color, indicating something precious. It was fluid and acidic, giving it the qualities of both water and fire, opposites that separated and united in the transforming opus. Urine was salty, thus it had kinship with seawater, and like seawater was a name for the miraculous vessel of the unconscious, the *aqua permanens*, the psychic matrix or "uterus" that gave birth to the perfected stone or divine child. It was also the living, changeable matter of the psyche that was being transformed and the solvent that was the agent of the transformation (CW 12:336ff). The "pissing man-ikin" thus embodied Mercurius, the familiar spirit of the entire process. His piss is not unlike the fertilizing rain of other creative deities, like Rudra, the Hindu "wild god of the world." An invocation to him in the *Rig Veda* reads: "May we obtain favor of thee, O ruler of heroes, maker of bountiful water ... Thou who blessest with the waters of thy body, be gracious to our children and grandchildren" (CW 5:322).

Urine belongs to the second chakra, the *Svadisthana*, to the kidneys, or reins, to the bladder, the pressure of instinctual urges and our awareness of them (Jung, 1087). It denotes the urgency of emotional and creative self-expression, the feeling-toned "yielding to or allowing the flow of what needs to come through one" (Whitmont, Perera, 146). Young children have been known to show love for beloved persons by peeing on them (Whitmont, 243). But embedded in our modern idiom, we find urine also representing affect that is hot, intense, personal and sometimes not ideally contained. We speak of a "pissing contest," a display of aggressive power; of being "pissed off," suggesting resentment or fury; of "pissing and moaning," as angry complaint; and "pissing in the well," a spoiling of a creative source through envy or rage. Countless dreams document needs, inhibitions, complexities and frustrations around urination—and the significance (and relief) of letting go of one's golden stream.

Bourke, John Gregory. *Scatalogic Rites of All Nations*. Washington, DC, 1891.
Collin de Plancy. *Dictionary of Witchcraft*. NY, 1965.
Horan, Julie L. *The Porcelain God*. Secaucus, NJ, 1996.
Jung, C. G. and Claire Douglas. *Visions*. Princeton, NJ, 1997.
Meadow, Mark A. *Pieter Bruegel the Elder's Netherlandish Proverbs and the Practice of Rhetoric*. Zwolle, NL, 2002.
Whitmont, Edward C. *The Symbolic Quest*. Princeton, NJ, 1991.
Whitmont, Edward C. and Sylvia Brinton Perera. *Dreams, a Portal to the Source*. London and NY, 1989.

1

2

1. Pointing out a universal human folly, Bruegel gave his 16th-century painted roundel the inscription: "What I attempt, I do not achieve. I always piss at the moon" (Meadow, 36).

2. The alchemical "pissing manikin" provides the basic substance—here imagined as urine—for the alchemist's work of transformation. From the alchemical manuscript *Speculum veritatis (Mirror of truth)*, Eirenaeus Philalethes, 17th century C.E.

Excrement

The filth that the goddess Tlazolteotl is seen endlessly swallowing and excreting in Aztec codices paradoxically polluted her and purified her, for her own bodily waste emerged as a flower, a Central Mexican glyph symbolizing female sensuality and, by suggestion, childbirth, over which she presided. The human waste that Aztecs collected to fertilize their fields decayed into humus or *tlazollalli* ("earth filth") that they believed generated in her bowels in the subterranean land of the dead, an unspeakable place that ironically gave birth to life-sustaining corn. Her name derives from the root *tlazolli*, meaning not just filth, but also vice and disease, since the Aztecs confessed their sexual misdeeds to her on their deathbeds, shameful stories that she greedily consumed in the form of excrement. The Aztec's word for disgrace literally meant to be smeared in excrement, yet their words for "gold" meant "divine excrement" or "the sun's excrement." With similar paradox, alchemy claimed, and psychology supports, that the gold of transformation "is found in filth," in those very aspects of one's substance the ego tends to dismiss as inferior.

Akin to Tlazolteotl is the Roman goddess of sewers, Cloacina (Bourke, 127). She was named after the stream Cloaca that flowed through the malarial marshes of the ancient Forum before it was dredged out to become Rome's principal sewer (Cloaca Maxima), a still-intact system that washed the waste of a million people into the sea (Horan, 11). Cloacina, whose name meant "Purifier," was eventually assimilated to Venus and cleansed sexual intercourse within marriage. Both these Aztec and Roman goddesses performed their transformation by taking in human-generated filth, thereby allowing for shameless sensuality in marriage, crowned by legitimate childbirth. Not all of our "shit" can be integrated, however; a portion belongs to psychic forces beyond the ken of conscious life and must be flushed into an abyss, rather than used to enrich ourselves or to fertilize our surroundings (Perera, 104).

Feces (Latin for "sediment" or "dregs") consist of excess fats such as cholesterol, dead mucous membrane sloughed off from the lining of the alimentary canal and protein debris shed by the intestinal bacteria that produce the sulfuric odors of flatulence. Their typical brown coloration is due to dead red-blood cells, which also cause the stools accompanying diarrhea to blacken. Young children often conceive scatological theories of childbirth, and see their excrement as proof of their own creative magic; psychotics are known to smear themselves with their feces or to swallow them (corpophagy). Because defecation is usually a deliberate act, its imagery has been linked to assertion, expression, willing, creative potential and transformation and also to compulsions having to do with control, domination and withholding (Whitmont, Perera, 146). Excretory images often evoke the circumstances and issues related to the channeling and appropriate containers for creative urges. We apply "constipated" figuratively when we feel creative stultification; what needs to come out can't or won't, and diarrhea symbolically supposes an abnormal, too loose, out-of-control discharge of one's substance. Even at the dawn of consciousness, and well beyond, our "droppings" were highly valued, as was the fertile excrement of revered animals like the elephant and cow. How extraordinary that from our most ancient ancestors to Freud and Jung, the divine nature of excrement has been intuited: "The lowest value allies itself to the highest" (CW 5:189) so that symbolically, one's shit really can smell like a rose.

Bourke, John Gregory. *Scatalogic Rites of All Nations*. Washington, DC, 1891.

Horan, Julie L. *The Porcelain God*. Secaucus, NJ, 1996.

Miller, Mary Ellen and Karl A. Taube. *The Gods and Symbols of Ancient Mexico and the Maya*. NY, 1993.

Perera, Sylvia Brinton. *The Scapegoat Complex*. Toronto, 1986.

Whitmont, Edward C. and Sylvia Brinton Perera. *Dreams, a Portal to the Source*. London and NY, 1989.

1. The Aztec goddess Tlazolteotl—known as the "Eater of Filth"—squats down to defecate in a traditional position for giving birth. Her excrement is shown falling from her rectum in the form of a flower.

2. This illustration of a fairy tale by Charles Perrault (1628–1703) depicts a magical ass that each day evacuated a fortune in gold, substituting one of nature's most despised elements for one of its most precious. Freud discovered in his patients' dreams that feces and gold were often interchangeable.

Ascent

A shamanic line drawing traces a path leading through a series of trials called the "swaying places" marked by water, sand and clouds, before bringing the shaman to the radiant face of his supreme god, White Ulgen. The Altaic shamans of Siberia inscribed recognizable shapes on such maps, which guided their ascent to the Upper World for the purpose of healing the sick or to retrieve a lost soul. The maps depicted an interior landscape of sufficient constancy from one shaman's experience to the next that each could venture beyond the familiar world to the supreme heights of the shamanic cosmos without becoming lost.

Gods and heroes of myth and religious lore also ascend to celestial realms representing glory, immortality or transcendent knowledge or spirituality, which they often share with those below. In the Christian narrative, when Jesus ascends to heaven, there is an expectation that he will return at an unknown time, sometimes depicted as an end-time of judgment. In the Hebrew Bible, figures like Abraham and Moses make mountain ascents to the presence of the Lord, whose laws or instructions they carry down to the people. At Jerusalem, the Dome of the Rock was built over the footprint of Būraq, the magical horse on which Muhammad was said to have ascended into heaven. Dante conveys the difficulty of obtaining spiritual heights and the unusual nature of their psychic access by portraying heaven as reached by climbing a seven-storied mountain, a world-tree, or a column of smoke.

Ascent, from the Latin *ascendere,* to climb, has to do with physical or psychical movement upwards. Ascent is associated with emergence, elevation, sublimation, freedom from what weighs one down. It is often depicted mythically as flight, wingedness, the birdlike eye taking in a greater perspective or spiritual expansiveness and release from the limitations of mattered life. Ascent is often paired with descent in initiatory rites and psychic processes of transformation. Here, it signifies one pole in a shifting between above and below, height and depth, the ups and downs of affect and mood or the movement between intellect and instinct as means of self-knowledge or in dynamics of separation and synthesis. Ascent can suggest the volatilizing of a solid, or the spiritualizing of matter. Symbolically, this would mean a making conscious of un-conscious projections that result in entrenched patterns of behavior or in the concretizing of something meant to be understood as a psychic factor requiring integration. On the other hand, descent can bring something suspended in the conceptual or potential into realized form.

Ascent evokes tree, ladder, mountain, sky and outer space, as well as elevators and stairs. It suggests gradual, step-by-step progression to the heights, a climbing to the summit or a more rocketlike "taking off." It depicts soaring thoughts and intuitions, and leaps of imagination. The other side of the coin is giddiness, disembodiment or inflation. One can live in the head, neglecting other sources of wisdom, or ascend to excessive heights and lose touch with reality, the humility, or "humus" that gives us a firm foothold in our earthy ground.

Ascension often posits a hierarchy of values. Something is seen as ascending from a lower, heavier, darker, more primitive state to something increasingly higher, lighter, more refined or more intelligent. In Gnosticism, for example, the *anima mundi,* the soul of the world, is trapped in *physis,* or nature, and redemption amounts to her release and ascent. Ancient rites of *solificatio* by means of ascent through the spheres of the seven planets symbolized the return of the soul to the realm of the sun from which it originated (CW 12:66). Many religions imagine a celestial sphere to which the soul ascends at death or in mystical states, freeing it from imprisonment in the body. Hell and the devil (and often the feminine) are, in many cultures, consigned to the lower, "inferior" regions. The chthonic is regarded with suspicion and fear as opposed to the heavenly. Yet in other symbolic systems, including alchemy, ascent must be followed by descent and vice versa, in an equalizing of unequal opposites toward the goal of the self's integrity. Indian yogis, who even mastered levitation, equated their apparent ascent with sinking into interior depths, clothing themselves invisibly in contemplation. And some shamans typically went into altered states wearing some token of their human identity, such as mittens, so that even in their confrontation with the spirits they still kept in touch with the bodily form and human consciousness to which they hoped to return.

1. Usha, the daughter of a prestigious asura (Hindu demon), dreamed of an amorous encounter with a stranger whom she later recognized in a drawing made by her companion, a woman with occult skills. Seeing that Usha had fallen deeply in love, Usha's companion ascended along a "mystic skyway" and flew back with the young stranger in hand. Miniature painting, detail, Bhagavata Purana, ca. 1820, India.

2. The map of a Siberian shaman's journey to the Upper World details his climb up the nine branches of the World-Tree that grows over his yurt and provides a passage through the heaven gate. Drawing, early 20th century, Altai region.

Descent

In Blake's illustration, death is depicted as an "under" world, to which the spirits of the dead initially descend before Hope illuminates the possibility of an eternal home. The mythic realms to which descent leads us are pictured variously as places of disembodied shades ruled by chthonic gods, fiery hells for the damned and kingdoms of hidden treasure within the bowels of the earth—rich soils, crystalline pools and precious metals and gems.

Descent takes us *down*: from above to below, heaven to earth, upper world to subterranean or watery depths. Gravity naturally pulls us down as mass and weight. We descend into solid reality, the burdens of responsibility; sensuality, pleasure and pain; cooling waters and volcanic fire. Descent into psyche's "inferior" and infernal regions is an essential aspect of initiatory process in almost every mystery cult and heroic journey.

Mythically rendered as acts of creation or divinity descending into earthly form, psyche's archetypal energies incarnate in symbolic avatars and conscious life. Descent coagulates and realizes. Through descent the things of the head become embodied. Volatile spirit acquires matter. Dream, idea, potential and the hovering images of intuition become concrete and are subject to corruption and end. We speak in both relief and disappointment of "coming down to earth" and "getting grounded." Descent can be deflation, crash, collapse, implosion, disenchantment and disillusion.

Descent is paired with ascent in the eternal cycles of nature registered in our psychic "ups and downs": Death and corruption lead to renewal, things dissolve and regroup; alchemy performs its "spagyric" medicine of analysis and synthesis, consciousness expands and gets embodied as experience. In these rhythms are the undercurrents of the great mystery religions and initiatory rituals that seek to separate above and below or to balance and unite them. The Mesopotamian goddess Inanna voluntarily descends to the realm of the dead ruled by her sister Ereshkigal in order to assimilate its great mysteries and then return. The Greek Persephone is abducted into Hades, found by mother Demeter, the goddess of the grain, and ever after moves between two worlds. Jesus descends into the death of crucifixion and the harrowing of Hell and then rises into eternal life. The alchemical savior ascends from matter into spirit, unites the opposites and once again descends to earth as the reanimating elixir. In a Cheyenne Indian myth, a coot swims down to the bottom of the primordial lake, and resurfaces with a ball of mud from which the earth is made.

While in these myths what goes down comes up, that is not always true of descent. One can get lost or stuck in psyche's lower regions, reflecting states of permanent decline or regression. Descent is thus a hook for devaluing fantasies of what is not conscious; we designate it as "subconscious." Yet myth and ritual from the oldest times attest to the transformative possibilities of descent. It is return to a transpersonal matrix for rebirth, the obtaining of treasured self-knowledge from realms of luminous darkness, or a boon of understanding that brings "up" to collective consciousness the genuinely profound.

The Descent of Man into the Vale of Death: "But Hope Rekindled, Only to Illume the Shades of Death, and Light Her to the Tomb," by William Blake, pen and gray ink and wash with watercolor, ca. 1805, England.

Falling

Subject to the stern law of gravity, everything in the world falls: snow, rain, leaves, unsteady toddlers. In our dreams, myths and fairy tales we fall from walls, trees, towers, airplanes, from the chariot of the sun and from heaven itself. We wish to rise, we yearn to fly; we fear falling. Perhaps we fear that like Humpty Dumpty, we could never be mended if we should fall.

Falling is not something sought for. Out of control, we are catapulted into a new state. Even slumbering is "falling asleep." Mysterious birth contractions forced us all out of the comfort of the womb as we fell into life. Unknown inner forces throw us about as we fall in love. At times, like Rapunzel in her tower, we know that our life is an imprisonment and the fall is a release, if a painful one. More often, though, the fall feels like a loss and a divine punishment, and our myths picture it, like Adam and Eve's loss of Paradise, as the result of disobedience.

We fall when we are above the ground, on head trips, above our natural human state. Getting up too high is risky. The view and the perspective are thrilling. We start to believe that we are more than we are—more special, wiser, more powerful, more important. Then the danger of falling looms. The angel Lucifer who rebelled against God's authority and was thrown out of heaven is an image of this. Pride, we say, goes before a fall. Humility is safer. Our religions tell us to fall to our knees or to the floor of the mosque, acknowledging powers greater than ourselves.

And yet, at times heroic arrogance is necessary. Otherwise we remain obedient children or largely un-conscious. Modern sporting enthusiasms reenact ancient fears of falling, ancient yearnings for flight. Skydivers (who refer to themselves as "fliers") plunge headlong from airplanes, giddily saved from crashing by releasing diaphanous parachutes. Falling bungee jumpers are snatched from disaster at the last instant by elastic lifelines. So in concrete form, we seek to assert our power over falling and over human limitations.

The heroes of myth and real life, from Prometheus to Columbus, Galileo and Einstein, cross the boundaries of the known and risk disaster. Sometimes they fall, are chained to mountain crags, are forced to recant their beliefs. Sometimes they increase their own knowledge and the consciousness of humankind. Moments of risk for the sake of new horizons appear in everyone's life and are often announced by dreams of snakes or of snakebites, harking back to the snake in the Garden of Eden and Adam and Eve's heroic disobedience, which initiated human consciousness (Edinger, 16 ff). "There is a deep doctrine in the legend of the Fall; it is the expression of a dim presentiment that the emancipation of ego consciousness was a Luciferian deed," observed Jung. "Man's whole history consists from the very beginning in a conflict between his feeling of inferiority and his arrogance" (CW 9i:420).

Edinger, Edward F. *Ego and Archetype.* Boston and London, 1992.

2

1. Young Phaeton tumbles down, felled by Zeus for his pride and ambition in driving the chariot of the sun. Engraving by Hendrick Goltzius, 16th century, the Netherlands.

2. *Fall of the Damned*, by Dieric Bouts the Elder, oil painting, ca. 1450, the Netherlands.

Play

Who knows what makes us play? The young of very many species, including our own, spontaneously chase, leap, twist, wrestle and cavort, promoting strength and endurance, instinct, social bonding and adaptation. Complex play with objects and goals is associated with more complex brains. But playing is also, apparently, just for the sheer pleasure of play. An aquarium fish will repeatedly leap in and out of a tiny waterfall. Ravens have been observed sledding on their backs down slopes of snow, and kea parrots toss rocks in the air. Elephants kneel to equalize play with a smaller playmate (Brown, 2ff). Cats, dogs and primates, among others, incorporate objects and obstacles in their play and often have favorite toys. Dolphins invite play with human swimmers. Play, in fact, is a principal way in which acquaintance is made with another.

Human games are often formalizations of play, framed by fixed rules, while allowing for individual strategies. Many of our most familiar games can be traced back to archaic rituals and myths the cosmology of which is embodied in the structure of the contest (EoR, 5:468ff). Hopscotch, for example, derives from myths of the soul's journey from earth to heaven through a labyrinth. Chess employs the hierarchy of medieval kingdoms. Games of chance are probably descended from divination rituals, and invoke the mythic forces of fate. In Hindu mythology, the spirit of *lila,* or divine play, is behind the infinite manifestations of the gods and their *maya,* or power of illusion. "The divine mother is always sportive. This universe is her play...her pleasure is in continuing the game," said Ramakrishna of the goddess Kali (Gupta, 136).

Artifacts of cultures thousands of years old reveal toy conveyances, miniature weapons, pull animals and human figures. Toys come alive through imagination and unconscious projection, reflecting in children the still-tenuous boundaries between inner and outer realities. Like the religious fetishes of antiquity, stuffed animals and dolls in particular reflect numinous facets of their possessor's unknown identity. They embody threshold guardians in developmental transitions. They are potent objects of comfort and companionship, expressed affects, urges and compulsions, protection, aggression and role-playing.

Natural forces outside their ken made our ancestors imagine they were themselves playthings of the gods. Contemporary computer-simulated games of sports, war, intergalactic conquest, evolution, urban planning and interactive doll houses transform the tactile experience of doll-playing and the hands-on making of models into a virtual experience in which enthusiasts play and are "played" by the unexpected components of the game (Seabrook, 97). Psychologically, consciousness and the unconscious interact and impact one another in all kinds of play. The reverie of play unveils feelings, aspirations, impressions, locked up pieces of experience and potentialities. Play can evoke the affinity and polarity between psychic opposites, and dynamics of exclusion and integration, separation and reunification. Alchemy described a part of the opus as "child's play" despite the arduous nature of the work of self-understanding, suggesting that psychic process requires an attitude of play and that the imagination was a primary tool of the adept. Jung played children's games of drawing, modeling with clay and *meditatio,* the dialogue with an unseen partner, as a means of engaging the unconcious aspect of psyche and bringing its contents into consciousness (CW 12:390). Dreams often utilize images of play. They reveal the stuff that supports or subverts our capacity for creative play. They illuminate a process related to contending in life, stepping up to the plate, going the distance, winning, losing, excelling. They invite play.

Lack of play, or abnormal play—sadistic, bullying, teasing play—is associated with abuse, abandonment, depression or sociopathy (Brown, 2ff). Play is frivolous, serious, consequential. There are sexual games, political games, war games. Game theory mathematically describes the seemingly unpredictable convergence of competing parties. Physicists play speculative "god-games" with giant particle colliders. Out of play emerges evolutionary change, self-awareness, scientific discovery, artistic composition, invention, pleasure, good friends of multiple species and the resolution of many questions. "The game's afoot," the legendary Sherlock Holmes would say when he had a lead to the mystery.

Brown, Stuart. L. "Animals at Play." *National Geographic* (186/6, 1994).
Gupta, Mahendranath. *The Gospel of Sri Ramakrishna,* New York, 1942.
Seabrook, John. "Profiles—Game Master." *The New Yorker* (November 6, 2006).

1. In time-honored style, a juvenile imitates the play of an adult. *Snow Monkeys Making Snowballs*, by Keren Su, photograph, 2003, Nagano, Japan.

2. Greek runners competing. Athletes (Greek *athlein*, "to contend for a prize") were associated in many cultures with the warrior, hero and immortal gods, signified in ancient Greece by the evergreen olive wreath that crowned the victor. Panathenaic prize amphora, ca. 530 B.C.E.

Swimming

Swimming returns us to our primordial origins in water. The mythologies of many cultures describe a watery chaos that precedes the creation of land, an allegory of our preconscious condition as fish swimming in the ocean of the unconscious. Darwinian evolution imagines life-forms beginning in water, floating, then swimming, then evolving over millions of years into struggling, amphibian creatures who venture tentatively onto solid ground. The body has an instinctive resonance with the sea of our beginnings, and the ego with the sealike depths of psyche.

When we swim we are encompassed by something greater than ourselves, an element fluid in nature, its conditions constantly changing—waves swell or a storm blows in, leaving the water muddy. If it is a lake, river or sea, the swimmer is aware of a great openness, the expanse of the water, the vast empty space above, the sheer depths beneath and an absence of boundaries. There is fear of being suddenly snatched and pulled under into the deep, and at the same time elation in floating above it. Likewise the ego self-navigates psyche's shallows or depths, contending with the rapidity and direction of affective currents that can carry it or oppose it, the shifting winds of circumstance, and the influence of life's turbulence and tidal activity. The attitude of the swimmer is all important because panic can come with the unpredictable or be incited by things we imagine, and the mysteries of submergence also carry the potential for dissolution. In alchemy, swimming is an aspect of *solutio*; in the saline waters of experience the ego's defenses are softened so that it can surrender itself to more flexible motility.

We float because our specific gravity is nearly the same as that of the water from which we evolved. The chemistry of our bodily fluid is remarkably similar to that of the sea. Swimming may stimulate the physical body's memories of its watery phylogeny; it has even been documented that human newborns tossed into water swim instinctively, an ability that disappears over time. Swimming allows playful movements that transcend more familiar possibilities. We gyrate, plunge, dive, progress rapidly at a crawl or on our sides or backs, and use our arms as wings and our legs as flippers. For humans, swimming is perhaps the closest thing to the freedom of flying, evoking the medium of the fluid, aerial imagination. In our dreams we often fly with swimming motions, buoyed by fantasy or intuition. Swimming may be experienced as an oceanic feeling of oneness with nature, uterine containment or rejuvenating immersion in the rhythms and flow of the source, like bathing or baptism. But if we find ourselves in too-deep water, are swept out to sea or in a vessel that is sinking, then swimming may represent our only means to get to the thing that can save us.

Indian girls swimming in a lotus pond, buoyed by airtight jugs. Watercolor on paper, ca. 1790, India.

Bicycle

The breeze-borne coattails disappearing toward the horizon in Georg Oddner's photograph *Towards the Light* single-handedly capture the exhilaration that the conquest of speed aroused in the nineteenth century, the frenetic era of expanding possibilities when the bicycle first became popular. Functioning without an engine, noisome exhaust or polluting noise, the bicycle is considered the most efficient invention ever devised for human propulsion, especially after nearly two centuries of experimental retooling. Like the airplane, it quickly found a lasting place in the popular imagination and in the landscape of dreams. In particular, the bicycle symbolically evokes a vehicle of psychic energy and progression (the bicycle doesn't move in reverse) that is personal rather than collective, and under the command of the individual ego. The exception is the old-fashioned "bicycle built for two" that intimates the movement of a romance propelled forward by the synchronized eros of the couple. For some, rhythmic pedaling or "pumping" a bike has suggested sexual energies that turn the wheels of life. Always the bicycle has signified independence and freedom in steering one's daily course and the byways of its occasional adventures. Susan B. Anthony—reflecting on its role in the disappearance of the bustle and corset—pronounced that "the bicycle had done more for the emancipation of women than anything else in the world" (Bly, 10). Now associated as well with professional racing and extreme sports, the bicycle, as an intimately personal set of "wheels," has also become emblematic of speed, daredevil challenges and the transcendence of the known limits of an individual's capacities. So accustomed are we to the bicycle's marvels that it requires the rare display of acrobatic finesse on a unicycle to remind us that bicycling is foremost a feat of balancing. Without momentum and balance between mind and body, a cyclist does not glide gently forward, but makes a bruising spill to the ground. The delight visible in a toddler's face taking its first steps is revisited in learning to master a bicycle: The initially unnatural sensation of finding balance on one's feet reawakens when a cyclist launches off on a wobbly virgin voyage, comically jerking the unfamiliar handlebars from side to side before finally rolling away with the elegant ease for which the ingenious bicycle was designed in a daring age of inventions.

Bly, Nellie. "Champion of Her Sex." *New York Sunday World* (February 2, 1896).

The distant horizon is suddenly within reach on the swift wheels of a bicycle—a liberating experience that has been poetically recaptured here. *Towards the Light,* by Georg Oddner, photograph, 1999, Sweden.

Car

The paradoxes of mass production were not lost on the pop artist Andy Warhol, or his 1962 serial repetition of the Cadillac's chrome-laden grill. The image reminds us that America's most prestigious car is a mass-consumer product created on assembly lines in the hundreds of thousands. "I like things to be the same over and over again," Warhol explained, seizing upon the Cadillac as the automotive counterpart to Marilyn Monroe and Jackie Kennedy, and reproducing all three celebrities in row upon row. At mid-twentieth century, the soaring fins and streamlined features of the yacht-like Cadillac reflected an apogee of car design that coincided with cheap gasoline, postwar prosperity and the fever pitch of America's love affair with the automobile. Although cars measured their might in "horsepower" they replaced our reliance on the horse in a generation. Henry Ford further revolutionized modern society by replacing custom-made production with massive assembly lines and pushed for gas stations and highways to be built nationwide, inventing the franchise system. Corporations could thus saturate the sprawling suburbs Ford's cars made possible, in order to market their own mass products.

In countless ways, psyche's conscious and unconscious have registered the impact of the automobile. There is its devastating effect on the environment worldwide—global warming, air and noise pollution, the disruption of wildlife habitats, oil consumption, traffic congestion and road rage. Sidewalks in many American suburbs were long ago dismantled to widen roads. A vast number of individuals live their lives between enclosed structures and the controlled, insular space of their cars, from which they make a "pass" at nature. The car, however, is associated with sexiness, power, speed, aggression, "drive." On the car is projected essential aspects of identity, or persona. Receiving the keys to the car in adolescence can represent the achievement of a developmental milestone, a perceived capacity for independence, following the rules of the road, displaying sound judgment and good instincts. Dreams reflect the analogy between types of vehicles and the way one lives psychic life, or moves forward in time, observed Jung (CW 12:153). The car would represent a specific instance of this, spelled out in the details. Whether, for example, the dreamer is firmly in the driver's seat. In the flow of traffic or in conflict with it. Moving with or without a sense of direction. Whether there is a feeling of confidence and right relation to the car's mechanics or difficulty with manipulating the brake, respecting boundaries, or maneuvering at intersections. Who's at the wheel, if not the dreamer, may reveal something about a driving force in the psyche that acts to help or to subvert the achievement of consciousness.

One of the most coveted consumer items, car is an expression of glamour, success, of "driving in the fast lane," of having "arrived." Cars and how we drive them can embody both individual movement and collective values, which undergo modifications in how car and driver occupy the road.

1. Vacantly smiling, a family of tourists watches an arid expanse of alien outback flash past them from their car. Australian artist John Brack reveals the deepening estrangement of human from nature. *The Car*, oil on canvas, 1955.

2. Nothing succeeds like excess, Andy Warhol seems to imply in *Twelve Cadillacs*, 1962, a silk-screen commissioned by *Harper's Bazaar*.

Train

The train has always seemed part animal, a huffing bull, a hissing snake, a great fire-breathing dragon, materializing with a prolonged, annunciatory *wail*. On-track, locomotive energy, it connects the points over sometimes vast distances toward a specific destination. "I think I can, I think I can," says the Little Engine That Could of the children's classic, while the sleepless novelist Arthur Koestler once heard the same clickety-clack as "I told you so, I told you so." The separate but linked cars that one can walk about, dine or sleep in while progressing through new vistas and constant change has suggested the movement of life that simultaneously engages the now and the timeless.

Railroads date back to 1550 when German miners built them as guides for horse-drawn carts filled with ore. "Train," from the Old French *trahiner*, "to drag," originally referred to a "train of carriages" pulled behind an engine, the way things can line up and be carried in an orderly way behind the leading energy. Building upon the first practical steam engine developed in 1769 by James Watt, passenger services were available in England by about 1825, contributing to the Industrial Revolution. The train brought together the eastern and western seaboards of the United States in 1859. Along with blackening billows of smoke from coal-fed engines, Victorian trains gave us silver dining vessels, immaculate linens and melancholy steam-whistles that sounded through the night. Streamlined twentieth-century diesel-powered trains preserved the glamour of speed while eliminating the finery, and French trains exceeding 350 mph using magnetic levitation have turned the train into a flying "bullet."

Trains combine such technological advances with a character inherently archaic, one of many reasons why they have found a lasting place in the psyche. Sigmund Freud, who compulsively minded timetables and often arrived at a train station an hour before his departure (Jones, 305), claimed that dreaming about missing one's train disguised a fear of dying (Freud, 243). The train's association with fate or death inexorably bearing down on the one who happens to be in its track has been grimly realized and artistically exploited. Trains have carried every kind of freight, from automobiles to human beings destined for concentration camps. Silent films endlessly portrayed the heroine roped to a train's tracks as it sped toward her. Later cinematic masterpieces built on the train's nervous suspense and featured trains at climactic moments. A train's scream parallels that of a murder victim, or our own horror as witnesses to the crime; a train glides into a dark tunnel suggesting sexual consummation. The train embodies immense energy, and reshuntings of energy, carrying one toward a goal and engaged on time, delayed or missed altogether. A train rarely deviates from its path, and we can clock the time by a regularly scheduled train. Train wrecks are usually spectacular, evoking equally shattering psychological derailments. Still, for many, the train most of all conveys a vehicle of mystery and magic, which, if we are receptive, might carry us anywhere.

Freud, Sigmund and A. A. Brill. *The Interpretation of Dreams*. NY, 1913.
Jones, Ernest. *The Life and Work of Sigmund Freud*. NY, 1953.

Trailing a cloud of smoke, a steam locomotive
approaches out of the snow-veiled distance of a bygone
era. *Train in the Snow*, by Claude Monet, oil on canvas,
1875, France.

Subway

We call the subway "the underground" and imagination often perceives it as the underworld. Dark and subterranean, its tunnels bring to mind caverns, catacombs and labyrinths. The subway is a separate realm to which we cannot gain entry except by descent and the paying of a toll. The turnstile allows us to go through only one by one, merging our individuality with a collective body. The trains approach the station like huffing bulls and pull away as agile serpents winding through their lairs. There are multiple paths and possibilities, destinations familiar and not, the rubbing of shoulders with ubiquitous and diverse strangers. We can choose which train we board or allow ourselves to be carried at random. The very first subway, London's, was realized in 1863. Later, Michel Verne's novel *"Un Express de L'Avenir"* ("A Great Transatlantic Subway") imagined passengers dashing between England and America beneath the ocean, an even bolder concept than the modern Chunnel that actually connects Dover and Calais. By the 1890s the London Underground, or "Tube," traveled daily beneath the River Thames. The New York City subway opened in 1904, as if the dreamlike stratification of the city above, with its soaring skyscrapers, required a corresponding push into the world below. The building of subways paralleled another nineteenth-century phenomenon, the fascination with the underground, dynamic energies of psyche, in order to arrive at the meaning of dreams, motivations, passions and powers. The two movements come together in the subway's easily animated, mythic qualities. However, what we fear about the mythic basement also applies to the subway: isolated, dimly lit, full of secret niches, scurrying rats and holding the possibility of danger and violation. The third rail by which most existing subway systems are powered can signify electrifying movement and potential annihilation. For some the subway means the underground, pumping arteries of urban life, and consciousness expanding in many directions; others find in it merely the claustrophobic sensation of being swallowed by anonymity and mass. Globally, subways will increasingly become computerized, driverless and equipped with sensors and camera eyes, conveying to an even greater extent an invisible reality with its own agency.

Unperturbed by the deafening roar of a train flashing
by, two New Yorkers chat nonchalantly in the bowels of
the world's largest subway system. *Grand Central
Subway Station*, by Konstantino Hatzisarros,
photograph, 20th century, United States.

Airplane

Filling the sky and forming a quaternity, Middendorf's airplane reflects his haunting memory of the Berlin airlift, which brought food and medical supplies to German cities leveled by Allied bombers. The neo-Expressionist image, painted long after the destruction of the artist's homeland, transposes the horrors of aerial bombardment into an organic fantasy of the creative self that can survive despite adversity, integrate devastation and overcome trauma by giving it aesthetic significance. The simple biplane of World War I evolved into the massive monoplane that ended the Second World War by dropping an atom bomb. Only a generation earlier, aviators first mastered taking off from the ground in their harmless biplanes, rising into the seemingly weightless air. With its awkward double tier of wings, the biplane was soon relegated to air shows and crop-dusting, while the monoplane was equipped with powerful jet turbines. During the war, airplanes also acquired a mystique—photographs of their nicknamed noses were pinned up by fiancées of pilots about to take off on no-return missions; or they were enshrined next to a boy's kite as a romance that later ripened into his profession as a commercial pilot. Gazing back at these photographs, we can still hear the drone of Amelia Earhart's aircraft disappearing into the void that lured early aviators away from terra firma. What began as a retooling of da Vinci's foot-powered aircraft in 1903 (when Orville Wright's biplane sustained flight for 12 seconds) soon evolved into sky-darkening bombers and the jumbo jets that routinely fly several billion passengers each year. Using merely the resistance of air molecules to gain lift under their wings, airplanes turned human attention to the skies, and beyond the clouds to outer space, as a medium for human travel. Psyche soon reflected these innovations, in dreams that replace Pegasus with Piper Cubs and Zeus' thunderbolts with the Blue Angels.

Our nightmares replaced medieval apocalypses with the terrors of aerial bombardment, accompanied by piercing air-raid sirens and earth-shuddering bombs—or the modern anxiety of a jet crashing to earth (or now, into office towers). Despite their statistical safety, anxious passengers staring down at farm fields miles below experience turbulence or a thrusting engine as a warning that their ascent has violated their natural place on earth. Ancient Greek stage managers invented deus ex machina cranes to lift actors playing deities into the air, but kept humans below on earth—anything else would signify hubris and, like Phaeton in his out-of-control sun chariot or Icarus with his melting wings, bring them plunging to earth. If we can calm these fears, the vision from an airplane window provides us with an objective overview that was once the sole prerogative of the gods. An ironic consequence of this sublimated perspective is that we are so far above the concrete realties below that *unlike the gods* we are impotent to act upon them.

As aviation became commonplace, filling our skies with its long jet-trails, the anxiety of missing flights, being stalled before takeoff or even skyjacked replaced metaphors that departed trains, lame horses and pirates at sea had expressed in earlier eras. Now, once their earphones are inserted and their eyes closed, even seasoned jet travelers may return to the same timeless dreams of flight that lured pioneering aviators into the cockpit. Peter Pan's summons to fly off to a wonderland and never grow up speaks to our longing to escape the tedium and tension of terrestrial life, even if we admire the "well-grounded" person who scoffs at our "airheaded" flights of imagination. Yet valid genius and inspired innovations do originate in the upward sublimation of our lower preoccupations, ultimately prompted by our innate urge to reclaim the inner heights from which we first came "trailing clouds of glory." Then our longing to fly finds its true pioneers in the shaman's magical flight, in the yogi's levitation and the swift angels of Islam and Christianity, recognizing in the airplane waiting to taxi down the runway no less a marvel than these legendary prototypes for having made flight a reality.

Helmut Middendorf's *Airplane Dream*, 1982, reawakens the trauma that followed the transformation of the miracle of flight into a nightmarish weapon.

Boat

The boat immediately evokes a passage and the containing vessel that carries one over watery depths. The soundness of the boat is important because its integrity comprises a boundary, sometimes between life and death. For this reason, in most cultures boat building has been surrounded by ritual practices, taboos and superstitions that have to do with the tension between forces that function to keep the boat afloat and those that would submerge it. The basic form of any boat is the empty space it contains as well as the "cavity" it makes in the surface of the water; the boat's resiliency depends on this small incursion into water's domain. The relationship and secret identity between the holding vessel and the deep waters that buoy it up and can also break it into pieces is nuanced and emotional, a linking with our first crossing into birth, with the uterus, the rocking cradle and the saving ark and with our last crossing in the ship of death "leading us back to the swaying, gliding somnolent rhythms of earliest childhood, of the primordial ocean and the night" (Neumann, 256ff). Thus the ship has often been experienced as an aspect of the great feminine, as mother or beloved, the strengths and vulnerabilities of whose holding body the captain or navigator must intimately know.

Crossing, odyssey, voyage—the boat or ship is the vehicle of our mythical peregrinations. The ancient Egyptians depicted the sun as conveyed each night in a bark over the abysmal ocean of darkness toward sunrise and rebirth, just as consciousness is conveyed over the nether seas of sleep. The lunar crescent, lending its curvature to the form of a hull, slips through the black ripples of space with its cargo of dews, or is portrayed as a ship of souls riding the clouds, serene and transcendent. The human ego is carried in vessels conscious and unconscious, ships of imagination, intellect, hope, faith, courage, illusion, fantasy and dream on psyche's shifting currents. All of our senses help us to navigate winds and tides, fathom the depths and take our bearings. We are moored, and loose our moorings, sail against the tide or with the tide in auspicious winds, are buffeted by storms, drift, circumvent the hidden reefs and glaciers or are wrecked by them. Is the vessel seaworthy? Has it an anchor or a sturdy pair of oars? Is its size and provision proportionate to the size of the waters?

So primal is the idea of the boat that holds us secure above the chaos that houses have been built in the image of a ship; so have Christian churches, with the cross as the mast. The boat denotes those things, material, spiritual, energic, that suddenly appear on our horizons and are brought to shore. Sailboats, cruise ships, battleships, ships of commerce, ferryboats, lifeboats, barges, canoes. The ship laden with goods, unexpected riches, or the fruits of long labor: "My ship has come in." Ships that carry the forces of terror, possession, piracy and war. Alchemy depicted its opus of psychological process as a circumnavigation to the four ends of the earth, and as a voyage in opposite directions at the same time, suggesting a destination of wholeness. The opus was also perceived as an odyssey, long, tedious, heroic and beset by dangers. One could easily get lost traversing those unknown waters, be swallowed by the things of the deep or get becalmed. The boat embodies the voyage of life, of coming full circle. And almost everywhere, the boat has signified the last journey, the reuniting one with the waters of the beginning, the passing over to the "yonder shore." Often it is a solitary journey, not always a bleak one:

Peace! Peace!
To be rocked by the Infinite!
Stanley Kunitz, *The Long Boat*

Neumann, Erich. *The Great Mother*. Princeton, NJ, 1972.

1

2

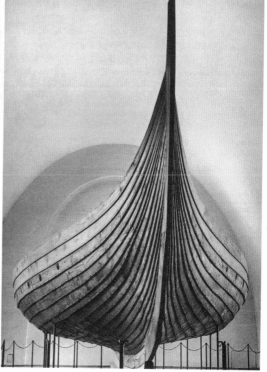

3

1. With the all-seeing Udjat Eye (Eye of Horus) hovering overhead, the bark of the sun makes its night-sea journey toward dawn. From the *Book of the Dead of Hor*, papyrus, ca. 300 B.C.E., Egypt.

2. A lifeboat carrying passengers from the sinking ship Titanic, photograph, 1912.

3. Shaped like the moon's crescent, the Gokstad ship, Viking ship, ca. 9th century C.E., Norway.

Shipwreck

… a brave vessel,
who had, no doubt, some noble creature in her,
Dash'd all to pieces.
Shakespeare, *The Tempest*, 1.2.8–10

A ship flails, its mast snapped in two like a matchstick, the bobbing heads of the drowning crew engulfed by the sea. The disappearing arm of one sailor eerily resembles a crab's leg, as if the doomed man were being reabsorbed into prehuman darkness so complete even his body is reduced to food for the creatures of the deep.

"Shipwreck" resonates in our terror of oblivion, of the absolute failure of vessels of containment in the encounter with the seas of life and the frenzy of their winds and waves. Among humankind's first organized ventures, perhaps the most daring was to construct ships to cross vast and perilous waters, a reflection not only of the heavenly bodies eternally traveling over the abyss of the dark night sky, but also of the ego itself mysteriously borne each night over psyche's unconscious depths to awaken at the light of day. If the ship with sails unfurled proudly skimming the sea evokes hope, deliverance, salvation, bounty, the heroic and adventuresome spirit of humankind, then shipwreck is their overthrow: a symbol of inundation, misfortune, the anger of the gods, terrifying descent into the churning waters of chaos or the unfathomable abyss of death.

The sinking of ships like the "unsinkable" Titanic becomes a moral example of the consequences of human inflation. Shipwreck is often portrayed as ordeal, a test of faith or courage, the defeat of an opponent, conflict between bonds of duty and the will to survive. Yet shipwreck is also about collisions with fate, unseen dangers, blinding fogs. A vessel designed to negotiate the unruly elements of nature, ship has been, symbolically, a figure for a system, vehicle or way toward transformation. Psychological process often borrows the metaphor of ship and voyage—setting a goal and steering a course, getting one's bearings in relation to the center; the mythic hero's journey that conveys conscious circumnavigation of the uncharted aspects of the personality. "Ship" has long been an analogy for a whole that depends on the cooperation of the parts and is governed by a "captain." Classical philosophy pictured the human body as a ship in which the reasoning soul is the helmsman. The state is depicted as a ship, in which good citizens cooperate in order to ensure its welfare. The Christian church is likened to a ship, whose mast is cross or steeple. Shipwreck, then, suggests a vessel pulled into the vortex of energies too overwhelming to withstand, or a vessel whose structure is inherently unstable or is shattered on the deadly rocks of malignant attitudes, the bad leadership of the "captain" or the ineffectiveness or anarchy of the "crew."

As the feminine figureheads on ships attest, ship catches the projection of containing and protective womb. Shipwreck is felt, and feared, as maternal defeat or betrayal, as womb become tomb, as coffin that carries the shipwrecked soul down and down and down.

A manuscript illustration of a passage from the *Divine Comedy* depicts shipwreck as the consequence of hubris. Dante relates the story of Ulysses' transgression of the boundaries of human knowledge established by the gods, invoking the whirlwind in which his ship is destroyed. Inferno XXVI, ca. 1400, Italy.

Path / Road

"Follow me!" says the road ahead, and so we do, confident that others have been this way before. Even when we cannot see the terrain clearly—in the dark of night or under the cover of snow—the road is a guide and a companion and an assurance that in time we will come to our desire, whether that is adventure and new territory or the familiarity of home.

According to the Biblical book of Job, however, there is "[a] path no bird of prey knoweth, neither hath the falcon's eye seen it ... " (Job 28:7). The high-flying bird sees the highway, the hiking trail, all the physical routes, but not the symbolic road, the path of wisdom. Such a symbolic path can be a religious idea or practice such as the Eightfold Path of Buddhism or the Tao of Laotzu "a natural guiding force that leads all things to their fulfillment" (Smith, 1053) or it might be expressed by Jesus' "I am the way, and the truth, and the life" (John 14:6). "The word 'way' means both a road and a method ... . the Christian way to heaven is to 'follow Christ,' with a double imagery of both treading in his footsteps and accepting his message" (MM 16:2145).

But the image of the path may also appear to any lost and bewildered individual in a dream of a road or of stepping stones, suggesting that there *is* a way to go, a path to follow, though he or she may not yet know what it is. In essence, "path" implies direction. In the face of chaos and a sense that the events of life are random, it offers something linear, a suggestion of meaning.

In many Native American cultures (Pima, Papago, Oglala, Hopi) the road has long been an image for the correct way of life (Gill, 256). In other religious systems there is an emphasis on two contrasting roads or paths; often the easy way is opposed by the steep, narrow and difficult one, which is the correct one to choose. The Buddha's "Middle Way" is an exception: It is neither the life of luxury nor one of asceticism and suffering. Our language embodies this symbolism. Whatever the situation, one can "be on the right track" or can "fall by the wayside," or, soberingly, be on the wrong path or on the way to a dead end.

The road can also simply stand for the natural course of one's life, with all its beauties, changes of direction, adventures and rough spots, and its eventual destination, death. Variously it is understood as "the path of duty"; the "open road" of adventure, release and freedom; the aimless track of man the wanderer, which leads back to its beginnings. Our times emphasize "going my (own) way," not the traditional way nor the way that is expected by others. Here is the potential for individuality, but also the danger of egotism and blind pride. Going into the unknown, where there is no path, is the task of the hero, the genius, the prophet, that may result in the discovery of a new path for stumbling humankind.

Gill, Sam D. and Irene F. Sullivan. *Dictionary of Native American Mythology.* NY, 1994.
Smith, Jonathan Z. Ed. *The HarperCollins Dictionary of Religion.* SF, 1995.

2

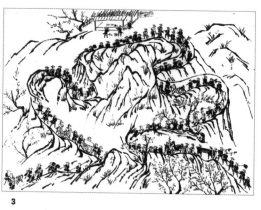

3

1. A road, like a pointing finger, directs the traveler into the unknown. *The Road West*, by Dorothea Lange, photograph, 1938, United States.

2. Walt Whitman describes the open road as "The long brown path before me, leading wherever I choose" ("Song of the Open Road"). *Winter Road I*, by Georgia O'Keeffe, oil on canvas, 1963, United States.

3. A Japanese procession twists along a mountain road, returning (almost) to where it began. *A Procession of Maeda, Daimyo of Kaga Crossing a Mountain Pass*, ink on paper, Edo period (1615–1868), Japan.

Weaving / Spinning

The warp was woven at noon,
The woof in the house of dawn,
The rest in the hall of the sun.

Golden gown woven for the moon,
Shimmering veil for the little sun.
Estonian song (Neumann, 228)

More rain with snow is being woven
on these great looms of early winter
Zbigniew Herbert, Song

A bird—the weaver of nests—is perched in a tree opposite a serene Mayan weaver, perhaps the moon goddess Ixchtel herself. A simple back-strap loom made of two branches joins tree and woman as she uses her body to hold the proper tension. In many cultures the upper crossbeam of the loom is called the "beam of heaven," the bottom representing the earth, as if in between the world is being woven into creation. In early myth Ixchtel was a spider, drawing the thread from her own body, and it was from her that humans learned the craft of weaving. Each morning her webs appear on earth, as magical as the drops of dew that cover them. When the Zuni see a beautiful piece of weaving they say, "Did you touch the spider's web?" (Wilson, 297)

In all myth, the art of weaving originated in the divine world and this is why some small mistake must be woven into the pattern, to remind us of the imperfection in all created life. Arachne, an unfortunate young weaver, learned this the hard way as she eventually was turned into a spider as punishment after winning a contest over Athena, the Greek goddess who taught humans weaving and all crafts. Arachnids, the family of spiders, still bear her name.

By drawing out the tangled fibers of plants or animals and twisting them, a continuous thread emerges. The crossing of two sets of interlacing threads—called warp and weft, woof or filling—is the underlying principle of all weaving. From these simple techniques fabric is produced of such complexity that weaving became an image for the mystery of existence. It is the crossing of time and space, where the visible and invisible worlds are woven together, each created form becoming a thread in the great tapestry of life. It is the crossing of the sexual union, and where the "tissues" of the child's body are woven in the womb of the mother (Neumann, 227). Weaving then means to create, to make something out of one's own substance. In a North African ritual, the weaver recites the same blessing when she cuts the threads of the finished cloth as the midwife utters when she cuts the umbilical cords of a newborn baby (DoS, 1093).

Cloth resembles language in many ways. The words form syntax similar to how threads produce fabric. "Text" and "textile" share a common root, meaning "to weave" (OED). In Dogon myth, weaving and speech are poetically combined to form a coherent cosmology. The mouth and the vocal cords of their ancestor figures Nommo were a loom from which not only words issued but also cloth. The Dogon people refer to the loom as "secret speech," and say "to be nude is to be without words" (Ginzberg, 261; Peek, 454). The designs woven into fabric are a form of storytelling where weaving, like song, imparts immortality. The women in the Odyssey acquire their voice through weaving. Helen, "she of the golden spindle," weaves the scenes of the Trojan war, turning her tapestry into an epic poem. Penelope defies her suitors by weaving dissent as she unwinds at night what she had woven in the day. When their households eventually return to order, these weavers become spinners, producing the thread for other women to weave their own stories (Pantelia, 495–7).

In the Norse poem *Völuspá*, a seeress sings the story of the world—poetry, like magic, being a "weav-

1. A simple loom is tied between a bird in a tree and a weaver, perhaps the Mayan moon goddess Ixchtel. The link between weaving and bird is ancient; Neolithic loom weights show signs and features of birds. An owl with human arms spinning wool is depicted on a series of Greek terra-cotta plaques (Gimbutas, 67–8). The link between divine and natural world is at the heart of weaving's transformative power. Negatively, matter becomes the web of Maya, hiding the divine realm. Terra-cotta figurine, ca. 600–800 C.E., Jaina Island, Campeche, Mexico.

ing, spinning, lacing, binding, fastening" (Neumann, 305). These are the activities of the Norns, the spinners of destiny seated at the roots of the world tree in ancient Scandinavia. Their names, Urd, Verandi and Skuld are variations of the word for "becoming." The Greek spinners of fate were also singers, according to Plato (p. 617). They were Klotho, "Spinner," who spins the thread of life; Lachesis, "Allotment," who measures it and Atropos, "Inevitable," who chooses when to cut it off. Destiny, the thread of life, is a certain period of time, long or short. Thread, like time, "stretches"—the original meaning of "spinning" to a certain length or span; everything ruled by time is subject to change, and thus fate. The moon measures time (and fate) as she changes from dark to full, corresponding to the cycles of women's menstruation (the word originating, like "month" and "measure" from the Greek for "moon"). Nature's rhythms resemble the pulse of shuttle and beam, the spinning motion of the spindle. And it all begins with a single thread, as Plato (p. 616) tells us, wound on the spindle of the revolving cosmos held in the lap of a woman, spinning the destiny of the world into being.

In ebb and flow,
In warp and weft,
Cradle and grave,
An eternal sea,
A changing patchwork,
A glowing life,
At the whirring loom of Time I weave
The living clothes of the Deity.
Goethe, *Faust*

Gimbutas, Marija. *The Language of the Goddess.* SF, 1989.

Ginzberg, Marc and Lynton Gardiner. *African Forms.* Milano, Italy, and NY, 2000.

Neumann, Erich. *The Great Mother.* Princeton, NJ, 1972.

"Text" and "Textile." *The Compact Edition of the Oxford English Dictionary.* 1987.

Pantelia, Maria C. "Spinning and Weaving: Ideas of Domestic Order in Homer." *The American Journal of Philology* (Vol.114:4, 2009).

Plato, Edith Hamilton and Huntington Cairns. *The Collected Dialogues of Plato, Including the Letters.* NY, 1961.

Peek, Philip M. and Kwesi Yankah. *African Folklore: An Encyclopedia.* NY, 2004.

Wilson, Eddie W. "The Spider and the American Indian." *Western Folklore* (10/4, 1951).

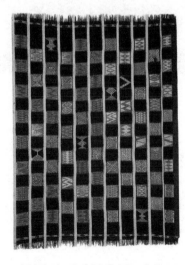

2

3

4

2. According to the Dogon people of Mali, the mouth and vocal cords of their ancestor gods formed a loom, producing both cloth and words. Cotton weaving, Africa.

3. In the image of the Virgin Mary holding spindle and thread, the archetypal structure is revealed: "She becomes the spinning goddess of destiny and her child the fabric of her body" (Neumann, 233). By the Master of Erfurt, panel painting, 15th century, Germany.

4. A woman holding distaff and spindle carved from ivory, her slender body resembling the shape of a spindle. Found in the foundations of the Temple of Artemis at Ephesus, Greek, 7th century B.C.E., Turkey.

Sewing

Alfred Stieglitz's photograph *Georgia O'Keeffe* elegantly suggests the essence of sewing—the creative "handwork" that brings the cloth together. The oldest needles from sharpened bone indicate that sewing began some 30,000 years ago (Yu, 1:19). Human fingers reached out of the darkness of unconscious life to contrive a rudimentary tool and stitch together animal skins and tendons for protective covering. In fairy tales and myths, sewing often represents the patient, stitch-by-stitch process that leads to redemption, repairs the rent fabric of the soul or mends the bewitched situation. Seamstress and tailor are psyche's embodiments of the humbly heroic, of detail and repetition; the ones wise enough to pick up the dropped stitches of potential wholeness. Sewing intricately fashions the costumes in which a culture clothes itself, symbolically evoking the garmenting both of social persona and individuality, illusion and flair, and reflecting societal patterns from which discrepant forms of experience are cut. Sewing is the tedium of assembly line piecework and the luxurious play of haute couture. We speak of the rich tapestries of life and the embroidering of language. Sewing is art and design, the surgeon's precise stitches, the knitting of wounds. At its source, sewing links us back, perhaps, to the fanciful idea of the body itself as "garment" of the soul, to the spinning of life and the threads of fate.

Weichao, Yu. Ed. *A Journey into China's Antiquity.* Beijing, 1997.

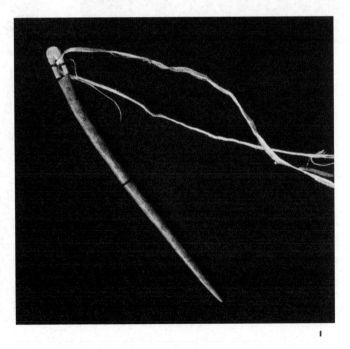

1

2

1. Needle, bone, about 18,000 years old, China.

2. *Georgia O'Keeffe*, by Alfred Stieglitz, photograph, 1920, United States.

Hunting

In the dawn of human consciousness, a Paleolithic hunter stalks an ostrich with bow and arrow. An antelope in the background suggests there is plentiful game, or a magical invoking of it. A female figure assumes a ritual pose, and there is a line of connection between her genitals and the man's. She may represent his wife, whose observance of rituals and taboos affects her husband's fruitfulness in the hunt.

Ancient rock engravings such as this one from Algeria evoke primordial hunting as a diffuse, instinctual reality of interconnection in which humans, animals, the landscape and invisible, supernatural forces participate in nature's predation. There is affinity, even a secret identification, between predator and prey, and reversals in which one becomes the other. Assimilation of the strength, ferocity and essence of the one slain is realized by the eating of its flesh and blood, in the making of clothing from skins, feathers or fur and the incorporation of bones into shelter and tools. Shamans, who in trance might shape-shift into animals, often mediated the relationship between their hunting group and the mythical Lady or Lord of the Beasts associated with the release or withholding of game. Shamanic energies were also employed in the importuning and propitiating of animal spirits and the imaginal sending, penetrating, magnetizing and luring that extended to the object of the chase.

The convergence of natural and supernatural in the hunt is perpetuated in countless myths and fairy tales where the hunt initiates a heroic quest, symbolically conveying both the wonders and ordeals of self-renewal and individuation. The pursuit of a rare and elusive beast (or a highly destructive one) glimpsed in an enchanted wood leads the hero or heroine into journey, adventure, danger and struggle, isolation and loneliness, the rescue of a captive princess or prince, the finding of treasure or the winning of a kingdom. Or, at the opposite pole, into wounding, disorientation or defeat. Such tales evoke processes by which fascinating new values in the psyche are intuited *in potentia* and arduously followed into conscious integration, transforming the soul of a culture or personality. Here, the skilled hunter is emblematic of the capacity to negotiate wilderness spaces, and to find and hit the mark.

The shadow aspect of hunting, lies, however, in the fact that early in their evolution, humans, with their numbers and weapons, became the deadliest predators on earth, often hunting indiscriminately and wastefully. Hunting is embedded not only in the drive for survival and the killer instinct, but also in the lust for domination, the pleasure of blood sport and the desire for trophies. The inequality between hunter and hunted may transcend any possibility for rapport. Human beings have also used the skills of hunting to headhunt, bargain hunt, job hunt and house hunt, to detect disease and track down criminals, in search and destroy missions, gang wars, sexual predation, stalking and serial killing. The hidden oneness between hunter and hunted suggests our vulnerability to psychic factors that if they become compulsive may pursue and seize us, sometimes doing us in.

2

1. *Stag Hunt*, attributed to Huang Zongdao, handscroll, ca. 1120, China.

2. A transcription of a rock engraving found at a prehistoric site in southern Algeria of a hunter in pursuit of an ostrich. Here, hunting is conceived as a convergence of interrelated forces, both natural and supernatural.

Sowing

*How Love burns through the Putting in the
Seed
On through the watching for that early birth
When, just as the soil tarnishes with weed,
The sturdy seedling with arched body comes
Shouldering its way and shedding the earth
crumbs.*
Robert Frost, *Putting in the Seed*

In one of the oldest collaborations between human
being and nature, Millet's *Sower* strides his ground,
scattering seed from a deep bag into the earth's fur-
rows. Vital, potent, he could well personify the "sturdy
seedling" itself.

The sowing of seed evokes every form of procreation. Primitive fertility rituals in which couples cop-
ulated in the fields on their wedding night or at the time
of sowing were sympathetic magic to assist germina-
tion in good soil, or, in other versions of such rites, ab-
stinence was thought to concentrate potency in the
sown ground. Nature has multitudinous ways of dispersing seed, imitated by human ingenuity.

Paradoxically, because the seed incubates invisibly in the dark earth, it has, since ancient times, caught
the projection of the "dead" fruit that in nature's cycle
of eternal return is reborn: "Unless a grain of wheat falls
into the earth and dies, it remains alone; but if it dies,
it bears much fruit" (John 12:24). Similarly, alchemy
saw the "dead stuff" of matter decayed and sunk into
the ground as also being the conception of the gold that
was the goal of the opus. The seed, however, never ac-

tually dies. Preserved by desiccation, it is merely dormant and not using oxygen, a state of suspended animation. Nor is sowing actually "planting" but rather the
act of dispensing seeds and hoping for the future—that
these germs of life will take root in receptive soil. Christ's
parable of the sower in Matthew 13 reflects the farmer's
dependence on good seed falling into good ground and
being blessed by rain and sun. From the Latin *semen*,
or "seed," derive the words insemination, seminar and
seminary, where words and ideas are sown in receptive
minds. The *logos spermatikos* is the source of creation
and sowing the seeds of the spirit in the body's earth
brings the two into potentially fruitful union.

However, though to some degree we "reap what
we sow," there is no guarantee that seeds will germi-
nate, nor what sort of fruit they will produce if they do.
Societies and individuals have wittingly and unwittingly sown seeds of hate, prejudice, violence, discontent; seeds of change, seeds of the future. Nature is impersonal and autonomous, full of variables outside of
human control. Ancient cultures propitiated gods of increase with animal and human sacrifices in order to
insure abundance, or followed sowing calendars arranged according to planetary influence. The alchemist
sowed the seeds of the opus only in "white foliated
earth," the "ash" that represented the painful burning
away of the dross of one's substance in order to reveal
its gold. Sowing requires both the release of the seed,
and, even with the best soil, a second letting go—of the
illusion that one can entirely control the outcome.

1

2

1. Man sowing large seeds in furrowed field. From the manuscript *Atalanta Fugiens*, by Michael Maier, 1617, Germany.

2. The image of fecundity, tiny seeds are silhouetted against the horizon as they scatter from the strong hand of a man sowing the earth. *The Sower*, by Jean-François Millet, oil on canvas, ca. 1850, France.

Mining

The pointed hoods and boyishness of the two miners in the whimsical illustration from an alchemical text identify them with mythical creatures like elves, cabiri, dwarves and dactyls. These were mercurial in nature, small, invisible and mysterious like the creative impulses of the unconscious that can guide us in mining our depths and point out, if we are respectful, rich lodes of potential, or if we are not conceal them. Mythically, such creatures are the children or helpers of divine smiths, metallurgists and alchemists associated with the transformation of base matter into what is precious, incorruptible and painstakingly formed. They serve the great mother in her function as mattered nature, live in her emblematic mountains and guard her mineral wealth.

While the alchemical image captures none of the hard realities of mining, it does convey something of the psychic background of mining that for so long has captured the imagination. Mining signifies the extracting of treasure from crude ore: the resilient metals of weapons and tools, mineral sources of heat and energy, gemstones that become crown jewels, diamonds that sparkle on wedding rings, gold that glisters as stature, riches or immortality. Human beings perceived in the bowels of the earth the mineral strata that mark the different levels of existence and the residue of the buried past. The metals of the depths were associated with celestial luminaries and planets, bringing together above and below, like silver and moon, gold and sun, copper and Venus, iron and Mars. The subterranean realm was a precinct charged with the supernatural and sacred presence of spirits, gods, ghosts and ancestors. Ancient peoples related to earth's depths as a vast maternal womb in which embryos of ore gestated and ripened into a perfected state over the endlessly slow progression of geological time. Religious rites and precautions circumscribed the sinking of a mine, a transgression of numinous ground and at the same time a human collaboration with nature in an "obstetrical" process (Eliade, 43ff). The mine was seen as a vaginal matrix from which one could extract the fetal ore and accelerate its growth in the artificial womb of the smelting furnace, just as the heat of psychic incubation can speed up processes of psychological change.

In all of our fantasies of mining is the intimation that embedded in nature is something of immense value, eternal, divine and luminous. Over the ages, the negative potential of such fantasies has confronted us in images of compulsive greed, depleted mines and disfigured mountains, the worn, dust-encrusted faces of mine workers, crippling hours in claustrophobic darkness, explosions, cave-ins and black lung. For the alchemists and their counterparts who excavate the psyche, mining resonates as dark descent, wearying, subterranean labor—and the possibility of discovered veins of gold. Psyche, too, can be mined in an attitude of exploitation and self-gain, a wrongful seizing of its natural resources. Depth matter worked hastily or brutally can leave the personality defaced and unfruitful. In the deep recesses of psyche's interior, consciousness is vulnerable to disorienting phenomena, wrong turnings, spurious finds and terrifying cave-ins of its defenses. That was why the alchemists learned to seek guidance from the homunculi, the imaginal little "metal" men who know their way around the deep regions, respect the greatness of nature and are masters of timing.

Eliade, Mircea. *The Forge and the Crucible.* Chicago, 1978.

1

2

3

1. Two miners excavate primordial matter, the body of crude ore in which is hidden the perfected stone. *Prima Materia*, illuminated manuscript from the alchemical text *Aurora consurgens*, early 16th century, Germany.

2. Henry Moore was the son of a mining engineer, and raised in a mining community. *At the Coal Face: Man Fixing Prop*, by Henry Moore, drawing, 1942, England.

3. Audacious descent for treasure or violation of nature's ground? *Sala Silvermine*, detail, by Johan Philip Korn, painting, 18th century, Sweden.

Potter

As long ago as 10,000 B.C.E. there existed potters. Primordial pottery-making was apparently woman's domain, a mystery sacral in nature, potent, dangerous and taboo. In some cultures, woman, especially an aged woman, was regarded as a natural sorceress, containing in her genitals the same fire as was believed to inhere in the piece of wood that friction from another turned into flame. Before the smith or the alchemist, the potter had mastery of fire, could control with the heat of live embers the passage of matter from one state to another, could harden with the transmuting agency of flame the shapes given to the moist clay (Eliade, 79, 80). Round and hollow, made of the earth with which the great goddess was everywhere identified, the clay vessels of the earliest potters were representations and attributes of her as cosmic womb that contains, protects, gestates, nourishes, gives gifts and gives birth. Primordial fingers shaped "mother pots," urns with the birdlike faces and arched, watchful eyes of the deity; pitchers made in the shape of the female breast; jars covered with breasts or potbellied, like a pregnant woman, some with a circle in the center signifying the navel of the world (Neumann, 122ff).

Later, but still ancient, cultures imagined mythic divine potters, creator gods sometimes female and sometimes male, like the Egyptian god Khnum, fashioning material being out of clay, which was then infused by means of divine breath with animation and psychic existence just as the flame actualizes the vessel. While some divine potters shape the universal forms with their hands, others are depicted with the emblem of the potter's wheel. The seventeenth-century alchemist Michael Maier compares the wheel to the circle the sun makes in its rotation, "the shining clay moulded by the wheel and hand of the Most High and Almighty Potter" into earthly substance in which the golden rays of the sun are manifest (CW 12:470). The symbolism of the divine potter and the material pot remind us both of the "earthenware" aspect of our being, and its divine spark, and the psychological tension between them. So, for example, the prophet Isaiah: Shall the potter be regarded as the clay; that the thing made should say of its maker, "He did not make me"; or the thing formed say of him who formed it, "He has no understanding?" (Isaiah 29:16). Or the beleaguered Job: Thy hands fashioned and made me; and now thou dost turn about and destroy me. Remember that thou has made me of clay; and wilt thou turn me to dust again? (Job 10:8–9). The figurative potter of alchemy intuited a psychic function that can creatively bring together the opposing elements of the personality, what is delineated and what is fluid, and temper them in a kiln of interior process, the affective heat of which strengthens the matter into a vessel that fire can no longer crack. "Let the work of the potter, consisting of wet and dry, teach you," instructed Maier.

Even today, the potter's art seems magically elemental. Is it the human hands kneading the earth, remembering themselves being shaped by nature? Is it the interaction between earth, water, air and fire? Is it the sense that just as fiery "breath" makes us physically and spiritually alive, so there is something living about the fired pot? The primeval forms and symmetries of the cosmos are its inspiration, linking us to ancestrally revered, mana-laden forces and animal and vegetative magic. In turn, the vessels of the potter's art have ever contained, secreted and poured forth what is vital and sacred: sacrificial blood and ritual offerings, ornamental flowers, seeds for sowing, harvest grains, fruits, herbs and spices, food and feast, water for drinking and ablution.

Eliade, Mircea. *The Forge and the Crucible.* Chicago, 1978.
Neumann, Erich. *The Great Mother.* Princeton, NJ, 1972.

1. Photographed a century ago, a Native American potter of the Hopi pueblo displays her materials and wares, including finished pots and raw clay and wood for firing the formed vessels. In her tradition, the secrets of the art pass from mother to daughter.

2. Khnum, the ram-headed potter god of ancient Egypt, creates the body and Ka soul of a king on his potter's wheel. The goddess Hathor extends the ankh, the sign of life, toward the new being. Drawing of wall relief, Hall of Birth, Temple of Amen, Mut and Khonsu, Thebes, 18th dynasty (1539–1295 B.C.E.), Egypt.

King/Queen

Like his kingly predecessors, Menkaure, the pharaoh of Egypt, was considered the adopted son of the sungod Ra, whose divinity he incarnated at his coronation. On this same occasion, it was believed, the goddess Isis nursed Menkaure's *ka*, or divine life-force and procreative power; her lap was Menkaure's first throne (Wilkinson, 33). His royal prerogatives included marriage to his sister, Queen Khamerernebty. The crown placed on his head incorporated a feather from Maat, the goddess of cosmic order, signifying the king's responsibility for the establishment of like order in the kingdom.

Every culture has its version of king and queen. They are the "crowned heads" of a people, traditionally individuals exalted on account of having seemingly great or singular mana, superior personalities or being first in powers or skills essential to the welfare of the tribe. They reflect what is sovereign within the psyche of an individual or a society, the principles and beliefs that hold sway. That these principles are partly under the dominion of consciousness and partly the unconscious is reflected in the ambiguous nature of king or queen. They are human, yet approximated to the gods. They are likened to the divine luminaries, sun and moon, in the celestial sphere, and to the precious metals gold and silver embodying the solar and lunar substance in the earthly sphere. Majesty is elevated by the throne and by wearing a crown or a headdress, suggesting the rayed corona of the sun, or its glinting wings or all-seeing eye. The ruler possesses the orb and scepter, signifying primacy over the worldly realm, and is cloaked in the jeweled mantle, suggesting the glittering firmament (CW 14:349). The sovereign's adamantine castle and flourishing, symmetrical gardens are evocative of the mandala or the sacred precinct encompassing the inviolate center. Often, especially in ancient times, the king or queen assumed the quasi-priestly role of mediating between the mundane and supramundane dimensions.

Always, the king and queen were (and are) perceived as the magical source of the fruitfulness and prosperity of the land, the king in particular identified with vigor, sexual potency and order; the queen with the attributes of the mother-beloved, including feeling values and virtues that inspire a kingdom (or an individual) to greatness. That such powers will inevitably wane, that rulers and ruling principles will grow old, sicken and die, fostered mythic fantasies about the barrenness and renewal of the kingship. In many fairy tales the queen is dead, childless, kidnapped or replaced by a wicked queen, suggesting something gone awry in relation to the feminine or to nature. In the Grail legends of the Middle Ages, the wounded fisher-king of the Grail Castle must be redeemed before the land will once again be physically and spiritually viable. In ancient times, the sense that the king must die for the sake of regeneration was ritualized in the "year-king" killing of the old king by the new, mirroring the dramas of light and darkness at the solstice. Mythically, there is often a period of chaos during the transition. The old king goes into the underworld, dissolves back into the elemental, the source of renewal, temporarily eclipsing the cosmic order. Primal, instinctual energies are rampant, depicted as snakes overrunning the land, or as human beings reverting to lawlessness until the new ruler is established.

Alchemy adopted these motifs to convey an intuition about psychic renewal, how dominant psychic factors no longer furthering adaptation undergo the fatality of the "old king" in the forms of immersion, incineration and decomposition of the stuff out of which the new king emerges. Another image of the fatality and regeneration of the king was the copulation of King Sol and Queen Luna, intimating a union of conscious and unconscious, by which both would be irrevocably mixed and changed, ending the old order. Thus, the conjunction was portrayed as a deathly embrace that was also the "conception" of the philosopher's stone, the dawning of a new ordering, regulating center of the personality.

Behind our fascination, even today, with reigning monarchs and their ceremonial opulence there stirs a recognition that they preserve a lost link to something royal, something greater than the familiar sphere of the ego, within ourselves. The psychic fields around the figures of king and queen have ever activated tensions, longings and quests, where high and low are equally agents of resolution. For in the stories, it is sometimes a humble subject who has the common sense or closeness to instinct necessary to accomplish the task or offer the boon to the sovereign that can replenish the ailing realm. And sometimes it is the royal figure that does the heroic thing, makes the essential sacrifice or finds a way back from exile.

Wilkinson, Richard H. *Reading Egyptian Art.* London, 1992.

1

3

2

1. The Pharaoh Menkaure (2532–04 B.C.E.) and his queen take a ceremonial step into their realm with the serene demeanor of gods, yet her light touch upon his arm and waist is entirely human. Stone sculpture, Egypt.

2. Rama, a Hindu incarnation of God, lounges on his throne beside Queen Sita, while his half-brother Lakshman cools them with a peacock fan. The monkey-god Hanuman massages the feet of the king that by royal custom must never touch the ground (MM 12:1572). Painting on paper, India.

3. The alchemical marriage of king and queen condenses a psychological process that begins with an initial hostility of opposites (Sol and Luna) and ends in harmonious union (the wedded pair join hands), all directed by a mediating spirit (the dove). Wood engraving from the alchemical text *Rosarium philosophorum*, 1550, Germany.

War/Warrior

When the ancient Greek philosopher Heraclitus wrote that "war is the father of all and the king of all" he was using war as a metaphor for the universal clash of opposites that rules natural processes of change. On the cosmic battlefield there may be temporary stalemates when the opposing forces achieve stability, but should the dominance of one side over another permanently prevail, the world, in the philosopher's view, would come to an end.

War, in the literal sense, does bring about profound change, for good or ill, in the ethos of an individual or a nation. Psychologically, war evokes the radical tension of opposites, sometimes breaking out in open conflict, that can, if its fury is not annihilating, ultimately engender dynamic process. The radically contradictory energies war constellates are evoked mythologically by the marriage of Ares, the hated and feared god of war, to Aphrodite, the goddess of love. Their offspring Phobos (Fear) and Deimos (Panic) reflect the terrifying emotions in a warrior's psyche, which in the extremes of war can nullify the humanity of the adversary, leading to atrocities as ancient as Achilles dragging Hector behind his chariot or as modern as My Lai or Abu Ghraib. Yet war can foster a sense of brotherhood, loyalty and shared suffering unparalleled in peacetime. Many who have been through war experienced the most intense aliveness because of the incessant proximity of death. Others have been pulled, disastrously, into the maelstrom.

There is hardly a person who does not dream of war, the "confusion" or "discord" that is the meaning of the Germanic word *werra*, from which our English word "war" is derived. We dream of bloody battles between usually unknown armies, suggesting violent conflict between opposing tendencies within ourselves, often unconscious. In the dream we might be aligned with one side or the other, or with neither, and yet appear to be in the line of fire. Occasionally even those who have never been soldiers dream of being soldiers, of needing soldierly discipline, courage and endurance in order to get through an ordeal or complete a particularly difficult task. Sometimes, too, we live as though our psychic territory were under the occupation of hostile soldiers; our truest substance asserting itself rarely and covertly, relegated to the underground "resistance." At other times, armies of liberation arrive at the critical hour to free us from the tyranny of entrenched forces.

If we consciously pay attention to the conflict within ourselves without "interfering with irritating rationality," observed Jung, "the opposites, just because they are in conflict, will gradually draw together and what looked like death and destruction will settle down into a latent state of concord," in which new dominant values and attitudes are gestated. If, on the other hand, the furious warring of elements in the individual psyche is merely unconsciously projected on a suitable host, it will likely be "reflected in the unleashing of primeval blood-thirstiness and lust for murder on a collective scale" (CW 14:506–10).

1

3

2

2. Model of soldiers found in the tomb of Mesehty, governor of Assiut, painted wood, 11th dynasty, ca. 2000 B.C.E., Egypt.

1. An Australian soldier crouches into the blind uncertainty of a smoke screen during the Battle of El Alamein, Western Desert, North Africa, in World War II.

3. The goddess Durga shown with weapons emerging from her head as an expression of her fierceness. Bronze sculpture, ca. 2nd century B.C.E., India.

473

Prostitute

All of a sudden, in the good-natured child the woman stood revealed, a disturbing woman with all the impulsive madness of her sex, opening the gates of the unknown world of desire. Nana was still smiling, but with the deadly smile of a man-eater ...
Emile Zola, Nana

I am the honored one and the scorned one.
I am the whore and the holy one.
Nag Hammadi Library, The Thunder, Perfect Mind

Where we find the prostitute now, female or male, is in the streets, worldly streets and the otherworldly streets of the inner mind, beckoning, servicing desire, perhaps predatory, unprotected, soliciting shadowneeds that do not survive the light of day. The ordinary, "profane" prostitute is typically an outcast, punished throughout history by stoning, branding, imprisonment or death, while her clients usually remain blameless. She is a source of shame and a source of salvation; as "the whore with the heart of gold" she carries the taint of redeemable sinfulness, or, like Mary Magdalene, is saintly when she renounces her sexuality. By contrast, at least ideally, the sacred prostitute is a vital figure of religious cult and sacred initiation, who serves and incarnates an aspect of the great goddess of love—Ishtar, Aphrodite, Inanna, Cybele, Isis, Shakti. Ishtar was sometimes represented as a prostitute named the "all accepting." She might also be thought of as fickle, lustful and undignified by those isolated from her sacred mysteries, but as Esther Harding writes, " ... because she was a goddess she must act according to her nature; and her nature is such that where she loves there must she give herself. For like the moon she can never be possessed. She is ever virgin" (Harding, 161). Celebrated as ecstatic physicality while also remaining eternally inviolate, she is an ever-renewing internal source of grace. Spirit and matter, from the sublime to the wild, are united in her being as living soul.

Cultic sexual activity was likely an essential aspect of ancient religions that regarded the great goddess as a mysterious power of life that generated and regenerated cyclically. The sacred prostitutes of the ancient Near East performed rites of holy marriage with their king. Through their sexual intercourse the sacred marriage of the goddess and her male consort was re-enacted such that the land and life were made fertile and regenerated by the transfer of sacred feminine power to the sovereign. There were as well sacred prostitution rituals performed as sexual initiation for young girls. Apparently in ancient Babylon young women sat in the temple of Aphrodite and a man, a stranger, would throw a coin into the lap of one as an offering to the goddess in exchange for the privilege of deflowering the girl of his choice.

However sacred prostitution was enacted in those ancient times, there is no possibility of its existing in a literal sense in our contemporary world or our consciousness, unmixed with the forces of power and commerce. Still, it is the goddess, desirer and devourer, who hovers in the background of the prostitute as psychic factor and symbolic form. The prostitute is a shadowy, liminal figure; art and reality depict her standing under a streetlight, glimpsed in a window, worshiped in the holy temple. One meets her within oneself outside of domestic roles and morals. She functions as the vessel of most intimate intercourse with the depths of desire, mediates the charged, sometimes dangerous longings of soul as they come into the body in unfettered erotic electricity and attraction. The prostitute is often a sympathetic figure, young or used, shy or tawdry, evoking the vulnerability of body or psyche to being coerced, abducted or degraded. At the opposite pole, she represents the capacity for promiscuity and predation. The prostitute materializes destructively whenever we disregard our deepest values, passions and gifts in exchange for momentary satisfaction, money or power. We can, however, be called by her image within to a deeper territory of eros and desire, to the value of exploring what is outcast and shadowed in ourselves or what is yet to be known and to which we are irrevocably drawn. Here is desire's feast with soul in it.

Harding, M. Esther. *Woman's Mysteries.* NY, 1972.

1

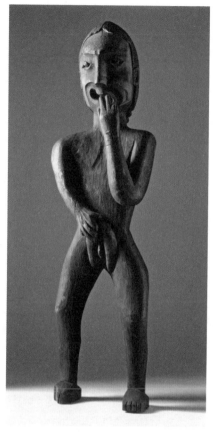

2

3

1. By the 20th century these prostitutes from Paris had become public women in a progressively fragmenting culture, and whoring was solely a social evil. *Prostitutes*, photograph, ca. 1900, Paris, France.

2. A Kwakwaka'wakw (Kwakiutl) figure fashioned for the purpose of ridiculing the family of a woman who had become a prostitute. With the increase of white settlement and the spread of syphilis among the native population, prostitution became rampant as a "profession" and associated with brutality, destruction of the gift circle, contamination and death. Wood, 19th century, British Columbia, Canada.

3. The woman at the window was a familiar motif associated with the goddess as prostitute. *Ishtar Kilili (She Who Peers Out)*, ivory panel, Phoenician, 9th–8th century B.C.E., Nimrud, Northern Iraq.

Beggar

... an old outcast, a beggar man,
leaning most painfully on a stick,
his poor cloak, all in tatters, looped about him.
Homer, *The Odyssey*, XVII

Like the weary Odysseus when he returns, disguised, from his wanderings, Goya's disheveled beggar is reduced to what he carries on his stooped back and, hat in hand depends on proffered coins. Bent into a question mark, his pitiable form elicits our musings: "Who are you, how did you come to such a pass, where are your friends and family?"

The beggar's staff was originally a white stick that designated persons forced to abandon their lands, prisoners of war and, like a white flag, those who had surrendered (Biedermann, 36). The figure of the beggar still implies the forced abandonment of vital resources, or a loss of access to the means of provision. Because they signify want, we have strong, often defensive reactions to beggars, identifying with or distancing ourselves from their straitened circumstances.

Mythically, gods and heroes come disguised as beggars, the thing of highest value hidden in the very low, simultaneously conspicuous and invisible. Li T'ieh-kuai, one of the Chinese Eight Immortals, assumes the form of a lame beggar to become a benevolent healer (MacCulloch, 8:120). Shiva as Supreme Beggar, his terrifying and transcendental form, signifies his breaking through time, his timeless immensity. Naked, skeletal, unfettered, the decapitated head of the creator Brahma stuck to one hand, a begging bowl in the other, he roams the world in expiation for beheading his father (Kramrisch, 286–7). Like Odysseus, the shattered Lear wears the mask of the beggar, tasting humility and testing the faithfulness of intimates. Holy beggars in India and mendicant saints in the West embody freedom from the ego, simplicity, chosen poverty and devout trust in divine compassion.

More destructively, we can beggar essential aspects of our psychic being, a kind of self-abandonment. What we disavow in our nature psyche may expose in the beggared figures of our dreams—vacant-faced derelicts, old women in rags, hungry waifs and friendless animals. Evoking the orphaned, rootless, marginal, unhomed and unmoored, the image of the beggar appears in the space between imagined self-sufficiency and our experience of the untoward things that set us low.

Biedermann, Hans. *Dictionary of Symbolism.* NY, 1994.

Kramrisch, Stella. *The Presence of Siva.* Princeton, NJ, 1981.

MacCulloch, J. A. *The Mythology of All Races.* Boston, 1932.

1. *Shiva, the Supreme Beggar (Bhiksatanamurti),* copper sculpture, 16th century, Nepal.

2. *Beggar with a Staff in His Left Hand,* by Francisco Goya, drawing, 1812–20, Spain.

Cripple

Bruegel painted his leprous cripples in 1568 as the outcasts and beggars of a Renaissance society that perceived them as grotesque. An old English word, *creopan,* meaning "to creep," is the origin of our word cripple. It suggests a perception of the cripple as one who is forced, by condition and society, to move differently in the world, and at Bruegel's time, perhaps furtively. Such perceptions collide with the reality of figures like the American President Franklin Roosevelt, who was crippled by polio. Nonetheless, cripple's etymological cousin implies a projection long hooked on the cripple as one who is physically or psychically "bent," impeding the mobility of potential.

Symbolically, cripple both deviates from and often purposefully compensates one-sided collective notions of wholeness. Crippled beggars remain a part of every culture, and even in contemporary times indigent infants and children are "modified" by crippling to make them more profitable as beggars. Yet, because of their exposure to the energies of the infernal, cripples are also depicted as mana-laden for creative and destructive ends. The "swollen foot" of mythic smiths and artisans, like Hephaistus, the Cabiri and Mani, represents the possession of a magical phallic power from psyche's chthonic depths (CW 5:183). Literature depicts the cripple both as irrevocably wounded and also as a wounded healer. While the superficial deformities of Tiny Tim and Quasimodo hide luminous natures, the missing leg of Melville's Captain Ahab "reaped" by the White Whale reflects a crippling attitude of hatred that sinks the whole ship. For many, "cripple" inevitably activates the ego's fear of constraint, for the reality of crippling challenges the illusion that anything is possible. Psyche, however, portrays the cripple in a differentiated way. Its images own the suffering implied and the implications of a physical or psychical disabling. But psyche also presents the notion that crippling limitation in one sphere can drive energy into another, awakening unknown sources of mobility.

2

1. Like many divine smiths, Hephaistus was often portrayed as a cripple. Cast out of Mt. Olympus, he later returned in triumph, his beautiful metalworks captivating even the high gods who once exiled him for his ugliness. Black-figured hydria from Caere, Ionic-Greek, ca. 525 B.C.E.

2. This painting of five men crippled by leprosy depicts them as outcasts of society. By Pieter Bruegel the Elder, 1568, the Netherlands.

Thief/Robber

Thieves and robbers are outlaws and despoilers, reminding us of the light-handedness, or much cruder violence, by which the material and spiritual valuables of our being can get snatched away. They embody those autonomous, disruptive forces that "break and enter" when we imagine our defenses secure. Time, Disease, Death and Eros have been depicted as thieves. So seriously do we regard the concrete act of stealing that those who do it have at times been punished by having their hands cut off, or by being disgracefully executed. Jesus was said to have been crucified between two thieves, emphasizing his supposed arrogation of kingly status. The pickpocket and cat burglar, even more so masked gunmen, pirates, bandits and highwaymen, violate us and violate our illusions of being "in full possession."

Yet, perhaps because of the inherently ambiguous nature of ownership, symbolism treats the thief or robber with relativity. The sacred thief is part of countless myths of transgression and blessing where a culture hero, god, animal or inspired mortal moves between divine and human dimensions, subverts authority and redistributes the hoarded wealth. Lord Ganesha's vehicle, the cunning rat, a master thief, shows us how to slip through the locks of the granary to get to the life-giving substance. The Scandinavian dwarf Loki obsessively steals from the gods, upending divine hierarchy and reconfiguring what appears to be immutable (Russ, 77ff). Hermes, the Greek trickster, guileful and deceptive, is patron of thieves, god of both luck and loss (Otto, 109). In morally neutral divine play, he transmutes thievery as power and violence into thievery as hermetic inventiveness (Kerényi, 72). Like the fire-boring that "wrested a secret from nature," the primordial appropriation of creativity is often depicted as an "unlawful intervention" that robbed the gods of something precious—the golden apples of the Hesperides, the golden bough of Diana's sacred grove, the herb of immortality, the spark of divine fire that Promethean theft planted in the soul of the individual (CW 5:250). Theft has a part in psychic processes of division and synthesis. Eve's mythic theft from the forbidden Tree of Knowledge breaks up paradisal unconsciousness, making us knowing participants in the fruitful and painful tension of opposites. Krishna, the mischievous, butter-stealing divine child of Hindu religion, is also the ravishing lover and supreme being within, stealing his devotees' hearts, and leaving them defenseless against spiritual union (Hawley, 9–10). In many fairy tales, theft is the *only* means of getting the "treasure hard to obtain," the goal of the initiatory quest or opus of transformation. For instance, a hungry protagonist's theft of a golden pear from the royal garden brings the redeeming prince or princess into the action, guided by the signal loss. Often the ultimate treasure is guarded by the like of witch, magician, dragon or serpent, with whose perilous energies the heroic thief is thrown into contention. Sometimes the task is beyond the capacity of the vulnerable seeker and requires help from the suprarational sphere embodied by the angel, wise old man or woman and magical animal.

To be sure, the motif of stealing by no means always comes down on the side of psychic gain: "The thief whom the police do not catch has, nonetheless, robbed himself, and the murderer is his own executioner," observed Jung (CW 14:202). Even worthy aspects of self requiring attention, if not paid it, will resort to stealing psychic libido, a loss of soul felt in states of melancholy, distractedness and inanition. In an alchemical text, a wicked thief "armed with the malignity of arsenic" represents more destructive forms of self-robbery, the ways we depreciate and betray the mysteries of the psyche, its winged possibilities and spirit of inner truth, which, portrayed as a shy and volatile youth, runs away, shuddering (ibid., 194–7).

Hawley, John Stratton. "The Thief in Krishna." *Parabola (9/3, 1984).*

Kerényi, Karl. *Hermes, Guide of Souls.* Putnam, CT, 2003.

Otto, Walter F. *The Homeric Gods: The Spiritual Significance of Greek Religion.* NY, 1978.

Russ, Lawrence. "The Cosmic Bee." *Parabola (9/2, 1984).*

1

2

1. Two accomplices pick the pockets of a naïve youth while an old gypsy woman tells his fortune. *The Fortune Teller*, by Georges de la Tour, oil painting, ca. 1625, France.

2. Robbers on the run, their ski masks enhancing the effect of an anonymous, thieving force.

Gossip

Two valets gossip, one whispering behind a cupped ear into that of his ready listener, who savors every tidbit. His eyebrows arch in delight, his smile expresses smug satisfaction at the news. In his painting, Daumier captures the power of gossip to bind its participants in a kind of feigned intimacy whose matter will no doubt soon leak abroad.

For all its pejorative connotations as malicious rumormongering, gossip is actually derived from the Old English *godsibb,* meaning god-relative or godparent, which can include friends and acquaintances (Barnhart, 325). Gossiping was another name for a christening feast, which primarily female friends and relatives of the mother attended in order to pray for blessings for the baby. Some of the same "gossips" would have also assisted at the childbirth. Their mythic counterparts are the wise women, fairies and witches of fairy tales who gather at the birth of a royal child. Each confers a blessing on the newborn, except for one, who curses the child instead. Evoking psyche's tendency to bring itself into balance by introducing what has been left out of the whole, the figure is usually the one excluded from the invitation to the gathering. Paradoxi-

cally, her unwanted presence, and her curse, imposes a trial on hero or heroine through which their unique destiny is fulfilled to the enrichment of the entire realm.

It is perhaps the age-old fear of the feminine and its association with fate, moon and the cooking up of things that surfaces in the projection on women as inherent gossips and on gossip as inherently bad. Gossip as rumor, especially of a sensational kind, feeds on envy and innuendo to defame character and ruin lives. But gossiping as idle chatter and report, the "buzz," is also the way news and advice of all sorts is exchanged among friends and colleagues. Journalism and history can be said to depend, in part, on the gossip of a time. Certainly, gossiping isn't the exclusive domain of women; the locker room, men's clubs and predominantly male political and corporate bodies are hotbeds of gossip—and they have given blessing and curse to the fates of many.

Barnhart, Robert K. Ed. *The Barnhart Concise Dictionary of Etymology.* NY, 1995.

AT·THE CHILDBED

2

1. A scene from a broadsheet depicts friends of the new mother, the "gossips," who have gathered for the birth of a child. *Tittle-Tattle; Or, the Several Branches of Gossiping*, detail, original plate, ca. 1560, England.

2. The two valets from Molière's play *Scapino, or the Trickster* share a delicious bit of gossip. *Crispin and Scapin*, by Honoré Daumier, oil painting, ca. 1864, France.

Orphan

The image of the orphan carries simultaneously both the discarded and the sacred. It is embedded in themes of absence, abandonment, rejection and exposure. Yet primal loss and the inherent vulnerability of the orphan exist alongside the potential for self-containment and self-sufficiency. The ancient Egyptian tomb figurine portrays a child sitting alone, naked, thin arms and knees pulled against the childish body, everything contracted in grief. It conveys one who is "bereft," the meaning of orphan (from the Greek *orphanos*), and anyone who has suffered the loss of his primary foundation or support, whether it is parents, homeland, religious identity or sense of worth, can recognize the abject loneliness depicted by the sculpted form. The image of the orphan, even the word, immediately elicits our compassion because of its linking with the young and small—a human child, a baby animal—left to the mercy and hardships of the world. Sometimes the orphan's history is one of miraculous beginning and intervention or adoption by deities or otherworldly spirits. To be orphaned is to be separated from one's origin, and so the orphan also portrays a psychological reality, how something within evolves toward independence, greater self-realization or wholeness: "It is only separation, detachment, agonizing confrontation through opposition that brings consciousness and insight," observed Jung (CW 9.1:286ff).

The orphan has held a special place in every culture. Moses is pulled from the river in a reed basket and adopted by the Pharaoh, Romulus and Remus are nursed by a she-wolf, Oliver Twist is born in a workhouse; Huckleberry Finn, Cinderella, Harry Potter, Bambi and Wilbur the pig are all famous and beloved orphans. Many creation myths involve an orphan who represents the initial emergence of consciousness from unconscious, and is faced with terrors that threaten to engulf and dissolve its tenuous infancy. Adam and Eve, like the ego, are orphaned in a feeling sense when having eaten the apple of "knowing" they are expelled from the paradisal garden of blissful unawareness. The tender age of the mythic orphan speaks, on the one hand, of littleness and helplessness but on the other hand of precociousness. He or she is very often a culture or light bearer, in possession of special gifts or capacities, persecuted by shadowy forces and difficult circumstances, and often aided by nature—wild animals, trees or plants, the sun, moon or stars, a fairy godmother, witch, magician or sorcerer. The childlike openness of the orphan is able to embrace unorthodox agencies of help, and while the orphan is naïve, he or she may also exceed the prevailing consciousness or wisdom. We can defensively isolate from the world, or the self, repudiating possibilities of integration. Quite different from this is the orphan as the authentic goal of individuation. Alchemy called its philosopher's stone "orphan," denoting the uniqueness of the individual self and also that its source is mysterious, an amalgamation of conscious and unconscious factors (CW 14:13). Orphan describes the "smaller than small, greater than great," ordinary-extraordinary quality of the self. However, to become singularly who one is may also mean a lonely going beyond the ruling spirit of a time or place. Thus the "achieved orphan" may be experienced both as a "solitaire," and as a solitary.

An Egyptian figurine representing mourning, found in an ancient tomb. Its posture captures both the youth and the aloneness of the orphan.

Stranger

Stranger. Etranger. While the word itself suggests uncertainty, the image of stranger evokes a visceral reaction. As the stranger appears in the doorway in Signorelli's painting we are called to ask, "Who enters? Friend or foe?" The mysterious other, this foreigner appears and time stands still. We are left not knowing whether to move toward or away from this "alien" being.

Stranger derives from the old French *estranger*, which means "foreigner" or "alien." The Latin is *hostis*, which means both "guest" and "host" and is the root of the word "hospitality." Culturally and religiously there developed over time a direct connection between these two concepts in, for example, the opening of hostels and hospitals, through the encouragement of Christ's words, "I was a stranger and you took me in" (Matt. 25:35).

In primitive cultures the stranger was seen as an enemy, a threat to the cohesion of the group or clan. Borders of territories were fiercely protected, and the stranger who entered was either captured or killed so as not to contaminate the group with his foreign spirit or magic. In Hebrew the word *sar* translates as stranger and is also the root of the word for "border." As cultures developed more cohesion, however, the role of the stranger changed from enemy to emissary. After ritual purification, he was allowed into the group as educator or as bringer of new energy.

The image of stranger as angel or God in disguise arises in the Old Testament. Abraham welcomes and feeds the strangers who are bringing prophetic information to the tribe (Genesis 18:1–16). Lot welcomes and defends the strangers from the angry crowd (Genesis 19:1–11). God in hiding also appears in the *Iliad* and *The Odyssey*. "For gods may wear the guise of strangers come from far-off lands; they take on many forms and roam about the cities; they would see if men live justly or outrageously" (Homer, 362). Janus-like, the stranger is the bearer of the new as well as the destroyer of the old. Thus he is to be both appeased and feared. In Ovid's *Metamorphoses*, Philemon and Baucis offer hospitality to Jupiter and Mercury disguised as strangers, and are thus saved from destruction.

In dreams, the stranger makes his appearance as a shadowy figure, an "unknown other" crossing the boundaries from the unconscious to the conscious. He appears as the bringer of change, which can be both fascinating and frightening, that which Rudolph Otto says is at the essence of the experience of "the holy." Jung described the unconscious as "the Unknown as it immediately affects us" and developed the technique of active imagination to deal with these alien images from our dreams (CW 8:p 68). In integrating these unknown parts we work toward wholeness, a way of going home to ourselves.

Psychologically, a stranger is the perfect screen for catching the projections of unknown parts of ourselves. When these strange parts of ourselves are left in the world as projections we are split apart, and this can be the making of prejudices and wars of all sorts. However, when we integrate these foreign parts, we are then more able to respect difference and otherness outside of ourselves. Then, as Francis Bacon said, "If a man be gracious and courteous to strangers, it shows he is a citizen of the world, and that his heart is no island cut off from other lands, but a continent that joins to them" (Bacon, 98).

Bacon, Francis and John Pitcher. *The Essays.* London and NY, 1985.

Homer. *The Odyssey of Homer.* Berkeley, CA, 1990.

1. The stranger standing in the portal stirs our imagination and urges us to ask, "Who is this and what is his intent?" As angel or god in disguise, he brings new energy for change, thus breaking through the boundaries of the old order. *The Birth of St. John the Baptist,* detail, by Luca Signorelli (1441–1523), oil on panel, Italy.

2. In Camus' *The Stranger* modern man's alienation is portrayed in Meursault's refusal to conform to society's rules. Photograph by Betsy Imershein, 1993.

3. In this haunting image of a stranger on a lonely road the Israeli-born artist Michal Rovner uses herself as a model on the military access road from Israel to Lebanon. *Border #8,* paint on canvas, 1997–8.

1

2

3

Ax

Ax links us to the awe-inspiring primordial experience of meteorite, stone and ore, of celestial matter that cleaved the earth and gave us "mystical solidarity" with heaven (Eliade, 19–20). Forceful, sharp and sudden, axes are emblematic of sky deities and their thunderbolts, like the Neolithic ax head that may have represented the Germanic sky and war god Tyr.

One of the oldest implements of humankind, the ax is also one of the few that functions as both tool and weapon. Aligned with the strong arm of pioneer and woodsman, axes have cleared wilderness forests for civilization. Evoking the same "force of lightning" that can split a tree, the ax was the chosen weapon of Bronze Age warriors in Eastern Europe, the formidable hatchet of Native Americans and the weapon wielded by the race of dwarves in J. R. R. Tolkien's *The Lord of the Rings*. But because the cleaving of the ax brings storm god and earth goddess into sacred union, the double ax of ancient Crete was linked not only with the thunderer Zeus, but also with the cult of the Great Mother. Numbers of such axes were deposited in her clefts and caves (Eliade, 21).

Not only does ax carry the force of nature, however, but the force of reason as well. Set on a haft, an ax resembles a human head. Its anthropomorphic shape and capacity to split with precision has made it an analogue of conscious judgment. As Pseudo-Dionysius wrote, "The battle-ax denotes the dividing of things unlike, and the sharp and energetic and drastic operation of the discriminating power." Such is embodied in the ruler's ax from Zaire, which portrays the conjunction of masculine and feminine potency in royal prohibitions and authority. The blade protrudes from the mouth, suggesting that it is the ruler's function to distinguish and pronounce right from wrong. In Tibet, the ax signifies the severing of all negative tendencies from the mind, and in the Roman Republic, the preeminent symbol of legitimate authority was the fasces, a bundle of rods surrounding an ax.

Perhaps it is the conflation of ax as human head and divine storm that confers its symbolic shadow. The ax is implicated in dismemberment and decapitation, in heinous crime and gothic tale. Hooded executioners and the monstrous guillotine have "axed" the offender. The notorious Lizzie Borden allegedly "took an ax and gave her mother forty whacks." The ax is the instrument of berserk rampage in countless stories from the fairy tale "Bluebeard" to modern crime novels. It is the "hatchet man" who kills for pay. The ax as fasces became the symbol of Benito Mussolini's National Fascist Party in the early twentieth century, perverting the ax's meaning as lawful republican government to that of the absolute power of right-wing despotism. Such realities serve to remind us that if the ax is wielded deftly, it is a superb tool of striking force—but the purpose of its cleaving is not always of like balance.

Eliade, Mircea. *The Forge and the Crucible.* Chicago, 1978.
Roy, Christopher D. *Kilengi.* Hanover, Germany, 1997.

1. A stone ax head from Neolithic Finland may be the image of a sky god and his lightning power.

2. A ruler's ax from southeastern Zaire, made of wood and iron. The female figure on the haft holds her breasts, which here signify the royal prohibitions of which the women in the chief's family are the ultimate guardians (Roy, 352).

3. In an ancient rock carving, an expressive figure conveys masculine power and readiness to fight, his ax raised and his phallus erect. Bronze Age (1800–500 B.C.E.), Finntorp, Sweden.

2

1

3

Knife / Dagger

That the bronze knife from ancient China is fashioned as a human hand gripping the hilt above the sharp blade serves to enhance the knife's character as emblem not only of human survival but also the sharp edge of human consciousness that carved out the structures of its civilizations. Stone Age hunters used the earliest versions of the knife to kill and skin animals of prey and render the skins into clothing and shelter. Their knives slashed through twisting roots and thick, impenetrable vines to open pathways, and eventually whittled at raw materials until they revealed their emergent forms. An essential implement in the fields of war, exploration and adventure, in the workshop, kitchen, art studio and operating room, the knife engages the killing instinct but also the energies of healing, creativity and cooking magic with intimacy and nuance.

Knife is no blunt instrument but embodies the efficacy and violence of a cutting edge. Mounted on a staff, the knife becomes a spear; extended in length, a sword whose smaller version is the dagger, especially designed for stabbing (*Enc. Brit.* 28:721–2; 3:846). Both knives and daggers are distinguished as weapons of stealth and proximity, able to be concealed on one's person. Used at close range where victim and attacker are no more than an arm's length apart, the knife evokes images of deadly hand-to-hand combat as well as bloody murders and mutilations, gang wars and decapitations, sudden cutting violence and betrayal from which derive the metaphorical "stabbing in the back" or "shooting daggers."

Its capacity for swift, precision cutting has given the knife a conspicuous place in the rituals and iconography of cultures as varied as the Hebrew, Celtic, Aztec and Hindu, where, as the implement for slaying sacrificial victims over sacred vessels, it released the libido of fertilization and renewal signified by the offertory blood. Traditional instrument of Abraham's ritual circumcision, the knife becomes the instrument of a symbolic sacrifice that since ancient times implies for the Jewish male the voluntary cutting away of an aspect of himself to join a larger, sacred covenant (Matthews, 112). In Tibetan Buddhism, the *phurba*, or magical ritual dagger, embodies the compassionate action of the wrathful deity Vajrakilaya. The *phurba*'s triple blade signifies the spiritual tools that sever the roots of ignorance, desire and hatred, which poison human existence (Beer, 246–7).

Knife continues both to serve and symbolically depict the human intellect that cuts through the superfluous and entangling, analytically separates and differentiates but is also capable of overbearing and soulless dissection. The knife is implicated in the perverse intimacy of compulsive self-mutilation and the seeking of aliveness through pain. Psychologically it gets embodied in the surprise attacks of unconscious dynamisms of affect and aggression, personified in the "breaking and entering" assailants that worry our dreams, or mythic figures like the Egyptian Set, whose attribute is the flint knife. Knife can represent an instrument of meaningless destruction but also a superb tool of deconstruction and adaptation. In T. S. Eliot's words, the mythic knife as the surgeon's scalpel, "questions the distempered part," a deft wounding that precedes synthesis.

Beer, Robert. *The Encyclopedia of Tibetan Symbols and Motifs*. Boston, 1999.

Matthews, Boris. *The Herder Dictionary of Symbols*. Wilmette, IL, 1993.

1. Knife as deadly weapon. Tin-plated bronze blade, Dian culture, ca. 2nd–1st century B.C.E., China.

2. The simplicity of a bread knife: knife in the service of kitchen, cooking and nourishment. Detail, oil painting by Gerard Seghers, Flemish, 17th century.

Sword

Viking warriors gave names to their ornately hilted and treasured swords—Battle-Snake, Sea King's Fire, Ice of Battle, Dog of the Helmet, Leg-Biter. Ancient Danes sometimes cast a sword into a peat bog at the demise of its owner, so identified was the personality of the swordsman with that of his sword and so much did the sword have a life of its own that it seemed advisable to put it out of reach (ARAS, 4Fg.027). Likewise, in Celtic Britain's great myth of kingship, the sword Excalibur, embedded in red marble, yields itself only to Arthur and is returned at his end to the magical Lady of the Lake.

Swordplay in the hands of a master has been compared to ice, lightning flashes, fire, gold and the sharpening of the "psychic power of seeing in order to act immediately in accordance with what it sees" (Suzuki, 148). The sword, a pointed, slender, elongated dagger of glinting metal, evokes something drastic and ensouled. Not a primitive weapon like the club or ax, the sword presupposes metallurgical refinement, skilled craftsmen to make it and elite training in order to practice its deadly art (ARAS, 4Fg.027). In Japan, which often painstakingly produced swords by laminating thin layers of metal, the swordsmith conducted his craft with religious soberness, inviting guardian gods into his workshop after roping it off to exclude evil spirits. Donning ceremonial robes and performing ablutions, he achieved a state of perfect concentration reflected in the design. The origin of the sword was the Bronze Age discovery that steadily sharpening a dagger produces a fatal point, and subsequently it served as a warrior's main weapon until modern firearms reduced it to the bayonet. But as the light-saber of *Star Wars'* Luke Skywalker attests, the phallic sword still burns with life.

Sword is emblematic of deities of war like Ares, Arjuna, Durga, warrior kings and heroes, nineteenth-century gentlemen-soldiers, as well as the Chinese sage and Zen Buddhist samurai. There is no contradiction in this because the sword's essence is to carve, thrust, divide, whether as the deathblow that slays an opponent, a decisive separation from worldly attachment or the separating out of consciousness from psyche's deep, unconscious recesses.

Alchemy portrayed the sword as the logos-cutting instrument of discrimination, dividing the primal egg into four elements—a cosmogonic act—so that matter can be delineated and identified, lending structure to its otherwise undifferentiated conditions. As such, the sword is associated with sacrifice in the service of clarity, with naming and categorizing, will and choice and the "dismembering of *participation mystique*" (Edinger, 189ff). The other side of this two-edged sword is the sowing of discord, schism, needless self-dissection and defensive splitting (ibid.).

Though the purpose of the sword is to cut, however, its effectiveness depends on union. Beyond technical brilliance, the best swordsman is the one who attains the capacity to engage the subtleties of the animating spirit of the sword, so that subject and object, mind and body are one, single-minded, resolute. There is an egoless letting go that transcends the attachment to a particular outcome, even the attachment to life or death.

Edinger, Edward F. *Anatomy of the Psyche.* La Salle, IL, 1985.

Suzuki, Daisetz Teitaro. *Zen and Japanese Culture.* Princeton, NJ, 1970.

1. Beyond its role as a supernatural-seeming weapon of war, the sword embodied justice and authority. Viking sword, iron, 800–1100.

2. The face of the Samurai warrior reflects the character of his elegant sword, an instrument of decisive action fearless of death. Fan print, detail, by Katsukawa Shunsho, 18th century, Japan.

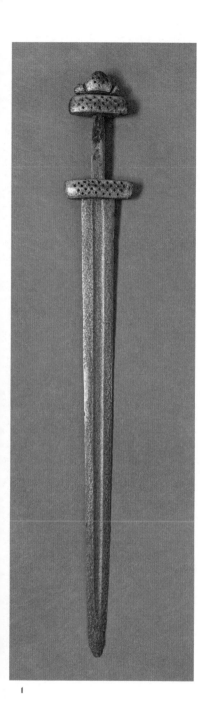

Spear

Engraved in rock more than 2,000 years ago, a small human-looking figure aims an immense spear. It is a simple image, but symbolically it has a forceful thrust. The dimensions of the weapon's blade and shaft dramatically elongate the figure's reach and accord him a capacity for survival that transcends his natural stature. Such a spear might dispatch a giant.

One of the earliest weapons of war and the hunt, the spear began in prehistory as a simple stick with a sharpened point or fitted with a stone blade. While the sword is often seen as divisive, cutting in two, the spear carries the sense of penetrating the vitals of something, piercing its essential core. Associated with a host of mythic figures like the Greek goddess Athena and Irish warrior Cuchulainn, the spear signifies courage, ferocity, martial nature or prowess in the hunt, but is also emblematic of the wisdom and creativity of the culture bearer. The Norse god Odin raged in battle with his spear "Gungnir." But in an act of divine self-sacrifice, Odin himself was speared and hung on the World Tree, Yggdrasil, for nine days: "I was stuck with a spear / And given to Odin / Myself given to myself." Pierced to the depths of his own substance, he acquired knowledge of the sacred runes, whose magical and poetic riches he offered to humankind (Davidson, 51, 143–4).

Evoking the erect phallus and the divine sun ray, the spear has embodied, in stories of cosmic creation, the energy that penetrates original wholeness in order that it can be given differentiated form. One such myth is that of Izanagi and Izanami, the brother-sister primordial opposites of Japanese myth. They stand on the Floating Bridge of Heaven with a jeweled spear, dipping its point into formless brine. Drops from the spear coagulate into the first island, to which the pair descends in order to continue their work of creation.

The spear can also represent the healing means by which things that are apart can be brought back into relationship. In religious lore, the spear has been associated with spiritual "woundings" through which divine spirit can enter and unite with the human soul, or consciousness can be linked once again to its transpersonal source. The ecstatic testimony of Saint Teresa of Avila, for example, describes a seraphic angel, whose golden spear pierces her heart, inflaming her with the love of God (ARAS, 1:220).

Psychologically, the spear has to do with our penetration of matter and of being penetrated by it. We can be pierced by the experience of an outer event, the pointed remark of another person or the significance of an interior content. We unconsciously project ourselves into others in idealizing or destructive ways. Consciousness has its spearhead in sharpened awareness and penetrating insight and can itself be on the receiving end of the unconscious psyche's projectiles. In either case, the symbolic spear can often breach formidable defenses or plunge to seemingly impenetrable depths.

Davidson, Ellis H. R. *Gods and Myths of Northern Europe.* Baltimore, MD, 1964.

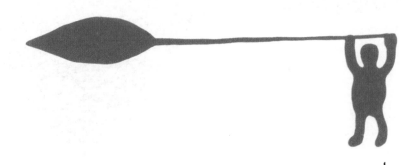

1. This image is believed to represent an ancient
spear-god. Drawing of a rock engraving, Bronze Age
(1800–500 B.C.E.), Östergötland, Sweden.

2. In this alabaster relief, the Assyrian king spears a
rearing lion during a hunt. The spear was traditionally a
sign of royalty and divine sun ray. *Ashurbanipal
Dispatching a Lion*, detail, 7th century B.C.E.

3. The divine primal couple of Japanese myth; their
jeweled spear initiated the creation of the Japanese
islands. *Izanagi and Izanami*, by Kobayashi Eitaku,
hanging scroll, ca. 1885, Japan.

Bow and Arrow

"Who shoots, and what is the mark?" asks a Japanese treatise on archery. Although an extension of the eye's vision, the arm's action, and the psyche's focus and desire, the bow and arrow is no longer the weapon of choice in either love or war. But released from its bow, like lightning leaping to its mark, the arrow that flies through the air and magically finds its target will remind us of the far-reaching and penetrating power of humankind's mental, physical and spiritual focus. The bow and arrow, with its beautiful and intelligent design, is a combination of feminine (bow) and phallic (arrow) shapes, which together symbolize penetration by light, love, death, perception and insight, a fundamental dynamic of psychological individuation.

As in Zen, where, egoless, archer and target become one, bow and arrow is associated with subtle and unseen powers that transcend space and time, hitting the mark without consciousness of self or goal. In ancient Oriental cultures shamans and mediums used the twanging of a bow to summon deities whose powers they wished to invoke, and a flight of arrows to exorcise evil spirits. Divination by means of arrows is cross-cultural, found in Arabia, Japan, ancient Greece and Native American cultures. In the West, the Greek understanding of "sin" referred to "missing the mark" in archery, and we still speak of "hitting the bull's-eye" in reference to getting something exactly right.

The bow and arrow is an attribute of the huntress Artemis, Mistress of Wild Things, whose arrows bring sudden death, and whose hounds can unerringly "sniff out" their unseen prey. Artemis moves between the boundaries of civilization and wilderness, and the bow and arrow as symbol bring together these aspects of the psyche. Artemis' twin, Apollo, god of solar light and prophecy, whose arrows drive away evil spirits but also bring devastating plagues, originally appropriated his power and knowledge by killing the deadly Python with a silver bow and golden arrows. The ascension of consciousness stands upon deep and unconscious sources of knowing. The bow and arrow represents and transcends humankind's duality: the unalterable consequences of aggression and death, opposed by the inner strength and unity deriving from correct use and development of the "killer instinct."

The attributes given to the constellation and ninth astrological sign Sagittarius, meaning "archer" in Latin, unite the animal and divine in human nature. Represented as a centaur, with the upper body of a man and the lower of a horse, the Sagittarian archer signifies philosophy, intuition, higher learning and wisdom. The progression of Sagittarius to the eighth constellation Scorpio, the underworld creature of death and transformation mysteries, symbolizes the evolution of aggression and desire into wisdom.

The art of archery is universally the weapon of royalty and manifests the virtues of a king. It requires concentration, poise, energy and accuracy. The phallic imagery of increasing and holding tension, taking aim, release and relaxation, which all combine to propel the arrow forward, is behind the use of bow and arrow as a test of manhood, but of a specific sort where fate and destiny are to be revealed. Only the young Buddha could draw the great bow of his ancestors, a theme echoed in the Homeric motif of Odysseus' bow, which no one else could draw, and whose arrows killed his enemies although Odysseus was by then an old man. The power of the bow and arrow derive not from brute strength, but rather from focused attention and spiritual maturity, where "less is more." The arrow and the archer are one, thus the arrows of the gods never miss, and only the warrior with a pure heart will immediately hit the bull's-eye.

Presumably the bow and arrow originally solved the ancient and pressing problem of killing game that couldn't be outrun. But throughout all cultures, from Paleolithic to modern, it represents an ascension symbol, the transformation of hunting magic by the sublimation of desire into penetration of the heart of the Self. In the same vein, the arrows of ecstatic love, erotic (Eros, Hindi Kaman, Sitar, Astarte) and divine (Buddha, the Lord) are imaged as piercing the human heart. Wounded by love, we also bow to passions that penetrate ego defenses, subject to the "slings and arrows of outrageous fortune" that create our path and reveal our destiny, thus unifying the personality. There is continuity between subject and object and an unbroken path toward a center mark inherent in the image of archery. The bow and arrow symbolize a dynamic tension of the individuation process as it outruns convention and the ego's boundaries to seek its mark.

1

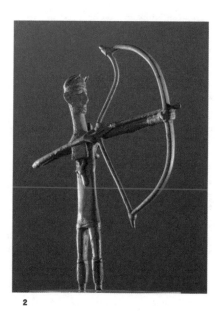

2

3

1. The goddess Artemis takes aim. Terra-cotta mixing bowl, detail, Athenian, 5th century B.C.E., Campania, Italy.

2. Statuette of an archer, bronze, 7th–5th century B.C.E., Sardinia, Italy.

3. Cave painting of bowmen and deer. Serigraphic transcription, 10,000–9,000 B.C.E., Los Caballos Cave, Fuentes de Leon, Spain.

Gun

The Pop artist Roy Lichtenstein (1923–97) forces us at gunpoint to consider what his painting is aiming at. After all, the gun plays an ambivalent role in the history of human survival and human carnage; hunting for food can be set alongside the extinction of entire animal species, the protection of home and hearth can be weighed against our staggering murder rates. From the ancient blunderbuss to the Remington rifle that helped to "win the West," from the lady's pearl-handled pistol that fits snugly into hand and handbag to the well-engineered AK-47, guns have emerged as astonishingly effective instruments and artfully crafted weapons of deadly power. Owing to a technical evolution that has ironically outpaced control of our impulse to fire it, the modern pistol has leapt far ahead of the projectile stone-throwers and catapults that were its archaic ancestors, aptly illustrated by "Lady Gunilda," the medieval stone-throwing engine from which "gun" is thought to derive its name (Partridge, 271). The power of the gun to easily terminate the conscious existence of another human being has placed gun ownership in the crosshairs of a debate over legislated gun control versus the psychological mastery of violence advocated by such ironic victims of fatal shootings as Mohandas Gandhi and Martin Luther King, Jr.

Like other weapons, the gun packs its own eros, embodied by the legendary gunslingers that stalk their victims across the old American West. Its automatic conferral of phallic one-upmanship in standoffs and its seemingly surefire self-protection make a gun's brass cartridges and intricate firing mechanisms especially seductive to men. Even a small boy understands what a gun does to its target long before he understands what death is. The pistol's fundamental maleness seems tacitly understood despite our campaign to shatter cultural constructs of gender, perhaps due to the widespread tradition of assigning hunting and fighting roles to males. Yet Annie Oakley (1860–1926) was a marks-woman par excellence, clipping the edge of a playing card or a dime tossed into the air, or even a cigarette held in her husband's lips 30 paces away (*Compt.*). The gun's thunderous discharge made it the climax at folk festivals originally performed to expel demons (Frazer, 568ff), the purpose behind China's invention of fireworks out of black powder (a concoction of saltpeter, sulfur and charcoal that became known as gunpowder after it was perfected by Arabs and Europeans). After this, a handful of Spanish conquistadors on horseback armed only with cumbersome harquebuses could overwhelm the Incas, perhaps due more to shock effect than bullets (Diamond, 76).

The megabusiness of global gunrunning, the pistol's explosive potency and its easy slippage into the hands of intruders and gangsters explain how the gun evolved its modern psychological mystique, as our tense modern idioms bear witness: We live "under the gun," we go "gunning" for our goals and figuratively "hold a gun" to someone's head. In both dreams and fantasies, the gun concentrates our fear of an unknown self or channels the aggression of violent complexes that threaten to annihilate our defenses, while bolstering the ego's capacity to master and depotentiate the constant menace of criminal violation. As our news-weeklies report, assassinations, suicides and murders increasingly overshadow the gun's other functions and eclipse the inventive craftsmanship that turned countless guns into collector's items. Lichtenstein's in-our-face handgun robs us of time to contemplate such complex meanings, confronting us instead with the mind-racing frenzy of a curbside holdup—one where the victims may or may not live to tell their story through arresting artwork, depressing actuarial tables and eyewitness accounts of the latest drive-by atrocity. The progressive mechanization of our innate primate violence sits balanced uneasily on a trigger; only the counterweight of human consciousness can determine if it will sometime be pulled at the target behind our eyes.

Diamond, Jared M. *Guns, Germs, and Steel: The Fates of Human Societies.* NY, 1999.
Frazer, James George. *The Golden Bough.* Oxford and NY, 1994.
Partridge, Eric. *Origins.* NY, 1958.

1. Pointing directly at a nation of anxious readers, Roy Lichtenstein's working drawing for Time magazine to accompany its cover story, "The Gun in America," on June 21, 1968, weeks after the assassinations of Robert Kennedy and Martin Luther King, Jr. © Estate of Roy Lichtenstein.

2. After an uprising in Madrid against his occupying army, Napoleon retaliated by executing thousands of partisans from dawn until past midnight. The Spanish painter Francisco Goya contrasted the despair, horror and defiance in the faces of those destined for a mass grave with the faceless soldiers mechanically firing 70-caliber flintlocks at point-blank range. *The Third of May 1808*, oil painting, 1814, Spain.

Hammer

Known as "crusher" and "murder-greedy," Mjoll-nir, the great hammer of the Norse god Thor, was crucial in fighting both the giants and the world snake, the primal chaos that threatened the gods. Magically, it returned to its master when it was thrown. Here reduced to less than an inch in size but still imposing in its effect, the hammer, in miniature, probably functioned as an amulet—a fertility charm for newlyweds, protection for the living and sanctification of the dead when placed on the grave (ARAS, 2:121–2). The hammer is one of our earliest implements, initially as much weapon as tool, likely a stone hurled or brought down with a forceful swing from a human forearm. Probably the sound of the hammer striking and its capacity to pummel things into small bits associated it with the shattering thunderbolt and lightning that opened the watery clouds, broke the prison that held the sun but also wrought destruction. Yet the hammer became the tool that "hits the nail on the head," bringing things precisely into place, and evoking mythic artisans and builders of the cosmic order. The Chinese P'an-ku used his hammer and chisel to carve the firmament; exacting human counterparts fashioned the structures of civilization (Baird, 261). Hammer is not only of the celestial and human realm, but also of the sooty bowels of the earth, volcanic fire and forge, alluding to psyche's daimonic creative center. With hammer and anvil, divine smiths like the crippled Hephaistus fashioned wondrous weapons, tools and ornaments of gold for heroes and deities, and revealed to human consciousness the mysteries of metallurgic transmutation. Like other primordial implements, hammer can evoke the force of violent impulse as well as of imagination and directed will. Hammer can be a mere "hammering in the brain" or an intentional "hammering out," not just of physical construction, but of mental constructs, due process and artistic form.

Baird, Merrily C. *Symbols of Japan.* NY, 2001.

Mjollnir, the Hammer of Thor, Viking, 10th century, Sweden.

Plow

Holding the reins of two yoked animals, a figure plows a field. This ancient image, engraved in rock, is full of evocative pairings: human and beast, phallus and tree, plow and furrow. By means of the pictograph, the artist has encoded the powerful magic that transfers the essence of vegetative fertility to the plowed field (Ström, 51).

The introduction of plowing into human culture some 9,000 years ago marked the transition from nomadic life to settled, agricultural societies and the dedicated cultivation of the earth. Always, plowing has been described in the language and imagery of sexuality. Its primitive form a stick piercing the earth, the plow mythically signifies the transcendent male seed impregnating the divine female soil (ARAS, 2:346). An ancient Sumerian hymn gives sensual and explicit voice to this *hierosgamos*, or "sacred marriage," between heaven and earth, whose progeny is the harvest. The goddess Inanna asks, "Who will plow my high field? / Who will plow my wet ground?" Her beloved, the king Dumuzi, responds like "the rising cedar." The passion of their lovemaking is such that, "Grains grew high by their side. / Gardens flourished luxuriantly" (Wolkstein, 37).

Erotic rituals at planting time echoed the cosmic plowing of the furrow in the sexual union of men and women, which symbolically canalized libido into the fructification of the earth (CW 5:151, n22). Many spring plowing festivals are thus associated with rain, which represents heavenly penetration and seeding. In folk traditions, farmers and their spouses made love in the fields or newlyweds made their bridal bed there in order to promote their own fruitfulness and that of the land (CW 5:151). The symbolic marriage of chieftain, king or conqueror with the land as divine consort was often celebrated in sexual relations with a human consort or a sacred hierodule to insure an abundant harvest and the fertility of the kingdom as a whole.

Yet, the original cleaving of the earth can also be seen as a wounding to the primal ground. Land that is repeatedly plowed and seeded, never conserved, can become exhausted and barren. Technology has, for some, distanced the intimacy between human, earth and beast imaged in the simplicity of the ancient pictograph. We speak of the spoiling of the earth and even of its rape.

Just as plowing represents humankind's wresting of the soil from its primal state for civilized cultivation, so does it evoke the wresting of consciousness from primordial psychic ground to be at the disposal of human endeavor (CW 8:148). The correlation between plowing and consciousness is conveyed in the alchemical motif where the adept begins to plow in the west, signifying the underworld to which the sun disappears, the land of the spirits, the darkness of the *nigredo*, and then moves toward the east where illumination dawns. But like the plowing of the land, the work of the opus, the interior turning of the soil, can't be sentimentalized; it is a process of wearying, steady labor, without knowing for sure that it will yield a harvest.

Ström, Folke. *Nordisk Hedendom: tro och sed i förkristen tid*. Göteborg, 1967.

Wolkstein, Diane and Samuel Noah Kramer. *Inanna, Queen of Heaven and Earth: Her Stories and Hymns from Sumer*. NY, 1983.

1. A Swedish rock carving depicts plowing as the transferring of the forces of vegetation to the earth. Petroglyph from the Bronze Age (1800–500 B.C.E.).

2. Sennedjem plowing the fields of Iaru, the dynamic hereafter of the Egyptians. He is followed by his wife Tutu sowing seed. Painting from the tomb of Sennedjem, Deir el-Medina, 19th dynasty (ca. 1295–1185 B.C.E.), Egypt.

Wheel

The sun wheel is a version of the mythic circle of totality and its hub, or eye, the ambivalent center manifest in the fiery, seed-germinating, creative rotation of the rim. The rayed spokes of the great solar wheels of ancient cultures divide the cosmic whole into measures of time or space, the four seasons, phases of the moon, elements or cardinal directions, the eight-petaled lotus, emblem of continuous renewal, the 12 months of the zodiac and their astral configurations and transits, the whirling of the changeable about the hub of eternity. The wheeling of the stars around the pole sets in motion the cycles of nature and the course of a life. Or in Tibetan Buddhism the Wheel of Life portrays rebirth as the succession of different states of existence, all in the grip of the monster of impermanence (*Enc. Brit.* 10:214). Tarot's Wheel of Fortune signifies turns of destiny, and "order, extension, time and duration" (Gad, 98). In the wheel-like circulatory process of the alchemical opus is implied mystic peregrination, ascents and descents, sublimation and coagulation, one moving into the other until synthesized at the hidden center.

Eventually bringing the heavenly wheel down to earth, humans discovered that logs or round stones could be made into sledges for moving heavy objects, that grooves and fixed axles in these primitive wheels increased their efficiency and stability. The oldest excavated wheel, from Mesopotamia, is approximately 55 hundred years old. But however we may take it for granted, the wheel still occupies a place between the concrete and imaginal—the potter's wheel that rotates formless matter into differentiated being, the millstone that once seemed to magically harness nature's power, but also evokes the intolerable heaviness of endless repetition; the spinning wheel that produces the threads of fate and belongs to both fairy godmother and murderous witch; the wheels of ordinary life—cars, trams, trucks, busses, bicycles and planes—reiterated in our dreams as vehicles of psychic motility and the grooves of progress, regression and routine.

In myths and life, the wheel has also been used as an instrument of torture on which one is fixed or stretched, suggesting the agonizing nature of psychic compulsion. Negatively, the wheel is emblem of being "stuck in a rut," or of endlessly turning the wheels of the mind, but getting nowhere. In Mahayana Buddhism, cause and effect is "the wheel that cannot be turned back." Some of the most intriguing of wheels are the giant medicine wheels of the Plains Indians of Alberta, Canada, and Wyoming, Montana and the Dakotas in the United States. Stone wheels, some as great as 12 meters in diameter, their center consists of piled rock from which extend spokes of stone. The precise meaning of the mysterious wheels is not known; they may have served as orientation for sun ceremonials or were used for rituals of healing. There are configurations of stone that seem to refer to particular stars, and some of the cairns are aligned with the light of the sunrise or sunset at the summer solstice, perhaps invoking its life-bestowing radiance.

Almgren, Bertil. *The Viking.* NY, 1975.
Gad, Irene. *Tarot and Individuation: Correspondences with Cabala and Alchemy.* York Beach, ME, 1994.

1. Wheel of the sun. Nearly ten feet in diameter, the
wheel of the sun temple of Konārak is one of 24
attached to two sides of the imposing structure. The
temple represents the divine chariot that carries the
sun god Surya across the heavens from dawn to dawn.
Carved sandstone, ca.1238–64 C.E., India.

2

3

2. Here, wheel suggests the turning of human fate and inevitability of change. *The Wheel of Fortune,* illuminated manuscript, ca. 14th century C.E., France.

3. The large, seemingly lumbering wheels of the Oseberg Wagon were purposefully designed to negotiate the uneven, often muddy roads of Viking times. This is the only complete wheeled wagon preserved from the Viking age (Almgren, 237ff). Wood, 9th century, Norway.

4. Perhaps signifying the unity of living things, the mysterious wheel, nearly 80 feet in diameter, is made of boulders. One of the wheel's outer cairns aligns with the sunrise of the summer solstice. Bighorn medicine wheel, ca. 700–1200 C.E., photograph by Courtney Milne, Wyoming, United States.

Calendar

In the very urge to carve intricate units of temporal human order on what must have seemed an ageless, indestructible 25-ton stone, the Aztecs sought to bring together time and eternity. The round calendar-stone, at one time placed on top of the great pyramid in Tenochtitlan, functions as a mandala reconciling opposites. A cycle of 250 *tzolkin,* or days, roughly equal to the period of human gestation, was divided into 13 20-day units synchronized by means of a unique numerical system with figures of gods and forces in the mythic cycle of the plumed serpent god Quetzalcoatl. The whole was correlated with the solar year and then reconciled at the end of a 52-year-long "Calendar Round," when, symbolically, the world met destruction and was created anew. This fateful event is captured in the face at the center of the calendar, which depicts the conjunction of the sun disk of light and the earth monster of darkness (Pasztory, 170).

Calendars of most premodern societies reflect the rhythms of a symbolic cosmos experienced within, that found correspondence in the cycles and seasons of the world without, the movement of its celestial bodies in relation to earth and ocean and the molting, rutting, migration and hibernation of its creatures. The monthly phases of the moon—easily observed and measured—mirrored a woman's menstrual cycle, and psyche's energies of fullness and emptiness, light and dark, pregnancy and birth. The fixed patterns of stars and the sun's yearlong passage of ascent and descent marked by the solstices told the archaic farmer when to plant and when to harvest, and resonated in his own being as intervals of potency and dormancy. By their seemingly magical regularity, the sun and moon served both the practical and symbolic needs of archaic cultures to measure time, leading to the development of counting, number and prediction—important foundations of consciousness and culture.

The moon—related etymologically to the words "month," "mind" and "measurement" (Cashford, 118)—was the basis for the earliest calendars, beginning with the Sumerians and Babylonians. Their lunar systems were absorbed into the Egyptian, Greek, Jewish and Islamic calendars, and survive also in the changeable date of the Christian Easter Day, determined in relation to the moon. The word "calendar" is derived from the Latin "calends," referring to the first of the month, the time of the new moon. The "ides" may derive from the Latin *iduare,* "to divide," or from Sanskrit roots that mean "to kindle" or "to light," referring to the moon. The Gregorian calendar, generally adopted in the West over several centuries, retains the ancient lunar-based division of the year into 12 months. But the number of days in a year, and in a given month, as well as a system of leap years, accommodates the timing of the earth's orbit around the sun. Another solar feature is the year's beginning in January, for Janus, a solar Roman god often depicted with two faces, looking backward and forward, the "hinge" of the door between the past year and coming year. In the twentieth century, the Chinese assimilated the Gregorian calendar into their celebrated 12-year cycle, which invokes symbolism particular to the animal for which each year is named, beginning with the Rat and ending with the Boar. The imaginative Mesoamerican counterpart includes the years of the "earthquake," "aquatic monster" and "the god who hunts with a blowpipe."

In the shift to a primarily linear or historical reckoning of time, and the privileging of consciousness over psyche's "round" totality, one can lack, felt Jung, the sustaining sense of recurring natural cycles. Counter to this shift are the traditional horoscopes that place the signs of their revolving zodiac around the earth at the center, or liturgical calendars that provide symbolic containers for the passage of ritualized, sacred seasons and "ordinary" time. The Aztec calendar, divinatory in nature, may have evoked the restoration of the *unus mundus,* often experienced in synchronistic events in which the realms of time and timelessness are meaningfully conjoined. While their reconciliation mythically brings on the destruction and rebirth of the world, the symbolic transition finds containment in the configurations of the calendar. The timeless center point is encircled by a rich "procession of gods which represent a qualitative aspect of time" unfolding in its seasonal variations (Zavala, 67ff), allowing one to perceive individual life in relation to ever-recurring constellations of process around an eternal hub.

Cashford, Jules. *The Moon: Myth and Image.* London, 2003.
Pasztory, Esther. *Aztec Art.* NY, 1983.
Zavala, J. F. "Synchronicity and the Mexican Divinatory Calendar." *Quadrant* (15/1, 1982).

1. The 10-foot-wide circular facade of the Aztec calendar-stone synthesizes the two principles by which the Aztecs ordered time—the solar year and a mythic cycle related to the plumed-serpent god, Quetzalcoatl. Ca. 1502–20.

2. Its standing stones aligned with the heavens, Stonehenge, one of the world's oldest astronomical calendars, may have aided ancient Celtic Druids to predict the annual path of the sun, moon and planets for ritual purposes. Ca. 2410–1240 B.C.E., Wiltshire, England.

3. A prehistoric Swedish petroglyph testifies to humankind's immemorial fascination with measuring the passage of time against the movement of celestial bodies. The human figure appears to be counting upon its fingers the twenty-eight days in a full lunar cycle. Bronze Age, 1800–500 B.C.E.

Compass

Mirrored in the human realm by its use in constructions of mathematical harmony and the imposing of form, the compass is depicted in a medieval manuscript as the attribute of the divine architect of the cosmos. Wisdom biblically tells of her presence beside the Lord when he "set a compass upon the face of the depth," establishing and delimiting the heavens, waters and foundations of the earth (Proverbs 8:27).

The compass (or dividers), a tool for measuring, drafting and drawing geometric figures, is emblematic of sciences like astronomy, architecture and geometry, which in part give form and scale to the unknown and express the relationship between things. William Blake's famous image of Urizen, the law-making demiurge who wields a compass, expresses through the instrument the extreme rationality that can restrict our imaginative horizons (Bloom). Alchemy, however, portrayed the compass as an essential tool of the imagination in the process of the opus. The adept used the compass to "square the circle," in other words to discriminate the original chaotic unity, or *prima materia*, into four opposing elements that, through the process of the opus, could be recombined into a more integrated whole (CW 12:124).

In the fantasies of sacred geometry, the compass, inscribing the perfect form of the circle, recreates the primal act of creation, starting with a center point, the origin of the cosmos. In the religious sense, the point is imagined as the divine, in the scientific sense as the moment of the Big Bang. Just as the second leg of the compass reaches outward from the stationary center, so existence expands in all directions. Where there was once only undifferentiated space, the compass draws a form that distinguishes inside from out. Equally, the act of drawing a circle with a compass describes the coordinates of individual life, origin and expansion, the fulfillment and circumscription of potential, the orbiting and circumambulations around what feels physically and psychically like "home." This notion is amplified in another kind of compass, the magnetic, which was invented at least a millennium ago by the Chinese, who used it for divination. The magnetic compass contains a piece of electrically charged iron that aligns itself with the earth's magnetic field and reflects its north or south poles. An invaluable tool of navigation on sea or land, the magnetic compass symbolically evokes the idea of navigating one's psychic course by conscious alignment with an invisible node. The magnetic compass is not, however, infallible. "The closer one gets to the magnetic pole, the stronger the vertical component and the weaker the horizontal component of the electro-magnetic field become, causing the needle to wander listlessly, east and west of magnetic north" (Lopez, 292). Similarly, the internal compass can be affected by the proximity between conscious and unconscious, sometimes causing states of extreme disorientation. And how one typically orients oneself may need to be permanently revised at the point where familiar and unfamiliar, or rational and nonrational aspects of life and personality come into polar conjunction.

Bloom, Harold. Exhibition Wall Text. *William Blake*. Metropolitan Museum of Art. NY, 2001.
Jobes, Gertrude. *Dictionary of Mythology, Folklore and Symbols*. NY, 1961.
Lopez, Barry Holstun. *Arctic Dreams*. NY, 1986.

God as the architect of the universe, rendering
primordial creation with the help of the compass.
Illuminated manuscript from the *Bible moralisée*,
ca. 1250, France.

Scale

Representing the tension between the forces of heaven and hell, the devil and the archangel Michael contend for souls of the departed, whose relative weight of evil and good is measured in the pan of a scales. Evoking the surreptitious nature of temptation, a demon attempts to tip the scales by pulling on the tail of a sinner who has already metamorphosed into the semblance of the devil.

A scale measures the weight of a thing and is associated with mass, gravity and balance. Scales have been in use since very ancient times to weigh primitive forms of currency before its standardization in coins and paper. The mythic *psychostasis*, or the weighing of souls in the afterlife, is a motif that occurs in many early cultures, suggesting the idea that even the attitudes and principles by which one lives and the way they are embodied have real substance. Images from ancient Egypt portray the rite of the weighing of the heart against the feather of Maat, the goddess of "order, the just measure of things, that underlies the world" (Hornung, 213). The monster Ammit waits below the scale, ready to devour the unbalanced heart. We do not know for sure what was considered the appropriate balance of lightness and heaviness that won entry into the afterlife; but the images attest to the significance placed on the harmonious functioning of the individual's heart, the symbolic center of psychic life. The Kabbalah says that before the Creation, the Ancient of Days held the scale of the universe from which was born the duality of all things (DoS, 832). Tradition-

ally an emblem of the balance of opposites, the scale is the attribute of Justice, often depicted blindfolded to signify impartiality in weighing the arguments that determine innocence or guilt before the law (Bruce-Mitford, 90). The astrological sign Libra is pictured as a scale, signifying the autumnal equinox when day and night are evenly balanced. An air sign, Libra suggests the element that mediates between heaven and earth, and the alchemical *sublimatio*, where one is able to rise above the personal and see things from a larger, more distanced, objective standpoint.

Symbolically, the scale evokes the balance or imbalance between psychic opposites like head and heart, or matter and spirit, and the way consciousness and the unconscious function in relation to one another in the service of equilibration. Psyche, it seems, demands that the energies of "heaven" and "hell" both get their measure. Developmentally, the scale cannot always be balanced; often, one or another aspect of the personality carries, essentially, greater weight. At the same time, psyche responds to gross fluctuations or real one-sidedness. *Enantiadromia*, or the sudden movement of a thing into its opposite, is psyche's tipping of the scale.

Bruce-Mitford, Miranda. *The Illustrated Book of Signs & Symbols.* NY, 1996.
Hornung, Erik. *Conceptions of God in Ancient Egypt.* Ithaca, NY, 1982.

1. An image from a Spanish altarpiece portrays the weighing of souls at the final judgment. Painting on wood panel, ca. 13th century.

2. An Italian miniature depicts the scales of Justice placed within the constellation of Libra. Manuscript illustration, 13th century.

3. *Weighing of the Heart,* papyrus with ink and pigment, ca.1050 B.C.E., Egypt.

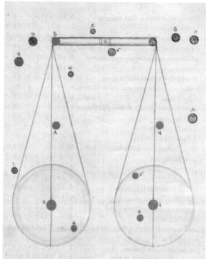

1

2

3

Chain

Often placed where there has been bloodshed or dispute, the *edan* bronze pair conveys the harmonizing force that brings duality into oneness. Linked by a chain, the couple becomes a single totem; it was given to initiates of the Oshugbo society within the Yoruba culture of West Africa. The male and female stand regally side-by-side, symbolizing the mystery and power found in the union of opposites (Fagg, 186).

Chain, derived from the Latin *catena*, "fetter," evokes the tensions and affinities associated with the notion of linking. The smallest particles of being engage in endless chain reactions of cause and effect. Evolutionary chains, and the pursuit of their "missing links," reveal sequential development, natural selection and unsuspected relationships. The reciting of a chain of names, or a chain of sacred narratives enhances generational continuity, and ties the tribe or group to the power of the ancestors (von Franz, 289). Early Christian theologians saw prayer as a luminous *aurea catena*, or "golden chain," extending to the Creator. Many traditions find cohesion in a lineage of teachings passed down through a chain of ordinations or initiations. Alchemy indeed conceived of magnetic chains binding all levels of existence, suggesting the mysterious links in the form of induction, projection, transferential phenomena and synchronicities that characterize activated psychic fields.

Chain reflects the ambivalence of interconnectedness, however, in its evocation of adamantine ties, of loyalty and love, but also fixation, imprisonment and the suppression of powerful, feared or obstreperous elements. Linking is associated with relatedness, support, mirroring, intimacy and transformation, and with dependence, encumberment and subjugation. Being bound in chains is defeat and punishment. The chained animal is in opposition to nature and instinct. The "ball and chain" are emblematic of the convict and slave. Zeus chained the mythic Prometheus to a rock where an eagle daily ate his liver as punishment for the Titan's stealing of divine fire as a gift to humankind. The Devil is portrayed as being thrown in chains into an abyss after the Day of Judgment. Chain suggests the weight of what is apparently fated and the intransigence of complexes and compulsions to which we seem bound. The breaking of chains is emblematic of liberation from servitude and tyranny. At the same time, the shattering of essential links to self or other can leave one feeling unmoored. Psychic process is itself a series of meaningful links—as memory, dream, fantasy, affect, desire, imaginal play and acquired experience—that serves to both loosen and bind.

Medieval alchemists spoke of a Homeric chain of wise men that links heaven and earth. The chain also represented the substances and chemical states that appear in the process of the opus (CW 12:148, n.24). The image of a far-flying bird like the eagle connected by a chain with a toad or land animal signified the spirit of imagination and its volatile intuitions, fantasies and aspirations that will fly away unless anchored to the solid matter of life (ibid., 148). In the individual existence Saturnian lead connects autonomous spirit with "heavy reality and the limitations of personal particularity" (Edinger, 86).

Edinger, Edward F. *Anatomy of the Psyche.* La Salle, IL, 1985.
Fagg, William Buller, John Pemberton and Bryce Holcombe. *Yoruba, Sculpture of West Africa.* NY, 1982.
von Franz, Marie-Louise. *Creation Myths.* Boston, 1995.

1. A chain binds together male and female, evoking the sacred power created from the marriage of opposites. Bronze sculpture, Yoruba, Africa.

2. The Persian alchemist Avicenna points to the necessity of spirit, represented by an airborne eagle, being chained to matter, signified by the earthbound animal. *Viridarium chymicum*, 1624, Germany.

1

2

Thread

Thread (from the old English *thrawan*, "to cause to twist or turn") denotes everything from lines of narrative to filaments of being like the weblike dark matter of space, the tiny, lashing cilia of unicellular organisms, or the double helix strands of DNA that signify both ancestral inheritance and individuality. Superstring theory has posited strings of energy a hundred billion billion times smaller than a single atomic nucleus, which vibrate in different patterns producing different kinds of particles.

A slender thread can become a whole fabric. Seemingly thin and delicate, threads of spider silk have greater proportionate tensile strength than steel. The solar spider of the Brahma Upanishad weaves his universal web with a single thread. The mythic Fates and Norns spin, measure and cut the threads of a particular life. Threads are lines of orientation in the labyrinths of psyche and invisible conductors of light, sound, emotion and memory.

Threads knot, evoking the interweaving of relationships and dependencies. The interlaced knot on which the small wooden figure from Gabon, Africa, is seated, indicates, along with her voluminous hair, that she is a feminine being of extraordinary potency, a *simbi* woman. The interlace suggests "the circle of life, mystic support, and the lap as foundation of instruction and human competence" (Weber, 186–7). Knots are loopings that seem to have no beginning and no end, suggesting evolution, reverberation and the force of destiny. Scandinavian and Celtic art portrayed oceanic waves as an intertwined series of knots to express the perpetual coiling of cosmic energy. Knots conjoin, but also entangle. Marriage is a "tying of the knot," or, as in a Swedish song, the "knotting of ribbons." The "knots of the heart," however, describe the compulsive desires that bind the self in ignorance. Psychic process often involves both unknotting and knotting as analysis and synthesis of the threads of the personality.

Threads of natural fibers and even metal, wire and plastic get twisted or braided into rope, which in religious imagery sometimes functions as a demarcation between the sacred and the profane, or as a path between them. The *shimenawa*, the Japanese sacred straw rope, is a traditional New Year's festival ornament for a Shinto shrine. Made in sizes from the massive to the modest, the *shimenawa* serves to prepare a seat for the deity that brings the New Year's blessings. Hung in an entryway or in front of a worship hall, it separates the ordinary world from the realm of the divine. The strands of rice straw are twisted atypically to the left rather than the right, imbuing the rope with mystical power to repel malevolent spirits and to honor the *kami*, the spirits of the household (Brandon, 47–52).

Associated with plant fibers growing upwards toward the sun, the rope is mythically solar and fertile. In Mayan iconography, ropes hanging from the sky signify divine semen falling from Heaven to bring the earth to life. Perhaps because it so easily resembles the uncanny snake or the vine snaking up the towering tree of our primordial experience, the rope has always been a tool of the shaman, suggesting ecstatic ascent to the celestial regions, a means of bridging and flight and the magical road on which spirits travel.

Helping us, ropes moor, tie and tether, which are functions that show their shadow aspect in forms of coerced constraint and the ultimate stricture of the hangman's noose. Yet the binding power of the rope is also that of the Zen Ox-Herding Pictures of the 12th century. Here, the rope signifies containment of the untamed mind, depicted as a bull, which must be found, caught and gentled, implying the encounter and recognition of one's own nature, the first step to achieving enlightenment.

Brandon, Reiko Mochinaga, Barbara B. Stephan and Honolulu Academy of Arts. *Spirit and Symbol: The Japanese New Year*. Honolulu, HI, 1994.
Weber, Michael John, Interviewer. *Perspectives: Angles on African Art*. NY, 1987.

1

2

3

1. Unwinding a ball of golden thread, which will show him the way back, Theseus descends into the labyrinth. *Golden Thread*, by Edward Burne-Jones, watercolor, ca. 1882, England.

2. Hook figure, Lumbo people, wood, Gabon, Africa.

3. This massive sacred rice-straw rope protects the entrance to a Shinto worship hall. A Japanese New Year's festival ornament, the *shimenawa* separates the realms of the sacred and the profane. *Shimenawa*, Suwa Grand Shrine, Nagano Prefecture, Japan.

Net/Web

The net is one of humankind's oldest tools, used for hunting and fishing even during the Stone Age (*Enc. Brit.* 8:614). Made up as they are of so little tangible material and so much empty space, nets tug at the imagination. How can something so slight be so strong? Perhaps there is magic involved? In a tale from Homer's *Odyssey* there is divine magic in the creation of an invisible bronze net. The smith god Hephaistus crafts it in order to catch his wife Aphrodite with her lover Ares, exposing them in flagrante delicto to the laughter of all the other gods.

Nets appear very commonly as symbols of more or less menacing capture, entrapment, entanglement, ensnaring, binding. But what is being captured and by whom? In some forms of Buddhism, physical existence itself is thought of as a net entrapping the human soul. A Buddhist poet-philosopher of the seventh century describes the terrible situation of human beings, who are "chased … into the net of birth" (EoR, 15:368). In the same vein, Sufism speaks of "the net of the body" (Attar, 1). In medieval Christianity, Satan was imagined at work with a great net to catch unwary souls (Tresidder, 144). But Christ also taught his disciples to be "fishers of men." We see Jesus in Duccio's painting, drawing the fishermen-disciples toward him, as if by a net. On the other hand, in ancient Persia, Sufi mystics were imagined as attempting to capture God with symbolic nets, the power of their devotion and surrender (DoS, 699).

More worldly entrapments are symbolized by more mundane nets such as "the silken net of matrimony" (William Blake). Depth psychology sees us as bound by nets made up of our past experiences and our unconscious complexes, and by our instincts and inborn patterns of perception, all of which limit our freedom of choice. This situation was envisioned by the ancient Greeks as Fate, and by the Roman Stoics as *Heimarmene*: the inexorable rule of the stars over human life.

At another level, the stretched-out net has been seen as an image of the physical universe, or of nature or, in modern physics, of "the fabric of space, warped and stretched by gravitational force" (Fideler, 300). The interconnectedness of the net comes into symbolic play here, as it does in the Taoist vision of the stars as knots in the "net of heaven," which binds together everything in heaven and earth and "is wide-meshed but lets nothing through" (Cirlot, 217). In myth, the Babylonian hero Marduk used a net to subdue the ancient chaos goddess Tiamat, suggesting that the net is an organizing power that contains and transforms conflicting energies.

This interconnectedness is basic also to the related idea of "network," whether it appears in a social, business or communication context. And of course it is the basic vision inherent in that most modern of human tools, the Internet, which was seen, at least in its early days, as a means to connect individuals in a vast invisible net over all the earth.

Attar, Farid al-Din. *The Conference of the Birds.* London, 1954.
Cirlot, Juan Eduardo. *A Dictionary of Symbols.* NY, 1962.
Fideler, David R. *Jesus Christ, Sun of God: Ancient Cosmology and Early Christian Symbolism.* Wheaton, IL, 1993.
Tresidder, Jack. *Dictionary of Symbols: An Illustrated Guide to Traditional Images, Icons, and Emblems.* SF, 1998.

1

2

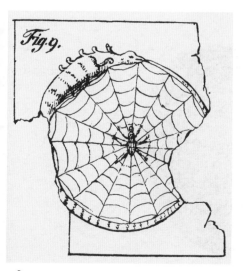

3

1. Jesus with fishermen at Lake Tiberias. Some are being drawn into the invisible net of discipleship; some are still absorbed with the concrete net of their trade. Oil on panel by Duccio, 13th–14th century, Italy.

2. This Egyptian image shows demons at work with the great net, which would trap the human soul after death. Papyrus vignette from the *Book of the Dead of Nestanebtasheru*, 21st dynasty (ca. 1070–712 B.C.E.), Egypt.

3. Maya within the circle of Time, her net becoming a spider's web, catching the unwise in the sensory world of illusion. Drawing from Indian Brahmanism.

Basket

Since earliest times, baskets woven from reeds and grasses have functioned as containers for gathered bounty like wild-growing nuts and berries and, with the advent of agriculture, for storing the harvest's surplus of fruits and grains. The weaving of a basket often incorporates symbolic patterns that are themselves a weaving together of the natural world, ancestral experience and spiritual teachings. The basket produced by Native American Maidu of Northern California, for example, bears the abstract "Geese Flying" pattern. For the Warao of the Orinoco Delta, the very act of making baskets eventually transforms an ordinary weaver into a shamanic craftsperson infused with the plant-ancestor spirit (EoR, 15:242).

Womblike in form, woven from and holding the vegetation associated with the great goddesses of cyclical life, death and rebirth, baskets are linked to the mysteries of eternal return. The basket that holds the threshed grain or mown corn carries both the seed for the next season's planting and, symbolically, the ever dying and ever reborn deity. In the Greek Eleusinian Mysteries, for example, a winnowing basket carried a mask or phallus representing the divine son of Demeter-Persephone. This most sacred object, cradled in the *likon,* may have in part revealed the unity of divine mother, daughter and child as the continuity of time extending backward and forward, evoking birth to the eternal (CW 9i: 316). According to Orphic legend, Dionysus was reared in the underworld by Persephone,

daughter of Demeter, and he awoke after three years in the mystic *vannus,* his winnowing basket cradle (ARAS, 3Pa.051). In one version of the Egyptian myth of Osiris, his sister Isis gathers the dismembered god's scattered limbs in a basket (DoS, 70). Further, baskets cradle culture bearers like Moses, who brings release and new life to his people. The Easter basket filled with eggs carries the promise of springtime rebirth, fertility and abundance. Picnic baskets share similar symbolic roots. Basket weaving as a healing therapy implicitly incorporates the ideas of maternal containment and the regeneration of matter and spirit.

The function of the winnowing basket to hold the grain separated from the chaff is perhaps what is associated symbolically with the Jump Dance or "world-renewal" ceremony of the Hupa, Karuk and Yurok Indians of Northern California. According to myth, a family of spirit beings was metamorphosed into nature's basket-making materials, which are thus seen as gifts of divine origin and emblematic of the interwoven character of family and village. Specially woven baskets used in the ten-day ceremony are considered to be alive and wanting to dance. In the culmination of the ceremony, a line of dancers "stamps out" sickness, natural catastrophes and bad thoughts, while an uplifted basket receives the spirit world's blessings (Lang, 83–5).

Lang, Julian. "The Basket and World Renewal." *Parabola* (16/3, 1991).

1. Basket with "Geese Flying" pattern, produced by Maidu Indians, ca. 1900, Northern California, United States.

2. Basket holding a mask of Dionysus, signifying the rebirth of the dismembered god. Red-figure vessel, ca. 500–475 B.C.E., Greece.

2

Purse

A female caryatid with a purse stands at the entryway of the temple palace of the ninth-century Aramean King Kapara. Apparently a member of the royal household, the woman was elevated to the role of a powerful guardian deity. She holds the small purse with a handle close to her body near the region of the womb. Similar vessels, made of copper, and also carried in the left hand, were used as buckets to carry water for deities to sprinkle on a tree of life, or on a king. The purse held by this watchful caryatid may contain sacred water for rejuvenating King Kapara (ARAS, 2Bt.600).

Purses are containers for valuable things like currency, identification and objects we might need at any moment: credit cards, driver's license, photographs, signatures, keys, checks, cosmetics, pens and personal talismans. While purses are often associated with women, historically they are gender neutral. For centuries, purses carried by men and women carried money, and thus became emblematic of the banker, the merchant and even of Saint Matthew, the tax collector (De Vr, 376).

Our word "purse" comes from the Old English *pusa* (bag) and Latin *bursa* and Greek *byrsa* (hide) (Barnhart, 620). In medieval Europe, purses hung from the belts of individuals of both sexes in lieu of pockets. Embroidered purses with long drawstring handles were associated with the female vulva in "shape, function and position on the body" (Camille, 64); in the art of love, the lady could convey the innocence of her flirtation, or her preference, by drawing the purse shut.

"Holding the purse strings" still refers to having control of the valuables. In the Gunter Grass novel *The Tin Drum*, a prostitute refers to her vulva as her "purse," and in a reversal of gender, the old Swedish word *pung* means both money-purse and testicles. The fourteenth-century religious visionary Julian of Norwich, however, delightfully located the purse in another part of the body: "A man walks upright, and the food in his body is shut in as if in a well-made purse. When the time of his necessity comes, the purse is opened and then shut again, in most seemly fashion."

Given its background, it is no wonder that, especially for a woman, a purse is an intimate object holding intimate things, and also an object of play. From the practical shoulder bag to the beaded, silk evening purse, there is remarkable versatility in the purse's design and adornment. In dreams, circumstances around the purse—the losing, or finding, of a purse; whether the purse is open, closed, messy or ordered—may suggest factors related to the containment or displacement of elements of identity, money (or psychic energy) and sexual boundaries. The stealing of one's purse can feel like a violation. The finding of a full purse may signify the potential for a fortuitous influx of wealth, or, if the purse's owner is known, a moral conflict over whom the riches belong to.

Camille, Michael. *The Medieval Art of Love: Objects and Subjects of Desire.* NY, 1998.
Julian of Norwich, *Showings.* NY, 1978.

A caryatid, or guardian figure, holding a small purse. Basalt sculpture, 9th century B.C.E., Syria.

Money

Money is currency, from the Latin *currere*, "to run" or "to flow," evoking liquid assets, circulation and commerce, from the simplest acts of bartering to the most sophisticated versions of buying and selling, lending and borrowing, profit and loss. Andy Warhol's *192 One-Dollar Bills* conveys the energic quality of money—the potency conferred on ordinary paper notes when by general agreement they represent a medium of exchange and a standard of value. For many the dollar bill is emblematic of America as the embodiment of capitalism, high finance, big spending, rags-to-riches opportunity and unimaginable wealth. Money is a descendant of those things early peoples deemed treasure, mana, fetish, what was perceived to have magical or talismanic properties or was suitable as offering to the gods (EoR, 10:50). Deities like the Greek Hermes personified the spirit of exchange of commodities and of the boundaries and crossroads where neighboring peoples carried on their trade (Covitz, 37). Beads, cowries and other shells were among the earliest forms of money in Africa, India, China, Europe and the Americas, but an immense variety of things have served: animals, especially cattle, and also goats, pigs, sheep, horses and reindeer, as well as pelts and woven cloths, teas, spices, grains and cakes of salt. In the Sumatran headhunting culture, human heads were a common form of currency. The Akan peoples of Africa designed abstract gold, stone or metal symbolic figurines of animals, geometric forms and spirits, the weight of which represented monetary values (Niangoran-Bouah, 44).

Metals, including gold, silver, bronze, copper, iron and brass have been in use as money for some 4,000 years, and standardized coins since 700 B.C.E., often stamped with the heads or figures of gods or animals evoking specific, powerful forces. China is credited with the printing of the first paper money in 1024 (Paludan, 8:128), but for centuries had offered paper as sacrifice to gods, ghosts and ancestors (EoR, 10:51). Money evokes psyche's currency, in the form of libidinal values coined in the multifarious images of psychic realities, telling us where energy is invested, accumulating or frozen, where there is wealth or impoverishment, depression or inflation, hoarding or bankruptcy. In psyche's treasury are "deposits of mythical fantasies" and "imaginal possibilities" (Hillman, 57). But whether or not we are able to avail ourselves of such treasure depends in part on the exchange among different aspects of the psychic economy, and the ways desire and fear direct our tendencies to save, spend or squander.

Covitz, Joel. "Myth and Money." *Money, Food, Drink, and Fashion, and Analytic Training.* Ed. John Beebe. Fellbach-Oeffingen, 1983.
Hillman, James. "A Contribution to Soul and Money." *Money, Food, Drink, and Fashion, and Analytic Training.* Ed. John Beebe. Fellbach-Oeffingen, 1983.
Niangoran-Bouah, G. *The Akan World of Gold Weights.* Abidjan, 1985.
Paludan, Ann. *Chronicle of the Chinese Emperors.* NY, 1998.

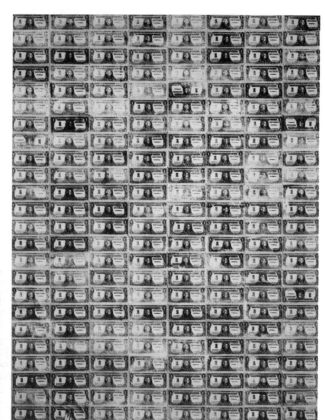

1. *192 One-Dollar Bills*, by Andy Warhol, silkscreen ink on canvas, 1962, United States.

2. Japanese gold coin, 1861.

3. A figurative weight resembling a Sankofa bird—San (to return), kô (to go), fa (to take or recover)—refers to the wisdom of looking back to know how to go forward. Not corresponding to a set unit of measure, such a weight would be placed on one side of a balance scale to verify the amount of gold dust on the other. Copper alloy, the Akan peoples, 18th–late 19th century, Ghana and Côte d'Ivoire, West Africa.

Comb

Some 3,500 years ago, a graceful comb was buried with a dead woman in a grave in Jutland. Combs were common Bronze Age grave gifts, and the comb was hung from the belt of the dead woman. The long, slender teeth of the comb, like rays emitted from the spiraling sun wheels along its rim, suggest that the comb was emblematic of the great light that would illuminate the dark way of death.

Comb has its name from the Indo-European *ghombos*, or "tooth," and the comb's teeth have long been associated with the light-giving, spermatic energies of the sun and sunlike consciousness. Like the grave gift, the red coxcomb of the dawn-heralding rooster suggests the sun's light penetrating the darkness. Indeed, the rooster was a form of the Roman god Mercury in his function as the psychopomp who can see his way to conduct the souls of the dead to the underworld. Rake and plough are combs that open the black earth for the sowing of seeds; in an Elizabethan play, a sacred head in a holy well sings, "Comb my hair and smooth my head. And every hair a stalk shall be" (Perera, 248). The comb's relation to earth's fertility extends to the timeless and sensual image of a woman combing her hair or having it combed by lover or maid—participating in the eros of unknotting, disentangling, smoothing, caressing and bringing light to the deep-rooted mysteries of psyche and nature.

One of the most potent depictions of the anima is the fishtailed mermaid whose attribute is a golden comb. Herself possessing the comb's magic, she controls how calm or chaotic the encounter will be. Her wild, sea-tangled hair evokes unfettered sexuality, feral desire and the captivating pull of unconscious currents. More dangerous, the unkempt ("uncombed") snaky locks of the Terrible Mother are reiterated in the matted, lice-ridden hair of dereliction and madness. In folktales, demons are deloused with combs as a form of exorcising the chaos from their heads.

A Greek word for comb, *kteis*, and its Latin equivalent, *pectin*, refer to the plectrum of the lyre and the comb of the weaver's loom, which separates out the warp from weft (Liddell, 1001), suggesting the discrimination of opposites that makes possible their synthesis. Another meaning, "fingers," reminds us that the comb, originating as long ago as the Stone Age, simulated human fingers pulled through the hair. Perhaps because the fingers also carried the numinous potency of enacting and shaping the creative ideas of emerging consciousness, the "fingered" comb has been seen as not merely functional but magical and talismanic. In Japanese shamanic rituals, a comb flung to the earth turns into bamboo or torch (Baird, 248). In a Siberian shamanic fairy tale, a woman throws a comb behind her when she is being pursued; turning into a forest, it creates an obstacle between pursued and pursuer (von Franz, 132).

Even in the hair, the comb can, if the combing is a rough, impatient ordering of the head, cause tangling where it would normally sort out. Likewise, if the comb of conscious discrimination is forced to serve a too critical, compulsive investment in making things neat, creative ideas may get hopelessly snarled. A surrender is required if the shape-shifting comb is to pull the hairs of the head together:

We must die to become
true human beings.

We must turn completely upsidedown
like a comb in the top
of a beautiful woman's hair.
Rumi, *Say I Am You*

Baird, Merrily C. *Symbols of Japan*. NY, 2001.
Liddell, Henry George and Robert Scott. *A Greek-English Lexicon*. Oxford and NY, 1996.
Perera, Sylvia Brinton. *Queen Maeve and Her Lovers: A Celtic Archetype of Ecstasy, Addiction, and Healing*. NY, 1999.
von Franz, Marie-Louise. *An Introduction to the Interpretation of Fairy Tales*. Dallas, TX, 1982.

1. This comb was found hanging from a woman's belt in a grave in Jutland, Denmark. The sun wheels on its rim are emblematic of the comb's solar symbolism. Bronze comb, ca. 1500 B.C.E.

2. Meditative, erotic, sensual—one of the most timeless of images. *Kamisuki (Combing the hair)*, by Hashiguchi Goyo, wood-block print, 1920, Japan.

3. An Eskimo walrus-tusk carving shamanically links the comb with the fingers of a hand and the figure of a man. *Comb-man-hand*, ca. 1000–1200, Cape Dorset, Canada.

Scissors

Fashioned from a single piece of silver, a pair of eighth-century Chinese shears displays exquisite ornamental detail. Yet the beauty and delicacy of the shears is discrepant with the way pop culture and even the spontaneous images of the psyche often picture scissors—as a tool of wounding, castration and violence. Scissors are essential to work as disparate as that of seamstress, physician, butcher, cosmetician, artist, craftsperson and landscaper. Scissors cut away excess, cut to shape something new from raw materials, cut to free one thing from another. Mythically, the cutting power is often wielded or guided by supermundane purpose, wisdom or cunning. Scissors also reflect, however, the darkest mysteries of the primordial feminine. Sharp and two-bladed, able to open and close, scissors suggest the severing jaws of death or the long beaks of seabirds that snatch their prey from the deep. With a pair of scissors, Atropos, the third of the Greek Fates, cuts the thread of life. Scissors are equally the emblem of the divine midwife who mediates the birth of the individual, cutting the umbilicus to the pleromatic womb, and of Kali, the Hindu goddess of time, matter and destruction. Scissors like the Chinese shears, with a spring connected to the handle for opening and closing, were first developed in the Bronze Age, while swivel-pin scissors date back to Roman times. In whatever way they are used, scissors are symbols of transformation. Like other cutting tools, they evoke the capacity of consciousness to limit, articulate, release and "cut to the core" (EoR, 2:237). But scissors also intimate that conscious life itself is vulnerable to simply getting snipped.

Scissors, Tang dynasty, 8th–9th century, China.

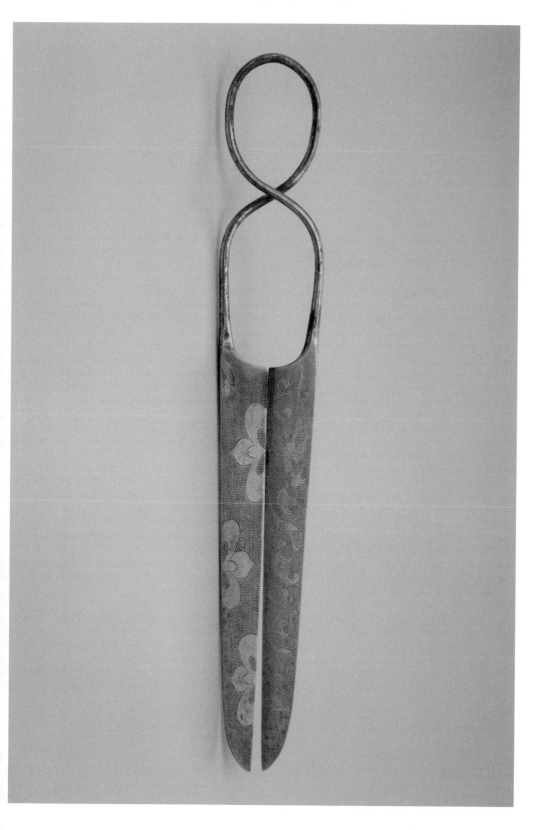

Veil

Veil basically refers to fabric used to hide or protect an object, especially to conceal the face (as we see in the ancient image of women in procession). But this sense has long been expanded, so that veil means anything that conceals, disguises or separates. We speak of a veil of silence, the veil of night, a veiled threat. Today, the symbolism of the veil stretches even farther, into theology and politics. From Buddhism to Sufism and from Plato to Shelley, world religions (and poets and philosophers) speak of our everyday material world, seemingly so real, so vivid, as a veil that conceals true reality. The poet Shelley writes of " ... the painted veil which those who live / Call life" ("Sonnet"). Buddhism, Hinduism and Islamic Sufism all tell us that truth or divine reality is hidden by a veil—by the fascinating clutter of everyday sense-life. Greek Platonism postulated an eternal realm of ideas and forms intelligible through the instrument of the mind, but opaque to the senses, which, caught in the flux of becoming, only perceive the reflection. Revealing, or revelation, would then constitute an "unveiling" of the transpersonal reality behind the sensate.

On the other hand, veiling may be necessary for protection or separation from what is psychically overwhelming or might tempt one into identification. Yahweh warns Moses not to look at him directly (Exodus 33:20–23). When Moses returns to the Israelites, his face is "radiant" from his encounter with the divine and he veils it (ibid., 34:35). Similarly, the prophet Muhammad is frequently pictured as veiled. Muslim lore has it that "the face of God is veiled by seventy thousand curtains of light and darkness, without which everything on which he gazed would be burned up" (DoS, 1063). "Taking the veil," once meant that a woman chose to cloister herself spiritually from worldly life, and "beyond the veil" signifies the transition between life and death.

But a veil is also a concrete piece of clothing, one with a long human history and many symbolic meanings, often contradictory. In ancient Greece, Assyria and Babylonia, wearing a veil marked a woman's high status, as it did for women in parts of the pre-Islamic Middle East (Bailey, 10). With the coming of Islam, the veiling of women increased in Middle Eastern countries, although the Koran does not require that the face be covered. In recent centuries, veiling has carried potent political symbolism in the tension between the discarding of the veil as an act of independence, progress and education, and veiling as a provision of religious and cultural identity, as well as liberation from exposure. In Western Christian cultures, veils were much worn in medieval times; vestiges remain in today's veiling of the bride, suggesting chastity, and in the mourning veil, giving privacy in sorrow. Yet the eighteenth-century Swedish woman of the Roslin painting shows that a veil can also convey a flirtatious invitation. Though veiling is generally associated with women, men also have concealed their faces in Arabia and parts of Africa; among the Tuareg, this is a sign of virility (El Guindi, 117, 125).

Psyche paradoxically veils, and unveils, itself in the enigmatic and sometimes archaic images that shape our dreams, fantasies and even our perceptions. What at first seems hidden, impenetrable, is, as if a portion of the veil were lifted, revealed in flashes of insight. Synchronicities that coincidentally conjoin inner and outer worlds are showings of our inherent and veiled soul stuff and its participation in the *unus mundus*. Conscious relationship to the unconscious is a process that unfolds in the sensed presence of potent, hidden forces and in glimpsed meanings that lead to self-knowledge, or more dramatic rendings of what obscures the unknown self.

Bailey, David A., et al. *Veil: Veiling, Representation, and Contemporary Art.* Cambridge, MA, 2003.
El Guindi, Fadwa. *Veil: Modesty, Privacy, and Resistance.* Oxford, UK, and NY, 1999.
Jung, C. G. *Dream Analysis: Notes of the Seminar Given in 1928–1930.* Princeton, NJ, 1984.

2. Half-concealing, half-revealing, the veil provokes the onlooker's interest, as seen here in a portrait by Alexander Roslin. Painting, 1768, Sweden.

1. Three veiled women walk in religious procession. Relief, detail, from the temple of Ba'al, 1st century C.E., Palmyra, Syria.

3. Perhaps it is in the eye of the beholder whether the veil is an instrument of oppression or protection.

Helmet

Suggesting the flowing mane of a great steed, and thus its strength and swiftness, a magnificent helmet crests high above the head of the warrior king of Sparta known as Leonidas. The helmet was originally an aspect of military accouterment. Its name derived from etymological roots meaning to conceal or cover, this protective headgear was constructed of durable materials like leather, metal or horn. Out of the ethos of military conflict as divinely inspired or ritual warfare, helmets have typically been embellished to convey the possession of intimidating magical powers, animal attributes or the patronage of a particular deity. One of the boar helmets prized by Swedish kings was endowed with the name of the goddess Freyja's golden boars, Hildisvin, meaning "Swine of the Battle"; a soldier who wore such a helmet came under Freyja's protection (Orchard, 84). Perhaps the most remarkable and creative helmets are the samurai *kawari kabuto* from sixteenth-century Japan. Each helmet was unique, temporarily transforming the warrior into a Shinto or Buddhist god, and endowing him with supernatural powers reflected in the particular ornamentation: auspicious animals, creatures with "body armor," natural forces like waves and mountains (Hall, 16–26). While many helmets are designed for maximum visibility in order to distinguish field commanders from rank and file, friend from foe or team from team, others protect by lending an eerie anonymity. Mythically, Hades, the Greek Lord of the Dead, is depicted wearing a helmet of invisibility, suggesting the unseen presence of death in life from which the helmet of the mortal is meant to protect (Herzog, 78–9; Hillman, 29). Shaped like the head and associated with the mystical powers attributed to it, a helmet can represent a coveted object and container of mana. Thus the confiscated helmet of the enemy represents the wreath of the victor and the first spoils taken from the dead.

Hall, John Whitney. "A Personal Image of Power: The Rise of the Daimyo Warlord." *Spectacular Helmets of Japan, 16th–19th Century.* NY, 1985.
Herzog, Edgar. *Psyche and Death: Archaic Myths and Modern Dreams in Analytical Psychology.* London, 1966.
Hillman, James. *The Dream and the Underworld.* NY, 1979.
Orchard, Andy. *Dictionary of Norse Myth and Legend.* London, 1997.

The Spartan King Leonidas, a warrior, wearing a helmet. Marble, 490–80 B.C.E., Greece.

Hat / Headdress

The bowler hat in René Magritte's witty and confounding painting bears a strange label, indicating that it is for "external use," as if it were a salve or liniment. Further tweaking our notions about the nature of a hat, this surrealist image is entitled *The Horrendous Stopper*. It suggests that something of the personality gets horribly "bottled up" under the societal conventions and roles that are often represented by the hat one wears.

Hats have the practical function of protecting the head from sun, rain, insects and injury. But hats, and headdresses, are more significant for the power with which they are invested by their association with the head—sometimes called the seat of the soul, as the mystical vessel of understanding and imagination. The hat encircles the head, reflecting the personality it covers and also imparting to the personality something of the hat's own significance (CW 12:53). The ten-gallon hat conveys the larger than life quality of the American cowboy; the veiled cloche, a woman of mystery and sophistication. The doctoral cap signifies academic accomplishment and the endorsement of a specific alma mater.

Hats hide, reveal and augment who one actually is. In accepting the monarchy's crown, the bishop's miter or even the baseball team's cap, the wearer sacrifices a measure of individuality to a larger, collective identity or exaltation. Warriors in many cultures have worn headdresses and helmets that made them appear more imposing and frightening to the enemy. Headgear adorned with symbolic metal objects signifying durability or magic mirrors or animal parts conferring the capacity to travel in many dimensions were aspects of the consecrated vestments of shamans and medicine people associated with states of altered consciousness and ecstatic flight. Individuals of all ages experiment with self-image and express their uniqueness by means of hats. Objects of play, eroticism and disguise, hats can evoke everything from the menacing to the seductive, and are often astonishing confections of bows, beads, veils, streamers, flowers, feathers, fruits and jewels regally encompassing or surmounting the head.

1. *The Horrendous Stopper*, by René Magritte,
oil painting, 1966, Belgium.

Mandalalike, hats can express our fantasies of wholeness and the nonego agency that helps to get us there. Hermes and his alchemical counterpart, Mercurius, wear the disc-shaped, winged cap that connotes the invisibility and volatile nature of the life spirit moving through psyche's realms as messenger and psychopomp of dynamic process. Fairy tales abound with magic hats that look worn and ordinary, but have supernatural powers assumed by the one who wears the hat. The pointed pileus of the seven dwarves and other homunculi signify psyche's phallic, creative impulses that are always working unconsciously and can be contacted by a receptive consciousness.

Its mysterious capacity to manifest not only familiar but also unknown and surprising elements of personality associates the hat with both shape-shifting and transformation. Hats can signify potential integrity, but they can also suggest possession by uncanny thoughts or fantasies. Even at the mundane level, hats are a daily part of idiomatic expression indicating attitudes or intentions. One doffs a hat out of respect, goes "hat in hand" as a supplicant, "changes hats" to assume a new role. Hats are constantly conveying information. So much so that when identity is undergoing change, a long favored hat may begin to look like a wilted chapeau.

2

3

2. A man of the Adis people of Arunachal Pradesh in northeastern India wearing a feathered headdress.

3. *Girl with a Red Hat*, by Jan Vermeer, oil on panel, ca. 1665, the Netherlands.

Wreath

A wreath of leafless, thorned branches from a dead tree encircles the Virgin Mary, robed in scarlet, and the infant Jesus in her arms. The peculiar nature of the wreath anticipates the wreath of thorns that will crown the head of Christ at his crucifixion, mocking his spiritual "kingship." Yet, like a bloom resplendent within the circle of death, Mary, herself the miraculous fruit of a barren woman, or "dry tree," holds the sweet fruit of divine promise: the Son who is crucified will be resurrected.

"Wreath," from an Old English word meaning "to twist," intertwines in a continuous loop flowers, leaves, tree branches, herbs and berries. Fingers idly touching the small wildflowers that carpet meadow and wood almost instinctively begin to weave them into wreaths, garlands or chaplets for the head, unconsciously intimating nature's majestically woven substance.

In ancient Greece wreaths were sometimes made of the leaves of a plant sacred to a particular god. The olive leaf was associated with Zeus, ivy with Dionysus, laurel with Apollo (Biederman, 390). The wreath of roses is emblematic of great goddesses like Aphrodite and Egyptian Isis as well as the Virgin Mary. The wreath that formally crowns the head that "crowns" the body thus confers something of the deity—particular honor, distinction or authority. The crown of thorns was a deliberate reversal of the wreath's symbolism, for the wreath typically serves as a "living" crown, surrounding the head like a halo with the vitality of plant life that has absorbed the celestial rays of the sun. Ancient emperors were crowned with wreaths signifying their status as incarnations of the divine. Animals wreathed for sacrifice to the gods were those considered "spotless" offerings. The athlete who won the victor's wreath had performed with transcendent power and grace; the poet awarded the laurel had been touched by Apollo's inspiration. Even the bride wearing her chaplet of flowers momentarily embodies the divine feminine at the *hieros gamos*, and the wreathed May Queen personifies the lovely Kore of spring.

Wreaths adorn dwellings and public structures, sanctuaries and burial grounds, evoking seasonal milestones and conjunctions of energies. The harvest wreath celebrates first fruits and marks the equinox that initiates autumnal waning. Solstice wreaths of holly and red berries refer to the evergreen spirit of nature that returns the germinating light at the darkest time of the year. Funeral wreaths celebrate the flowering of life, commemorate a specific life and signify rebirth. And though the organic elements that constitute a wreath inevitably dry out and wither, it is only another allusion to the circular continuity the wreath evokes. Like the Year King the wreath once crowned, old will be replaced by new in unending order.

Ainsworth, Maryan, et al. *Petrus Christus: Renaissance Master of Bruges.* NY, 1994.
Tresidder, Jack. *Dictionary of Symbols: An Illustrated Guide to Traditional Images, Icons, and Emblems.* SF, 1998.

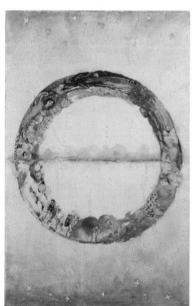

1. A wreath of tree branches surrounds the Virgin Mary and Jesus, forming a crown of thorns that intimates the future Crucifixion. The "dry tree" on which Mary stands alludes to her mother, St. Anne, who miraculously conceived though she was barren (Ainsworth, 162). *Our Lady of the Dry Tree*, by Petrus Christus, oil on panel, ca. 1450, the Netherlands.

2. *Wreath*, by Ami Ronnberg, collage on fabric, 1991, United States.

Crown

Anyone who has ever seen the crown of a monarch cannot fail to be struck by the majesty emanating from the soft luster of precious gems and coronal radiance of gold. A coronation is a *solificatio*, for the crowned head is identified with the sun and its force of life and fertility, which, in the crowning of a sovereign, is conferred on the whole kingdom. Nature preceded us, not only with the sun, but the lovely, yellow coronas in the center of flowers, the brilliant, crown-like plumage of many birds, and the horns on animals. Two thousand years ago Gnostic gems portrayed the seven or 12-rayed crown of light on the head of Agathodaimon, the tail-eating serpent of wisdom (CW 14:6). In the alchemical fantasy, earthly metals and gems corresponded to the distinct qualities projected on planetary and sidereal luminaries. The crown was emblematic of the goal of the opus to synthesize these elements with the sun, or at the psychological level to integrate the diverse properties of the totality of the self with sunlike consciousness. The crown exalts one who is lowly, such as the Virgin Mary, the humble "handmaiden of the Lord," who, crowned by the angels, becomes the regal and compassionate Queen of Heaven. Or the *Anima Mundi,* alchemy's Soul of the World, who wears the diadem that conveys the august reunion of matter and spirit. Yet the crown can be weighty, more than merely a halo of splendor. In Shakespeare's *Henry the IV* (Part 2), the king laments, "Uneasy lies the head that wears the crown," (3.1.33) and Prince Hal reiterates the woe of his diminished father, "O polish'd perturbation! Golden care!" (4.5.27). The crown of thorns pierces the brow of Christ on the cross, mocking his earthly "kingship" while elevating his suffering to spiritual majesty. Corona Borealis, the mythic Ariadne's breathtaking crown, also represents the inescapable ring of her destiny of love, seduction, abandonment and death. Nevertheless, children in their make-believe, beauty queens, athletic victors and royal heirs still seek the crown, whose lofty ritual and ancient symbolism secure its glory.

Virgin Crowned by Angels, detail, workshop of Stefan
Lochner, oil on wood, ca. 1450 or later, Germany.

Necklace

Anything that shimmers as if "otherworldly" holds a special attraction for us. This fascination is as old as human existence to judge by the finds in the earliest burial sites: iridescent shells, powder of red paint, animal teeth or bones, all offering some special "magic" and sometimes shaped into an ancient artifact, like a necklace made of double-breasted ivory beads (as if promising eternal nourishment).

In myth, the necklace is an attribute of the goddess, highlighting her beauty, her ability to attract, as well as her fecundity. The circular necklace indicates the underlying unity of her world, while the many beads, pearls or chains represent the diversity and multiplicity of manifest life. A Norse myth tells the story of how the goddess Freyja got her famous necklace Brísingamen. One day she happened upon the four dwarves who had made the treasures of the gods as they were forging a gold necklace. She asked if she could have it. The dwarves agreed on one condition: that she promise to spend a night with each one of them. Nothing could come more easily to a goddess of love and Freyja got her necklace. In Greek myth it was Hephaistus who made special treasures for the gods. Although a god, he was deformed, his feet crippled and he was so ugly when he was born that his mother Hera threw him down to earth, where he learned the art of the smiths. Later it was Hephaistus who married Aphrodite, the most beautiful of the goddesses. These stories seem to embody the union in all creative acts between the goddess as source and its manifestation in earthly reality by the craftsman as her partner.

A special necklace or collar (sharing the same symbolism) called *menat* belonged to Hathor, the Egyptian goddess of joy, love and fertility. In fact, Hathor was believed to be manifest in the necklace and was sometimes called "She of the Menat" or "The Large Menat." By touching or wearing her necklace, a stream of life was passed as a divine fluid, offering pleasure, fertility or rebirth. The underworld, or the destructive aspect of the life cycle, is expressed by Hindu deities like Shiva or Kali wearing necklaces made of skulls or snakes. Priests, priestesses or shamans of ancient societies would take on the power of a totem animal by wearing a necklace made of its teeth, bone or feathers. Some of this survives in the chains of office, medals of military orders or sports achievements. Negatively, wearing a necklace or a collar can be subjugation to someone more powerful, sometimes with erotic overtones, or even enforced like a prison, slave or animal collar.

Like all jewelry, the necklace also protects. Worn around the neck, the necklace safeguards the vital link between the head (mind, psyche, spirit) and the rest of the body; often a larger bead or stone or a symbol like the cross guards the throat as the seat of the voice, breathing and swallowing (EoR, 8:28). By covering the heart, a pendant also protects its symbolic meanings such as courage, love and life itself. In Egypt a special pendant in the form of a scarab was placed over the heart of the deceased to secure the passage through the underworld. The scarab was believed to help raise the sun in the morning, and in the same way it guided the pharaoh toward rebirth and eternal life.

In dreams then, receiving or losing a necklace can have many meanings, depending on its origin and emotional value. The breaking of a necklace might suggest that a relationship to someone or something needs to be broken; or perhaps it is a warning about a loss of order, protection or something of great value. Should someone be stealing one's necklace, there is even more reason to review the motifs: Is the necklace a bond to an unconscious power complex or an authentic link to our true self?

1

2

1. Eight double-breasted beads, mammoth ivory, probably once strung into a necklace, 30,000–18,000 years old, Dólni Věstonice, now Czech Republic.

2. Life-giving fluid is transferred to Seti I as he touches Hathor's menat necklace. Painted limestone relief, 19th dynasty (1292–1190 B.C.E.), Egypt (ARAS, 2Am.031).

Earring

The striking Woodabe girl would have had her ears pierced for the first time around the age of four, and as she grew added hoop upon hoop, elongating the lobe and enhancing her beauty (Beckwith, 67). As with many nomadic peoples, her earrings form part of her portable wealth, a sign of abundance in the sparse existence of a tribe that strives against the fierce droughts of the Niger steppe.

The earring is an ornament of stupendous variation that in many cultures also signifies a rite of passage or an aspect of identity. For many young women, it marks the achievement of sexual maturation, the piercing of the earlobe corresponding to the breaking of the hymen. This initiatory ritual is less formally but just as meaningfully enacted amongst high school girls or in college dorms. The ear is an erogenous zone associated with the feminine genitals since it has an opening likened to the vulva and a deep inner chamber or "womb." In one of the African languages, the same word refers to both earring and vulva.

The Indonesian ear pendant resembles a vulva. Associated with the clan's founding ancestors, they were given to a woman upon her engagement as bride wealth, or used as funeral ornaments at the end of her life (Pal, 241, 346). With similar allusion to the sanctity of feminine sexuality, the Aures women of Algeria wear earrings called *Töbularwah* or "soul-carriers" from puberty to menopause (DoS, 330–1). The wearing of earrings is not, however, restricted to women. As a fashion among men, they may suggest sexual orientation or a statement of individuality.

Earring also has religious significance. For the ancient Mexicans, it was a sign of penance because of its association with piercing the flesh. Especially in the East, the earring is related to the idea of spiritual "hearing." For example, as part of the initiation of the Khanphata yogis, Indian religious men, the guru makes a long cut in the ear. After the wound heals, the yogi inserts earrings weighing over two ounces, made of agate, horn or glass (ERE, 12:835). Khanphata literally means "slit ears," and the group is also known as "Darsanis" after *darsana* or "earring." The heavy earrings stretch the earlobes, symbolically enlarging the ear in order that it may better receive religious wisdom.

Beckwith, Carol and Marion van Offelen. *Nomads of Niger.* NY, 1983.

Pal, Pratapaditya and Stephen Little. *A Collecting Odyssey: Indian, Himalayan, and Southeast Asian Art from the James and Marilynn Alsdorf Collection.* NY, 1997.

1. On the earrings of a West African Woodabe girl are clusters of amulets. They protect her ears from bad influences and evil spirits (ARAS, 2:189).

2. Earring known as *mamuli*. According to the Sumbanese, the shape of the pendant represents the vulva. Gold, 19th–20th century, Sumba, Indonesia.

1

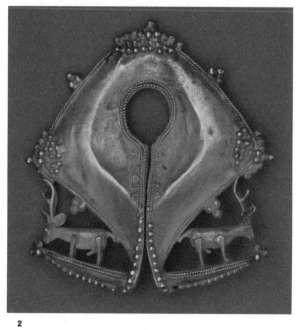

2

545

Ring

In a ring, the divine form of the circle is made tangible, brought into the everyday. A ring has no beginning and no end, is unbroken and unchanging, so it is an image of eternity and infinity. Yet at the same time, its closed form suggests completeness, enclosure, permanence. Enclosure is also implicit in a variety of rings: the boxing ring, the smuggling ring, the circus ring, as well as the ring on one's finger. Perhaps because of the odd pairing of endlessness and enclosure, rings are used to symbolize bonding, binding, promises, vows, covenants. Since Roman times, betrothals, as well as the promises and the binding of marriage, have been marked by finger rings. (A wedding ring is worn on the third finger of the left hand because in former times, it was believed that a vein or nerve runs from this finger directly to the heart.) A nun wears a ring as the spouse of Christ. The "Fisherman's Ring" of the Roman pope, showing the apostle Peter casting his net, testifies that the pope, a successor of Peter, is bound to the Church; this bond, and the ring that symbolizes it, is broken at the death of each pope (*Enc. Brit.* 4:800).

But rings' bonding and binding symbolism goes further even—toward enslavement. The origin of the finger ring, according to the Roman historian Pliny, lies with the mythical Greek Prometheus who was chained to a rock by Zeus as punishment for his reckless daring in stealing fire from heaven. He was released before his sentence was completed, but was required to wear a link of his chain with a fragment of the rock set in it, as a ring. This symbolized that he was still bound to the rock, and bound in submission to Zeus. This was the first time a ring had ever been worn and in honor of Prometheus, men also began to wear rings (Avery, 935). The ring of legendary King Polycrates, set with a magnificent emerald, was cast by him into the sea when he began to suspect that his extraordinary run of good fortune would be followed, inevitably, by bad. The bad luck of losing his cherished ring was intended to avoid the greater woes that he feared. However, the ring was returned to him when the fish that had swallowed it was caught and the ring found, and later he was captured and crucified, demonstrating that one is bound by, or a prisoner of, one's fate and cannot escape it (Avery, 909). In earlier times, the rings of the dying would be removed so that they could be released from bonds to this life.

Rings are a sign of power and also a magical source of it. On the hand of king or sage, they symbolize authority, which can also be symbolically given to another person in the form of the ring: "And Pharaoh said unto Joseph, See, I have set thee over all the land of Egypt. And Pharaoh took off his signet ring from his hand and put it upon Joseph's hand … " (Genesis 41:42f). The wisdom of Solomon was said to derive from his magical ring (EoR, 8:30) and the success of Joan of Arc on the battlefield from hers (MM 17:387). In former times, a king's ring was supposed to have healing powers derived from the king's own person, and there were other rings with curative and protective magic: the plague was warded off with rings on which the Holy Family was pictured; in medieval England, "crampe rynges," made of silver blessed by a priest, cured epilepsy and "convulsions and fits of every kind" (Opie, 327).

Fairy tales abound with magic rings that give the wearer untold power. In some tales, this power is quite concrete: " … [he] moved the ring from one hand to the other, and three hundred strong men and a hundred and seventy knights jumped out and asked: 'What do you order us to do?'" (*Guterman*, 33). The fairy-tale heroes benefit from the power of their magic rings, but more modern symbolism focuses on the dangers of such magical power. In recent centuries, Richard Wagner (in the opera cycle *The Ring of the Nibelung*) and J. R. R. Tolkien (in *The Lord of the Rings*) have given us popular epics on this theme. These modern rings, symbolizing the human power drive, are cursed at their source, and bring moral corruption and disaster to their owners and potentially to the world. Although these ring-wearers believe that they have control over all of man and nature, it becomes clear that they themselves are the slaves of their own demonic addiction to power (DoS, 808). As well as divine wholeness, it seems, the ring can also signify this devilish power-love.

Avery, Catherine B. *The New Century Classical Handbook*. NY, 1962.

Opie, Iona Archibald. *A Dictionary of Superstitions*. Oxford and NY, 1989.

Guterman, Norbert. Tr. *Russian Fairy Tales*. NY, 1973.

A woman in Turmi, Southern Ethiopia, shows the rings
on her fingers. Photograph by Susan Liebold, 2005.

Apron

The "apron" of the body, the abdomen and pelvic area that contains the organs of generation, lends its shape and potency to the apron of costume. The curve of the apron over the skirt of the Minoan snake goddess is emblematic of her generous sexuality and fecund womb, her proudly sensual nature further emphasized by full, rounded breasts. The lozenges that decorate the border of the apron are ancient symbols of fertility. Aprons have been associated with feminine figures as far back as the Upper Paleolithic period in Europe. A bone Venus figurine was discovered at Lespugue in France wearing an apron of twisted strings suspended from a hip band at the back, dating from around 20,000 B.C.E. (Davidson, 91).

Apron takes its name from the Latin, *mappa*, in Old French *naperon*, Middle English *napron*, meaning napkin, cloth or covering. As such, the apron may have been the first piece of clothing humans ever wore. This is true of the Biblical Adam and Eve. When the mythic couple became conscious of their nakedness after tasting the fruit of knowledge from the forbidden tree in Eden, they "sewed fig leaves together and made themselves aprons" in order to hide their genitals (Genesis 3:7). In certain African tribes, men wore aprons when venturing outside their village as a means of protecting their genitals from evil spirits that might be abroad. Like the girdle, aprons have long been worn to signify the sexual status of a woman, the virgin often wearing a simple string or beaded apron, the woman who was betrothed or married one that was more elaborate or of woven fabric (Stepan, 60).

Perhaps because aprons are so associated with the genital area of the body, to which has been attributed, especially in women, natural fire, heat and magical creativity, aprons have been part of the vestments of ritual practice, from Siberian shamanism to modern-day Freemasonry. Their purpose was surely not only to protect but to enhance and display the occult powers of their owner. The Tantric sorcerer of Tibet, for example, wore an apron of human bones hanging from a cloth belt. Glowing in the dark, the bone fragments, possibly amulets, were often carved with human figures, faces, flowers and other designs, interspersed with colorful beads of semiprecious stones (DoS, 37). The apron can also suggest the idea of humble service; for example, Jesus girds himself with a towel in order to wash the feet of his disciples before his last supper with them.

Cooks, bakers, artists and artisans wear aprons to protect them from the materials of their work, but such aprons also carry the evocation of a chthonic, generative "fire," which, consciously employed and directed, transforms matter into differentiated forms. Emblematic of both mother and crone, the capacious apron of the great maternal can, of course, also suffocate or bind. One can be "tied to the apron strings" of the mother, meaning a tendency to infantilism or a lack of adequate differentiation between consciousness and the unconscious matrix. For many, however, "apron" resonates nostalgically, in memory or fantasy, with the image of abiding nurturance.

Davidson, Hilda Ellis. *Roles of the Northern Goddess*. London, 1998.
Stepan, Peter. "Ijogolo Bridal Apron." *Africa*. Munich and London, 2001.

1. Ancient emblem of the great feminine and her fertile earth, an apron covers the heavy skirt of a Minoan goddess. *Snake Goddess*, faience, polychrome, ca. 1500 B.C.E., from Palace of Knossos, Crete, Greece.

2. Well-protected by an apron, C. G. Jung fills a kettle in his workshop.

3. This shaman's ceremonial apron is made from moose hide painted with human and animal figures and a fringe hung with deer dewclaws. Sixty amulets of bone or teeth are sewn to the center, some of which are carved to represent spirits. Tlingit apron, ca. 1830–60, Alaska.

1

2

3

Shoe

When, as primates, we came down from the arboreal realm and touched ground, our feet encountered briars, sharp rock, hot sand and frigid streams. Coverings made of tree fiber or animal pelt offered protection. These early prototypes of the shoe may have been among the first creative innovations toward the shod foot of civilization. Yet imagination remained supernaturally mobile, shoeing itself in the seven-leagued boots of northern European folklore, or more elegantly, in the winged sandals of Hermes who travels between seen and unseen dimensions. The magical sense of the shoe's independent agency and divine connections is embodied in popular rituals of leaving a pair of shoes at threshold or hearth on special holidays in hopes of finding it filled with gifts.

As human culture developed, shoes became associated with authority, ownership, sexuality and status. To claim property, one might place shoes upon it or walk its perimeter. Rank and social standing were conveyed by specific features of the shoe: the elaborately beaded buckskin moccasin of a native American chief, for example, or the bright-red sandal of a Roman senator. On the opposite end of the spectrum is shoelessness, widely associated with poverty. In many sacred traditions, the removal of shoes signifies a casting off of worldliness, or a reversal of standpoint.

The sensitivity of the foot to touch, its vaguely phallic shape and the hollow receptacle of the shoe fostered the shoe's erotic connotations. Shoes are common objects of sexual fetishism. The custom of throwing a pair of shoes at newlyweds or tying a miniature pair to their departing carriage expressed the sexual pairing of the couple. The four-inch long "lotus shoe" that fit the foot of a Chinese woman who had undergone foot-binding, and the severely pointed toe of the Western stiletto pump, both denote an idealization of the erotic feminine coupled with its crippling confinement in the standards of beauty or fashion that define it.

In dreams, shoes can evoke the nature of one's standpoint and its relative authenticity. Does the shoe fit, or are the shoes too small or too large for the wearer's true size or potential? Or too tight or too loose for what stability or mobility requires? Does one shoe oneself in the practical, whimsical, sexy? Badly worn shoes might suggest a stance that requires renewal, new shoes a fresh beginning. Sometimes the shoes may even seem to have a life of their own. In the fairy tale "The Shoes That Were Danced to Pieces," the daughters of the king secretly descend each evening to an enchanted, underground realm where they dance all night with phantom suitors. They return home exhausted with their shoes in pieces, reminding us that too much investment in a fantasy world can be at the sacrifice of sure footing in reality. The red shoes of Hans Christian Andersen's moralistic tale represent the restless vanity of a young girl, which drives and ultimately maims her. The ruby slippers in *The Wizard of Oz*, on the other hand, embody psyche's magical power to carry one away into the dark journey of initiation, but also to bring one back to earth. And the glass slippers from the fairy godmother that only fit Cinderella indicate something greater in the personality that ultimately shoes the impoverished young woman in her noble uniqueness.

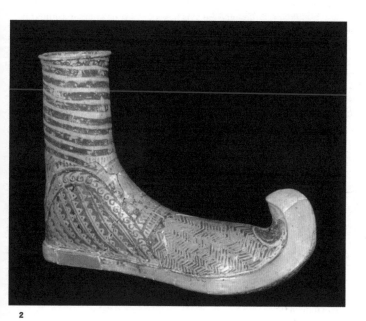

1. King Tutankhamun's gold thongs on whose interior surface are burnished complete portraits of the enemies upon whom Egypt had trod. From the tomb of Tutankhamun, 1332–23 B.C.E., Egypt.

2. Vessel in the shape of a winged boot, ceramic, 14th–11th centuries B.C.E., Attica, Greece.

Umbrella/Parasol

A Chinese bronze depicts a kneeling man holding a parasol that resembles the stalk of a large leaf and provides cooling shade for an unseen dignitary. This act of protection is a traditional gesture of honor and respect for both secular and ecclesiastical authority in the East and West (*Enc. Brit.* 26:870).

The word parasol is derived from the Latin word meaning, "to hold off the sun," while umbrella, from a diminutive of the Latin *umbra*, "shade" refers to the portable shelter carried in case of rain (Beer, 178). Symbolically, the parasol brings together the ideas of divine and human, deity and king. The parasol suggests the curving dome of the sky; an allusion to heaven's protection of the king. Its finial represents the axis mundi that, like divinely ordained kingship, links heaven and earth. Invoking perhaps the sheltering presence of both gods and ancestors, Asante African festival occasions were dominated by brightly colored state umbrellas of diverse, imported fabrics; the finials of those belonging to a chief carried the motifs of ruling clans and culture heroes. In early Indian Buddhism, the parasol's spokes radiated from a still, central point, suggesting the hub of the great wheel where the Buddha sits.

Buddhism, in fact, gives special significance to the parasol. Buddhist shrines, or stupas, often display a series of parasols on a single pole, symbolizing a succession of extracosmic levels of existence. Held over the head of the Buddha, the parasol represents spiritual protection from the heat of suffering, desire, illness and all other obstacles to human happiness, or, in Vajrayama Buddhism, is deified as the thousand-armed goddess Sitatapatra, "the white umbrella" that protects all beings from all fears (Beer, 176–7). Similarly, in Hinduism, the body's spinal energy channel, with its series of wheel-like chakra points, culminates in the crown chakra, conceived as a parasol with a hole in the center.

Making a comparatively late appearance in the West, the umbrella was used by a few women in Britain in the seventeenth century and not at all by men until the late eighteenth. One man who appeared with an umbrella in the London streets of 1778 was subjected to jeers and hoots (MM 16:2605). Now a ubiquitous and gender-neutral accessory, the umbrella is also an object of superstition, especially the idea that the inopportune opening of an umbrella brings the "foul weather" of bad luck. Umbrella can be said to connote the imaginal axis between psyche's personal and transpersonal spheres that offers the ego relative shelter from psychic downpours. Nevertheless, as in outer reality, there are some storms that turn the umbrella inside out.

Beer, Robert. *The Encyclopedia of Tibetan Symbols and Motifs*. Boston, 1999.

1. In Asia, the parasol has been a traditional emblem of power and majesty. Bronze, Western Han dynasty (206 B.C.E.–8 C.E.), China.

2. A scene of modern urban life in which the umbrella plays a functional and fashionable part. *Paris Street, Rainy Day*, by Gustave Caillebotte, oil painting, 1877, France.

3. Working along the river, three men crowd under an umbrella during a rainstorm. *Shower on the Banks of the Sumida River at Ommaya Embankment*, by Utagawa Kuniyoshi, wood-block print, ca. 1834, Japan.

1

2

3

Telephone

A marriage of the phallic and the feminine—of sending and receiving—Andy Warhol's retro *Telephone* conjures us to connect. The telephone gets its name from the Greek *phone,* "sound," and *tele,* "far off," which refer to the telephone's capacity to transmit and receive the sound of the voice over distance. Alexander Graham Bell got the patent for the telephone five years after the death of his brother, with whom he had once made a pact that whoever died first would attempt to communicate with the other (Bruce, 66ff). We can only speculate if the two things were related, but certainly the telephone catches the projection of being magical and supernatural.

Vastly expanding the thrust and speed of spoken communication, the telephone has become the ubiquitous image of deals in the making, a direct line to authority and the slender thread between an individual in need and saving help. Invoking family ties, close friendship and the reassurance of a loved one's voice, Bell Telephone's famous ad invited us to "reach out and touch someone" virtually anywhere in the world.

Both a link and a boundary, no telephone is an island unto itself: One phone necessarily implies the absent presence of another. In its refusal to ring a silent phone can exaggerate loneliness. A ringing telephone, however, asserts an immediate hold on one's attention, targeting its signal to the instinctive, reactive mind. It evokes a prerational response—annoyance, excitement, anticipation or dread. Indeed, like Warhol's rendering of it, which seems alive with possibilities from the playful to the sinister, the telephone is capricious in what it calls up. Phones can be used to intimidate and harass. Countless thrillers have implicated the phone as an instrument of seduction, espionage and murderous scheming. Telephone hotlines once offered services as diverse as suicide intervention, prayer, astrological readings and phone sex. Telemarketing once inundated us with sales promotions. The cell phone, answering the need to be connected all the time, may compensate a collective sense of isolation. And while a technological hero of emergency and disaster scenes, it has become for many the embodiment of intruding, compulsive chatter.

Symbolically, the image of the telephone evokes psychic lines of communication that can get confused by the static and crossed wires of conflicting attitudes and desires. The telephone is a common image in the dreams of modern individuals, sometimes connoting the psyche's "ringing up" of consciousness to deliver an important message, even a warning; it behooves us to listen.

Bruce, Robert V. *Bell: Alexander Graham Bell and the Conquest of Solitude.* NY, 1973.

Telephone, by Andy Warhol, acrylic and pencil on canvas, 1961, United States.

House/Home

The little ceramic Chinese house from 2,000 years ago, with its rudimentary windows and door, conveys the essence of house as containment and shelter. A house is one embodiment of home; "home is where the heart is," a feeling state of belonging, safety and contentment. Physically, our earliest home is the maternal womb in which we are gestated, and like the animals who instinctively make their homes in nests, burrows in the earth, the hollows of trees, caves and clefts, many of the first homes of our devising were intimate, encompassing womblike structures. All over the world, cave drawings attest to our primordial presence. Mud huts in parts of Africa are still fashioned in the form of the female torso, with vaginalike slits as doors. The tepee of the Great Plains Indians, the triangular tents of the nomad, are circular at the base, suggesting the alpha and omega of existence that begins in the womb, and the eternal cycles of nature. Home is the sacraments and rituals of relationship, conjunction, solitude and nakedness, enacted in the house's kitchen, bedroom, bathroom. To be unhoused is not necessarily to be homeless. On woods, desert, the moon, a ship at sea, a beloved friend, a particular city, a set of circumstances, is projected "home." These correspond to, or contribute to something within, the experience of a vital center of both fixity and freedom,

rest after striving, being fully oneself. Homelessness is associated with dereliction, dispossession, instability, rootlessness, restlessness, emptiness and chronic longing. For some, home seems unattainable in the here and now. Death is then emblematic of homecoming, the fantasy of ineffable origin and return. In dreams, psyche is often depicted as a house. Sometimes there are different levels, representing a continuum of time. There may be familiar rooms, and others unknown, hidden, revealing multivalenced potentialities. The structural soundness of the personality, the relation between its personal and transpersonal aspects is also suggested in the depiction: Is the house solid or tawdry, is there symmetry between vertical and horizontal, or disproportion? Is the space pinched or spacious? The outer manifestations of home are subject to countless variables. Home has been idealized. In mythologies all over the world our first home is a paradise of oneness, a time before consciousness and its conflicting discriminations. Home can be a prison or a haven of avoidance. One is homebound, or a homebody. In house and home are domestic harmony and domestic violence. Home can represent the nurturing of the self, and also its violation. We escape home, outgrow home, return home, seek home. Home is the goal of epic odysseys, spiritual quests and psychic transformations.

1

2

1. House, ceramic, ca. 25–220 C.E., China.

2. *Home*, child's drawing by Tassos Bareiss, 2001, United Sates.

Gate/Door

Gates beckon: "Come in!" says the beautiful gate of our first image. But they can also bar us and convey "no admittance!" Gates stand between here and there, between the known and the unknown. At a psychological level, gates are found between the inner world and the outer, between sleeping and waking: We labor to bring a half-remembered dream through the gateway between sleep and the daylight (Hillman, 181). We may also search for "doors in the wall" (as H. G. Wells called them)—openings from everyday consciousness to the transcendent—through ecstatic states, meditation, hallucinogens (Huxley, 62f). So gates are places of transition from one state to another. A mother's body is the gateway opening to this world, the tomb the gateway to what comes after death. In ancient Egypt, a "doorway" in the tomb was built to allow free passage—in and out—to the soul. In Judaism, death was called a door to Sheol, the underworld (Psalm 9:13).

In our everyday world, gates and doors protect the house and the life of the family from strangers. Cities and nations erect gates and barriers at their borders. In ancient times, the two-faced god Janus protected both entrance to and exit from Roman cities (MM 11:1483–4). Gates of temples separate the profane and the sacred and protect the interiors and the holy presence within. Mythical gatekeepers watch over entrances to holy places: Saint Peter over the pearly gates of heaven, the great dog Cerberus over the gate to the Greek underworld, the god Ganesha over entrances to the shrines of India. Sometimes gates are intended to keep inhabitants from leaving: Greek Hades was known as "he who closes the door" (Hillman, 180) to make sure that the shades stayed in the underworld.

The gate-doorway is a dangerous and numinous place, rich in protective rituals and superstitions. Offerings and prayers are made; shoes are removed before entering. A bride is carried over the threshold. One must step carefully over a threshold, usually right foot first, and should not sneeze, sit, linger or suckle a baby there (ERE 4:846ff). Doorways are also magically protected from evil influence and powers by sprinklings of salt or the presence of iron objects such as a horseshoe. Sacred symbols are found there—images of protective gods or demons, crosses, Jewish mezuzahs (de Vr, 143). Our image shows sculptured human heads protecting an ancient cathedral doorway in Ireland. In Japan, approach to Shinto shrines is signaled in advance by freestanding gates called torii.

On the other hand, sometimes doors and gates must be opened to release what is too confined inside. Thus the "doors of fancy's flight"—imagination—are released by education or religion (Goodenough, 4:103). Similarly, the seven liberal arts are referred to as "the seven gates" (de Vr, 211). More concretely, in folklore of the British Isles, house doors are to be opened when someone is dying, "to ease passage of the soul." And in Indonesia, house doors were opened during childbirth, magically making for the baby's easier emergence (Leach 1:321).

The Virgin Mary has long been a Christian personification of the holy gateway, closed in virginity but open as the channel for Christ's crossing from heaven to earth. A twelfth-century hymn describes her:

> Sancta Maria
> Closed gate
> Opened at God's command—
> Sealed fountain,
> Locked garden,
> Gate of paradise.
> (CW 5:577fn)

Goodenough, Erwin R. *Jewish Symbols in the Greco-Roman Period*. Princeton, NJ, 1954.
Hillman, James. *The Dream and the Underworld*. NY, 1979.
Huxley, Aldous. *The Doors of Perception and Heaven and Hell*. NY, 2004.
Leach, Maria. Ed. *Funk & Wagnalls Standard Dictionary of Folklore, Mythology and Legend*. NY, 1949.

1. The gate in Ross Bleckner's painting seems to be an invitation to the green Eden behind it, rather than a barrier. *The Gate*, 1985, United States.

2. Door as the threshold between physical or imaginal rooms. *The Dining Room*, detail, by Justus Lundegård, oil painting, 1919, Sweden.

3. This 13th-century Irish cathedral door is protected by carved stone foliage and flowers, and also guarded by carved human heads. The heads are linked to pre-Christian symbolism of the head as the place of the immortal divinity within human beings (ARAS, 2:82).

Lock

Carved in the form of a female figure, the wooden lock from Mali is crossed horizontally by a bolt that signifies the woman's husband and strengthens closure. Together, lock and bolt suggest not only the physical "locking" or conjunction of opposites in the sacred union of marriage, but, as well, the way the intimate commitment to each other protects the privacy and faithfulness of the couple from intrusion by the outside world (Bargna, 23). Like the lock that protects the granary containing nourishment for the body, the apotropaic figure wards off threats to the marriage, a social contract that the Bamana culture regards as a nourishing element in the community (Bamana).

The lock is a practical device that in many forms has secured home and treasure for at least 4,000 years (Schlage's History of Locks, 2). Lock is also a venerable symbol, activating a wide field around its function of keeping in or keeping out. This includes sexual metaphor related to virginity, intercourse and even the violence of rape as forced entry. The romantic lock is also implicated in one's getting literally locked out of the dwelling as a signal that a relationship is over, or figuratively "locked out" of access to the other's feelings.

What a collective keeps under lock and key says something about its fears as well as its mores. Being locked behind prison walls may connote justified incarceration or signify a regime's repression of political dissent. On the other hand, the locked arms of a protesting crowd have effectively defied authority. The locked wards of mental institutions have been seen as both a protective container for the insane and "back wards" where society locks away its disordered. In countless stories, the clink of key or bolt in lock may represent the ominous sound of imposed confinement, and/or the reassurance that one is contained.

Access to what is locked away may be contingent on finding the key that fits the lock, like an intuition that brings new knowledge into consciousness. Psychic defenses can act as locks on unconscious contents, but whether to leave them locked or loosen the bolt requires discrimination. There are fairy tales, for example, where one is forbidden to unlock a particular door or ask a particular question that might unlock a dark secret. In some cases the "unlocking" results in saving revelations that serve integrity; in other cases, the unlocking is merely destructive. In myths, the unlocking of places of deepest initiatory mystery often requires the mediation of a transpersonal guide who holds the key.

Protecting everything from the trunks of immigrants crossing the ocean to jewel boxes and diaries, cars and bank vaults, locks signify ownership, value and enticing secrets. Repressive lockdowns as well as the indiscriminately open door may be equally faulty relationships to the lock. Similarly, breaking a lock can represent a necessary forcing in or out, or merely a violation. Like the Bamanan figure of husband and wife, the lock is a "fastening" that imposes boundaries.

Exhibition Wall Text. *Bamana: The Art of Existence in Mali.* Museum for African Art. NY, 2001/2002.
Bargna, Ivan. *African Art.* Milano, Italy, 2000.
Schlage's History of Locks. http://www.locks.ru/eng/informat/schlagehistory.htm.

The lock configured as a woman and the bolt signifying
her husband together evoke the protective force of
matrimonial union. Door lock, wood, Bamana culture,
Mali, Africa.

Key

Knowing he will soon die, Jesus hands over to his disciple Peter the "keys to the Kingdom of Heaven" (Matthew 16:19). In Perugino's solemn depiction, Peter's expression and the greatness of the key he clutches to his chest convey the weight of this symbolic transmission: the impending death of his master and the burden of responsibility he must assume when the master is gone. Exegetes have understood this metaphorical key and its capacity "to bind and loose" to mean Peter's authority to interpret the laws that regulate the community of the faithful (Laymon, 630). Some have seen it as a proof text for the primacy of the Roman Church, which Peter is said to have founded before his martyrdom in Rome. Imagination, however, has made of Peter the gatekeeper of heaven, his golden key signifying the saint's power to absolve sin and open the door to eternal life, and the silver, to lock out from heaven the souls unworthy of heaven's gate (EoR, 8:278).

Keys function to let us in or out, to lock or unlock everything from storerooms of provisions to houses, prisons, hospital wards, diaries, caskets of jewels, drawers of old letters, knowledge, memories and hidden or forbidden dimensions of psyche. Pandora's legendary box of worldly woes would seem to need permanent locking, but, like most locked things, provokes us to use the keys at hand. Likewise, the "locked room" of many fairy tales, reflecting psyche's defended spaces, nevertheless bids one to key in to what it conceals of possibility, and also danger. Unlocked, such rooms reveal treasure, secrets, dismembered bodies, demons, captives—or nothing at all. Sacred realms of death, rebirth and transformation have often been regarded as locked regions, protected by deities that possess the keys, or their priests and priestesses who mediate the initiate's entry into divine mysteries. Keys belonging to the mythic witch Hecate secure the Greek under-world of Hades. In the Book of Revelation, an angel holds the keys to the abyss where the devil is chained (Leach, vol. 2, 575). The Babylonian goddess Ishtar bears the keys that open the locks of heaven (ERE 10:122). Her counterpart Cybele locks up the earth each winter and opens it to growth and flowering every spring (EoR 8:277).

Keys evoke the tension between seeking and finding, restricting and releasing, withholding and giving, prohibiting and admitting. The individual with the "key" momentarily becomes threshold guardian and opener of the way. Human consciousness perpetually searches for the key that will give it access to the object of its longing—self-discovery, peace of mind, the enigmatic heart of the beloved. The difference between being shut out and getting in seems as tantalizingly simple as an antique key sliding into a keyhole. The key's pattern of slots matches up precisely with the projections inside the lock (*Enc. Brit.* 7:433), a conjunction that finds analogy with sexual coitus. There are keys unique to complicated locks and there are "skeleton" keys, like the fundamental laws of physics. Key to the alchemical opus was the imagination, which made meaning of what happened in the alembic. Psyche offers keys to its conundrums in the form of symptoms and symbols. Key is mercurial, however. Knowing what is "key" often requires the trying of many different keys before the hoped-for yielding of the bolt.

Laymon, Charles M. *The Interpreter's One Volume Commentary on the Bible.* Nashville, TN, 1971.
Leach, Maria. Ed. *Funk & Wagnalls Standard Dictionary of Folklore, Mythology and Legend.* NY, 1949.
Marijnissen, Roger H. and Peter Ruyffelaere. *Hieronymus Bosch: The Complete Works.* Antwerp, 1987.

1. *Christ Hands the Key of Heaven to Saint Peter,* detail, by Perugino, side fresco in the Sistine Chapel, 1481–3, Rome, Italy.

2. The artist's vision of Hell. A sinner's avarice hangs on a key, perhaps representing both the man's locked-up riches and his anxiety about them, which he is never without (Marijnissen, 89–90, 134). *Garden of Earthly Delights,* detail, by Hieronymus Bosch, oil on panel, ca. 1504, the Netherlands.

1

2

Window

Through a mullioned window fleeting sunlight breaks into an empty room, illuminating the dust motes. Who knows what life sometimes fills the silence here. Is it a schoolroom? An empty house? A place of merriment, or dream, or contemplation?

Window is a transparent threshold. It is an opening in a wall of matter that lets in air, moonlight and sunlight, the colors of the world, the dark of night. The window is where inside and outside meet and cross, bringing together two worlds and their elements. Wind rattling the windowpane. The streaking of raindrops. Passing, one sees through a window an intimate domestic scene. At the same window, another looks out "experiencing longing, the lust for travel or escape" (Appleton, 78).

Eyes have been called the windows of the soul and windows the eyes of a house. The "third eye" of imagination is a window on the inner world of possibility. The word "window" is derived from the old Icelandic *vindr*, "wind," and *auga*, "eye." The wind-eye was "originally a mere hole in the wall protected by branches or a curtain and exposed to the wind" (Barnhart, 883). Over the centuries the opening in the wall was screened or filled with marble, alabaster, rice paper or, sometimes, thin panes of mica or horn as substitutes for glass. Eventually able to open and close, windows contributed to the regulation of heat, light and air and acquired the meaning of an interval of time in which something can occur. A launch window in aeronautics is an opening in the earth's atmosphere for a spacecraft's safe passage. There are weather windows and windows of opportunity. We say, hopefully, "There is a window in the clouds." The window, unscreened, enables us to see through clearly. Windows of glass insulate while allowing us to observe what's on the other side. But the window's transparency also draws the voyeur or the spy, stealing information and intimacy. There are those who feel that "glass-box" high-rises, with their walls of windows, embody the erosion of urban character and architectural aesthetic (Wolfe, 1ff).

Yet, the "wind-eye" also evokes a spirit laden "looking" and exchange. Windows are a framing of images resonant with psychic potency. The fairy tale "Snow White" begins in the winter with a childless queen looking out an ebony-framed window at the snow-covered ground and wishing for a child. Ancient priestesses of ritual prostitution in honor of the goddess Astarte were often represented by the image of a woman in a window. In the Middle Ages, the Virgin Mary, humbly bearing the son of God, was depicted as being receptive as a window allowing light to pass through. The icons of eastern Christianity are windows opening on the divine, a form of meditation and revelation that "shows a cosmic version of events seen in eternity" (Kala, 26). Stained-glass windows also engender inspired perspective. By the thirteenth century, the stained glass technique made possible the creation of the great rose windows of Paris cathedrals. "Roses full of fire," brilliant with light and color, these round windows are mandalas (Cowen, 7ff), intimating transcendence, perfection, totality and paradisal restoration. In ancient cultures all over the world, a window was opened at the time of death to release the soul to immortality. The "opening in the plane" that shamans experienced in trance was a window on the spirit world, a linking of visible and invisible realms.

Dreams, memories, fantasies are windows on psyche's timeless reality and the complexes and potentialities of the dreamer. Alchemy intuited such in Gerhard Dorn's notion of the "*spiraculum*." This "breathing-hole," or window on eternity, was a spiritual expansion through which the soul engaged the matter of psyche's unconscious dimension, the "divine influx" that brought self-knowledge (CW 14:670ff).

Appleton, Jay. *The Symbolism of Habitat: An Interpretation of Landscape in the Arts.* Seattle, 1990.

Barnhart, Robert K. Ed. *The Barnhart Concise Dictionary of Etymology.* NY, 1995.

Cowen, Painton and Jill Purce. *Rose Windows.* SF, 1979.

Kala, Thomas. *Meditations on the Icons.* Middlegreen, 1993.

Wolfe, Tom. "The (Naked) City and the Undead." *The New York Times* (November 26, 2006).

1

2

3

1. *Sunbeams*, by Vilhelm Hammershoi,
oil painting, 1900, Denmark.

2. Allowing no view inside, the windows in a high-rise
cityscape appear impersonally as flat shapes in a
geometrical design. *Windows*, by Charles Sheeler, oil
painting, 1951, United States.

3. Colorful patterns made of rice paste create a
"curtain" above these windows. In the rural Indian
village, where much of life is spent out of doors, the
windows are designed to admit not light, but air.
Photograph by Stephen P. Huyler, from *Painted
Prayers*, 1994.

Stairway

Built without mortar of half-ton stones, the Nuragic towers of Sardinia defy gravity as they rise 70 feet in the air, enclosing spiral staircases that sentries once mounted to reach their lookouts. Like all stairs, these massive steps consist of horizontal treads and vertical risers (but lack the handrails prudently required by modern building codes). The etymology of stairs—drawing on the Old English words *stigan* (to climb) and *staeger* (riser)—suggests that stairs are primarily perceived as going up rather than in two directions, furnishing a symbol for ascents in slow stages and transitions through difficult steps. We see this externally in the long staircases ancient Babylonian, Mayan and Roman architects placed on the facades of their ziggurats, pyramids and temples in order to bridge earth and heaven, and in the stepped pyramids of ancient Egypt whose stairways provided a transitional zone between life and death (Wilkinson, 151). The Egyptian god Osiris, whose throne was a set of stairs, watched the dead climb a stairway to their Last Judgment, including the weighing of their hearts against the feather of Maat, goddess of cosmic order. In ancient Rome, Mithraic priests led initiates up a Stairway of the Seven Planets, each step of which was cast from a different metal paired to one of the seven known planets. The gold tread at the top corresponded to the sun; reaching it, the initiate underwent *solificatio*, the soul's sublimation back to its source.

But staircases not only ascend, they also go down. The bottom step of the Mithraic Stairway was made of lead, signifying the limitation and heaviness of saturnine depths. Yet, in myth, fairy tales and dreams, staircases, like ladders, descend into realms of mystery, magic, treasure and initiation. Psychoanalysis has taught us to search our own descents for meaning.

Freud used the delightful French phrase esprit d'escalier ("wit of the staircase") to refer to the repartee that occurs to us belatedly as we depart after an argument. The gain of creative wit by reclaiming our "lower" nature through psychoanalysis led Freud to reject what he considered the pretenses of sublimation. Jung once dreamed of the psyche as the different levels of a house linked by a sequence of staircases. The stairs descended from a rococo salon on the upper floor to a fifteenth- or sixteenth-century ground floor to a basement with vaulting that placed it in Roman times. Then, after he lifted the ring of a stone slab, narrow stone steps took him down into the depths and beyond, into a cave with scattered bones and broken pottery, an image of "the primitive man within myself." Jung said that the dream led him to the concept of the collective unconscious.

Esoteric spiritual traditions of descending stairs point us toward a world beyond the opposites suggested by a staircase, especially alchemy with its fundamental axiom "as above, so below," referring to the correspondence between spirit and matter. Medieval manuscripts depict the alchemist standing before a staircase of transformative stages that evokes the extension of self-knowledge through height and depth, as well as the affective "ups and downs" experienced during the opus. It made no matter that the sequence of the stages (such as *calcinatio*, *solutio*, *coagulatio*), varied from text to text. Not only do up and down lose their absolute distinction in these mysteries, but any fixed order dissolves in the dynamic passages that lead in opposite directions to places where opposites vanish.

Wilkinson, Richard H. *Reading Egyptian Art.* London, 1992.

1. This set of stone stairs winding up an ancient Sardinian tower is lit by sunlight above and darkened by shadows beneath—a reminder that every staircase leads in two directions at once. A 1999 photograph by Sandra D. Lakeman; stairs ca. 1500 B.C.E.

2. Rembrandt's *Philosopher in Meditation* anticipates the optical inventions of his compatriot Escher. Both Dutch artists used staircases to illustrate the relativity of ascending and descending when viewed from a philosophical perspective. Oil on panel, 1632, the Netherlands.

3. Burdened with bags of grain, servants (whose lesser status is shown by their size) trudge up a flight of stairs leading from the Nile docks to their master's rounded granaries. Sarcophagus of Ashait, from the temple of Mentuhotep II, 11th dynasty (ca. 2008–1957 B.C.E.), Deir el-Bahari, Egypt.

Ladder

The ladder derives its template on the one hand from the mythical axis mundi connecting heaven and earth, and on the other, from branching tree limbs that encouraged climbing and niches in rock that gave foothold. Covered with sacrificial materials like millet and blood, the miniature log ladder of the Mali (Dogon) people of Africa imitates its life-size counterparts but traditionally leans against a clay jar set on a household altar. The jar contains the soul of the head of the family and when he dies, the ladder enables his soul to climb to the hereafter where the ancestors reside (Ginzberg, 286).

An often portable succession of rungs between two uprights, which typically leans or hangs, the ladder is a means of ascending or descending to places otherwise inaccessible. The ladder reaches to rooftop, tree house and the upper stories of burning skyscrapers; likewise underground into manholes, wells and shafts. Ordinary and magical, the ladder's specific character evokes the sense of climbing through space, suspension above an abyss and the linking of disparate realms.

Pueblo cultures embodied equally the ladder's practical and symbolic significance. Hopi women reached from ladders to build the sandstone walls of their ancient dwellings. Ladders led to the entranceways on the lower roofs and up and down to the multilevels of the structure (Nabokov, 370). The kiva, or religious house, was designed to symbolize the mythic place of emergence. Its tilting entry ladder, which the Acoma people saw as the rainbow, linked the levels representing the present world and the ancestral underworld.

In the shamanic traditions of India, Tibet and Siberia, the ladder has an affinity with bridge, stairway, rope and tree as an implement for transcending the limits of time and space. The ladder is associated with magical flight in trance or ecstasy, the initiatory "difficult passage" or "narrow way" and the opening of the plane into the transpersonal spirit world of possession and healing (Eliade, 487–94). Analogously, the rope ladder of folk and fairy tale materializes to offer escape from confinement or access to an unknown dimension. In the Biblical Genesis, the Hebrew patriarch Jacob dreams of a ladder between earth and heaven, the rungs of which form a kind of vertical highway for angelic emissaries.

To climb a ladder is to make vertical progress up or down one step at a time, each involving a temporary destabilization and rebalancing. Christianity, Islam, Mithraism and Orphism saw in the ladder gradations of spiritual development, mystical ascent and salvation. Depictions of a mythic Judgment Day show righteous souls ascending a ladder to a celestial host, while demons cause sinners to fall off. Alchemy employed the image of the ladder as the stages of the journey through the planetary spheres of the opus.

1. Replicas of utilitarian ladders for home or granary, the miniature Dogon ladders are spiritual objects for the ascent of the soul (Ginzberg, 286). In other cultures, like the Egyptian, similar ladders were ancient grave gifts. Wood, Mali, Africa.

Psyche's ladder of process evokes sublimation and grounding, the spiritualizing of matter and the earthing of spirit, affective ups and downs and the risk of both hubris and fall. As a human tool, ladder suggests the sequences of conscious development that effect practical adaptation, mastery and reach. But like the miniature of the Dogon, ladder extends much further, to embody the symbolic rungs of continuity between conscious and transconscious realms—footing that once initiated, can profoundly shake our imagined equilibrium.

Eliade, Mircea. *Shamanism.* NY, 1964.
Ginzberg, Marc and Lynton Gardiner. *African Forms.* Milano, Italy, and NY, 2000.
Nabokov, Peter and Robert Easton. *Native American Architecture.* NY, 1989.
St. Lars Museum and Lunds konsthall. *Särlingar Från St. Lars Museum Utställning i Lunds Konsthall.* Lund, Sweden, 1989.

2

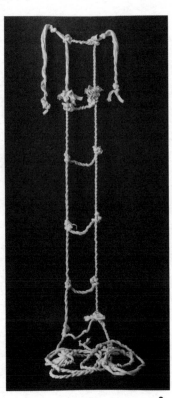

3

4

2. Emblematic of the rainbow, a ladder provides entry into a Pueblo kiva, or ceremonial house. Sometimes the braces of the ladder, whose poles reached into the sky, were ornamented with cloud symbols (Nabokov, 376–7).

3. A rope ladder of sheets, 16 feet long, used in 1910 for the first of several escapes by a patient at St. Lars mental hospital in Sweden.

4. A ladder signifies the 30 rungs of monastic ascent to heaven. Christ welcomes the victorious; devils drag others into the mouth of hell. Icon, Byzantine, late 12th century, Sinai or Constantinople.

Attic

The attic of the eighteenth-century Dutton House is a space of filtered light and shadow, trapped air and gathered dust, serendipitous discovery and the poignancy of things forsaken. Here, a child's stroller and a sturdy wooden horse await the animating fantasies of a chance visitor or a former playmate. Other objects, familiar and curious, are half-revealed behind the slanted roof beams.

Attic, the part just under the roof, evokes stored memories of childhood, "bits of our personality still alive, which cling round us and suffuse us with the feeling of earlier times" (CW 12:81). It is accumulated treasures and trash, the residues of faded life and clues to family skeletons. Attic suggests the idea of things removed but not discarded, nor, perhaps, resolved. It is storage space and sometimes living space, and also hidden space. One may go to the attic as a place of solitude or as a means of avoidance. The fugitive can find temporary deliverance there and unknown intruders be concealed. Murder, incest and suicides have happened in the attic.

Literature has immortalized the attic as the pinched quarters of the servants, the garret of the struggling artist, the room of a lonely child or a sanctum sanctorum giving refuge from the noisy bustle of familial life. In Charlotte Brontë's *Jane Eyre,* the attic of Rochester's mansion signifies both the forbidden suite where his mad wife Bertha is secretly confined, and the tormented space of Rochester's mind to which Jane has no access. The classic mystery play *Gaslight*, portrays the attic as a dissociated recess of unsolved murder, which holds the key to a lamp's repeated dimming and the heroine's flickering sanity.

Like its literal counterpart, psyche's attic contains things known and unknown, but available for discovery, though not necessarily revealed. The attic's diminished verticality suggests that its contents are not so much of an impersonal nature, but rather an often-cluttered museum of personal and familial deposits. The attic requires an ascent, for it suggests the head, but also demands, in the crawlspaces of its territory, that one get down into experience as well, engaging the life of generations that is particular, small, human and perhaps untidy.

For some, the cherished belongings in the attic elicit reverie and unembarrassed regression. For others, dread ghosts inhabit its dark corners. One can put things in the attic almost unknowingly, forget, return and memory is reawakened. Attic fascinates, repels and invites. What is it that is "once removed?" Do we let it lie? Or do we enter the attic—to sort, explore, imagine, shed light on the matter and give it play.

Time seems eerily suspended in the attic of a house.
Dutton House, built in 1782, Vermont.

Basement/Cellar

Built in Prague around 1200, the Palace of the Lords of Kunstát and Poděbrady was reconstructed in the Gothic style in the fifteenth century atop these well-preserved Romanesque pillars in its cellar—a visible reflection of how modern Europe rests upon a layered heritage of medieval and ancient Roman culture. Visitors are often surprised to discover that European castles surmount vast cellars, and that cathedrals conceal sprawling undercrofts that allow them to wander into the lower foundations of this older world.

Cellars originated as storerooms for perishable foodstuffs, from the farmer's root-cellar that preserves fruit and vegetables at a temperature that neither freezes nor overheats to the expansive undercrofts of palaces and cathedrals, in whose forests of pillars and vaults are stored provisions, entombed bodies and the detritus from above. The Latin derivation of "cellar" from *celare*, to hide or keep secret, is also that of the *cella*, a granary, stall, chamber, cell or the place in a temple where the image of the deity stood. Thus the cell where the monastic absorbs the fruits of spiritual cultivation has a natural analogy to these underground repositories of harvested goods. "In Islam, too, the cellar in which is stored the wine of divine knowledge symbolizes the secret chamber to which the mystic withdraws" in order to accomplish union with God (DoS, 172).

The cellar or basement is the lowest part of a building and absorbs the earth's energy of cool darkness, concealment and insularity, giving it affinity with the womblike underworld and the sacred mysteries of the dying and reborn deities of vegetation. In the house, the basement has become a container, too, for the implements of humble, essential activities—laundering, carpentry, repairs—that support the life in the upper regions. Basements are also places of descent into privacy, recreation and isolation. Grounded and often windowless, the cellar is the prairie farmer's safe haven from tornadoes, and the fallout shelter from nuclear explosion. The cellar's function of preservation extends to the sunken remnants of former ages, ancestral traditions and symbolic life, which lie in the subterranean depths of newer physical and psychological structures. Jung once observed that under every medieval church, "there is a secret place where in old times the mysteries were celebrated" (CW 18:254). In the depths of Chartres there is both a labyrinth and a well that is today consecrated to the Virgin Mary, but was earlier dedicated to a Celtic goddess. Alchemy nourished itself on what had been discarded in the basement of the Western Christian psyche, like the cult of the Great Mother and her son, and ancient Egyptian rituals of death and transformation.

What is "abased," can both ripen and molder, and the basement carries far cruder associations with the underworld than being the storehouse for the grain. In earlier times, human victims, sometimes merely unconscious from inebriation, were immured in the foundation of a building, in order to ensure good fortune for its occupants. The shadow aspect of basement associates it with every kind of degradation: captive and dungeon, sexual abuse, child pornography, kidnappings, torture, murder and violence. Among the visceral-looking furnace ducts and boiler pipes, basements have housed the evidence of hideous stored up impulses and secret arsenals of weapons and bombs. Basement bivalently signifies the foundations we build upon—evolutionary, developmental, instinctual, psychical. Basement attests to the correspondence between lowest and highest; in dreams as in waking, what thumps in the cellar may need investigation, or demand engagement, or require arrest.

1. Electric spotlights banish the aged shadows from a Romanesque cellar, allowing visitors to explore the masonry vaulting that supports the ponderous weight of the Gothic edifice overhead. Palace of the Lords of Konstát and Poděbrady, built ca.1200, enlarged in the Gothic style in the 15th century, Prague.

2. An artist's collage reveals the disorder in the basement of our minds—a dustbin of dim memories and inexplicable fantasies. But the shaft of light directed into this underworld also illumines sacred ancestral relics that enter the dreams of the woman sleeping in their midst. *Dreamer in the Crowded Cellar*, by Gayle Homer, collage, 1981, United States.

Kitchen

The meal may be over, or not yet prepared, but Monsieur F.'s small French kitchen gives the impression of readiness, familiarity and seasoned use. Here are the essential tools of cooking: stove, matches, salt box, knife, coffee grinder, pots and kettle blackened by the repetition of fire. It's not hard to imagine how the kitchen and the operations that take place in it—chopping, roasting, boiling, seasoning, mixing—make their way into our dreams, evoking transformation not just of foodstuffs, but of ourselves, the events of our lives, all that we take in, digest and metabolize. In the searing heat of loves and hates, our psychic matter gets "cooked," nourishing the possibility of change or stability, development and growth. Sometimes the steely, sharp edge of the intellect is called for to separate reality from fantasy or divide chunks of experience into manageable slices. Sometimes there is mixing, as memory, desire and unforeseen happenings come together, fizz up, and bring about surprising new awareness.

Wherever the kitchen is in the house, symbolically it evokes the center, for its origin and correspondence is in the hearth and magic cauldron, the body's stomach, the alchemical retort, the psyche's creative core. Like these, kitchen represents a container in which diverse ingredients undergo processes of chaos and order, merging and separation, heating, cooling, decoction, distillation and transmutation. Literally and symbolically, kitchen is a magnet and hub for the convergence of energies: talk, argument, play, gossip, laughter, creativity and nourishment. Kitchen is never merely serene, however, for its implements and operations are potentially deadly, and the cook has the capacity to both nurture and poison. The kitchen entrance and "kitchen talk" allude to the humble, servile, common or crude. Yet, Zen Buddhism calls a fully realized life "the supreme meal," and the Zen cook is one who "knows how to plan, cook, appreciate, serve, and offer" such a meal, including spirituality, study, productive work, social action, relationship and community (Glassman, 4, 7). Like the hearth, the kitchen is often associated with the feminine as vessel and source. Even the Chinese kitchen god that links the family with heaven grew out of the pre-Buddhist tradition of the feminine hearth spirit. The burning of wood in its flames was a "sacrifice to the old women who are dead," the souls of departed cooks (CW 5: 663).

Glassman, Bernard and Rick Fields. *Instructions to the Cook: A Zen Master's Lessons in Living a Life That Matters.* NY, 1996.

1. *Interior of Monsieur F., Merchant, Rue Montaigne- the Kitchen*, by Eugène Atget, photograph, ca. 1910, France.

2. *The Kitchen*, from *A Home*, by Carl Larsson, watercolor, 1890s, Sweden.

Hearth

Fire, the "brilliant guest" (ERE 6:561) comes from the gods, but we must build the hearth to hold it. This union of the flame and its container has been the image of "home" through the ages: "hearth and home," we say. The blazing fire in the hearth is the symbol for the living center—of the family, the community and the nation—even though we no longer depend on it as we once did for warmth, light, protection and the cooking of food.

This long experience with the hearth fire has left an imprint that is more than a memory of the physical structure of the hearth. Concretely, the hearth has changed from a primeval stone slab or clay pit at the center of a cave or a one-room dwelling, moving in medieval times to the house wall and, since the sixteenth century, including a grate (MM 9:1253). The structure of the hearth changes, but its spirit is still felt when family intimates gather around lively centers: the holiday table, or even a ball game on the television set.

For millennia the wood-burning fire on the hearth required someone's constant tending, which gave rise to the sense of a spirit of the hearth, something that presides over the family or community gathering, mediates and integrates differences of the members, patiently and devotedly prepares for and guards the gathering. This spirit stood for "the sanctity to be found in the most ordinary and familiar things ... " (EoR, 6:308) Traditionally, it was seen as feminine, and most famously as the Greek goddess Hestia, whose origins are so archaic that she was not usually imagined in a human form, but as the hearth itself. This spirit, expressing the continuity and stability of the centered group, large or small, was given great religious devotion by the Greeks (and in a related form, as Vesta, by the Romans). Hestia was always offered the first and last prayers and sacrifices on any occasion, even taking precedence over the great Zeus. Her hearth, in the form of a fire-filled altar, was the center of each Greek city, the place of civic ceremony. Hestia's hearth was felt to be the fiery center of the planet and of the universe.

More individually, the hearth spirit is invoked by attending to one's own psychic center, linked as it is to many "hearths," such as one's familial, community, regional and national origins (Edinger, 40–1). These form one layer of the center. Others appear with patient tending to dreams, inner voices and promptings, which lead to knowing and becoming "what one is" (Huffington,168). Connected to this internal center one feels "at home" rather than "off base," "in balance" rather than "off center," "at rest" rather than "unable to settle down" (ibid., 169). Passion and spirit can then flame up into creativity. They will not leap out to consume the house; chaos from the outside will not invade and contaminate them; they are protected and supported by consciousness, by the watchful hearth.

Edinger, Edward F. *The Eternal Drama: The Inner Meaning of Greek Mythology.* Ed. Deborah A. Wesley. Boston and NY, 1994.
Huffington, Arianna Stassinopoulos and Roloff Beny. *The Gods of Greece.* NY, 1983.

A medieval family, its diverse members held together by the warmth of the hearth. *Confabulator (conversation),* manuscript from *Tacuinum Sanitatis,* 14th century, Medicina, Italy.

Lamp/Candle

Aladdin's legendary lamp might well have been a version of the simple clay lamps shown here, the original oil lamp of the ancient world. In the famous tale from the *Arabian Nights*, the magic of the lamp was a wish-fulfilling genie that materialized when the lamp was rubbed. "Lamp" is derived from the Greek root meaning to give light, shine, beam, be bright, brilliant, radiant. The lamp's "genius" is to be a container for a small quantum of cosmic light. From the haloed single flame of the candle in the candlestick to the oil lamp, gas lamp and electric light, lamp embodies the ability to strike a spark and keep it burning. Circumscribing its illumination of darkness, lamp has been associated with consciousness and its capacity to sustain the flame of life, hope, freedom, creativity and the sacred and divine. Perpetually lighted lamps in temple, mosque, synagogue or church are a sign of divine presence suffusing the ordinary world. The Paschal candle of western Christianity is ritually lit each year at Easter from the "new fire," and represents the light of Christ. Eternal flames at gravesites suggest the continuity of life, death and rebirth. Lamps placed on top of Buddhist pagodas are "lighthouses of the Dharma," the sacred order of a life determined by its nature. Release from the cycle of rebirths, achieving Nirvana, is the blowing out of the lamp. In the Berber culture of North Africa, when a child was born women would light a lamp and place it near the baby's head, the lamp's clay signifying the body, the oil the life principle that animates the body and the flame the divine spirit that glows within. Lamp faithfully iterates the longed for resurgence of light in a wintry season: "The showers beat / On broken blinds and chimney-pots, / and at the corner of the street / a lonely cab-horse steams and stamps. / And then the lighting of the lamps" (Eliot, 23). With the progression a century ago from the oil lamp to the electric, to footlights, headlights, stadium lights, we have tended to identify with the great genii of the lamp, as if we owned the night and had the freedom to light up the darkness any way we want. But lamp is also evocative of subtler illumination in accord with nature. Psyche's luminosity, for example. The dawning of an idea. The moment of clarity (CW 14:128). There is the Greek philosopher Diogenes, who symbolically carried a lamp, searching for an honest man. Or the tarot figure of the Hermit, whose lantern signifies the solitary, dedicated seeking of one's authentic path and the luminous wisdom of introspection.

Eliot, T. S., "Preludes." *Collected Poems, 1909–1962.* London, 1974.

1. Three ancient Roman terra-cotta oil lamps.

2. *Two Candles,* by Gerhard Richter, oil painting, 1982, Germany.

1

2

Oven

The oven, like the womb, has transformative powers. This identification is so essential that the earliest ovens we know of, dating back to Neolithic times, were shaped like a mound with a knoblike protrusion—the female belly with umbilicus. Through the oven, raw material, whether dough, fetus or corpse, is transformed into a different state and emerges "newborn" as food, infant or soul. The oven exemplifies one of the feminine mysteries in which transformed nature becomes human culture (Neumann, 285).

In Neolithic times, the bread oven was the main feature of Old European shrines and considered to be the incarnation of the Grain Mother. The bread that emerged from these ovens was considered sacred and used as offerings in the rituals that were part of the agricultural mysteries (Gimbutas, 147ff). The connection between oven and womb survives even into modern times, where a pregnant woman is said to have "a bun in the oven," while "the oven will soon cave in" describes a woman about to give birth. An old proverb states it directly: "The oven is the mother" (Neumann, 286). Some of these ancient ovens were entirely anthropomorphic in form, complete with eyes and an open mouth. They suggest also the more sinister, devouring aspect of the oven/mother embodied in the form of a witch in fairy tales like "Hansel and Gretel." It is Gretel who overcomes the witch by pushing her into the oven being prepared for the two children. The heat from an oven bakes and transforms but it can also immolate, just as the dual mother gives birth and sustains but also devours and pulls her creation back into death. Thus the oven came to carry all of the awe associated with death as well as life. Crematory ovens reduce the dead to ashes. In Southern Europe, some of the tombs dating back as far as 4000 B.C.E. were shaped like an oven, suggesting the hope that burial in the oven/womb would ensure that even the dead would be "baked," to be born again like the reaped and milled wheat that rises as bread (Gimbutas, 200–1, 218–19).

As the Mother creates, sustains and transforms both the living and the dead, she holds opposites together and signifies the perpetual change in which one continually moves into the other. Connected with both fertility and death, with the food that is the "staff of life" as well as the fire that reduces all to ashes, the oven is an emblem of her ambivalent powers. As such the oven even functioned as an oracle, a potent vessel of domestic life that invoked the goddess as arbiter of destiny (Neumann, 286).

Gimbutas, Marija. *The Language of the Goddess.* SF, 1989.
Neumann, Erich. *The Great Mother: An Analysis of the Archetype.* Princeton, NJ, 1972.

This model of a bread oven is shaped like the pregnant belly of a woman. Terra-cotta, 5000 B.C.E., Hungary.

Table

The table in Domenico Gnoli's painting, covered by a white cloth, is emptiness that invites "setting" by the imagination. Table is potentially a medium for animated life, gathered company and relationship, whether of harmony or discord. Family meals around a dining table evoke the actualization or pretense of cohesive family life that extends to the ritual and sacramental use of table, for example as the altar around which the family of Christian believers gathers to receive the Eucharistic meal. The circular table, in particular, like that of alchemy, around which the four elements are combined, or the solar table of the orphic mysteries, or the Round Table of the legendary King Arthur and his knights, points symbolically to the perfection of the *rotundum*, and the bringing of things together in an integrated whole (CW 14:7). The angled table, on the other hand, allows for the tension of oppositional, competitive and hierarchical seating. Table is the potent object of delimiting, joining and setting apart at every kind of corporate meeting. One "draws up a chair" to the table in order to be included in the whole, or "brings to the table" some capacity or contribution that supports the collective endeavor. Tables used for séances may even knock with the energies of unconscious spirits activated by hopeful participants. Countless tête-à-têtes of romantic and conspiratorial nature have taken place at the table. And while the solitary individual seated at a table can suggest life digested in loneliness or a waiting for an "other," it may alternatively imply a peaceful "just being with myself."

Without Still Life, by Domenico Gnoli,
painting, 1966, Italy.

Chair/Throne

The original throne is the lap of the Great Mother, the imaginal and infinite womb of nature in which all is conceived, and the cosmos, within and without, in which, upon emerging, each thing gets "seated." Physically her lap is echoed in hill, mountain, tree branch, rock clefts and the smooth surfaces of huge boulders. Neolithic depictions of the large-thighed goddess emphasize the vastness of her lap and its capacity to support, encompass, steady, comfort, hold or hold fast. Later, goddess and throne are brought together, as in the ancient Philistine figurine "Ashdoda." Even ordinary chairs carry her presence in their arms, legs and back. Chairs made of wood, grasses and reeds, horn or hide, chairs carved with feet ending in claws, or the backs carved in the images of sun, moon, flowers or animals, further reflect the goddess's natural forms and manifestations.

For peoples accustomed to sit on the ground, a chair signifies the elevation accorded by power or status. The throne is often further elevated by being placed at the top of stairs, conveying a bridge between heaven and earth and the distinction between the one who is entitled to mount the stairs and those below. Sovereign, religious leader and dignitary are enthroned, and the divine protection embodied in the throne bestows on them the perceived gifts of divine right, wisdom, strength, fertility, mystery and infallibility. This is as true of the professor who possesses the endowed academic "chair" as it is of the Roman Catholic pope whose word is considered infallible if he speaks ex cathedra, or "from the throne." Pharaohs in ancient Egypt were understood to be enthroned in the lap of the goddess Isis, whose name was synonymous with "throne"; she is typically portrayed wearing a throne as her crown. There is a legend that the throne of King Solomon first belonged to the Queen of Sheba, but a female jinn stole it for him along with the queen's books of magic (DoS, 999). Medieval Christian art seats the Virgin Mary in the *Sedes Sapientiae,* the Throne of Wisdom, where, simultaneously, she enthrones the divine child on her lap.

Throne, and its humbler embodiment, the chair, figuratively evoke how we are seated in life, and, in the larger sense, what or who gets "enthroned" as ruling principles. Is one, for example, on the edge of the seat, tentative, or anticipating, or ready for flight? Is one rigidly, or formally seated, or slumped, sleepy, infantile, or flexibly, comfortably, authoritatively in one's seat? The throne is often portrayed with mandalalike quaternary forms. The Hindu god Shiva's throne is borne by four animals corresponding to the four ages of the world. In Christianity and Islam, eight angels aligned with the eight points of the compass support the throne of God (DoS, 998). In Sufism, the throne of God is found in the heart of the mystic and Buddha's throne corresponds to the Tantric Lotus of the Heart. In these images, throne implies a seating that transcends the personal, is more sizable than the ego, a "lap" that encompasses both what is conscious and transconscious. Here, throne signifies not only the seat of cosmic unity combining feminine and masculine forms, but also the seat of potential oneness within the individual.

1

2

3

1. The merging of woman and throne as the seated lap of the goddess. Terra-cotta figurine, nicknamed "Ashdoda," after the city Ashdod in Philistine where it was found, 12th century B.C.E.

2. Probably a king's throne carved in the form of a kneeling female figure who supports the seat. Usually this kind of stool was not functional but served as a receptacle for the king's spirit during his reign and continued to do so after his death. Wood, Zulu, Eastern Zaire, present-day Democratic Republic of the Congo.

3. The Egyptian goddess Isis, crowned by the throne that is the hieroglyph for her name. In her lap were enthroned the rulers of Egypt. Carved stone, 18th dynasty (ca. 1550–1295 B.C.E).

Glass

Glass is translucence, transparency, refraction. A pair of spectacles that bring into focus words on a page, a glass of wine that invites unhurried sipping. So many things are visible through glass. Light striking a prism in a radiance of color, perfumes and spices, the pungent, mysterious medicaments of itinerant healers: "A wave of glass, an archangel, all the ointments within the bottles warmed from the sun ... " (Ondaatje, 9). Glass lenses of telescopes and microscopes have bent light into heavenly, Galilean perspective, revealed the brilliant self-destruction of stars, the cellular delineations of a marigold, and the microbes of disease. Heat-resistant, insulating glass retorts, beakers, flasks, test tubes, barometers, thermometers and compasses disclosed revolutionary secrets of knowledge and navigation between the middle ages and the nineteenth century (ScienceWeek.com 2005). Glass has given us liminal windows on the temporal world, and stained glass, glimpses of eternity.

Dualistic and mercurial, glass looks like a solid, but has the properties of a supercooled liquid, a fluid state at high temperatures brought to below freezing so quickly that, solidified, its molecules remain amorphous instead of forming into crystals. Yet molten glass can be rolled, blown, molded, drawn or cast into all the shapes of creation, so that glass is associated with both chaos and form, randomness and precision, spirit and matter. The main ingredient of glass is sand, silica, to which additives of limestone, mineral salts, potash or metallic oxides contribute durability and color. Nature produces glass autonomously. Lightning, striking desert sand, can leave in its electrical path a tube of pure glass. Some volcanoes produce obsidian, a natural form of glass with dark-hued impurities, from which Native Americans made tools and carvings (Turner, 12:780–1).

Human beings were making glass over 4,000 years ago in Mesopotamia and Egypt. Syria invented glassblowing of hollow objects at the end of the first century C.E. In the West, Venetian technology produced glass of rare brilliance and made possible the mass production of glass for industry and science. Stained-glass art reached its zenith in Europe in tints made from powders of crushed glass, pulverized minerals and metallic oxides mixed with wine and other liquids (Compt.).

Glass is durable, odorless, nonporous, impervious to the corrosion of most acids, able to shield against radiation, capable of being made sterile and airtight. Medieval alchemists, fascinated by glass, made it an emblem of their opus of transmutation. Glass referred to the transparent "vessel" in which processes of transformation at many levels were taking place. The raw material of glass, the "batch," suggested the amorphous nature of the *prima materia*, the "undifferentiated lifemass" with which the adept began (CW 12:242). Glass was associated with salt and ash, symbolically the distilled residues of physical and psychical processes of calcination, sublimation and purification. Glass embodied the *albedo*, or whitening, the moonlike waxing of potential into being, and consciousness imbued with the luminous, hidden fire of the self.

Yet the dual nature of glass induces bivalent fantasies. Glass conveys beauty, ornamentation, purity, delicacy, but also extraordinary fragility as a substance that can be shattered into minute and cutting shards. Glass suggests both tempered exposure and excruciating transparency. The insulating nature of glass that allows light to pass through but protects from the elements evokes discriminated receptivity to possibilities of exchange, and also isolation, insularity and brittleness. "Glass-box" high-rises are prized for their views and censored for looking cold and impersonal. The glass mountain of fairy tales is removed from life, dissociated, the end of the world, the land of the dead, the dwelling place of supernatural, shape-shifting forces personified as ogres, witches and swan maidens (Leach, 1:456). Suggesting loss of soul and the arduous journey to find it, a princess is often captive in the glass mountain, which can only be penetrated by her true love.

In our contemporary world, glass is ubiquitous, mass produced, utilitarian—and nevertheless still magical in its powers, loveliness and psychic resonance. The electric light bulb, for example, which depends on glass, is one of the most common images of the "light going on" symbolically. It expresses the vitreous ability of consciousness to contain and transmit the hot filaments of creative illumination—not just in service to intellectual expansion, but also self-understanding, clarity, insight, vision.

Leach, Maria. Ed. *Funk & Wagnalls Standard Dictionary of Folklore, Mythology and Legend.* NY, 1949.
Ondaatje, Michael. *The English Patient.* NY, 1992.
Turner, Jane. *The Dictionary of Art.* NY, 1996.
ScienceWeek.com. 2005 (SW050715-3).

Here, glass objects give transparency to the mood and
rhythm of an informal afternoon. *The Sisters*, detail, by
Ivar Nyberg, oil painting, 19th century, Sweden.

Mirror

Mirror is a reflective container whose source of power is light. The elegance and sophistication of this Bronze Age Celtic mirror's back, the intricacy and detail of its design, attest to the value placed on the object by its creator. The pattern, a well-wrought optical illusion, suggests the roiling of cosmic seas, the eternal, the never-ending. The image embodies a mesmerizing energy, a feeling of mystery and portent. The mirror's significance as a magic tool is conveyed by its artistry.

Mirrors have always existed. Before the use of metal, they were the reflections on the waters collected in the earth's indentations. Early peoples believed that in such reflections the soul element could be perceived and even today the fantasy persists that the mirror can steal one's soul. The association of the mirror with the essential nature of a thing is carried in the ancient Egyptian hieroglyph for life, the ankh, which was also one of the words for mirror. The mirror represented the solar disk as the source of light that contained life's essence. Mirrors were placed in burial chambers and were also cult objects in the worship of Hathor, goddess of abundance, joy, music, dance, cosmetics and self-beautification, which brought one into harmony with the divine (ARAS, 2Ak.191).

Our English word "mirror" comes from the Latin *mirari*, to wonder or marvel at. The wondrous nature of the mirror is how it draws our imagination into its seeming depths, the sense that beyond the mirror image of our immediate reality might be seen something entirely different. In Lewis Carroll's famous story, the world of dreams lies "through the Looking-glass." Personifying the unconscious and its compelling capacity to reflect the unknown and potential, alchemy attributed to its figure, Sulphur, the possession of "a mirror in which the whole world is to be seen. Whosoever looks into this mirror, can see and learn therein the parts of the wisdom of the whole World ... " (CW 14:137, n108). At the same time, the more destructive aspects of the unconscious, like consuming appetites and "lunatic" tendencies, were projected on the changeable and cyclically dark Luna, "the great poisonous mirror of nature." Yet as the illuminating speculum or "looking glass," Luna could also mediate self-knowledge and the face she showed was affected by the receptiveness or resistance of the adept to the insights she offered.

What do we see when we look in a mirror? To "reflect" means to bend back or around, suggesting a linking. Attuned mirroring of the infant and young child

1

2

1. Bronze mirror, Celtic, Iron Age, 50 B.C.E.–50 C.E.

2. A self-reflective Mary Magdalen gazes at a luminous candle flame, reflected in a mirror. The skull on which her hands rest suggests the hollowness of vanity in the face of inevitable death. *The Penitent Magdalen*, by Georges de la Tour, oil painting, ca. 1638–43, France.

contributes to the bringing of their substance into being. Derangements in mirroring have been associated with pathological narcissism, borderline states and chronic depression. In the Greek legend of Narcissus, the youth, divinely spellbound by his own reflection, wastes away. Two twentieth-century women, Virginia Woolf and Freud's patient, Anna O, testified to the traumatic experience of seeing a beast or monster in their looking glass—projections, perhaps, of the distorting effects of mental illness. Every day, we confront mirrors in the reactions of others to our behavior. Saint Paul saw the mirror as an analogue to our experience of the divine here and now as opposed to the afterlife: "For now we see in a glass darkly, but then face to face" (1 Cor. 13:12). Schopenhauer, however, compared the human intellect to a mirror. In its magical aspect, the mirror is a trickster's tool, an implement of illusion, often making us appear as more, or less, than we are. But the mirror as an emblem of our capacity to reflect is also an instrument of salvation. In the myth of Perseus, it is only by looking at the reflected image of what is too dangerous to absorb directly, that the hero is able to slay the snake-headed Medusa.

Freud, Sigmund, et al. "Studies on Hysteria." *The Standard Edition of the Complete Psychological Works of Sigmund Freud*. London, 1964.
Lewis, Charlton T. *A Latin Dictionary*. Oxford, 1996.
von Franz, Marie-Louise. *Projection and Re-Collection in Jungian Psychology Reflections of the Soul*. La Salle, IL, 1982.

3

4

3. A cult object and funeral treasure, this Egyptian mirror represents the sun and the divine solar power of light. Mirror with a female handle, bronze cast, ca. 1500 B.C.E.

4. A golden-haired, goddesslike adolescent views herself in a mirror. Here, the mirror may imply self-absorption, feminine wile, enchantment, fantasy and consciousness. *Nu au Miroir*, by Balthus, oil painting, 1981–3, France.

Carpet

The intricately woven carpet transports us to a Persian garden by a wide, rippling stream alive with fish swimming in synchronized precision. The main watercourse and two crossing streams flow around islands studded by flowering trees. The formal garden beds are full of blooms, protected from the outside world by a wall bordered by red flowers. The patterned motifs, fitting together within a rhythmic geometrical order, transmute the ephemeral into an image of everlasting abundance.

The fine carpets of the Sufi Islamic tradition are pictures of God. Each carpet "tries to show a pattern which is the infinite domain" seen through a window, the border of the carpet, which is also "made of the infinite pearl-stuff." Embedded, however, in a much older (possibly prehistoric) tradition, the carpet is, as well, "an animal presence," and the images of God and the animistic being "exist together and reflect each other in the actual substance of the carpet" (Alexander, 21).

In their crude dwellings, early hunters laid down animal skins, whose softness and warmth were retained in later woven and knotted carpets (*Enc. Brit.* 21:499). The nomadic peoples of central or western Asia fashioned the earliest of Oriental carpets for the earthen floor of their tents, bringing their own "ground" to the ground of their wanderings. According to legend, the first Persian garden carpet was created in the sixth century at the command of the ruler Khosroes I. A colossal carpet was woven to furnish his cold winter palace with a garden perpetually at full springtime bloom, an image of paradise celebrated in the Koran: "And for those who believe and do righteous works, we will cause them to enter gardens beneath which rivers flow, and to dwell there eternally" (ARAS, 6Ad.080).

In a number of religious traditions, the carpet constitutes a *templum*, a place that is made holy, separate from the profane world (DoS, 159). The carpet may be a personal space for meditation or devotion, such as the small woolen carpets used by Buddhist monks in Tibet, or the Muslim prayer carpet, echoing the mihrab niche. The carpet can be used for worship as a substitute for a mosque, whose niche, orienting prayer toward Mecca, is incorporated in the rug's design (EoR, 14:413). In the secular realm, too, the carpet can set one apart, as in the "red carpet" laid out for a visiting dignitary.

The patient, intricate, devoted work required in the making of a carpet is also what it takes to achieve the paradoxical capacity to transcend consciousness and at the same time to hold one's ground. The two come together in the magic carpets described in both the Egyptian and Tibetan *Book of the Dead*. In Tibetan Tantric belief, a paper carpet could be constructed that would glide an adept over a ravine. The wonders of the imagination to carry us beyond where we are is evoked in *The Arabian Nights* tale of "Prince Ahmed and Periebanou," where the prince's brother Houssain acquires a flying carpet on which he can be transported in an instant to wherever he wishes to be (Goodenow, 160). Even in the exquisite carpets that stay earthbound, there is centeredness, depth and fantasy. The purpose of many of the most splendid carpets of the eastern world is to create "a profound religious wholeness" (Alexander, 30). Nevertheless, it is also said that the wise artisans, reflecting how human longing, however great, must fall short of attaining oneness with the divine, wove a single, tiny mistake into their dazzling and harmonious compositions.

Alexander, Christopher. *A Foreshadowing of 21st Century Art: The Color and Geometry of Very Early Turkish Carpets*. NY, 1993.
Goodenow, Earle. *The Arabian Nights*. NY, 1946.
Pope, Arthur Upham. *Masterpieces of Persian Art*. NY, 1945.

1. The dyed-wool carpet from northeastern Iran depicts a paradisical garden of the type known as "Four Gardens." The name refers to the square garden beds full of blossoms and flowering trees, divided by intersecting canals. Garden carpet, detail, ca. 18th century.

2. After drinking the elixir of immortality, the Chinese immortals gained the ability to fly, which is here poetically shown as a flying carpet where even food and drink as well as books are provided. Screen, detail, by Fūgai Honkō, 1832, Japan.

Broom

Almost invisible among the slender, multiple trunks of a Banyan tree in India, a broom propped against the tree is illuminated and even ensouled by a mysterious play of light. In much the same way, our fantasies confer supernatural vitality upon this simple tool for sweeping made of wood and straw. Throughout the world, the sweeping of house or shop with a broom is one of the first acts in the ordering of the day; it is reality and ritual. Zen Buddhism embraces the broom as an emblem of the sage, signifying contact with the world that must accompany pureness of thought. Broom suggests simplicity through the elimination of what is unnecessary—the sweeping away of the illusions, strivings and attachments that clutter consciousness—and alludes to the emptiness in which unforeseen possibilities of enlightenment can spontaneously emerge. Its association with the humble work of daily life and keeping house often puts broom in the hands of the feminine, where it has particular potency. A veiled woman performs the menial task of road sweeping and our imaginations are swept into the living matter of broom rooted in the dark earth of psyche with which woman is seen to have an affinity. Like the feminine as anima or self, the broom can transform a space or disturb it, stirring up the dust, pulling cobwebs out of dark corners. The rhythmic motion of the broom and the phallic broomstick easily move our projections to broom as an autonomous, devilish vehicle of psyche's shadowy ground. Broom evokes sorcery, magic, sexual lewdness and lust, volatility and disinhibition. Full of uncanny energies, broom, unnoticed at the back of the broom closet, bristles with a life of its own; sweeps, dances, flies.

1

2

3

1. On a church wall, we see what may be the Norse goddess Frigg riding on a broomstick. Painting, 12th century, Schleswig Cathedral, Germany.

2. A broom leans against a banyan tree. Photograph, India.

3. A lower-caste Hindu woman performs the menial task of road sweeping. Photograph, India.

Bed / Bedroom

In a letter to his brother Theo, Vincent van Gogh described a painting he had made of his bedroom in Arles, France, where he was taking an "enforced rest" for exhaustion. "This time it's simply my bedroom, only here color is to do everything, and giving by its simplification a grander style to things, is to be suggestive here of *rest* or of sleep in general. In a word, looking at the picture ought to rest the brain, or rather the imagination" (letter from Vincent van Gogh to Theo van Gogh, Arles, October 16, 1888).

Distanced from the pressures and activities of daily life, the bedroom can be a timeless place, a haven of stillness. Here, one might be closest to one's private self, shed one's clothes, go to sleep and dream, perhaps make love or simply rest and recuperate from the pressures of the outside world.

But bedroom can also be associated with exposure, nightmare, fear of the dark and supernatural visitation. One can be confined to the bedroom, even imprisoned there. In the bedroom are enacted incest, misalliance and conjugal war. Gnawing anxieties can fill the space emptied of the day's welcome distractions. The bedroom houses sickbed and deathbed.

Because of its personal and intimate nature, the bedroom is often situated farthest from the entrance to a residence and removed from the more active kitchen and living room. The word *chambre* in French and the related older English term bedchamber emphasize the concept of protection and enclosure, as contrasted to the public *sale*, "salon" and "hall" (Duby, 173ff). The more romantic term boudoir derives from the French word for "sulk," and was originally designated as a room where a lady could retire from company and be alone with her private feelings (ibid., 204, 218ff). Indeed, bedroom can evoke feminine mysteries, the world of the yin, seduction and generation. The English word "bed" has a semantic connection with "dig" as a hole or a ditch to lie in or soft earth to lie on. Although this meaning disappeared long ago in the Germanic cognates, the connotation of fertility in the word survives, as in a garden bed for plants. The horizontal nature of bed activities is explicit in the French word for the bed, *lit*, which is derived from the same root as "lie" and "layer."

Bedroom also evokes for some the experience of the feminine womb as both regression and revivification. In the rhythms of sleep and waking or in sexual surrender, there is a ritual continuity of symbolic death and rebirth. Healing or admonishing voices from the "spirit world" are activated in the lunar darkness. The bedroom can be said to be a liminal space where one's defenses and persona yield to the vulnerable humanity of the naked self. The nocturnal journey of consciousness into the "underworld" of psychic depths echoes the cyclical movement of the sun, its light extinguished in its setting, only to be renewed at dawn. Just so, in the morning one rises from the horizontal space of sleep and dream, dresses and makes the bed, closes up the night in the bedroom and enters the vertical world of day.

Duby, Georges and Arthur Goldhammer. *A History of Private Life: Revelations of the Medieval World.* Cambridge, MA, 1988.
Melville, Robert. *Erotic Art of the West.* NY, 1973.

1. Lit by early morning sunlight and protected from the outside world, the artist's bedroom in Arles was meant to be a place of "inviolable rest." *Vincent's Bedroom in Arles*, by Vincent van Gogh, oil painting, 1888, France.

2. In an unfinished etching (note the extra left arm of the woman), the artist portrays bed as the medium of the erotic. It is uncertain whether the lovemaking couple represents husband and wife, young people having sex out of wedlock or a tryst with a prostitute, but the man's feathered cap on the bedpost is suggestive (Melville, 118–9). *Ledikant*, by Rembrandt van Rijn, 1646, the Netherlands.

1

2

Cradle

For the child, poet or visionary artist the world is full of wonder: The crescent moon becomes the foot of a cradle and the stars the lamps of the sky. In this image, the Virgin Mary as the Queen of Heaven, is surprisingly depicted seated in a domestic setting, her foot tapping the crescent moon, as if recording time, while cradling her radiant child, whose birth coincides with the returning light of the sun. Her breath and heartbeat are the rhythms of nature, like the cycles of the sun and the moon and the waves of the sea. The womb of the mother is the child's first cradle, from which it is born. The cradle complements the coffin, which carries the dead to the afterlife. Mythically, it is the cosmic barque on the primordial ocean. All life once emerged from the sea, "out of the cradle endlessly rocking" as in the famous poem by Walt Whitman. The fertile land between the Euphrates and the Tigris rivers in the Near East is called the "cradle of civilization," where the yearly rounds of labors gave birth to culture. The recurring familiar movements of the cradle soothe us like a lullaby (also called cradle song) and reassure us that we are safe. At each turn, however, there is a moment when everything stands still, when the cradling arm may lose its grip, the wave bring us under or the night swallow us up. This is probably how ritual was born—to carry us through the uncertainties before any new undertaking. We pray then that Mother Nature will continue to hold us and protect us in her cradle.

I am going to sleep, nurse, put me to bed.
Put a lamp at the headboard;
a constellation, whichever one you like;
they're all nice; turn it down a little.
...
a celestial foot is rocking you from above
and a bird is tapping out some rhythms ....

Alfonsina Storni, *I'm Going to Sleep*

The Virgin cradling the Christ Child in her arms.
The crescent moon at her feet goes back to Isis as the
Queen of Heaven. Painting, Flemish, 13th century.

Toilet

"Toilet" is the receptacle for the body's waste matter. The immense age of the lavatory chair (over 3,000 years old) attests to our long concern with the appropriate, hygienic containment of human urine and excrement, around which so much psychological symbolism has evolved in contemporary times. This ancient Egyptian toilet would have belonged to an upper-class person, whose bathroom might also have included a shower unit.

The simplest form of toilet, still utilized in less developed parts of the world, is a hole dug in the earth or over a cesspit. In the European Middle Ages, human waste was emptied from chamber pots into the street and as late as the nineteenth century raw sewage fouled rivers like the Thames, the stench of which at times closed down sessions of Parliament. The fastidious disposal of human waste is a development reflecting the tension between the natural and cultural, for the body imposes its need to "relieve" itself as a necessity that often won't wait.

The names we give the toilet reflect our attitudes toward the products and process of elimination. "Toile," the French word from which toilet is derived, is a cloth that protects the shoulders during hygienic activities, and lavatory and latrine are both from the Latin "lavare," meaning to wash. "Comfort station" suggests the convenience of public bathrooms with toilets, which offer the traveler relief when necessity calls. "Throne," a name for toilet from the German nursery (Whitmont, Perera, 146), conveys the relation between appropriate toileting and the development of the ego, the "ruler" of the personality's conscious sphere, including deliberate willing. The value that Freud gave toilet training implicates the toilet in the primary experience of control, dominance, letting go or withholding the raw instinctual matter of affects, activities and urges that are potentially creative or transformative (ibid., 146–7). "Privy," from the Latin privo, a verb meaning "to deprive, free, release or deliver," perhaps best incorporates the symbolic richness of toilet, for "privatus,"

the adjectival form, means "pertaining to an individual, private." The toilet in this sense represents a container for coagulated soul stuff in its preliminary form, and an alchemical vessel of putrefactio into which shadow matter of the personality can be discharged. For more than a few, the toilet represents a "seat" of meditation or distress, of inhibition or freedom. The complexities around toilet are mirrored in psyche's countless dream images, suggesting whether one has available, appropriate containers for one's substantive "piss and shit" or not. All too often the toilets of dreamscapes reflect the latter; are clogged, overflowing, filthy or exposed; or, in public restrooms, are unavailable or malfunctioning, suggesting conflict between fundamental elements of individuality and the collective's capacity to receive them.

The toilet and its plumbing, connecting to larger sewage systems whose pipes run underground, symbolically lead us into the underworld spheres of stench and darkness, the collective shadow of the human species or an aspect of one's own particular psychic hell (Hillman, 184–5). The perceived potency and the veneration accorded excretory substances in many cultures, however, attest to their being experienced as more than mere waste. Toilet evokes the processing and containment of this "base and noble" prima materia.

Hillman, James. *The Dream and the Underworld.* NY, 1979.

Horan, Julie L. *The Porcelain God a Social History of the Toilet.* Secaucus, NJ, 1996.

Lambton, Lucinda. *Temples of Convenience.* NY, 1979.

Laporte, Dominique. *History of Shit.* Cambridge, MA, 2000.

Whitmont, Edward C. and Sylvia Brinton Perera. *Dreams, a Portal to the Source.* London and NY, 1989.

1. An early incarnation of the toilet, this Egyptian version was found in a tomb in Thebes. For centuries, toilets have evoked individual expressions of potency, will, shadow and creativity. Lavatory chair, wood, ca. 1539–1295 B.C.E.

2. This wooden outhouse from East Anglia, England, with its communal seating, suggests that the contemporary emphasis on bathroom privacy is only one part of a spectrum of cultural attitudes toward the toilet. Two-seat privy, early 18th–late 19th century.

3. Known as the king of the water closets, this highly decorative "wash-out" was an early ceramic flush toilet produced in Birmingham, England (Lambton, pl. 86). The "Dolphin," early 1880s.

Bath/Bathing

The symbolism of the bath extends far beyond a simple scrubbing at the end of the day. It reaches into religious rite and psychic transformation, such as we see in the sculptured Greek goddess of our image, arising in beautiful freshness from her ritual bath. Historically, the bath, as an immersion in a pool or natural spring, was long known in Greece, as well as in ancient Egypt, Mesopotamia and the Asian world. In imperial Rome, communal bathing was a popular recreation; during the fourth century C.E., the city of Rome alone supported some 800 public baths (Grant, III, 1700), which were also centers of social life and hedonism: drinking, eating and freewheeling sexuality. Ascetic early Christianity turned against the Roman bath as a temptation to debauchery. But Christian baptism, with its commitment to the life of the spirit over that of the flesh, was in itself a bathlike immersion, originally meant to symbolize drowning, and representing death to the old life and one's rebirth as a new being. Baptism's Jewish ancestor, the ritual bath or *mikveh*, is a symbolic purification.

In the early Christian Middle Ages, bathing of the whole body was still viewed with suspicion as a sensual temptation, especially in Christian monasteries. Some orders sanctioned only two hot baths a year for monks, and Saint Benedict regarded an unwashed body as a "temple of piety" (Croutier, 89). Ultimately, of course, the bath again became acceptable, even virtuous: "In the minds of many people frequent washing may have assumed the same spiritual value as frequent confession" (Duby, 600)—or, as the folk saying has it, "Cleanliness is next to Godliness."

Many traditions (Native American, Muslim, Greek Eleusinian Mysteries, Jewish) have required bathing or washing as symbolic purification before approaching the deity in prayer or ritual. Some have even immersed statues of the gods themselves in ritual cleansing baths, symbolizing renewal of the connection between god and the faithful. Cleaning of the worshipper's mouth and ears is emphasized in Islam in order to "sanctify [one's] ... prayers and open [one's] ... hearing to the will of God" (EoR, 12:96). In other cultures such as the Japanese, communal bathing is a secular setting for social life, relaxation and a sense of balance with the forces of nature (Croutier, 80).

Beyond these meanings of purification and healing, the bath stands for a place of spiritual change or transformation. Ritual baths mark major life milestones: marriage, burial, birth. In medieval alchemical symbolism, " ... bath, submersion, drowning and baptism are synonymous and symbolize the breaking down and cleansing of old outmoded states of being, leading to the birth of the rejuvenated illumined man" (Abraham, 18). Depth psychology finds this same symbolism in modern dreams in which swimming, bathing and showering are seen as an immersion in unconscious forces that can dissolve the dreamer's cramped outlook and bring the possibility of change. Such change, of course, may lead either to growth, renewal, creativity—or to psychic dissolution and disaster. If the submersion leads to loss of conscious values and standards, primitive energies may be released. Legend often pictures these energies as erotic. The hero's exposure to a beautiful feminine being in her bath leads to his own regression and/or destruction: David sees Bathsheba and compromises his integrity; the Elders spy on Susanna and enter into perjury and disgrace; Acteon stumbles on Artemis bathing and is killed by his erotic reaction in the symbolic form of his own hounds.

But dissolution of the personality in unconscious waters is not confined to legend. Consider attempts to escape the pain of one's struggles and conflicts through numbing alcohol and other addictions. Or the loss of one's bearings by psychic immersion in a group, be it a religious cult, a sports mob, a gang bent on ethnic cleansing. Or the gradual erosion of reality-connection, which can lead to psychosis, and is suggested by our image of the woman in her bath, dissolved to a point almost beyond recognition.

Clearly, entry into unconscious waters can be treacherous and is not for the naïve or the ungrounded. And yet, it must be said that even in frenetic modern life, descent of one's body into a bath leads to a moment out of time, to a kind of oblivion but also to a state in which anything can be imagined, and the seeds of new possibilities can come into being.

Abraham, Lyndy. *A Dictionary of Alchemical Imagery.* Cambridge, UK, and NY, 1998.
Croutier, Alev Lytle. *Taking the Waters: Spirit, Art, Sensuality.* NY, 1992.
Duby, Georges. *A History of Private Life: Revelations of the Medieval World.* Cambridge, MA, 1988.
Grant, Michael and Rachel Kitzinger. *Civilization of the Ancient Mediterranean: Greece and Rome.* NY, 1988.

1

2

3

1. A Greek goddess is helped to rise up, renewed,
probably from regenerating waters below. She may be
Aphrodite, Hera or possibly even Persephone returning
from the underworld. Marble relief, 460–450 B.C.E.

2. Over the 50 years of their life together, Pierre
Bonnard showed his wife Marthe in her bath in a
number of paintings, her body always young and
beautiful. A troubled woman, increasingly beset by
depression, she seems in this portrait at age 70 to be
disappearing, dissolving in the bath. *Female Nude in a
Bath Tub*, 1937, France.

3. A medieval alchemist endures being "cooked" in the
hot bath of his own emotions and fantasies. Though the
bath water is still dark, the appearance of a white dove
suggests that a lightening and brightening process has
begun. An illustration from the alchemical manuscript
Splendor Solis, or "Splendor of the Sun," by Salomon
Trismosin, school of Nuremberg, ca. 1531–2, Germany.

Pool

This image of an Egyptian garden pool is thought to have adorned a tomb. But death seems to have no power in this domain; it abounds with life. Ducks, fish and flowers fill the pool, which is surrounded by sheltering trees laden with figs and dates.

The pool in the painting is the centerpiece of an earthly paradise, adjacent to a home or a temple. It not only represents the best of mortal life, ease and abundance, but also the promise of a happy afterlife. The sacred nature of this setting is indicated by the presence of the goddess in the painting's upper-right corner. She is Hathor, the mother goddess, emerging from a sycamore tree with a plate of fruit and a pitcher of water (ARAS, 2Ak.171). She bears these for the deceased, who is permitted in the afterlife to emerge from his tomb to cool himself in the shade, walk along the bank and to drink each day from the pool.

This image of eternal enjoyment is deepened when we consider that the waters that fed Egyptian garden pools came from the Nile. The river, its waters and its yearly flooding were each deities, and were regarded as the waters of life, the source of all creation (ARAS, 2Ak.171). Water itself, along with light, fire, earth and air, was a manifestation of the supreme god, with the created world an island in the primordial ocean (Betrò, 163).

Thus, the pool in the Egyptian image is both domesticated nature and a small reservoir of the infinite brought into the midst of ordinary life. The product of human culture, the pool's rectangular sides are a temporary collect for the ever-moving energies of both water and the spirit. There are many images in religion, psychology and myth that evoke a simple pool that contains the waters of continual renewal. These are the "still waters" of the 23rd Psalm, where amid green pastures God "restores my soul." Isaiah enjoined "everyone that thirsts, come to the waters" for the soul's refreshment (Isaiah 55:1). The baptismal font is a kind of miniature pool holding holy water for the sanctification of a child. Similarly, pools are used for the full immersion baptism practiced by some Christian denominations. The pool at Bathesda (John 5), when troubled by an angel, became a healing bath for the first person who immersed himself in it. At that site Jesus performed a miracle, making an infirm man whole.

The aphorism "Still waters run deep" hints at meanings far beneath the pool's placid surface. In the symbolism of psychology, a pool of water represents the wellspring from which all psychic life flows (Whitmont, 72). These waters can be a perpetually replenished source of revivification or, left neglected, they can become a stagnant pool. For Narcissus, the figure of Greek myth, missing the pool's depths proved ultimately tragic. A beautiful, androgynous youth, Narcissus looked into a pool, saw his own reflection and fell in love with it. Pining for his unreachable beloved, he died, and was turned into the flower that bears his name (ARAS, 3Pa.115).

Betrò, Maria C. *Hieroglyphics the Writings of Ancient Egypt*. NY, 1996.
Whitmont, Edward C. *The Symbolic Quest Basic Concepts of Analytical Psychology*. Princeton, NJ, 1991.

1. Pools like the one depicted here have symbolized the promised refreshment of a happy afterlife as well as the presence of both sacred and psychic depths in ordinary life. Tomb painting, 1539–1295 B.C.E., Egypt.

2. The swimming pool brings together man-made container and natural element for recreation, sport or even the exhibition of one's opulence. Psychologically, it suggests a consciously contained "pooling" of psychic energy in which the ego can propel itself imaginally. *A Bigger Splash*, by David Hockney, acrylic painting, 1967, England.

1

2

Fountain

Whatever is arid will find refreshment from the brimming fountain in Venus's splendid garden. The lush, dewy flora and exotic birds are emblematic of her watering; for those who honor the goddess of love, she is *fons*, moisture, pleasure, feeling, the eros that gives rise to the flourishing of things.

Fountain is water pressing up from a hidden spring. The animated quality of the fountain, the play of sunlight or moonlight on its silvery water, the melodious tinkling on pebbles and leaves has timelessly intimated the presence of nature spirits and psyche's magical "upwellings." Fountain conveys the mysterious source of fecundating life, often personified as a form of the eternal feminine, like the Lady of the Fountain or the enchanted Castle of the Fountain in Arthurian romance (Zimmer, 98ff). Universally, the fountain is an image of the "living waters" that restore the soul parched of meaning, creativity or joy. The fountains of mosque, cloister or temple suggest the flowing center of the divine primordial garden, reflecting the numinous, life-giving center in one's innermost self, the linking with which is the goal of processes of religious seeking and initiation.

The alchemical imagination engages the fountain at many levels of the opus. The moon in whose dominion are all waters, including springs, is called the "fount of the mother," personifying the psyche as a bath of renewal, in which the personality is transformed (CW 14:75; 193). The ever-flowing fountain expresses the flow of interest toward the unconscious, a kind of "devotion" that facilitates, in turn, the crossing of unknown contents into consciousness, benefiting the psychic balance and enriching the psyche as a whole (ibid., 193). Yet fountain also represents, initially, the "chaotic waters" of the unconscious bubbling up into consciousness with the possibility of submerging as well as fertilizing it with erotic fantasies and the pressing desires of unlived life. Later, the fountain represents the cooling and moistening of passions and affects through reflection and feeling. The fountain is a form of Mercurius, the fluid medium in which the transformation is to take place, and the animating spirit of the work, always moving and changing. The "circular distillation" by which the water flows in an endless circle suggests how the personality is sustained and watered by the exchange between unconscious and consciousness. The sacred "fount" in the midst of a hidden "Judea" corresponds to the imaginal center of the personality from which issue fructifying ideas, fantasies and dreams (CW 14:341ff).

Out of such intuitive imagery, we have projected on fountain the properties of miraculous healing, eternal youthfulness, immortality and rejuvenation, oracular powers and poetic inspiration. Like the ancient image of a spring originating within the abysmal roots of the Tree of Life to become the rivers that flow to the four corners of the world, fountain intimates an irrigated, fruitful totality, a mandala that is also the "bath of Venus" in which warring opposites are ultimately united by love.

Zimmer, Heinrich Robert. *The King and the Corpse: Tales of the Soul's Conquest of Evil*. Princeton, NJ, 1948.

1. Fountain as the proliferating effect of the goddess of love. Mural in the house of Venus, 1st century C.E., Pompeii, Italy.

2. The three spigots represent alchemy's spirit Mercurius manifested in the inorganic, organic and spiritual realms, suggesting how psychic energy enlivens all the domains of human experience. *The Mercurial*

Fountain, from the alchemical manuscript *Rosarium philosophorum*, 1550, Germany.

3. Evoking the saving waters in a dry land, a depiction of the great goddess as water-carrier; fish swim in the streams flowing down her skirt. Fountain as Goddess with a Vase, limestone sculpture, ca. 1779–61 B.C.E., Syria.

1

2

3

Well

Life-giving water issuing from the dry earth: a miracle. No wonder that wells, springs, fountains—where this miracle occurs—have long been seen as holy places, the homes of spirits, sources of wisdom and healing. Wells, particularly, have a special place in our imagination since—unlike a natural spring—a well is created by both nature and by human labor. Since the Stone Age, humans have been digging, boring and drilling into the earth to make contact with springs of living water and underground aquifers where groundwater from rain, snow or surface streams has seeped into cracks and pores in the rocks, and into the minute spaces between grains of sand. When the groundwater finally sinks to a watertight layer of rock, it is held there and can be reached by the shaft of a well.

A deep well is uncanny. Looking straight down into the dim interior, we catch the glint of water far below, feel the chill, damp air, and hear odd echoes. We are connected, it seems, to another mysterious realm, underground, underworld, evocative of our own, unknown, reflective depths, a psychic matrix perhaps infinitely extensive. Wells may be relatively shallow or hundreds of feet deep. But always they have been perceived as holy places, the homes of spirits, sources of wisdom, healing, prophecy, renewal and the fulfillment of wishes. The digging for the living moisture issuing from the earth, the round, eyelike shaft of the well left open so that we can draw up, again and again, the delicious water—all this has intimated our conscious linking with psyche's wellsprings of feeling, imagination, dream and idea.

Mythic feminine entities—nymphs and maidens, the triple moon-goddess, the Virgin Mary—have personified the yin qualities of the well and access to its life-giving waters. The Greek goddess of the grain, Demeter, exhausted from wandering after Hade's rape of her daughter Persephone, rests at the Well of the Virgin in Eleusis. Here, in ancient times, initiates danced around the well built to commemorate its mythic counterpart, and entered into the Mysteries of the sacred precinct (Kerényi, 37). In the Grimm's fairy tale "Mother Holle," the well is a portal to the domain of the mercurial earth mother, her submerging waters and fruitful, flowering, sunlit fields. In her subterranean house are enacted processes of incubation from which, potentially, one may emerge in possession of gold.

The well is quintessentially an image of nurturance. The oracular *I Ching* compares the wooden poles used to haul water from the well to the life of plants, "which lift water out of the earth by means of their fibers" (Wilhelm, 185). In the Hebrew language, the word for "well" has the meaning of "woman" or "bride" (DoS, 1095), and the Torah is described as a well of fresh water. The square, brick-lined well is an Islamic image of Paradise. Norse mythology tells of the god Odin giving one of his eyes in order to drink from Urd, the well of wisdom, and the Irish Salmon of Wisdom lives in a holy well.

Well has other aspects, however. There are Japanese legends of encounters with both gods and monsters at wells. One can fall into a deep well and drown; suicides have thrown themselves into wells. A well can become contaminated. From antiquity to the present day, human beings have even maliciously poisoned the wells of their neighbors and enemies, a disaster especially in the driest lands where a well may be the only source of water. Equally, psyche's well of possibility can get contaminated by destructive attitudes, or its imbibed energies experienced only as toxic. Though mythic wells are inexhaustible, in reality a well can dry up, and may have to be infused with water from above in order for the well to regenerate below. Symbolically, the required infusion of conscious attentiveness toward a creative "welling up" from the depths is beautifully put by an alchemical text: "If thou knowest how to moisten this dry earth with its own water, thou wilt loosen the pores of the earth ... " (CW 14:189).

Kerényi, C. *Eleusis Archetypal Image of Mother and Daughter*. NY, 1967.
Wilhelm, Richard and Cary F. Baynes. *The I Ching or, Book of Changes*. Princeton, NJ, 1977.

1. Miniature replica of a Chinese Han dynasty wellhead, terra-cotta, 20 inches high.

2. This ancient Greek well at Delphi (now walled-in) is the mythic spot where the goddess Demeter was met as she rested during the search for her abducted daughter Persephone.

3. An Indian well supplies the water of life during a severe drought in 2003.

1

2

3

Castle

Pristine and dreamlike, the soaring turrets of the Château de Saumur display the fleurs-de-lis that signify the late September grape harvest, which peasants gather in sight of the castle's protective walls. The chateau was one of many belonging to Jean, Duc de Berry (1340–1416), who commissioned the Flemish Limbourg brothers to create his *Very Rich Book of Hours* not only to guide prayer, but to feature his splendid castles in glorious form, rich in gold and exquisite pigments made from lapus lazuli and crushed flowers.

To the imagination, of course, every castle seems enchanted. The castle is where the sovereign power resides and, massively walled, evokes a vessel of wonders concealed by narrow apertures and impregnable stone. Originating in Normandy, the earliest entrenched fortress (Latin *castrum*) or fortified village (Latin *castellum*) was considerably cruder than Jean's; a ditch beneath a wall protected a single tower, the "keep" or *donjon* from which our "dungeon" was derived. The epochal development of the castle produced elaborate, Byzantine-influenced turrets, rings of walls and the portcullis, an immense gate approached on a drawbridge lowered over a moat. In the great banquet hall tapestries thwarted the chilly damp, and while venison and boar roasted over huge spits, the company was entertained by jugglers, strolling troubadours and games of chess in which the "castle" made its characteristic protective moves. Predating the age of guns, the castle, like its playful counterpart in chess, *was* the means of defense, and during lengthy sieges its enclosed gardens, courtyards, chapels and stores gave refuge and provision to the surrounding populace.

What was intimated in all this but a mysterious structure within ourselves that won't allow the sovereign value to be assailed? Children build sand castles and fantasy castles where the innermost self can live, especially if the outer circumstances are very unfavorable (von Franz, 65). Deep, watery moats and intricate bridges regulate comings and goings and secure the cas-

tle boundaries. The sixteenth-century Christian mystic Saint Teresa of Avila compared the soul to a crystalline castle of concentric circles leading to the principal chamber at the center where God and the soul are united. She noted that many go no further than the outer walls or courtyard and fail to explore the delights of the interior rooms or who dwells in the midst of the castle.

Fairy tales and the stories of knightly romance often depict the soul as a beautiful princess or queen whose presence is the fountainlike, animating spirit of the castle. Yet the shadow aspect of the castle is that the defenses that insulate can also constrain. Often the lady is spellbound by a father-magician or threatened by a wicked stepmother, or barren, haunted, dispirited or asleep until the knight of virtue can extricate or awaken her. Grail castles with their revolving walls, vanishing hosts and hidden entrances evoke the disorienting strangeness of the invisible realms of psyche, and the struggles and illusions that must be negotiated through knightly awareness if one is to claim one's soul. But awareness is not just reason: Kafka's last novel, *Das Schloss,* meaning either "castle" or "lock," describes an enigmatic castle on the edge of town that withstands every siege upon its inner truth, resisting our rationalistic attempts to unravel the soul's mystery (Carotenuto, 108). Earlier, alchemy had depicted the hermetically sealed vessel as a castle that not only defends its contents from invasion, but prevents the premature escape of the volatile stuff that might eventually coagulate into golden substance.

Carotenuto, Aldo. *The Call of the Daimon.* Wilmette, IL, 1994.

von Franz, Marie-Louise. *Shadow and Evil in Fairy Tales.* Irving, TX, 1980.

Phoebus Apollo in his sun-chariot adds glory to an already majestic castle as Virgo completes the summer cycle and Libra ascends. Illuminated manuscript from *Très Riches Heures du Duc de Berry*, Limbourg Brothers, ca. 1416, France.

City

Poised between the earthly and the ideal, the "eternal city" of Rome is envisioned in a fifteenth-century illuminated miniature as a jewel-like, circular totality contained within a golden wall. Here, past and present converge in the flowing of the Tiber River, and we have the impression of something timeless, hallowed and cosmic.

In the first place, cities delimited civilization from wilderness and solidity and continuity from nomadic wandering, as they still do for the individual or group that seeks the place of belonging. "Dig and dream, dream and hammer, till your city comes," wrote Carl Sandburg. Cities are the goals of pilgrimage, and embody our projections of possibility, reorientation and rebirth. Cities have personalities, genders, names and nicknames: the Windy City, the City of Light, the Big Apple. Cities are brides and harlots. Cities sleep and wake. We are seduced and infatuated by a city, we fall in love with it. A great city anywhere in the world is, for someone, a defining destination expressing a crystallization of sorts, evoking one's innermost recesses, wherein is to be found the inviolable center, divine spark, immortal point or self. Sacred mandalas of which the center is the focus are sometimes configured as cities, and the city is also an image of the alchemical lapis, signifying sanctuary, integrity, symmetry, balance, the marriage of heaven and earth or of Sol and Luna. Like their symbolic counterparts, actual cities are often quadratically oriented in the angled, discriminated forms of sacred geometry as rectangle, square, diamond and cross. Their main thoroughfares radiate out in the cardinal directions, channels for the ebb and flow of life, and the reception and expulsion of multiple influences. In the past, rites and ceremonies at a city's inauguration honored and propitiated the more unpredictable of these; omens were ritually read, the city's boundaries were furrowed and sanctified, the central hearth was lit with sacred fire. Sacrifices of fruits, vegetables or blood might be offered to the uterine earth, the spirits of the infernal regions and the deities of destruction. The oldest cities were hieratically realized around an emblem of the cosmic center—a temple, ziggurat, mountain or pyramid, a beautiful garden, the palace of the monarch or a statue of a goddess who wore the mural crown signifying her correspondence with the walled metropolis or "mother-city" that "harbors the inhabitants in herself like children" (CW 5:303).

Celestial cities depict the dwelling place of divinities, of perfection or completion that transcends (or excludes) all the oppositions of the worldly sphere; they can represent a different level of consciousness, or a new spirit of understanding. But ordinary cities also infiltrate our dreams and nightmares, recalling the structures, thoroughfares, familiar and unfamiliar neighborhoods of our psychic adaptation and the sections of our lives that are undergoing construction, change or disintegration. Soaring urban skyscrapers have become the emblems of our aspirations and our overreach. The infrastructures of a city, massive systems of water pipes, electrical wires and railroad tracks, vast sewers of collective excrement, subway lines of snaking energy hint at mythical, underworld elements of linking, motion, shadow and drive. Layers of history, cities are often built over the remains of other cities, incorporating the visible landmarks and invisible spirits of another time. Cities are pictures of our conscious attainments and cultural evolution, and every city contains the means of its own demise.

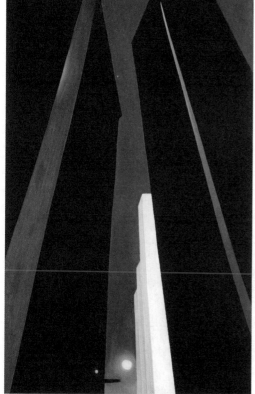

1. Map of Rome, illuminated manuscript from *Très Riches Heures du Duc de Berry*, Limbourg Brothers, ca. 1416, France.

2. The celestial reach of vertical motifs is posed against the pristine beauty of a moonlit sky. *City Night*, by Georgia O'Keeffe, oil on canvas, 1926, United States.

3. *Townscape Madrid (Stadtbild Madrid)*, by Gerhard Richter, oil painting, 1968, Germany.

Temple

A temple is the dwelling place of a god, a shrine set apart from the secular world, hence its name, from the Greek *temenos*, "a secluded realm." From the mysterious circles of Stonehenge to the soaring minarets of an Islamic mosque, the temple has found a multitude of expressions down the ages. Yet the simple austerity of this tiny Mexican sculpture perfectly conveys its universal symbolism and meaning. Standing four-square, it is a building that bridges earth and sky, with steps leading up to its entrance, and a conical top on its roof. The figure on the threshold stands in an attitude of profound stillness, perhaps with his arms in a position of prayer. His expression is inscrutable, focused on an inner dimension that will remain forever unknown to us. Held between the worlds above and below, he perhaps communicates with the gods of each. Perfectly positioned between two pillars, he balances the polar energies of the world of opposites. He is at the sacred center of his universe.

Although this icon comes from an obscure region of western Mexico, carved by an unknown hand, its vertical structure is found throughout the ancient and medieval world, symbolizing the primal threefold cosmos of Underworld, Earth and Sky. The original Temple of Jerusalem was divided into three parts: the court, symbolizing the lower regions and the sea; the sanctuary, the earth, and the curtained inner chamber called the Holy of Holies, Heaven. The ceiling of an Egyptian temple was painted with stars and sacred birds, while plant life seemed to spring to life up its carved pillars (Hall, 89). A tree with its threefold structure of roots, trunk and branches formed a central feature of pagan temples in Northern Europe—which seems to have been remembered centuries later by the builders of Gothic cathedrals whose soaring columns and fan vaulting evoke a mighty forest, frozen in stone.

Yet a temple is even more than the earthly residence of a deity and a template of universal order. For it calls us forth on pilgrimage—a journey in the shape of a prayer, which requires the full participation of body, mind and soul. A visit to a temple can engage us at the deepest levels, even if we know little of its historical context. Temples, such as those in Mesoamerica (EoR, 14:388ff), may be built upon hills or artificial mounds, requiring us to consider the meaning of ascent. In European churches, we traverse three stages: from the nave, through the quire and up three steps to the high altar, moving ever further from the periphery to the inner sanctum of our lives. In these churches, we enter by a western door and walk eastward into the light of a new morning. Some eastern shrines, including Byzantine churches, Islamic mosques and Buddhist temples, have domes, recalling the protective vault of heaven—or they may be egg-shaped, evoking the possibility of new beginnings. Many temples, East and West, are built according to the patterns of sacred geometry, and radiate the harmonious energy of a three-dimensional mandala. Beyond cultural and religious differences, beyond language and time, a temple invites us into the dynamic stillness that lies at the heart of the turning world, and reminds us of our place in the divine order of things.

Hall, James. *Illustrated Dictionary of Symbols in Eastern and Western Art.* NY, 1994.
Jones, Julie, et al. *Houses for the Hereafter: Funerary Temples from Guerrero, Mexico.* NY, 1987.

This pre-Columbian temple model is carved from green metamorphic rock, and stands only five inches tall. Unique to the Guerrero region of Mexico, its design recalls the pyramid temples of the Aztecs (Jones, 26).

Niche

The concave, snug resting place of the niche is designed to act as a refuge uniquely suited to the contours of the statue or object to be placed therein. It is a special space hollowed out from the vertical plane according to the exact dimensions of its ideal complement. It is a symbol of the perfect fit, the female side of the *conjunctiones mystica,* the receptive angle of potential fulfillment.

As a feminine French noun (*la niche*) derivative of the Latin verb *nidicare* or "to nest," one speaks of nestling down or "finding one's niche in life." This nestling imagery was no more prevalent than in the aesthetic conventions of Chinese landscape painting, where the "perfect fit" between the Confucian scholar-official and his government appointment was illustrated by swallows happily nesting in their little niches among the sprawling branches of the government tree. Those birds (scholar officials) that had not yet found their niche in life were depicted as still in flight, searching for a suitable branch of the bureaucracy in which to make their nest.

In temple architecture, the niche is often employed to interrupt the neutrality of a basilica's flat wall by furnishing special decorative or devotional spaces. In the niche, the object of veneration receives a three-dimensional frame, which literally and figuratively lends it depth and dimension. In other words, by consecrating a separate space for the figure or devotional object, that object is thrust into high relief and becomes as profound as the sacred space it occupies. Paradoxi-

cally, the effect of light in this sacred space is extraordinarily effective, for rather than highlighting the figure by means of a luminous halo or aureole, the niche's very absence of light dramatically silhouettes the object of worship. The devotional niche par excellence then is the Muslim mihrab or sacred niche facing Mecca, which houses nothing other than the lantern perpetually lit with the light of Allah. This is described in the Koran as "His light is like a niche in which a lamp is set."

In the case of domed architecture, the corner niche provides the necessary transition from the hard angularity of the square base to the arched expanse of its soaring circular dome. Here then, the niche softens and curves the four sides of the structure's lower walls into the one single unifying line of the upper domed register, indicating again the presence of the Divine Unity. Thus the constructive and symbolic potential of the niche's negative space is paradoxically powerful. As the space becomes more profound, so too does the meaning.

For these reasons, the rendition of illusory niches was one of the favorite conceits of the eighteenth-century rococo trompe l'oeil painters as they successfully "tricked the eye" into seeing three dimensions in a two-dimensional plane. By giving the illusion of depth to their paintings, they endeavored to create not "a window onto nature," but rather a deeper glimpse into their vision of an idealized world.

The writing in the center of the Islamic prayer niche or mihrab states that "the mosque is the house of every pious person." Ca. 1354, Iran.

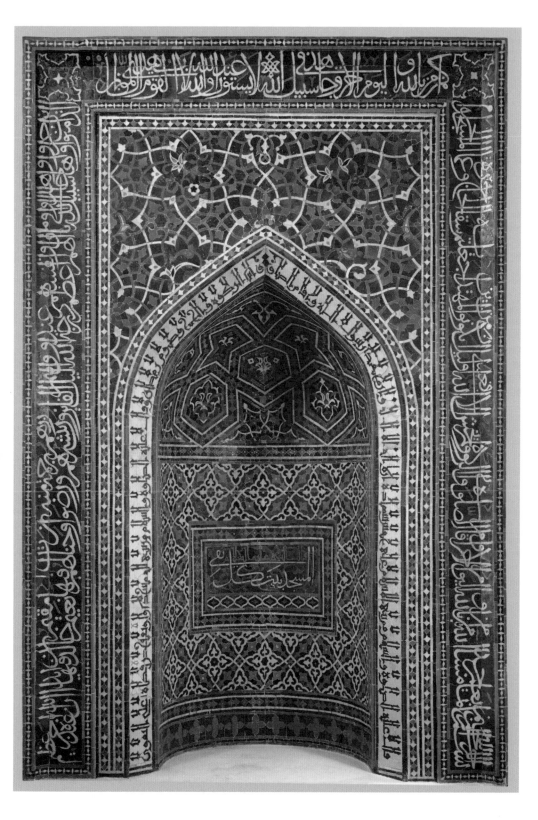

Cloister

A cloister is an enclosed walkway attached to a cathedral or abbey, designed to protect the seclusion of monastic life. This fifteenth-century example displays the typical features of a cloister: a covered arcade with an interior colonnade, often filled in with tracery or glass, opening onto a quadrangular garden. A cloister's four walls conceal the garth (a central garden) from the outside world, often with a well or rosebush at its center to recall the Garden of Eden.

The cloistered life of monks and nuns was not only isolated, but it also limited physical exercise. Medieval architects wisely included these protected spaces for walking within the precincts, uniting the functions of the community. A cloister is usually attached to the southern wall of a church. Adjoining the eastern walkway is a chapter house (where the community gathered to hear a chapter from scriptures), perhaps an infirmary, a parlor for conversation otherwise prohibited, and workrooms and dormitories. Along the southern walkway may be a heated gathering place (or calefactory), the refectory for meals and guest quarters. Along the western walkway were cellars and stores, and to the north scribes worked in the library.

A cloistered person may voluntarily choose isolation to concentrate upon the stillness that may be otherwise drowned out by the external world. The Latin root of the word cloister—*claustrum*—means an enclosed place with the implied rigors of solitude. It is not a blind maze, however, as the corridors of the cloister face out onto a sunlit center, always to be contemplated as an image of eternity. Among the Carthusians, each monk resides in a separate hut opening onto a great common cloister. But even here the monk privately tends his own enclosed garden, cultivating the fruits of deliberate privacy.

Walking along formal pathways is an ancient practice in sacred traditions worldwide. While a Buddhist monk deepens his meditation by slowly winding around a stupa, so does a Christian nun find that her spiritual center is mirrored in the labyrinth she treads in a cathedral undercroft. Such geometric exercise includes the body in a reordering pattern and through the fourfold form of a cloister reinforces a sense of wholeness.

One can live a cloistered life outside of a monastery. The American poet Emily Dickinson drafted her poems in insular seclusion, even shielding herself from callers by visiting them behind a half-open door. Psychologically, "cloister" reflects the dedicated circumambulation of one's interior, transpersonal center, in the service of enlarging consciousness. There were many in the Middle Ages who found the cloistered life to be the container in which their potential could bloom; they have their counterparts in contemporary individuals who give religious attention to their psychic totality.

Nevertheless, the shadow side of cloister is suggestively preserved in our modern term "claustrophobia," derived from the same root. A cloistered existence can be imposed by circumstance or culture, suffocating desired life, or represent a defensive circumscribing of consciousness out of fear of life's demands. Jung was firm that the *circumambulatio* was active engagement of the psyche and not escape into an Eden-like innocence that avoided the tension of opposites. The unity in multiplicity then revealed as the transcendent self is beautifully embodied in the image of the garden at the center of the interior "cloister"—perhaps what Augustine intended by his admonition to the dawning Middle Ages: "Go not without, remain within, truth dwells with the inner man."

The Cloisters, a branch of the Metropolitan Museum in New York City, was mainly reconstructed from the French 15th-century convent of Trie-en-Bigorre. The cloister's character is preserved by its remote location at the northern tip of Manhattan, overlooking the Hudson River.

Tower

Lacking entrance and without a visible horizon, the enigmatic vision by de Chirico still conveys the essence of a tower as a human-made construction rising toward the sky.

Ziggurats, pyramids and stupas are ancient towers created in the image of the cosmic mountain. They stand at the center of the world as an expression of the universal desire to reunite with the heaven, as it was at the beginning of time (EoR, 14:583). The Luba people told the story this way: The High God and the humans were living together in the same village. Finally the creator tired of hearing the endless quarrels and sent the humans down to live on earth where they came to know sickness and death. A diviner advised them if they built a tower they could return to the sky and find immortality. A string of round towers across Southern Africa is believed to be connected with the widespread tower myths in southern Africa, seeking to unite above and below (Willis, 273). Church spires and minarets likewise pierce the heavens at the center of their spiritual worlds from where the sounds of bells and prayers mark sacred space and time.

The strong walls of towers once served as protective fortresses from where enemies could be discovered from afar. Gradually, cities grew up around the towers and anything beyond was considered wilderness. Symbolically, these "towers of strength" have become the structures of society, where its organizations protect us from the return of chaos that always seems to threaten at a distance. The skyscrapers of modern cities continue to be the proud signs of civilization, allowing for a concentration of people, culture and commerce. At times, though, we may reach too high, searching for merely false gods of profit and empty progress. The Biblical story of the Tower of Babel warns about the hubris of building too close to heaven and the consequences of going beyond human limitations. The fall of the Twin Towers at the World Trade Center in New York City and the financial collapses, past and present, eerily seem to echo the age-old story. The tower of the Tarot deck is shattered by lightning, while the falling sparks of the divine fire also suggest the seeds of new creative life.

The erect shape of the tower makes it an obvious phallic symbol; its vertical structure expresses hierarchies of higher and lower, power and powerlessness. The tower's interior evokes the feminine container, where the dark dungeons below—which once held the imprisoned outcasts—seem compensatory. Sometimes the entire structure, like the Tower of London, served as a prison. Here the movement is turning inward, also allowing for reflection and study. Being out of touch with the ground, like living in an ivory tower (which originated in the purity of the Virgin Mary as a mandala-precinct), has come to mean self-absorbed isolation. In the story of Amor and Psyche, the heroine is able to complete her last and most difficult test by applying those aspects of the tower, which at times are necessary—of being far-seeing, having emotional distance and a sense of discrimination (Neumann, 110–11). In many fairy tales a tower also plays a role in the trials of the heroine. The young girl or princess finds herself imprisoned in a tower, situated in the middle of a forest or some abandoned war-wasted land. In this case, the tower suggests the need for a different kind of far-seeing view, one of patient endurance in solitude, which may feel like imprisonment. Throughout life, when our soul feels impoverished by our striving to reach the top, we may once again have to learn to perform our task by humbly turning inward and look for a tower deep in the forest and patiently wait for new visions.

Neumann, Erich. *Amor and Psyche*. Princeton, NJ, 1971.
Willis, Roy G. *World Mythology*. NY, 1993.

1. *The Great Tower*, by Giorgio de Chirico, oil painting, 1913, France.

2. *The Tower*, from the tarot deck by A. E. Waite, drawn by Pamela Coleman Smith.

3. The aspirations of humankind exceed their nature in an edifice built to scale the heights of God. *The Tower of Babel*, by Pieter Bruegel the Elder, oil on panel, 1563, the Netherlands.

1

2

3

Pillar/Column

Strikingly, both this ancient Athenian temple and twentieth-century African house use the human form as a pillar. So does the medieval French cathedral at Chartres. Of the many forms of architecture, the tall slender pillar and column come closest to human body proportions. " ... [The pillar] is a monumental version of our own stance on the landscape" (Lawlor, 84). As part of a building, columns are the essential supports, the source of its stability. If they are compromised, the building itself is in danger. Pillars also function as the vertical axis of a structure and tie together the different levels of a building. And within the body itself, the bony spine, known of course as the "spinal column," has the same function. Symbolically then, pillars and columns have come to represent basic stability and strength. They support the building, the organization (we speak of a person as "a pillar of the community"), the body.

Pillars and columns have a long history with us, symbolically as well as structurally. This is especially true of the freestanding pillar or shaft, often a monument. The Djed pillar of ancient Egypt (Djed was the hieroglyph meaning "stability") had an especially rich history. It was originally a fertility symbol and always related to generative phallic energy (like other monumental shafts such as the Hindu lingam and the Greek herm). The Djed pillar later came to stand for the resurrecting god Osiris and was imagined as his backbone. The huge Djed pillar was hoisted upright as the climax of the crowning of a new king, suggesting the rebirth of the former king and "the establishment of stability for the new reign and for the cosmos itself" (Wilkinson, 165).

The upright pillar also carries the symbolism of an upward thrust toward the heavens, the realm of the spirit. Even the gods themselves have been imagined in this form: Consider Old Testament Yahweh who, in the form of a pillar of cloud by day and a pillar of fire by night, led the Israelites out of Egypt (Exodus 13:21–2). Or the Hindu Shiva, pictured as a "cosmic pillar of fire extending between heaven and earth." Early images of the Buddha represented him as a pillar long before he was pictured in human form. The pillar also serves to elevate sacred things above the ground of everyday reality. The tops of pillars were used as places of sacrifice. The ascetic pillar saints of fifth- to twelfth-century Syria and Palestine lived for years on tiny platforms atop high pillars, never descending to the ground.

Probably the origin of the pillar image lies in mankind's experience of great trees—their overwhelming height, long lives, great strength, their rootedness in earth and apparent reach into the sky. In this way the pillar is symbolically related to the world tree, the symbolic axis that connects earth and heaven and allows travel between the two realms.

Lawlor, Anthony. *The Temple in the House: Finding the Sacred in Everyday Architecture.* NY, 1994.
Wilkinson, Richard H. *Reading Egyptian Art.* London, 1992.

1. These finely worked caryatids in a line of six have supported the porch roof of a small Greek temple on the Acropolis for 2,500 years.

2. A 20th-century Yoruba king's house in western Africa was the site of this carved wooden pillar showing the seated king, his monumental senior wife and other wives and attendants upholding the verandah roof. Olowe of Ise (died 1938).

2

Bridge

Seeming to overarch the rising moon, a bridge connects the ascending cliffs on either side of a river, bringing into relationship clusters of huts, fishing boats and majestic nature. Bridge is structure and pathway, a linking of opposing sides of a landscape often separated by a void. The latter may take many forms: the depths of river, lake or waterfall; a chasm in the earth, the gap between two people, given differences in language, personality or goals; the mythologized breach between heaven and earth, conscious and unconscious, time and eternity. To the ancients, a river or its equivalent represented a natural divide, a divinely ordained boundary setting apart territories in the possession of different forces. The building of a bridge was *contra naturam*, and required sacrifices to resident spirits and deities. Bridge still carries the potency of transgression and abyss. Despite its anchoring, a bridge looks suspended, is subject to collapse and associated with hangings and suicides. The motif of the "perilous bridge" is very widespread. Only gods can traverse the rainbow bridge; humans must pass under. Or, in shamanic traditions, it is the initiated shaman, as master of death and retriever of the soul, who alone can bridge into the spirit world and return to human embodiment. In medieval romances, the drawbridge of the magic castle leads into mortal dangers that test the virtue of the knight. Islam, Hinduism, Christianity and Zoroastrianism all have variants of the bridge to Paradise. Exemplary lives of faithfulness or sacrificial gifts bestow a worthiness that wins safe passage; unworthy individuals fall into Hell or the hands of the Evil One. Psyche appears to support the separation of conscious from the unconscious, but also a bridging that brings them into creative relationship. The ego, unwilling to sacrifice hard-won defenses and fearing the dangers of the void, is often chary of such a bridging. Yet psyche offers guidance in the crossing: unconscious projections that compel libido toward conscious goals; dreams that illuminate the background of interior experience and outer event, the moonlike nature of feeling that blurs unequal opposites into correspondence and parity.

The Monkey Bridge, detail, by Katsushika Taito II,
wood-block print, ca. 1833, Japan.

Tunnel

Emerging from the dense blackness of a tunnel, white lines of train track curve to an opening and disappear in a blast of daylight, the proverbial "light at the end of the tunnel." This experience of dramatic immersion in darkness and reentry into light has evoked the straitened passage of struggle before resolution, despair preceding hope and the birth canal to life and afterlife.

The earliest recorded man-made tunnel was built in Babylonia some 4,000 years ago beneath the Euphrates River. Increasingly refined technology has associated the tunnel with the ambitious burrowing of human beings, often underground or underwater, to create conduits through which to move their vehicles, sewage and fluid resources. Yet countless species of animals from the ant to the mole preceded human beings in creating tunnels or burrows—as snug home or hidden storehouse, a safe haven from predators or a trap for prey. "Tunnel" is etymologically derived from the middle English *tonel*, a tube-shaped net, and is akin to *tonn*, skin or hide, and the Latin *tondere*, to shear, shave or prune. Thus tunnel is a passageway through something massive, tangled or dense, whether it is a mountain or the wooly coat of a sheep, or a psychological complex that obstructs libidinal movement. Healing and initiatory rites have sometimes included an individual's being pulled through the flayed skin of a sacrificed animal as a sign of death and rebirth. In accounts of near-death experiences, individuals have described being pulled through a dark tunnel, sometimes at great speed. Intuiting the symbolic nature of tunnel as itself an animal "body" or arched ribcage conveying psyche's uncanny aliveness, the Tikigak Inuit built their igloos with a subterranean entrance-tunnel articulated with the ribs, jaws, vertebrae and scapula of whales. Storm shed, cold trap and meat cellar, it was also a transitional space where death, birth, danger, initiation and shamanic shape-shifting might occur (Lowenstein, 30 ff).

The tunnel as a numinous *transitus* is employed in films, books and art to convey regressions or progressions into potent psychic dimensions like aboriginal "dream time," parallel universes, past or future. Lured by an intriguing draft, cave explorers have literally tunneled on hands and knees into the interiors of cliffs that revealed dazzling galleries of prehistoric cave art. But while tunnel offers the hope of successful passage in and out, its compressed nature also assumes the phobic-making possibilities of suffocation, stillbirth, getting stuck or getting lost. A means of attempted escape from every kind of captivity, tunnel is fraught with its own dangers. Wells, mine shafts and rat-infested sewers are all forms of tunnels. Tunnels can magnify, mute or fuse stimuli, be disorienting and claustrophobic, evoke a narrowing of vision or the terrifying mental confusion of dementia, amnesia and fugue states. Nevertheless, tunnel attests to the instinctive urge to make a way in, under, through, to penetrate, dig and perhaps link opposite realms of experience and potential.

Lowenstein, Tom. *Ancient Land, Sacred Whales.* NY, 1994.

The light at the end of a tunnel.
Photograph.

Street

Giorgio de Chirico's 1914 painting *The Mystery and Melancholy of a Street* surprises us by its absence of the throng. Instead, elongated shadows and a girl playing with a hoop are the sole figures in the street. The possibility of loneliness in this shadowy cluster of humanity gives the painting its resonance. Here, the street is depicted as a press of buildings, all bearing an infinite sameness and offset only by its lone player—an enigmatic meeting of quotidian reality and inner, psychosomatic life.

Streets are the circulatory system of entire cities and towns. They regulate traffic, give access and organize the orderly flow of life. Often evolved from footpaths, streets are frequently the first component of city planning, taking into account the potential for commerce, traffic and the stable presence of residents. A good city street, writes Jane Jacobs, achieves a balance between the determination for privacy and the desire for differing degrees of contact (Jacobs, 59). Abutted by sidewalks and buildings where people shop, live and meet, streets represent the intersection of our domestic and communal engagements, a place where the practical, routine functions of life are invigorated by chance. As such, they convey the spontaneity of the unexpected, as well as the familiar "walks" of collective culture, including its squalor, crime, industry, learning and romance. The ill-lit and isolated streets of dream and reality are places where "anything can happen."

The character of a street may change radically from one era to another in terms of the prevailing ethnicity of its residents, its social or economic status, its specialty shops and businesses. Nursery rhymes preserve the memory of bygone streets: hubs of activity where carriage horses jostled pedestrians and vendors hawked their wares. As Baudelaire remarked, "The streets of a city provide a vantage point on which to observe the entire traffic of history." So, too, they viscerally evoke the personal history of the individual in its detailed unfolding.

But while street may resonate with a poignant sense of belonging, the image also conveys an opposition to the state of being "homed." One who has none is "out on the streets" and makes his rude and temporary dwelling there. The streets are where outcasts and urchins furtively interact with the society that neglects them; the "streetwise" among them are those who know how to negotiate the perilous urban "jungle" and survive. Streets are where the criminal loses himself, the runaway hides or is preyed upon. Warring street gangs transform their street territories into zones of violence where "chance" becomes threatening. The "voice of the street" as popular opinion or shared belief can take on the momentum of revolutionary change.

Like the "mystery" and "melancholy" of de Chirico's street, the symbol of a street is often ambiguous. The street of one's childhood may evoke a sense of both security and limitation, of the "way" from here to there, or a dead end to nowhere. A street may bring people together, or separate those who live on one side from those who live "on the other side of the street." But while the character of a street is determined by the caprices of nature and the human life that flows through and around it, the sameness and surprises of the street in their turn shape, determine and transfigure the lives of those who traverse them.

Baudelaire, Charles. *The Painter of Modern Life, and Other Essays.* London, 1964.
Jacobs, Jane. *The Death and Life of Great American Cities.* NY, 1993.

A surprisingly alienated world is depicted where we normally expect the distractions and interactions of daily life. *The Mystery and Melancholy of a Street*, by Giorgio de Chirico, oil on canvas, 1914, France.

School

The ironic title of Peter Tillberg's rendering of an elementary school classroom in Sweden speaks of the tension between imposed, collective expectations and the caprices of individuality. It is a classroom that might haunt our dreams. The globular ceiling lights hang like fixed balloons, pictures are tacked neatly to the bulletin board; desks are aligned in perfect rows. Shadowed in the tenuous light of a cloudy day, the spirit of learning seems to overbear the young schoolchildren, who look like small captives of its order and regimentation. Few venues of human experience invite the same chaos of feelings, memories, blessings and curses as school, for so much of our identity is linked to it. School evokes prized opportunities for learning, equated with freedom, stature and creative potential. School is instruction, literally a "building up" of a body of knowledge that in turn contributes to the structuring of consciousness and adaptation. From Latin and Greek roots, the English word school originally denoted "leisure time" for discussion, disputation or lecture, and like the Greek "gymnasium" whose purpose was the training and exercise of the body, contributed to the formation of the virtuous life. Yet school also conveys a whole spectrum of involuntary "lessons" about authority, structure, aggression, competition, achievement, self-image and self-esteem. There are those who at times have been prohibited from even attending school—women, slaves, ethnic minorities and the poor—assigning them to an inferior status within the society. Novels, autobiographies and newspaper articles associate school not only with the fertilizing exchange of ideas, but also with scapegoating, sexual violation, racism, sexism and random violence. Psyche exploits the resonance of school. Dreaming, we find ourselves back in primary school, suffering anxiety over unfinished homework or an impending exam, wandering unfamiliar corridors of classrooms. Or, at the opposite pole, we are tutored by the visiting spirits of venerable masters, receive academic laurels or vanquish the class bully. Such subliminal returns and regressions illuminate points of developmental arrest that now have the potential for movement, or old, unresolved conflicts of identity manifesting in new guises. They reveal the value of our seeking new corridors of inquiry for the needful expansion of inner and outer worlds. They make us aware of "incompletes" in self-understanding that may require periods of interior schooling at a sometimes painfully elementary level. Symbolically, school expresses many things about our relation to learning and how knowledge, of all different kinds, can promote integrity, and dismantle it.

Will You Be Profitable, My Dear?, by Peter Tillberg,
oil painting, 1972, Sweden.

Prison

Like many of his late-nineteenth-century contemporaries, Redon depicted for us the existential imprisonment of the individual. His hollow-eyed convict is a figure so compressed by the death of meaning that he is rendered little more than a mummy. That the prison bars resemble a window frame only serves to emphasize the prisoner's lonely insularity.

Few things engender such fear as the thought of prison or such misery as the reality of it, for living things, breaking out of seed or egg or womb, innately strive for freedom. Prison (from the Latin *praehendere*, to take, seize, capture) means to be confined—in a radical, sometimes an ultimate sense, with no hope of liberation. And almost anything can become a prison. Whatever seizes us, arrests us, by way of desire, impulse or fascination. As an outsider may feel constrained by the withering scrutiny of a repressive state, so do we find ourselves imprisoned by intractable, incomprehensible forces. We imprison ourselves by choices embedded, unwittingly, in coercive fears and inhibitions. Many consider the body a prison, given the impediments it represents compared to the seemingly unfettered flights of the intellect. Gnosticism thought of the luminous *anima mundi,* or soul of the world, as being imprisoned in matter. Alchemy depicted Saturn as the governor of the prison in which Sulphur, the motivating spirit of both will and compulsion, was bound. Saturn is associated with lead, cold and the darkest time of the year, implying the weight of limiting circumstances by which our soaring aspirations are shackled.

In the most literal sense, prison represents punishment for criminal acts, and the protection of society by the containment of destructive tendencies. Dreams about prison reveal many things. Accountability the dreamer is evading, for example, or repeated offenses against the integrity of the self. Or paradoxically, the experience of consciousness being encompassed by the largeness of the self. *Nigredo*-like, encapsulating withdrawal or enforced periods of reflection can seem like prison, as Van Gogh conveys in his painting of a prison round where he placed himself at the center, made during his stay at the Saint-Rémy mental hospital.

At the bleakest level of the symbolism of prison, however, is nothing more than the soul's getting trammeled—not only by incarceration, but by degradation, violation and false arrest. History offers us no end of examples. "If subjects are confined without light, odors, sound, or any fixed references of time and place, very deep breakdowns can be provoked," remarks a historian of CIA black site (secret prison) experiments in interrogation techniques (Mayer, 51). The Swedish poet Tomas Tranströmer describes the deadening monotony of a young offender's prison: "More noise than need be / just to startle time into / getting a move on" (Tranströmer, 45). And Rilke writes of the anguish of the caged panther: " … It seems to him there are / a thousand bars, and behind the bars no world" (Rilke, 25).

Mayer, Jane. *A Reporter at Large: "The Black Sites." The New Yorker.* (August 13, 2007).
Rilke, Rainer Maria. *The Selected Poetry of Rainer Maria Rilke.* NY, 1989.
Tralbaut, Marc Edo. *Vincent van Gogh.* NY, 1981.
Tranströmer, Tomas. *The Great Enigma: New Collected Poems.* NY, 2006.

1. *The Accused*, by Odilon Redon, charcoal on paper, 1881, France.

2. Painted after an engraving by Doré at the asylum at St. Rémy where van Gogh stayed during the last years of his life. The face of the prisoner in the center, looking toward the viewer, is the artist himself (Tralbaut). *Prisoners' Walk*, by Vincent van Gogh, oil painting, 1890, France.

1

2

Color

Imagination built fantasies on the developing science of color, from Aristotle's mixing of elemental hues to Newton's prismatic splitting of a sunbeam into a spectrum of seven primary colors (correlated with the seven planets and the heptatonic musical scale), and Goethe's insistence on the importance of shadings. Colors convey feeling values, relationships and contrasts, dramas and tensions, the nature of matter and its processes and transmutations. They can suggest temperament, class, vocation and hierarchy. Colors define, differentiate and blend. While color is a means of expression, it evolved as a factor of survival. The retina of the eye has millions of light-sensitive cells with different color sensitivities. Colors tell us about climate and season, and when vegetation is ripe and edible. They signal mating opportunities and the presence of prey or predator. Protective coloring allows some animals to become invisible, and others to be made conspicuous, their gaudy pigments warning of defensive toxins. Particular flowers and flower markings, some of them reflecting ultraviolet light undetectable by human eyes, attract particular insects and birds, inviting and guiding pollination. Most mammals are color-blind, including some humans, but color-blind vision more acutely perceives different textures and camouflage. Color-blind RAF pilots in WWII were used in reconnaissance flights because they could detect camouflaged camps and vehicles (Ball, 74).

Alchemy put colors at the very core of the opus. Paradoxically, it was the bitterness of life that produced the colors, a "poison" that tinctured. What the alchemists meant by this is that the chaotic mass of the personality's affects, unmet desires, moral impurities and disappointments got heatedly activated and burnt off in the process of self-understanding. The residue, imagined as white salt or ash, signified both the corrosive scourings of these warring elements and the released hermetic spirit of transformation that differentiated and synthesized them into a unified spectrum of the soul's "colors" or qualities (CW 14:116ff). The welcome appearance of the colors took the form of the iridescent dawn, peacock's tail, rainbow or iris. Chinese alchemy associated specific colors with seasons, elements and directions, intuitively orienting the adept on the way. Western alchemy assigned three or sometimes four colors to stages of the process: the *nigredo* or blackening, suggesting the matter "in the dark"; the *albedo*, or whitening, a state of introverted reflection

that brought into conscious awareness what had been hidden; and the *citrinitas*, or yellowing, and *rubedo*, or reddening, that had to do with the application of the insights to embodied life.

The mysteries of color are not resolved. Yet much has unfolded since Maxwell's discovery in the nineteenth century that light is a vibrating electromagnetic field, the frequencies of which increase from the infrared to the ultraviolet ends of the light-color spectrum. Colors are generated by the play of light in many ways. The pigment of an object is made up of chemical compounds; the frequencies of light these pigments reflect (reject) rather than absorb ascribe to the object a specific color (Murphy, 20). Air molecules in earth's atmosphere scatter shorter wavelengths of visible light (violet, indigo, blue) more than longer wavelengths (green, yellow, red), so the sky looks blue (ibid., 90). The interference of light by submicroscopic, overlapping scales and ridges in wings and feathers creates the vivid coloring in moths, butterflies and birds (ibid., 78). Impurities of colored "transition metals" like chromium and copper transform certain colorless minerals into gorgeous sapphires, rubies and emeralds (Ball, 69). Chlorophyll gives the verdant hues to plants, but decays in the autumn. The carotenoid pigments in some vegetables, flowers and leaves are then unmasked, producing the golden yellows, reds and oranges of harvest time (ibid., 70).

Color is a neural response, a biochemical reaction and a psychological phenomenon and also has to do with complexities of culture and language (Olin, 1). Color affects us, resonating in memory, instinct, the body and all of the five senses. Each of the seed sounds of Indian Tantrism is also experienced as a color, for example. Artists fashion and create colors aesthetically, bringing us the pigments of sensate reality as well as the tones of invisible dimensions. Alchemy hinted that the mythic "painter of all the colors" was no less a figure than Mercurius, the revelatory light of nature and the very spirit of the opus.

Ball, Philip. "Seeing Red." *Natural History* (March 2002).
Murphy, Pat and Paul Doherty. *The Color of Nature.* SF, 1996.
Olin, Dirk. "The Way We Live Now: Crash Course; Color Cognition." *The New York Times.* (November 30, 2003).

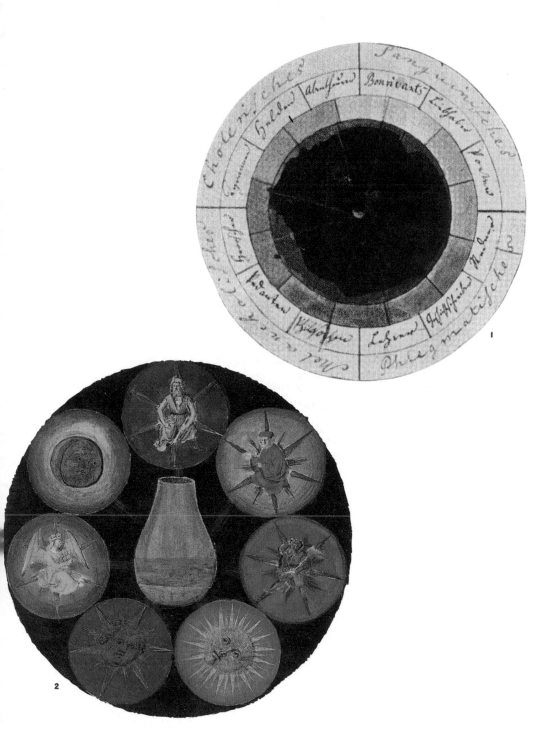

1. German poets Johann Wolfgang von Goethe and Friedrich Schiller collaborated on this version of Goethe's color circle. The four categories of the human temperament each correspond to a specific quadrant. *Rose of the Humors*, painting, 1799, Germany.

2. The changes in the color of the matter in the alembic symbolically expressed the stages, or "operations," of the alchemical opus. Illustration from the alchemical text *Aurora consurgens*, late 14th–early 15th century, Germany.

Red

If color is the music of the eyes (Portmann, 158), then red would be the sound of trumpets (Theroux, 161). Concretely, red is evoked in humans by radiant energy of specific wavelengths, which increase muscle tone, blood pressure and breath rate. For some animals it is sexually arousing. These effects occur also in blind humans and animals, so "red" is not purely an experience of the eye but something more like a bath (Portmann, 138ff).

Symbolically, red is the color of life. Its meaning relates, at bottom, to the human experience of blood and of fire. In primitive thinking blood was life: When the blood left the body, it took life with it (Edinger 1992, 227). At the same time, the red flow of blood was a danger signal. The glow of fire was our great comfort and protection, but, out of control, a threat of annihilation. Red attracts us, conveying vitality, warmth, excitement, passion, but also warns of danger, calls for attention, says "stop!" In China, as well as in Stone Age Europe, red pigment was buried with the bones of the dead for renewal of life (Portmann, 140).

The color red stands at the center of our images of libido—life energy—whether sexual passion or aggression and rage. The slinky red dress, the scarlet-robed Whore of Babylon, the Scarlet Letter (of adultery), the red hearts on valentines, "red-light district," all strike the sexual chord. But we also "see red" when we are enraged and connect the "red planet" Mars with the god of war. In Africa, the warrior has red eyes (Portmann, 64), and the vengeance-seeking Erinyes of the Greeks did too. Red stands for murder, anarchy and war, fierce energy and destruction.

In Roman times, red meant war and a call to arms. The red flag was carried as a sign of defiance in European battles as early as 1600 (Barnhart, 644). More recently, revolutionary activists are "reds."

In many cultures, red is associated with fiery intensity, ardor, daring, bravery, which can move into fury and cruelty. This aspect of red is expressed in African symbolism both by the color and by the idea of *nyama*, the potential force in all things and the bodies of all beings, especially in the blood. This potent energy fills witnesses with both wonder and fear (Portmann, 64). Red was the color of the alchemists' sulfur, the burning energy of human desirousness.

1. Chaim Soutine's red image faces us with the tension between life-giving food and bloody death. *Side of Beef and Calf's Head*, oil on canvas, ca. 1925, France.

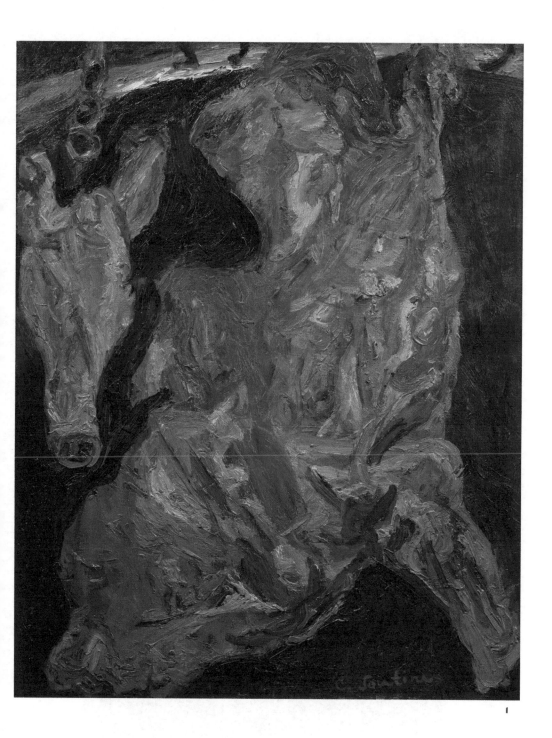

The fierce energy of red is so widely felt that even red hair has been seen as related to a hot temper, irascibility, choleric temperament. By the principle of like protecting from like, a red ribbon over the doorway or a red spot painted on the forehead was protection against devils. The Christian devil, of course, was red too. Red coral protected against the evil eye (Theroux, 202ff).

And, to the alchemist, *rubedo* or reddening was the last stage of the long process of making gold or, psychologically, integrating the personality. It meant nothing less than bringing spiritual realization into full-blooded reality, lived out fully in everyday life (Edinger 1995, 296).

Barnhart, Robert K. Ed. *The Barnhart Concise Dictionary of Etymology.* NY, 1995.

Berger, Patricia, et al. *The Legacy of Chinggis Khan.* London, 1995.

Edinger, Edward F. *Ego and Archetype.* Boston and London, 1992.

Edinger, Edward F. *The Mysterium Lectures.* Toronto, 1995.

Portmann, Adolf, et al. *Color Symbolism: Six Excerpts from the Eranos Yearbook, 1972.* Zurich, 1977.

Theroux, Alexander. *The Primary Colors.* NY, 1994.

2

3

2. Not all reds have the same punch. In this painting, even red achieves harmony and balance. *Red No. 5*, by Mark Rothko, oil painting, 1961, United States.

3. Red as the raging fire of ferocity: The Tibetan ritual-dance mask from Mongolia was worn by one of eight Sword Bearers in the retinue of Begtse, the war god who became the guardian of the Dalai Lama (Berger, 166). Papier-mâché, 19th century.

Orange

A hemisphere of orange, Ellen Krüger's untitled, abstract watercolor suggests the rising or setting sun, the succulence of orange and cantaloupe, or the glow of molten lava and igneous rock. Orange is a mixture of red and yellow and in the light spectrum of color stands between the two. Orange extends into the realm of gold, the incorruptible and everlasting, and into the realm of blood, vigorous, active and mutable. The lambent saffron of the East brings the two together, evoking flame and arousal, the physical and subtle body energies of the second chakra, the tantric unity of opposites, and the sacral fragrance and flowering of life. In the Buddha's time, prisoners wore orange and the Buddha was said to have adopted a robe of saffron as a sign of compassion for the dispossessed and condemned. Bold and visible, orange still signifies detention, warning and protection, from the jumpsuit of the American prisoner to the vivid markings of the monarch butterfly that tell potential predators its body has toxins that make it lethal prey. Orange colors the ascent, descent and burning of the sun, associating its hues with processes of emergence, heat, growth and perfection, and the coagulating intensity of desire. The Roman bride wore the *flammeum* or flamelike veil of Aurora, the goddess of the dawn. Divine Jupiter was said to have presented an orange, round, seedy and fecund, to Juno on their wedding day (Inman, 18). Sendivogius, a seventeenth-century alchemist, intuited in the sun-ripened orange an emblem of psyche's transmuting heat sufficient to cause the nature of a thing to bring forth its vital spirit, come to fruition and produce its seed. Orange is then maturation and harvest, the brilliance of the turning leaf, the russet, autumnal moon, ingathering and completion. But the warmth of orange also becomes emblematic of nature and psyche's more searing transformations, sudden and drastic—the quality of forest fire, volcanic explosion and nuclear blast.

Inman, W. S. *An Essay on Symbolic Colors in Antiquity, the Middle Ages, and Modern Times.* London, 1845.

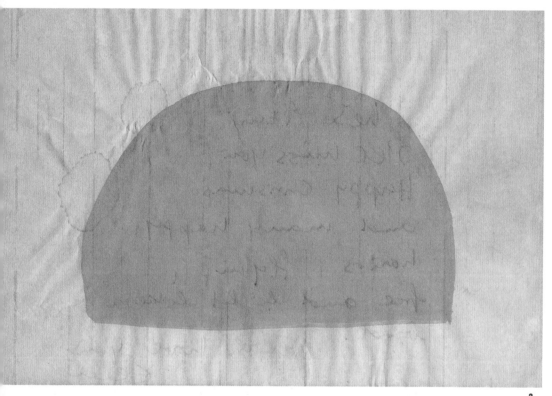

2

1. Buddhist and Hindu monks of India and Southeast Asia typically wear saffron-colored garments, Laos. Photograph.

2. *Untitled*, by Ellen Krüger, watercolor, 1997, United States.

Yellow

Yellow is "a color capable of charming God" (Theroux, 146). So wrote Vincent van Gogh from his yellow house in sun-drenched Arles. Preparing a room in his house for his friend Gauguin, he made a series of yellow sunflower paintings but judged only two to be fine enough to hang (www.vangoghmuseum.nl). Van Gogh's yellow is exultant, radiant with the energy of the sun in the blue sky. The Maya of ancient Mexico used the word *Kan*, yellow, for the god who held up the sky (Theroux, 86). Traditional Chinese belief has also linked yellow with the highest things—with the sun as the center of the heavens, with the emperor (whose emblem was a yellow dragon) as the center of the universe (DoS, 1138). During the Ch'ing Dynasty (1644–1911), only the emperor was allowed to wear yellow clothing (Theroux, 90). *Huang*, the Chinese word for yellow, also means "radiant."

In China, yellow was also the color of fertile soil and used for hangings on the bridal bed, to ensure the fertility of the marriage (DoS, 1138). Chinese refer to themselves as golden, not yellow (Theroux, 112), and of course yellow is closely linked to gold in Western symbolism, from the halos of the saints to the bones and flesh of Egyptian gods, which were thought to be of gold.

Islamic culture saw yellow in two ways: Golden yellow stood for wise and good advice; pale yellow for betrayal and deceit (DoS, 1139). This pale yellow is the color of sulfur, which belongs to the devil's realm. There is a host of unflattering yellows: The doors of traitors were yellowed in the sixteenth and seventeenth century as were the houses of bankrupts in medieval France. In the 1200s and within recent memory, Jews have been forced to wear yellow insignia on their clothing as a form of persecution (DoS, 1139). A familiar personality type for centuries, a choleric person was thought to have an excess of yellow bile and to be "yellow-faced, lean, proud, ambitious, shrewd and quick to anger" (Theroux, 126). Then there is the yellow of cowardice ("yellow-bellied," "yellow streak up your back"). A (yellow) "canary" is an informer. "Yellow journalism" is cheap and sensation-driven.

More practically, yellow is highly visible; chrome yellow can be seen at a greater distance than any other color. So yellow has become a color of warning: on heavy machinery, life preservers, as the sign of quarantine against deadly disease, as a cautionary traffic light.

Yellow is also a stage in a process. Aging is yellowing: the paper of old books and the leaves of autumn trees, the teeth of old animals and humans. After summer green comes yellow and then brown, a slow process of decay. To the medieval alchemists, yellowing (*citrinitas*) was a phase in the long process of making gold, or, metaphorically, of arriving at psychological wholeness and integration. It was a transitional stage, coming after the (black) chaos and despair of the beginning had given way to (white) reflective awareness and quiet. Yellow was a reenergizing and a returning of interest in the outside world—on the way to a full (red) involvement with life (Hillman, 83–5).

Hillman, James. "The Yellowing of the Work." *Personal and Archetypal Dynamics in the Analytical Relationship. The Eleventh International Congress for Analytical Psychology.* Einsiedeln, Switzerland, 1991.

Portmann, Adolf, et al. *Color Symbolism: Six Excerpts from the Eranos Yearbook, 1972.* Zurich, 1977.

Theroux, Alexander. *The Primary Colors.* NY, 1994.

1. *Vase with Fourteen Sunflowers*, by Vincent van Gogh, oil on canvas, 1889, France.

2. Yellow warbler on a branch, photograph by Ron Austing.

645

Green

The miracle of green spreads softly over the winter-brown landscape, thrusts up from a dry wrinkled seed, draws water and earth and light together in hidden chemistry to appear as new, green plant life. This holiest of mysteries, on which our survival depends, has been imagined over the eons in the form of a divine being who is often green-skinned. The deity, like the Egyptian god Osiris shown here, may suffer seeming death, yet returns to life full of vigor, just as green plants sprout again, bud and blossom in the spring. The Christian crucifix, representing the dying and resurrecting Christ, was also pictured as green. This vibrant life energy that infuses plants also flows through us: "The force that through the green fuse drives the flower / Drives my green age ... " wrote Dylan Thomas (Thomas, 10).

The link between "green" and plant growth is built into the word itself: "Green" is related to the Old English word *growan*, meaning to grow or cover with green (Barnhart, 329). Green affects the body by lowering the blood pressure and dilating the capillaries, a restful effect used against both insomnia and fatigue (Portmann, 139). But beyond physical-life energy, green also stands for hope, for the promise of reaching one's precious goal beyond the blackness of discouragement (CW 14:623–4).

Green's relationship to life can easily swing over to a connection with life's opposite pole. Then green is found in images of death and decay and illness: slime, mold, poison, pus, nausea; also in the threatening faces of witches, the bodies of extraterrestrial enemies, dinosaurs, monsters. In the psyche, too, there is the green-eyed monster of jealousy, and being "green with envy."

More positively, green is linked to the creative, fertilizing power of the Christian Holy Ghost and to the Greek goddess Aphrodite, who oversaw love and fertility. As well, it is sacred to Islam, the color of Muhammad's flag, of the dome and interior of his tomb and the green and white flags of his descendants (Theroux, 280). In ancient Egypt, green was a symbol of growth and of life itself and "to do green things" was an expression for positive, life-producing actions, as opposed to "red things," which were evil (Wilkinson, 108).

In our time, "green" implies being ecologically aware, caring for the organic life of the planet. This adds a modern note to the old meanings of green as fresh, moist, pliable (like green wood), not rigid. To twelfth-century Saint Hildegard of Bingen, *viriditas*, greenness, came when "Those who approach Christ the living vine and drink there become green and fruitful from him ... " (Fox, 93). Though green can imply freshness, of course it can also carry the notion of immaturity, inexperience, awkwardness, unripeness—the "greenhorn."

Just as green is complementary to red in color theory, fresh, moist greenness is often associated with fiery red. The serene Green Tara of our image appears beneath a small red Buddha and above a fierce love goddess (Leidy, 10). To the Greeks, fruitful green Aphrodite was the lover of fierce red Ares. The highest value is often the green vessel containing the red substance: the alchemical green lion's rose-colored blood, the emerald chalice of the grail containing the holy blood of Christ. A psychological reading (Bishop, 15) might say that the endless serene cycling of green needs and holds the shocking energy of passionate red.

Barnhart, Robert K. Ed. *The Barnhart Concise Dictionary of Etymology*. NY, 1995.

Bishop, Peter. *The Greening of Psychology*. Dallas, TX, 1990.

Fox, Matthew. Ed. *Illuminations of Hildegard of Bingen*. Santa Fe, NM, 1985.

Frazer, James G. *The Golden Bough*. NY, 1958.

Leidy, Denise P. and Robert A. F. Thurman. *Mandala, the Architecture of Enlightenment*. NY, 1997.

Portmann, Adolf, et al. *Color Symbolism: Six Excerpts from the Eranos Yearbook, 1972*. Zurich, 1977.

Theroux, Alexander. *The Secondary Colors: Three Essays*. NY, 1996.

Thomas, Dylan. *The Collected Poems of Dylan Thomas*. NY, 1953.

Wilkinson, Richard H. *Symbol and Magic in Egyptian Art*. London and NY, 1994.

i.

i. Van Gogh's painting embodies what St. Hildegard of Bingen called the "blessed greenness" and alchemy the *viriditas*—the lush, fertile verdancy of nature. *Flowering Chestnut Tree*, 1887, France.

2

2. The resurrected Egyptian god Osiris, of whom it was proclaimed, "The world waxes green through him" (Frazer, 442). Pigment on papyrus, 1403–1365 B.C.E., Egypt.

3. A Tibetan Green Tara is enthroned amongst leaves and flowers bursting with life. Ink and opaque watercolor on cloth, 17th century.

Blue

Goethe wrote that " ... a blue surface seems to recede from us ... it draws us after it" (Hillman, 133). Also, into it—into the wild blue yonder, into the deep blue sea. It is not quite of earth, this blue, which apart from sea and sky is the rarest color in nature. Given the unearthliness of blue and living as we do below the vast blue heavens, we have colored our gods blue—Kneph, Jupiter, Krishna, Vishnu, Odin—and our goddesses too: "Blue is the color of Mary's celestial cloak; she is the earth covered by the blue tent of the sky" (CW 11:123). Blue is linked with eternity, the beyond, supernatural beauty, religious transcendence, the spiritual and mental as contrasted with the emotional and physical and with detachment from the earthly.

When this celestial blue appears in everyday language, its symbolism becomes less clear, but often points to the special, the highest, the most valued. Thus, a blue ribbon for first prize, a blue-ribbon (elite)

committee, blue-chip stocks (those of the most valuable, most profitable companies), a blue blood (patrician), this last said to derive from the veins showing through the skin of fair-complexioned aristocrats (*American Heritage Dictionary*, 207).

In the course of physical evolution, mankind has been able to perceive (and so to name) the colors at the warm end of the spectrum before the cool ones (Portmann, 132). Blue is a latecomer. Homer had no word for blue, referring to the sea as dark. In a majority of the world's languages the same word means both "blue" and "green" (Theroux, 56). Blue was seldom used in prehistoric art or by nonliterate peoples for lack of the raw materials with which to produce blue pigment (Biedermann, 44). The original ultramarine blue pigment was produced from a finely ground semiprecious stone, lazulite, the source of lapis lazuli, and was so expensive that it was reserved for important

2

1. The Brahman section of the old city Jodhpur in India is almost entirely painted bright blue.

2. Blue draws us into a meditative mood. Yves Klein was a French painter known for his patented color, filed under the name IKB (International Klein Blue). *Blue Sponge-Relief*, relief, 1957–9.

paintings, and for images of spiritual beauty and perfection (Theroux, 39).

At the same time, blue feels cold. It cools and calms. It is the color of moonlight. Blue light slows the heart rate, lowers blood pressure and retards the growth of plants. It is the color of bruises, melancholy, isolation, "the blues." Pablo Picasso's paintings from his "blue period" show poor laborers, beggars, café sitters in states of lethargy and despair, all painted in blue tones to convey their hunger, cold and sadness (Theroux, 31f). The blues as a musical form arose from the poor, black rural American South and predated jazz music, mixing sadness and humor as the singer laid out his travail. The blue note, a flatted note dropped into a melody in a major key, is a hallmark of jazz, which, despite its exuberance, still has the ruefulness of the blues.

Psychologically, blue can be seen as midway between black despair and the white of hope and clarity, suggesting a state of reflection and detachment. Linked to shadows and darkness, blue brings depth (Hillman, 133).

American Heritage Dictionary.
Boston and NY, 1996.
Biedermann, Hans. *Dictionary of Symbolism.*
NY, 1994.
Hillman, James. "Alchemical Blue and the
Unio Mentalis." *Spring 54* (June 1993).
Portmann, Adolf, et al. *Color Symbolism:
Six Excerpts from the Eranos Yearbook, 1972.*
Zurich, 1977.
Theroux, Alexander. *The Primary Colors.*
NY, 1994.

3

4

3. In ancient cultures, the fish was both despised for its voraciousness and venerated as an image of the soul floating, similar to the idea of the soul-bird flying. *Oxyrynchus*, sacred Egyptian fish, wearing the crown of Hathor. Blue glass, New Kingdom, (ca. 1000 B.C.E.).

4. *Blue Lady* sits enthroned on her totem animal, just like an archaic goddess. By Suzanne Nessim, acrylic on canvas, 1987, Sweden.

Purple

Francis Bacon's imaginal pope is a figure both of grandeur and diminishment, cloaked in the ambiguity of majestic purple. Besides the regal hue of spiritual and secular royalty, purple possesses in itself a whole spectrum of color. Nature offers us in its fruits and flora lavender, lilac, violet, plum, grape and eggplant. There is the purple of livid wounds and the washed purples of the dying sun.

Fascination with a rich, vibrant color called "purple" goes back so far in history that we are not sure what the precise hue of ancient purple really was. Probably Biblical purple, used in the clothing of Hebrew priests and in tabernacle furnishings, was what we would today call crimson. The ancient Greek purple, too, was a dark reddish color thought suitable for appeasing and honoring the dead and the fearsome gods of the underworld (Harrison, 249). Hugely admired by the Romans, a color known as "Tyrian purple" came to represent wealth, worldly position and honor, and was worn exclusively by the famous and powerful. Ultimately, by law it could be worn only by the Caesars themselves. The Tyrian dye, precious and costly, was painstakingly made from a Mediterranean sea snail. This purple—a very dark color that was most valued—was described by ancient authors as the color of congealed blood (IDB 3:969). The sense of extravagance of the Roman purple lives on perhaps in our term "purple prose," used for rich showy writing, full of ornate phrases.

Outside the Western tradition, a purple dye made from mollusks appears in other seacoast cultures, too, notably in the Tehuantepec area of southern Mexico and in Japan, where purple cloth is used by Shinto priests to enclose the most sacred objects of the temple ritual (Finlay, 381). The color was also associated with royalty and divinity in China, where it was connected with the emperor (Eberhard, 242), and was a royal color for the Aztecs and Incas of the Americas (Cooper, 40).

The color purple is a mixture of the primary colors red and blue. Beyond kingly splendor, much of its symbolic meaning comes from the fact that it brings together opposites. For instance, purple can stand for the red of passion balanced by the blue of reason, or the real by the ideal, or love by wisdom, or earth by heaven, or, psychologically, for union of opposing energies within an individual. In Taoism, it is a transition between yang and yin, active and passive (Stevens, 150). Purple, or violet, in which blue predominates slightly over red, is the last color of the rainbow, and can be thought of as "the end of the known and the beginning of the unknown," bringing it into connection with dying (Finlay, 356). In medieval times, the "precious purple tincture" was a term for the alchemists' goal, signifying the successful outcome of the work, the final union of opposing substances—or energies—into a whole, evoking the image of majesty: "The king puts on the purple robe," they said, at the climax of the alchemical process (Abraham, 160). Jung translated the alchemical fantasy into the idea of a spectrum. At the infrared end is the dynamism of instinct. At the ultraviolet or "mystical" end is the archetypal image of the instinct, numinous and fascinating. It is through its mediation that instinct can be realized and assimilated in the service of integrity, hence the "purple robe" (CW 8: 414ff).

Christian symbolism similarly relates purple to spiritual process and growth. It signifies martyrdom as a devoted "witnessing" and is used on the altar at penitential seasons of fasting and sober reflection such as Advent and Lent. At the same time, Christian art pictures Jesus in a purple robe at the time of the Passion, symbolizing once again a paradoxical union: the mystery of divine and human nature combined in one being. Here, as in many other symbol systems—the alchemical, the Roman, the Aztec and Incan, the Chinese—we find that the highest, most sacred values are represented by purple.

Abraham, Lyndy. *A Dictionary of Alchemical Imagery*. Cambridge, UK, and NY, 1998.
Cooper, J. C. *Symbols*. London, 1978.
Davies, Hugh and Sally Yard. *Francis Bacon*. NY, 1986.
Eberhard, Wolfram. *A Dictionary of Chinese Symbols*. London and NY, 1986.
Finlay, Victoria. *Color*. NY, 2002.
Harrison, Jane Ellen. *Prolegomena to the Study of Greek Religion*. Princeton, NJ, 1991.
Stevens, Anthony. *Ariadne's Clue*. Princeton, NJ, 1999.

1

2

1. The first of Francis Bacon's three paintings of an imagined pope, a paraphrase of Velasquez's ornate 16th-century portrait of Pope Innocent X (Davies, 23). *Pope I*, 1951, England.

2. Nature's purple: a modest bunch of violets. German School, formerly attributed to Albrecht Dürer, watercolor and tempera on paper, late 16th century.

Brown

The variant browns of fallen leaves mingle, decomposing, with autumn's damp soil, shavings of bark, the residue of nuts and berries, animal scats and tiny, indistinguishable insect life. Brown carries the bustling, fecund substance of earth, and its dissolutions. The vast majority of animals are brown, blending protectively with woods, rocks, dirt and desert, or submerged in the muddy sediment of rivers and ponds. Brown is both rich and humble, evoking softness, warmth, depth and respite, the sepia tones of coming darkness, the duskiness of skin, the sumptuous brindling of fur and feathers. Brown is produced by the mixing together of many colors, its reds, yellows and grays elegantly asserting themselves as chestnut, bay, roan, sorrel, walnut, oak, heather, chocolate, coffee, mocha. Brown can also represent colorlessness or discoloration—rust, and dried blood, drought, brownouts of electricity or creativity, blandness, boredom or muddle. Service and military uniforms capitalize on brown's capacity to merge the individual with the herd, reinforcing collective identity and dependence. Nazi soldiers were known as "brownshirts." Brown evokes the formless, chaotic liquidity of muck, slops, waste, vomit, feculence and sewage. It is desiccation and mummification. Yet brown is also emergence, the shapes and boundaries of dry land surfacing out of watery abyss, the dormant vitality of seeded fields, the mothering support of firm ground and good earth.

Autumn Leaves, by Christopher Gallo, photograph, 1992, United States.

Black

Black envelops and swallows, is cave and abyss, the holes of space and the bowels of the earth, night, melancholy and death. Mourning sinks into black and rests in its muffled sadness. The widow's veil of separation and loss, the judge's robe of sober authority, are black. The black vestments of the cleric renounce the bright-hued pleasures of the sensual, material life; the black elegance of eveningwear engages them. There is bible black and ebony black, and the black of scarab, crow and cat.

Black is foulness, decay and dirt. But the black dirt can be the soil itself, the fertile covering of the earth from which life arises. In Ancient Egypt black evoked death but also life, as the black silt of the inundating Nile brought fertility; the resurrecting god Osiris was sometimes depicted with black skin, sometimes green. Black encompasses the terrors and beauties of the underworld and its tenebrous precincts of healing and initiation. The "black" deities are ambiguous, chthonic and fateful. Divine smiths are black with the soot of volcanic forges in psyche's fiery, creative depths. The dark ground of Kali, the Black One, absorbs the blood of sacrifice and nature's slaughter and nurtures the seeds of return. Black Mary, Isis, Persephone, Artemis, Hecate possess the black womb of uncanny darkness and new moon.

The Navajo see in black the sinister, but also, because it confers invisibility, black's capacity to protect (Reichard, 194). Black comes from the north, the direction of danger, but also from the east (ibid.), the place of sunrise. In parts of Africa, black is also traditionally the color of the north, but here it signifies the direction from which come the dark clouds of the rainy season, vegetation and water (Portmann, 63). Black connotes the "seasoned" individual's achieved social maturity and authority, patience and the ability to wait (ibid., 73–4).

Black and white are often in tension with each other, especially where the one is perceived as a deficiency of the virtues of the other: white as blandness and coldness, and black as richness and warmth, or black as benighted and white as enlightened. We are not always sure what to call black—a color, or the absence of any color, or as the Sufi mystic poet Rumi described it, "the consummation of all colors," the state of beatitude in which the godhead reveals itself, ravishing the initiate (De Vr, 93). From the Heian period of Japan (800–1100 C.E.) derives the notion that in black is expressed the "sublimation and purification of all emotions" realized by the individual who has plumbed the depths "of the sadness of human existence" (Portmann, 172). Black is primeval chaos, the polar heart, hidden center and locus of emergence.

Black is primary to many forms of transformation, the imaginal hue of individual *metanoia*, a turning away, or a turning inward, or even a "dark night of the soul," the luminous darkness of self-understanding. In the alchemical opus black signifies the eclipse of familiar patterns of identity and meaning. The *nigredo* is a state of disorientation, exhaustion, self-doubt, depression, inertia, confusion and disjunction. The alchemists described it as a "black blacker than black," black sun, widow, orphan, *caput corvis* or "head of the crow." Yet, the alchemists found the *nigredo* not cause for dismay, but for rejoicing; it expressed conjunction with psyche's illimitable, teeming potential in which could be conceived the golden embryo of self.

Portmann, Adolf, et al. *Color Symbolism: Six Excerpts from the Eranos Yearbook, 1972.* Zurich, 1977.

Reichard, Gladys, A. *Navaho Religion: A Study of Symbolism.* NY, 1963.

1. A window on black. *Ultimate Painting No. 6*, by Ad Reinhardt, oil painting, 1960, United States.

2. Blackness as a stage in the alchemists' work, here pictured as a black alchemical vessel labeled "Crow's Head." The black container is set against a strip of flourishing life-green, the hoped-for conclusion of the darkness. *Putrefactio philosophorum*, illustration from a collection of alchemical extracts, mainly by Arnold of Villanova, 15th century, Germany or Austria.

3. Nineteenth-century village women in their Sunday black, which has the effect of disembodying and eliminating individuality. *At the Sermon*, by Theodule Ribot, oil painting, ca. 1890, France.

1

2

3

White

White evokes pristine, monotonic landscapes—the endless, undulating sands of Arabia's desert, or the Arctic's crystalline glaciers and frozen ground. The polar "whiteout" erases even shadows, eliminates the horizon and deceives our perceptions of scale and depth (Lopez, 239). Yet white is also newness and beginning, harboring color. The briefest white of predawn yields to rose and saffron. A field of impeccable snow absorbs the hues of hovering sky and shifting sun. White suggests mist, vapor and ether, and the fantasized emptiness and silence just preceding the first sound-colors of the discriminated world. Baptismal candidates and the initiates of ancient mysteries clothed themselves in the white vestments of rebirth, simplicity and restoration. Delicate white blossoms of apple, pear and orange trees are emblems of springtime, renewal and wedding vows; the trumpeting, translucent blooms of the Easter lily announce resurrection. Equally, at the other end of life's spectrum, white connotes infirmity and disembodiment, a lack of red-blooded vigor or a failure of courage. White is the pale horseman of death, the pallor of the corpse, bone stripped of flesh, shroud and wraith, and the dove or seabird as the soul departing.

White plays between opposites. It is incandescent heat and frigid cold or a merging of fire and ice. The mythic Snow Queen of the north is captivatingly beautiful and wintry of nature; the pallid vampire is bloodless in its passion. White receives the projection of all or nothing. The psychologist Rudolf Arnheim observed that white is "a symbol of integration without presenting to the eye the variety of vital forces that it integrates, and thus is as complete and empty as a circle" (Riley, 302). In his poem "Adonais," Shelley speaks of "the white radiance of eternity." For Melville's Captain Ahab, however, the great white whale Moby-Dick conveys the indefiniteness and impersonal vastness of the universe, and human fears of annihilation (Melville, 194). Yet the milky, maternal ocean of Hindu myth is the source of all the fundaments of the cosmos. From its waters emerge saps and elixirs, the white cow of all desires, and the moon-white elephant Airavata, emblem of the Vishuda chakra, the throat or "void" in which all the elements intermingle. White Buffalo Cow Woman, dressed in white buckskin, is the dazzling, mysterious presence that gives to the Sioux the gift of the sacred pipe and all the holy rituals honoring Grandmother and Mother Earth (Brown, 3ff).

Where fantasy identifies white reductively with light, white can be forced into polarizing opposition to black. Here, white becomes purity, virtue and innocence versus black as turbid, lustful and evil; white as the unblemished lamb of sacrifice versus black as the derelict scapegoat of sin.

Alchemy projected on white an essential aspect of the opus. On the one hand white was childlike naivety, unawareness, immaturity and a lack of experience. One might need to sacrifice such whiteness and tincture one's matter with substance and individuality. On the other hand, white represented the ash or salt of bitter suffering and hard-won wisdom, and the white hair of the knowing old man or crone. Indeed, primary white gave way symbolically to melting, blackening, burning, flooding and separation—a discrimination of one's nature that preceded synthesis. The second whitening or *albedo* was conceived as a state of illumination or the dawning of the unknown personality in consciousness. Some deemed the *albedo* the attainment of the goal. Others believed the opus reached fulfillment only when dawn turned into the ruby brilliance of sunrise, the roundness of an integrated, creatively embodied life.

Ball, Philip. "Seeing Red." *Natural History* (March 2002).
Brown, Joseph Epes. Ed. *The Sacred Pipe.* NY, 1971.
Lopez, Barry Holstun. *Arctic Dreams.* NY, 1986.
Melville, Herman. *Moby-Dick.* NY, 1926.
Riley, Charles A. *Color Codes.* Hanover and London, 1995.

1. The artist observed that white is "the ultimate color, the true, real, concept of infinity"(Ball, 74). *Suprematist Composition: White on White*, by Kazimir Malevich, oil on canvas, 1918, Russia.

2. Polar white on white. A bear merges with the ice. Photograph.

1

2

Gray

Gray is a mixture of black and white, but also, as anyone with a watercolor paint box knows, it results from mixing any of the color opposites: green and red, yellow and violet, blue and orange. Because of this, it has a peculiar position at the center of the color world. Despite the attraction of the vivid primary colors, gray is essential: " ... that fundamental grey which distinguishes the masters and is the soul of all colour," wrote the painter Redon (Gage, 185). Gray is present to some degree in almost all colors, and this common note ties together in harmony the various hues in a painting (Gage, 215).

Human newborns do not, as we once thought, see only gray. Though they are not able to focus as well as adults, so that objects are fuzzy, their eyes possess color vision. As we develop, gray, neither bright nor bold, takes on particular meanings. Probably by association with graying hair, gray stands for old age and all that is associated with it: retrospection, inaction, narrowing of libido—but also wisdom and serenity. In Christian symbolism, it is the color of mourning, of the ascetic time of Lent, of humility—and of resurrection of the dead. Medieval paintings show Christ in a gray cloak at the Last Judgment (DoS, 456). Gray evokes saturnine "lead" and the moods that leadenness conveys: sadness, inertia, melancholy, indifference or boredom. Gray is linked with the sackcloth and ashes of penitence and with the symbolism of ashes in general. Despite the association of ashes with defeat and failure, however, in alchemy ashes symbolize the immortal part of the personality that has survived the confrontation with primitive desires and emerged purified (Edinger, 139). Gray is neutral, an in-between place. Opposites balance there or are yet undifferentiated. Mythically, dead persons and spirits moving between the realms are gray. A "gray area" is not certain, one way or the other. There is indefiniteness about gray, embodied especially in gray clouds and fog, which adds to its ambiguity and its place as a mediator.

The varying usages of gray as a symbol suggest that it has differing meanings, depending on one's temperament. To the outward-directed personality, which seeks excitement and stimulation, gray stands for all that is burdensome and limiting. In an 1899 speech, Theodore Roosevelt proclaimed, "Far better it is to dare mighty things, to win glorious triumphs, even though checkered by failure, than to take rank with those poor spirits who neither enjoy much nor suffer much, because they live in the gray twilight that knows not victory nor defeat" (Gable, 30). By contrast, the American poet Paul Engle, writing of his experience as a student at England's Oxford University, remembered that: "The tense American nerve relaxed. I lived / with a gray quietness that let the mind / grow inward like a root."

Edinger, Edward F. *The Mysterium Lectures.* Toronto, 1995.
Engle, Paul. *Corn.* NY, 1939.
Gable, John Allen. Ed. *The Man in the Arena: Speeches and Essays by Theodore Roosevelt.* Oyster Bay, NY, 1987.
Gage, John. *Color and Culture.* Berkeley and LA, 1999.
Kertess, Klaus. *Brice Marden: Paintings and Drawings.* NY, 1975.

Brice Marden's quiet gray painting is rich with the colors it has absorbed. "It is the painting's very reticence which compels our involvement" (Kertess, 19). *Wax I*, oil and wax on canvas, 45 in. x 56 in., 1966, United States.

Flute

"When the first full moon of autumn approaches and the jasmine is in bloom, the shrill, soft sound of the flute penetrates the rooms. It is Krishna calling" (Calasso, 281). In the beloved Hindu story, the music ravishes the *gopis*, the milkmaids of Vraja, whose butter and hearts are stolen by the mischievous god. Abandoning their half-milked cows, leaving their families with food still cooking on the fire, the women are irresistibly drawn to the blissful melody. Human ears respond, and divine as well, for even the gods are transported. Clouds and rivers cease their movement, and all creation harkens to the sound of the flute (Kinsley, 34–39).

Flute is wood, reed, wind, breath. In myth it is associated with nature gods and spirits, as if, in the flute's haunting, birdlike notes, the god breathes on the listener and infinite and finite are momentarily experienced as one. The flute conveys the elemental, uncanny essence of nature, something invisible, pervasive, everywhere and nowhere, which seizes upon us. In Greek mythology, it is the instrument of Dionysus and his intoxications, Eros, and the sylvan, goat-god Pan who invents the panpipes from the reeds into which a fleeing maiden transforms herself (Avery, 809). The sound of the flute is mocking, playful, seductive and beautiful, calling one to one's own fate (Neumann, 156), and fate may take the form of ecstasy, revelry, wantonness or captivation. The Pied Piper of Hamlin, for example, plays on his flute in order to enchant away the rats that are overrunning the town, but the children, charmed by the piping, also disappear.

Courtesans, magicians and tricksters are depicted with the flute. Yet, in the hands especially of the shepherd, the flute evokes the capacity to restrain the passions, quiet the appetites, tame what is unbridled within and harmonize the chaos of its force. In Mozart's opera *The Magic Flute*, it is the magical instrument the Queen of the Night bestows on the reluctant hero Tamino; the flute subdues the lions guarding the way to the mysteries of transformation.

1. Krishna with his flute; its music was irresistible to the milkmaids. Miniature painting, ca. 1760, India.

When Krishna, playing his flute, dances with the *gopis,* he multiplies himself, manifesting in countless forms so that each of the milkmaids perceives the god as dancing with her alone. The clear, pure notes of the flute tell a similar tale of psyche—that something apart from consciousness, paradoxically vital and preexistent, wants union with the soul. And the soul, devotedly answering, finds itself renewed in this eternal Other intimately present and never able to be possessed.

Avery, Catherine B. *The New Century Classical Handbook.* NY, 1962.

Calasso, Roberto. *Ka.* NY, 1998.

Kinsley, David R. *The Sword and the Flute.* Berkeley, 1975.

Neumann, Erich. *The Fear of the Feminine and Other Essays on Feminine Psychology.* Princeton, NJ, 1994.

3

2

2. A fragment of a Roman marble relief depicts a hetaera, or courtesan, of ancient Greece, playing double flutes. Detail of the *Ludovisi Throne,* 460–450 B.C.E.

3. A Peruvian boy playing a flute. Photograph by Werner Bischof, 1954.

Trumpet/Horn

At the lips of a great New Orleans jazz musician, trumpet is declarative, strutting, syncopated, bluesy. Louis Armstrong made solo improvisation primary in the art of jazz. Here, as if his essence might be distilled in a golden horn, he plays the trumpet in Carnegie Hall in 1947.

Trumpet has a multifaceted voice. It reverberates with nature: the elephant's roar, the bellowing of apes, the high-pitched soundings of the whale and dolphin, the trumpeting of the wild horse. Mythically, the Greek god Poseidon, embodying the dynamism of the sea, is heralded by a thunderous trumpeting of the sea creatures on which he rides the waves. The Neolithic ancestor of the trumpet was a lip-vibrating wind instrument made from animal horn, conch shells, bone, wood or metal. The trumpet has taken the form of the *dung chen,* a Tibetan version that can measure up to 16 feet in length, or the gourd trumpets played in South America. In medieval paintings, angels are depicted blowing the double-bend precursor of the modern, valved brass instrument known to symphony orchestras, jazz ensembles, battlegrounds, parade routes and athletic fields at halftime. The trumpet has called to arms battle-ready troops and rallied retreating soldiers. It can be heard at great distances, clamorous, urgent, warning, triumphant. It speaks of what stirs life and what obliterates it.

In the music of pageant and processional the trumpet evokes sacred time and space, the majestic and revelatory. The trumpet fanfare for kings and queens echoes the glory of the gods of which the ruler was perceived to be image or incarnation. Greatest of the Jewish ritual instruments, the *shophar,* made from the horn of a ram or mountain goat, signaled the holiest Day of Atonement, as well as war and peace, the new moon, the beginning of the Sabbath, approaching danger or the death of a dignitary (Youngblood, 871).

Angels, prophets and priests blow the trumpet, invoking an agency of transpersonal reach, which consciousness perceives in the dissolution of old forms, reversals and disintegrations. At the legendary battle of Jericho, the priestly circumambulation of the city and trumpeting on seven rams' horns precede the tumultuous shout of the army that brings the walls of the city down (Joshua 6:8ff). Heimdall, the watchman of the gods in Norse myth, sounds his trumpet at the end of the world (MM 21:2897). In the Book of Revelation, when the seven angels of the Lord blow their trumpets one by one, the earth is thrown into a chaos of fire, smoke, earthquake, lightning and hail, and both heaven and hell are opened. Yet, the trumpet is also angelic herald of glad tidings. Echoed in the silent, jubilant trumpeting of lilies in the spring, it announces resurrection, and in the darkest times, mythically proclaims divine birth, dawn's light and nature's awakening.

Youngblood, Ronald F., F. F. Bruce, et al. *Nelson's New Illustrated Bible Dictionary.* Nashville, TN, 1995.

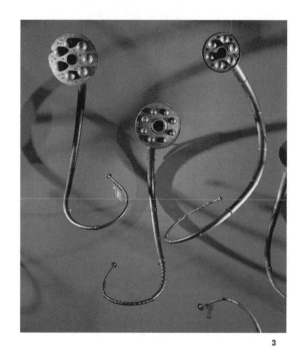

1

2

2. An angel playing a trumpet with a double bend; trumpet as the instrument of celestial proclamation. *The Linaiuoli Triptych*, detail, by Fra Angelico, tempera on wood, ca. 1433, Italy.

3. Several of these bronze lurer, or trumpets, measuring about four feet long, were found in Danish bogs. They may have been played during rituals and then sacrificed. Ca. 800–700 B.C.E.

1. *Portrait of Louis Armstrong, Carnegie Hall, NY, 1947,* photograph by William P. Gottlieb.

Harp / Lyre

In the long ago, maybe seated in a place of honor by the fire, a tribal bard sings his epic tales of gods, heroes, wars and odysseys, accompanying himself on the lyre. Its curved, horn-shaped sides recall the bull worship of ancient Crete and evoke the engendering nature of lyric forms and poetic recitation. These open us to memory and empathy, releasing the liquid notes and deep vibrations of the heart. The lyre was the most honored ceremonial instrument of Greece and Rome. Its cousin the harp was known to the peoples of Mesopotamia, Egypt and Europe. Mythically, the two, like many musical instruments, were perceived as objects of earthly stuff and divine invention, bringing together material and nonmaterial realms. The infant Hermes, trickster and thief, later the messenger of the Olympian gods, slayed a tortoise, made the lyre from its patterned shell and gave it to Apollo as a gift after stealing his cattle. The Celtic god Daghda carved his magic harp from a sacred oak, sealing in it the four seasons, laughter and sadness, darkness and light (White, 56). Angels as well as poets play harps, expressing states of bliss beyond fixed patterns and troubling oppositions. The ordered tuning of the harp's vibrating strings embodied a ladder between above and below. By the playing of his harp, David, in the Bible, soothes the "distressing spirit" of madness that possesses King Saul. The rippling, waterlike sound of the harp intimates the soul's refreshment and the world's reanimation. Equally, the lyre was associated with solar gold and Apollonian harmony. And when Orpheus, Apollo's son, played the lyre, everything distempered was tamed, even the heaving shadows of the underworld.

White, Thomas. "Epicycle: The Oak and the Two Blossoms." *Parabola* (5/2, 1980).

Bard with Lyre, bronze statuette, ca. 900–700 B.C.E., Crete.

Bell

We'll take refuge in bells, in the swinging bells,
in the peal, the air, the heart of ringing.
We'll take refuge in bells and we'll float
over the earth in their heavy casings.
Adam Zagajewski, The Bells

The massive bell of King Seongdeok was cast in bronze for the Pongdok Temple in eighth-century Korea. Rung throughout the day, it summoned the Buddhist monks to periods of devotion. On the bell's body are images of *apsaras,* celestial nymphs (Sørensen, 18:347), and its rim is shaped like an eight-petaled flower (*Korean Overseas Information Service,* 268).

From the deep resonance of a ritual bell like the Seongdeok or the sonorous tolling of the hour bell of the Great Clock of Westminster, to the silvery tinkling of the little bells adorning the ankles of Hindu dancers and Hindu gods, the crystalline emphasis of the *sanctus* bell and the cow bell's more earthy comfort, bells awaken the senses and the spirit. Bells ring out glad tidings of victory and celebration, warning's urgent clamor, the "joyful noise" of praise, the cadenced voice of mourning. Hindus identify the bell's echo with the primordial vibration of the universe (DoS, 81), and scientists confirm that "the early universe rang like a bell" (Cowen). Similarly, the Japanese Zen sage Dōgen evokes the image of a bell when he compares meditation to the melodious sound made by striking emptiness—an endless sound, both preceding and following the moment the hammer hits (Okumura, 54).

The tonal properties of bells have made them the expression of the harmony of the spheres, the cosmic unity that the Greek philosopher Pythagoras saw in the fundamental patterns of numbers and ratios (EoR, 12:14). In magical folk practices bells bring rain, ward off storms and protect animals from malign spirits (MM 2:238), and attempt to insure nature's harmonic

balance with human life. In Russian history the tolling of church bells is credited with turning the human heart away from its most destructive intentions, or bringing the hard-hearted to repentance. In Russian Orthodox Christianity, bells are animated beings, with names, feelings and bodies; they are not tuned to major or minor musical chords, because the bell is considered "not a musical instrument, but an icon of the voice of God," and each bell is prized for its deep, rich, untuned individuality (Batuman, 22–23).

The bell's rounded, hollow shape likens it to the female form, while the clapper and the handle both suggest a phallus (de Vr, 44). These sexual connotations play a role in the symbolism conveyed in the Tibetan Buddhist ritual bell and *dorje* (a small scepter) often used together (Berger, 258). The bell, which has a half-scepter handle, represents the wisdom of emptiness, a feminine aspect, while the *dorje* signifies the masculine aspect of universal compassion (Thurman, 104); together they represent the enlightened mind.

Batuman, Elif. "The Bells Harvard and a Russian Legacy." *The New Yorker* (April 27, 2009).
Berger, Patricia, et al. *The Legacy of Chinggis Khan.* London, 1995.
Cowen, R. "Sounds of the Universe Confirm the Big Bang." *Science News* (April 28, 2001).
Korean Overseas Information Service.
A Handbook of Korea. Seoul, Korea, 1979.
Okumura, Shohaku. *Shikantaza: An Introduction o Zasen.* Kyoto, Japan, 1985.
Sørensen, Heinrich H. "Bells and Gongs."
The Dictionary of Art. Ed. Jane Turner. NY, 1996.
Thurman, Robert A. F. and Barbara Roether.
Inside Tibetan Buddhism: Rituals and Symbols Revealed. SF, 1995.

1. This Korean bell, one of the largest in world, is over 12 feet in height and weighs 19 tons. *The Divine Bell of King Seongdeok*, bronze, 771 C.E.

2. These bells, the largest continuous bell-chime from the Chinese Bronze Age, were found in a tomb in Henan Province. Each bell has the ability to emit two notes, depending on where it is struck. *Twenty-six Bronze Zhong Bells*, ca. 550 B.C.E.

3. Pythagoras uses bells and water glasses to determine the numerical values of musical notes. Woodcut, Renaissance.

Drum

The tranquil expression on this carved, wooden drummer's face, the characteristic oval shape favored by the Nkanu of Zaire, reveals his absorption in the primordial language of his drum. Equatorial Africa is home to two entirely different types of drum: the "slit-drum," made of a scooped-out cylinder of wood, split on one side and beaten with a stick; and those made by stretching animal hides over a wooden tube, a hollow pot or calabash, and struck with the palms, fingertips or baton. Throughout the Congo, the resonant vibrations produced by a drum mimic the tonal quality of the local spoken languages, allowing the drum to communicate messages of abbreviated speech up to 20 miles away. Its ability to echo the pitch, pauses and accents of the human voice engendered the fantasy that the drum understood the tribal languages and possessed a soul of its own. The enslaved descendents of the Congolese peoples devised such Afro-Caribbean innovations as the bongo drum, the larger Congo drum (accompanying the irresistible conga dance) and closely guarded vodou drumming rituals.

Drums are among the most ancient musical instruments. Neolithic drummers stretched fish, snake or other animal skins over wooden frames to create the earliest drums; pastoral herds later made goat and sheepskin and cattle hides more practical. The animal's spirit was thought to return with the beating of its skin, which the drummer often decorated with images of celestial bodies or protective guardians. Priestesses and devotees of the great goddess in Mediterranean cultures beat hoop-shaped, handheld frame drums in her sacred rituals, inducing trance states for healing and prophecy. The drum beat was the reflection of the "rhythmic web" of plant, animal and human life, the pulse of the blood, heart and world, invoking elemental powers, articulating processes of creation and linking the individual to the rhythms of moon and cosmos (Redmond, 10ff). Bells and rattles attached to the inside rim amplified the capacity of the drum to purify and dispel. The striking of the drum embodied for the ancients the fertilizing power of thunder that preceded rain; its sound could offset destructive earthquakes and eclipses and exorcise demons. The latter function developed into the military ritual of dismissing a wayward soldier to the staccato tattoo of drums, and the "drumming out of town" of undesirables. The drum's visceral booming has heralded the start of battles, the fall of the executioner's axe and the firing squad's volley of bullets.

The English word "drum" comes from the Old Germanic *trumpa,* a parallel to the Norse *trumba,* meaning "echoic," from which "trumpet" and "trombone" are also derived (Partridge, 741). Yet the drum has perhaps a special affinity with the notion of "echoing," attuned to the beating heart of the universe but also reverberating with the immediacy and rapture of a sphere transcending the boundaries of the universe. Indeed, the sacred drum of the Siberian shaman was envisioned as the cross section of the world-tree that visionaries ascend to the realm of spirits. The round edge of the drum's taut surface mirrored the horizon beyond which the drummer journeyed, his drum now the horse, reindeer or boat that carried him away to other worlds. The drum's steady monotone may have induced an alternate state of consciousness characterized by theta brain-waves, but at the same time sounded the mortal world to which the shaman would return from ecstatic flight. And what unimaginably distant place does our Nkanu drummer hear, and answer, lending him his lithe equipoise, and echoed in the buried, steady drumbeat of his body.

Partridge, Eric. *Origins.* NY, 1958.
Redmond, Layne. *When the Drummers Were Women: A Spiritual History of Rhythm.* NY, 1997.

1. The carved wooden drummers of the Nkanu tribe of the Democratic Republic of the Congo (Zaire) memorialized rites of initiation. Their human counterparts pounded drums to give courage to young initiates undergoing circumcision and tactfully smother their cries.

2. A maenad tosses her head back in ecstasy at the rhythmic sound of her tambourine. In Dionysian processions, sacred intoxicants and the drum's steady beat transported these devotees into orgiastic frenzies. Marble relief, Roman, ca. 100 C.E.

3. The sheer delight of beating a drum is visible in the merriment of this 2,000-year-old Han Dynasty ceramic figurine. Chinese drums produce eight orderly sounds reflected in the eight sources of their various composition: metal, stone, silk, bamboo, wood, skin, gourds and earth.

1

3

2

Silence

There are silences and silences. The woman in Odilon Redon's painting invokes silence, and in her meditative appearance she seems to seek more than a personal silence in which something is better left unsaid, more even than the awed silence in which we might sit at the lip of the Grand Canyon on a quiet evening. She calls us instead to that deepest silence in which the voice of the Wholly Other may be heard. At the symbolic level, silence is a part of every sacred tradition, for each knows that profound mysteries may address us only in silence, as the monastic rules of silence in the West encourage. In a Quaker meeting, a sustained silence may work mysteriously to bring members together; a word spoken as a call or leading from within the silence may evoke a higher truth. The Holy Spirit is the companion of silence.

"A philosopher once asked the Buddha: Without words, without the wordless, will you tell me the truth? The Buddha kept silent. Since real silence is beyond both words and wordlessness, by this answer the philosopher was freed from delusion" (EoR, 13:323).

Silence, by Odilon Redon, oil and gesso on paper,
ca. 1911, France.

SPIRIT WORLD

MYTHICAL BEINGS

**ANGEL, GANESHA, DAKINI, QUETZALCOATL,
SIREN, FURIES, MERMAID, UNICORN, CYCLOPS / GIANT,
VAMPIRE, WITCH, DRAGON**

680

RITUALS AND
SACRED SYSTEMS

**DOT / BINDU, ZERO, ONE,
MANDALA, LABYRINTH, CROSSROADS, SPIRAL,
MASK, INCENSE, ASHES, BLESSING**

706

SICKNESS
AND DEATH

**DISEASE, WOUND, VOMIT, MEDICINE, POISON, DROWNING,
CRUCIFIXION, HANGING, MURDER / SLAYING, SUICIDE,
BURIAL, COFFIN, CREMATION, MUMMY, DECOMPOSITION,
DISMEMBERMENT**

732

SOUL AND PSYCHE

**SHAPE-SHIFTING, METAMORPHOSIS, TRANSFORMATION,
CHAKRAS, CRACK, PEARL, GHOST, ANCESTOR**

770

Angel

Whatever the nature of their "overshadowing," angels fatefully alter our lives. Within the fire of their love lies the latent power for igniting terrifying judgment. We can wrestle with the angels, lose or find ourselves in their cascading glory, shudder at their prescient declarations. Though not always benign and often portrayed as morally ambiguous, they are irresistible. Lucifer ("light-bearer") illuminates the paradoxical association between rebellion and the fall into consciousness. The angels in Genesis 6:2 seduce human women and sire destructive giants, yet in the Book of Enoch they also teach humanity the secrets of horticulture, metallurgy, astrology and jewelry making. Angels may embody the potentially saving or the potentially annihilating.

Who or what they are we do not know, but they have stirred the imaginations of artists, writers, mystics and ordinary individuals of virtually every age and culture. Their name deriving from the Greek *angelos*, denoting "one who announces or tells, a messenger," angels are agents of supernatural revelation, proclamation, aid and guidance. They approach us as emissary dreams, visions and meditative states; manifest as celestial voices or choirs, human or animal shapes, male, female or androgynous, star, cloud or fire. Their great wings are tokens of access to supernal regions of knowledge and information unavailable to ourselves except in the bedazzling angelic moment. They enthrall us with the lovely subtle stuff of their "corporeal incorporeality" and "unearthly voluptuousness" (Zimmer,

1

2

1. Colorfully attired angels compose a choir of celestial
bridesmaids attendant upon the
Virgin's assumption into heaven. *Angels Dancing in
Front of the Sun*, by Giovanni di Paolo (ca. 1403–82),
oil on panel, 15th century C.E., Italy.

2. An unknown Italian artist depicts this "messenger"
from transpersonal realms
as a being neither human nor god, animal nor force of
nature, yet incorporating aspects
of each of these orders. Fresco,
early 14th century C.E., Northern Italy.

120). We delight in images of seraphic aerodynamics, the sweet rapture of child angels at the manger, the glorious assemblage of angelic hosts in a night sky.

Their guardian images surround us. You see them anywhere you go: engraved in an ancient rock wall, looking out serenely or militantly from the stained-glass windows of a church, painted in ancient tombs or etched on a gravestone. Hindu or Buddhist *apsaras*, Tibetan *dakini*-angels, the winged attendants in Indian carvings, or *ba*-figures in Egyptian myth evoke them. They appear as flying spirit men in the great vision of Black Elk. Alchemists depict angelic guides in their illustrations. Winged figures of Sleep and Death escort pagan souls beneath the earth. The angel Gabriel commands the illiterate Muhammad to "Read!" and thus to assume a preeminent role as Allah's messenger. In near-death experiences, angelic "beings of light" have lovingly encompassed the dying, returning them to life. The profound nature of angelic encounter is one of numinous insight or immediate, portentous intimation of possibilities consciousness scarcely comprehends. Angels trumpet us to religious and creative awakening; herald sacred birth and psychic unfolding. And, as shattering in-breakings of ecstasy and overflow, they "dictate" the passionate words of philosophers and poets:

> Who, if I cried out, would hear me
>   among the angels'
> hierarchies? and even if one of them
>   pressed me
> suddenly against his heart:
>   I would be consumed
> in that overwhelming existence.
>   For beauty is nothing
> but the beginning of terror, which we
>   still are just able to endure,
> and we are so awed because it
>   serenely disdains
> to annihilate us. Every angel is terrifying.
> **Rilke, "The First Elegy," *Duino Elegies***

Rilke, Rainer Maria. *The Selected Poetry of Rainer Maria Rilke*. NY, 1989.
Zimmer, Heinrich. *Myths and Symbols in Indian Art and Civilisation*. NY, 1946.

3

4

5

3. With animated faces, two Islamic angel scribes write the names of the blessed in the *Book of Life*, suggesting angels' ongoing and attentive interest in human affairs. *Recording Angels*, book illustration, 1280 C.E., Wasit, Iraq.

4. The fallen angels who defied their creator in pursuit of radical self-determination become inverted intermediaries between Lucifer and humankind. *Fall of the Rebel Angels*, detail, illuminated manuscript from *Très Riches Heures du Duc de Berry*, Limbourg Brothers, ca. 1416, France.

5. An angel prods Adam and Eve into exile, his demeanor evoking uncompromising adherence to divine law. *Expulsion from Paradise*, detail, from the *Cortona Altarpiece*, by Fra Angelico, tempera on wood, ca. 1432–3, Italy.

Ganesha

Ganesha, perhaps the favorite among the Hindu gods in contemporary India, is a study in contradictions and conjunctions, as the large elephant's head on his pot-bellied childish body instantly makes clear. There are, says Paul Courtright, "more than seventy myths" (p. 20) of his origins and history, which, in the Indian way, include many contradictions, but the conjunction of animal and human, of wise, mature, elephant head and dwarf or toddler's human stockiness in this eleventh-century relief is characteristic. Here, Ganesha "stands in the graceful 'triply flexed' pose on a lotus pedestal. His head is crowned with the matted, piled-up coiffure of an ascetic, while serpents and strings of pearls serve him as ornaments. The bells on his feet indicate that he is a dancer. Ganesha holds objects in each of his four hands: a broken tusk, a rosary, a bowl of sweets, and an elephant goad ... and his vehicle, the rat, gazes up at him" (ARAS, 1:111).

In one common myth of Ganesha's origins, he is the offspring of Shiva and Parvati, but in an unusual way. Shiva, the powerful deity of both destruction and restoration, the ascetic and yet also actively erotic god whose consort is Parvati, has refused to give her the son she desires. When he is absent in ascetic retreat, Parvati makes her own son from the dirt of the earth rubbed off her body, and loves him passionately, for he is solely hers. As the boy grows up, she appoints him guardian of her private and sacred bath, and instructs him to keep out all visitors. When Shiva suddenly returns and desires to join his consort, Ganesha opposes him, angering him until in fury he beheads the youth with his sword. Parvati is so distressed that Shiva is compelled to seek the first head he can find to restore the youth to life, and thus Ganesha owes the elephant half of his being to Shiva. But his human body is so young he is no sexual threat, despite Parvati's ambiguous attraction to him; this is suggested additionally in this sculpture, as in many others, both by the curved rather than erect shape of his elephant trunk and by the broken left tusk whose end the figure holds.

Having had his dual origin as guardian of a threshold, Ganesha is the Lord of Beginnings, invoked at the start of every new endeavor. He is called Gatekeeper, and his image is placed at the doorways of homes and temples, mediating the realms of sacred and profane space. He is "Lord of Hosts" (the multitudes of Shiva's deities), the remover and the placer of obstacles. While Ganesha is generally propitious, he must be attended with offerings, especially of the sweetmeats (*modaka*) he loves with childlike gluttony. Hearing the prayers of all, his large ears are likened to winnowing fans that sift out the true and essential from the false and inessential. His gifts include the head powers of the elephant—wisdom, memory, feeling—rather than those of the natural or wild body. His intelligence suits him as the deity of writers (his broken tusk is sometimes used as a pen). His vehicle or mount (*vahana*) is the rat, who, as Heinrich Zimmer points out, represents on a smaller scale Ganesha's elephant skill, for "the rat makes its way through all obstacles into the security of the granary, there to consume the rice stores of the village household" (p. 183).

Ganesha's compromised body, lacking the phallic authority of adult masculinity, has probably contributed to his popularity. Though he is demanding of attention, he conveys a childlike neediness or human woundedness more than the awesome terror of a distant god. As both animal and human he is a true *monstrum*, a wondrous but appealing conjunction of multiple potentialities. Yet as watcher at the threshold of sacred space, he emphasizes both the dangerous difference and the opportunity to cross over between the worlds of human and divine.

Courtright, Paul B. *Ganesa: Lord of Obstacles, Lord of Beginnings.* NY, 1985.
Zimmer, Heinrich. *Myths and Symbols in Indian Art and Civilization.* NY, 1946.

1. A sublime "monster," Ganesha, the beloved elephant-headed god of Hinduism, is at once threshold guardian, remover of obstacles, teacher, scribe and childish glutton for sweets. The thumb and index finger of his lower right hand touch in the vidarka mudra, a gesture evoking knowledge. Relief, schist, 11th century, Orissa, India.

2. An unusual depiction of Ganesha as an infant being breastfed by Parvati resembles similar scenes of the Virgin Mary and the Christ Child. Opaque watercolor on paper, ca. 1820, Jaipur, India.

Dakini

This little figure is stripped of all but her most essential characteristics. Naked but for her ornaments, she stands in dancing pose, her right foot grounded, her left leg raised over her left arm to expose her vagina—the source of her creativity and power. Her vagina, in Buddhist Tantric tradition, is the gateway to the womb, symbolic of the spacious emptiness that is the source and end point of myriad human forms.

In Tibetan Buddhist practice one concentrates on an image such as this and meditates on its esoteric meaning. The *dakini's* body is lithe, active and very beautiful. Her face, serene at this moment, displays passionate intensity and concentration. In her left hand she offers her skull cap bowl (*kapala*) that traditionally contains either *amrita*, representing the white energy of semen, or red blood, representing feminine life force, lust, passion and the capacity to give birth: "the burning interior power of women" (Allione, 33–4).

In her right hand, this tiny evocation of active potency holds a hooked knife, or *kartik*, with a "thunderbolt" handle, or *vajra*, combining skillful means with the hook of compassion. This traditional implement of the *dakini* "pulls one forth from suffering, chops up the ego-centered self and is guided by the diamond clarity of the *vajra*" (Allione, 33).

Originally, the *dakini* was associated with the terrifying aspect of the Indian goddess Kali and was taken to be a witch, a flesh eater and a demon. But as traditional folk demons became integrated within an increasingly sophisticated religious canon, the role of the *dakini* rose to be one of the most powerful and multivalent symbols in Tantric Buddhism; women, concurrently, became accepted as teachers, mystics and practitioners in their own right. Until recently, the *dakini* has been best known for her usually secret role as teacher and consort to the great Tibetan wise men and leaders. Lately, however, Buddhist scholars have recovered the *dakini* as an archetypal representation of a potent and many-faceted feminine self (Allione, 25–38; Shaw, 3).

Contemporary writers such as Nathan Katz make a comparison between the *dakini* and the Jungian concept of the anima—usually seen as the feminine side of a man, which in its undeveloped form (the demoness) leads to moods, sulks, rants and rather hysterical behavior, but in its developed form serves as a teacher, a balancer and a bridge to the unconscious and larger self. For women, the symbol of the *dakini* integrates traditionally masculine attributes—her activity, passion, leadership and yang energy—with feminine being that is playful, wild, mercurial, creative and deeply wise. "She may appear as human, taking a variety of forms, from crone to virgin or sexual consort. Her name literally means sky or space goer" (Campbell, viii).

Though one can summon the *dakini*, she will arrive if and when she wishes. One beseeches her with longing and reverence. She can bring fear, delight, awe and great challenge when she appears. But the *dakini* cannot be pinned down nor made subject to the ego's demands. In her sky-dancing form, her garments speak for her: They flutter around her on her little cloud of bliss as fragrantly as a gentle breeze, as delicately as a butterfly. Beware not to grasp at her nor ignore her lest the *dakini* vanish leaving at most a faint scent—an ashy dusting of once brilliant possibilities—in your empty hands.

Allione, Tsultrim. *Women of Wisdom.* London and Boston, 1984.
Campbell, June. *Traveller in Space: In Search of Female Identity in Tibetan Buddhism.* NY, 1996.
Katz, Nathan. "Dakini and Anima—On Tantric Deities and Jungian Archetypes." *Self and Liberation: The Jung-Buddhism Dialogue.* Eds. Daniel J. Meckel and Robert L. Moore. NY, 1992.
Shaw, Miranda Eberle. *Passionate Enlightenment: Women in Tantric Buddhism.* Princeton, NJ, 1994.

The artist has stripped his statue to her essence in the way a Brancusi, Picasso or Arp eliminates or abstracts in order to intensify. Dancing *dakini*, gilded bronze, 17th–18th century, Nepal.

Quetzalcoatl

Quetzalcoatl, a serpent ("*coatl*") feathered with the iridescent green plumes of the quetzal bird of tropical Central America, winds its way like a bright thread through almost 1,500 years of Mesoamerican history. Through the rise and vanishing of empires, great migrations and conquests, the sacred image was carried and reimagined as new civilizations arose, gaining new meanings yet maintaining its form and its benevolence. The image of Quetzalcoatl married the snake and the bird, earth and heaven, the devouring, germinating powers of earth and the fertilizing, ordering powers of sky.

The earliest images of Quetzalcoatl, before 900 C.E., link this green dragon with the fertility of the plant world and the springtime, when the earth, like the snake's scales, is covered with feathery green. The earth was feathered with sprouting cornstalks, which miraculously sprang from seeds placed in the cold dark ground. The earth's great maw was thought to swallow seeds, and also to devour the setting sun and the stars, yet they returned as corn and other food-giving plants, and as the sun at daybreak and the rising stars. Ensuring this miracle of new life arising from death required continuing blood sacrifice to the underworld powers (EoR, 12:152–3). Quetzalcoatl is an image of the divine incarnated in temporal life-forms, delivering and suffering birth and death (Campbell, 2:254).

Later civilizations combined new meanings with the image of the plumed serpent. He became the wind god of earlier traditions and was known as the fertilizing wind that sweeps before the rains. In the later cultures Quetzalcoatl also became one with the planet Venus, which had long been a wonder to Mesoamerican astronomers for its periodic disappearances from earth's view, "dying," and returning now as morning, now as evening star. One of the planet's periods of absence would last eight days, which was equated with the eight days the planted corn seed remained hidden in the earth before the green sprout appeared. Venus as the morning star was envisioned as a fiery warrior, shooting darts at the rising sun until overcome by its brilliance. As the evening star, it led the sun into the jaws of earth for its nightly self-sacrifice.

Now empowered with the forces of earth and sky, fertility, rain and of the luminous star, the plumed serpent became an image, like the mighty dragons of eastern mythology, of the power and majesty implicit in the joining of opposites of heaven and earth. His image became the emblem of king, emperor and high priest, carved into great temple columns and undulating around the walls of palaces.

The long flowering of native Mesoamerican cultures and kingdoms was ended in 1521 when Moctezuma II, the Aztec ruler of the last great civilization, welcomed a band of invading Spanish conquistadors into his capital, believing them, the stories say, to herald the prophesied reappearance of Quetzalcoatl, who had disappeared centuries before on a raft of braided serpents, promising to return.

Campbell, Joseph. *Historical Atlas of World Mythology.* NY, 1989.

Florescano, Enrique. *The Myth of Quetzalcoatl.* Baltimore, MD, 1999.

Markman, Roberta H., Peter T. Markman and Jay I. Kislak Reference Collection (Library of Congress). *The Flayed God: The Mesoamerican Mythological Tradition.* SF, 1992.

Tompkins, Ptolemy. *This Tree Grows out of Hell: Mesoamerica and the Search for the Magical Body.* SF, 1990.

An Aztec sculpture of Quetzalcoatl as the plumed serpent, his scales covered with feathers and his human face visible between the serpent's open jaws. As a serpent, which repeatedly sheds its skin and emerges renewed, Quetzalcoatl embodies the basic natural image of death and rebirth. Stone, ca. 1325–1521.

Siren

It was the witch Circe, on whose island Odysseus was marooned for a time following the Trojan War, who foresaw that as he continued to sail home he would face many dangers, including the haunting song of the Sirens. Circe warned Odysseus to have himself bound to the mainmast of his ship so that he could hear their irresistible singing and yet not abandon himself to their clover-covered shore. His crew must stop their ears with wax, ignore their captain's pleading to be set free and keep rowing out of harm's way of these embodiments of "the impulses in life as yet unmoralized, imperious longings, ecstacies whether of love or art or philosophy, magical voices calling to a man from his 'Land of Heart's Desire'" (Harrison, 206). The Siren is one of psyche's deadliest anima aspects, luring the ego overboard, pulling consciousness off course, obliterating the memory and means of getting to where one needs to be. Addiction, delusion, seduction's disintegrating madness, she is a daughter of a river god and a muse (Padgett, 74), so that her divinely exquisite voice is combined with powers of dissolution. She is unearthly, only partially of human form. She wears a human face and sometimes the breasts and arms of a young woman, while her body is that of a bird, clawed, winged and feathered. She is volatile, fleeting, primor-dial, preying especially on consciousness becalmed in windless weather (and it seems it is she who lulls the sea), so that nothing of the vital or creative is stirring. The Sirens are specifically the temptation of music, a deadly shadow of the beauteous soundings of the spheres; diabolical muses and musings—omniscient, prophetic, spellbinding. A later addition to the story of the Siren was that if one resisted her singing, she was compelled to cast herself into the sea, where she would be transformed into a rock (Avery, 1014). Similarly, resisted self-destructive longings remain somewhere in the landscape of the psyche, but depotentiated and mute. Homer's answer to the Siren song is the mainmast, a lashing to the center within that transcends unmooring desires and keeps the vessel together.

Avery, Catherine B. *The New Century Classical Handbook.* NY, 1962.

Harrison, Jane Ellen. *Prolegomena to the Study of Greek Religion.* Cambridge, UK, 1908.

Padgett, J. Michael, William A. P. Childs and D. S. Tsiaphake. *The Centaur's Smile: The Human Animal in Early Greek Art.* Princeton, NJ, and New Haven, CT, 2003.

Siren holding a pomegranate and a syrinx
(pan flute). Greek *askos* (oil container),
bronze, ca. 470–460 B.C.E., Italy.

Furies

That they could treat me so!
I, the mind of the past, to be driven under
the ground, outcast like dirt!
The wind I breathe is fury and utter hate.
Aeschylus, the furies in The Eumenides, 837–40

Unceasing, relentless, implacable, ever-grudging, the archetypal affects of the Furies avenge all betrayals and sins against primal relationships with a pitiless, ruthless intensity. They are found at the interstices of all kinship conflicts; those initiated by willful disregard of the humanity of others through envy or greed, and even in those unintentional insufficiencies of love, and genuine struggles between relationship and independence (Salman, 235).

In Aeschylus' *Orestia*, Orestes, who has committed the most heinous crime of all, matricide, is not mad but at his most sane at the moment he recognizes that his mother's Furies are in pursuit (Nussbaum, 41). Fury, vengeance, madness and guilt are psychological realities that can't be denied, but must be suffered through to their deeper meaning. The gods hound us; the pursuit of Orestes by the Furies enacts a deep ethical response in the psyche to take ownership and responsibility for one's totality: for death, guilt, fear, despair, pain and all that appears hostile to the ego's life. Madness dismembers and is a first step in the fertility magic where dissolution provides the seeds of rebirth. The ancient Greeks struggled with the problem of containing fury's madness, as we do today, searching for a pact with the Furies that would express meaningful contact with the archaic life of the unconscious, not just the triumph of reason over the darkness of our deeper selves.

When the Greek god Cronos flung the severed phallus of his father Ouranos toward the sea, the Furies were born from the blood that fell onto the earth, while the phallus received by the sea fathered Aphrodite. The Furies embody the dark side of the binding power of eros, the madness of blood betrayed, the primal affective cry when one's substance and identity are denied. They are imagined as three winged, whip-wielding sisters with serpentine hair and deadly claws, beastly predators when enraged. They emerge from their underground lair in dreadful Tartarus to punish the most heinous crimes, particularly murder, particularly blood-guilt within a family, and especially matricide. Their names mean "unceasing," "vengeance"

and "strange dark memory." The Furies are also conceived as the unpurified spirits of the dead. Their frightful wailing was called a "binding hymn," and like the Sirens' song, had the power to grip its victims, weaving a curse, casting a spell, reaching into the blood and driving its victims mad.

Fury, revenge and the madness it brings seem built into the fabric of our cultural unconscious. We merely seem to turn up, or down, the volume. What might it serve beyond compensatory omnipotence and destructive grandiosity? Consciously suffering fury's madness, its wounds kept open, may lead to a recognition of our own suffering soul, and to empathy for the other. As dynamisms of the Self, the Furies aim to "correct," both in their defensive aspect, where their destructive bloodlust for revenge blocks access to our own shadow, and in their prospective dismemberment, moving eventually toward wholeness.

If stripped entirely of their function, hidden in Athena's logos and "the rules of engagement," the deeper claims of catabolic, destructive processes, like fury, become more, rather than less, unconscious. They eventually erupt. But consciously drinking the dregs of fury's rage, our own and that of others, may become part of the psyche's move toward wholeness, leading us below into an underworld initiation, whose dark fruit is the blood-bond of communion. As highly ambivalent mana figures, the Furies both abase and transform. The difference lies both in a recognition of this, and in a willingness to let the archetype unfold and fulfill its potential to "lead us below and set things right" (Aeschylus). As mythology and world events have repeatedly illustrated, if not given their due, the Furies will always have the last word in vengeance, even if it brings the whole house down.

Aeschylus. *Aeschylus I, Oresteia, Agamemnon, the Libation Bearers, the Eumenides.* Chicago and London, 1953.
Nussbaum, Martha Craven. *The Fragility of Goodness: Luck and Ethics in Greek Tragedy and Philosophy.* Cambridge, UK, and NY, 1986.
Salman, Sherry. "Blood Payments." *Terror, Violence, and the Impulse to Destroy: Perspectives from Analytical Psychology: Papers from the 2002 North American Conference of Jungian Analysts and Candidates.* Einsiedeln, Switzerland, 2003.

1. A large and powerful angel appears capable of confronting the Furies. *The Angel at the Gate of Dis*, by William Blake, from Dante's *Divine Comedy* (*"Inferno"*), pen, ink and watercolor, 1824–27, England.

2. One of the Furies rising up from underground to punish Agrius, who had seized his brother's throne. Red-figured vase, Greek, 360–320 B.C.E., Paestum, Italy.

Mermaid

Her upper half is the form of a beautiful, human woman with flowing hair and glistening, naked breasts; her lower half the iridescent scales of a fish. Figured in stone relief on a wall of a monastery in Ireland is a mythical mermaid. From her underwater niche she invites engagement, delicately fingering her favored mirror and comb. Two curious fish swim nearby, a reflection of her sea nature. While the mermaid plays a cautionary role in Christian symbolism, she descends from much earlier traditions. Here, she warns of the enticements of the flesh personified by the feminine as sensuality, fluid, unconscious depths and instinctual life (O'Brien, 222).

To the men who gaze upon her at their peril, the mermaid is both beguilingly human and very alien. As a personification of the sea's and psyche's generative waters, the mermaid represents the prospect of sexual love, pleasure and wish fulfillment, and she also possesses the gift of prophecy. The mermaid's habitat is the open sea, the rocky shoreline and an underwater world of unbelievable luxury, which she sometimes shares with a merman, her masculine counterpart (MM 13:1812). Yet, attraction and danger are inseparably intertwined in the mermaid. Like her predecessors, the Sirens of Greek mythology, the mermaid can lure sailors to their destruction, or imprison them in her watery domain (Leach, 2:710). For many cultures, the mermaid has embodied fears of the dissolution of consciousness as well as fears of woman who gets identified as its agent because of her imagined fickleness, hiddenness, engulfing eroticism and captivating allurements.

Although the mermaid is a quasimortal, she is related to a worldwide pantheon of water gods and goddesses, nymphs and tritons and like them represents the potency of seas, rivers and all profound, watery realms in their abundance and unpredictability. Among her earliest ancestors can be counted Oannes, the beneficent Babylonian half-fish, half-man sun deity, and Atargatis, the mermaid goddess whose violent anger conveys the destructive aspect of erotic energies (Gradwell, 94). Mermaids belong to the lineage of Aphrodite, the sea-born Greek goddess of love (MM 13:1812). Alchemy regarded the mermaid as Melusina, the water creature who is a variant of the mercurial serpent, embodying the spirit of the unconscious. She was said to have seduced Beelzebub into practicing witchcraft, and was descended from the whale that once held Jonah, associating her with the unconscious as "womb of mysteries" and with the innocence of Paradise (CW 13:179ff). In the alchemical fantasy, Melusina "lives in the blood," suggesting she has reality in the interior substance of a man, and that, calling to him from the depths, she longs for a soul and redemption; the unconscious soul stuff wanting to be humanized by being made conscious.

But the mermaid is ever elusive, and in some tales, when the man discovers her fishtail, evoking his own unconscious instinctuality, he is repulsed; rejected, she disappears back into the unconscious. In Hans Christian Andersen's tale "The Little Mermaid," the water nymph is brought into the upper world, but though she acquires human feet, every step she takes cuts through her like a sword, attesting to the difficulty of bringing unconscious matter into consciously integrated form. The dual nature of the mermaid, both soulful and cold-blooded, is a reflection of the nearness and remoteness, the contact and separateness that we experience in relation to the things of psyche's world. "Mermaid" is mercurial, magical, shimmering, gorgeous—and impersonal. She can be encountered, related to and even transformed. But as an embodiment of the unconscious, she herself wields an extraordinary fascination. The danger lies in losing one's self in one's longing.

Gradwell, Lois E. "The Mermaid." *Journal of Sandplay Therapy.* (1:2, 1992).

Leach, Maria. Ed. *Funk & Wagnalls Standard Dictionary of Folklore, Mythology and Legend.* NY, 1949.

O'Brien, Jacqueline and Peter Harbison. *Ancient Ireland: From Prehistory to the Middle Ages.* London, 1996.

The image of a mermaid carved on a wall of
Kilcooley Abbey in Ireland served to warn the
Cistercian monks about the sins of the flesh.
The mermaid is known for luring sailors to their doom
with her beauty and haunting songs. Stone relief,
Late Middle Ages, 1400–1600 C.E.

Unicorn

How is it that the unicorn, that "beast ... that never was" (Rilke, 79), has such a place in our imagination—even now, 3,000 years after first appearing in Chinese myth? Why is he still alive in our minds? Umberto Eco answers: "The Unicorn ... is like a [foot] print. If the print exists, there must have existed *something whose print it is ...* it is the print of an idea" (Eco, 317). The idea embodied in this imaginary animal appears in different images at various times and places, yet some threads run through them all: He is a wild, solitary animal of great strength and swiftness, bearing a single horn in the center of his forehead. He cannot be captured alive except by trickery. He has magical powers.

Unicorns were of special fascination in the West during medieval Christian times. But centuries before that, the Hindu epic *Mahabharata* told of a human-bodied unicorn called "Gazelle Horn," lured from his solitary forest life by a king's beautiful daughter, because it was foretold that rain would not fall in the kingdom until the unicorn came to the royal palace. The Chinese unicorn, *Ch'i-Lin*, has an animal form and also lives alone in the forest. His body gives off light and he has a voice like a monastery bell. He harms nothing—not even plants. He embodies benevolence, wisdom and long life. (He lives one thousand years.) He is rarely seen, and then only when virtuous men rule the kingdom.

By contrast, consider ancient Western images: the Greek physician Ctesias (400 B.C.E.) wrote of seeing unicorns in Persia whose horns were taken and used to cure epilepsy and poisoning. Megasthenes (300 B.C.E.) described the terrible roaring voice and wild belligerence of unicorns in India (Gotfredsen, 19, 21). When the Hebrew Bible was first translated into Greek (in about 250 B.C.E.), the Greek word for "unicorn" was used to express the Hebrew word *re-em*. (This usage continued until the twentieth century.) This Biblical "unicorn" was an image of the spiritual power and fierce destructive energies available through Yahweh.

Two of our images show what happened to this wild unicorn during the Christian Middle Ages: He is contained—in the arms of a pure maiden in one view, and in the other, in a fenced flowery garden. Both of these enclosures look too slight to hold him. Evidently he is there by choice. Christian symbolism combined the unicorn's fiery, penetrating spiritual nature with a loving benevolence; he was imagined as a metaphor for Christ. His legendary attraction to the scent of virginity (he was said traditionally to lay his head in a virgin's lap, or suckle from her breast, and so allow himself to be captured) was interpreted in terms of the spirit's willingness to be incarnated through the body of the Virgin Mary. His pursuit by hunters and his bloody death were seen as an image of the Crucifixion; his ultimate containment, tethered by the chain of love and enclosed in a garden, was an image of Christ's resurrection and of the transformation of a wrathful divinity into a loving one.

Throughout this period and after, the unicorn, and especially his horn, was thought to have magical powers: to detect poison, to purify contaminated waters so that other animals could safely drink, to heal wounds and illness. In our time, the unicorn retains his mystery and his fascination. Now we may think of him as a visitor from the inner world, the psychic realm, and feel his strangeness, his intensity, which is somehow combined with the power to heal and to counter the poisons of life. This beautiful spirit animal lives in the dark hidden places of human nature, what we might today call the unconscious, and only appears fleetingly and apparently reluctantly in our ordinary day-lit world. He is known to creative people, who welcome his powerful dynamic energy that is penetrating and single-focused, like his one perfect horn.

Eco, Umberto. *The Name of the Rose.* San Diego, CA, 1983.
Gotfredsen, Lise. *The Unicorn.* NY, 1999.
Rilke, Rainer Maria. *The Sonnets to Orpheus.* NY, 1985.

1. A unicorn, alert yet calm, contained in the embrace of a maiden. Painting, 15th century, Veneto, Italy.

2. Here, the unicorn, reborn after his pursuit and death at the hands of hunters, lies in tranquility in a fenced flowery garden. *The Unicorn in Captivity,* the last of a series of seven tapestries, 1495–1505, Brussels.

3. A contemporary sculpture by Marston Smith suggests that the power and dynamic spirit of the unicorn continues into our time. Bronze, 2008, United States.

1

3

2

Cyclops/Giant

The artistry of a tiny, two-inch-high terra-cotta head is such that it conveys to the imagination the great size and brutal strength of the Cyclopean giant it portrays. The rough texture of the face, the humanlike and yet incompletely human features, the single-sighted eye in the forehead, suggest something that has an affinity with the human, yet is still in the form of a force of nature, and brutal, appetitive and suffering.

The Cyclopes (from the Greek *Kyclops*, or circle-eyed) are distinguished from other giants by the single eye in the middle of the forehead. They are first described by Hesiod as three gigantic sons of Gaia and Ouranos, earth and sky. Metal smiths associated with thunder, lightning and brightness, they made thunderbolts for Zeus and thereby enlarged his power (Hesiod, lines 139–46). But the best-known early story of a Cyclops is in Homer's *Odyssey*, where, in their travels home from Troy, Odysseus and his men arrive at an island inhabited by these one-eyed giants, who in this case are shepherds and children of the tempestuous sea-god Poseidon. Odysseus describes the Cyclopes as "lawless brutes" who never plant or plow; yet unsown, the earth teems spontaneously with all they need (Homer, 148).

Odysseus' encounter with a particular Cyclops, the loner Polyphemos, goes badly—out of what might be called a violation, on the part of both, of the Greek code of hospitality. Odysseus assumes he will meet "a towering brute ... a wild man, ignorant of civility" (Homer, 151). Terrified on seeing the vast size of the giant's cave, the men want to steal the Cyclops' cheeses, lambs and kids, and make their escape before he returns with his rams. Odysseus recklessly refuses their pleadings. When the giant does come home, he closes the mouth of the cave with an enormous stone, discovers his small guests (having already feasted on his cheeses) and scorning the stranger's right begins devouring them two by two. Odysseus devises escape for the remainder of his band by making Polyphemos stuporous on potent wine, thrusting a burning stake through the giant's single eye to blind him and getting out of the cave strapped to the bellies of the great sheep as the giant releases them to pasture at daybreak.

Told that Odysseus' name is "Nobody," the Cyclops' cry for help is ignored: "Nobody's tricking me, nobody's ruining me!" he nonsensically yells (Homer, 153). The trickery that undoes the giant points both to Odysseus' famed capacity for clever deceit and to the characteristic crudeness of the giants, who lack rational intelligence. The monstrous image of a single eye amplifies this weakness for the Cyclopes cannot see in depth.

Nevertheless, the Cyclopes represent the attunement to fruitful nature as well as the brute instinctual powers that are the biological foundation of human as of animal being. One does well to approach such energies with something other than temerity and contempt. Psychologically, they point to the residue in ourselves of "that unconscious wholeness at the beginning of mental development that is full of life and has the potential for consciousness, but is as cruel, as uncivilized, as nature itself ... and has a tendency to swallow its own product" (ARAS, 2:141). The terra-cotta figure suggests that both conscious and unconscious suffer from such devouring.

Hesiod and Richard S. Caldwell. *Hesiod's Theogony.* Cambridge, MA, 1987.
Homer. *The Odyssey.* Garden City, NY, 1963.

The characteristic single eye of a Cyclops is rendered as
an open eye above the seemingly empty eye sockets on
either side of the giant's nose. The sculptor seems to
suggest that though the Cyclops sees with one eye, he is
at least half-blind. Terra-cotta, Greek, 4th century
B.C.E., Smyrna, Turkey.

Vampire

A suave man encompasses a beautiful, swooning woman in his batlike cape and draws her close as if for a kiss. But wait!—his look is feral and predatory, his eyes those of a deathly lover. To our gasps of horror and fascination, a vampire is about to sink his fangs into the neck of his hapless victim and drink her blood.

The photograph of a movie still from 1931 is pure Hollywood; the origin of the image older and darker. The vampire is a monster of both genders that drains the blood of a living person. The English novelist Bram Stoker popularized the vampire in his 1897 *Dracula*, from which the film version was made. But the centuries old vampire lore especially of Central Europe is echoed in the legends of bloodsucking demons throughout the world.

The vampire is a strange phenomenon of the imagination, a shapeshifter, hypnotist and captivator, erotic and chillingly repugnant at the same time. He or she is often ravishingly, irresistibly seductive. That the vampire is also represented as a form of were-animal, fanged and nocturnal, suggests that as a psychic factor it shuns the light of consciousness, manifesting in the twilight of the subliminal as a sexual compulsion or another form of raw, insatiable hunger that cannot be put to rest and eventually takes possession of the whole personality. Psyche portrays the vampire as one of the most compelling and libido-draining aspects of the inner "other" and part of its paradoxical attraction is that it is potentially dangerous. Some have compared the vampire to the "hungry ghost," the revenant of unmetabolized deprivation and trauma, which obsesses us, keeping us out of life. The most deadly aspect of the classic vampire is that with each attack it replicates its condition in the victim, who becomes one of the melancholy, exhausted or restless "dead."

More contemporary portrayals have idealized the vampire as a being of pale, lunar beauty, soulfulness, wisdom and magical powers combined with exhilarating animal instinctuality. In this version, because the vampire lives forever, it can teach us the lessons of history. The human and vampire lovers of the popular *Twilight* series reflect the youthful romance between consciousness of process and change and the alluring fantasy of physical perfection, immutability and immortality. But though the vampire can never again become human, a human can become a vampire, suggestive of our vulnerability to the wholly absorbing nature of desire.

1. In this film adaptation of the 1897 Bram Stoker novel, Bela Lugosi established the modern image of the aristocratic, cape-wearing vampire with a taste for blood. *Dracula*, 1931.

2. The female vampire is an updated version of a succubus, a beautiful female demon who visits men in their sleep. As a femme fatale, she symbolizes the fear of female sexuality. *Vampire II*, by Edvard Munch, lithograph, 1895, Norway.

1

2

Witch

All has been consecrated.
The creatures in the forest know this,

the earth does, the seas do, the clouds know
as does the heart full of
love.

Strange a priest would rob us of this
knowledge

and then empower himself
with the ability

to make holy what
already was.
Saint Catherine of Siena

Nature in its occult aspect, the craftly uncanniness behind the semblance of things, is embodied in the witch. She creates illusions, is a caster of spells, a mistress of disguise. She baffles, confounds, veils—and unveils—her beautiful, enchanting, hideous, poisonous, magical, sexual and deathly secrets. Witches in ancient Thessaly used to ritually "draw down" the moon to obtain from its rays subtle and malignant powers. The witch's crystal ball, circular cauldron and magic mirror are emblems of her lunar eye. She sees with "second sight," mediating sacred realities inaccessible to conventional faculties of perception. The witch communes with the dead, looks into the past, foretells the future, though she may tell it in riddles. As cultural form and psychic factor she is priestess, medium, sibyl, necromancer, sorceress, herbalist, healer and midwife. Mythically, she inhabits the densest part of the forest, the secret nadir of wells, gloomy hollows and isolated byways, associating her with marginal, "suspect" and auspicious territories of experience.

The image of the witch most familiar to us, perhaps, is the crone, often in a peaked sorcerer's hat, her features pointedly disfigured, her beaklike nose sniffing out possibilities for mischief. Other depictions emphasize the young and lustful enchantress of black magic, sexual abandon and sexual pleasure, who flies to the moon on her phallic broomstick. English poet Edmund Spenser in 1590 vilified the witch as one who "did dwell in loathly weeds ... choosing solitary to abide" in order to hide "her devilish deeds" and "hellish arts" from her (civilized) neighbors. No doubt the witch can be dangerous. In Apuleius' *The Golden Ass*, the hero Lucius naively pursues magic, the manipulation of nature, and is turned into an ass by a witch's spell until redeemed by true devotion to the divine witch Isis. Homer's Circe captivates men with and then turns them into the likenesses of their beastly appetites, over which she is mistress. The witch in the fairytale gingerbread house embodies the enticement of maternal sweetness that in its hideous aspect seduces what it will eventually devour.

Nature is at home with its polarities; patriarchies and their priestly cults not always so. The native ground of the witch is the mysteries of the great and terrible Mother, triple-headed moon goddess, lady or lord of the animals or plants, horned god and shaman. In the witch trials between 1450 and 1700, a time noted for its misogyny, probably as many as 100,000 "witches" died. The persecution began at the height of priestly supremacy in Christian Europe, when the Church was idealized in the image of the denatured, spotless Virgin, and its rejected shadow fell on the witch. A Dutch play of the 14th century relates how a chaste Christian girl is accosted in the dark by the devil. She agrees to become his mistress in return for being taught necromancy, or at least the seven liberal arts, including alchemy (Petroff, 355–72). Less humorously, it was this perception of the witch as whore to the diabolical that fanned the flames of the stake.

Yet even at her most frightful, even as the cackling, tornadic Wicked Witch of the West in the film classic, or the terrifying Baba Yaga who pulverizes the stuff of the world with her mortar and pestle; even as the ubiquitous "wicked stepmother" or venomous crone of so many fairy tales, the witch is always at the vital center of things. She brings us to our true nature. She breaks stasis, or purposefully creates it. She sets things in motion, stirs the pot, is instigator and matrix of fateful odysseys and transformations. And if she manifests in our stupefying tendencies—the regressions and fascinations that arrest possibilities of growth—she is also the weird earth of our restoration. She makes things so intolerable that we are forced to break the lock. She scares the life into us.

Petroff, Elizabeth. *Medieval Women's Visionary Literature.* NY, 1986.

1

3

2

1. Francisco de Goya's 1798 etching of an old and a young witch suggests by its ironic caption (*Linda maestra*, "a fine teacher!") that the crone will introduce the young woman to a life of prostitution. Above them flies an owl, or *buho*, a slang word for a streetwalker. Spain.

2. The young woman hoping to catch a husband is not identified as a witch, but such innocent rites in the Middle Ages hooked the Church's fantasies of female sorcery. *The Love Potion*, oil on panel, Flemish School, 15th century.

3. Sharp-featured and malicious, the Wicked Witch of the West, famously portrayed by the actress Margaret Hamilton in the 1939 film classic *The Wizard of Oz*.

Dragon

A master of the Chinese technique of splashed ink, the Sung Dynasty painter Chen Rong intended his *Nine Dragons* to reveal the waterlike nature of the Tao, the way of the universe. Becoming, it seems, a dragon himself, Chen Rong painted by spitting water, dipping his cap in ink, and smearing it across his 50-foot scroll to form swirling rain clouds. Against this nebulous background, he sketched his dragons with the "nine resemblances" established by the canons of Chinese calligraphy: a pair of stag horns, a camel head, a serpent neck, the belly of a clam, the scales of a carp, tiger feet, the ears of a cow and outstretched eagle claws that reach for an elusive moon-pearl by which the dragon's flashing eyes are captivated. Intimating something subtle, intrinsic, gripping the dragon was also perceptible—at play in the vines encircling tree trunks, plunging to earth in the waterfalls of autumn, rising to heaven in the clouds of spring and in the steam from cooking pots (Charbonneau-Lassay, 414). Of the dragon's charged, arousing summer aspect, the Japanese poet Okakura wrote: "He unfolds himself in the storm clouds; he washes his mane in the blackness of the seething whirlpools. His claws are in the fork of the lightning .... "

Long ago, the dragon began as a winged or flying serpent, expressing the primal harmony between the subterranean and aerial dimensions. This fabulous creature is chthonic, darkly reptilian and birdlike, lofty and expansive. As an image of the unconscious, the dragon moves in and out of psyche's darkness, showing only parts of itself, evanescent. One of its aspects is the "beneficial" demon that causes the rising of life-giving nourishment from the vegetative realms and contains in its head the secret of regeneration. The Greek *drakon* signifies aliveness, gleaming light and the eye that flashes fire and sees keenly, like the figurative "eye" of the unconscious. One of alchemy's oldest emblems is the dragon. It is a version of the *uroborus*, the self-fertilizing and self-devouring serpent, expressing the tendency of the unconscious to initiate and sponsor the opus of renewal on its own matter.

The perils of the dragon are inherent in the multiple powers, principles and elements its mythic form displays: water, air, earth, fire, light, wind, storm, electricity; these have their terrifying aspects—as do the immense head and great mouth of the dragon, its rap-

torial talons, its sinuous, muscular coils, the way it fills infinitely abysmal caverns and stretches to the highest heavens, visible, invisible, able to surprise, fascinate, immobilize, consume, encapsulate, eclipse, poison, crush and devour. Legendary heroes and saints, perceiving the dragon as the swamping, primeval mother-world of nature and instinctuality, slay and dismember the dragon or surmount its chaos with ladders to heaven. Alchemy describes its mercurial dragon as active, fiery, sulphurous, corrosive, light and dark, poison and *medicina*. Yet the toxic vapors at the beginning of the work have the potential to become the healing "sublimates" through which eventually one glimpses the pearl of wisdom. Winged and wingless dragons fight, cavort and compete throughout the opus, evoking the violent conflicts and creative play between material and nonmaterial, concrete and symbolic, volatile and embodied.

As the divine "round," with its head in eternity, the dragon encompasses, guards and gestates the treasure of the self. The winged dragon represents the visionary experience of the alchemist on which depended the achievement of the opus. Unconscious projections lent a compelling character to the operations applied to the matter in the *vas*. Dreams and dream visions "allied themselves to the alchemical work" and were sources of revelation (CW 12:356). Imagination grasped inner facts and depicted their truth in images. All this "illusion" had informing power, bringing substance from potentiality into manifestation. One of the most singular products of the image-making faculty of psyche *is* the dragon, which gave birth to itself in ancient times as the "star-glittering, damp-fiery-cold Spirit" invoked by the pagan Magic Papyrus, and these thousands of years later still symbolically discloses what would otherwise be inexpressible.

Charbonneau-Lassay, Louis and D. M. Dooling. *The Bestiary of Christ.* NY, 1991.

Okakura, Kakuzo. *The Awakening of Japan.* NY, 1904.

Shuker, Karl. *Dragons: A Natural History.* NY, 1995.

Wilhelm, Hellmut. *Heaven, Earth, and Man in the Book of Changes: Seven Eranos Lectures.* Seattle, 1977.

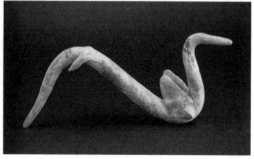

1. Chen Rong's *Nine Dragons* is often considered the greatest dragon painting of all time. Detail, Southern Song Dynasty, 1244, China.

2. Here, enemy of the spirit and jailer of the soul, the dragon is portrayed as the embodiment of the primeval, complete with batwings and a serpent's tail. *St. George and the Dragon*, by Uccello, tempera on canvas, ca. 1465, Italy.

3. A 2,000-year-old winged dragon weds the opposites of airborne flight and earthbound locomotion in its graceful ceramic curves. In China, the dragon rises to heaven and falls to earth with the cycle of seasons. Ceramic, Eastern Han dynasty or later, 25–220, China.

Dot/Bindu

We know it by a dozen names, this tiny spot that Jung calls "the symbol of a mysterious creative center in nature" (CW 14:40). It is referred to as dot, point, jot, tittle, monad, *bindu* and even mustard seed. In purely formal terms, it is the smallest visible mark. It has position but no extension in space. As well as small size, dot can imply short duration and intense focus (Liungman, 132).

As the smallest, it is the first, the beginning point. It can be seen as an image of infinity, "of the completely formless principle from which all beings and all matter originated" (DoS 306), which we can only represent in concrete terms as a visual pattern, as a dot. But it can also mean the very first material incarnation of such formlessness, the starting point from which all things arise. " ... The universe is conceived as unfurling itself from the *bindu*" (Khanna, 102). The dot is pure potentiality. "Out of this little point," said alchemist Gerhard Dorn, "the wisdom of God made ... the 'huge machine' of the world" (CW 14:41). As the starting point, it is called "bud" and "seed." As the source of everything, it is imagined as the creative force in the cosmos. In Tantrism, as *bindu*, it is symbolized and concretized in the body as male semen, the source of new life (Walker, 152).

But there is still more to dot. As the center and source of everything, the dot is imagined as giving rise to all opposing tendencies: above and below, male and female, hot and cold. And it is also the place where they can be reconciled, the still place at the center of life's multiplicity. This still place is known to Tantric mystics as "the ideal mid-point, the balancing of all polarities" (Khanna, 130), to the poet T. S. Eliot as the "still point of the turning world" and to alchemy as " ... the simplest symbol of wholeness, therefore the simplest God-image" (CW 13:457). Dorn said that "nothing is more like God than the center, for it occupies no space, and cannot be grasped, seen or measured" (CW 13:186). The dot can also be connected with the tiny mustard seed growing into a huge bush, which Jesus likened to the kingdom of heaven (Matthew 13:31–2).

Other traditions speak of the dot as the potent spot of the divine within man. Monoimos, a second-century Gnostic, wrote: "Seek him [God] from out thyself, and learn ... whence is sorrow and joy, and love and hate, and waking though one would not, and sleeping though one would not, and getting angry though one would not, and falling in love though one would not. And if thou shouldst closely investigate these things, thou wilt find Him in thyself, the One and the Many, like to that little point, for it is in thee that he hath his origin and his deliverance" (CW 9 II:347).

Khanna, Madhu. *Yantra, the Tantric Symbol of Cosmic Unity.* London, 1979.
Liungman, Carl G. *Dictionary of Symbols.* Santa Barbara, CA, 1991.
Walker, Benjamin. *Hindu World; an Encyclopedic Survey of Hinduism.* NY, 1968.

A Tantric image of the recurring cycles of the universe. Out of the most minute point, the universe expands. The three *gunas*, the stuff of intelligence, energy and matter, combine and separate into the diversity of the phenomenal world. When the cycles are complete, the universe recedes back to the primary source to begin again. Painting on paper, ca. 18th century, Rajasthan, India.

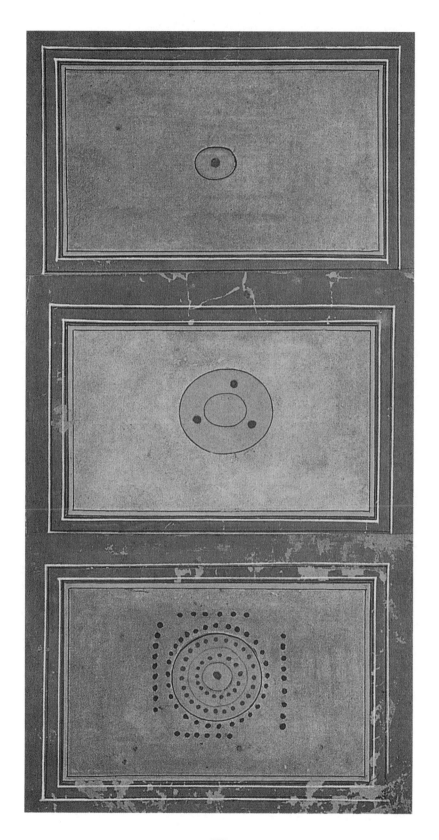

Zero

Jasper Johns has painted a zero, the numeral that indicates the absence of value, as rich and vital. This sign for nothingness scintillates with the energy of brilliantly colored brushstrokes. Here, zero's firm ring has begun to fragment, becoming a porous membrane between space and the reservoir of emptiness held within.

In his painting, Johns has captured some of zero's paradoxical mystique, the void that is powerfully present, the number that is both ordinary and absolute. The invention of zero has been considered one of humankind's greatest achievements (Seife, 12), but central to its significance is the radical effect that zero has had upon human thought.

Zero's history hints at the deeply philosophical nature of this numerical concept. Zero began in Babylonia, and in the Mayan culture, as a placeholder in writing numbers indicating that a unit of value was nil, a function that remains the same today (*Enc. Brit.* 22:312; 23:604; 26:12). It was in seventh-century India that the true genius of zero began to reveal itself, allowing progress from the concrete world of geometry to the abstractions of algebra and purely mathematical calculations (Seife, 67–71).

In Sanskrit, zero was *sunya*, emptiness, with its implication of a qualityless layer that exists behind all appearances. Its root, *vi*, to swell, connotes that it is a receptive womb, a pregnant void with the potential to give birth to all things (Kaplan, 59). Like the Cosmic Egg, zero is the fecund feminine principle, paired with the number one, the male animating force. (LaVigne, 9).

From India, the new number entered the Arabic-speaking world, where it was called *sifr* (root of both zero and cypher), from whence it spread to Europe around the year 1000 (Seife, 73). That it took another 650 years for zero to be fully adopted attests to its profoundly unsettling nature (Schmandt-Besserat, 33). In the Middle Ages, zero was considered the Devil's work, introducing the horror of nothingness into the fullness of God's creation (Kaplan, 190).

While a frightening reminder of the primal void, zero had both logic-defying mathematical properties and the power to suggest the abyss of infinity (Seife, 20ff). The Rennaisance discovery of perspective's infinite space was found in the zero vector of the vanishing point (ibid., 85). And for Descartes, the proof of God could be sought at the meeting of the void and the infinite, for there lay zero, the balance point between negative and positive, the crossroads of coordinates that made a common language of number and form (ibid., 93).

Modern physics has discovered in zero its own portal to the infinite, with absolute zero the theoretical freezing of all molecular movement, the zero space of the black hole, the limitless zero point energy of quantum mechanic's vacuum, and the cosmic zero of the big bang theory, the cataclysmic creation of the universe from nothingness (ibid., 160ff). All the contemporary wonders of the computer, telephone and television depend on the infinitely transformable binary code of one and zero (Kaplan, 203).

In a psychic sense, zero holds all the terrors of nullity, nonexistence, death. In a society that often counts its blessings in dollars, a string of zeros can mean the millions of a blockbuster success; a single zero can be ignominy. To be a zero is to be the lowest of the low, a social nonentity, a loser.

Therefore, it behooves us to remember that whatever our material fortunes, we begin our lives at the zero hour, delivered at our own ground zero, an unknown value in the calculations of this world. We live our lives as if traveling a great circle, returning to our naked beginnings, having created for a while our own small space within the infinite.

Kaplan, Robert. *The Nothing That Is: A Natural History of Zero*. Oxford and NY, 2000.
LaVigne, Eric. "Creation by Numbers." *Parabola* (24/3, 1999).
Schmandt-Besserat, Denise and Michael Hays. *The History of Counting*. NY, 1999.
Seife, Charles. *Zero: The Biography of a Dangerous Idea*. NY, 2000.

The gestural brushstrokes of the painting suggest that zero, the numerical sign for nothingness, is actually a full and energetic presence. Zero's logic-defying mathematical properties, throughout history, have challenged humanity's conceptions of the divine, infinity and the cosmos. *Figure Zero*, by Jasper Johns, oil and collage on canvas, 1959, United States.
© Jasper Johns/Licensed by VAGA, New York, NY

One

"One, two—buckle your shoe; three, four—shut the door; five, six—pick up sticks .... " we chanted as schoolchildren. "One" was just a number, not different from the others, except for coming first. Western scientific thought also sees One in this light: a unit in a series of units making up the chain of numbers. But other times and other peoples have seen One differently. As far back as the Pythagoreans—500 B.C.E.—One was thought of not as a numeral but as a philosophical idea: as the unity from which all things arise and as the source of all the numbers. Very early on, One became an image for divine unity. So Angelus Silesius wrote, in the seventeenth century, "Just as unity is in every number / thus God the one is everywhere in everything" (Schimmel, 45). The *unus mundus* or imaginal "one world" of alchemy becomes two in the division of heaven and earth, bringing the "one" world out of the state of potentiality into reality and multiplicity (CW 14:659). This belief, that all things are really one thing, and that this one thing underlies the seeming variety of things in the world, is basic to much of religious and mystical thought. This image from India conveys such belief. The symmetry and unbroken line of the design unite all of its varying forms into unity, into the One.

The sacred One has been named variously Tao or the Great Monad (in China), the Single One (by the Mayans), Brahman (in Hinduism), God (in Christianity), the Most High (in Judaism), the One God (in Islam). The aim of the mystic is to become one with this divine whole. The myriad things of the world are seen by many traditions as mere offspring or reflections of the One or as deceptions, which veil the One from human awareness. Visually, One is represented by the point, and is related in symbolism to the circle as an image of wholeness and unity.

One has other symbolic meanings, as well. In the West, beginning when One took on the form of the Arabic numeral "1" about 1000 C.E., One was seen as phallic, aggressive, active and as a symbol of man as *Homo erectus*, the only species to walk upright. Images of the staff and the standing stone reflect this symbolism. In materialistic cultures of today, One suggests the individual, the first, the most powerful or successful (or richest or most beautiful), the winner.

Psychologically, the experience of oneness is a natural state before the child becomes aware that he or she is an individual. Feelings and fantasies may appear at first as belonging to other people or to things in nature as much as to oneself. Such experiences of fusion are lost with increasing age and awareness, with the necessity to develop a clear sense of self and individuality (Neumann, 266ff). Yet the sense of the deeper connectedness of all things, that "the multiplicity of the empirical world rests on an underlying unity" (CW 14:767), can return in maturity when it may be sensed that male and female, spirit and body, inner and outer, consciousness and the unconscious, the I and the Thou, are One.

Huyler, Stephen P. *Painted Prayers.* NY, 1994.
Neumann, Erich. *The Origins and History of Consciousness.* Princeton, NJ, 1971.
Schimmel, Annemarie and Franz Carl Endres. *The Mystery of Numbers.* NY, 1993.

A woman of southern India completes a "visual prayer,"
a freehand drawing in powdered rice on the pavement
near her home. It will not outlast the foot traffic of the
day, but it gives eloquent expression to the idea of all-
embracing unity, the sacred One.

Mandala

The mandala is one of the best-known symbols associated with Tantric Buddhism. Tibetan Buddhist literature speaks of three closely interwoven levels, the so-called outer, inner and alternative mandala. The outer mandala comprises the outward appearances of the whole human environment, i.e., the universe. The inner mandala is made up of those who live in this environment, human beings. They correspond exactly in composition, construction and inner periodicity to the outer mandala. The other or alternate mandala is the teaching of these analogies and correlations as well as the resulting yoga practices.

Mandalas can be two-dimensional or three-dimensional and may be constructed out of a range of materials including paper, pigments, metal, cloth and even colored powder. Mandalas may also serve a variety of functions as contemplative aids in visualization meditation, as instructional tools, as ritual objects and even as protective talismans, to name just a few.

Almost all mandalas (Tibetan: *dkyil-'khor*) familiar today display one or more concentric circles (*'khor*) in the center (*dkyil*). About a round, central disk, in the middle of which there sits or stands a deity—sometimes with a partner—an even number of deities are set in an additional circle. These figures are the assembly or entourage of the central deity of the mandala.

In the great majority of mandalas the innermost sacral area is surrounded by a square. This is none other than a building or the ground plan of a palace. In its structure, the mandala palace recalls the religious architecture of India. The Indian temple offers an image of the world, a complete *imago mundi*. In drawing the basic lines of a Tantric Buddhist mandala these classical Indian instructions are still followed today. Because of its perfect form and content the mandala serves as a frequent model for temples and monasteries in the Himalayas and Tibet, but also the Borobudur in Indonesia has a clear mandala structure. Each sidewall of the palace corresponds to one of the cardinal directions and displays its characteristic color. The center is considered to be the fifth cardinal point.

In a popular mandala pattern each of these directions is associated with one of the so-called Tathagata Buddhas. Though they seem to be five different buddhas, they are all one and the same. They just symbolize different aspects of the one experience of Enlightenment. As the white light contains different wavelengths resulting in different colors, equally white Vairocana, who is often seen in the middle of the mandala, contains and embraces all the abilities and qualities of the four other Tathagatas.

According to his character, disposition and destiny, a meditator selects one aspect of Buddha nature, one divine being out of the virtually innumerable throngs of Buddha manifestations, each of which belongs to one of the five Buddha classes. Once chosen, the deity becomes one's personal protective and meditational deity.

This personal deity plays an important role in the so-called deity yoga (*deva-yoga*; *lha'i rnal-'byor*), in the course of which one imagines oneself as an ideal, altruistic being in the shape of a Buddha. The practices of deity yoga make great demands on the practitioner's powers of imagination; particularly complicated is the visualization of multiple deities arranged in mandalas—clear geometric patterns in space and forming whole groups. That is why pictures of the relevant deities are readily used as an aid, as mental supports. The meditator hangs such pictures up in front of him or herself, or—in the case of mandalas made of colored powder—sprinkles them on a flat surface.

The most important function of mandalas is their use in initiations during which the initiates are guided step-by-step through the entire mandala. The practitioner has to purify himself in a progressive process and attains the body, speech and mind of a Buddha. The mandala initiations with the visualization of deities should foster this process; for whoever visualizes a deity and assumes its form—which is endowed with a high degree of purity—is close to the state in which the false view of things is abolished. In its stead the realization dawns that nothing exists of itself.

The Five-Deity Mandala of Amoghapasha,
ground mineral pigment on cotton, 16th century, Nepal.

Labyrinth

The labyrinth of the Cathedral of Notre-Dame is set into the central axis of the nave in such a way that the great rose window would, if folded down, almost overlap it (Doob, 131), and one cannot approach the main altar without becoming entangled in its turnings. Between the outer, spiky, coglike shell and the scalloped petals of the central flower lie intestinelike coils, circling around and back and forth in a regular pattern which moves from quarter to quarter and then from half to half, thereby tracing a cross within the circle in the form of a mandala. The cross, symbol of the death and resurrection of Christ, leads to the center, occupied by the six-petalled flower emblem of the Virgin Mary (to whom the cathedral is dedicated), as the feminine principle. The journey of transformation involves a discovery of that reality (ARAS, 1:67).

The labyrinth is an ancient symbol whose convoluted form, found naturally in seashells, animals' intestines, spider webs, the meandering body of the serpent, the eddying of water, the internal structure of underground caves and the whirling galaxies of space, has always been highly suggestive to the imagination. Spirals and meanders, precursors to the labyrinth, have been found among the cave paintings of prehistoric peoples, often incised on or near goddess figurines, carved animals, cave walls and thresholds. These labyrinthine spirals indicate the symbolic passageway from the visible realm of the human into the invisible dimension of the divine, retracing the journey souls of the dead would have taken to reenter the womb of the mother on their way to rebirth (Baring, 24–5).

The themes of weaving and spinning, evident in the image of the creator god Siuhu's house, whose protectively surrounding labyrinth is woven, weblike, directly into the pattern of the basket it adorns, are congruent with the idea of the fateful unfolding of life's twists and turns. Ariadne's golden thread, which Theseus unwound along his descent to slay the Minotaur, provided the "clew" that would allow him to find his way out again. In the Upanishads, the thread (sutra) is described as linking "this world to the other world and all beings" (Stevens, 4). In Mercurial fashion, the movement through the labyrinth veers back and forth, round and round, creating a dance whose steps eventually weave a vessel strong enough to hold what was at first intolerable experience. A transcendent pattern eventually emerges, which lifts one to a new vantage point, like the wings Daedalus fashioned to escape the labyrinthine prison of his own creation (EoR, 8:411–12).

The purpose of the labyrinth's frequent inclusion in initiatory rites is to temporarily disturb consciousness to the point that the initiate becomes confused and symbolically loses his way, or his rational, linear frame of orientation. The oldest known Chinese alchemist, Wei Po-yang (2nd century C.E.), speaks of a region "closed in on all sides, its interior made up of intercommunicating labyrinths," wherein Chen-yen, the whole or true man, is concealed in the darkness. To attempt to enter this region rationally is "not pleasing to the tao of the feminine principle (yin)" and will lead to great danger. The proper attitude for approaching this hidden divine spirit requires the complete cessation of thought and worry (CW 13: 433).

The essentially dual, paradoxical nature of the labyrinth is both circular and linear, simple and complex, historical and temporal. Contained within a compact space, a long and difficult path constantly doubles back on itself, leading circuitously to a mysterious and invisible center. From within, the view is extremely restricted and confusing, while from above one discovers a supreme artistry and order. Thus the labyrinth simultaneously incorporates confusion and clarity, multiplicity and unity, imprisonment and liberation, chaos and order (Doob, 1–8). This paradoxical duality reflects the psychotherapeutic purpose of groping one's way through suffering, darkness and confusion, with the aim of building a capacity for greater insight and perspective, thus enlarging the personality. On the journey through the labyrinth, once the center, or goal, has been reached, the way back will always be utterly new.

Baring, Anne and Jules Cashford. *The Myth of the Goddess: Evolution of an Image.* London and NY, 1991.

Doob, Penelope Reed. *The Idea of the Labyrinth from Classical Antiquity through the Middle Ages.* Ithaca, NY, 1990.

Robertson, Seonaid M. *Rosegarden and Labyrinth: A Study in Art Education.* Dallas, TX, 1989.

Stevens, Anthony. *Ariadne's Clue.* Princeton, NJ, 1998.

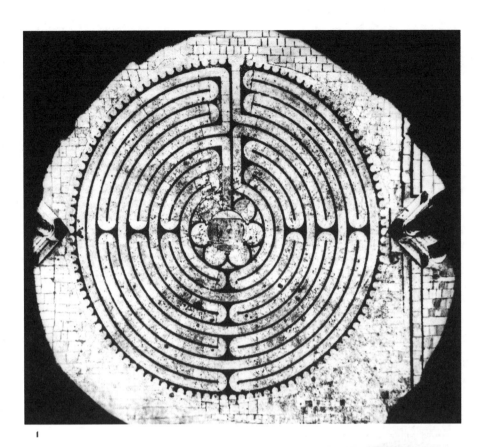

1

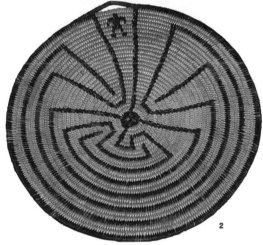

2

1. The labyrinth of the Cathedral of Notre-Dame (1220–30 C.E.) in Chartres, France, is made up of a path of large, white paving stones on a dark-blue ground, tracing out 11 concentric circles superimposed by a cross, leading to a floriform center, suggesting that if the world of sin is traversed in the Christian spirit, it will lead to the heavenly Jerusalem (ARAS, 1:66–7).

2. This willow tray depicts the house of Siuhu, the legendary creation deity who was said to have brought the people by way of a spiraling path from the center of the earth to its surface. The labyrinth surrounding his home served as protection from enemies while still allowing him to come out to help his people in times of great need (ARAS, 1:71–2). Tohono O'odham tribe, 1964, United States.

Crossroads

Kalfou, the Haitian vodou spirit of the crossroads, is the "hot" equivalent of Papa Leġba, typically depicted as a ragged old man hobbling on crutches, who conveys the idea of venerable years, wisdom and the highway (Galembo, 4). In both aspects, as Kalfou and Papa Legba, this Congolese deity is associated with red, emblematic of the heat and intensity of the crossroads. Heat is suggested in the burning red eyes and red arms, and even in the bottle of rum hanging around the neck of the cruciform figure. His red, horizontally extended arms might suggest either prohibition or guidance or the more sinister possibility of the crossroads drawing the wayfarer into a state of confusion or panic.

Crossroads, the intersection where disparate paths converge, has always been viewed as a locus of extreme potency and ambivalent gods able to contain and synthesize opposites flowing into one another. To the crossroads are essentially related the journey, the highway, "the ancient world of the path" including the snakelike, winding "wet paths" of the sea (Kerényi, 46) or the psyche. Cities that embody the crossroads of the world, like London, Mumbai and New York, teem with commerce, enterprise and the mingling and collision of alien elements. At the crossroads one confronts the necessity of choice and the immensity of fate. Crossroads is a matrix of union, and also of separating, parting, splitting, of meeting and farewell (CW 5:577). Ancient travelers offered sacrifices at a crossroads in recognition of the invisible agencies that affect life's transitions. Oedipus laments, "Oh three roads, dark ravine, woodland and way / Where three roads met: you, drinking my father's blood, / My own blood, spilled by my own hand: can you remember / The unspeakable things I did there, and the things I went on from there to do?" (Sophocles, 72)

In ancient Greece, a junction of three ways was dedicated to Hecate. The marker of three faces looking in three directions signified her dominion of the three realms of the physical world—sea, sky and earth—and the three phases of the moon, and night with its lunar intimations and terrifying obscurities. Here, on the branching roads, the bodies of executed criminals where thrown (CW 5:577), for the crossroads was an opening to the underworld, of which Hecate was mistress. Hermes, too, was honored, especially at quadratic crossroads. Like Hecate, he is a psychopomp, guiding the spirits of the dead to the underworld. Both are emblematic travelers of the highways. Hecate arrives at the doorways of those laboring toward birth, a midwife mediating that crossroads of becoming or obstruction. Hermes, with his winged feet, his mantle and staff, is a "skilled highwayman, deceiver and bandit," the spirit of the unconscious, as of the night, "which can terrify the solitary man and lead him astray, can also be his friend, his helper, his counselor" (Kerényi, 56, 95).

A crossroads represents the possibility of many ways and also commitment to the individual path. Legendarily, the crossroads is where a pact with the devil is made, suggesting a juncture where consciousness must regard the unconscious, and be accountable to the whole self in all its Luciferian ambivalence. At the vodou altar, Legba must be invoked first. As the crossroads, he is lord of the gate between the material and spirit worlds (Galembo, 4), where "mortals may contact *les invisibles.* … "

Galembo, Phyllis. *Vodou: Visions and Voices of Haiti.* Berkeley, CA, 1998.
Kerényi, Karl, *Hermes: Guide of Souls.* Putnam, CT, 1995.
Sophocles. *The Oedipus Cycle.* NY, 1949.
Stevens, Anthony. *Ariadne's Clue.* Princeton, NJ, 1998.

1. An altar honors the fiery trickster and opener of the way, Kalfou, the vodou spirit of the crossroad. Ounfò (vodou temple) of Oungan (vodou priest) Guy Bata, Léogâne, Haiti, photograph by Phyllis Galembo.

2. This floor sculpture made of stones evokes the mystery of the crossroads where we both meet and part ways. The sacred joining of paths, where opposites are reconciled, represents a crucial place of transition in our lives (Stevens, 243–4). *A Crossing Place,* by Richard Long, 1983, England.

1

2

Spiral

Georgia O'Keeffe's *Pink Shell with Seaweed* exemplifies the golden or logarithmic spiral that is the most widespread shape found in the natural world. It is the form of embryos, horns, whirlpools, hurricanes and galaxies, the path that energy takes when left alone, the path of unfettered yet balanced growth.

Spiral motifs appear worldwide in the symbolism of religion, art, dreams, folktales and mythology. Mathematically, a spiral is simply a line that grows continuously toward or away from its own center. But its symbolic power is in its evocation of an archetypal path of growth, transformation and psychological or spiritual journey. Based on the direction of its spin, whether expanding outward and larger, or tightening inward and smaller, a spiral is a cosmic symbol that may represent one or the other of several dualities: growth or decay, ascent or descent, evolution or involution, waxing or waning, accumulation or dissolution, increasing or decreasing, expanding or contracting, offering or receiving, revealing or hiding. The double spiral combines both opposites in one glyph.

There are three main types of spirals. Coiled snakes, ropes and labyrinthine paths are Archimedian spirals, where the distance between coils remains constant. The way clinging vines wrap around stems and branches, the double strands of DNA and the twining serpents of the caduceus are examples of the helix configuration. In the logarithmic spiral, also called equiangular, the distance between coils continuously increases or decreases.

Logarithmic spirals indicate that a clash of opposites has been resolved and transcended. We see how these spirals are formed in nature when rising smoke meets the air. The cool air forces the hot and therefore lighter smoke to turn aside again and again, resulting in a rhythm of graceful whorls. The spiral is the path that resolves conflict, allowing for balanced movement and natural unfolding; thus harmonious transformation can proceed. These spiral processes in nature form a language evoking the mythic journey, regeneration and awakening—as fronds and flowers whorl open to the light—by ascending to a higher rung. Mirroring the

I

2

1. A spiral galaxy in Antlia (NGC 2997), Anglo-Australian Observatory, Edinburgh, Scotland.

2. *Pink Shell with Seaweed*, by Georgia O'Keeffe, pastel on paperboard, ca. 1938, United States.

way of the wind and whirling galaxies, spirals describe a path of travel not only of shamans, genii and spirits, but also of psychological development in general, as if the inner development repeatedly comes round to the same point again, but at a different level.

Spirals extending infinitely in two directions make the path of ascent and descent between heaven and earth. Deities and humans communicate with each other along spirals. It is the sacred way of commandment and prayer, the spiral voice of God and the sacred call to God. Various deities speak through spiral whirlwinds and through columns of whirling dust, smoke and fire. Humans pray to deities along the same spiral paths by making offerings with ascending smoke spirals and by blowing through spiral conch shells and ram's horn trumpets. Each natural spiral has a center of balance or calm eye (the eye of the storm) around which all motion and turbulence revolves. The spiral's eye evokes one's own center, divine source, "I am" and seed of consciousness. It suggests the eye of wisdom that observes all but is never entangled in the turbulence.

Purce, Jill. *The Mystic Spiral: Journey of the Soul.* London, 1974.
Schneider, Michael S. *A Beginner's Guide to Constructing the Universe.* NY, 1994.

3

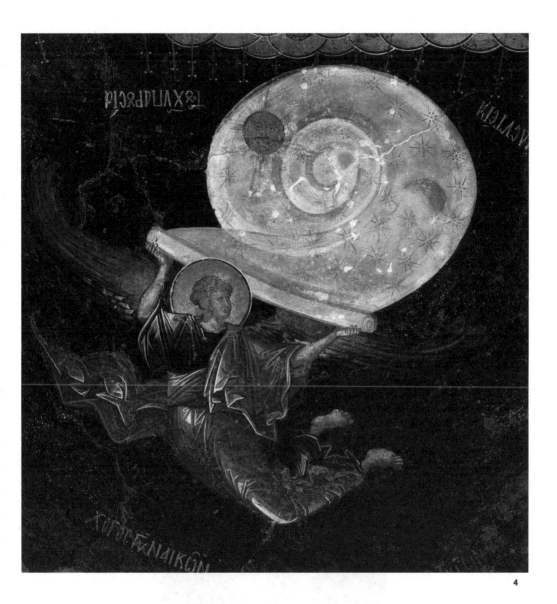

ΤῼΧ ΥΝΡϹΙΑ

4

3. As shown in a coiled snake or rope, the distance between the coils remains constant in the Archimedean spiral. In Tantric tradition, the kundalini (energy) is represented as a coiled snake before being aroused. Miniature painting, India.

4. An angel rolls up the heavenly vault. Detail of the *Last Judgment*, fresco, 14th century, Church of St. Savior, Chora, Istanbul, Turkey.

Mask

What did your face look like before
your parents were born?
Zen koan

A mask is the face imagination gives a god. Reaching back into Paleolithic history and still in use today, the mask may be a quintessential genre of human psychological expression. Masks portray the human "life drama" in all its manifold aspects, especially the compelling, ambiguous, sometimes revelatory and often treacherous search for the "real self" behind our more familiar self-images. As the human wearer of a mask becomes obscured, he or she is transformed into the archetypal patterns the mask evokes. These enduring archetypal images are brought into the context of the present, and serve as models for social and psychological life.

Used for worshipping the gods, for healing, for initiation, to maintain collective authority and social mores, and also to escape that authority, masks belong to the mythic arts of drama and storytelling. These, in turn, trace their lineage back into shamanism and, by extension, into a sacred sensibility toward the mystery and depth of human experience. Distillations of powerful archetypal emotions—love, fear, rage, disappointment, joy—are given impersonal artistic form in a mask, which supports paradoxically both catharsis and disidentification. The mask, far from merely concealing its wearer, provides a bridge, opening psychological experience toward the "spirits," the instinctual, archetypal factors of the personality, by providing "temporary housing" for those "gods."

Since the mask stands between one's self and the world, it has a dual nature: It looks both in and out. A mask can disguise, cover, veil, lie, capture, release, reveal, project, protect, disown, recollect, deceive, dissociate, embody and transform. The best Noh theatrical masks have the ability to "change emotions," appearing differently depending upon how the light strikes the mask, capturing both the "essential" and "changing" nature of emotional and psychological life.

This shape-shifting aspect of the mask provides ritual access to levels of experience not ordinarily available to the conscious mind. This can be both enlivening and terrorizing. The terrorizing aspect of tribal or cultic initiation rituals is designed to discipline and lock in behavior so as to maintain collective stasis.

1

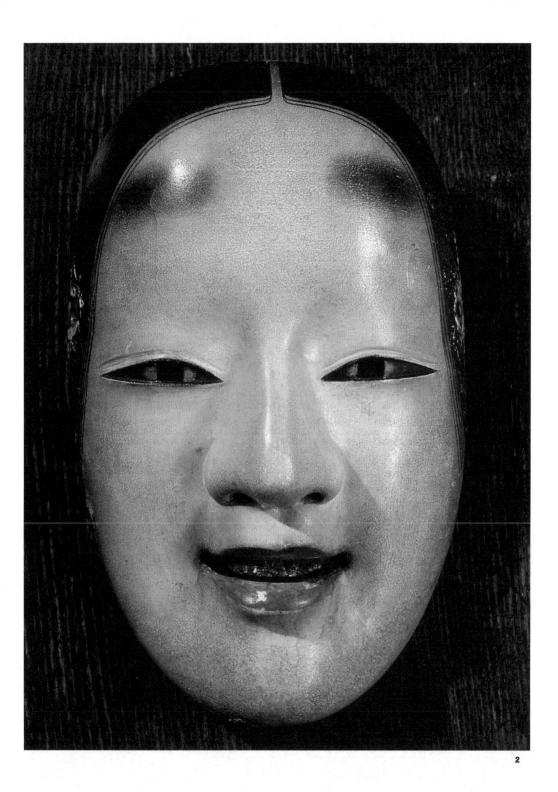

1. Bare-chested Navajo man wearing mask of Haschebaad, a benevolent female deity. Photograph by Edward S. Curtis, ca. 1905, United States.

2. "Ko-omote" ("small face") of a smiling female, one of the 10 types of Japanese Noh theater masks worn by men. Kongo School, Kyoto Prefecture, Japan.

There is a similarly terrorizing aspect to being identified with one's persona, with our contemporary "tribal roles"—the masks through which we enter and live in the world, such as "spouse," "doctor," "artist," "mother."

These masks also stand between subjectivity and the collective, and are influenced by collective authority. At the same time, they reflect the underlying archetypal drive toward adaptation and participation in collective life, toward incarnation of the "gods."

Sorting this out, in other words becoming aware of one's masks and identifications, the living "masquerade," what is hidden and what is revealed, what is unduly pressured by conformity, and what is emergent and true, is part of the work of individuation. If a persona-mask is a face for an archetypal image, then identifying with it is tantamount to possession. Alternatively, having no personae can make one overly vulnerable and in some cases may reflect failures of psychological development.

The etymology of "mask" traces back to Arabic, meaning "buffoon," then into the European "masquerade," and the modern meaning "to hide or protect the face." This nuance within masking speaks to feelings of vulnerability in the face of the transpersonal, to human suffering and to "saving face." A mask provides protection from the powerful affects of archetypal states, and affords an indirect relationship with emotions and psychological patterns, which might be overwhelming if experienced directly, "in your face."

"Man is least himself when he talks in his own person. Give him a mask, and he will tell the truth," observed Oscar Wilde. On the other hand, there are those who are most themselves when they finally remove the mask.

Shefer, Elaine. "Masks/Personae." *Encyclopedia of Comparative Iconography: Themes Depicted in Works of Art.* Ed. Helene E. Roberts. Chicago, 1998.

4

3. *Intrigue*, by James Ensor, oil painting, 1890, Belgium.

4. Initiates wore this helmet mask with scars and filed teeth at their coming-out ceremony into adulthood. Makonde culture, Mozambique, Africa.

Incense

For thousands of years, the aromatic smoke of incense (from Latin *incendere*, "to burn") has ascended, symbolically merging material and nonmaterial realms of being in its diffuse, spiraling, vaporous cloud. It has signified the fragrant eros of that conjunction in ceremonial, meditation and rites of worship: "Let my prayer be set forth in your sight as incense, the lifting up of my hands as the evening sacrifice" (Psalm 141). Two of the three precious gifts the Magi mythically presented to the infant Jesus were incense: frankincense, emblematic of his divinity; and myrrh, his future death on the cross. Frankincense and myrrh are obtained from the dried sap of two different species of a botanical family of plants common to present-day Somalia. Both resins were extraordinarily prized in ancient Mesopotamia, Africa, Egypt and India for religious ritual and healing. At Sinai, God was said to have commanded Moses to have frankincense and myrrh blended with spices into fine oils for anointing and consecration (Exodus 30:37). The ancient Egyptians used frankincense as an antidote to hemlock and as an essential ingredient in cosmetics. Daily worship of the sun god Ra included burning golden resin at dawn, myrrh at noon and at sunset a compound of frankincense, honey and wine, symbolic of harmony. Myrrh, which is softer than frankincense and has antiseptic and antiinflammatory properties, was an ingredient in the Egyptian embalming and deification mysteries of the dead. Greek soldiers carried supplies of myrrh into battle as a medicinal for cleaning wounds and preventing infection.

Myrrh's association with both death and cleansing is carried in Ovid's *Metamorphosis*, where Myrrh, the maiden whose incestuous love for her father produced Adonis, is transformed into a tree whose weeping sap is her repentant tears. The sensual and sacred qualities of incense have made it an aspect of cultic rites throughout the world. Copal resin is burned in domestic and religious rituals of Mesoamerica. In China, the burning of *hsiang* was a part of ancestral cults, and accompanied writing and the performance of music. On the Mexican Day of the Dead, the burning of incense guides the spirits to their former homes. Christian churches make ritual use of incense as purification. The fragrance of incense evokes the presence of the divine and the flowering gardens of Paradise. Pungent fumes of ritual incense rose over the effigy of Babylonian Tammuz, Ishtar's beloved, in order to awaken him from the sleep of death so that the earth could be regenerated each spring. Similarly, the phoenix fabricates her nest of frankincense and myrrh, ultimately to be reborn in its perfumed smoke.

Detienne, Marcel. *The Gardens of Adonis: Spices in Greek Mythology.* Princeton, NJ, 1994.
Genders, Roy. *Perfume through the Ages.* NY, 1972.
Rahim, Habibeh. *Incense. The Encyclopedia of Religion.* NY, 1987.
Schiller, Gertrud. *Iconography of Christian Art.* Greenwich, CT, 1971.

Smoke rises from a burning stick of incense.
Photograph by Karen Arm, 1999, United States.

Ashes

The familiar litany of "ashes to ashes, dust to dust" forebodes our decomposition and return to origin. Through the agency of fire, flesh, bones and other matter turn into the mixture of carbonates and oxides we call ash. Whether flames have licked away a log on the hearth, or consumed a human body on a funeral pyre, this colorless, odorless silt is "all that remains." On ash we project finality, irrevocability, what has gone cold after the heat and light of desire, hope, creativity or generation has been extinguished. Ash is holocaust, the devastation of bombs, the end of love, a gutted structure. Sackcloth and ashes clothe the figure of remorse, sorrow or abasement. Yet ash is also associated with the sacred and the essential. Ash is the extract from a completed life or an achieved process, the substance that can undergo no further decomposition. Folk customs and religious rites express the symbolism of ash as fertilizer of physical and psychic earth, which fosters the emergence of new matter and gives rise to the phoenix of rebirth. Farmers sprinkle their fields with ashes before planting and blend them with stored grain to prevent rot. The Nahuatl people of ancient Mexico rubbed infants with ashes to give them strength. Other indigenous peoples mixed funeral ashes with a liquid and imbibed the virtues of the deceased. Ascetics throughout India smear wet ashes, food from the god of fire, over their bodies. Such "baths" from their own or a temple's sacred fire or a cremation fire signify immortality, a sacrificing of the self and a burning of karma in the fire of austerity (Hartsuiker, 85). Lamas in Tibet combine the ashes of a holy man or woman with clay to make figurines of the Buddha to place in shrines. Ash Wednesday initiates the penitential season of Lent that culminates in the Easter resurrection. Alchemy perceived ash, like salt, as an emblem of the *albedo,* the "white foliated earth," resulting from the burning-off of impurities—desire freed from compulsion, bitterness become wisdom. It was the substance of the "incorruptible body" or "diadem of the heart," the paradoxical simplicity of self-knowledge.

Hartsuiker, Dolf. *Sadhus: India's Mystic Holy Men.* Rochester, VT, 1993.

"Despise not the ashes for they are the diadem of thy heart and the ash of things that endure." Quote from Morienus in *The Rosarium;* illustration from the alchemical manuscript *Donum Dei,* 15th century, France.

729

Blessing

In Rembrandt's painting of Jacob's blessing of Ephraim, Joseph's second son, many of the essential elements of the symbolism of blessing are brought together. Nearing death, Jacob conveys Yahweh's favor to Joseph's two older sons, both in words and with the classic gesture of the right hand. But he lays it on the head of Ephraim, the younger of the two. Over Joseph's protest, Jacob declares that the younger will be the greater one, even as he adopts Manasseh, making both symbolically not grandsons but sons; they too will father tribes of Israel, like Joseph and his brothers.

In so blessing Joseph's sons, Jacob invites the transfer of sacred power or energy that is the hallmark of a blessing. We are aware of the irony that Jacob has himself stolen Isaac's blessing from his older brother Esau as Isaac lay dying many years earlier, but we also know that each of these events has its origin in the unfathomable will of the divine authority—one that goes against the rules, but may also have taken human talents into account.

Throughout the world, the transcendent power that blesses—the mana of the Polynesians or the tao of the Chinese—may express itself directly, but very often it is conveyed through mediation in words, gesture or ritual by a prophet, priest or king. Here, holding his right hand tenderly over the head of the human beneficiary, the family elder affirms the divinely ordained priority of his descendants.

Jacob Blessing the Sons of Joseph, by Rembrandt van
Rijn, oil painting, ca. 1656, the Netherlands.

Disease

Though this terra-cotta figure from Mali probably portrays a woman, it is difficult to tell, so much has disease obliterated the delineations of being. The swollen (or pregnant) belly, shrunken chest and stippled skin, the emaciated limbs and gaunt face speak of extreme suffering (Vogel, 15). The figure's neck is twisted in agony and worms are already beginning to possess the tortured flesh. Disease, or the dis-ease of vital functioning within an organism, represents both natural process and aberrations of nature. Disease is malady, ailment, morbidity and discontent. We speak of the disease of societies and nations as well as of individuals. We associate disease with an organic wearing out or breaking down, but also with invasion, surfeit, lack, disorder, imbalance and corruption. Disease is sometimes the first, terrifying intimation of mortality. Psyche images disease as visitation by an ominous stranger, the faltering of the daemonic animal or the ruin of lush vegetation, a fissuring of containers of identity, self-image and self-control. Disease belongs to the realm of deities of death and destruction, like Kali with her necklace of skulls, Shiva of the serpentine locks, Artemis aiming her sickle-shaped bow. But at the same time, disease is of the essence of their reverse, for Kali is also the ground of rebirth and infinite process; Artemis nurtures the newborn; Shiva's beloved spouse awakens in himself as the active, vibrating Shakti. "Symptom" shares with "symbol" the *sym* that evokes the "throwing together" of a thing and its meaning, and is warning and portent, somatic analogy of psychic conflict. Early peoples, intuitively expressing psyche's experience of disease, depicted it as the lost or stolen soul, the activation of evil spirits, ritual impurity, transgression of taboo or wrong relation to a deity; and, as divine possession, shamanic vocation, initiatory process, alchemical transmutation and the harrowing of hell. Regardless, disease is affliction. And while it can be experienced as meaningful, revelatory passage, it is, as well, a just-so participation in nature's vast, cosmic energies—intricate, impersonal and ever-shifting.

Vogel, Susan M. *African Aesthetics*. NY, 1986.

Terra-cotta figure, Djenne, Mali, Africa.

Wound

A "wound," from the Old English *wundian*, is a laceration or a breach (Barnhart, 889) in the physical body or psychic tissue. Wounding of every sort is a "trauma," the Greek word for wound, which also meant the hurt or damage of things, and heavy blows, or defeat, in war (Liddell, 1811). From the Latin *vulnus*, wounds represent cuts, holes, rents, cracks and misfortunes; visible and invisible, they reveal and expose our vulnerabilities (Lewis, 2016). Wounds are eruptions and disruptions in what is otherwise continuous and developing (*Enc. Brit.* 12:762). Wounds are embedded in narratives, and often change the narrative in critical and permanent ways.

Mythically, the wound as opening is also a gateway to potential transformation, and a window on encapsulated history. Freud's psychoanalytic technique relied in part on the revelations of hidden traumas. Collective wounds, like the World Wars, or the Holocaust, or the 9/11 bombings of New York's Twin Towers, are intentionally kept open by memory and memorial as a means of illumination, mourning and conscious reflection. The image of the open wound of Christ, from a thirteenth-century psalter, appears as a neat, clean slit, perhaps mirroring the precise, thin penetration of the sword that caused the infliction. But its form also suggests the feminine vulva, and in Christian iconography evokes the womb from which Christ gave birth to the church. Jung saw the image as intimating "Christ's androgynous nature that the traditional church suppresses" (CW 8:313). Saint Augustine thought of the wound as a symbol of eternal life, a place where the sacrament flowed forth (ARAS, 5Ek.573).

Through psyche's wounds, new dimensions of being may similarly come to birth. Psychic process involves both the healing of wounds and the causing of wounds as those "lesions to the ego" that inevitably result with expanded self-knowledge (CW 16:472). Alchemy depicted this as the nigredo, a wounding of sun, king or lion—all symbols of the reigning attitudes of consciousness. Likewise, when the Biblical patriarch Jacob wrestles with the angel of God, he suffers a wounding to the thigh, a dislocating encounter with the divine. Indeed, wounds may be the passage into an initiatory drama or represent a numinous site where the relationship between self and other coagulates on new terms (Slattery, 7). Wounds are the apertures through which the ambivalent energies of the deep structures surface into conscious awareness, or, on the other hand, possess the personality with bitterness and despair.

We must look into a wound, not neglect or evade it. A wound has to be evaluated, attended to, cleansed, perhaps knit together or gently probed. Wounds are subject to infection, and can fester and poison the integrity of the whole. The genital wound of the Grail's Fisher King, for example, is witness to the affliction and sterility of both king and kingdom. Healing and renewal require that a questing knight acknowledge his participation in the unfolding story by asking the quintessential question: "What is it that troubles you, oh king?"

Barnhart, Robert K. Ed. *The Barnhart Concise Dictionary of Etymology.* NY, 1995.
Lewis, Charlton T. *A Latin Dictionary.* Oxford, 1996.
Liddell, Henry G. *A Greek-English Lexicon.* Oxford, 1996.
Slattery, Dennis P. *The Wounded Body.* Albany, NY, 2000.

Wound of Christ, illuminated manuscript from *Psalter and Hours of Bonne de Luxembourg*, ca. 1349, France.

Nous monstre tres dous dier vie
trelquant laigesce.
Quant uouliltes pour nous
souftur tant de destresce.

Vomit

The image of a Greek youth on the inside of an ancient drinking cup may have been meant as a caution against excess. So true is the depiction that we can almost feel the aching of the young man's ivy-wreathed head, which a slave woman gently steadies against the violence of his stomach's regurgitation. Supporting himself with the help of a knotted stick, he vomits a stream of red wine, which he has perhaps overimbibed.

Few things are as miserable as the sensation of the body's convulsive disgorgement of the stomach's contents. Vomiting is aptly described by words like spew, eject, retch and heave. Vomiting is the body's mostly involuntary reaction to diverse phenomena: the poisons of illness and chemicals of healing, overindulgence of food or drink, putrid odors, motion sickness and head injuries, the roiling hormonal changes of pregnancy, and psychic shock or trauma. Muscles in the intestines and stomach contract spasmodically, causing the abdominal muscles and diaphragm to compress the stomach and force its contents into the esophagus and out through the mouth (*Enc. Brit.* 12:429).

Originating in the belly, the mythic seat of the passions, vomiting is associated with psyche's tumultuous affective spewing from the depths, like so much volcanic lava. But the belly is also the locus of devouring, holding and incubation, so that vomiting becomes symbolically related to the energies of initiatory process,

transformation and dramatic emergence. Vomit evokes the stuff that can't be contained, as well as what must be let go in the service of evolution. Vessel of psychic birth, Rainbow Snake surfaces from the bottom of the cosmic sea to spew out primordial human life, and the great whale of psyche's night-sea journey swallows, incubates and disgorges the heroic individual into consciousness. Rites of purging, purification, ordeal and healing have long employed emetics to induce vomiting in order to flush out physical and psychic toxins, or to empty and disembody for visionary flight. The poison oracle determined the guilt or innocence of one under suspicion in the belief that innocence would spontaneously reject the ingested poison. Before ritual acts, shamans sometimes used emetics or curved spatulas to self-induce vomiting as a means of expelling food contents that might pollute the soul's bodily shelter and obstruct its communion with the spirit world. Eating disorders adopt almost identical symbolization to express through rituals of vomiting the suffered corrosions of instinctual ground—appetite, sexuality, aggression—and the tensions around control and freedom. Body and psyche convey meaning through nature's dire expulsions; vomiting is a kind of gut-wrenching "knowing" at the core.

Bercht, Fatima. Ed. *Taino: Pre-Columbian Art and Culture from the Caribbean.* NY, 1997.

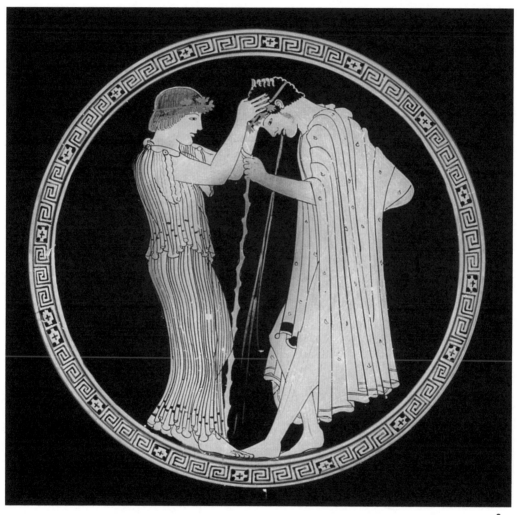

2

1. Curved to fit down the throat, a spatula employed by shamans in the Taino culture induced vomiting as a means of purification before shamanic rites (Bercht, 119, 138). Manatee bone, 1200–1500, Dominican Republic.

2. Depicted on the inside of an ancient Greek drinking cup, the realistic image of a youth vomiting wine would have been gradually revealed as the drinker downed the contents of the cup. From Vulci, ca. 490 B.C.E.

Medicine

A preternatural creature is seen in a vision, recognized as an emissary from the divine realm and its physical likeness procured to become a container of healing energy. The eagle medicine bundle of the Crow Indians of southern Montana could not present a more striking contrast to the medicine of multicolored capsules, chemotherapies and synthetic drugs. Yet the medicine of both has its origin and potency in nature—the vital force of animals, embodied in skin, fang, talon, feather, horn and fur, the paradoxical *pharmakon*, both remedy and poison, the curative properties of minerals and plants. Human beings discovered by trial and error nature's vast cornucopia of palliatives and made infusions from leaves, roots and oils, unguents to rub on fevered skin or salve a wound, and mysterious and effective decoctions. Spirit as much as substance, medicine was also the felt bivalent power of particular objects and individuals—medicine people, shamans, witches, herbalists, midwives and physicians—and the deities that directed them. Chiron, the centaur and wounded healer of ancient Greece, expresses consciousness rooted in the body, and reveals the medicinal seeds of light in the psychosomatic darkness. Asclepius evokes the healing bite of psyche's daemonic "snake" as dream, reflection, meaning and insight. Egyptian Isis mediates the transmutation of venom into antidote. The healing principles of the East unfold in the transformation of subtle body centers, the nuanced shifting of organic fluids and the restoration of balance and flow. Alchemy's *medicina* is seeding and emergence, occult understanding and the mystery of dead matter becoming new psychic tissue. Medicine is coincidence and correspondence, lapis and goal, the panacea, elixir or balm. But medicine is also the stuff that's hard to take but must be swallowed, can sicken before it relieves, must be survived before it can save.

Eagle medicine bundle, Crow Tribe,
Plains Indians.

Poison

Almost concealed in the semidarkness of a church niche, a golden eucharistic chalice brims with the liquid curves of a slender snake. Anticipating the later art of still life, this singular detail from a Christian panel painting portrays poison symbolically as viperous sin that can only be contained by the sacraments of faith. Hinduism's *Mahabharata* perceives poison as one of the original elixirs of creation. Shiva, importuned by the gods, takes the form of a sacred chant and holds the poison in his throat (turning his neck blue) before the fumes can engulf the emerging cosmos. Countless myths and fairy tales depict poison as the dissociated underside of all that is idealized. The little toad of mortality lurks, unnoticed, in love's verdant entanglements. The fatal, pricking spindle of the Terrible Mother nips in the bud what hopes to blossom. The baby Krishna drinks milk from the poisoned breasts of the infant-eating demon Putana, disguised as a beautiful woman.

Poison, from the Latin *potiere*, "to drink," evokes the venom we imbibe with life, despite our instinctive recoiling. Poison is what we experience as harmful, malignant or evil, the "hostile element" that erodes our possibilities of "any decent adaptation" (Jung, 1988, 1320). Nature's toxins, from the Greek *toxon*, "bow" (Liddell), produced by the stingers, spines, teeth, roots, leaves and extracts of animals and plants incarnate the lethal projectiles of mythic archers like Rudra and Artemis, who rule the primordial wildernesses. The venom molecules of snakes become "intimate assassins" when they enter prey, locking onto cell receptors and proteins in the bloodstream (Zimmer, 4). Caustic and necrotic, psyche's pernicious aspect manifests in energies of self-hatred, betrayal, paralyzing inhibitions, rancorous words and malefic tendencies that corrode integrity or cause fatal dysfunction.

Yet poison is not merely destructive, but represents an essential aspect of nature's balance, a means of discouraging competition, dispatching enemies and securing prey (*Enc. Brit.* 25: 895). Poison has the quality of the *pharmakon*, the ancient Greek word that denoted a drug, whether healing or noxious, a remedy or medicine, enchanted spell or philter (Liddell). Arsenic has been used to treat diseases ranging from asthma to leukemia and African sleeping sickness (Newman, 8). Medical research is discovering that snake venoms may treat illness such as congestive heart failure (Zimmer,

1). Our chemotherapies and psychotherapies are *pharmakons*, intimating the pre-Christian configuration of snake and cup that once belonged to the mysterious domain of Asclepian healing. Curative dreams emerged from psyche's coiled depths to address the malady of the sleeping patient, who spent the night in the sacred precinct where a living serpent was resident. The serpent represented the daimon of Asclepius, the physician god of the ancient Greeks and embodied his potent soul substance, the "venom" that made his medicines, signified by the cup, effective (Jung, 1965, 112ff). Psychologically, painful insights that hit the mark, internal conflict actively engaged, corrosive sadness, bitterness or remorse both sicken and heal. "All substances are poison," observed Paracelsus, the 15th-century physician and alchemist; what makes the difference in their effect is the dosage.

Throughout the world the mediation of poisons, the nuances of titration and methods of ingestion were early entrusted to individuals thought to be gifted at the magical manipulation of nature and spirit for good or ill—the sorcerer, witch, shaman, herbalist, midwife and medicine person, and finally the physician—in all of whom the energies of healer and poisoner were combined. Alchemy depicted its spirit Mercurius ambivalently as poison and *medicina*, the agent of the "dissolve and coagulate" dynamics that characterized the opus and reflect psyche's self-equilibration. Fantasies of venomous creatures, stinking putrefaction or the new moon eclipsing the sun expressed the unconscious psyche's "poisonous" countering of the conscious standpoint and the virulent affects and baneful moods that possessed the adept. However, the self-same poison drunk to the dregs released the "hidden wind" of salutary mysteries and potential change.

Jung, C. G. *Spring*, 1965.
Jung, C. G. *Nietzsche's Zarathustra*. Princeton, NJ, 1988.
Landsberg, Sylvia. *The Medieval Garden*. NY, 1995.
Liddell, Henry G. *A Greek-English Lexicon*. Oxford, 1996.
Newman, Cathy. "12 Toxic Tales." *National Geographic* (May 2005).
Zimmer, Carl. "Open Wide: Decoding the Secrets of Venom." *The New York Times* (April 5, 2005).

1. Two young lovers succumb to the venom of a toad hidden in a sage bush. In the background softly twisting vines contrast vital beauty to untimely death (Landsberg, 50). Illustration of a story by Boccaccio, ca. 1440.

2. In a contest with devotees of a pagan deity, John was said to have made the sign of the cross over a cup of deadly poison, rendering it harmless, just as Christ had redeemed a poisonously sinful world. *Chalice of St. John the Evangelist*, by Hans Memling, altar panel painting, 15th century, Germany.

Drowning

Drowning is suffocation caused by immersion in fluid. The lack of air is fatal; water is only an instrument, yet in the human imagination, overwhelming depths of water are the cause of drowning. Drowning can occur (face down) in an inch or two of water, as well as in such great waves as those of Noah's flood, which Genesis tells us rose more than 20 feet above the highest mountain peaks and drowned almost all life on earth. Biblical floods and mass drownings occur as God's punishment of a degenerate humankind (Genesis 7) or his destruction of the enemies of his people, as the Egyptian army drowned pursuing the Israelites through the Red Sea (Exodus 14).

Mythology and literature often picture drowning as suicidal, a result of despair or of loss in love. Ophelia comes to mind. Like the waters, love itself overcomes us. In some cultures, drowning has been seen as the work of revengeful human ghosts who lure people to watery deaths or as being taken by a spirit of the water. Certain rivers were thought to require a yearly victim. After the first drowning, others were safe (de Vr 182). Similarly, it was said to be unlucky to save one drowning at sea. The one who saves another will soon be drowned himself, as the sea must have its quota of the drowned (Opie, 127).

Beyond the concrete and physical, "drowning" has come to mean being engulfed by anything overwhelming. We speak of being drowned in emotion or paperwork. In our psychological age, drowning in dreams and fantasies conveys the softening, weakening or the complete dissolution of the personality. This can be catastrophic; for example, it may signal the emergence of a psychosis—or it can refer to something more positive, such as an individual's loosening or opening to the possibilities of personality growth. Medieval al-

chemical symbolism suggested that transformation was not possible until the original material (imagined as a metal) was altogether dissolved. Depth psychology builds on this symbolism: "The fixed static aspects of the personality allow for no change. They are established and sure of their rightness. For transformation to proceed, these fixed aspects must first be dissolved. This is done by the analytic process, which examines the products of the unconscious (dreams or fantasies; they are the dissolving 'water') and puts the established ego attitudes into question" (Edinger, 47ff). Of course, the established ego resists and fears such a change. It fears losing its customary standpoint, its footing, its ground, and hence "drowning" (Hillman, 152ff). Other experiences— falling in love, religious or political conversion, major life changes, exposure to intense emotion—can also have a dissolving effect, which may be enlivening and fruitful, or destructive, depending on the strength of the personality.

This imagery is also implicit in Christian baptism. The initiate was originally fully submerged in water, experienced a symbolic death by drowning, and emerged transformed, as one newborn. This was a birth into a community of religious believers—a new world, perhaps reminiscent of the new, cleansed world awaiting Noah as he emerges from the ark after his ordeal by water.

Edinger, Edward F. *Anatomy of the Psyche.*
La Salle, IL, 1985.
Hillman, James. *The Dream and the Underworld.*
NY, 1979.
Opie, Iona A. and Moira Tatem. Eds.
A Dictionary of Superstitions. Oxford, 1989.

1. Perhaps the mini-flood of tears will dissolve her rage, and save her from drowning in it. *Drowning Girl*, oil and synthetic polymer on canvas, by Roy Lichtenstein, 1963, United States. © Estate of Roy Lichtenstein.

2. Men, giants and horses drown in the flood sent by God because of human wickedness. Unseen, Noah, his family and his animals are safe in a tightly enclosed ark built to God's specifications. Medieval manuscript, early 5th century, Spain.

Crucifixion

Like many depictions of the Crucifixion, this sixteenth-century version adds an allegorical company of mourners. Despite their presence, the isolation of the anguished figure on the cross, nailed in suspension above the earth and wracked by the gravity of his body, seems absolute. The isolation begins in the agony of Gethsemane, where Jesus ultimately agrees to drink the cup of suffering to the dregs, and is given voice at the end in his derelict cry from the Cross, questioning whether even God has not forsaken him.

Even outside the Christian context and faith-based messianic understanding of the death of Jesus of Nazareth, the image of the crucified one has resonated as one of the dominant symbols in the world, particularly in the Western psyche, for over 2,000 years. Historically, crucifixion was practiced in some form as early as the seventh century B.C.E. For about a thousand years thereafter it was a widely used form of capital punishment primarily applied to slaves, foreigners and political or religious enemies of the state. Apparently, the condemned was first stripped and scourged. Then his outstretched arms were fastened or nailed, probably through the wrists, to a horizontal beam that was raised to cross an upright stake. Suspended one to several feet above the ground, the victim was "evil food for birds of prey and grim pickings for dogs" (Brown, 2:951). Death, most likely from dehydration and loss of blood, followed within a day or two, sometimes hastened by piercing the body or breaking the legs.

The symbolic equivalent to the reality of crucifixion could only be the most drastic, excruciating forms of psychic tension, where harrowing dualities and oppositions rend body and soul, eliciting from the sufferer, as crucifixion once did, "screams of rage and pain, wild curses and outbreaks of nameless despair" (ibid., 1044). Indeed, moral idealism begets unbearable tension with the drives and desires of the natural person and the vitality of animal energies. The ego's intimation of permanence and infinite potential is in tension with the terrors of the body's disintegration and the limits of incarnate life. The longing for happiness and meaning is in conflict with uncontrollable events, rank disparities and the shattering inevitability of suffering and loss. Moreover, crucifixion evokes the razor's edge of psychic process, the ego's lonely bearing of the mandates of the self.

Depicted as redemptive self-sacrifice and atonement between human and divine, the Christian Crucifixion has affinity with mythic stories that are part of a broad symbolic field. Germanic mythology's Odin willfully hung impaled on his sword from the World Tree Yggdrasil for nine days and nights, in the course of which the runes, the divine, magical roots of expressive creative life, were revealed to him, and he in turn revealed them to humanity. Alchemy found in crucifixion an image of the voluntary sacrifice of a former state of consciousness in the service of a dynamic reconfiguration. Here, the suffered crucifying tension between opposites becomes the vessel in which one is liberated *from* the opposites.

The image of crucifixion, whether it is the agonized body on the cross, or the simplicity of the empty cross, has been ennobled by its immense significance as a religious symbol; the cross itself is emblematic of suffering ennobled and meaningful, and the promise of resurrection. But while the crucifixion experiences of life may, finally, admit of meaning and redemption, it isn't always so. Sometimes they are experienced as the merely punishing conflicts imposed by the cruelest arbiter of fate. Crucifixion is torture and its inevitable end is death. And that symbolically evokes a radical, permanent reversal of the way things were, and an equally radical shift, for better or worse, in the consciousness that mediated them.

Brown, Raymond E. *The Death of the Messiah.* NY, 1994.

A 16th-century painting of the Christian Crucifixion.
At the foot of the cross are the allegorically portrayed
Virgin Mary (supported by the disciple John), Mary
Magdalene, the Lamb of Christ bleeding into a chalice
and John the Baptist. Center panel of the Isenheim
altarpiece, by Matthias Grünewald, ca. 1515, Germany.

Hanging

I know that I hung on a windy tree
Nine long nights
Wounded with a spear, dedicated to Odin
Myself to myself
On that tree of which no man knows
From where its roots run.
"Hávamál," *the Poetic Edda*

The tree on which the Norse god Odin sacrificed himself was called Yggdrasil, "the horse of Odin," and it grew at the center of the world. In its roots were hidden the runes, the alphabet of poetic divination. Suspended from its branches for nine long nights, Odin "rode" the tree and obtained its secrets. Reflecting Odin's "hanging," it was a Norse custom to sacrifice men and animals to the god by hanging them in trees; therefore Odin was known as Hangatyr ("God of the Hanged") and Galgatyr ("Gallows God"). The motif of a mysterious place beneath the gallows reappeared in medieval legends of the mandrake, a potent healing root that sprouted from semen falling from a hanged man who was in fact innocent.

Medieval tarot decks captured the enigmatic significance of hanging and the gallows in the Hanged Man card, which portrays a man hanging upside down, tied by one foot to a branch, with one leg positioned across the other. The card is thought to illustrate an initiatory inversion, the self-surrender of outgrown limitations to achieve spiritual maturation. The man's limbs crossed within a triangle may signify the alchemical completion of a stage of the great work (Nichols, 214–27). In

one account of the Christian crucifixion, however, Judas Iscariot hangs himself out of self-loathing for his betrayal of Jesus. Medieval artists portrayed demons crouching beneath his gallows, waiting to carry his soul to hell for the double sin of betrayal and suicide. Saint Peter, who defended Christ with his sword at Gethsemane, but then denied him, at his own crucifixion pleaded to be suspended upside down to prevent his martyrdom being compared to Christ's more significant death.

Ironically, the long agony brought on by crucifixion contrasts with the supposedly painless death caused by hanging from a rope, which is still a legal punishment in some American states. When this is performed carefully, a hanged person drops with a force that prevents strangulation or beheading, by dislocating the third or fourth cervical vertebra, bringing instant death. If it is performed recklessly, the limbs of the victim may thrash wildly, as the victim of mob violence suggests, shown in the photograph with one shoe tightly laced and the other kicked onto the ground. The hanged man was a town drunk who was lynched, on September 26, 1913, for the presumed assault on a young girl; a witness later conceded that he had only harmlessly stumbled into her path (Allen, pl. 39).

Allen, James. *Without Sanctuary: Lynching Photography in America.* Santa Fe, NM, 2000.
Nichols, Sallie. *Jung and Tarot: An Archetypal Journey.* York Beach, ME, 1980.

I

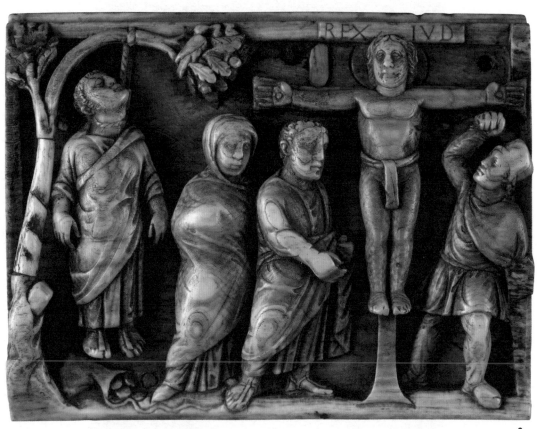

REX IVD

1. This relief is thought to be of the Norse god Odin hanging from the World Tree Yggdrasil, a self-sacrifice that yields the wisdom of the runes. Stone, 8th century, Gotland, Sweden.

2. A symbolic counterpart to Jesus hanging on a cross, Judas hanged himself in remorse for betraying Christ to his persecutors. Relief from the side of a small casket, ivory, Roman, ca. 425 C.E.

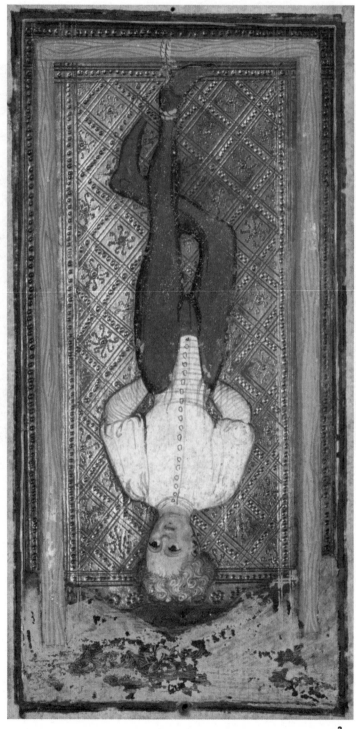

3

Leitchfield Ky   Sept 26° 1913

4

3. Suggesting transformation more than torment, the Hanged Man, the 12th Major Arcana card in traditional tarot decks, dates back to the late medieval period. The Visconti-Sforza deck, 15th century, Italy.

4. *The Lynching of Joseph Richardson* documents the execution of an innocent black man in Leitchfield, Kentucky; such hangings inspired the immortal verses sung by Billie Holiday: "Southern trees bear a strange fruit / Blood on the leaves and blood at the root / Black bodies swinging in the Southern breeze / Strange fruit hanging from the poplar trees." "Strange Fruit," 1913.

Murder/Slaying

With Abel lying murdered at his feet, Cain forfeited whatever vestige of innocence his fallen parents, Adam and Eve, had left to him, leaving theologians to debate the relative innocence of crimes of passion versus cold-blooded premeditation. The agonizing process of weighing a murderer's intentions continues in municipal jury rooms, along with international war-crime tribunals confronted with tens of millions of victims of genocide. Ironically, such grim drama is not the least unsettling to the readers of modern murder mysteries, a genre of thrillers initiated by Poe's "The Murders in the Rue Morgue," which often relies on actual police cases such as the never-apprehended serial killer Jack the Ripper. Murder witnessed on stage or screen has mesmerized audiences from the ancient Greeks (as Clytemnestra slays Agamemnon on entering his bath), to Elizabethans (virtually all the major characters of *Hamlet* lie slain by the final curtain), to the stunned first viewers of Hitchcock's *Psycho*. Oedipus' shocked reaction to the discovery that it was his own father whom he had knifed to death has an echo in modern police statistics—the majority of all murders occur within the family (and unlike Oedipus, the murderer is generally well-known to the victim). Murder strikes home and we cannot turn our eyes away from its gory images.

That Freud reached back to the Greeks for his central patricidal complex reveals the ancients' insight that such imagery nestles at the core of our psyche: the Greek Furies (or Erinyes) were avengers of spilled blood, relentlessly pursuing murderers like Orestes, whose matricide of Clytemnestra avenged his father's bathtub slaying. Blood feuds—tribal killings in revenge for murdered relatives—show how inbred the prompting to kill is, despite our wish to keep aloof from the fate of being either slain or slayer. Some biologists claim that such primal aggression is as fundamental to us as hunger or sexuality. That we nevertheless torment ourselves for it is illustrated nowhere more pointedly than by Dostoevsky's *Crime and Punishment*, when after weeks of self-agonizing the protagonist Raskolnikov turns himself over to the police to be punished for axing two elderly women pawnbrokers to death. Dostoevsky derived the name Raskolnikov from the Russian *raskolnik* ("schismatic, divided") to illustrate how split off from our primordial nature we moderns are when we imagine ourselves beyond primordial good and evil—Abel's shed blood cries out from the ground not only to God but to our own inescapable Furies, to seek vengeance for the outrage as much to our lost integrity as to our slain kin.

In his autobiography, Jung describes a dream about his nearly fatal struggle with a shadow figure in the guise of a princely Arab: " ... I was not prepared for the existence of unconscious forces within myself which would take the part of these strangers with such intensity, so that a violent conflict ensued. The dream expressed this conflict in the symbol of an attempted murder" (Jung, 242 ff). Of course, Cain, who succeeded with *his* murder, is the sole survivor of the pair of brothers and is therefore our own shadowy ancestor. Our naive wish to deny consanguinity with him endangers the cohabitants both within our homes and within our psyche who can perish as permanently by our stabbing remarks and brutal repressions as in a pool of blood. When God marks Cain's forehead with a special stigma, it is for his own protection against avengers. For he, like us, must live the full measure of his days with the knowledge that, no longer innocent, he must master his hot blood with awareness.

Jung, C. G. *Memories, Dreams, Reflections.* NY, 1963.

1. A massive pile of American bison skulls. The wanton slaughter of millions of buffalo contributed to the genocide of the American Plains Indian, for whom the great buffalo had enormous significance as means of life and as symbol. Photograph, 1870s.

2. Humanity's earliest homicide (according to Biblical accounts) occurred within the first generation after creation. This relief on the Orvieto Cathedral portrays Cain slaying his brother Abel out of jealousy that God unaccountably preferred Abel's sacrifice of a sheep to Cain's own sacrifice of fruits and grain (Genesis 4:2). By Lorenzo Maitani, 14th century, Italy.

Suicide

Unassailable on the battlefield of the Trojan War and the bulwark of the Greek army, the hero Ajax met his untimely end at his own hands. He and Odysseus both claimed the armor of the fallen Achilles, and the dispute was settled in favor of Odysseus. Frenzied with disappointment, Ajax plotted a night raid on his comrades, but Athena thwarted it by driving Ajax mad so that he killed a flock of sheep instead. Shamed and remorseful, Ajax committed suicide by falling on his sword.

While the voluntary taking of one's own life would seem, at one level, to be an agonizingly private matter, its often shattering ramifications for the survivors of the victim, and the implications it has for law, philosophy, medicine, religion, ethics and politics, have since ancient times made suicide a subject of public debate and controversy. The Roman Stoics perceived suicide as an acceptable and dignified way to deal with the unbearable misfortunes of life. Christian writers since the fifth century have condemned it as an appropriation of the prerogative of God. Jewish tradition forbade taking one's own life except to avoid specific threats of idolatry, murder and sexual immorality (Unterman, 190). In Japan, hara-kiri, ritual suicide, is practiced in response to failure, loss in love, as a means of shaming one's enemies and as a way to show loyalty to a dead superior. In Hindu India, suicide was generally frowned on, but honored and at one time required in sati, the self-immolation of widows on their husbands' funeral pyres, a practice outlawed only in the nineteenth century (MM 20:2733). Buddhism and Islam formally reject suicide, but Buddhist monks have immolated themselves as a form of political protest, and Muslims have self-destructed in suicide bombings as instruments of holy war.

As the ancient story of ignominy and self-annihilation depicted on the Greek vase attests, however, suicide, for many, conjures the sharp, punishing sword of self-judgment that mortally penetrates the place of insufferable vulnerability. Whether it is an issue of honor, loneliness, defiance or despair, the sense of an unredeemable past or a future that offers no possibility, suicide often represents a flooding in the psyche of obliterating force. Passive as well as active, suicide may harbor within its violence the desire for transformation, or may signify an evasion of it. There are suicides that can be understood as an unconscious effort at compensating what is "hopelessly inefficient in the personality" (CW 14:149). There are accidental deaths that ensue when, unconscious of what's at stake, one refuses psyche's fateful demand for a figurative "death" as self-knowledge that dissolves the fixed attitudes of consciousness (CW 14:674ff).

Suicide can also be experienced as an act of eros. In the grip of a suicidal impulse, the idea of killing oneself can take on the fascination and power of a sacred image and become a symbol for the self (von Franz, 55). The mythic "deathly lover" can seduce a woman into an act of suicide as consummation; likewise, the anima soul can lead a man into insurmountably dangerous acts of passionate boldness and posthumous glory.

Literature has often depicted the ghost of a suicide victim as desultory or vengeful. In Dante's *Divine Comedy*, suicides are relegated to the inferno. Such images are derived, perhaps, not only from religious taboo, but also from the haunting feelings many are left with in the wake of a loved one's suicide. Or they may reflect an innate tension within the psyche itself between the striving for survival and consciousness, and the energies that pull toward an oblivious letting go.

Unterman, Alan. *Dictionary of Jewish Lore and Legend.* NY, 1991.

von Franz, Marie-Louise. *The Psychological Meaning of Redemption Motifs in Fairytales.* Toronto, 1980.

1. Driven to suicide, the Greek hero Ajax self-inflicts a mortal wound. Red-figure vase (calyx-krater, wine bowl), Etruscan, from Vulci, 400–350 B.C.E.

2. A young Buddhist monk kills himself by fire in a protest against anti-Buddhist policies of the 1963 Saigon government.

3. In mad despair over her father's death and her estrangement from Hamlet, Ophelia accidentally falls into a brook. "Incapable of her own distress" (*Hamlet* 4.7), she does nothing to save herself from drowning. *Ophelia*, by Sir John Everett Millais, painting, 1852, England.

1

2

3

Burial

Second Fool: *"Who builds stronger than a
mason, a shipwright, or a carpenter?"*
First Fool: *" … a gravemaker: the houses
that he makes last till doomsday."*
Hamlet, 5.1.19, 28

The elegantly reconstituted skeleton in the image
from Bulgaria depicts with macabre realism the common end of mortal beings. The gold penis-sheath and
others of the 990 different gold objects and adornments
buried with the grave's occupant, as well as copper and
flint weapons, may suggest prestige and wealth, but the
bare bones of this human ancestor yet reveal the de-
nouement to the story of Everyman.

Like the somber cadence of a tolling bell or the funereal drumbeat for a fallen leader, burial most immediately evokes an utmost sense of finality. Although
death and life will continuously merge and separate in
the grave, burial nevertheless marks the terminus of a
particular existence or embodiment. The setting apart
and consecration of this vanished life establishes the
ultimate boundary between the "quick" and the
dead.

At the grave, the living must irrevocably surrender the last bodily vestiges of the beloved's once animate, inspirited presence to the silence and mystery
of the "underworld." Bodies (or the ashes or bones of
bodies) may be buried in the depths of the sea, in caves
or trees, in the walls or floor of a church or even in the
belly of the human being or animal that eats them.
Since the Stone Age, however, burial in the earth (Latin
humus or *terra*) has been a natural and efficient way
for numerous cultures to dispose of a dead body. In*hu*-
*mation, inte*rment, is rendered colloquially as "planting" the dead, with all the implication and dark humor
attendant upon the inevitable decomposition and
decay of organic matter:

"That corpse you planted last year
    in your garden,
"Has it begun to sprout?
    Will it bloom this year?
"Or has the sudden frost disturbed its bed?
T. S. Eliot, *The Waste Land*

The idea of burial as a planting, however, alludes
to the mysteries of descent and resurrection. The image
evokes not only ultimate submersion in the body, but
also the fertilizing humus of psychic depths and the
dissolutions that release rich elements of transformation.

For some, burial is most evocative of sleep. Sheltered in the encompassing womb of Mother Earth a
spouse slumbers peacefully, or a dead child, buried with
her favorite toy, is gently cradled until a future, otherworldly awakening. "Sometimes I stand among the
stones and wonder," writes the poet and undertaker
Thomas Lynch. "Sometimes I laugh, sometimes I weep.
Sometimes nothing at all much happens. Life goes on.
The dead are everywhere" (Lynch, 99).

Detective fiction and the investigations of anthro-
pologists have long accustomed us to the revelatory aspect of burial. Opened graves conjure up ancestral secrets, telltale clues to unsolved crimes or even long lost
treasure, the dark stuff that has been repressed and revealed. Above ground, the grave markers suggest, much
as Shiva's provocative stringing of skulls, the movement
of generations through endless cycles of life and death.
In his role as Bhuteswara, haunter of cemeteries and
cremation sites, Shiva embodies the opposing energies
of creation and destruction, the erotic and the austere,
which hover at the grave.

Alchemically, the imagery of burial belongs to the
dark melancholy of the *nigredo*. Just as the corrupt-
ible body goes into the earth and putrefies, so the dead
matter of the psyche—the outgrown desires and tendencies that informed the old life—is surrendered and
ceases to exercise its potency. In the liminal space and
time of the metaphorical tomb, the old way of being
decomposes, while the new has yet to emerge. The
waiting, however, is not merely stasis. Descent is also
restoration of contact with the mother ground, where
loss is the seeding of the "golden grain," and death is
conception.

Ions, Veronica. *Indian Mythology*. London, 1967.
Lynch, Thomas. *The Undertaking*. NY, 1997.

1

2

3

1. The reconstituted bones of a man about 45 years old, buried ca. 4000 B.C.E., articulate past life for those in the present. Grave 43 in the Copper Age cemetery at Varna, Bulgaria.

2. This family portrait, at once charming and grotesque, portrays what appears to be an unremarkable daily activity. The Indian god Shiva, smeared with white ash, strings human heads with the assistance of his consort Parvati and their sons, elephant-headed Ganesha and six-armed Karttikeya. The white bull Nandi, Shiva's animal embodiment, gazes placidly from behind a tree while in the foreground, jackals dig for human bones among the fires of a cremation site (Ions 29). Kangra painting, 1810, India.

3. Stones in the shape of boats surround Viking graves in this 7th-century Scandinavian grave-field. Evocative of the seamanship central to Viking life and culture, the stone "boats" also suggest continuity between life and death in the passage of the dead to the "otherworld."

Coffin

Thou art given to thy Mother Nut,
In her name Coffin;
She embraces thee in her name
Sarcophagus;
Thou comest up to her
In her name Sepulcher.
Pyramid Texts, Utterance #616 (Piankoff, 21)

Nut, the covering sky, in her night aspect, completely fills the inner lid of an Egyptian sarcophagus, conveying that coffin is not only a receptacle for the dead, but a vessel of passage. For in Nut's body, the stars rise and set and rise again in everlasting continuity. So does the orb of the sun pass into her mouth at sunset and is reborn from her vagina at dawn.

Before the use of coffins, the dead were buried in jars, baskets, shrouds, animal skins or sometimes simply exposed (Colman, 77). Coffins came into use to preserve the dead from predators and evil spirits, protect the living from the dead person's ghost and as a form of status or honor. Coffins are usually oblong wooden boxes, caskets their rectangular equivalent; a sarcophagus is a stone coffin sometimes holding a wooden coffin within it. Materials used for coffins range from hollowed-out logs to glass and metal, ceramics, plastics and cement, while gold and jewels were often reserved for royalty. An artist in Ghana creates coffins in whimsical shapes and brilliant colors to provide personalized, stylish "vehicles" with which the dead may enter the afterlife. Some of the most elaborate and beautiful, the coffins of ancient Egypt began as simple wooden boxes, which, along with the temple, "housed" the soul of the king, and evolved into the anthropoid-shaped coffins of the Middle Kingdom that conformed to the shape of the mummified corpse.

The attention given to coffins, and the "fantasies of permanence and protection" they evoke, have to do with the precious nature of their contents, like other things such as heirlooms and jewels that we put into "caskets" (Lynch, 182ff). This is carried in the motif of the glass coffin of fairy tales, in which is preserved the sleeping princess, a potentially revitalizing principle of feminine spirit that must be heroically claimed. The infant and orphaned divine child or culture hero is often fetched up from the sea in a glass coffin or casket that both protects and allows the vital content to be seen. The coffin was a symbol for the alchemical *vas* in which "dead matter" was reanimated by the dew of understanding and transmuted into incorruptible gold.

No doubt, coffin reminds us of ineluctable finality, burial, loss and absence, and, in more ghoulish depictions, of assailing worm and restless dead. Yet coffin, like its earliest forerunners, also intimates a containment of life. In the so-called *Coffin Texts* of ancient Egypt, the ritual lowering of the lid over the sarcophagus symbolized the sacred copulation of Nut with her spouse Geb, the earth on which the sarcophagus rested. The corpse became their symbolic offspring, a hoped-for rebirth out of time into the eternity of the gods. Thus the sarcophagus—meaning (from the Greek) "flesh-eater"—became the womb in which, an old form of life extinguished, one was gestated into the new.

Beckwith, Carol. *African Ceremonies*. NY, 1999.
Colman, Penny. *Corpses, Coffins, and Crypts:*
A History of Burial. NY, 1997.
Lynch, Thomas. *The Undertaking*. NY, 1997.
Piankoff, Alexandre. *The Shrines of*
Tut-Ankh-Amon. NY, 1955.

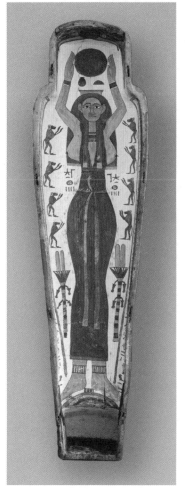

1. African Ga "fantasy coffins" represent some aspect of the identity or dignity of the deceased person. This coffin of a wealthy merchant is a Mercedes-Benz; a fisherman might be buried in one shaped like a sardine (Beckwith, 2:332–57). Photograph, Ghana.

2. Her arms upraised to cover the entire undersurface of a sarcophagus lid, the goddess Nut, as the night sky, hovers protectively over the dead. Ca. 664–332 B.C.E., Egypt.

Cremation

In Bali, before the crematory pyres are ignited, the priest encourages the dead to find embodiment in the cosmos:

Thy hair will return to the bushes,
thy skin to earth, thy flesh to the waters,
* thy blood to fire,*
thy sinews to roots, thy bones to wood,
* thine eyes to Sun and Moon,*
thy head to the sphere, thy breath to the wind.
(Daniel, 52)

It is a prayer of dispersal and reconstitution, for once the body is burned there can be no illusion of inside or outside, or of identity separate from the elements.

Ritual cremation is, above all, a treatment of the body and not merely a means of discarding it. In the cremations of the Balinese and the Hindu, the soul is delivered up in smoke just as the physical vehicle is returned to ash. Many cultures believe that fire dries out the life liquid, the psyche, before the soul rejoins its ancestors and the period of mourning is ended. Only through fire, it is felt, are the fiery passions, desires and attachments of the soul consumed and released. In Homer, too, cremation is purification and a leveling. Trojan War heroes Patroklos and Hector, though on opposite sides, are honored together in a public burning on an erected pyre, the flames of which symbolically destroy antagonistic forces and extinguish mortal aims.

Cremation is, however, often not the last, but rather a preparatory, step in funerary rites. In India, Nepal and Thailand, the ashes and fragments of bone are cast into a river. In India, the Ganges is identified with the goddess Ganga who is capable of giving birth to a new body. The Yanoama Indians of Venezuela grind and consume the cremated bones of their warriors, reintegrating into the tribe, perhaps, the courage and power the bones represent (EoR, 5:457). The Maiduan Indians, in a ritual that was later suppressed, positioned the corpse in a fetal position in a large basket surrounded by animal skins that was either cremated or buried (Dobkins, 76). The womblike image suggests the idea of the corpse being reborn within the skin of the animal, while the fiery colors evoke the incinerating core of the earth that lays final claim to the old body. In contrast, Christianity banned cremation for centuries because the burning of the dead seemed to oppose the doctrine of the resurrection of the body.

Cremation links us with the physical and psychic mysteries of fire and smoke: mortality, transience, sublimation, transcendence, essence and substance. The shadow of cremation has shown itself in holocaust and genocide. At the opposite pole are the images of the cremation of the Buddha, his body conveyed to the cremation site after ceremonies with dances and offerings of flowers, the flames igniting spontaneously into the golden red of release and awakening.

Daniel, Ana. *Bali: Behind the Mask.* NY, 1981.
Dobkins, Rebecca J. *Memory and Imagination: The Legacy of Maidu Indian Artist Frank Day.* Oakland, CA, 1997.
Eiseman, Fred B. *Bali: Sekala and Niskala.* Berkeley, CA, 1989.

1. Flames lick a Balinese sarcophagus in the form of a bull, or lembu, connoting that the deceased is a male of highest caste. The bull is emblematic of the divine Siwa, symbolizing death, destruction and the recycling of the spirit (Eiseman, 1:118).

2. The funeral pyre ignited spontaneously on the arrival of Mahakashyapa, one of Buddha's great disciples. Stupas were erected over the relic bones. *The*

Cremation of the Buddha, relief, schist, ca. 2nd century C.E., Pakistan.

3. One of the earliest burial paintings by Frank Day, a Konkow Maiduan Indian, showing a body ready for cremation, placed within a large woven basket surrounded by animal skins. Oil on paper, 1963, United States.

2

1

3

759

Mummy

The jackals seen prowling at twilight and sniffing at bones around ancient Egyptian necropolises provided a natural source for the image of the god Anubis, the jackal-headed psychopomp of the dead and overseer of Egypt's nearly 4,000-years-long experiment in human mummification. Anubis may derive his name from the bandages that were wrapped around mummies like the horizon wrapped around the visible world—the threshold to the invisible land of the dead in the west where the sun sank into the underworld. Here Osiris ruled; to survive in his blessed realm, the physical body itself had to be preserved just as the body of Osiris had been preserved in ancient myths; failure to do so doomed the deceased to annihilation.

The prehistoric inhabitants of the Nile Valley had long observed that the desert naturally preserved the dead, virtually petrifying their skin and bones after three-quarters of a corpse's weight was absorbed as water into the Sahara's dry sand and heated air. But once the corpses of royalty and aristocrats came to be entombed in coffins, their recognizable features were dissolved in putrefaction, horrifying the Egyptians who believed that for the departed ba-soul to return to re-animate the body, it must be able to recognize its own physical counterpart. Proceeding by trial and error, priestly morticians therefore slowly perfected the art of mummification, so that even today it is a recognizably human face that stares back at mesmerized museumgoers. During the 70-day procedure, all the visceral organs subject to decomposition were removed (except the heart, since it was believed to be the seat of wisdom and intelligence) and stored separately in canopic jars. The brain was drained or removed through a hole made at the top of the nostrils, while the body cavity was purified with aromatic spices, palm wine and oils. Finally the body was laid on a bed of natron ("divine") salt as a drying agent.

The now-desiccated limbs and face were padded out with substances at hand, such as lichen, sawdust or rags, to give the mummy a lifelike plumpness and to complement the wigs, artificial eyes, jewels and cosmetic coloring that adorned men and women alike. Linen strips soaked in resin were tightly wrapped around the corpse to keep it intact; their blackening over time created the impression of bitumen (hence the etymology of mummy: Arabic mummiya, bitumen). Royal mummies were often given masks of imperishable gold before the coffin was closed for eternity (barring thieves or archaeologists). Although food and even board games were provided in the tombs, after the climactic Opening the Mouth Ceremony, the now-radiant dead were believed fully able to walk into the Land of the Blessed where the bountiful pleasures of Egypt could be enjoyed forever.

The desire to preserve the human body after death was not confined to ancient Egyptians. Beyond their natural preservation in peat bogs, human mummies have been preserved deliberately in China and especially Incan Peru with its royal mummy cult at Cuzco. In the Old Testament, Joseph ordered the body of his father Jacob to be mummified (Genesis 50:1-4). Priests of the esoteric Buddhist sect Shingon mummify themselves as a form of self-sacrifice. Ascetical practices have included the ingestion of purgative poisons that desiccate the body and kill bacteria that would cause decay (Newman, 26).

Symbolically, mummification suggests a preparation for psychic rebirth. The ego's former way of being, its sovereign strivings mortified, has been rendered inanimate and immobilized. A delicate psychic process begins, a synthesizing of old and new, visible and invisible, light and darkness, conscious and unconscious. Alchemically, the mumia refers to the Anthropos, the original human being, a fantasy of wholeness that intimates the potential emergence of a new, "incorruptible" center of the personality (Edinger, 162-3). The passage to its actualization demands utmost precision and the tightest containment. It is a deeply introverted state in which occurs the coherent re-membering of things informed by unconscious energies and yielding, ultimately, to the "breath" of a reconfigured engagement with life.

Edinger, Edward F. Anatomy of the Psyche. La Salle, IL, 1985.
Newman, Cathy. "12 Toxic Tales." National Geographic (May 2005).

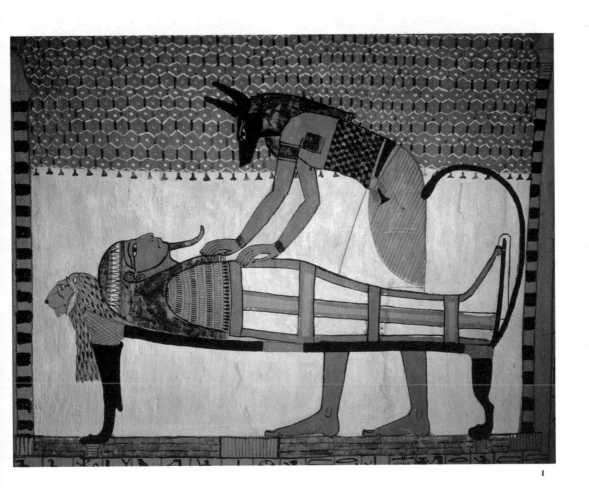

1. An Egyptian priest preparing the deceased has
assumed the form of Anubis, the jackal-headed lord of
the necropolis, while the corpse has assimilated the
form of Osiris, god of the underworld. Just as Osiris was
re-membered and reborn after his fatal
dismemberment, so through the process of
mummification could each of the dead become an
"Osiris," with the potential for resurrection. Wall
painting, 18th dynasty (1550–1295 B.C.E.).

2

3

2. Draped in layers of a surprisingly well-preserved cotton garment, a thousand-year-old Peruvian mummy seems to echo the words spoken by a skeleton on a well-known Italian altarpiece: "I was once that which you are, and that which I am you also will be." Photograph by Brooks Walker.

3. Snugly swaddled in layered linen squares, a cat mummy gazes into eternity with lifelike eyes painted onto its modeled head. Egyptians not only preserved animals sacred to various deities, but also provided the deceased with animal mummies as food in serving-sized coffins (Ikram, 131ff). Mummy of a cat, Upper Egypt Roman period, perhaps 1st century, Abydos.

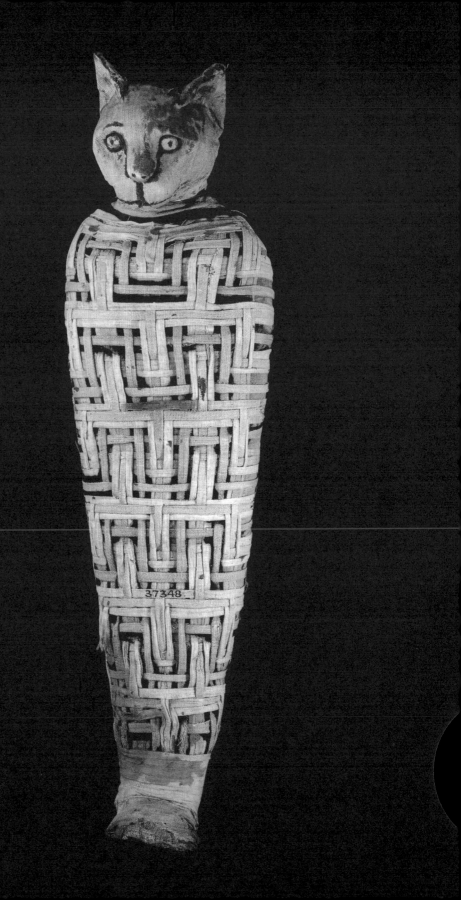

Decomposition

The medieval alchemists, who often referred to decomposition as *putrefactio,* performed their work inside a glass vessel. To modern readers, their arcane manuscripts portray a bewildering combination of metaphorical and natural objects inside the vessel. The human couple in the image would seem to be metaphorical, but the putrefaction they symbolized was so physical that the alchemists complained that the couple's sulphurous stench recalled the grave. As a symbol of the conscious and unconscious aspects of the psyche joined together, the pair was somehow imagined as having entered a stage of real decomposition in a glass sepulcher.

Decomposition is the breakdown of something into its constituent elements. It is disintegration, division, separation, reduction and distillation. Organic matter dies and decomposes, leaking malodorous compounds and volatile acids that, in turn, support new life. The carrion of one creature is food for another. In a symbiosis between cadavers and insects, corpses quiver with maggots that hatch and feed on the bloated, liquefying remains, and honeybees swarm over bodily openings searching for eggs that blowflies have laid (Osborne, 106–7). Composts of withered, rotting flora supply living plants with foods, retain rain and improve soil structure (*Enc. Brit.* 15:1039). Even dying stars decompose, shedding their outer layers in clouds of gas and dust over thousands of years, in their last moment collapsing into black holes.

Broadly, however, decomposition refers to activities ranging from psychoanalysis (the breakdown of an individual into underlying complexes) to more natural processes of digestion and decay. Typical dream images such as rotting food, corpses or gangrenous sores signify a downward movement in the psyche, often by descending into a grave or cesspool, or the enclosing wetness of swamps or quicksand. At the climax of "The Facts in the Case of M. Valdemar," Edgar Allen Poe transforms Valdemar into a "liquid mass of loathsome, of detestable putridity." Few of us can conceive anything to redeem such transparent reminders of death, but the alchemist's texts patiently counseled, "wait and see." The disgust aroused by decomposition's telltale odor is a way of bringing the imagination into the body, especially the lower tracts, the bowels of the earth, and finally the underworld itself. In these depths, the elements commingle; boundaries blur in an unsettling way; opposites find their common ground in human emotion. And in this repulsive mire they are reborn.

In the medieval period, when the alchemist experienced his psyche through projection into literal chemical changes, his spirit sank into a despondent state during this stage, generally known as *mortificatio.* He felt the death of his experimental substance to be a humiliating failure; a collapse of his hopes to animate matter with spirit. Once the beaker's content had fully decomposed, however, disintegrating into the primal substance that alchemy posited at the root of matter, the "couple" in the beaker seemed to revive. It was not until the Enlightenment, when it was demonstrated that flies do not rise spontaneously from rotten food sealed in a jar, that this belief in literal reanimation was abandoned.

Depth psychologists, the modern heirs of alchemy, equate putrefaction with the waning of an artist's creative power or with clinical depression. In psychotherapy, it is the projection of psychic contents onto the outer world that dies. The glass beaker, a metaphor for the therapeutic relationship, serves as a container for taking one's conflicts inside, whereupon after a listless period that follows the loss of such an emotional investment, black depression transforms into renewal. Shamanic candidates in circumpolar Siberia and Canada undergo a comparable process. In terrifying initiatory visions, their eyes, ears, and tongues and their internal organs and bones are stripped away in the beaks and claws of fierce spirits. Yet once the candidates are dismembered, they are given extraordinary new body parts, eyes of clairvoyant crystal and bones capable of flight.

Osborne, Lawrence. "Dead Men Talking." *The New York Times Magazine* (December 3, 2000).
Watts, Alan. *The Two Hands of God.* NY, 1963.

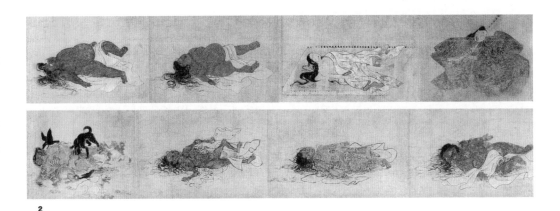

1. A significant alchemical stage known as decomposition is well-illustrated by a glass beaker filled with black "aqua," or putrid water, where inside we see a man and woman suspended in a lifeless embrace. Illustration from the alchemical manuscript *Donum Dei*, ca. 15th century, France.

2. In the Far East, the stark progression of physical decay depicted in a Japanese picture-scroll from the *Kusoshi emaki* is merely one phase in the cyclical play of opposites. Chuang-Tzu writes, "Therefore all things are one. What we love is animation. What we hate is corruption. But corruption in turn becomes animation, and animation once more becomes corruption" (Watts, 60). 12th–14th century.

Dismemberment

Dismemberment is a mythopoetic rendering of the process of fragmentation and dissolution, which may lead to differentiation and renewal. Belonging to the family of "death mysteries," dismemberment calls forth fertility and resurrection, freeing libido by breaking down defensive structures until only the bones of the personality remain, upon which a new body is created. The magic of this process is gained by the sacrifice of finitude and stability. Surviving dismemberment initiates one into the intimacy between sacrifice and creation, suffering and transformation.

Depicted in the image of Watakame's dismemberment, development out of wholeness is a death, a dismemberment that creates as-yet-unknown forms of life. The myth of world creation by dismemberment of a primordial being is universal: the flesh of Icelandic Ymir became earth, his bones became rocks, teeth became gravel, skull became sky. In Greece the dismembered phallus of Ouranus created Aphrodite, while his blood spawned the Furies. In Babylonia, the hero Marduk dismembered the goddess Tiamat, and created sky and earth from her body.

The dismembered remains of sacrificial victims, an "ultimate ancestor" or the individual who stands in for him, are usually formally distributed and then buried or eaten, giving rise to the various hierarchies (from head to foot) of both "corporate" society and the "organic" cosmos. Each act of dismemberment recapitulates the Creation. When the 1,000-headed-and-footed Indian god Purusa was dismembered, the parts of his body created the various castes. In Indonesia staple foods were imagined as growing from the body of a beautiful and wealthy princess, dismembered by jealous villagers. "You are what you eat" takes on symbolic significance as the assimilation of various psychological attributes projected onto the body, which are "eaten" in order to reanimate ourselves. Divine scapegoats such as Jesus were symbolically dismembered in order to effect renewal: by ingesting the "body and the blood" to save the spirit and identify with the ideal ancestor.

In the image of the goddess Coyolxauhqui, primordial wholeness also gives way to dismemberment, but like the cycle of the moon, wholeness arises again. Psychologically, nothing is ever "lost," but rather we are transfigured through the dismembering effects of loss. The Many arises out of the One, but the One is re-created from the Many. Gods personifying the dynamics of dismemberment, such as Osiris, Dionysus and Kali, personify the prospective potentials of this archetypal experience: violence, loss, grief, catastrophe, privation, illness, despair, envy, fury and ecstasy induce altered states that dismember by delinking the personality from its habitual moorings. Egyptian Osiris is dismembered and scattered by envious Set, but re-collected and reintegrated at another level by his sister/wife Isis. In his "new body" he fathered Horus the son-king, assumed rulership of the underworld and the buried parts of his old body "sprouted" into various sites of worship in Egypt. The fruits of dismemberment are both a broader and transcendent perspective and a deep connection to unconscious processes. As archetypal process, dismemberment is an "undoing," which effects transformation on a different register than rational understanding. Dionysus, personifying the dismembering frenzy of ecstasy, possession by unconscious manias and obsessions, opening of boundaries and being "torn-up," symbolizes many forms of "madness" that dismember as a first step in the fertility magic where dissolution provides the seeds of rebirth.

1. The primordial farmer has died. His body pulls apart. Organs disintegrate, but metamorphose into flowers and plants. From a peyote vision, the painting renders the process of dismemberment leading to differentiation and renewal. *The Dismemberment of Watákame*, by José Benitez Sánchez, yarn painting, Huichol, 1973, Mexico.

2. A defeated and murdered moon goddess is dismembered, killed every month by the sun, her adorned and severed body parts arranged to suggest life and motion on a round disk, dismemberment and wholeness. *The Goddess Coyolxauhqui*, eight-ton stone disk, Aztec, ca. 1325–1521.

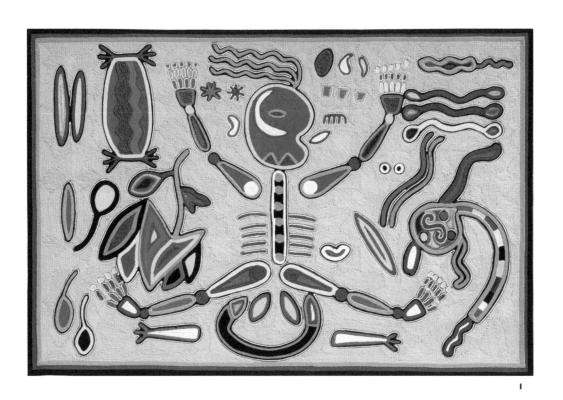

1

2

Dismemberment is characteristic of the tradition of shamanic initiation across cultures (Central Asia, Siberia, Australia, Indo-Tibetan, North and South Americas, Norse). Inflicted by other shamans, demonic spirits, illness, dreams and madness, or "chosen" as autoinitiation by oneself by withdrawing into solitude or privation, the dismemberment of the future shaman's "old body" (ego death) acts as a return to a state of primordial chaos, which allows for a new, "supernatural" body, a new self to be born. A radical dissolution of the old persona returns one "to the bones," the essentials of being. This is a form of psychological development, more than just renewal or participation in nature's cycle of death and creation. Notes Eliade: "The spirits cut off his head, which they set aside, for the candidate must watch his dismemberment with his own eyes." After dismemberment of the body, its parts and organs are fed to the spirits of the diseases, which the shaman will encounter: acknowledgment that the imperishable world inside that of time and change imparts the power to heal. The "supernatural" body created after dismemberment allows the shaman to move between these worlds, finding lost souls and curing disease.

Dismemberment as initiation is echoed in western medieval alchemy. In the image from the manuscript *Splendor Solis*, the *nigredo*, the decapitated head, seems to be watching the dismemberment of its body while it also turns its gaze inward. This emphasizes the separation of the earthbound body, which participates in the cycles of death and renewal, and the "golden head," the soul, which has a different perspective. As "Children of the Golden Head," the alchemists also explored the fact that to be made whole includes being torn apart first. The text, held by the dark executioner, says: "I have killed thee, that thou mayest receive a superabundant life, but thy head I will carefully hide, that the world may not see thee, and destroy thee in the earth; the body I will bury, that it may putrefy and grow and bear innumerable fruit" (Fabricius, 100).

Eliade, Mircea. *Shamanism*. NY, 1964.
Fabricius, Johannes. *Alchemy*. Copenhagen, 1976.

3. The god dances, wreathed in vines and leopard skin, brandishing halves of a fawn he has torn apart. *Dionysos Mainomenos (the Mad One)*, terra-cotta vessel, Hellenic era, 490–80 B.C.E., Greece.

4. Kali, the annihilating aspect of Chandi-Durga, the Loving and Protecting Mother. Kali the destroyer stands on wounded men, surrounded by severed heads and holding a sacrificial sword. All is in motion, including her bloody tongue; the creative aspect of dismemberment and destruction. Painting, ca. 18th century, Rajasthan, India.

5. In front of a palace, a dark man holds a sword, a piece of paper and the golden head of a dismembered white corpse, which lies at his feet. The image signifies separation of body and soul, torment, the nigredo, sacrifice and dismemberment of the king or usurper. Illustration from the alchemical manuscript *Splendor Solis*, or "Splendor of the Sun," by Salomon Trismosin, school of Nuremberg, ca. 1582, Germany

3

4

5

Shape-Shifting

In the very earliest time,
when both people and animals lived on earth,
a person could become an animal if
*   he wanted to*
and an animal could become a human being.
Sometimes they were people
and sometimes animals
and there was no difference.
All spoke the same language.
That was the time when words
*   were like magic.*
The human mind had mysterious powers.
....

Nobody could explain this:
That's the way it was.
Translated from Inuit by Edward Field

Encompassing both dangerous borderline confusion, and the transcendent experience of the essential unity of being, shape-shifting symbolizes psyche in flux and the coincident psychology of altered states of consciousness. The world is interconnected and always changing; shape-shifters amplify, reveal or hide this process; that is their magic. Shamans, tricksters, witches, jinns, druids, gods and heroes with an affinity for "deconstruction and reconstruction" share the ability to separate and regroup elements of psychological process, ultimately in service of renewal.

This is expressed in the ancient and ubiquitous belief in humanity's power to change into animals at will or at junctures in the cycles of nature. This can be actual bodily change, or passage of the soul into an animal, while the human body remains in an altered state of awareness, asleep or in dream time. Werewolves and witches' familiars exemplify this ritual assumption of animal instinct, as do shamans and practitioners of altered trance-states. In one image a were-jaguar rises in the ecstatic trance of shamanism, partaking in the unity of human and beast (Furst, 68ff). Herein, one can accomplish the seemingly impossible: stalk lovers as did Zeus in swan or bull form (EoR, 13: 225), or escape enemies by transforming into magical salmon or selkies of Celtic myth. One might become invisible, or create strategic confusion or deception like Native American trickster Coyote, or experience elements hostile to humans: air, fire and water. The Norse Odin obtained unusual information from the Otherworld as a bird. The Celtic hero Cuchulainn transformed himself into a raging beast to fight more effectively for his countrymen. A less threatening and more usual shift is into the West African "bush-soul," one's animal spirit. Although part of the amoral, nonrational psyche, which escapes the ethics of relatedness, shape-shifting carries responsibility and consequences. Wounds suffered in the animal body are thought to be reproduced correspondingly in the restored human body.

Unlike metamorphosis, in shape-shifting there is no progressive development, but a fluid slide into one or another aspect of psyche; temporary, protean and intended to hide as much as to reveal. Unlike complete transformation, shape-shifting doesn't alter essentials, but portrays the pluralistic, polymorphic, "alternative reality" of what exists. In fact, shape-shifters have antipathy to the "truth" of static form, preferring dark, mercurial, mediumistic venues, frightening to the ego seeking permanence and object constancy. "Catch me if you can," says the shape-shifter, and the hero's task is often just that: wresting meaning and consciousness from the flux of psychic process. Proteus, the "Old Man of the Sea," was sought by heroes because of his gift for prophecy. He assumed every conceivable form in order to elude their grasp, until caught and held fast he was forced to tell the truth. The goddess Thetis also assumes multiple forms to avoid marriage to a mortal. But King Peleus manages to secure her, symbolizing an exchange and binding of power.

Shape-shifting has a transcendent dimension as well, both dark and light. A deceptive union was central to the birth of King Arthur of Britain, when Merlin gave Uther Pendragon the form of Ygranne's husband, tricking her and conceiving the beloved Once and Future King. Many creatures from the "dark side"—ghosts, demons, comic-book heroes like Spiderman, even Satan himself—are shape-shifters, symbolizing depth experience, compensating the rational psychological attitude. In the supremely popular *Harry Pot-*

1. This human-animal composite may depict the supernatural kinship of human and animal that is experienced in the ecstatic trance of shamanism. Rock painting by the San Bushmen, South Africa.

ter series young wizards-in-training learn shape-shift-ing spells in their quest for knowledge rather than for propitiation of the nonrational psyche. The Hindu gods Vishnu/Krishna were prodigious shape-shifters assuming numerous avatars in their battle with evil. And the Greek Tiresias and Dionysus shape-shift into female form, knowing the mystery of love and eros as the Other (EoR, 13:226–8).

"In the beginning was the word, and the word was with God, and the word was God … and the word was made flesh and dwelt among us, and we beheld his glory," begins the Gospel of John. In the sacred tradition of Taoism the path to liberation is also a form of eternal shape-shifting, following a path of endless change, at one with the flux of existence (EoR, 13: 227).

The image of shape-shifting suggests that life always eludes stasis; the more genes we discover the more alteration and myriad forms of life are revealed. A mythopoetic acknowledgement of experience with no boundaries, distinctions or forms, the image expresses possibilities, potentials, daemons and shadows, the protean aspect of psychological process. Those who retain this underworld initiation—mystics, shamans, healers, sorcerers, devils and the mentally ill—inspire both awe and fright as shape-shifting both expresses and threatens the very nature of our being.

Furst, Peter T. "Shamanism, Transformation, and Olmec Art." *The Olmec World: Ritual and Rulership.* Princeton, NJ, and NY, 1995.

2

3

4

2. Drawn during his confinement in the psychiatric clinic of Heidelberg, the art metalworker Franz Karl Bühler may have depicted the permeability of identity and the shape-shifting of the inner world, most pronounced during mental illness. The Prinzhorn Collection, 1909–16, Germany.

3. The jaguar, lord of the forest, and Olmec ruler or priest rise to reveal their supernatural kinship in the sacred turmoil of ecstatic shamanism. Were-jaguar, dark-green serpentine with red pigment, Olmec, 900–300 B.C.E., Mexico.

4. Affronted at being ordered to marry a mortal, the sea-goddess Thetis attempts to escape by turning successively into fire, water, lion and serpent. King Peleus wrestling Thetis, by Peithinos, painting at the bottom of a cup, 6th century B.C.E., Greece.

Metamorphosis

"When Gregor Samsa woke up one morning from unsettling dreams, he found himself changed in his bed into a monstrous vermin."

Thus begins Kafka's *Metamorphosis*, a chilling vision of modern man's transformation into a state of irreparable estrangement and alienation. Gregor was a man whose inner being had become completely alien to him, a burden threatening his existence. This psychological rift caused a terrifying metamorphosis, a destructive transformation of the self into something totally "other," where what should house the creative imagination had become a brittle carapace, a mere façade. From the Latin "meta" (to change), "morphosis" (form), metamorphosis, a powerful symbol of transformation, reflects one aspect of psyche's encounter with its development: radical changes in form, function, character and state of being. Usually evoking the notion of soul or psyche's liberation or true incarnation, the symbol itself rests on an ancient vision of the essential unity of being, reflected in the multiplicity of form and structure that psyche and matter can assume. While shape-shifting expresses the fluid, temporary, Protean aspect of this vision, metamorphosis reflects the differentiated, permanent, prophetic qualities that arise. Metamorphosis often takes place hidden from sight, attesting to unconscious dynamics at work. Under a cloak of invisibility, at the behest of a god, in the alchemist's laboratory, at night under the influence of "unsettling dreams" or wrapped up in a cocoon, the radical changes wrought by metamorphosis come about through an intense incubation and release of libido.

Images of this process have themselves undergone successive metamorphoses as in the image of a caterpillar undergoing metamorphosis into a butterfly. This is an example of our scientific understanding of metamorphosis as part of a normal developmental process reflecting the progressive unfolding of inherent, genetic potentials and structures. This process may be gradual (tadpole into frog), or achieved abruptly in the butterfly. Here, organs important to the juvenile disintegrate during an incubating, pupal phase, while those important to the adult are created from embryonic tissue. Remarkably, this process of dissolution and coagulation, of disintegration, regression and individuation was prefigured in the archetypal imagination of the ancient, classical and Renaissance periods.

In early Egyptian, classical and Celtic mythology metamorphosis meant transformation by magic or sorcery, often the result of punishment, revenge or reward by the gods. Mythology abounds with stories of gods changing other beings into humans, animals, even trees, rivers and flowers. These transformations gave shape to a variety of psychological dynamics, as in Ovid's tale of overweening pride, where the master weaver Arachne was changed into a spider by Athena as punishment for daring to challenge the goddess to a contest of skills. They also depict the personality in the process of individuation, as in the lovely story of Pygmalion and Galatea, Ovid's tale of metamorphosis wrought by love and art. In our image we see the renowned but unhappy sculptor Pygmalion, who finally fell deeply in love with his beautiful, lifelike creation, Galatea. He worshiped and adorned her, but despite his talented efforts she remained just a statue. In the throes of passion and despair he prayed to the goddess Aphrodite to bring her to life. As reward for his devotion to love and beauty, the goddess answered his prayers (Ovid, Book Ten, 313–71).

1. Development of a large-winged butterfly. Features of the adult butterfly are present in the larval caterpillar in the form of "imaginal disks," reserve cells regulated by non-species-specific hormones, which unfold into the adult butterfly. Photographs by A. Weaving.

During the medieval and Renaissance periods, alchemy, the "divine metamorphosis" referred back to classical imagery to express the idea of transmutation, the creation of gold from lead, of mystical man from earthly man (Abraham, 128). Traditional religious symbolism echoes the transmutation motif: the transfiguration of Jesus the man into Christ, the son of God, can be seen as a process of successive ascending metamorphoses toward deity.

In our time, the image of metamorphosis is embedded in variations—from the sophisticated unfolding and alteration of the genome to the children's series *Power Rangers,* adolescents who "morph" into superior beings at the touch of a button through the transformative energy of technology. But whether it is at the behest of the gods, or through the devotion and works of man, metamorphosis symbolizes the revelation of essential qualities and radical transformations of destiny.

Abraham, Lyndy. *A Dictionary of Alchemical Imagery.* Cambridge, UK, and NY, 1998.

Kafka, Franz. *The Metamorphosis.* NY, 1915.

Ovid. *Metamorphoses.* NY, 2004.

2

3

2. In Canto 13, vol 1., of the *Inferno,* Dante describes the "Violent Against Themselves": suicides who are planted as trees, immobilized by their life-denying, self-pitying surrender to despair. *Wood of the Suicides,* by Gustave Doré, engraving, 1868, France.

3. Crowned Zeus on an altar with sword and thunderbolt facing seven nymphs in stages of metamorphosis into trees. *Seven Virgins Being*

Transformed, by Béroalde de Verville, woodcut, from *Le Songe de Poliphile,* 1600, France.

4. Pygmalion's workshop, where he and his creation Galatea embrace as she is brought to life by Eros, son of Aphrodite. The bottom portion of her body is ivory, the top has already changed into rosy human flesh. *Pygmalion and Galatea,* by Jean-Léon Gérôme, painting, ca. 1890, France.

Transformation

Formation, transformation,
    eternal spirit's eternal re-creation.
Goethe, *Faust*, part II, act I, scene 5

Transformation may be the one immutable fact of life. As such it is also a quintessentially psychological process: both natural and instinctive, but also a "work against nature," the *opus contra naturam* of individuation. Although related to the images of shape-shifting, metamorphosis and rebirth, transformation psychologically understood is different in that it suggests a relatively permanent and new solution, while also preserving continuity of person and process. This is akin to the way in which the genetic material contained in DNA is released from one cell, taken up and incorporated into another, resulting in genotypic changes. The psyche also initiates its own transformation, and that capacity is a sine qua non of psychological health. Pathology might be defined as the failure to initiate and respond to transformation, and the central question of depth psychotherapy—"how do people change?"—addresses the processes of transformation, rather than simple symptom substitution or sublimation.

In Goethe's *Faust*, the ever-mercurial Mephisto proclaims the secret of life and creation as "Formation, transformation, eternal spirit's eternal re-creation." Similarly, in the "Returned from Heaven" mythology of the Northwest Coast Native Americans, ancestral heroes descended from the heavens and are transformed into humans and animals as they land on earth. In turn, these beings depart this world and are transported back to the heavens, from whence they return to materialize again in recognizable forms. Back and forth it goes, in a cycle of ongoing regressions and progressions, as the process of transformation is also imagined here to be the link between human and divine (Macnair, 95).

Such "transformation masks" were often used in initiation ceremonies, which themselves serve to transform one phase of life into another, i.e., childhood into adulthood. Archetypal antagonists, masked and thus transformed into sacred animals or deities, torment the initiate, whose "death" and rebirth transform him permanently. These ceremonies and rituals were designed to control the psychic injury liable to occur during critical transitions, and avert negative transformations such as splitting of the personality or death. Modern depth analysis also functions as such a container for transformational processes.

It is in the nature of psychic energy to transform, to redistribute and differentiate one form into another. Alchemical symbolism also illustrates this process: Lead becomes gold, the stone becomes the philosopher's Stone, the *massa confusa* becomes the elixir of life. Basic substances and elements, which symbolize unconscious processes, are transformed by "torture" into incorruptible psychological states of mind. Likewise, the psychological conditions and mechanisms of transformational processes are often torturous: Vulnerability, loss, rage, depression, anxiety and shifts in hormonal chemistry and body integrity all transform.

This transformation from darkness to renewed life is depicted in the alchemical operation. A black substance obtained from mixing mercury with melted sulphur (the "Ethiops" or "Moor") was baked until it gave off a vapor, which was condensed into a valuable blood-red pigment, vermilion or cinnabar. If the vapor wasn't captured correctly, all that remained was a black residue. Psychologically, the shadow and other difficult passages, depicted as the black river, have to be worked until their underlying spirit is released (Henderson, 83–8). Complete immersion and "cooking" of inertia, indifference, rejection and even evil can transform such conditions into material available for life and growth when assisted by faith in their transcendent and relational dimensions. This paradigm of transformation, from *nigredo* (blackening) into *rubedo* (reddening), repeats itself throughout life as part of the ongoing process of conscious and creative differentiation. Transformation, although it symbolizes true and lasting change, is not a once-in-a-lifetime achievement, but rather a means by which we move toward wholeness. As the alchemists said "The goal is the art."

Henderson, Joseph L. and Dyane N. Sherwood. *Transformation of the Psyche the Symbolic Alchemy of the Splendor Solis.* NY, 2003
Macnair, Peter L., et al. *Down from the Shimmering Sky: Masks of the Northwest Coast.* Vancouver and Seattle, 1998.

1. A tri-colored man in the process of transformation emerges from a muddy stream to accept a robe offered by a peacock-winged queen. "The Regeneration of the Ethiopian," an illustration from the alchemical manuscript *Splendor Solis*, or "Splendor of the Sun," by Salomon Trismosin, school of Nuremberg, ca. 1582, Germany.

2. A transformation from bird, to man, to cosmos and back again, is revealed as this mask is opened and closed. Wood, hair, twine and paint, Nuxalk Indian, ca. 1865, British Columbia, Canada.

Chakras

Although we do not fully understand the mysterious inner phenomena of the chakras, they are imagined to be the centers for the essential life force surrounding, permeating and emanating from within particular parts of the human body. In India this force is called *prana*; in China, chi; Pythagoreans called it luminous body light; and in the Middle Ages, Paracelsus spoke of *illiaster*, the vital force. Chakras metabolize different kinds of energy, transmitting them to appropriate places within the auric field. Each chakra acts like a vortex of energy whirling at different rates of vibration, which range from gross (very slow) to subtle (extremely fast), depending on the specific chakra and the individual person.

Optimally, each chakra is open and moving in a clockwise direction. If chakras are congested, closed or reversed, the energy is unable to flow freely, potentially impacting well-being. There are seven major chakras, starting with the first or base chakra located at the perineum, which informs and supports all others up to the top of the head (called the crown chakra). In addition, there are approximately 23 minor chakras located throughout the body, such as on the palm of each hand, the bottom of each foot, behind the knees, etc. Hundreds of minuscule chakras spread throughout the body are called acupuncture points. All of them contribute to how we act intrapsychically and interpersonally with the world around us. We continuously influence the chakras and are influenced by them throughout our lives through psychological efforts, physical activity, diet, meditation and quality of life.

Each major chakra can be actively engaged for the purpose of awakening greater consciousness. Colors, sounds, numbers, elements, deities and animal entities associate each chakra with its symbolic meaning. Archetypal energies manifest very differently through different chakras. The second chakra, for example, is associated with the water element, the whale or leviathan, the bladder and with impulses and urges, including the sexual. The third chakra is associated with the solar plexus, the fire element and the ram; the fourth with the heart, the element air and the leaping, light-footed antelope.

The first chakra represents the foundational basis of human existence that we share with other animals, psyche meeting soma. It is associated with the perineum, the earth element and the elephant, the mass, solidity, gravity on which all else rests. If this base is jeopardized, all other chakras will be compromised and unable to function optimally. It is here that the dynamic polarization of feminine/masculine, represented by the Hindu goddess and god Shakti/Shiva still lies dormant. The Kundalini, or "serpent energy" of Shakti, is coiled at the base of the spine until it begins to be unleashed and travels upward through the spine. The heat and energy released in this process manifest the awakening of consciousness.

Whereas the base chakra at the bottom of the spine is holding the as-yet-unawakened, latent potential of Kundalini, the seventh, or crown chakra, represents the awakened psychic possibilities of self-realization, the gods conjoined. The crown chakra signifies the ultimate refinement and differentiation of expanded consciousness for an embodied human being. Because of its highly refined energetic activity the crown chakra is sometimes symbolized as a thousand-petaled lotus. The slow, dark, unconscious earthy realm of the base chakra has now fully evolved up through all the other chakras into the heavenly flowering of full consciousness in the crown chakra. We literally embody the potential of bringing together heaven and earth within ourselves.

Armstrong, Polly. *The Archetype of Muladhara.* Unpublished thesis. NY, 2002.
Saraswati, Satyananda. *Kundalini Tantra.* Munger, Bihar, India, 1984.

1

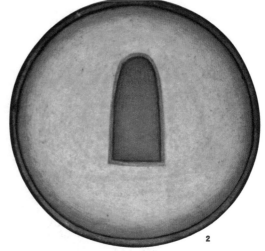

2

1. A glimpse of what a yogi might see: the ordering of subtle body energies within the seven major chakras. Kangra painting, ca. 1820, Himachal Pradesh, India.

2. An unconventional depiction of the first chakra, or wheel of energy, that lies at the base of the spine. The vertical shaft, or lingam, representing the Hindu god Shiva, is centered within the Kundalini energy of Shakti, the goddess whose dynamism activates the world. Muladhara chakra painting, detail, ca. 18th century, Rajasthan, India.

Crack

The glacier knocks in the cupboard,
The desert sighs in the bed,
And the crack in the tea-cup opens
A lane to the land of the dead.
W. H. Auden, *"As I Walked Out One Evening"*

A crack can be an opening into the world of imagination, like in Auden's poem, while the crack in the ordinary teacup makes it a leaky container, no longer safe. The original meaning of the word comes from the sound it makes, as if something is breaking, the connotations often negative. Cracks evoke dryness, like the barren earth in Edward Weston's photograph, the dry lips of fever or a house no longer cared for. Psychologically, a crack in the façade suggests a false persona. The splitting experience of mental illness is often felt as if one's whole world is breaking apart, concretely envisioned in the poet Weldon Lee's words: "The crack is moving down the wall." Our voice cracks in a moment of insecurity, but we may be restored by "cracking up" as we burst out laughing.

Then there are the cracks of magic, usually unexpected, which lead to other realities, to the "land of the dead," beyond earthly boundaries, as through a crack in time. Or the reverse, the light in Georgia O'Keeffe's dark painting suggests spirit entering the dense world of matter as through a crack. Leonard Cohen describes it in song: "There is a crack in everything / that is how the light gets in." The new day arrives at the crack of dawn with all its potentials—a gateway between night and day where mythic heroes descend through the horizon into the underworld or where prayers travel up to heaven.

The word "crack" is also used for decoding an ancient alphabet or a secret language, as if the alchemists' spirit Mercurius opens doors of knowledge. Hermes, or Mercury, his Greek or Roman counterpart, was the only god who could travel freely between the worlds and perhaps it is he who guides us through the narrow passageways that easily get unnoticed, like Freud's famous slip of the tongue, in order to retrieve some surprising insight. When something falls between the cracks it is forgotten or lost, and it may be our fear of falling into the chaotic abyss that gave rise to the superstition of avoiding walking on cracks in the sidewalk. And like Auden's teacup, the crack in the door, neither inside nor outside, may open up to the liminal place where poetry is born.

Between what I see and what I say,
between what I say and what I keep silent,
between what I keep silent and what I dream,
between what I dream and what I forget:
poetry.
Octavio Paz

1

2

1. *Cracked Earth, Borrego Desert*, photograph
by Edward Weston, 1938, United States.

2. *Dark Abstraction*, by Georgia O'Keeffe, oil painting,
1924, United States.

Pearl

I send you a box
Of glowing pearls.
Wear them with irises
And orange blossoms.
Yakamochi

A single, natural pearl from its source, the oyster is considered a treasure. Whatever is most valued, most beloved, most beautiful, from a child to the Kingdom of Heaven, we have called "pearl." Pearls have filled the coffers of royalty, and ornamented the vestments of queens, kings, sultans and popes. Pearls are mythically guarded in their deep-sea abodes by mermaids, water nymphs and snake genii. Strands of pearls, threaded orbs of light, adorn the sensual bodies of deities: "On Me all this (universe) is strung, / Like heaps of pearls on a string," says the god Krishna to Arjuna (Edgerton, 38). Chinese symbolism depicted the Tao as the pearl of the sage. Celestial dragons retrieve the pearl of wisdom out of the mists of chaos, and are themselves the form of the pearl's effulgence. Chinese alchemy called its divine water, the fluid, quicksilverlike psyche, "the flowing pearl" (CW 14:317).

That a jewel can begin as an irritant is part of the pearl's fascination. A grain of sand or a bit of organic matter enters the shell of an oyster and can't be extruded. Concentric rings of a calcium carbonate coating known as nacre build up layer by layer around the foreign body until it is eventually covered, and this creates a pearl. The pearl's shape may be round, oblong or irregular, and its color range from pale to dark, but most common is a soft, iridescent pastel. The delicate, pristine nature of the pearl has made it an emblem of virginity, purity and youthful love, a gift of betrothal and a bridal necklace. In earlier times, it was ground into a fine powder for elixirs of healing.

Yet the pearl is self-made in the fleshly oyster, intimating something singular and of inestimable worth luminously hidden in the psychic darkness of our fleshly nature, a "pearl" that could be discovered by chance, actively sought or mysteriously shown. In Persian mysticism the pearl became an image of the immortal soul within the mortal body. For alchemy, the pearl represented the "arcane remedy," an inherent "virtue" or tendency in the unconscious to restore what has been compromised in the self to its essential integrity. In the Gnostic Hymn of the Pearl, the pearl is the gnosis or "self-acquaintance" that reunites the soul forgetful of itself with its divine origin (Layton, 367). Pearls have been likened to drops of rain that bring moisture and renewal to the sere land, and to teardrops that are the priceless emollients of bitter sadness. So, too, the pearl evokes the "irritant" that can't be extruded, the grain of suffering that gathers to itself layers of living matter, to reveal in time, as meaning, its pearly substance.

The Bhagavad Gita. Cambridge, MA, 1972.
Kunz, George Frederick and Charles Hugh Stevenson. *The Book of the Pearl; the History, Art, Science, and Industry of the Queen of Gems.* NY, 1908.
Layton, Bentley. *The Gnostic Scriptures: A New Translation with Annotations and Introductions.* Garden City, NY, 1987.
Taburiaux, Jean and Jean-Paul Ehrmann. *Pearls: Their Origin, Treatment and Identification.* Radnor, PA, 1985.

1. The eternal soul gleaming within the material body is one symbolic rendering of the pearl within its humble shell.

2. Tao as the pearl of the sage and conjunction of yin/yang. *Nine Dragons*, detail, by Chen Rong, handscroll, 1244 C.E., China.

1

2

Grail

Hidden from the impious, a perfect rose blossoms out of the Grail in the middle of an enclosed garden. In this simple, elegant form, the artist of some five centuries ago has conveyed the ideas of wholeness, center, vessel and source. The word "grail" is derived from the French *graal* and medieval Latin, *gradale,* "in stages," the name given to a serving dish on which courses were brought in turn throughout the meal. The earliest stories of the Grail portray it as a version of the great goddesses' Cauldron of Plenty, the inexhaustible provision of whatever food and drink is most desired. Christianized, the Grail was associated with the vessels of Communion or with the mythical story of a chalice in which Joseph of Arimathea caught drops of the blood of the crucified Christ. In medieval literature, the Grail became the mystical goal of the knightly quest. Grail's etymology also suggests a gradual process of psychic integration and transfiguration, "a coming together and offering up of all things to a higher state of being" that conforms to the numinous object ultimately revealed (Matthews, 94). The quest for the Grail is long and arduous, often involving the "strange detours and wrong turnings" known to the alchemists in their opus, and requiring both humble courage and divine grace. Evoking the complexities and dangers of the psychic terrain, there are perilous bridges to be crossed, obstacles breached and monsters subdued. While the Grail has often been portrayed as a cup, it can take many forms corresponding to the individuality of the inner life of the seeker. The Grail participates in the symbolism of the night-sea journey, the treasure hard to attain and the alchemical stone that is elixir and panacea. In medieval Grail romances such as von Eschenbach's *Parzival,* it is only the Grail that can heal the wound of the Fisher King and restore fertility to his kingdom. Such stories seek to describe the effects of the longed for contact with one's soulful essence, "the consummation of heart's desire, its root and its blossoming—paradisal, transcending all earthly perfection!"

Matthews, John. *The Grail: Quest for the Eternal.* NY, 1981.

In a paradise garden blooms the rose within the Grail,
an image of Eden restored within the human soul.
Printer's mark, 1655, Europe.

Ghost

The dejected ghost of a woman named Oiwa looks up with one eye; the other is swollen shut and she has also lost part of her hair. Her story was the subject of one of Japan's most popular nineteenth-century kabuki plays (Addiss, 29–33). Oiwa's husband wanted to be rid of her so that he could marry the granddaughter of a well-to-do neighbor. He tried to kill Oiwa by means of poison, but it served only to disfigure her. Aware of her husband's betrayal, Oiwa died of anger and returned to haunt him as a terrifying ghost.

Everywhere in the world there is the concept of ghosts, spirits of the dead that return to haunt the living. Typically, ghosts make themselves known as shrouded or wraithlike apparitions, disembodied heads or hands or through our sensory experiences of sudden chills, the autonomous disturbance of furniture and objects and in strange knockings or tappings. Jung speculated about a "consciousness without the brain" of which ghosts would be the manifestation (Shamdasani, 15). Ghosts also reflect our age-old fascination, fear and bewilderment in relation to death. Feelings, once bound to the living person, slip into the unconscious at his death and become uncanny, tinged with the archetypal and externalized, hovering between the material and spiritual. Unresolved grief and persistent attachment to the dead may overwhelm the living, a danger reflected in countless tales of East and West peopled by ghosts who behave as vengeful, malicious shape-shifters. Shamans, spiritualists and exorcists have long been summoned to cure states of possession by the dead or a "loss of soul" to the underworld.

Yet, the derivation of the word "ghost" links it with root words that convey mixed qualities: spiritual being, angel, devil, fright (Barnhart, 316) and also fury, wounding or tearing in pieces (EoR, 5:547). In our imaginations, ghosts may return for many reasons: to complete unfinished business, to bring messages of import or offer care and protection. There are tender ghosts—infants who return to console their grieving parents, drowned mothers who come back to suckle their children (Jones, 199). But others—especially those who have died untimely or violent deaths—are restless, unhappy, demanding vengeance or retribution. We mollify and honor the spirits of the dead on All Hallows' Eve, the Day of the Dead and All Souls' Day, and in prolonged periods of ritual mourning and offerings at the grave. An African custom was to paint the head of a corpse in bright colors so that the ghost could be recognized (EoR, 5:548–50). In China paper boats bearing images of deities or lotus-shaped lanterns were set upon the water to guide the way of the dead across the river of transmigration.

The dead appear in our dreams, apparently as personifications of unconscious complexes and vital energies undergoing processes of change, conflict or integration. Thus, these ghosts are sometimes reinvigorated or they are shadowy, waning. They may be removed, disengaged, loving, needy or menacing. Often they appear for poignantly brief reunions to show us something not available to our conscious sight, or to remind us of something of value we've forgotten or to acquaint us with eternity.

Addiss, Stephen, et al. *Japanese Ghosts and Demons*. NY, 1985.
Barnhart, Robert K. Ed. *The Barnhart Concise Dictionary of Etymology*. NY, 1995.
Jones, Alison. *Larousse Dictionary of World Folklore*. Edinburgh, 1995.
Shamdasani, Sonu. "The Boundless Expanse: Jung's Reflections on Life and Death." *Quadrant* (38/1, 2008).

1. Behind the ghost is a ball of fire, also called will-o'-the-wisp and many other names, an eerie light that often appears in marshes or cemeteries, associated with the soul of the dead. *The Ghost of Oiwa*, by Shunkosai Hokushu, wood-block print, 1826, Japan.

2. From the Northwest Coast, Kingcome Inlet, these Kwakwaka'wakw (Kwakiutl) puppets depict a ghost and its two children. Wood, 19th century, British Columbia.

1

2

Ancestor

With intimate care peoples all over the world have preserved the cherished relics of their ancestors—bits of native soil, ritual objects or personal belongings, bones of the dead that they washed, rocked, sang to, prayed to or blessed. In part, these relics serve to mitigate the pain of separation between living descendents and their revered departed. In another sense, they represent the luminous and powerful essence of the departed, like that embodied by the reliquary guardian of Punu ancestral sacred objects, shown here, whose efficacy extends even to the packets of herbs she holds under her arms.

The ancestors possess this in-between quality of the flown soul and the hovering presence. They seem to have a kind of materiality and exalted awareness; they also display an immateriality, a repose and introspective serenity that suggest they inhabit a timeless dimension. We imagine the ancestors as residing in the Island of the Blessed, the Land of the Dead, the Spirit World, Underworld, Night Sky or West, mythic conceptions of the sacred place of origin. The ancestors are those who have "gone before" (from Latin *antecedere*), all the life that has ever been, leaving behind the traces of kinship. Something in the buried self, for example, lovingly recognizes the excavated bones of the diminutive "Lucy," our anthropoid matriarch. Or, watching the gliding of a bird, we are aware of the primeval within us, resonating somatically, remembering flight.

How would we have survived had we not been carried on the shoulders of the ancestors? How would we have found our way had we not been guided by the psychic deposits they have left us as signs? By what means would we hold in balance the worlds of natural and supernatural if not for their occult mediation? The ancestors arrive at the threshold of consciousness in the sheaths of dreams and imagination to ask questions, impart knowledge and to peel away the multiple skins of our identity. They visit us in familiar patterns of behavior as well as inexplicable phenomena, inviting our curiosity and engagement. They manifest as animal and human spirits of surpassing intelligence and adaptability. They are the stars in the night sky of our unknown being, emitting the light of millions and billions of years ago. As prototypical instruments like the harp, bow or drum, they convey the vibratory, rhythmic structures of the cosmos and their underlying harmony. Sagacious, uncanny, oracular, they are the legendary elders and immortals who belong to the past, to dreamtime, to the primordial "time outside of time," and nevertheless impinge eternally upon present and future, affecting the innate disposition of their descendents and participating in everyday affairs.

The ancestors are not only felt as benevolent. They are also fierce, terrifying, atrocious. They possess, impel, dismember us. They can act in our psyches as malign ghosts, critical and shaming. They haunt us if neglected, disturb our equilibrium, impose themselves as fixed beliefs and fear of change or reinterpretation. In some cultures they represent the way to spiritual liberation, in others the endless procession of rebirth. For good and ill, they are "the custodians of the source of life" whence derives our vitality, sustenance and renewal (Clark, 119). The great goddess Mnemosyne, said Kerényi, "is *memory* as the cosmic ground of self-recalling which, like an eternal spring, never ceases flowing" (p. 68). So, instinctively, we follow religious intimation and psychological process that lead us into psyche's veiled precincts and bring the awakened mythopoetic images to light, reuniting us with the ancestors. For these are the emblems of their accumulated experience and existential riches

the washed colors of the afterlife
that lived there long before you were born
W. S. Merwin, "Rain Light"

Clark, R. T. Rundle. *Myth and Symbol in Ancient Egypt.* London and NY, 1991.
Kerényi, Karl, *Hermes: Guide of Souls.* Putnam, CT, 1976.
Morphy, Howard. *Aboriginal Art.* London, 1998.

1. A reliquary guardian at the summit of a roped bundle of ancestral bones, her face painted white to convey her luminous nature. Sculpture, wood, paint, hide and other materials, Punu, late 19th century, Gabon, Africa.

2. As custodian of the Wanjina, Charlie Allungoy (Numbulmoore) repaints these ancestor figures in order to ensure the rejuvenation of nature in Ngarinyin culture. *Wanalirri Wanjina*, ochre on bark, Aboriginal, 1970, Australia.

APPENDIX

Index

Chrysalis, as alchemical
vessel, 234-5
Church. *See* Temple
Cignani, Carlo, *346*
Circe
and mandrake, 180
and Odysseus, 690
as witch, 702
Circumambulation, and
cloister, 620
CITY, 614-5
CLAM/OYSTER, 216-7
Claustrophobia, and clois-
ter, 620
CLAW/NAIL, 386-7
Cloacina, goddess of
sewers, 428
CLOISTER, 620-1
CLOUD, 58-59
COBRA, 198-9
COCKROACH, 224-5
Cockscomb, as sunlight, 328
COFFIN, 756-7
alchemical, 74
COLOR, 636-7
COMB, 526-7
and mirror, of mermaid,
694-5
COMET, 34-35
Communion, and grail, 786
COMPASS, 510-1
magnetic, 510
Compassion, and tears, 356
Conception, of Buddha and
queen Maya, *266*
Conch, shell as trumpet
and ear, 212
Conscious and unconscious
and beach, 122-3
and incest, 416
couple in alchemical
vessel as, 764-5
symbolism of sexual act,
414
Consciousness
and angel, 680
and hand, 380-1
and marsh, 120
and seeing, 352, 354
and sun, 22-23
beginning of, as island,
124
without a brain, 788
Cornell, Joseph, *248*
Cornucopia, from horn of
Amalthea, 318
Correggio, *59*
Cosmic egg, 14-15, 17
Cosmos
aboriginal,and brain,
344-5
and soul and fire, 84
as sperm and egg, *411*
compass, attribute of
constructing, 510-1

cycles of, *707*
man and bird mask
depicting, *779*
mandala as, 712
turtle supporting, 192-3
Vishnu as, *377*
Couple
Ask and Embla, 132
chained together, *515*
clasped hands of, *380*
in alchemical vessel,
764-5
Izanagi and Izanami, 72
king and queen, 470-1
kissing (*mithuni*), 374-5
Krishna and Rada, 158-9
lovers kissing and butter
fly, *235*
lovers poisoned, *741*
Peleus and Thetis, 770,
773
Pygmalion and Galatea,
774, 777
sexual union, 414-5
vampire and victim, *701*
Covenant, rainbow as, 72-73
COW, 304-7
cow goddess, Hathor, *373*
cows and milk of goddess
Usas, 88
COYOTE, 276-7
CRAB, 210-11
CRACK, 782-3
wound as, 734
CRADLE, 600-1
Creation
and destruction, and
flood, 50-*51*
and incest, 416
and scarab beetle, 236
and spark, 86-87
and spear of Izanagi and
Izanami, 494-5
dot as beginning, 706-7
God using compass, *511*
honey-making as, 228
spider as creator, 220,
222
through egg, 14-*15*
through licking, 304
through masturbation,
412
through Vishnu's breath,
16-*17*
Creation god, Siuhu, in
labyrinth, 714-5
CREMATION, 758-9
fire of, *82*
CRESCENT, 30-*31*
CRIPPLE, 478-9
CROCODILE, 200-1
Crone, and witch, 702
Cross
as tension of opposites,
745

within circle, of
labyrinth, 714-5
CROSSROADS, 716-7
CROW/RAVEN, 248-51
CROWN, 540-*1*
Crucifix, vision of, in stag
antlers, 286
CRUCIFIXION, 744-5
Crystal
salt, *115*
snow, *79*
Cup/Chalice, and poison as
snake, 740-*1*
Curtis, Edward S., *315,*
722
Cybele
Agditis and pomegranate,
176
Attis and pine tree, 136
CYCLOPS/GIANT, 698-9
da Vinci, Leonardo, *133,*
395, 425
Daghda, celtic god, and
harp, 670
DAKINI, 686-7
Dance
dancing Dakini, *687*
dancing Ganesha, *685*
of Kali on Shiva, 418
of Shiva Nataranja, 418
DARKNESS, 100-3
Date palm, 138-9
Daumier, Honoré, *483*
DAWN, 88-89
goddess of
- Aurora, *642*
- Eos, 74-5
- Marichi, as pig, *326*
- Usas (Usus), *416*
Day, Frank, *759*
De Chirico, Giorgio, *623,*
631
de la, Tour, Georges, *481,*
591
De Maria, Walter, *71*
Death, Aztec lord of, *335*
DECOMPOSITION, 764-5
DEER, 284-7
Demeter
and ancient pig sacrifice,
324
and Persephone, and
pomegranate, 176
horse-headed, 314
well at Delphi, *611*
Diseases, from tears of
Death maiden, 356
DESCENT, 432-3
DESERT, 116-7
Set, god of, 316
Devouring
and teeth, 370
crocodile as a symbol of,
200
darkness, 100

eclipse as, 32-33
whirlpool Charybdis as,
46
Devouring father, Saturn
and his son, 364, *367*
Devouring mother
Medusa, 372-3
spider as, 220
DEW, 74-75
Dietzsch, Barbara Regina,
167
Dionysius
and pine tree, 136
and dismemberment, *769*
and flute, 664
as embodiment of
phallus, 406-7
(Bacchus) and grapes,
174-5
born from thigh, *420*
bull and cult of, 310
god of tragedy as goat
song, 320
mask of, signifying
rebirth, *521*
Directions, four
and mandala, 712-3
East and West, 54-55
goddess of the West, *173*
snakes as, 60-61
DISEASE, 732-3
from tears of Death
maiden, 356
DISMEMBERMENT, 766-9
Divination
and femur, 420
and liver, 398-9
Djed. *See* Pillar
DOG, 296-9
and mandrake, 180-1
DOLPHIN, 206-7
DONKEY, 316-7
Door. *See* Gate/Door
Doré, Gustave, *119, 776*
Dot
center of compass circle,
510-1
dots on Neolithic breast,
389
dotted horse in Pech-
Merle, *381*
flame-point of fire, 82
one as, 710
spark as, 86-87
worm as point of divine
life, 186
See also Egg, Star, Sun
DOT/BINDU, 706-7
DOVE, 244-7
as mediating spirit, *471*
DRAGON, 704-5
green, Quetzalcoatl as,
688
guarding pearl, 784
train as, 444

Samson and Delilah, *346*
Sanchez, José Benitez, *767*
Sanchi, stupa and Yakshi, 144-5
Sandover Kngwarreye, Lily, *41*
Sarcophagus. *See* Coffin
Satan
  horned, portrayed as he-goat, *318*
  imagined as fly, 232-3
Saturn
  devouring his son, *367*
  governor of prison in alchemy, 634
SCALE, 512-3
Scapegoat, 318
SCARAB, 236-7
Scarification, 338-9
SCHOOL, 632-3
Scintilla. *See* Spark
SCISSORS, 528-9
Scorpio, astrological sign, scorpion as, 218-9
Scorpion goddess, Selket, Chamunda, 218
SCORPION, 218-9
Seed
  and sowing, 464
  mustard, 706
  Ishtar carrying seeds, 30
  See also Dot/Bindu, Masturbation, Sperm
Seeing. *See* Eye
Seghers, Gerard, *491*
Sekhmet, lion goddess, 82, 116, 268, *363*
Selene, moon goddess, 28
Selket, scorpion goddess, 218-9
Sengai, *191*
Senju, Hiroshi 76-77
Set
  Egyptian god as donkey, 316
  flint knife, attribute of, 490
  god of the desert, 116
Sewers, Cloacina, goddess of, 428
SEWING, 460-1
SEXUAL UNION, 414-5
  and plowing, 502
  eclipse as, 32
  of earth and sky, 400
  of Sol and Luna, *417*
SHAPE-SHIFTING, 770-3
  fox becoming human, 278, *281*
Sheeler, Charles, *565*
SHEEP, 322-3
SHELL, 212-5
Shepherd, as guide, 322
Ship. *See* Boat
SHIPWRECK, 452-3

and dolphins, 206
Shiva and Parvati, parents of Ganesha, 684
Shiva
  and family on burial ground, 754-5
  and Ganges River, 40
  as supreme beggar, *476*
  as zebu bull, 308
  lingam as fiery pillar, 118, 408
  swallowing poison, 376
SHOE, 550-1
Shu
  and Tefnet, 412
  god of air, 54-55
Shunkosai, Hokushu, *789*
Signorelli, Luca, *487*
SILENCE, 676-7
Singing/song
  and mermaid, 694
  of birds, 240
  of Sirens, 690
  Shiva as chant, 740
SIREN, 690-1
Skeleton, Zapotec lord of death as, *335*
SKIN, 338-9
  blue, of river god, *43*
  blue throat, of Shiva, 376
  blue, of Krishna, *159*
  blue, of woman, *653*
  green, of Osiris, *648*
  green, of Tara, *649*
  shedding by snake as renewal, 194
Skull
  and crossbones, 334
  necklace, as cycles of life, 754-5
SKY, 56-57
Sleipnir, Odin's eight-legged horse, 314
Smith, Kiki, *403*, *411*
Smith, Marston, *697*
SNAIL, 184-5
SNAKE, 194-7
  Ananta, 16-17
  and Bacchus, *175*
  and churning of Milk Ocean, 38
  coiled, as Kundalini, *720*
  feathered, as wind, 60-61
  feathered, Quetzalcoatl, 242
  hair of Medusa, *373*
  of Asclepius, 740
  shedding skin, as renewal, 338
  Snake goddess, Minoan, 548-9
  See also Bird and snake, as opposites
Sneezing, losing divine essence, 340

SNOW, 78-81
Sobek, crocodile god, 200
Sodom and Gomorrah, *84, 115*
Solar plexus, and sunrise, 90
Soldier. *See* War/Warrior
SOLSTICE, 92-93
Sophia, and milk of wisdom, 388
Soul
  as a crystalline castle, 612
  as Ba bird returning to body, *241*
  bird, symbol of, 238
  bush-soul as animal spirit, 770
  butterfly image of, 234
  Ka, of king created by Khnum, *469*
  located in head, 340
  lost or stolen, 732
  metamorphosis of, *774*
  pearl image of, 784
  star as, 18, *21*
  substance, nails as, 386
  weighing of, 512-3
Sound
  coming into being, and throat, 376
  existing before light, 358
Soutine, Chaim, *639*
SOWING, 464-5
SPARK, 86-87
  fish eyes as sparks in matter, 202
SPEAR, 494-5
SPERM, 410-1
Sphinx, and Oedipus, *417*
Spider, (arachne) membrane in head or brain, 344, *397*
SPIDER, 220-3
  as weaver, 456
  web of, as Maya's net, *519*
SPINE, 336-7
Spinning, symbol of, in spider myths, 220
  See also Weaving
SPIRAL, 718-21
  cyclical time and snail, 184
Squaring the circle, 510
Squirrel, Ratatosk, 130
Staff, white, sign of beggar, 476-477
STAIRWAY, 566-7
STAR, 18-21
  ancestors as stars, 791
  stars as knots in net of heaven, 518
  stars as sparks of consciousness, 56-57
Stieglitz, Alfred, *461*
STONE, 104-7

birth from, 404-5
  gaze of Medusa turning victims into, 372-3
Stone. *See also* Alchemy, philosophical stone
Storm god, Mexican, 67
STORM, 66-67
STRANGER, 486-7
STREET, 630-1
See also Path/Road
Styx, river, 42
Su, Keren, *437*
SUBWAY, 446-7
Sugimoto, Hiroshi, *101*
SUICIDE, 752-3
  suicides as trees, 776
Sulphur. *See* Alchemy
SUN, 22-25
  black sun, *103*
  crowned head identified with, 540
  disk, mirror as, 590, *592*
  eagle as solar bird, 256-7
  egg as sun-point, 14-*15*
  night-sea journey of, 450-1
  swallowed by toad, 188
Sun and moon
  and breasts, 388
  eyes of Horus as, 252
  union of Sol and Luna, *417, 470-1*
Sun god
  Horus-of-the-Horizon, *24*
  Mexican, sacrifice of heart to, 392
  Surya, wheel of, *505*
Sun goddess
  Ameratsu, in a cave, 112
  Australian, with lover, 96
Sun woman, 25
SUNRISE, 90-91
  Khepri raising solar bark, 236-7
SUNSET, 96-97
SWIMMING, 438-9
Swing, and solstice, 92
SWORD, 492-3
  and lily, 156
TABLE, 584-5
Tara, green-skinned, enthroned, 646, *649*
Taurus, astrological symbol of, as bull, 310
TEARS, 356-7
  and drowning, *743*
  of God, humans born from, 352
TEETH, 370-1
Tefnet, goddess of moisture, 412
TELEPHONE, 554-5
TEMPLE, 616-7
THIEF/ROBBER, 480-1
THIGH, 420-1

of Jacob, wounded by
angel, 734
Third eye, 352
THISTLE, 166-7
Thor
and oak tree, 132
beard, and hammer, 368-9
hammer Mjollnir of, 500-1
Thoth
as ibis, lays cosmic egg, 14
moon god, 26
wise baboon-god, 262-3
THREAD, 516-7
golden, Ariadne, in
labyrinth, 714
golden prayers as thread,
364
of fate, 458
Throat. See Neck/Throat
Throne
mountain as, 108
See also. Chair/Throne
Thulin, Anne, 345, 423
Thunder god, Raijin, 68, 69
THUNDER, 68-69
Thunderbolt, and Thor's
beard, 368-9
ax emblem of, 488
Tiger, as warrior, king, yin,
270-1
Tillberg, Peter, 633
Time
and calendar, 508-9
ant as unit of, 226
four cosmic ages (yugas),
304
Kali Yuga, dark age, 100
Tjamalampuwa, 25
Tlazolteotl, goddess of filth
and childbirth, 428-9
TOAD, 188-9
TOILET, 602-3
TONGUE, 372-3
Tonsure, of St. Francis,
350-1
TOWER, 622-3
of Babel, 622-3
TRAIN, 444-5
**TRANSFORMATION,
778-9**
Traylor, Bill, 317
TREE, 128-31
and backbone, 336-7
moon tree, Sumerian,
30-31
suicides in Hell as trees,
776
Tree goddess, Isis, 129
Tree of life, and human
blood-system, 396-7
Tree spirit, Yakshi, 144-5
Tree woman
seven virgins as, 776
St. Anne as dry tree, 539
Tremorin, Yves, 339

Triangle
inverted, and vulva, 405
sign of Odin, 746
Trickster
coyote, as, 276
crow or raven as, 248
fire as, 82
rabbit as, 288
spider as, 220, 223
TRUMPET/HORN, 668-9
Trunk, of elephant, 362
TUNNEL, 628-9
Turner, J.M.W., 67
**TURTLE/TORTOISE,
192-3**
Tusk, broken, as pen of
Ganesha, 684-5
Uccello, 705
Ueda, Kako, 397
Ultraviolet, spiritual pole of
spectrum, 654
**UMBRELLA/PARASOL,
552-3**
Unconscious
and black sun, 103
and comet, 34
and cosmic egg, 14-15
and lake, 44-45
and ocean, 36-39
dragon image of, 704-5
farther shore of river as,
42
Underworld
and snake, 196
and subway, 446
cave as entrance to,
112-3
descent into, 432-3
Field of Rushes, 120-1
UNICORN, 696-7
URINE, 426-7
Uroborus, dragon as, 704
Utagawa, Kuniyoshi, 553
Utnapishtim, and cosmic
flood, 50
VALLEY, 110-1
VAMPIRE, 700-1
Vampire bat, 294-5
Van Eyck, Jan, 323
**Van Gogh, Vincent, 20,
135, 141, 599, 635,
645, 647**
**Van Huysum, Jan, 173,
184-5**
Vehicle
body as, 758
coffin as, 756
VEIL, 530-1
Venus, planet, Quetzalcoatl
as, 688
Vermeer, Jan, 537
Virgin Mary
and Christ child in crown
of thorns, 539
and rose, 165

Annunciation, 157
as spinning goddess, 459
cradling Christ child, 601
pregnant, 401
Vishnu
as the universe, 377
as turtle supporting the
world, 193
Vishnu, creating the
universe, 16-17
Vodou spirit, Kalfou, of
crossroad, 716-7
Void, zero signifying, 708
VOMIT, 736-7
Von Wright, Ferdinand, 245
VULVA, 404-5
and ear/earring, 544-5
and wound, 734-5
divine, and ears, 360
exposed of Dakini, 686-7
shell as, 213-4
War god, 641
War goddess, Durga, 473
Water. See Flood, Lake,
Ocean, River, Whirlpool
WAR/WARRIOR, 472-3
**Warhol, Andy, 363, 443,
525, 555**
Warrior
fly as emblem of soldier
in Egypt, 232-3
society, and eagle
warrior, 256, 259
wearing helmet, 533
WATERFALL, 48-49
Waves
of sea and psyche, 39
tidal wave, Poseidon, god
of, 122
**WEAVING/SPINNING,
456-9**
Web
of Maya, 457
of spider, as matrix of
life, 220
Wedding ring, as binding,
546
Weighing. See Heart, weighing of, Soul weighing of
WELL, 610-1
of Mimir, 130
Weston, Edward, 782
WHALE, 204-5
WHEEL, 504-7
of energy, chakras as,
781
WHIRLPOOL, 46-47
Whistler, James Abbott
McNeill, 123
WHITE, 660-1
and red, semen and
blood, 410, 686
WIND, 60-61
fertilizing, Quetzalcoatl
god of, 688

WINDOW, 564-5
Wine. See Grape/Wine
Winged being
dragon, 704-5
Eos, goddess of dawn,
74-75
Furies, 692
Wings, symbolism of, 240
Wisdom, and salt, 114, 356
WITCH, 702-3
and Snow White, 170
WOLF, 274-5
WOMB, 400-1
as spacious emptiness,
686
Church born from, 734
house or chamber, and
phallus, 407
oven as, 582-3
zero as, 708-9
Words, as woven cloth,
456, 458
Work
ants symbolizing, 226
worker bees, 228
World tree. See Tree
chapter
WORM, 186-7
WOUND, 734-5
Wounded healer, Chiron,
738
WREATH, 538-9
of olive leaves, 118
of thorns, and heart, 393
Writing
Ganesha god of, 684-5
recording angels, 682
Xolotl, Mexican underworld
dog guide, 298
Yahweh, as pillar of cloud,
624
YAKSHI, 144-5
Yan-Hui, Haichan 189
YELLOW, 644-5
Yggdrasil, 130
Odin hanging on, 746
Yogini, on owl, 255
Yoni, adoration of, 404-5
Yoshitoshi, 281
Zapotec, lord of death, 335
ZERO, 708-9
Zeus (Jupiter)
and oak tree, 132
and Io, 59
as bull, and Europa, 311
giving birth to Dionysus,
420
nurtured by she-goat
Amalthea, 318
worshipped in his snake-
form, 195
Zokosky, Peter, 306
Zongdao, Huang, 462
Zotz, Mayan vampire bat
demon, 294-5

Credits

Picture Credits

AR = Art Resource, NY
ARS = Artist Rights Society
BAL = Bridgeman Art library
Names of actual image suppliers are set in bold

© The Estate of the artist licensed by Aboriginal Artists Agency 2009. The Holmes à Court Collection: 41; **AKG-images, London**/Museum der bildenden Künste, Leipzig: 184-5; **Alamy:** Ancient Art and Architecture: 417:2/Classic Image: 119:2/Elvele Images Ltd.: 257:2/Interfoto: 776:2/© Susan Liebold: 547/David Lyons: 105/Mary Evans Picture Library: 75/© Wonderlandstock: 225:1; **AlaskaStock.com**/© 2009 Bill Watkins: 273:2/© 2008 Mark Newman: 661:2; **Alinari Archives:** 157:2, 420; **Allard Pierson Museum:** 177; **American Museum of Natural History Library:** 475:2/Photo: Bobby Hansson: 233:3/Photo: Stephen S. Myers: 209:2, 549:3, 789:2; **Anatomisches Institut der Universität Basel:** 401:2; © **Ancient Art & Architecture Collection Ltd:** Ronald Sheridan: 349; **Andreas von Einsiedel © Dorling Kindersley:** 785:1; **Anglo-Australian Observatory**/David Malin Images: 718; **ARAS:** 325, 549:2; **Archaeological Museum, Varna, Bulgaria:** 755:1; **Archaeological Survey of India:** 405:3; **ARDEA:** © Jean-Paul Ferrero: 283:2/© M. Watson: 315:3/© Alan Weaving: 775; © **Karen Arm:** 727; **The Art Archive:** 473:1/Archaeological Museum Sparta/Gianni Dagli Orti: 533/MGM/THE KOBAL COLLECTION: 703:3/Museo del Templo Mayor, Mexico/Gianni Dagli Orti: 212, 767:2/Victoria and Albert Museum/Sally Chappell: 377:1/Gianni Dagli Orti: 297:1, 721; **Photography © The Art Institute of Chicago:** 26-7, 46-7, 53:1, 365, 529, 545:2, 625:2, 627; **Art Resource, NY:** 497:3, 599:1, 645:1, 705:2 / Adoc-photos: 35/Alinari: 579/Bridgeman-Giraudon: 63, 129, 506:2/Bridgeman-GiraudonARS/SABAM, Brussels: 724/© DeA Picture Library: 509:2/Werner Forman: 17:2, 139:1, 149, 194, 243:2, 273:3, 275:2, 275:3, 307, 373:2, 415:2, 567:3, 723, 739/© 2009 C. Herscovici, London/ARS: 535/© Gilles Mermet: 203:3/The Newark Museum: 525:2/Nimatallah: 157:1, 549:1/The Pierpont Morgan Library: 599:2, 748/The Philadelphia Museum of Art: 399:1, 577:1/Tate, London: 67:1, 753:3 © 2009 Estate of Pablo Picasso/ARS: 357:1/John Bigelow Taylor: 259/Vanni: 275:1/© 2009 The Andy Warhol Foundation for the Visual Arts/ARS:

443, 555, 525:1; **Arthur M. Sackler Foundation, New York:** 421; **Ashmolean Museum, University of Oxford:** 413:2; **Asia Society, NY:** 379:2; © **Asian Art Museum of San Francisco:** 687; **Ron Austing Wildelife Photography:** 645:2; **Austrian National Library Vienna, Picture Archive:** 51:1, 73:1; © **2009** The Estate of Francis Bacon/ARS/DACS, London: 299; **Scala/AR/** 655:1; Photo © **1985 Dirk Bakker:** 3, 222:4, 383, 685:1, 736; **Courtesy Fabrice Balossini:** 720; © **2009 Banco de México Diego Rivera & Frida Kahlo Museums Trust/Collection of Museo Dolores Olmedo, Mexico:** 390; **Photo: Ina Bandy:** 531:1; **Courtesy of Tassos Bareiss:** 557; **The Walter & Molly Bareiss Collection of African Art:** 263:1, 489:2, 587:2; © **Bayerische Staatsbibliothek:** 682; **Carol Beckwith/Angela Fisher/Photokunst:** 757:1; **Photo: Dawood Bey. Courtesy the Tilton Gallery, New York:** 80; **Bible Lands Museum Jerusalem:** 352; **Biblioteca Apostolica Vaticana:** 29, 109:2, 165, 397:3, 427:2, 429:1, 453; **Biblioteca Nazionale, Florence:** 131:3; © **Bibliothèque de l'Arsenal:** 207, 245:2, 513:2, 729, 741:1, 743:2, 765:1; **Bildarchiv Preussischer Kulturbesitz/AR:** 157:3, 167, 195, 230, 261:3, 327, 407, 459:3, 759:2, 773/© 2009ARS/SIAE, Rome: 585/© 2009 ARS/VG Bild-Kunst, Bonn: 203:1/© 2009 Kate Rothko Prizel & Christopher Rothko/ARS: 640; **Hans von Boxel:** 28; **Photo, Reiko Mochinaga Brandon:** 517:3; **Bridgeman Art Library:** © Ashmolean Museum: 255:2/Egyptian National Museum: 353/Fitzwilliam Museum, UK: 553:3/Giraudon: 237:2/The Illustrated London News Picture Lib., UK: 451:2/© Isabella Stewart Gardner Museum: 123/Musee de l'Orangerie, France/Peter Willi/© 2009ARS/ADAGP, Paris: 639/Museum of Fine Arts, Boston: 465, 495:3, 785:2/National Gallery, UK: 286, 375:2/National Gallery of Art, US: 537/Thyssen-Bornemisza Collection, Spain: 539:1/Victoria & Albert Museum, UK: 471:2/Worcester Art Museum: 49/Yale Center for British Art:187/Private Collection/Photo © Heini Schneebeli: 271:4/Private Collection/© Fondazione Giorgio e Isa de Chirico, Rome/© 2009ARS/SIAE, Rome: 631; © **British Library Board:** 59:2, 163:2, 227:1, 464, 515:2, 605:3, 659:2, 769:5, 779:1; © **The British Museum:** 15:3, 43, 228, 271:3, 371:1, 451:1, 482, 495:2, 517:1, 519:2, 693:2/AR: 87:2, 231, 233:1, 237:1, 301, 357:2, 373:1, 433, 475:3, 497:2, 527:2, 675:2, 747, 753:1/BAL: 85 ; **Brooklyn Museum:** 61, 161, 191:1, 205:2; **Photo: Emil Brunner:** 117:2; © **Buffalo Museum of Science:** 342; **Burton Historical**

der Psychiatrischen Universitätsklinik Heidelberg: 772:2; **The San Antonio Museum of Art.** Photo/Peggy Tenison: 255:3; **San Diego Museum of Art:** 203:2/© 2009 Georgia O'Keeffe Museum/ARS: 719; **San Francisco Museum of Modern Art:** 461; **© Sarl la Crypte, France:** 715:1; **Scala/AR:** 151, 153, 175:1, 209:1, 243:3, 318, 319, 323:1, 323:3, 335:1, 341, 346, 347, 351:1, 369:2, 384, 427:1, 513:1, 519:1, 563:1, 625:1, 635:2, 648, 669:2, 683:4, 751:2/Scala/Ministero per i Beni e le Attività culturali: 311; **Seattle Art Museum:** 250-1/Excavated in 1982 from Xindu Sanhexiang Majjiashan, Xindu County Bureau of Cultural Relics/Photo: Paul Macapia: 675:3; **Fuji-san Hongu Sengen Taisha, Japan:** 109:1; **© Hiroshi Senju, Courtesy of Daitoku-ji Temple, Japan:** 76-7; **© Shelburne Museum, Vermont:** 573; **Sirot-Angel Collection:** 475:1; **Skira, Milan:** 160:2; **© Kiki Smith/Courtesy PaceWildenstein, NY:** 403:2; **Courtesy Marston Smith:** 697:3; **Smithsonian Institution: Art and History Collection, on loan to the Arthur M. Sackler Gallery:** 235:2 /**National Museum of the American Indian:** 152, 298:4, 363:1, 715:2, **National Museum of African Art**/Photo: Franko Khoury: 525:3/**Department of Anthropology:** 303:4/Photo: D.E. Hurlbert: 520; **South Australian Museum, Adelaide:** 25:4, 283:1; **Spencer Museum of Art:** 789:1; **Staatsbibliothek zu Berlin-Preussischer Kulturbesitz-Handschriftenabteilung:** 329:3, 467:1, 637:2; **Stadtbibliothek Mainz.** Photo: Arno Garrels, Berlin: 143; **© Saul and Marsha Stanoff Collection:** 289:2; **State Hermitage Museum:** 97; **Stiftung Weimarer Klassik, Weimar:** 637:1; **Photo: Allan Stone Gallery, NY:** 265:1; **© Hiroshi Sugimoto:** 101; **Sun Tree Publishing:** 556, 611:1, 705:3; **Courtesy of the artist/ Collection of Charles Taylor:** 37; Photo: Eberhard Thiem: 380; **Tips Images/Guido Rossi:** 193:1 ; **Tokyo National Museum/TNM Image Archives:** 69, 137; **© Topic Photo Agency/age fotostock:** 629; **Courtesy of Michael Tracy, Texas**/Photo: Christopher Gallo: 393; Yves Trémorin/la mère/1985-adagp: 339:1; **Courtesy of Lyle Tuttle:** 222:3; **U.S. Fish and Wildlife Service:** 279; **U.S. Library of Congress, Prints & Photographs Division, Edward S. Curtis Collection:** 315:4, 722; **© Universität Heidelberg:** 757:2; **Universitätsbibliothek Mannheim.** Photo: Arno Garrels, Berlin: 103, 241:4; **The Stanley Collection, University of Iowa Museum of Art:** 515:1; **© University of Tübingen:** Photo. H. Jensen: 238/Photo. J. Lipták: 409; **Van Gogh Museum Amsterdam:** 647/Giraudon/BAL: 141:2; **© Photo. Jean Vertut:** 113:1, 381; **Victoria and Albert Museum:** 38, 139:2, 305, 431:1, 755:2; **Vitlycke Museum, Sweden:** 503:1; **Wadsworth Atheneum Museum of Art/© 2009 Georgia O'Keeffe Museum/ARS:** 128, 217; **Photo: © Brooks Walker:** 762; **Reprinted by permission of International Creative Management, Inc. © Marina Warner, 1994:** 429:2; **Wheelwright Museum of the American Indian, Santa Fe.** Photo: Addison Doty: 64, 99:2; **© Patrick Wiggins:** 33:1; **From Without Sanctu-**ary Collection: 749; www.worldreligions.co.uk/G.B. Mukherji: 227:2; **© Yale Center for British Art:** 235:1; **© Yunnan Provincial Museum, China:** 553:1; **Zefa Pictures:** 339:2, 545:1; **The Zimmerman Family Collection/Photo © John Bigelow Taylor:** 360:2; **© Peter Zokosky:** 306

We wish to express our gratitude to everyone who provided us with images for *The Book of Symbols*. Complete credit information can be found on our website, www.aras.org. Despite every effort, the copyright could not be established in all cases. We would welcome any further information.

Poetry Credits

ANONYMOUS: From *A Haiku Menagerie*, by Stephen Addiss with Fumiko and Akira Yamamoto, © 1992 by Stephen Addiss. Shambhala Publications Inc. www.shambhala.com. **APPLEWHITE, JAMES:** *River Writing*. © 1988 Princeton University Press. **AUDEN, W.H.:** "As I Walked Out One Evening," © 1940 & renewed 1968 by W.H. Auden, from *Collected Poems*. Random House, Inc. and Faber and Faber Ltd. **BARCLAY, LILIAN, E.:** "The Coyote: Animal and Folk Character." *Coyote Wisdom*, J. Frank Dobie, Mody C. Boatright, Harry H. Ransom, eds. Publications of the Texas Folklore Society, No. XIV. Dallas: SMU Press, 1938. 58. **BUSON/ADDIS:** From *A Haiku Menagerie*, by Stephen Addiss with Fumiko and Akira Yamamoto, © 1992 by Stephen Addiss. Shambhala Publications Inc. **CATHERINE of SIENA/LADINSKY:** "Consecrated", by Catherine of Siena, trans. Daniel Ladinsky, from Penguin anthology: *Love Poems from God*, © 2002 Daniel Ladinsky and used with his permission. **DANIELS, ANA:** From *Bali: Behind the Mask*, Random House, 1981. **DICKINSON, EMILY:** Trustees of Amherst College from *The Poems of Emily Dickinson*, Thomas H. Johnson, ed., Cambridge, Mass.: The Belknap Press of Harvard University Press, Copyright © 1951, 1955, 1979, 1983 by the President and Fellows of Harvard College. **ELIOT, T.S.:** Excerpt from "The Waste Land: Burial of the Dead", from *T.S. Eliot Collected Poems* 1909-1962. P. 53-55. Faber and Faber Ltd., 1963/Excerpt from "East Coker" in *Four Quartes*, © 1940 by T.S. Eliot and renewed 1968 by Esme Valerie Eliot, Houghton Mifflin Harcourt Publishing Company and Faber and Faber, Ltd./Excerpt from "Ash Wednesday" in *Collected Poems* 1909-1962, © 1930 and renewed 1958 by T.S. Eliot, Houghton Mifflin Harcourt Publishing Company and Faber and Faber, Ltd. **FIELD, EDWARD:** "Magic Words", translated/adapted by Edward Field from the Inuit, from *Poetry in Motion: 100 Poems from the Subways and Buses*, W.W. Norton & Company. © Edward Field. **FRANKLIN, ARETHA:** "Spirit in the Dark" written